Property in Europe: Law and Practice

General Editor: Anthony Hurndall, MA (Oxon), Solicitor, FRSA

Butterworths
London, Dublin, Edinburgh
1998

United Kingdom	Butterworths a Division of Reed Elsevier (UK) Ltd, Halsbury House, 35 Chancery Lane, LONDON WC2A 1EL and 4 Hill Street, EDINBURGH EH2 3JZ
Australia	Butterworths, SYDNEY, ADELAIDE, BRISBANE, CANBERRA, MELBOURNE and PERTH
Canada	Butterworths Canada Ltd, TORONTO and VANCOUVER
Ireland	Butterworth (Ireland) Ltd, DUBLIN
Malaysia	Malayan Law Journal Sdn Bhd, KUALA LUMPUR
New Zealand	Butterworths of New Zealand Ltd, WELLINGTON and AUCKLAND
Singapore	Butterworths Asia, SINGAPORE
South Africa	Butterworths Publishers (Pty) Ltd, DURBAN
USA	Michie, CHARLOTTESVILLE, Virginia

A CIP Catalogue record for this book is available from the British Library.

ISBN 0 406 01309 8

Printed and bound by Mackays of Chatham plc

List of contributors

Austria
Mag. Ivo Deskovic

Denmark
C Bennetsen

England and Wales
D A Hurndall

Finland
Kaj Swanljung, Susanne Mattsson

France
Maître Philippe Dubois

Germany
Gerhard Wegen, Stefan Lingemann, Wolfgang Spoerr, Edgar Joussen, Dirk Wasmann, Eckhart Schweyer and Christopher Kuner

Greece
S Karaiskakis, C Metaxotou, I Anastassopoulou, A Anghelakos, A Katsiavou, M Sergakis, H Hristakou

Italy
F Ago

Luxembourg
A Schmitt

Netherlands
Cornelis Slangen, Evert Wiggers

Northern Ireland
Laurence Mahood

Norway
L O Askheim and C Rødsæther

Portugal
Luis Vinhas, Isabel Garcia, Ana Menéres

The Republic of Ireland
Colin Keane

Scotland
Christine McLintock, Pat Hawthorn and Brandon Nolan

Spain
Victoria Llavero

Sweden
Rolf Johansson

Switzerland
D Hochstrasser

Co-ordinating Editors
Alexandra Stanton and Lara Crellin

To S, T, B and F

Preface

Warnings should always be listened to but fortunately they do not have always to be acted on. We were right to press on despite the cautionary tales. The need was clear. A European business simply could not get basic, user-friendly guidance on the law and practice involved in buying, building or leasing property elsewhere in Europe. This was even truer of businesses from overseas. The developer could not find out what planning, environmental, tax and construction hurdles he would have to clear. The investor did not know what restrictions he would face, what security of tenure and rent controls there might be. The banker did not know what security he would get, how effective it would be and how he could enforce it. What business vehicles could be used? What restrictions were there on inward investment or repatriation of profits?

The language and cultural barriers were enough, without the variations in industry, legal and professional practice. Even the professional adviser had no ready sources. He would have to scour volumes of periodicals and a variety of books to find that there was still no comprehensive summary. He would collect fragments and try to piece them together, only to find they conflicted, or were out of date, or both.

Any fuller guide was usually in the local language and assumed a working knowledge of the system. Going to the local property professional or lawyer often confused, because professionals are apt to assume a greater knowledge in their clients and professional colleagues than is safe. Unfamiliar terms and concepts were used as though they were common knowledge, or worse still, familiar terms one thought one could relax with, were found to have an entirely different meaning.

The problems were too common: too much misunderstanding, too many delays, too many negotiations breaking down and too many damaged relationships. There had to be a basic guide which enabled a business or professional to enter any country in the EU, and its neighbours, with a preliminary understanding of the issues and with confidence they were not in totally unknown territory.

So we hope this is it. The aim has been to use a common format, so that the reader can go from one country to another and find the same information in the same place in each chapter for each country. The terminology has been kept the same, but the local term is also given where this will help. The guide is in English, the international business language. It has been written with the assistance of a top property practice in each country. It does not cover Eastern Europe because of the new and fast-changing economic and legal structures being developed there, which would have made the book too cumbersome and quickly dated. It is hoped to include coverage of these countries in later editions.

We believe all subjects likely to be of interest are covered. This ambition has been its own burden, and it has taken four years to bring the project about.

My apologies are owed to all those who have waited patiently for the result and to all the prompt contributors who have had to provide updates to make up for stragglers and the occasional loss of momentum. There will perhaps have been mistakes in approach and the choice of topics covered. I hope these will be forgiven and that readers will be quick to write in to suggest improvements for the future.

The book is written for all in industry, commerce and the property business, and not simply the professionals. It must be remembered though that it is only a guide and specific advice should be obtained before any actions are taken or investments made.

I will keep the list of those to be thanked brief: above all the contributors themselves, whose details are at the front of each chapter and who have made this book a pleasure to put together; Richard Thomas who has suffered a similar fate, survived, and like me, enjoyed the experience; my former managing partner, Jeff Morgan; my secretary, Dana Taylor; all at Butterworths; and, of course, my two London sub-editors who ensured we kept going despite the odds: Alexandra Stanton (text and editorial) and Lara Crellin (text and promotion).

DAH
February 1998

Contents

Preface ix

Chapter 1 Austria
1 OWNERSHIP OF LAND 3
2 OTHER INTERESTS IN LAND 6
3 TITLE TO LAND 9
4 TRANSACTIONS IN LAND 11
5 LEASES AND OTHER RIGHTS OF OCCUPATION 14
6 FINANCE AND INVESTMENT SOURCES 16
7 FORMS OF SECURITY 18
8 PLANNING AND BUILDING REGULATION 20
9 ENVIRONMENTAL MATTERS 22
10 DEVELOPMENT 25
11 TAXES 27
12 GRANTS AND INCENTIVES 30
13 COMPANIES AND BUSINESS ENTITIES 30
14 INTERNATIONAL 32

Chapter 2 Belgium
1 OWNERSHIP OF LAND 37
2 OTHER INTERESTS IN LAND 39
3 TITLE TO LAND 42
4 TRANSACTIONS IN LAND 43
5 LEASES AND OTHER RIGHTS OF OCCUPATION 47
6 FINANCE AND INVESTMENT SOURCES 51
7 FORMS OF SECURITY 53
8 PLANNING AND BUILDING REGULATION 54
9 ENVIRONMENTAL MATTERS 56
10 DEVELOPMENT 57
11 TAXES 60
12 GRANTS AND INCENTIVES 63
13 COMPANIES AND BUSINESS ENTITIES 63
14 INTERNATIONAL 66

Chapter 3 Denmark
1 OWNERSHIP OF LAND 71
2 OTHER INTERESTS IN LAND 74
3 TITLE TO LAND 77
4 TRANSACTIONS IN LAND 78
5 LEASES AND OTHER RIGHTS OF OCCUPATION 81
6 FINANCE AND INVESTMENT SOURCES 83
7 FORMS OF SECURITY 86
8 PLANNING AND BUILDING REGULATION 88

9 ENVIRONMENTAL MATTERS 91
10 DEVELOPMENT 94
11 TAXES 97
12 GRANTS AND INCENTIVES 100
13 COMPANIES AND BUSINESS ENTITIES 100
14 INTERNATIONAL 102

Chapter 4 England and Wales
1 OWNERSHIP OF LAND 107
2 OTHER INTERESTS IN LAND 110
3 TITLE TO LAND 113
4 TRANSACTIONS IN LAND 114
5 LEASES AND OTHER RIGHTS OF OCCUPATION 116
6 FINANCE AND INVESTMENT SOURCES 118
7 FORMS OF SECURITY 121
8 PLANNING AND BUILDING REGULATION 123
9 ENVIRONMENTAL MATTERS 126
10 DEVELOPMENT 128
11 TAXES 132
12 GRANTS AND INCENTIVES 135
13 COMPANIES AND BUSINESS ENTITIES 138
14 INTERNATIONAL 140

Chapter 5 Finland
1 OWNERSHIP OF LAND 143
2 OTHER INTERESTS IN LAND 146
3 TITLE TO LAND 149
4 TRANSACTIONS IN LAND 150
5 LEASES 155
6 FINANCE AND INVESTMENT sources 158
7 FORMS OF SECURITY 160
8 PLANNING AND BUILDING REGULATION 162
9 ENVIRONMENTAL MATTERS 164
10 DEVELOPMENT 166
11 TAXES 169
12 GRANTS AND INCENTIVES 173
13 COMPANIES AND BUSINESS ENTITIES 173
14 INTERNATIONAL 175

Chapter 6 France
1 OWNERSHIP OF LAND 179
2 OTHER INTERESTS IN LAND 181
3 TITLE TO LAND 184
4 TRANSACTIONS IN LAND 185
5 LEASES AND OTHER RIGHTS OF OCCUPATION 188
6 FINANCE AND INVESTMENT SOURCES 191
7 FORMS OF SECURITY 193
8 PLANNING AND BUILDING REGULATION 194
9 ENVIRONMENTAL MATTERS 198
10 DEVELOPMENT 201
11 TAXES 204

12 GRANTS AND INCENTIVES 207
13 COMPANIES AND BUSINESS ENTITIES 208
14 INTERNATIONAL 209

Chapter 7 Germany
1 OWNERSHIP OF LAND 213
2 OTHER INTERESTS IN LAND 215
3 TITLE TO LAND 219
4 TRANSACTIONS IN LAND 220
5 LEASES AND OTHER RIGHTS OF OCCUPATION 223
6 FINANCE AND INVESTMENT SOURCES 226
7 FORMS OF SECURITY 229
8 PLANNING AND BUILDING REGULATION 230
9 ENVIRONMENTAL MATTERS 234
10 DEVELOPMENT 237
11 TAXES 240
12 GRANTS AND INCENTIVES 243
13 COMPANIES AND BUSINESS ENTITIES 244
14 INTERNATIONAL 247

Chapter 8 Greece
1 OWNERSHIP OF LAND 251
2 OTHER INTERESTS IN LAND 253
3 TITLE TO LAND 256
4 TRANSACTIONS IN LAND 257
5 LEASES AND OCCUPATIONAL RIGHTS 260
6 FINANCE AND INVESTMENT SOURCES 263
7 FORMS OF SECURITY 265
8 PLANNING AND BUILDING REGULATION 267
9 ENVIRONMENTAL MATTERS 270
10 DEVELOPMENT 273
11 TAXES 277
12 GRANTS AND INCENTIVES 280
13 COMPANIES AND BUSINESS ENTITIES 281
14 INTERNATIONAL 283

Chapter 9 Italy
1 OWNERSHIP OF LAND 287
2 OTHER INTERESTS IN LAND 290
3 TITLE TO LAND 293
4 TRANSACTIONS IN LAND 294
5 LEASES AND OTHER RIGHTS OF OCCUPATION 297
6 FINANCE AND INVESTMENT SOURCES 299
7 FORMS OF SECURITY 302
8 PLANNING AND BUILDING REGULATION 304
9 ENVIRONMENTAL MATTERS 308
10 DEVELOPMENT 310
11 TAXES 313
12 GRANTS AND INCENTIVES 316
13 COMPANIES AND BUSINESS ENTITIES 316
14 INTERNATIONAL 320

Chapter 10 Luxembourg

1 OWNERSHIP OF LAND 323
2 OTHER INTERESTS IN LAND 325
3 TITLE TO LAND 329
4 TRANSACTIONS IN LAND 331
5 LEASES AND OCCUPATIONAL RIGHTS 333
6 FINANCE 336
7 SECURITY 338
8 PLANNING AND BUILDING REGULATION 340
9 ENVIRONMENTAL MATTERS 343
10 DEVELOPMENT 345
11 TAXes 348
12 GRANTS AND INCENTIVES 352
13 COMPANIES AND BUSINESS ENTITIES 353
14 INTERNATIONAL 356

Chapter 11 Netherlands

1 OWNERSHIP OF LAND 359
2 OTHER INTERESTS IN LAND 361
3 TITLE TO LAND 364
4 TRANSACTIONS IN LAND 365
5 LEASES AND OTHER RIGHTS OF OCCUPATION 368
6 FINANCE AND INVESTMENT SOURCES 371
7 FORMS OF SECURITY 374
8 PLANNING AND BUILDING REGULATION 377
9 ENVIRONMENTAL MATTERS 380
10 DEVELOPMENT 382
11 TAXES 385
12 GRANTS AND INCENTIVES 389
13 COMPANIES AND BUSINESS ENTITIES 390
14 INTERNATIONAL 392

Chapter 12 Northern Ireland

1 OWNERSHIP OF LAND 397
2 OTHER INTERESTS IN LAND 399
3 TITLE TO LAND 402
4 TRANSACTIONS IN LAND 403
5 LEASES AND OTHER RIGHTS OF OCCUPATION 405
6 FINANCE AND INVESTMENT SOURCES 409
7 FORMS OF SECURITY 409
8 PLANNING AND BUILDING REGULATION 410
9 ENVIRONMENTAL MATTERS 413
10 DEVELOPMENT 416
11 TAXES 417
12 GRANTS AND INCENTIVES 417
13 COMPANIES AND BUSINESS ENTITIES 419
14 INTERNATIONAL 419

Chapter 13 Norway

1 OWNERSHIP OF LAND 423
2 OTHER INTERESTS IN LAND 425

3 TITLE TO LAND 428
4 TRANSACTIONS IN LAND 430
5 LEASES AND OTHER RIGHTS OF OCCUPATION 432
6 FINANCE AND OTHER INVESTMENT SOURCES 434
7 FORMS OF SECURITY 436
8 PLANNING AND BUILDING REGULATION 437
9 ENVIRONMENTAL MATTERS 440
10 DEVELOPMENT 443
11 TAXES 446
12 GRANTS AND INCENTIVES 448
13 COMPANIES AND BUSINESS ENTITIES 450
14 INTERNATIONAL 452

Chapter 14 Portugal
1 OWNERSHIP OF LAND 457
2 OTHER INTERESTS IN LAND 460
3 TITLE TO LAND 464
4 TRANSACTIONS IN LAND 466
5 LEASES AND OTHER RIGHTS OF OCCUPATION 469
6 FINANCE AND INVESTMENT SOURCES 472
7 FORMS OF SECURITY 474
8 PLANNING AND BUILDING CONTROLS 476
9 ENVIRONMENTAL MATTERS 479
10 DEVELOPMENT 481
11 TAXES 484
12 GRANTS AND INCENTIVES 487
13 COMPANIES AND BUSINESS ENTITIES 487
14 INTERNATIONAL 489

Chapter 15 The Republic of Ireland
1 OWNERSHIP OF LAND 493
2 OTHER INTERESTS IN LAND 495
3 TITLE TO LAND 498
4 TRANSACTIONS IN LAND 500
5 LEASES AND OTHER RIGHTS OF OCCUPATION 503
6 FINANCE AND INVESTMENT SOURCES 505
7 FORMS OF SECURITY 508
8 PLANNING AND BUILDING REGULATION 509
9 ENVIRONMENTAL MATTERS 512
10 DEVELOPMENT 514
11 TAXES 518
12 GRANTS AND INCENTIVES 522
13 COMPANIES AND BUSINESS ENTITIES 523
14 INTERNATIONAL 526

Chapter 16 Scotland
1 OWNERSHIP OF LAND 529
2 OTHER INTERESTS IN LAND 534
3 TITLE TO LAND 540
4 TRANSACTIONS IN LAND 542
5 LEASES AND OTHER RIGHTS OF OCCUPATION 546

6 FINANCE AND INVESTMENT SOURCES 549
7 FORMS OF SECURITY 550
8 PLANNING AND BUILDING REGULATION 552
9 ENVIRONMENTAL MATTERS 553
10 DEVELOPMENT 555
11 TAXES 556
12 GRANTS AND INCENTIVES 556
13 COMPANIES AND BUSINESS ENTITIES 557
14 INTERNATIONAL 557

Chapter 17 Spain
1 OWNERSHIP OF LAND 561
2 OTHER INTERESTS IN LAND 564
3 TITLE TO LAND 568
4 TRANSACTIONS IN LAND 569
5 LEASES AND OTHER RIGHTS OF OCCUPATION 571
6 FINANCE AND INVESTMENT SOURCES 574
7 FORMS OF SECURITY 576
8 PLANNING AND BUILDING REGULATION 577
9 ENVIRONMENTAL MATTERS 580
10 DEVELOPMENT 582
11 TAXES 586
12 GRANTS AND INCENTIVES 589
13 COMPANIES AND BUSINESS ENTITIES 590
14 INTERNATIONAL 593

Chapter 18 Sweden
1 OWNERSHIP OF LAND 597
2 OTHER INTERESTS IN LAND 601
3 TITLE TO LAND 604
4 TRANSACTIONS IN LAND 605
5 LEASES AND OTHER RIGHTS OF OCCUPATION 608
6 FINANCE AND INVESTMENT SOURCES 612
7 FORMS OF SECURITY 614
8 PLANNING AND BUILDING REGULATION 616
9 ENVIRONMENTAL MATTERS 619
10 DEVELOPMENT 621
11 TAXES 625
12 GRANTS AND INCENTIVES 628
13 COMPANIES AND BUSINESS ENTITIES 629
14 INTERNATIONAL 630

Chapter 19 Switzerland
1 OWNERSHIP OF LAND 635
2 OTHER INTERESTS IN LAND 637
3 TITLE TO LAND 641
4 TRANSACTIONS IN LAND 642
5 LEASES AND OTHER RIGHTS OF OCCUPATION 645
6 FINANCE AND INVESTMENT SOURCES 648
7 FORMS OF SECURITY 650
8 PLANNING AND BUILDING REGULATION 652

9 ENVIRONMENTAL MATTERS 655
10 DEVELOPMENT 656
11 TAXES 660
12 GRANTS AND INCENTIVES 663
13 COMPANIES AND BUSINESS ENTITIES 664
14 INTERNATIONAL 667

Index 669

CHAPTER 1

Austria

Mag. Ivo Deskovic

Partner, Weiss-Tessbach, Vienna

CONTENTS

1 OWNERSHIP OF LAND 3
2 OTHER INTERESTS IN LAND 6
3 TITLE TO LAND 9
4 TRANSACTIONS IN LAND 11
5 LEASES AND OTHER RIGHTS OF OCCUPATION 14
6 FINANCE AND INVESTMENT SOURCES 16
7 FORMS OF SECURITY 18
8 PLANNING AND BUILDING REGULATION 20
9 ENVIRONMENTAL MATTERS 22
10 DEVELOPMENT 25
11 TAXES 27
12 GRANTS AND INCENTIVES 30
13 COMPANIES AND BUSINESS ENTITIES 30
14 INTERNATIONAL 32

CHAPTER 1

Austria

1 OWNERSHIP OF LAND

Austria has a codified system of law. For property, the main sources of law are:

(a) the Austrian Civil Code (*ABGB*, for general property and lease matters);
(b) the Rent Control Act (*MRG* for most types of apartments, offices and shops); and
(c) the Condominium Act (*WEG* for condominiums).

An important distinction is made between moveables and immoveables. Moveables are objects which can be removed without damaging their substance. Land and all items which are legally a part of land (which are all items that are permanently attached) are considered immoveables. The difference mainly concerns acquisition of title, as rights concerning immoveables can only be transferred by an entry in the land register, which is not required for the transfer of moveables. The principal form of land ownership is absolute ownership which creates a right in or against the land itself (a right in rem).

1.1 Types of tenure

1.1.1 Absolute ownership

Absolute ownership – which is by far the most common form of tenure – carries with it the right to own, occupy and dispose of the land and any buildings on the land, provided this does not conflict with third party rights or statutory provision. Any building or structure on the land will be treated as part of the land unless the right over it has been granted to someone other than the absolute owner (see 2.1.3). Therefore, moveables are considered immoveables if they form part of the land, ie when they are permanently affixed. However, there is an exception to this rule: where buildings are erected on land by persons other than the owner with the intention of removing them at a subsequent stage, they are considered to be moveables (*Superaedifikat*) under the Civil Code. These buildings are not considered part of the land and are subject to special property laws (see 2.1.3). Absolute ownership carries with it the right to the soil below and the air space above. However, certain minerals (such as salt which belongs to the state, and uranium, silver, gold, platinum which belong to the finder) are excluded.

1.1.2 Leasehold

Austrian law does not recognise the concept of leasehold as a right in rem or interest in land as in some common law countries. However, there exists a concept of building rights under the Building Rights Act (*Baurechtsgesetz*). These building rights (which should not be confused with the *Superaedifikat* dealt with in 2.1.3) may be granted where a right less than absolute ownership of a building or of land is intended, such as a right to occupy land for a limited period, but it confers greater rights of ownership and security than the usufruct described at 2.1.2. It will grant the exclusive right to use and occupy the property and is fully transferable; the grantee will own the building for the duration of the building right. Building rights are not common in Austria, and, until a reform of the Building Rights Act in 1990, they could only be established over land owned by the federal government, the states, the municipalities, or other public bodies, and for a fixed period of between 30 and 80 years. Since 1 July 1990 they have become available over all types of land and for periods of between 10 and 90 years but are still not popular, mainly because they are not a traditional form of ownership. (For further comment on building rights granted over private land, see 2.1.3.) Building rights are created by a contract (to be notarised) between a landowner and building right owner, which needs be registered in the land register in a similar way as absolute ownership. The usual arrangement closest to that of a lease is the tenancy (*Miete*); the terms on which tenancies are granted and other aspects of tenancies are dealt with more fully in section 5.

1.1.3 Joint ownership

Property may be owned by two or more persons (*Miteigentum*). Each joint owner may (without the other owners' consent) encumber the land in proportion to his share or dispose of it. Joint ownership is created either by agreement or, very often, as a result of inheritance. The joint owners will only be entitled to a notional part of the land and not to certain physical parts. The administration of jointly owned land is carried out by the owners together, or by an administrator appointed by simple majority. Decisions for the ordinary course of business are taken by simple majority (or by an administrator, if appointed). Other decisions require unanimous vote. Each of the joint owners has the right to request the termination of the joint ownership and where this is possible the estate will be divided between the joint owners in proportion to each share. The other owners will have no pre-emptive rights. Frequently, however, one owner will buy the other shares to save the property from being auctioned. Where the division is impossible, the joint owners' request will result in the sale of the property in a public auction and the distribution of the proceeds of sale.

1.1.4 Condominia

Condominium ownership (*Wohnungseigentum*) occurs where a building is divided into privately owned units. Every owner owns a notional part of the building with an exclusive right to use, possess or even dispose of one particular apartment. The common areas of the building belong to all owners together. The rights over the common parts combined with the absolute rights over the individual units are not separately disposable and together constitute the two elements amounting to condominium ownership, which itself is fully transferable. Condominium ownership is created by a (notarised) contract and its registration in the land register. As for the administration of condominiums, the same rules apply as for joint ownership (ie ordinary business is decided by simple majority or the appointed administrator; extraordinary matters require the decision of all owners unanimously). Condominium ownership is available for all types of property, regardless of the use to which the individual unit may be put.

1.1.5 Lesser rights of occupation

The only lesser rights of occupation that can be created are the *Leihe* where the land is lent to someone free of consideration for a certain period of time, or the *Precarium*, which is similar to the *Leihe*, but the owner retains the right to cancel the agreement and repossess at any time without notice. Both can be created by an informal agreement where the borrower makes no payments other than the ordinary maintenance costs. The various rights to use and enjoy land not amounting to rights of absolute ownership are dealt with in sections 2 and 5.

1.2 The role of the trust and the distinction between legal and beneficial ownership

The Civil Code provides for a concept of trust, which should not be confused with the Anglo-American institution. It is based on an agreement (usually informal) between trustee and trustor. It has no effect on third parties, who for all purposes can regard the person who is registered as owner in the land register as the real owner, who will also remain liable towards third parties (in many cases also to tax authorities). The trust system consequently plays little role in Austrian property.

1.3 Restrictions on ownership and dealing

1.3.1 There are few restrictions on the ownership of land, and these mainly concern foreign residents and foreign-controlled entities which must obtain authorisation before acquiring an interest in land (see section 14). These restrictions will remain at least until the end of this century even after Austria's accession to the EU, as the Accession Treaty provides for a five-year interim period, allowing Austria to amend the relevant provisions gradually. Minors and mentally disabled persons require a judge's approval to own or transact land. Companies (domestic or foreign) are not restricted from owning land. There are some legislative restrictions on the extent of the rights of landowners, which are mainly aimed at protecting the public interest and include planning regulations, rights of access, and compulsory purchase. There are also restrictions aiming at protecting private interests such as laws regulating the rights of neighbours.

1.3.2 There are certain restrictions on the disposal of agricultural and forestry land or sales to foreign individuals or foreign-dominated companies, which require prior approval by the local authorities without which any sale and registration in the land register will be void (see section 4).

1.4 Adverse possession and acquisitive prescription

Acquisitive prescription (*Ersitzung*) creates title in the possessor after 30 years' uninterrupted possession of land by the possessor in good faith. It creates a positive title even before it has been registered in the land register. It is therefore (apart from acquisitions in public auctions and as a consequence of inheritances) one of only three situations where title to absolute ownership is acquired before registration in the land register. The importance of the concept of acquisitive possession is in fact limited in practice as all land is registered in Austria. Consequently there is only very limited room for taking possession of third-party land – particularly in good faith, where such land is registered in the name of someone else in a public register. It arises mainly in agricultural areas, where the physical borders between the plots of land by frequent use of agricultural machinery may have moved from their original place.

2 OTHER INTERESTS IN LAND

There are various interests in land which confer rights less than absolute ownership or possession. These may be public or private. The most common are servitudes, usufruct, building rights, *Superaedifikat*, mortgages, rights of pre-emption and local land charges.

2.1 Servitudes or easements, usufructs, building and dwelling rights

2.1.1 Servitudes

A servitude (*Dienstbarkeiten*) is the right to use or enjoy the produce of another's land. The servitude imposes an obligation upon the landowner to tolerate or to abstain from certain activities for the benefit of the holder of the right. It can never call for a positive obligation. It is necessary to distinguish between real and personal servitudes. The real servitude (*Felddienstbarkeiten*) is a right in rem over land such as the right of way, the right to drive cattle across land or the right to graze livestock (*Weidedienstbarkeiten*). The creation of all servitudes requires a notarised agreement between the parties and registration (see section 3) in order to be valid and enforceable. As with absolute ownership they may also be created by acquisitive prescription (after 30 years, see 1.4). A servitude is always for the benefit of the owner from time to time of other land and will therefore pass with the ownership of the dominant and servient tenements. They are made in perpetuity.

2.1.2 Usufruct

The most important (non-transferable) personal servitude (which is also a right in terms of binding the owner from time to time of the land), also known as usufruct (*Fruchtgenuß)*, enables the holder of the right to use and possess the property belonging to another for a period of time provided the holder does not treat it in a manner inconsistent with the landowner's substantive rights of ownership; unless otherwise agreed the beneficiary will not therefore be able to alter the use of the land. The usufruct is usually made for the lifetime of the beneficiary.

2.1.3 Building and dwelling rights

An alternative, but not a very popular way of owning buildings, is the *Superaedifikat*. This is one of the rare cases (the building right granted over publicly or privately owned land being the other) where the ownership in a building and the land it stands on, do not coincide. This is only available for buildings which are not built to be there in perpetuity. It is therefore commonly available for buildings at fairgrounds or exhibitions (even if built for some number of years). The *Superaedifikat* is frequently used for buildings (such as office buildings) above railway stations. In these cases the railway operators still have the ownership of the land required for the rails and the station, but the office developer owns the office building. The creation of a *Superaedifikat* is comparable to the right to build described in 1.1.2. The building right granted over privately owned land distinguishes itself from the *Superaedifikat* in so far as the buildings constructed over it are intended to be there in perpetuity and once the right comes to an end, the building will become the property of the landowner. The *Superaedifikat* is instead rather more akin to the right to place one's building upon the land of another and to subsequently move that building and place it elsewhere. Other personal servitudes, including dwelling rights, are created by agreement between the parties (and sometimes by will) and registration (see section 3). They are usually created for the lifetime of the holder or for a certain term. They only give the holder the right to personally occupy the property, or certain designated parts of it.

2.2 Restrictions on use and other restrictions

Absolute owners may enter into restrictions on the use of one piece of land to protect the amenities and value of another piece of land. It is possible to impose positive obligations, in the form of burdens, on land so as to bind absolute successors in title, eg the payment of annuities. It is necessary to distinguish between real burdens imposed on the owner from time to time of the land and burdens imposed upon specific individuals. Both types of burden require registration. (Public law restrictions under planning and other legislation are commented on at section 8.)

2.3 Mortgages

There are several types of mortgage which can be secured on land, which include the 'running account' mortgage (*Höchstbetragshypothek*) and the 'composite' mortgage (*Hypothek*) on which specific comment is made at section 7. Courts can make charging orders to secure judgment debts. Other private rights in the nature of security, eg the seller's lien for the unpaid purchase price on sale of a property, can only be secured as a composite mortgage.

2.4 Contracts and options

A preliminary contract for sale will not give the buyer an interest in the land before its registration even if there is an unconditional contract for sale. The same will happen when there is only an option or right of pre-emption. These contracts only give the (potential) buyer an obligatory right against the contracting party(ies). The right of pre-emption (*Vorkaufsrecht*) enables the holder of the interest to be given the opportunity to purchase the property against which the interest is registered at the price which was offered by a third party. The holder of the interest must make his decision within 30 days. The right to repurchase (*Wiederkaufsrecht*) grants the seller the right to repurchase the land under the conditions of the original sale contract. The right is not transferable. The registration of the right entitles the seller to enforce the right not only against the original buyer but also against subsequent buyers of the land. Where the right to repurchase is not registered, it will only be enforceable against the original buyer with whom the agreement was entered into. If it is sold to another party who in good faith believes in the unencumbered ownership of the seller, the beneficiary of the non-registered right will only have a claim for damages against the seller.

2.5 Public or municipal charges

Properties are encumbered with obligatory liens with respect to payment of property tax. Other public charges may be registered in certain situations, such as registrations of safety areas in the close neighbourhood of airports.

2.6 Other interests

There are no relevant interests in land, other than those already noted.

2.7 Liabilities attaching to the land

There may be liability under the provisions of the Civil Code regulating the rights of neighbours for the unreasonable use of one's land to the detriment of an adjoining owner. Obligations are also imposed under the Historic Sites Protection Act (*Denkmalschutzgesetz*) for the repair and preservation of buildings designated as being of interest. The owner of land is strictly liable for environmental damage under the Water Act, if the person who actually caused such damages cannot be found or otherwise cannot be made liable. There is further strict liability for damages following an accident that a person has using a street, path or similar (such as a bridge). Here the owner of the land on which the street or path is situated will be liable, unless the injured person had no right to use the street (eg streets which have been closed off to the public). Finally, there are fiscal liabilities which attach to the land. General comments on tax are made in section 11.

2.8 Legal and beneficial interests

There is no distinction between legal and beneficial ownership in Austria.

2.9 Protection of interests

A number of interests (such as mortgages, usufruct, securities, dwelling rights, building rights) cannot be enforced against the land and subsequent buyers unless protected by some form of registration (see section 3). Private (ie not registered) interests will be enforceable without registration only between the parties who entered into the agreement, and not against successive landowners. Tenancies do not require registration to be protected.

2.10 Priority of interests

Priority between interests will depend on the date that an application for registration was made, so that the first in time prevails. There are no exceptions to this principle.

3 TITLE TO LAND

3.1 Proof of title

Title to land may only be established by registration in the land register (*Hauptbuch*) which covers the whole of Austria. Every transfer on sale of ownership will require registration. Other interests requiring registration are servitudes, burdens (see 2.2), building rights, mortgages as well as rights of pre-emption and of repurchase. Tenancies do not require registration. Until the transfer of land is registered, the buyer's legal title is insecure. If a fraudulent seller sells the land more than once, the buyer who registered the transfer first is considered the owner. The only remedy open to the other buyer would be to claim compensation against the seller. The 'principle of determination' requires all rights registered with the land register to be clearly determined rights, attached to one determined piece of land only and each piece of land registered must have clearly ascertainable rights attached to it. Therefore, where there is an assignment of the total assets owned by one person, title of ownership must be transferred individually for each single piece of land by registration in the land register. The only disposals of land not requiring registration are those by way of succession, which will be evidenced by the probate document (*Einantwortungsukunde*) issued by the court, and sale by public auction or acquisitive prescription. The land registers are open for inspection by the public.

3.2 Land registry and the land registers

The land register is kept by the local lower court (*Bezirksgerichte*).

3.2.1 Plans

All parcels of land within a district carry a specific register number (*Grundbuchseinlage*). They are described by plans. The boundaries shown are definitive. Searches can be made by reference to the land, street number or to the parcel number, but only the owner has a right to search by reference to his name.

3.2.2 Content

The register consists of the document collection (*Urkundensammlung*). The document collection contains certified copies of the documents which serve as the basis for the entry into the register. The register is further subdivided into three folios. The A-folio (*Gutbestandsblatt*) describes the actual address and plots forming part of the land, as well as those plots which have been added to or separated from the property. The B-folio (*Eigentumsblatt*) shows the owner or owners of the land as well as previous owners. The C-folio (*Lastenblatt*) shows any encumbrances on the land such as mortgages, servitudes, real burdens and rights of pre-emption. Applications for registration in the land register must be accompanied by the relevant documentation showing valid legal title and executed in the form of a legal transaction, either by notarisation or by court order. If the interest has been transferred several times without registration following every transfer, the party which eventually acquires ownership should apply for registration of title by producing the contractual documents relating to each previous transfer prior to his acquisition of the land or interest.

3.2.3 Errors

There is a presumption that the content of the land register is accurate and that all rights and obligations connected with the land in question have been included. If it is established that an error has been made in the register, there are provisions for compensation and/or rectification.

3.3 Passing of title

Until the legal transfer of ownership has been registered in the land register, the parties' rights are merely contractual. Although possession may pass early (eg under the terms of the sale contract) this will never give the buyer any absolute rights. Once registered, the transfer of the interest will be binding upon third parties, as well as between the parties to the agreement. Therefore legal title only passes upon the registration being completed.

4 TRANSACTIONS IN LAND

The most common transactions in land are the sale and purchase of the land, and the creation of a mortgage to secure a loan.

4.1 Procedure

4.1.1 A typical transaction begins by the parties negotiating the principal terms (eg the exact definition of property to be sold and the purchase price). In many cases the results of such negotiations will be subject to contract or due diligence. One of the first steps that a lawyer will undertake in a transaction is the title search. Where there are reasons to believe that an environmentally difficult question may arise, an environmental investigation is usually undertaken after the parties have agreed the principal terms such as the purchase price. However, at this stage the parties are usually not fully bound. Once these investigations have been finalised (and the buyer has found sufficient financing) the parties' lawyers will negotiate the details of the contract. Once these details have been established the parties are fully bound (even before signature on the contract document).

4.1.2 The next step is the execution of the purchase contract which requires notarisation. At the same time the seller will hand over to the buyer a 'priority statement' (*Rangordnung*), which is registered in the land register on a particular date and allows the buyer to enter his name in the land register once the contract is fulfilled in all other respects, with retrospective effect from the date on which the priority statement was issued. If the seller sells for a second time and the second buyer is registered between signing and registration of the first contract, the first buyer with the priority statement can claim for deletion of the second buyer from the register. This gives him full protection for the time between signing and closing. Very similar procedures apply to mortgages, where the lender can also be protected by a priority statement. At the date of signing the purchase price is usually deposited with the buyer's lawyer as escrow agent with instructions to release the funds to the seller as soon as the ownership of the buyer (with the retrospective date of the priority statement) has been registered. This escrow agent will also hold the purchase contract and will be responsible for the registration of the ownership of the buyer.

4.1.3 If there are rights of pre-emption or rights to repurchase, the contract is usually made conditional upon the beneficiary of such rights not having exercised them. The beneficiary is then given the opportunity to exercise his rights between signing and closing. A contract may also be conditional upon approval by the land transfer commission (for agricultural property or where a foreigner purchases). This authorisation must be sought before application to the land register for registration is made.

4.2 Contract terms

4.2.1 Under general Austrian contract law the seller will always have to warrant (without explicit statement in the contract) the usual characteristics of the property sold. In many cases he will undertake further warranties, such as the existence of a building permission. Other warranties may be for the lack of environmental liabilities, or where buildings are divided ino a number of existing apartments, that particular apartments are at the point of sale free of any leases or other encumbrances. A warranty as to title is usually given although the buyer will be able to rely on the land register. Warranties as to size are very rare, as the buyer will rely on what he has seen or investigations made by his surveyors. Sellers may, however, contract out of all warranties. This will be restricted by the general principle of good faith which will not allow the seller to exclude warranty as to defects of which he has positive knowledge. Usually no deposit is payable as the full amount will be paid, upon signature of the agreement, to the agent lawyer who then holds the amount in escrow.

4.2.2 Contracts usually provide for the relevant date for transfer. This is then usually the date when possession is handed over (although ownership will not be transferred until registration), and that is also the date on which risk, expenses and income will pass to the buyer. Very often this date is taken as the first of the month following the transaction for ease of calculation. Insurance usually remains with the property and therefore is transferred to the new owner, although the new owner will have a right to terminate existing insurance with a short notice period. If one party fails to complete, the other party will have the right to insist on completion (and charge for all damages incurred by reason of the delay, such as interest), or will have the right (after a reasonable notice period) to rescind the contract. Warranty claims for land have a three-year limitation period. However, the contract may provide otherwise, and frequently does.

4.3 Formalities

All contracts for the sale of an interest in land must be in writing and the signatures of the contracting parties must be legalised by a notary public or by court order. It is important that the contracting parties are clearly identified by their name, address and date of birth (or in case of companies, by their registration number). However, a contract to sell land can be valid if it is not in writing. Austrian law extends the recognised principle of oral contracts to include the sale of land. However, for the purpose of registration of ownership (and the buyer will not be the owner before his name has been entered into the land register) a written and notarised contract is required. Failure to formalise such a contract will give the buyer a right to sue the seller for his notarised signature. In this case he will have to prove that a full agreement (in every detail) had already been reached orally. The signatories may also be represented by their agents, in which case these agents will require a notarised power of attorney for the purpose of registration.

4.4 Fees, costs and taxes

4.4.1 The buyer will usually pay the land transfer tax, the notary fee, the registration fee, and the fee of the lawyer drafting the contract and acting as escrow agent. In many cases the seller will not have to pay the estate agent's fee (although this depends on his agreement with the estate agent). Unless otherwise agreed the estate agent has the right to collect three per cent of the purchase price from either party. Usually only the seller instructs an estate agent, but sometimes both seller *and* purchaser instruct agents. Estate agents' fees are only chargeable in the event of successful transactions.

4.4.2 The fees of the notary will depend on the purchase price and follow a relatively complex fee structure. It is possible for only one notary to be instructed, acting for and paid by the buyer. Normally, however, the seller also instructs a lawyer, seller and buyer paying their own legal fees (unless otherwise agreed). Lawyers' fees depend on the value of the transaction, again following a complex fee structure. In property matters it is rare that a lawyer will agree to hourly rates and the total combined legal and notarial fees will range between 2.5 and 5 per cent of the transaction costs (high value transactions will normally entail a smaller percentage of fees).

4.4.3 Transfers of land are subject to a land transfer tax, under the Land Transfer Tax Act (*Grunderwerbsteuergesetz*). The tax is charged on a transfer of absolute title or usufruct, and when all shares of a company that owns land are transferred to a single owner. Land transfer tax is charged at 3.5 per cent of the purchase price (reduced to two per cent where the transfer is between close relatives), although under special circumstances it may be charged on the actual market value of the land itself. The transfer agreement will stipulate which party will bear the cost of the land transfer tax, and often imposes the obligation on the buyer. The contract must be filed with the tax office within one month of signing the contract. All the parties involved, including their lawyers, are obliged to ensure that the filing formalities are complied with. The tax is assessed usually within one or two months and payable within one month after the assessment is served (usually on the buyer). Failure to pay in time will result in fines up to the amount of tax due.

4.4.4 A further registration fee of one per cent of the consideration is due to the land registry.

4.4.5 In total the fees of a property transaction (including taxes) usually amount to between seven and ten per cent.

4.4.6 The lawyers', notary's and agent's fees will attract 20 per cent value added tax (VAT), which may be recovered as pre-tax by companies. This applies whether the parties to the transaction are EU nationals or companies.

4.5 Professionals' roles

Estate agents are usually instructed to market and sell land. The chamber of estate agents, the Real Estate Agent Order (*Immobilienmakler Verordnung*), regulates the principal rules on how estate agents should conduct their businesses. Usually both parties will employ their own lawyers. The involvement of surveyors is not common. A notary will be required to legalise the signatures of the parties. Only one notary is involved.

5 LEASES AND OTHER RIGHTS OF OCCUPATION

A tenancy (*Miete*) is the typical contract for occupation where the occupier is not the absolute owner. A tenancy is a personal contract which only in very rare situations is registered in the land register. The traditional tenancy is for an indefinite period of time, but this may change as a result of changes in the law effective from 1 March 1997. The Rent Control Act (*Mietrechtsgesetz*), which applies not only to residential but also to commercial premises, regulates rent and imposes restrictions on the landlord's ability to terminate the tenancy agreement (see 5.3). Short-term leases used to be rare. If a lease for a term was permissible (eg in buildings constructed after 1953 without government subsidy) the usual term was three or five years. In some cases a 10-year term could also be agreed. The recession of the 1990s had a very negative impact on the Austrian rental market. Subsequently landlords who can agree a term lease (eg in houses which were built after 1953) now try to agree short terms to take advantage of possible increases in rental value as soon as possible by obtaining vacant possession of the premises and finding a new tenant. Under the new legislation it is expected that term leases will become more common.

5.1 Rent and other terms

5.1.1 The usual lease contract will contain a rent review clause linked to the Austrian consumer price index. The landlord is prohibited from imposing rent increases higher than the consumer price index (unless it concerns a building which does not fall under the Rent Control Act in which case the landlord has the right to terminate the lease or to increase the rent). The Rent Control Act determines the amount of rent payable, and the parties are usually not free to negotiate. Exceptions to the Rent Control Act are very limited but include garage space, hotel rooms, company flats (ie flats owned by the employer and occupied by employees in connection with their contract of employment), lease agreements for a term of less than 12 months, high standard apartments, offices or other business premises (within market value limits) and weekend and holiday homes (for further details, see 5.3 on rent control). Rent reviews (which work either way) are linked to the Austrian consumer price index. Usually the contract excludes movement of the index amounting to less than five per cent; in some cases the amount is 10 per cent. Rent is usually payable monthly in advance. Rents by reference to turnover are not common. Usually any assignment, subletting or disposal is prohibited. Internal repair is usually paid for by the tenant; external repairs by the landlord. Insurance is paid for by the landlord. The Rent Control Act does not impose a standard form of lease contract, but governs many other aspects of the lease (such as certain repairs and the right of use of common parts in the house). Usually the tenant will have to give a deposit amounting to three months' rent. Where a corporate tenant sells his business the lease rights will be attached to the business and acquired by the buyer without the need for landlord's consent. However, such a sale, as well as the sale of the majority of shares in a corporate tenant, will trigger the possibility for the landlord to increase the rent to fair market value.

5.1.2 The Rent Control Act also limits the amount of maintenance cost for the entire building that the landlord can charge to the tenants. In principle, anything that is common, eg supply of water to the building, lighting in the common parts, as well as the lift, insurance against fire and theft, the costs of a caretaker and a reasonable sum for service charges may be charged to the tenants as maintenance costs on top of rent. Internal repairs will normally be carried out at the tenant's expense, whilst external repair costs will be borne by the landlord. The tenant will have to obtain the landlord's consent if he wishes to undertake anything beyond minor alterations. In the event of default by the tenant or on its becoming insolvent the Rent Control Act entitles the landlord to terminate the lease. For recovery of possession, see 5.3.

5.2 Privity of contract and estate

The landlord and tenant will in general not be personally liable on the obligations of a lease once they have ceased to be the landlord or tenant.

5.3 Rent control and security of tenure

5.3.1 The Rent Control Act separates property into three different categories:

(a) property which is fully regulated;
(b) property which is partially regulated; and
(c) property which is not regulated.

Only limited types of property are unregulated by the Rent Control Act, and these are discussed at 5.1. Partial regulation involves both regulation of the length of the term and provisions as to termination. This regulation is extended to buildings built after 1953 without government subsidy, apartments in buildings which only have two self-contained units, condominium units in a building constructed after May 1945 and rented out by the owner of the unit, and buildings in a business park. By an amendment to the Rent Control Act effective from 1 March 1997, the freedom of the landlord to agree term leases has been increased. Any term is now possible for: buildings built without government subsidies after 1967; buildings with not more than two flats; premises in business parks; condominia in buildings built after 1953; and business premises in condominia. Condominia in buildings built before 1953 can be let for a maximum of three years. All other premises may be let on a term of between three and ten years. Subleases can now be made for a term of up to five years, and student leases may be for up to five years, or until the end of the student's studies. It is possible in some cases to append a number of term leases one after the other, as long as the total time limit is not exceeded. If a term lease is agreed, the landlord can only terminate the agreement early for cause, whereas the tenant will be free to terminate the lease at an early stage, although will usually have to stay at least one year. Termination for cause in this respect will include non-payment of rent, substantial adverse use of the premises, etc. Normal termination clauses require a notice period between one and six months.

5.3.2 Where the Rent Control Act does apply to a particular lease agreement, it restricts the parties' freedom to agree its terms and the circumstances under which it is permissible to terminate the lease. Permissible grounds include default by the tenant, unauthorised assignment of the lease to a third party and the death of a tenant (provided there are no surviving dependants wishing to exercise the option, under the terms of the original agreement, to take over the lease). Where the Rent Control Act regulates the agreement, rent increases are determined by statute. Rents will normally be increased where the consumer price index has grown by over five per cent. The consumer price index is published by a regulation of the Austrian Minister of Justice. Where the Rent Control Act does not apply, similar rent review clauses are usually agreed to.

5.4 Other legislative restrictions

The Rent Control Act also includes other restrictions such as an obligation for the landlord to do certain repairs (eg if the apartment was rented out with existing heating, it is the landlord's obligation to keep the heating running, and to deal with necessary repair; he will not, however, have to pay for the energy costs).

5.5 Method of measurement

Measurement is regulated by law. It is by reference to internal areas only and will exclude any common areas, lobbies, lavatories and other non-usable areas, ie what is commonly referred to as the 'net' internal area in other countries.

6 FINANCE AND INVESTMENT SOURCES

The most common way of financing property investment is by way of mortgage. Sale and lease-back has become increasingly popular.

6.1 Loan finance

The most common sources of loan finance are the clearing banks, saving banks and building societies. Most banks are privately owned (or publicly listed). This will soon also apply to Austria's second largest bank, Creditanstalt-Bankverein, which is in the process of being privatised. All large Austrian banks are specialised in property lending. The Austrian banking market is characterised by a universal banking scheme. This means that most banks have a licence to do all types of banking business (including property lending). Banks will usually not have such a strong relationship with their borrowers as to have a representative on the board. However, they will always lend on a full recourse basis, holding the borrower liable for any amounts they may not be able to get from a sale of the property. Property loans are usually made for 10, 15 or 20 years. Repayments will be on the basis of fixed and equal instalments over the term of the loan where the instalments are amortised, ie involve payments consisting of a mixture of interest and capital repayment in which the interest element decreases and the capital element increases during the period of the loan. Interest rates will usually be fixed. However, under current conditions, where interest rates are low, a variable interest rate may also be agreed. In this case the interest rate will usually be linked to one of the indices (such as the Secondary Market Yield) published by the Austrian National Bank. Security in the form of a mortgage is usually required before the bank pays the money to the borrower. For this purpose an escrow agent (a lawyer) will be involved to ensure that the loaned amount is used for the purchase price and at the same time that the mortgage is registered in the land register. Syndicated loans are not common and are only given for large property developments, although such developments have increased in recent years. Generally, banks will not lend above 80 per cent of value even when the creditworthiness of the borrower may justify this.

6.2 Investment or equity finance

Usually, equity finance is provided by private investors. However, in recent years, the number of property investment funds (including also some which are structured as listed corporations) has increased. These investment funds are usually organised by banks and are often listed on the Vienna Stock Exchange. Investors include institutional investors, private investors and banks as well as other financial institutions.

6.3 Mezzanine or mixed funding

Mezzanine or mixed funding is rare, and will usually only be found in large property development projects.

6.4 Sale and lease-back

Most larger businesses (in particular in the manufacturing industry) will own and occupy their own premises. In the recent past (not least for tax reasons) sale and lease-back of property has been used more often.

6.5 Tax leasing

For larger businesses, the property of the business is commonly owned by a separate company, or in case of a family business by a partnership formed by the owners of the company. The owner will then lease the premises to the operating company and give the operator either the right to build the required buildings, or to use them where the buildings already exist. This way the operating profit of the operating company can be decreased, and the income of the owner can be increased. The owner will therefore pay income tax but the corporation will pay less corporate income tax. If the corporation is also the landowner this would increase the income of the corporation on which the corporation would have to pay corporation tax, and, upon distribution of the dividends, the shareholders would have to pay further income tax. The structure of separate landowner and operator therefore minimises the exposure to a double tax charge.

6.6 Other types of property finance

As already noted the property investment fund has become increasingly popular. Other than that, there are no further types of property finance that have not been mentioned in the previous paragraphs.

6.7 Institutional investment

It should be noted that insurance companies, pension funds and banks are large property owners on the Austrian market. They usually have a preference for residential property or commercial property in prime locations. They often make a straightforward investment to purchase absolute ownership. Institutional investors favour a prime location, and therefore possible future value increase, more than the current income of the property.

6.8 Other investors

Other typical investors include private owners buying residential property to cover their own dwelling needs but with a view to renting out the other parts of the property, or to secure a safe and long-term investment to be inherited by future generations.

7 FORMS OF SECURITY

Security is usually required in property transactions. Only for larger creditors, for whom the property transaction only forms a very small part, will lenders not require security. The most common form of security is the mortgage. The emphasis on taking security does not seem to be undergoing any change.

7.1 Mortgages

7.1.1 There are two principal types of mortgage: the running account mortgage (*Höchstbetragshypothek*) and the fixed mortgage (*Hypothek*), both of which are rights in rem, require notarisation and registration, and cannot exist independently of a debt. Mortgages are confined to charges over land. The fixed mortgage is for a fixed amount which will be registered in the land register together with a certain amount of interest (usually specified as a percentage), a separate amount (also expressed as a percentage) for default interest and a sum for additional fees (such as the cost of enforcing the mortgage). The fixed mortgage is used when the borrower wishes to raise a specific amount needed for a single specific purpose, and which he wishes to draw down at a single point in time. The running account mortgage will have a maximum amount, specified in the land register. No additional interest rate or supplementary costs will be registered or secured. The accumulated interest and other expenses must be included in the maximum amount which is registered. The running account mortgage is usually resorted to by a borrower requiring a credit line which he may call upon at different stages or repay (in part) and call upon again (in part or in its entirety). The credit line will therefore usually be at least 10 to 20 per cent below the amount of the registered mortgage. The composite mortgage may be extended to both fixed and running account mortgages. The composite mortgage will merely state that the type of mortgage is registered against more than one property belonging to the same or to different owners. The different properties will then provide security for one (or more) credit line(s). In case of default by the mortgagor, the composite mortgagee may choose any of the charged properties in part or in full, to satisfy the claim, thereby granting greater security to the mortgagee. There is a one per cent stamp duty on mortgages and a one per cent registration fee upon registration in the land register.

7.1.2 The mortgagor will not be entitled to the property until it is sold at auction. The only way to enforce security is for the mortgagee to apply to a court, who will first have to render a judgment on whether the mortgagor is really in default, and then proceed by public auction organised by the same court. For the priority of mortgages, see 2.10.

7.2 Floating and other charges

Floating charges are not known in Austrian law. A general charge over all the assets of a borrower is also very unusual, and would not include land unless registered as a mortgage. However, any creditor of a landowner can have his claim secured by an enforceable mortgage, after he has received a final judgment by a court. He could subsequently proceed with the same auction procedure that would be required for a mortgage. To secure sums such as mezzanine loans, security is sometimes taken over a bank account. An assignment of rents can also be taken which can be registered at the land registry.

7.3 Performance bonds and guarantees

Guarantees and performance bonds are virtually unused in property transactions.

7.4 Credit insurance

Whilst available, credit insurance is also very unusual, as most lending is performed by Austrian banks, who do so on their own credit ratings.

8 PLANNING AND BUILDING REGULATION

The development and use of land is regulated by the Regional Planning Act, and each of Austria's nine provinces enacts local regional planning law.

8.1 Planning authorities

Ultimate control of all matters relating to town and country planning rests with each of the nine provincial governments (*Landesregierung*). On a local level decisions are taken by the municipality (*Gemeinde*) for its area. The provincial governments and the representatives of the municipality are elected representatives, so town and country planning is based strongly on political considerations.

8.2 Development plans

Each of the nine local governments pass regional planning laws which establish an overall utilisation plan for its province, attributing specific uses to each area. There will therefore be zones designated for, amongst others, residential, retail, office, industrial and recreational use. Based on these overall utilisation plans, the municipalities prepare a more detailed plan (*Flächenwidmungsplan*) for the development and use of land in the local area by dividing and subdividing it into the different selected zones in order to indicate where development may take place, including which form it should take to comply with the use designated within a particular zone, and where development is forbidden. This means that a use which does not conform with the plan will not be permitted. Public consultation takes place before plans are finalised.

8.3 Planning control and planning procedure

Planning control is based on the provisional Building Acts (*Bauordnung*) which are enacted by the nine Austrian provincial governments. They are different to some extent in each province. A building permit (*Baubewilligung*) under the relevant provincial Building Act is required for any construction, alteration or demolition. Permission is also required for engineering, mining or similar operations and any material change of use. There are provisions exempting minor alterations (ie if no material parts of the building, such as supporting walls and drains, are affected).

8.3.1 Where a building permit is required, the person who wishes to carry out the development has to file an application with the building control department of the municipal authority (*Baubehörde*). The applicant need not have an interest in the land, but in that event must obtain the owner's consent before applying for permission. Full details of the proposal supported by a construction plan showing the changes must be given. If changes to the initial proposal are made whilst the application to obtain the building permit is still in progress, the plan can be amended. The *Baubehörde* will in all cases (except for minor changes) decide after a first instance hearing has taken place on site. Neighbours are invited to that hearing and can raise their objections. Where the proposal does not contradict or violate any of the regulations contained in the relevant provincial Building Act (*Bauordnung*), objections by neighbours will not be successful and the building authority will have to grant the building permit.

8.3.2 The statutory period in which a permit must be granted is six months from the initial application. However, licence procedures frequently last longer although in simpler cases of minor alterations they can be quicker. There is no effective means by which the applicant can force the building authority to expedite the process, even where the authority exceeds the six-month period. The application can only be refused if the proposal contradicts the local *Bauordnung*. Conditions may be attached to the permit to ensure the proposal complies fully with that Act. If the application is turned down, the applicant has the right of appeal, which will be to the *Baubehörde*'s chamber of second instance. The appeal will have to determine whether the application was fully in compliance with the Building Act. There is no room for political discretion in this decision. A successful application may be challenged by neighbours, again on the grounds that it is not in compliance with the Building Act, and that development authorised by the permit would have a negative impact upon their own property (eg the building is too near the border line between the two plots or the building is higher than permitted by the local Building Act).

8.3.3 The permit attaches to the land. Development has to commence within a three-year period, otherwise the permit will become void, and the *Baubehörde* may issue an order for completion of unfinished developments. If the permit has lapsed, the applicant may apply for a renewal immediately. If a building has been erected without proper approval, the authorities can demand its removal but also have the power to demand reinstatement where unauthorised development has taken place. Developments have to be completed, otherwise the permission lapses.

8.3.4 In theory, there is no time limit for the enforcement of breaches, although a failure to enforce certain breaches may act as a bar to enforcement. In case of breach of any planning control which is regarded as an administrative matter, the *Baubehörde* can request and enforce an immediate halt to works, can require an unauthorised building to be removed, and if not removed by the applicant, the authorities may instruct a building firm of their choice with the removal costs to be met by the builder who carried out the unauthorised development. The same applies to unauthorised changes. In addition, the *Baubehörde* can levy fines on people who develop land without approval. Any decision of the *Baubehörde* can be appealed against in the *Baubehörde*'s chamber of second instance, which is also a government department. An appeal against the decisions of the second instance may be lodged in the Constitutional Court or the Administrative Court.

8.4 Building standards and supervision

The procedure for compliance with building standards will be part of the same process as the application for the building permit, and will take place at the same time. Building regulations deal with the design and construction of the building and the provision of services, fittings and equipment. They also require compliance with current technology and with the applicable health and safety, structural and fire regulations as well as provisions regarding sound and thermal insulation. Plans for the proposed work must be filed with the local authority for approval prior to building work being undertaken. Building control department officials have the power to inspect buildings to examine compliance with building regulations, and for this purpose may not be denied access to any part of the building. Owners and occupiers of the building are under an obligation to provide department officials with any information in relation to the building which is required.

8.5 Protection of buildings of special interest

The regulations dealing with the preservation of monuments aim to prevent the deterioration of monuments (or component parts of monuments or buildings) having special architectural, historic, scientific or other value, the preservation of which is in the public interest, and to ensure that alterations or demolitions are only carried out where special consent has been obtained from the Federal Office for the Preservation of Monuments (FOPM). There is a list of protected buildings and monuments; the obligation is to maintain the building as at the time of listing and does not extend to restoring it to its original authentic state. Subsidies and tax privileges are available for the preservation of monuments. The transfer of publicly owned monuments or buildings may only be carried out after the approval of the FOPM has been obtained. Privately owned buildings also require consent prior to sale and there is an obligation to provide the FOPM with information regarding the prospective buyer.

8.6 Expropriation or compulsory purchase and compensation

It is possible to expropriate land in full or in part in the public interest, eg for the purpose of construction of major infrastructure facilities. Expropriation of part of the land will always be in respect of a geographical part and never by way of lease. Very rarely it will be by way of a servitude over the land owned (eg where a pipeline for water or oil is driven). A public authority or a public utility, such as a railway corporation, may initiate expropriation proceedings. Compensation is at market value, assessed by an independent valuer. Expropriation and compensation procedures can take time, mainly due to valuation questions. Private developers cannot initiate proceedings.

9 ENVIRONMENTAL MATTERS

As has been the case throughout Europe in the last few years, there has been an increased awareness of environmental issues. Neighbours' rights have existed for many years which have led to liabilities for pollution. In addition to this, there has been an increase in specific environmental legislation introduced to protect the environment in a number of important areas and regulation extends to matters including soil, ground water and water contamination, air and noise pollution. The main sources of environmental liability can be found in the General Civil Code as well as the Water Act. A General Environmental Liability Act is currently pending in the Austrian parliament, but so far has not been passed for lack of agreement after heavy criticism from Austrian industry.

9.1 Protection against atmospheric and noise pollution

9.1.1 Under the provisions governing the rights of neighbours under the General Civil Code, a landowner may prevent emissions such as smell, noise, vibration and fumes from neighbouring land exceeding those which are reasonable in the locality and likely to affect the ordinary enjoyment of the property. There is a right of action where there is an emission. The affected landowner has a right to demand that the activity causing the nuisance cease and to claim compensation for the damage incurred. Where the emissions emanate from a licensed plant, the landowner may only claim compensation, although the liability on the operator of the plant is strict. This is a civil claim of one neighbour against the other to be decided upon and enforced by the ordinary courts. Standards in this case are set by independent experts, such as medical experts, etc. The Combustion Plant Clean Air Act (*Luftreinhaltegesetz für Kesselanlagen*) sets emission limits for combustion plant. The standards for other air pollution limits are to be found by reference to Austrian (or sometimes German) norms such as the *TA-Luft*. Violation of the Clean Air Act for Boilers or other standards will primarily result in liability of the polluter. This is again a civil claim by one neighbour against another. The term neighbour is a wide concept, such that a neighbour can also be a person living far away, as long as the pollution would affect his property or health. Violation of the Clean Air Act for Boilers can result in an administrative fine.

9.1.2 There are no specific statutory limits in respect to noise. This is dealt with by independent experts in the general licence procedure for plant or buildings. Otherwise noise may equally result in a civil claim from one neighbour against another to be determined by independent experts (in particular medical experts). The liability will rest with the polluter.

9.2 Water pollution

The major source of water protection can be found in the Water Act (*Wasserrechtsgesetz*). In 1959 strict liability was introduced against anybody whose machinery caused, or whose actions or omissions resulted in water pollution (including ground water). The emission limits are set in a general Water Emission Regulation (*Abwasseremmisionsverordnung*) passed by the Minister of Agriculture. For each branch of industry there is a special Water Emission Regulation, containing special emission limits for this type of industry. The strict liability under the Water Act results in the polluter being liable to clean up the polluted water at his own expense, whether it was the result of exceeding emission limits or not. Since 1990 the landowner can also be made liable, if the original polluter cannot be found (or in particular where companies involved have ceased to exist, eg following liquidation). However, the landowner is only liable if he had knowledge, or should have had knowledge, of the polluting activity (whether he knew that such activity was creating pollution or not). If the pollution is in respect of a large area of land or affects a large number of people, this can result in a criminal liability, and may trigger custodial sentences.

9.3 Waste storage and disposal

The storage, transportation, disposal and treatment of waste require licences. Each of these licences is obtained under the Waste Treatment Act (*Abfallwirtschaftsgesetz*). The breach of the licence requirements or conditions set by the licence can result in an administrative fine as well as civil claims by a neighbour (again under the wider concept of neighbours). Local authorities are under an obligation to provide landfills for refuse disposal under the Waste Treatment Act.

9.4 Contaminated land

Only in the recent past has it become usual to include a property enquiry regarding pollution of the land in transfer transactions. Therefore it is not yet usual to make enquiries about nearby landfills. Under the Polluted Area Restoration Act (*Altlastensanierungsgesetz*), the provincial governments are under an obligation to notify a central register (*Altlastenkataster*) about existing polluted areas. However, this list is in no way conclusive as special investigations were undertaken only to a limited extent. The reason for collecting this information is that under the Polluted Area Restoration Act, a scheme of financing the restoration of such areas had been introduced. However, the funds for such activity are very limited. Under the Water Act there is an obligation to clean up contaminated water, which also includes the cleaning up of contaminated land that contains polluted water. There is no special rule for cleaning up polluted soil as such. If the polluter or the landowner cannot be found or their liability cannot be enforced due to factual reasons (such a lack of funds), the authorities are under an obligation to clean up at their own expense. The Austrian government will pay for this but will try to recover costs from the polluter or landowner, if at all possible. A draft bill is pending on the introduction of a General Environmental Liability Act. It would introduce strict liability for all polluters, including liability for polluters to prove that they are not the cause of the pollution (rather than for persons suffering damage to prove that the damage was caused by the defendant). The bill is under heavy scrutiny in particular from Austrian industry which perceives it as an unnecessary burden on the Austrian economy.

9.5 Environmental impact assessments

On 1 January 1995 the Environmental Impact Assessment Act (*Umweltverträglichkeitsprüfungsgesetz*) was introduced. It is basically in line with European

Directives in this area. For the construction of larger infrastructure projects, the application to obtain the appropriate licence must contain an environmental assessment focusing on the impact the project has on humans, animals and plants, water, soil, air and climate, biotopes and eco-systems, landscape and cultural resources. At the same time the Act introduced the possibility for environmental power groups (where there are 200 people living in the community in which the project is planned or a neighbouring community) to raise their objections and appeal against approvals (including a second appeal to the Constitutional or Administrative Court).

10 DEVELOPMENT

10.1 Development projects, structures and vehicles

The simplest development project will involve the purchase of a site by an owner and the construction by the buyer of the premises he requires using his own builder. In many cases, however, the developer and owner will not be identical. The law distinguishes between a landowner constructing on his own premises using building materials belonging to another, constructing on premises belonging to another with one's own materials and building on premises belonging to another with another's materials. A buyer may sometimes approach a developer to arrange both the site and development, but it is more common for developers to find a site and build on it for their own risk and benefit. There are also a number of construction firms that own property development companies or initiate developments. Construction firms will often form a joint venture (*ARGE*, which in Austria will not have a legal standing separate from the members) to coordinate their different skills and workforce. The joint venture structure will involve an agreement between its members coordinating the tasks. Although the joint venture may trade under a separate name, its members will be regarded as contracting parties with suppliers or sellers to the joint venture. Consequently, all members will assume all liabilities for the joint venture. Large developments will commonly be funded by syndicated loans and an equity part contributed by the developers.

10.2 Building contracts and appointment of professionals

10.2.1 Typical forms of building contracts

The typical form of building contract is a contract between the owner (or developer) of the property with a building firm that takes overall responsibility and subcontracts to the necessary specialists. A fixed price is usual, but there will always be an allowance for the main contractor to charge for extra (unexpected) work. It is not unusual that, in spite of a fixed price contract, the final costs exceed the quoted price by 10 per cent or more. The liabilities of the contractor will be regulated according to the Civil Code and the provisions of the contract. The main contractor takes responsibility for all of the work undertaken, including that of subcontractors. The only person who generally contracts directly with the owner (developer) is the architect, who takes responsibility for the structure and design. Construction firms usually give a fixed price for the overall development which is based on an estimate of the overall size of the project (eg by cubic metres), which will include their fee as a profit margin. The fee of the architect is based on the financial volume of the project.

10.2.2 Common terms

The terms of the main contract usually provide that the owner pays in instalments (usually monthly) during the period of the project being built. They also provide for a final computation and invoice after the end of the project. Five or ten per cent of the cost is normally retained to secure the making good of defects. The architect will supervise the stages of construction. There is usually a date by which the project should be finished containing penalty payments in case of delay. Termination of the contract is usually only provided for in the event of default.

10.2.3 Standard form of contracts

There are no standard forms of contract.

10.2.4 Appointment of the professional team

The architect is usually responsible for the design and supervision of the building. In many cases he will also take care of tendering procedures to identify the best construction firm, and be responsible for any other professional expertise which needs to be brought in. The fee of the architect is usually defined as a percentage of the building costs.

10.3 Those involved and their roles

In larger developments the owner of the land instructs a separate development company and/or appoints a development manager. An architect is instructed to undertake the design and to prepare the application for the building permit. He will supervise the project and certify completion. Either the architect or the development manager will carry out competitive tendering procedures to obtain the best offer from construction firms. Construction firms then appoint their subcontractors (whose selection will usually involve the developer and the architect).

10.4 Defects and remedies

10.4.1 The developer has a remedy in respect of defects in design, workmanship and materials for repair against those who took contractual responsibility. If repair is not undertaken within a reasonable time the developer can instruct someone else with this task and claim damages to cover the further costs and the consequential damage arising from the delay such as loss of income and the costs of alternative accommodation.

10.4.2 Subsequent owners will usually have to turn to their seller for defects, who in turn may be reimbursed by the constructor or architect. In some cases the subsequent owner may have a direct claim against the construction firm (such as if the building becomes uninhabitable).

10.5 Defects insurance

Defects insurance, as a simpler and more viable alternative to suing the contractor and the professional team, is not generally available.

10.6 Copyright

Copyright in the design of the building is not protected.

10.7 Fees

Professional fees usually account for somewhere between 5 and 25 per cent of the overall cost of the project, varying according to the type and size of the project.

10.8 Taxes

Value added tax (VAT) is imposed on all construction at a rate of 20 per cent. In addition to this, the Taxation of Building Sites Act (*Bodenwertabgabegesetz*) imposes a tax payable on vacant plots which might be used for development and is dealt with in more detail at 11.2.

11 TAXES

11.1 Corporation tax

Companies resident in Austria are liable to corporation tax on their worldwide profits. These include capital gains. The liability, however, is subject to double taxation treaties available in the country where the profits originate. Companies incorporated in the Austrian Companies Register will be regarded as resident in Austria. Foreign companies may be regarded as having a branch, and therefore resident, if they have actual operations in Austria.

11.1.1 Tax rates

The rate of corporate income tax is 34 per cent. This rate applies to all companies regardless of size. There is a minimum tax of ATS15,000. The tax applies whether the company made a profit or not, and is therefore also payable if the company made a loss.

11.1.2 Computation and administration

In calculating its profits, a company may deduct expenses of a revenue or recurring nature (rather than a capital nature). These will have to be wholly incurred for the purpose of the trade of the company. Interest that is paid for financing the company's operations can be deducted. Corporation tax is administered by and paid to the *Finanzamt für Körperschaften*. Calculation is assessed on the basis of yearly tax returns or special inspections by the tax inspectors. Decisions can be appealed against to the *Finanzlandesdirektion*. The tax payer can then further appeal to the Constitutional or the Administrative Court. While it is open to the tax payer to arrange its affairs in such a way as to minimise tax, tax avoidance and any unlawful non-payment or evasion of tax are criminal offences.

11.1.3 Depreciation/capital allowance

The Income Tax Act (*Einkommenssteuergesetz*) provides a structure for deduction by way of depreciation of capital assets. This is computed in accordance with the useful life of the asset in question and standards have been set for most types of assets. The useful life of an asset will be admitted within the following ranges: 20–50 years for buildings, 5–10 years for plant and machinery, four to five years for office equipment and eight years for motor vehicles. Land cannot be depreciated. For property leased for residential or office use there are provisions for the deduction of irregular repair costs (ie not occurring annually) from income over a 10-year period. Regular repair and maintenance costs can be offset against the income of the year during which they occur. All depreciation will apply on a straight line basis. As a further incentive, an investment allowance in the form of additional depreciation of nine per cent (formerly 20 per cent) of the costs of depreciable fixed assets may be made. Prior to 1996, taxable profits arising from leases of land could be carried forward as an untaxed reserve for a 10-year period and set-off against later costs on repair and maintenance. Recent budget reforms not only revoked this mechanism but also required those who had accumulated such reserves in recent years either to make repair and maintenance related investments in their property by the end of 1998 or pay tax for the entire profit in the year of 1998. This rule has created a substantial incentive for home owners to invest in their property over the next two years.

11.1.4 Withholding tax

A withholding tax levied at a rate of 25 per cent applies on certain capital income, such as dividends, interest from securities and bank deposits where payment is made to residents and non-residents alike. This withholding tax constitutes a final tax settlement. Additionally, for other income from sources other than trade or business received by non-resident corporations and individuals, a withholding tax on gross receipts is imposed. There are many exceptions to this rule, primarily under double taxation agreements. No withholding tax applies to the payment of rent. As elsewhere in the EU, dividends from an Austrian subsidiary of a company in another EU member state are exempt from withholding tax if the parent has owned a minimum of 25 per cent of the subsidiary's shares for a period of two years.

11.2 Taxes on development value

The Taxation of Building Sites Act (*Bodenwertabgabegesetz*) imposes a tax payable on vacant plots which might be used as building sites. The purpose of the tax is to put higher charges on unused building sites to favour the sale of such plots to developers or encourage the owner to develop the same by himself. Therefore, potential commercial development sites are subject to the building sites tax, although vacant building plots with a fixed value of less than ATS200,000 are exempt. The building site tax rate for vacant building sites amounts to one per cent of the value of the site; as in the case of property tax, building site tax is also calculated on a yearly index.

11.3 Taxes on capital gains

The sale of land within 10 years of its purchase by the same owner will trigger speculation tax (capital gains tax) for resident *and* non-resident owners. Capital gains realised by a resident company are treated as ordinary business income and taxed at the regular corporate rate (34 per cent), unless exempt from tax under the participation exemption which applies to resident companies owning at least 25 per cent of the nominal share capital of a foreign corporation for at least 12 months. There is no tapering or reducing relief for length of ownership.

11.4 Taxes on owner of property

The property tax (*Grundsteuer*) under the Property Tax Act (*Grundsteuergesetz*) is a tax levied by the municipalities on the ownership of all property, payable by the owner (who may require reimbursement from the occupier under the tenancy agreement). The levy is calculated in accordance with the provisions of the Evaluation of Real Estate Act (*Bewertungsgesetz*). The basis for evaluation for each property is its fixed value, which is calculated in accordance with the Act. On the basis of the fixed value, a property tax index is calculated by reference to a statutory general tax index, which enables the municipalities to set an annual tax rate, payable in quarterly instalments. The property tax amounts to less than one per cent of the fixed value, and will therefore comprise only a negligible amount of the total cost of maintaining the property.

11.5 Taxes on occupier

Usually, the owner will require the occupier under their contract to reimburse the property tax. There are no other taxes chargeable on the occupier.

11.6 Taxes on land transfer

All transfers of land are subject to the transfer tax, payable by the transferee (see further 4.4.3). This is charged on the consideration paid at 3.5 per cent, although this is reduced to two per cent where the transfer is between close relatives.

11.7 Wealth taxes

There are no taxes on the wealth of individuals or companies.

11.8 Value added tax (VAT)

Businesses providing goods or services over ATS300,000, a year will charge value added tax (VAT) on the value of those supplies at a rate of 10 or 20 per cent. VAT is calculated on the amount of the consideration for the goods or services. It is regulated and paid to the *Finanzamt für Körperschaften*, the decisions of which are subject to the usual appeal (see 11.1.2). All rents will attract VAT and the rate is 10 per cent for residential property and 20 per cent for business premises.

11.9 Local and other taxes

There are no local taxes or taxes of general application other than those described.

12 GRANTS AND INCENTIVES

There are only a few grants available, mainly for the protection of preserved historic sites or for individuals building their own homes. The latter differ very much from region to region, and there are very few government incentives available in Vienna. Grants are usually only for limited amounts and only for smaller houses or apartments (eg less than 100 square metres).

13 COMPANIES AND BUSINESS ENTITIES

13.1 Limited and unlimited companies

13.1.1 A company may be a limited liability company or a joint stock corporation (also known as a public limited company). Lawyers are not allowed to limit their liability by entering into a company with limited liability. Other professions, such as accountants, auditors and civil engineers, are able to form limited liability companies; however, each of their members will retain unlimited liability for their own work. The other shareholders will not assume this liability. Where the company's members' liability is limited by shares, the members will not be subject to liability for the debts and liabilities of the company beyond the amount which they have to subscribe for their shares.

Usually, the company will have one or more executive directors. In larger companies (as well as in stock corporations) there will also be a supervisory board, which consists of supervisory board members, who do not intervene into the day-to-day business of the company. Directors are liable for fraudulent or wrongful trading and supervisory board members are also liable for their actions. However, supervisory board members have no power to represent the company and therefore will very rarely be in a position where they will be found liable for fraudulent and wrongful trading.

13.1.2 If a company limited by shares is not a public limited company (*AG*), it will be a private limited company (*GmbH*). The main differences between limited liability companies and public limited companies are the share capital (ATS500,000 for *GmbH* and ATS1,000,000 for *AG*) and the existence of a supervisory board for public limited companies, consisting of at least three members. Further, there are no share certificates for limited liability companies. The transfer of its shares can only be effected by a notarial deed executed in Austria. A public limited company will have share certificates which can be bearer instruments, freely tradeable. A public company may also be listed in the Vienna Stock Exchange subject to a number of further conditions.

13.1.3 The company is a separate legal person from its shareholders and directors. It has its own assets and liabilities. It will be taxed under different rules. The articles of incorporation set out what the company may or may not do. However, this does not make contracts outside the objects clause void, although it may entail the directors being liable to their shareholders. The procedure of incorporation requires a notarial deed and registration in the Companies Register.

13.2 Partnerships

A partnership exists where two or more persons carry on business in common, with a view to profits. Partnership is regulated by the Commercial Code (*Handelsgesetzbuch*). It can be created informally, without the need for a notarial deed or even a signed agreement, although the relationship of the parties will be regulated by the partnership agreement. The partnership does not have a separate legal persona for its individual members, but can acquire rights and liabilities, can be registered as owner in the land register and can sue under its name or be sued. Partnership agreements do not require formality, however the partnership should be registered in the Companies Register. Each partner is liable for all debts of the partners. Indemnities from the other partners are usually agreed.

13.2.1 A limited partnership can be set up under which certain partners have general liability (the general partners) and the other partners have their liability limited to a fixed financial contribution to the partnership. A company may validly be made into the general partner, liability of which is unlimited to the outside world, but whose members have only limited liability under usual company law principles. Under these circumstances, the limited partners will usually not have the right to take part in the management of the business or to bind the business. The directors of the company which is the unlimited partner (who can be identical to the limited partners) will manage and represent the partnership.

13.3 Other types of business association

Companies and partnerships are the principal forms of association recognised by law. Other unincorporated associations do not have legal recognition.

13.3.1 Trusts

Trusts in the Anglo-American sense are not available under Austrian law. However, in 1991 a *Privatstiftungsgesetz* came into force, which introduces a similar institution to the Liechtenstein *Stiftung*. It is a registered entity (in the Companies Register) that can hold assets contributed by the founder and on behalf of certain beneficiaries named in the forming document. It is gradually becoming an important vehicle for wealthy individuals, as it can accumulate income without taxation, although any distributions to the beneficiaries will be taxed at the time of distribution. The relatively high Austrian inheritance tax can thus be avoided.

13.3.2 Joint ventures

The joint venture is not a legal mechanism under Austrian law.

14 INTERNATIONAL

14.1 Restrictions or consents required for inward investment

Non-residents are under an obligation to obtain consent from the authorities before acquiring an absolute interest in land, a right of usufruct or applying for a building permit. The conditions with which a non-resident must comply are rigorous and authorities will only grant approval if the acquisition of the rights by the non-resident is compatible with, or in the economic, social, cultural or political interest of the country as a whole, or of the respective state or municipality. This restriction will remain in force for another five years following Austrian's accession to the EU. The Accession Treaty granted this period of grace to facilitate the adjustment of Austrian legislation. In some provinces (those where foreign ownership has no major impact) liberalisation has already been introduced (such as in the Burgenland).

14.2 Exchange controls

Austrian exchange control has been totally liberalised since 1989. The only means of control that remain are notification requirements for certain types of foreign transfers. However, failure to comply with the transfer notification requirement will not make the transaction void. Usually, it will not even result in a fine.

14.3 Restrictions and registrations on carrying on a business

Any business conducted in Austria will require a licence from the appropriate trade licensing authority. Any company wanting to obtain such a licence will have to nominate a person as the trade licence responsible person. This person must fulfil certain educational and practical experience criteria, and in particular must be an Austrian or EU citizen. Other citizens may be granted the same status under exemption rules. Foreign (non-EU) companies cannot obtain a licence since Austria's accession to the EU, although all EU companies and all EU nationals can obtain a licence under the same conditions as Austrian nationals or companies. Foreign (non-EU) companies having a registered branch office in Austria (registered in the Companies Register) may obtain a licence under the same conditions; however, they must nominate an Austrian or EU citizen as their trade licence responsible person. Again, exemptions are available for other foreigners.

14.4 Repatriation of income and proceeds of property trading and development

There are no consents or restraints involved in the repatriation of income and proceeds.

14.5 Withholding tax

Withholding taxes have been referred to at 11.1.4.

14.6 Double taxation relief

Austria has separate double taxation treaties with a number of countries.

CHAPTER 2

Belgium

CONTENTS

1 OWNERSHIP OF LAND 37
2 OTHER INTERESTS IN LAND 39
3 TITLE TO LAND 42
4 TRANSACTIONS IN LAND 43
5 LEASES AND OTHER RIGHTS OF OCCUPATION 47
6 FINANCE AND INVESTMENT SOURCES 51
7 FORMS OF SECURITY 53
8 PLANNING AND BUILDING REGULATION 54
9 ENVIRONMENTAL MATTERS 56
10 DEVELOPMENT 57
11 TAXES 60
12 GRANTS AND INCENTIVES 63
13 COMPANIES AND BUSINESS ENTITIES 63
14 INTERNATIONAL 66

CHAPTER 2

Belgium

1 OWNERSHIP OF LAND

Belgium has a codified system of law and the Civil Code is based on the Napoleonic Code. Property law deals only with rights in rem which are rights to the thing itself as distinct from a right to claim against a third party, ie a right in personam. In relation to the objects of a right in rem a further distinction is made between moveables and immoveables and this chapter deals only with immoveables. There are three types of immoveable: immoveables by nature (ie the land, the subsoil and vegetation), artificial immoveables (buildings and their appurtenances) and immoveables by destination (eg equipment and machinery in the nature of fixtures).

1.1 Types of tenure

1.1.1 Freehold or absolute ownership

The most important and frequently exercised right in rem is absolute ownership (*eigendom/propriété*) . It gives the right to use, enjoy, occupy and dispose of the land and any buildings on it, provided such use is not incompatible with legislation or third-party rights of ownership. An exception to the normal Civil Code rule that anything attached to the land is deemed part of the land is where buildings are owned under the building or surface right (*recht van opstal/droit de superficie*), see further 2.1.3. Under this, it is possible to own a building or part of a building itself separate from the land, unlike in common law jurisdictions. Minerals generally belong to the owner of the land although special regulations exist in certain areas and in relation to mines.

1.1.2 Leasehold

Leasehold in the Anglo-American tradition does not exist but the nearest equivalents are the right of *emphyteusis* and the surface right (see 2.1.3), which are rights in rem, and the rental agreement or tenancy (*huur/bail*) which is a right in personam. The right to build under a surface right will grant the beneficiary of the right full ownership of any structures he constructs on the land for the duration of the surface right, although the landowner will retain title to the land (see further 2.1.3.1). The rental agreement or tenancy (*huur/bail*) is a contractual agreement only and is dealt with in section 5; possible types are defined by statute and include civil, residential and commercial tenancies.

1.1.3 Joint ownership

When a property is owned by two or more persons, they are in a state of *indivisum*, by which each has a share in the property. This can occur accidentally, voluntarily or involuntarily. Accidental joint ownership occurs, eg when property passes to two or more heirs in the case of intestacy. As with other cases of accidental joint ownership, this cannot continue indefinitely other than by agreement of the parties. *Indivisum* may also be involuntary or imposed in which case it will be permanent, and the joint owners cannot request termination. This will apply whenever there are common parts of a building in multiple ownership. When different buyers acquire the property by agreement for common use, their joint ownership will be voluntary. They will agree the arrangements regulating the *indivisum*, including those for its termination. Each joint owner will have to bear a part of the charges, according to his use; each joint owner can freely dispose of his part; each joint owner has the use of the property; and all joint owners must agree to the transfer of any part. Any joint owner can apply to the court for sale, although the parties can dissolve the joint ownership by mutual agreement. There are special rules under the Civil Code regulating the arrangements for common ownership of walls between adjoining buildings.

1.1.4 Condominia

Condominium ownership occurs when units in a building, not necessarily residential, are privately owned by different owners, who will each be a co-owner of the common parts, and since 1995 condominium ownership may probably also apply to estates of buildings. The parties must agree a specific set of rules (*basisakte/acte de base*), and the different bodies which will govern the condominium. In the absence of an agreed set of rules, arrangements are implied by law. The rights over common parts combine with the absolute rights of ownership of the individual units, to constitute the parcel of rights making up the condominium ownership.

1.1.5 Lesser rights

Rights in rem to use and enjoy land less than a right of absolute ownership are dealt with in section 2.

1.2 Legal and beneficial ownership

The distinction between legal and beneficial ownership as found in common law jurisdictions does not exist, but there is a mechanism for issuing certificates allocating shares in the economic ownership of properties (see 13.3.3).

1.3 Restrictions on ownership and dealing

Both natural persons and legal entities, resident or non-resident, may own land. There are special provisions for certain categories such as children, the mentally incapacitated and municipalities. Originally, ownership was considered by the draftsmen of the Civil Code as an absolute right, in the true sense of the word. Over time, however, and due to economic, social and political concerns, ownership has been made subject to a number of public law limitations. These will include rights of expropriation, public rights of way, and planning and other restrictions as well as rights of pre-emption of a private nature and in favour of public bodies.

1.4 Adverse possession or acquisitive prescription

Long-term possession can lead to acquisition of the right of ownership of a property (*usucapio*). It will be necessary both to have possessed the premises and to have intended to keep them as one's own, not to have merely held them on behalf of another. Possession is enough but must be continuous, undisturbed, unequivocal, public and in good faith. If the claimant has no title, the period is 30 years, but if he does have title which for some reason is defective, eg through lack of formality, the period may be 10 or 20 years depending on whether the other party is resident in the same area.

2 OTHER INTERESTS IN LAND

There are interests in rem which confer rights less than those of absolute ownership over the land of others. These include servitudes, usufruct, (*superficies*, *emphyteusis*) and the right of use.

2.1 Servitudes or easements, usufruct, building and dwelling rights

2.1.1 Servitudes or easements

A servitude (*erfdienstbaarhede/servitude*) is a right in rem over one piece of land for the benefit of another piece of land. There will be a dominant and a servient tenement. Servitudes will arise by will, deed, prescription of 30 years and by designation of the pater familias. Apart from those rights arising from prescription and by will (in which case the right is often integrated in the will which will usually be notarised), servitudes created by deed and designation will require authentication by a notary. They will need to be entered in the register (see section 3), if they are to be enforceable against third parties. The most common are rights of access, rights of drainage, rights of passage, and rights of light and air. Transfer of the dominant tenement automatically transfers the benefit of the servitude, although third parties coming to the servient tenement will only be affected once the servitude is registered. Servitudes are in principle granted in perpetuity.

2.1.2 Usufruct

A usufruct (*vruchtgebruik/usufruit*) is a right in rem granting the beneficiary the right to use and enjoy property that belongs to another, and to receive its profits for a limited period of time provided he does not alter the nature or use of the land. It will arise upon inheritance but is otherwise rarely used except possibly for tax purposes. If created by deed, it will have to be notarised if it is to be enforceable against third parties. It will be for a fixed period of up to 99 years and may be transferred unless the parties agree otherwise (see also 2.6 describing the right of use).

2.1.3 Building, emphyteusis *and dwelling rights*

2.1.3.1 The right to build (*recht van opstal/droit de superficie*), or *superficie*, enables the holder of the right to build on another's land and own the building for the duration of the right, as the building right is a right of ownership of the building for a fixed period. It is a right in rem and limited in time to a statutory maximum of 50 years. Renewal may be agreed. The right may be granted for no payment or for a capital or rental payment. Unless otherwise agreed, all constructions or buildings erected by the holder of the right on the land will become the property of the landowner upon expiry but subject to compensation for the superficiary. *Emphyteusis* is similar and grants the holder a right in rem, who may enjoy the use of the land and its produce as if it were his own for a limited period of time in return for the payment of a fee (*canon*), often equivalent to a market rent. The holder may erect constructions and buildings which will be considered to be his property and which he may sell, rent out or use to raise a mortgage. On expiry of the *emphyteusis*, any structures which the holder has built will become the property of the owner of the land without compensation, unless otherwise agreed. However, if the agreement did not oblige the holder to construct, the holder will be entitled to remove such structures on expiry of the *emphyteusis*. This temporary right of ownership is a right in rem and can last for a minimum of 27 years and a maximum of 99 years. *Emphyteusis* is a slightly more extensive right of temporary ownership but in practice is very little different to the *superficie*, although the *emphyteusis* may be granted for a considerably longer period and will always be for consideration. In order to bind third parties, both the *emphyteusis* and the *superficie* must be notarised and entered in the register. The *emphyteusis* is a popular instrument in private development, and public authorities also often use it for the completion of important projects if funds are low and private investment is required.

2.1.3.2 The dwelling right is the right of a person to live in the house of another. It differs from the usufruct because the party granted the dwelling right may only use the house for his residence or that of his family. The dwelling right is a right in rem although it is not transferable. It will be enforceable against successors in title provided it has been notarised and entered in the register. It is very rarely used in practice.

2.2 Restrictions on use and other restrictions.

Private restrictions on land can be created, eg restricting the use of the land to agreed purposes although these will only be enforceable between the original parties. There are various public law restrictions. Planning law restrictions are described in section 8.

2.3 Private mortgages, privileges and charges

Monetary liabilities can be secured on land in a number of ways. Both privileges (*voorrechten/privilèges*) and mortgages (*hypotheken/hypothèques*) are rights in rem and grant the beneficiary a prior right to the sale proceeds of the land charged. Comment is made on mortgages in section 7. Privileges, which do not give a right to compel sale, simply give certain creditors the right to be paid in priority to other creditors out of the proceeds of certain assets. They are a form of preferential debt or lien. They will be either special, attaching to specific assets, or general, attaching to all assets of the debtor. To bind third parties, special privileges will need to be transcribed or registered. Special privileges for example protect loans made for the purpose of purchase, architects' and contractors' fees, and can protect a seller by securing payment of the purchase price in a similar way to a lien.

2.4 Contracts and options

Sale contracts and options do not grant a right in rem and are not enforceable against third parties (see further section 4 where these are dealt with in more detail and other types of contract are explained).

2.5 Public or municipal charges

Taxes may be treated as privileges, enforceable against the proceeds, but these are not necessarily charges on the property. There are no registers keeping a central record of all administrative and public law charges, orders or restrictions.

2.6 Other interests

The right of use (*gebruik/usage*) merely gives the right to receive as much of the natural profits from another's property as is necessary to satisfy the personal needs of the user or those of his family. Unlike the usufruct, it does not give the right to enjoy and occupy the land. The right of use is not transferable and is rarely used for immoveables. There are no other material rights in rem.

2.7 Liabilities attaching to land

The Civil Code provides that the person in possession of buildings is liable for any damage suffered by third parties caused by defects in the buildings or by lack of maintenance. Liability is strict and the damage need not have been foreseeable, but if the owner proves that it resulted from some other cause, eg an act of God, he will not be held liable. The third party always has the burden of proof as to the defect. There is a general duty of care to third parties in respect of any other injury or damage arising from negligence or lack of foresight on the part of the owner or occupier. There is further liability under environmental law (see section 9) and the laws of nuisance *(burenhinder-nabuurschade/troubles de voisinage*). Under the latter liability can arise where there is fault or an unreasonable use of land, or abuse of rights, or even where there is no fault in certain circumstances to preserve the balance between adjoining properties. Fiscal liabilities relating to land are described in section 11.

2.8 Legal and equitable interests

There is no distinction between legal and equitable interests.

2.9 Protection of rights and interests

Most interests in land must be entered in the register to be enforceable against third parties. The system of registration is explained more fully in section 3.

2.10 Priority of interests

This generally depends upon the date of entry at the register. Privileges generally take priority over mortgages.

3 TITLE TO LAND

3.1 Proof of title

The transfer of land as between the parties does not require registration. However, the transfer will only be enforceable against third parties after it has been copied or transcribed into the registers kept by the registrar (see 3.2). Only an authentic deed (*authentieke akte/acte authentique*), incorporating the terms of the private contract between the parties and recorded before a notary, or sale agreements notarised or recognised by a court judgment, may be entered in the register. All real rights in land and all leases of more than nine years must be entered in the register in order to bind third parties. The registers are open to the public, who may apply for a certificate regarding the status of the land. It should be emphasised that the registry is of deeds and not of title, although it will include the name of the present owner as indicated by the deeds.

3.2 Registration of land

There is one registry office per district (*arrondissement/arrondissement*), kept by the registrar of mortgages (*hypotheekbewaarder/conservateur des hypothèques*), and each one shows the transactions in relation to property in that district. The registry also keeps a daily register into which all deeds delivered and to be copied are recorded immediately, and a general register. There are separate cadastral registers (*kadaster/cadastre*) kept by the Ministry of Finance for fiscal purposes, where parcels of land are divided into cadastral units and registered under parcel numbers in a land survey register. They can be useful for anyone seeking specific information on a plot of land, eg plot size or the identity of the owner.

3.2.1 Plans

Plans of the cadastral units registered under parcel numbers in the land survey register are kept at the land registry offices. The plans are only indicative, but the cadastral units are used for a number of purposes.

3.2.2 Content

All real rights in land and all leases of more than nine years must be copied into the *overschrijvingsregister/registre de transcription* and all mortgages and privileges (see 7.1) over property will be entered into the *inschrijvings-register/registre d'inscription*. Other important issues relating to the property will be entered in the margin of the register eg a claim before the court for rescission of a purchase agreement.

3.2.3 Errors

Unlike some other countries, the registrar is not obliged to check on the validity of the transfer, and because the registry is one of deeds it carries no guarantee as to title. The entry in the register will only give evidence of transfer.

3.3 Passing of title

As between the parties the buyer becomes the owner from the date of the sale agreement (*verkoopcompromis/compromis de vente*), see section 4. This is to be distinguished from the moment the purchase becomes enforceable against third parties which will be from the moment of entry in the register of the authentic deed, not the date of the deed.

4 TRANSACTIONS IN LAND

The most common transactions in land other than rental agreements are the sale and purchase of land, the grant or assignment of surface rights and the creation of mortgages.

4.1 Procedures

4.1.1 For there to be a binding sale all that is strictly necessary is agreement or consensus on the main terms; no formalities are required. The agreement will be perfected from the moment the parties agree, even verbally, upon the object, price and principal terms. For evidential reasons, however, it is highly desirable to enter into a written contract to record the main details of the sale. This is commonly referred to as the private sale or preliminary agreement (*onderhandse verkoopcompromis/compromis de vente*), which will be fully enforceable between the parties. It will record the main details of the sale. The purchase will only stand against third parties, however, after it has been the subject of a formal contract entered into before a notary public in one of Belgium's official languages and in the form of an authentic deed (*authentieke akte/acte authentique*) and been transcribed in the registers (see section 3). The authentic deed will usually incorporate as faithfully as possible the terms of the private sale. Where the parties choose to authenticate the agreement, subsequent entry in the register must take place within four months and there will often be a clause in the private agreement giving an undertaking to this effect. It is possible to by-pass the private sale agreement and proceed directly to the notary and the authentic deed.

4.1.2 During the negotiation of any purchase (and of any building contract) it is usual to carry out an investigation as to title, any encumbrances (and the obtaining of any certificates from the registrar of mortgages) and burdens over the land, zoning matters such as permitted use, development rights and restrictions and environmental matters (see further section 9). Where the purchase is of a building, the buyer should obtain a rent roll review, the schedule of service contracts and check insurance matters.

4.1.3 Both options and offers are in common use. The offer is a unilateral promise which binds the promisor and gives the promisee the legal right to demand performance provided the offer is definitive, known to the promisee, and contains details of offer and price. An offer made to a specific party may only be withdrawn following reasonable notice. If the offer was made to all the world, it can be withdrawn without notice. As soon as an offer is accepted, the contract will be concluded. The option, on the other hand, is a contract entered into by both parties, eg where the seller agrees to sell to the beneficiary on the conditions stated in the agreement. The option differs from the offer in that it involves reciprocity at the outset. Completion of the sale will only depend upon the owner of the option. The parties must, therefore, agree the object and the price and include all the necessary terms for the transfer of land. It must also include the date of expiry and the formalities required for exercising the option. Often, the beneficiary of the option agrees to pay a premium to the seller if he does not exercise the right. If no time is specified, the option will be valid for a 30-year period and may only be dissolved by giving reasonable notice. Both offers and options are valid in the form of a private agreement and do not require authentication. It is important not to confuse these with agreements subject to 'suspensive' or 'dissolving' conditions.

4.1.4 The right of ownership can be granted, or acquired, subject to conditions. The agreement transferring ownership can be subject to different types of condition; the 'suspensive' condition, or condition precedent, must be fulfilled before the contract comes into force, typically the obtaining of a building permit or loan facility. The contract will only be triggered once the condition is fulfilled, and this cannot be within the sole control of one party alone. The sale can also be subject to termination on the occurrence of a 'dissolving' condition whereby the contract will come to an end if an event occurs.

4.1.5 There are a number of other specific contracts relating to the sale of land. The right of first refusal (*voorkeurrecht/droit de préférence*) is an agreement whereby the owner of the land grants a right of purchase to a specific person before accepting an offer by a third party. This will usually be ancillary to another agreement, eg a tenancy, where the landlord agrees to give the tenant the right of first refusal. By way of contrast with the option, the price and other terms need not be determined in advance. Another type of contract, the *verkoop met handgeld/vente avec arrhes,* provides for the payment of a sum by one party as security, but either party may waive the agreement. In the event of waiver by the payer, the other party will be entitled to forfeit the *handgeld/arrhes* sum. Where the party in receipt waives the agreement, he will have to compensate the paying party with twice the amount of the *handgeld/arrhes.* In practice, the payment is usually used as evidence of the agreement and as an advance payment on the purchase price to be forfeited to the seller in the event of breach by the buyer. Another type of contract, the *verkoop met recht van wederinkoop/vente à réméré*, gives the seller the right to repurchase the property within a set time and upon repayment of the purchase price and additional costs specified in the Civil Code. In the event of the right to repurchase being exercised, the original sale agreement will be dissolved and no new transfer agreement will be required. Finally, there is the sale under annuities (*verkoop op lijfrente/vente contre restitution d'une rente viagère*) by which the buyer pays the price by way of annuity.

4.2 Contract terms

Contracts will differ according to whether the property is residential, commercial or industrial and whether the premises are occupied. There are certain terms, however, which are common to all. There will normally be a detailed description of the property. It is usual for the buyer to insert a clause acknowledging that he has seen a copy of the owner's title and for the seller to include a clause stating that the property is sold unencumbered by debts, privileges or mortgages of any kind. A guarantee may be given as to the state of the property and a warranty may be extended by the seller as to defects (latent or visible) in the building, land or subsoil. Unless otherwise agreed, the seller will generally be liable for hidden defects which would render the property unfit for the use intended which is normally specified in the contract. A deposit of up to 10 per cent of the purchase price is usually paid when the private sale agreement is entered into, with the balance to be paid upon authentication by the notary of the sale agreement with penalties for failure to pay the balance. Both parties are entitled to appoint notaries if they wish, but must name both notaries in the contract. If there are two, the buyer's notary will be the 'instrumenting notary'. The private sale agreement must also state the date on which the authentic deed should be executed. A transfer of property and possession clause will be included which will usually provide for transfer from the date of execution of the authentic deed subject to the payment of the purchase price. There will also be provisions to determine the payment of taxes attaching to the property, which will usually be pro rata from the date of transfer. The contract will deal with existing rental agreements, fiscal liabilities and any existing management or maintenance agreements. The private sale agreement will usually state that the buyer will insure from the date of agreement or the date of transfer, although the law requires insurers to cover the property for 15 days after the transfer. Special attention should be paid to building contracts for residential property, and agreements to purchase buildings not yet constructed or under construction. Separate legislation governs these contracts and imposes a number of compulsory conditions to protect the buyer.

4.3 Formalities

There are no formalities required for an agreement to transfer land to be valid and enforceable between the contracting parties (see 4.1). However, to be enforceable against third parties, the agreement must be entered in the register of mortgages by a notary public. Before the entry can be made, the sale agreement should be executed in an authentic deed before the notary. Otherwise the agreement can take any form but must include details of the property for sale and the price to be paid. If the contract is for the sale or construction of buildings, and not just land, the contract must be in writing. Any long-term lease of more than nine years must be recorded before a notary if it is to bind third parties.

4.4 Fees, costs and taxes

4.4.1 The buyer will usually pay the notary's fees, the costs of the authentic deed and the property registration tax, but if the buyer fails to pay, the seller will by held liable as technically they are jointly responsible. Agents' or brokers' fees are usually paid by the party who instructed them and will range from two to three per cent of the value of a sale transaction and amount to approximately 15 per cent of the rent for rental agreements. Lawyers' fees will be paid by the instructing party. However, in certain sales (*vrij op naam/acte en mains*) it is common for all costs to be paid by the seller (except for the lawyer's fee) and to be included in the price.

4.4.2 Lawyers' fees will mostly be based on a combination of value and time spent. Lawyers may not charge on a contingency basis. A rough indication would normally be between 0.1 and 1 per cent. If more than one notary is appropriate, the notaries will usually split the single statutory fee.

4.4.3 Registration duty (*registratierechten/droits d'enregistrement*) is charged at 12.5 per cent of the purchase price, or of the objective market value (*venale waarde/valeur vénale*) when the tax administration considers that this is higher than the sale price agreed between the parties, and is to be paid upon registration within four months of the authentic deed. There is a reduction to five per cent for property traders and six per cent for small rural properties and small private houses. A fine of twice the duty may be payable for any misdeclaration of value. Leases, subleases and transfers of leases are subject to a tax of 0.2 per cent of the cumulative amount of rents and charges for the duration of the lease or, if this is indeterminable, to a tax of two per cent of the annual amount. Registration duty may be levied instead of value added tax (VAT) under certain circumstances (see further 4.4.5 and 11.8).

4.4.4 Total costs will range generally between 13–14.5 per cent of the value of the transaction.

4.4.5 All agents', but not lawyers', fees currently attract VAT at a rate of 21 per cent. Sales will also be subject to VAT at 21 per cent instead of registration duty if the contract is for sale of a new building or a building still to be erected, and if the seller is in the building industry or fulfils certain conditions (see further 11.8).

4.5 Professionals' roles

Many sales are still negotiated directly between parties who may then ask a lawyer (or a notary public) to prepare the sale agreement once they have agreed the terms. It is however the notary who will prepare the authentic deed and process the entry in the register (see 4.3). Both parties are entitled to appoint notaries, and it is advisable for each party to seek separate representation (unlike the position in other countries such as France). The notaries will then split the statutory fee. Important sales are often conducted by estate agents, however, and the terms and conditions of sale drawn up by qualified legal advisers. Since 1993 the estate agents profession has been strictly regulated by law.

5 LEASES AND OTHER RIGHTS OF OCCUPATION

5.1.1 Rental agreements or tenancies (*huur/bail*) are personal contracts which do not grant rights in the land itself. These are invariably granted at full market rent and not for a premium or capital sum in the Anglo-American tradition. The right of *superficie* and of *emphyteusis* are more like the common law long lease (see 2.1.3.1). The Civil Code contains a number of general non-mandatory provisions regulating both oral and written tenancies which will apply in the absence of other agreement. In addition, the Civil Code also contains mandatory provisions for residential, commercial and agricultural rental agreements. Negotiations increasingly involve lawyers even for smaller properties. Commercial buildings are those used primarily for retail purposes and they are governed by the general provisions of the Civil Code and the specific and mainly compulsory provisions of an Act of 1951. These also apply to other parts of a commercial building and might include, for example, the apartment above a shop. Industrial and warehouse rental agreements are governed by the general Civil Code provisions and are not subject to any specific compulsory regulations. The rules laid down by an Act of 1991 regarding residential rental agreements have severely restricted the rights of landlords to set their own terms. Rental agreements of agricultural land and buildings are strictly regulated by an Act of 1969 as amended in an Act of 1988. In principle, the duration of the rental agreement may be freely agreed between the parties as long as it does not exceed 99 years. The most common duration for most rental agreements is nine years with break clauses for one or both parties at the end of each three year period (known as the 3/6/9 lease). Where the tenant is still in occupation at the end of the agreement, the agreement will be automatically renewed for a further period of time which will be the same as the period which has just expired

5.1.2 The parties to all rental agreements are in principle free to negotiate the basic rent, which will usually be payable in advance each month or trimester. Exceptionally, however, yearly or half-yearly payments may be agreed. Automatic review clauses are common for all types of agreement, and the parties are free to select the criteria against which the adjustment is measured (eg foreign currency or the gold standard). If indexation is expressly excluded, the provisions of the Civil Code will be used, although most agreements will usually refer to an indexation clause. The agreement will usually provide for break clauses by either one or both of the parties. Rented premises must be provided in good condition and the landlord will be liable for all necessary structural repairs and repairs of the external areas of the rental building (eg roof, walls, chimneys, stairways) and for any damage caused by his neglect. This requirement may be altered by agreement. Generally, the tenant will by contract not be allowed to assign his rights or sublet the premises without the prior consent of the landlord. The tenant will take out insurance for his personal liability to the landlord and to third parties, and the landlord should ensure the tenant's insurance cover includes the direct consequences and damage resulting from fire for which the tenant is liable, as well as any consequential loss. Even tenants who are of first-class financial standing will generally be required to provide security to guarantee their obligations, which can be provided in various forms, such as stocks and shares, bank guarantees (used in residential and commercial rental agreements) or money deposited in a blocked bank account (popular for offices, industrial and warehousing rentals). The security will amount to the equivalent of three to six months' rent (plus charges).

5.1.3 Where the building occupied by a tenant is sold, the new landlord will have to honour the rental agreement if it has a 'fixed date' (eg one which has been registered or transcribed in an authentic form), and there is no eviction clause incorporated into the agreement, or if the purchase agreement provided that the new landlord will have to 'maintain' the existing rental agreement. The new landlord may evict the tenant if the contract has no fixed date, or where the contract with a fixed date provides an eviction clause. If the rented premises are the subject of a compulsory purchase order, the rental agreement will end by virtue of law and the tenant must claim damages from the expropriating authority as he is not entitled to compensation from the landlord. The landlord must, therefore, involve the tenant in the negotiations with the authorities or else he may be liable to pay the tenant compensation himself.

5.1.4 Value added tax is not payable on rental agreements. It is possible for the landlord to pass on property taxes to the tenant but by reason of the Act of 1991 the prepayment levy (*onroerende voorheffing/précompte immobilier*) referred to at 11.4 cannot be passed on to a residential tenant.

5.2 Residential rental agreements

5.2.1 The 1991 Act applies to all rental agreements where the premises are occupied as a main residence. A rental agreement of residential premises must be entered into for a fixed period of time which will usually be nine years. Should the parties agree to an indefinite period, the contract will automatically be construed as a nine-year rental agreement. (A long-term rental agreement extending beyond the nine-year standard term must be recorded before a notary in order to be enforceable against third parties.)

5.2.2 The standard residential agreement of nine years will automatically be renewed for a further three years unless either party has given the other at least six months' notice before the end of the term. Automatic renewal is subject to two exceptions: the parties may either conclude a short-term rental agreement (ie for a maximum of three years), or they may enter into an agreement which is for a term longer than nine years, provided in either case it is in writing. The latter will also need to be notarised to stand against third parties. The short-term rental agreement cannot be terminated before the end of the term by either party giving notice. Automatic renewal of the short-term tenancy may only be avoided by giving one month's notice prior to the end of the rental agreement. Where a short-term rental agreement has been renewed once or twice, thereby exceeding its three-year period, it will automatically become an agreement for nine years Where one of the parties to a long-term rental agreement (ie one over nine years) subsequently wishes to terminate the rental agreement, he will have to serve six months' notice at the end of the first period beyond nine years.

5.2.3 Any agreement may be terminated at any time by mutual agreement or dissolved by the court (*ontbonden/résolu*) in the event of default. Standard rental agreements and long-term rental agreements may be terminated by the tenant, by giving three months' notice and paying an indemnity of up to three months' rent if the notice is given during the first three-year period of the tenancy. The agreement may be terminated by the landlord for purposes of personal occupation (at any time, by six months' notice), structural works (at the end of the first or second three-year period, by six months' notice), or without any reason after the expiry of the first or second three-year period subject to paying an indemnity of six months' rent. Under exceptional circumstances, the court (*vrederechter/juge de paix*) may extend a rental agreement under which notice has been served.

5.2.4 For all residential rental agreements, the rent is indexed automatically on each anniversary of the agreement, unless this is expressly excluded by the parties, and the formula provided for in the Civil Code will be applied. It is also possible to review residential rents every three years.

5.2.5 The tenant will usually bear all charges (either by way of a lump sum payment or in payment of actual costs incurred), except for withholding tax on land which must be borne by the landlord (see 11.1.4). Most residential rental agreements provide for a guarantee to be given by the tenant as security for his performance; either as a sum of money or as a guarantee by a third party, often in the form of a bank guarantee. Residential premises may only be partially sublet by the tenant, and this is subject to prior approval of the landlord, and to the additional requirement that the principal tenant continue to occupy the remaining property as his main residence.

5.2.6 Any property let for residential purposes must be fit for occupation as a residence and satisfy all other relevant regulations such as those relating to health and safety.

5.3 Commercial rental agreements

5.3.1 Parties to a commercial rental agreement (ie one relating to retail premises or those with a principal retail use) will usually be free to negotiate the rent. Most commercial agreements will provide for an indexation clause. The tenant may adapt the building for his own specific needs provided he does not breach the terms of the agreement. A clause prohibiting the assignment of the lease will be void if the rental agreement is transferred with the sale of the business. The provisions specifically relating to commercial leases are to be found in an Act of 1951.

5.3.2 The minimum duration of a commercial rental agreement is nine years and the term is renewable. The agreement may be terminated by the tenant at the end of each three-year period by giving the landlord six months' prior notice. The landlord may also terminate the agreement at the end of each three year period by giving one year's prior notice, but only where this is expressly provided for in the contract, and provided certain conditions are met. The parties may terminate the lease at any time by mutual agreement, but the termination must be recorded before a notary or competent judge *(vrederechter/juge de paix)*. After the first nine-year period, the commercial tenant is entitled to three agreement renewals (which must be formally applied for using a registered letter or by writ), and each may be for a period equal to the duration of the original rental agreement, ie a nine-year rental agreement will entitle a tenant to ocupation for a maximum of 36 years. Where the tenant has applied for renewal, the landlord may within a three-month period either expressly accept the request, or abstain from replying, in which case the agreement will be renewed on the tenant's proposed terms. Alternatively, the landlord may refuse to renew the terms with or without specifying reasons, or he may accept the renewal but on different terms to those proposed by the tenant, in which case the tenant will have to bring the case before the judge within 30 days. There are certain statutory grounds on which the landlord may refuse to renew the agreement subject to the payment of compensation (eg one year's rent for reconstruction). Where the landlord refuses to renew without reason, the tenant will be entitled to compensation equal to three years' rent.

5.3.3 As to rent review, the parties have the right to file a claim at the end of each three-year period requesting a rent adjustment if it can be shown that due to external circumstances the normal rental value has increased or decreased by at least 15 per cent. This claim may only be brought before the competent judge during the last three months of every three-year period. In the event of renewal, the parties may renegotiate the rental value, and where they fail to agree, arbitration will take place before the judge. Where a building is sold, the new landlord is under an obligation to recognise an existing rental agreement which has a 'fixed date' (see 5.1.3) unless the right to evict is expressly provided for in the contract, for certain limited statutory reasons. The landlord must give 12 months' notice within the three months following the transfer of ownership. Where the rental agreement has no 'fixed date', it may be terminated by giving 12 months' notice within three months of the transfer of ownership for one of the statutory reasons, whether the contract expressly provides for termination or not. The termination is subject to the payment of compensation.

5.4 Industrial and warehousing rental agreements

Industrial and warehousing rental agreements are generally entered into for nine years with the right to terminate by both parties at the end of each three-year period as is common with other leases. There are no specific statutory provisions or protections.

5.5 Methods of measurement

It is usual for the area of a property to be calculated on a gross external basis.

6 FINANCE AND INVESTMENT SOURCES

6.1 Loan finance

The most common sources of loan finance are the national or foreign banks, and those specialising in the finance of land and development projects. Loan finance can also be obtained from the public credit institutions such as those belonging to the *Algemene Spaaren Lijfrentekas/Caisse Générale D'Epargne et de Retraite* holding group and the *Gemeentekrediet/Crédit Communal* holding group. Banks will scrutinise each proposal, examine the risks involved and will seldom provide the full amount of the loan. Projects will often be funded by syndicated loans involving a number of banks, in order to spread the risk. In addition to this, the investor will be required to provide part of the finance from his own funds (eg 15 per cent). The duration of the average loan will range between 2, 10 and 15 years. Loans are generally flexible and will combine a variety of techniques to accommodate the expectations of the different parties (eg matching, forward rate agreements and interest rate futures).

6.2 Investment or equity finance

The principal investment vehicles are the Belgian corporation, which has certain advantages in terms of speed and ease of set up, and the Luxembourg or Dutch holding company, in particular the closely held company or *besloten vennootschap BV*. 'Real estate' certificates play an important role in equity finance (public or private). The holder has the right to the earnings, revenue and sale price of one or more immoveables. The holder is neither owner nor co-owner of the property, but he can, nevertheless, make a claim which gives him a position close to ownership in relation to the property. The leading investors tend to be the investment and insurance companies and to a lesser extent the public.

6.3 Mezzanine or mixed funding

Banks seldom provide 100 per cent of required funds, and generally projects will be financed by several banks, in order to spread the risk. Loan finance often consists of 70 per cent from the prime lender, 15 per cent from the mezzanine lender, and 15 per cent from the borrower. Mezzanine loans usually require a higher return to reflect the greater risk involved for a second ranked creditor and can therefore be expensive.

6.4 Sale and lease-back

Although less successful than in other countries, the sale and lease-back technique is gaining increasing popularity. The seller of the property sells it to an investor who will then grant him a lease-back at a market rent. This creates an income for the investor and releases the seller's capital for use in other projects rather than being tied up in property ownership.

6.5 Leasing

Although driven to a lesser extent by tax concerns, leasing is common. The lessor usually agrees to build, buy or furnish a building in accordance with the specifications of the lessee. The lessee then makes periodic payments covering the capital and interest costs of the project to reimburse the capital invested by the lessor. 'Real estate leasing' is not regulated by the Civil Code; there are merely indirect references to it in the laws on value added tax (VAT) and accountancy. It is, nevertheless, quite popular, since the lessee need not use his own funds and he can instead invest elsewhere whilst the development is carried out to his own specification. The lessor also has responsibility for any problems during construction and there are also tax advantages, in particular VAT, which will be spread over the entire leasing period, which create greater incentives to enter into such agreements. Alterations to the VAT laws in 1993 have reduced these benefits.

6.6 Other types of property finance

In addition to the vehicles already mentioned, securitisation and asset-based securities are recognised and regulated by the Civil Code but not commonly used. The hire-purchase arrangement (*onroerende leasing /leasing immobilier*) is more common and may also be used where capital and rental payments are made throughout the term of the agreement with an option to purchase at the end.

6.7 Institutional investment

As is the case throughout most of Europe, institutional investors, particularly insurance companies and investment companies, perform a vital role in property investment, not only because they provide finance themselves, but also because they set trends and the criteria for the market.

6.8 Other investors

Foreign investors are increasingly common, especially in Brussels in the light of its position at the heart of Europe and, to a lesser extent, Antwerp. Private investors are also increasing in importance.

7 FORMS OF SECURITY

7.1 Mortgages

7.1.1 A mortgage gives the mortgagee the right to priority payment from the proceeds of sale or to enforce the mortgage and to demand payment from the mortgagor and subsequent owners and buyers. It does this without dispossessing the owner. There are three main categories of mortgage; the contractual mortgage, the legal mortgage and the mortgage created by will.

7.1.2 In the case of the contractual mortgage, the mortgagor must be the owner of the mortgaged estate and have power of disposal over it, which will not be the case after he has been declared bankrupt. Where the property is the family residence, the spouse's consent will also be required. The contractual mortgage may be granted over land and buildings, over the *emphyteusis* and *superficie* but not the dwelling right or the right of use as these rights are not transferable. The mortgage must be in writing in an authenticated form drawn up by a notary; it must also specify the land to which the mortgage attaches as well as the sum, interest and costs secured, although there are statutory limitations on the amount of future interest which may be covered by the mortgage. Under certain circumstances, it may be possible to secure future or contingent liabilities. Mortgages created by will are rare and need not be drawn up in authenticated form. Legal mortgages are created automatically by implication of law and arise in specific circumstances, eg the state has a legal mortgage on all tax payers' assets to secure the payment of taxes listed by the Treasury. The creation of this type of security will not require the consent of the debtor or authentication by a notary public. However, all three types of mortgage require registration to be perfected and enforceable against third parties.

7.1.3 The creation of a mortgage will incur a fee of one per cent of the amount secured in addition to a mortgage duty of 0.2 per cent. Cancellation of mortgages will attract a penalty of 0.2 per cent of the same amount. The mortgage will cover the whole property, whether or not the mortgagor subsequently divides the property. A mortgage will not transfer possession and the mortgagor may continue to use the property or may rent or sell it. If the borrower defaults, the mortgagee may enforce and require the sale of the asset. He can also oppose a transfer of the property to a third party. Priority of mortgages is determined by date of registration. Registration takes place in a local register and will be effective for 30 years. Upon expiry of 30 years, registration will require renewal. Note should be made of the role of privileges (see 2.3 and 2.10), in relation to preferential debts, and these will take priority over a first mortgage

7.2 Floating and other charges

The floating charge which creates a charge which does not attach to the assets until the charge crystallises upon insolvency or default does not exist. However, a similar concept exists in promises to create a mortgage (*hypotheekbelofte/ promesse d'hypothèque*). These give the creditor less security than the mortgage or the privilege, as they are simple contracts to mortgage a specific piece of property at a later stage as security for payment of a specific amount. They may be created by private deed, but not authentic deed. They may be valid even if there is only partial identification of the property. In the event of default, the mortgagor will only be entitled to damages and any intervention of the court requires the existence of a certified deed. They must however indicate specific assets and cannot float over or attach to all and unspecified assets. Privileges are described at 2.3 and will generally take priority over mortgages.

8 PLANNING AND BUILDING REGULATION

Regional regulations regulate planning control and zoning. Despite the apparent diversity of regulations between the three regions of Belgium (Flemish, Walloon and Brussels-Capital), the principles that govern planning and building are normally identical and zoning and planning in the three regions are regulated by a set of plans showing the authorised use for each area (eg agricultural or industrial).

8.1 Planning authorities

The institutional reform of 1980 devolved planning regulation upon the three regions. Each has its own regulations for construction permits, zoning and planning certificates, construction regulations, partition permits and partition regulations. These are dealt with by the municipal authorities.

8.2 Development plans

Plans exist at various levels, regional, sectorial and municipal, and the plans passed at a lower level must conform with those passed at a higher level. These plans and regulations provide the regulatory framework which controls all development (see 8.3). Each authority has the power to pass specific plans which determine land use by demarcating different zones within an area, including housing zones, rural zones, green zones and industrial zones. The plans which most affect private individuals are the particular allotment plans (*plans particuliers d'aménagement*) and the *plans particuliers d'affectation du sol* in the Brussels-Capital region, which are municipal plans covering most municipal territory. For the time being, a number of zones are not actually regulated by a municipal allotment plan, and in its absence, reference must be made to allotment carried out at sectorial level for the zones in question, as the sectorial plans cover the whole country. Where no particular allotment plan is in force for a particular zone, the opinion of a regional official must be sought on the subject of the proposed development. Only negative opinions will bind the authority which considers the application whether to grant permission. The conformity of a proposed development with the relevant plan and regulations does not however carry with it automatic permission. The municipality will retain the power to refuse permission for a specific project, even if it conforms, on the grounds that it is deemed incompatible with the 'proper planning of spaces'. Its decision is discretionary.

8.3 Planning control and procedures

In all three regions, a construction permit will be required for any works, as defined by law, ie construction, demolition, reconstruction or transformation of a building (not normal repair and maintenance) and significant changes to the surface appearance of certain land. Additional consents may also have to be obtained (see eg section 9).

8.3.1 The application will be made to the municipal authority. Depending on the nature of the proposed development, a public investigation, study and the consultation of a special commission may be required.

8.3.2 The application procedure can range in duration from two weeks to more than 12 months. There is a prescribed time limit beyond which the decision of the authority is deemed unfavourable, enabling the applicant to lodge an administrative appeal with the regional government. If the latter also fails to deliver a decision within a specified period, its decision is deemed to be favourable (sometimes mistakenly referred to as a 'tacit permit'). The applicant has the right of administrative appeal against a refusal or permit subject to conditions which must be brought before the permanent deputation of the province. In the event of a negative decision or one subject to conditions by the provincial authority, a second administrative appeal is available to the regional government. The regional government's decision may be appealed against in the final instance in the administrative court (*Raad van State/Conseil d'Etat*). Where the municipal authority chooses to exercise its discretion to refuse consent for the permit even where the proposed development complies with the plan on the grounds of 'incompatibility with the proper planning of spaces', its decision may only be reversed by the administrative court. Those aggrieved by the grant of a permit, eg a neighbour affected by proposed development, may lodge their complaints immediately with the courts, such as the court of first instance or the state council.

8.3.3 Authorised development must be carried out within one or two years of the grant of the permit. An extension of time is possible but exceptional.

8.3.4 Violations, eg building without a permit, can lead to imprisonment or fines (often equivalent to the added value that the property has acquired through the unauthorised works or changes) or both. In addition, the party who has violated the permit may have to restore the building to its original condition or to complete the planning work.

8.4 Building standards, control and supervision

In addition to obtaining a construction permit, the developer must also comply with building regulations and standards of construction, materials, acoustics and the like, laid down by the municipal authorities. Compliance with construction requirements will be examined at the time of the application for the building permit and the planning and building procedures are dealt with together. In general, these regulations will be the same in all the regions but occasionally the individual regions will create extra requirements.

8.5 Protection of buildings of special interest

There are special provisions governing buildings and areas of, eg architectural and historic importance.

9 ENVIRONMENTAL MATTERS

After a slow beginning, Belgian environmental law is now developing fairly rapidly. Responsibility for environmental protection has been transferred to the three autonomous regions, the Flemish, Walloon and Brussels-Capital regions. However, production standards, minimum standards for drinking water and the transportation of all waste and nuclear power currently remain under the control of the national authorities. It is often necessary to establish which is the competent authority for the area in question in order to obtain the necessary permits. National legislation will only remain applicable on a matter under the control of one of the regions if the regional authorities have not yet enacted special legislation. The process for obtaining a permit in each area may vary. In Flanders, the environmental system has been regrouped so that it is possible to apply for one permit which will cover a number of authorisations. The installation will be classed as a first, second or third-class risk, depending on the threat of pollution which it presents. The only other permits which will be required concern construction and the extraction of underground water. In Wallonia, however, a site may require several permits covering various possible forms of pollution. Two classes of inclusive exploitation permits are available for a site but separate regulations exist for the various types of pollution. Penalties for infringement of environmental provisions include administrative sanctions (fines, prohibitions on use of certain equipment, suspension orders); criminal sanctions which can be imposed on both individuals or corporate bodies (imprisonment and fines or both, suspension of production and confiscation of the profits resulting from the infringing activity); liability in tort (restitution or damages) and strict liability. Procedures and sanctions will also vary between the regions. As to private law remedies, the Civil Code provides in relation to nuisance/neighbourhood law (*burenhinder-nabuurschade/troubles de voisinage*), that if a neighbour interferes with the use and enjoyment of adjoining land or is responsible for a nuisance, he may be liable to rectify the damage if he was at fault. Liability without fault is also possible where the balance of interests between two properties requires this. The regions are also given responsibility for hunting, shooting, fishing, forestry, parks, the green zones and the preservation of nature.

9.1 Protection against atmospheric and noise pollution

Noise and air pollution is regulated by the regional authorities which are responsible for setting standards and enforcement, the national legislation being set out in Acts of 1973 and 1964 respectively.

9.2 Water pollution

Water pollution is regulated by the regional authorities. In Wallonia, it is necessary to obtain separate licences for discharge or for the extraction of water to purify it for drinking purposes. The material legislation consists of two Acts of 1971, separately dealing with surface and groundwater, and one of 1974 dealing with water pollution.

9.3 Waste storage and disposal

The regional authorities regulate waste policy although the transportation of waste, and particularly radioactive waste, remains under national control. It is necessary to obtain either a national or regional licence for authorisation of the transport, import or export of waste. The regional decrees all aim to prevent unauthorised dumping of general or toxic waste.

10 DEVELOPMENT

10.1 Development projects, structures and vehicles

A simple development project typically involves an owner/occupier who purchases a site intending to construct his required premises using his own builder. However, it is increasingly common for developers to find a site, construct a building and then seek to sell the land and the building at a profit either to property agencies or to private individuals. In both cases, the developer will need to contract with a number of different parties. A building contractor will have to be found to execute the plans, and he will often be assisted by a number of specialised subcontractors. In the case of larger projects, the developer may appoint a project manager. However, notwithstanding the number of potential parties involved in a project, the principal contract will be between the developer and the contractor, and most legal conflicts will arise between these two parties. Developers differ from building contractors, in so far as they combine the three essential factors enabling completion of a development project, namely land, labour and finance. The developer will wish to enter into an agreement with a buyer to sell a plot of land together with the development. This can arise typically either where the developer sells the proposed development which at that particular moment in time only exists on paper, ie off plan, or he may agree with the buyer to erect a building to the latter's specification and to deliver it on a turn key basis, ie fully equipped and ready to be occupied. Public tenders and private contracts are both common.

10.2 Building contracts

10.2.1 Typical forms of building contract

The building contract, which is relatively flexible in terms of assessing the actual cost of development, is concluded between the developer and the building contractor and may be for 'fixed price', 'unit price' or for 'no price'. Fixed price contracts exist when the parties agree that the work will be performed for a definite, or relatively fixed, price. Often, however, the figure is only fixed for certain tasks involved in the project, whilst reserving the price of others. Unit price contracts involve agreed figures for the price of materials and labour but leave the quantities required unspecified. No-price contracts ('open account') arise where the builder is not bound to any limitation on cost but is placed in a position of trust, and has an open account in which to determine the quantity and quality of labour and materials he will use. If the quantity of labour is to be the most important factor in the contractual arrangement, the parties may agree that the work will be paid for per metre or square metre. Subcontractors will normally deliver their specialised services on an independent basis. However, they may still be held liable under the contract they have entered into with the building contractor. The developer/employer will not normally have a direct contractual relationship with the subcontractors, and where the employer has contracted with a contractor the latter will assume liability for the default of subcontractors. The process usually starts with the contractor being approached to enable him to give an estimate of the work required to achieve the result and he will make an offer without engagement.

10.2.2 Common terms

The contractor must demonstrate the necessary skills and gather the requisite information regarding the site for the proper execution of the work. The work must be delivered within an agreed or reasonable time limit and there may also be a penalty clause for late completion. The developer/employer must pay for the construction work at the appropriate stages or on final completion. If, for any reason, he has to cancel the project, he may do so provided he compensates the building contractor for his expenses in connection with the work, and for any reasonably foreseeable profits. The contract will guarantee that suitable materials are being used. Damage discovered prior to delivery must be rectified by the contractor at his own expense. Under the estate developer's contract, the developer is legally considered a professional salesperson, which means he is under the obligation to safeguard against defects, including those of a latent nature. This will be in addition to the existing architect's and the contractor's defects insurance (see 10.5) which will run with the development notwithstanding passage of title.

10.2.3 Standard forms of contract

In principle, building contracts are freely negotiable and standard form building contracts are not generally used. No formalities are required. It should be noted however, that the House Building Act 1971 was enacted to give extra protection to the owner/occupier as well as the building contractor. It applies to any contract for residential construction which stipulates payment before completion. It is not possible to contract out of these provisions.

10.3 Roles of the various parties

It is common for the party initiating the development project to contract with several other parties, such as an architect, a building contractor, subcontractors to perform specialised work, a quantity surveyor to determine the required labour or materials if the task is more complicated, quality controllers and/or structural engineers. For large or complex developments a project manager may be appointed who will organise daily operations for the duration of the development project. For smaller developments, the most important relationship will be between the contractor and the owner/developer. If an architect has submitted the plans for the building but the main contractual relationship is between the developer and a building contractor, the contractor must, nevertheless, allow the architect to supervise the work and must follow his instructions. If the contractor does not execute the plans with due care he will incur liability. The architect will have a greater responsibility when the contractor is bound by a no-price contract, since he has the additional task of protecting the developer against excessive billing by the contractor. Not only must the contractor carry out and complete the work, he is also under a duty to exercise due care and to gather basic information regarding the site which is required to carry out the development.

10.4 Defects and remedies

10.4.1 Remedies of employer in respect of design and materials

The employer will not normally have a direct contractual relationship with the subcontractors, but in the event of defects for which they are liable, he may recover damages from them. Otherwise, he will be able to recover damages from the contractor who will assume liability for all defects (see 10.5).

10.4.2 Remedies of subsequent owners/occupiers other than the contractual employer

For the position of those who come to the property subsequently, see 10.5.

10.5 Defects insurance

The 'decennial system' is used to regulate defects liability insurance by the architect and building contractor. Both will be liable for 10 years for complete or partial damage to the building caused by negligent construction or the unsuitability of the land. This warranty is contractual but is imposed by operation of law and cannot be excluded by the contract. It will apply to any building project, irrespective of the nature of the contract and the benefit will pass to subsequent owners.

10.6 Copyright

The building owner will need to consider the copyright implications if he needs to have future access to the original drawings.

10.7 Fees

The parties are entirely free to negotiate fees. The architect will assess his fees on the basis of the value of his services and the value of the development as well as the type of building in question. The fees will be calculated on the basis of the actual value of the work taking the size of the project and the architect's reputation into account.

10.8 Value added tax

Value added tax is the most important tax in the construction industry and is currently charged at a standard rate of 21 per cent.

11 TAXES

11.1 Corporation tax

Resident companies (ie companies having their registered office, principal establishment, head office or effective management in Belgium) will be taxed on their total income derived from business activities and from other sources, including foreign sources. Conversely, where the company is managed abroad and only has a branch in Belgium, it will be subject to non-resident income tax on profits derived from the local activity only.

11.1.1 Tax rates

The current rate of corporate income tax for the tax year 1997 ranges from 28 per cent to 42 per cent. Occasionally, however, the lower tax rates will be unavailable (a) when more than half the shares in the company are held by another company; (b) when the distributed profits are higher than 13 per cent of the fully paid up capital; and (c) when the company is a 'financial company'.

11.1.2 Computation and administration

All reasonable expenditure and charges incurred during the taxable year which relate wholly and exclusively to the trade of the company are deductible from gross income if accompanied by supporting documentation or other evidence and provided the amount is not unreasonable. Depreciation relating to organisational expenses and intangible and tangible fixed assets of definite duration, forms a deductible business expense. The most important deductible expenses include organisational expenses, interest and royalties, taxes other than Belgian income taxes, depreciation and amortisation, obsolete equipment and some capital losses.

11.1.3 Depreciation and capital allowances

Depreciation of tangible and intangible fixed assets with a life of definite duration may be made and land (whether developed or not and buildings constructed over the land including any fixtures and fittings) is considered to be a tangible asset for this purpose. The assessment of depreciation is complex but is based on the acquisition or investment cost and related costs such as turnover tax, registration duties, notary fees and so forth. Depreciation is normally computed on a straight line basis, eg office buildings at three per cent, industrial buildings at five per cent, and plant and equipment at 10 to 20 per cent.

11.1.4 Withholding tax

Where no double taxation treaty applies the withholding tax rates are, for dividends, 25 per cent, for interest and royalties, 15 per cent.

11.2 Taxes on development value

There is no tax payable on the development value or value attributable to zoning or permission for development.

11.3 Taxes on capital gains

Capital gains are taxable at the same rate as income.

11.4 Taxes on owner of property

When corporate income tax is imposed upon property income, a prepayment (*onroerende voorheffing/précompte immobilier*) is levied on the value of the cadastral income of the property relating to the annual rental value as attributable to the property by the land registry offices (see 3.2). There is a national prepayment based on the cadastral income and a municipal sum as well. Within certain limits the prepayment may be credited against the corporate income tax. The prepayment is never refundable but any amount of tax which cannot be credited can be deducted as a business expense if the property is used for trade or business purposes. In certain cases reductions in the prepayment may be allowed.

11.5 Taxes on occupier

See 11.4.

11.6 Taxes on land transfer

Property transfer tax takes the form of the registration duty (*registratierechten/droits d'enregistrement*) and is charged at 12.5 per cent of the purchase price or of the objective market value (*venale waarde/valeur vénale*) when the tax administration considers that this is higher than the sale price as agreed between the parties. If the parties' valuation is seen as an attempt to commit fiscal fraud, they may be liable to pay extra duty and fines. In addition, some parties try to avoid payment of the registration duties altogether by merely selling shares in a company to which the property was previously transferred. The tax authorities may, however, challenge this as a sham, particularly if the property is the sole asset of the company. There are rebates for resales generally within two years. Authorised property dealers (*marchands de bien*) benefit from reduced registration duty of five per cent. There is also a reduction whereby only six per cent is paid for small rural properties and small private houses. (Value added tax may be levied instead of registration duty under certain circumstances, see further 4.4.5 and 11.8.)

11.7 Wealth taxes

There are no wealth taxes.

11.8 Value added tax

Value added tax (VAT), rather than registration duty, is charged on sales when the object of the transaction is a new building or a building still to be erected and if the seller meets certain requirements (ie he performs a role in the building sector or various administrative roles). This is also charged on construction. The leasing or renting of immoveable property is exempt from VAT. The rate of VAT is 21 per cent.

11.9 Local and other taxes

See 11.4. Note should also be made that any contribution to the capital of companies is in principle subject to a registration duty of 0.5 per cent (exemption exists under certain conditions for the contribution of all assets of a company into another company).

12 GRANTS AND INCENTIVES

12.1 Subsidies, grants and loans

Large companies may apply for a range of special grants that are generally based on research and development or activities involving high levels of technology. Smaller and medium-sized companies (ie commercial companies of a maximum of 40 employees, or craft, tourist, service or industrial businesses with a maximum of 70 employees) may apply for aid for interest payments on loans, accelerated depreciation or capital grants.

12.2 Tax allowances and reliefs

There are some tax advantages available for multinationals who wish to set up a company or branch in Belgium. These extend to their coordination centres, distribution centres, and to foreign sales corporations.

12.3 Other public schemes and incentives

Any business choosing to set up within the Greater Brussels region is eligible for aid which will vary according to the size of the company and the nature of the proposed business.

13 COMPANIES AND BUSINESS ENTITIES

Company law is regulated by the Commercial Code.

13.1 Limited and unlimited companies

13.1.1 Naamloze vennootschap *(NV)*/société anonymc *(SA)*

This is one of the most widely used forms of business entity for investment. The NV/SA is incorporated either by contributions in kind or in cash from the shareholders or by public subscription (in which case special regulations under the Company Act and Royal decree of 1935 must be observed), and is a mechanism akin to the UK public limited liability company and the US joint stock corporation. Certain information must be included on incorporation including a financial plan confirming the availability of sufficient working capital and confirmation that a separate account has been opened for any contributions in cash. A report from an independent auditor (*bedrijfsrevisor/ reviseur d'entreprise*) valuing any contributions in kind must be prepared and filed with the commercial courts. If, within three years, the company goes into liquidation, the founders may be held liable if it can be shown that the share capital was insufficient to carry out the proposed business activities during the first two years. The articles of incorporation must be executed in a notarised deed signed by a minimum of two founders or shareholders and then published in the Official Gazette (*Belgisch Staatsblad /Moniteur Belge*). They must also be registered in the trades register and with the VAT administration. Such companies can be either of limited or unlimited duration. The minimum capital of BEF1.25 million must be fully subscribed and paid up, and at least 25 per cent of each share must be fully paid up by the date of incorporation. Prior authorisation is not required for the setting up of the NV/SA. In principle, shareholders' liability is limited to their contributions, unless a single person holds all the shares for a minimum of a year, in which case he will be held liable for all commitments of the company whilst he was the only shareholder and until another shareholder is found or a decision to wind up the company is published in the annexes to the Official Gazette. Shares can be freely transferred once they have been paid up to 25 per cent of their value. Bearer shares simply require transfer of title, but registered shares require notification of the transfer in the shareholders' register (to notify third parties). These rules may not apply if the articles of association state otherwise and still comply with the provisions of the Company Act (ie do not prevent shares from being transferred for more than three months). The company will be managed by a board of directors (*bestuurders/administrateurs*), with a minimum of three directors, shareholders or non-shareholders, resident or non-resident, individual or corporate. They will be appointed for a maximum of six years by resolution during a general meeting and can be dismissed at any time following a majority vote.

13.1.2 Besloten vennootschap met beperkte aansprakelijkheid *(BVBA)/* société privée à responsabilité privée *(SPRL)*

Most of the requirements for the BVBA/SPRL are the same as for the NV/SA but there are a few differences. The BVBA/SPRL must also be incorporated by notarial deed and excerpts of it must also be published in the Official Gazette. The minimum share capital is BEF750,000, fully subscribed, with at least one-third of the minimum stated share capital (BEF250,000) paid up. Unlike the NV/SA, the the shares of a 'closely held limited liability company' have to be registered and can only be transferred on specific conditions. Capital in excess of the minimum stated share capital and subscribed for cash must also be fully subscribed, but only 20 per cent must be paid up at the time the BVBA/SPRL is formed. Contributions may be in cash or in kind. Any contributions in kind are also appraised by an independent accountant. Since an Act of 1991, it has not been necessary to have a minimum of two founders. The same regime and procedures as for the NV/SA apply to the BVBA/SPRL. Founders are personally liable for incorrect incorporation. A financial plan must be submitted. Shares must be in registered form, have a minimum value of BEF1,000 and all be of equal value to ensure no differentiation in rights. A SPRL/BVBA may neither publicly offer its shares nor issue bonds. Credit is only available from banks, which often request a personal guarantee from the shareholders. One or more managers (*zaakvoerders/gérants*) are appointed by the general meeting of shareholders or by the articles, for an unlimited period. Only individuals can act as managers in a BVBA/SPRL and they are directly responsible to the company for their actions. The requirements for establishing a branch of a foreign company are dealt with in 14.3.

13.1.3 Coöperatieve vennootschap *(CV)*/société coopérative *(SC)*

A simple form of corporation is the *coöperatieve vennootschap* (CV)/*société coopérative* (SC). This requires a minimum of three shareholders and must be registered at the register of commerce. The transfer of shares is strictly regulated. Although legal provisions regulate the administration and operation of a CV/SC, the founders are free to choose most of the rules to govern the company. Annual accounts must be filed with the commercial court. The CV/SC may take different forms: with limited liability; with unlimited and joint liability; and in each case with or without participation. A CV/SC with limited liability has a minimum capital of BEF750,000 of which BEF250,000 must be paid up. A CV/SC with unlimited liability has no minimum capital threshold and the capital can be increased or decreased freely. The CV/SC is normally constituted for an indefinite duration. On the whole, the CV/SC with unlimited liability is the most flexible form of business entity, but it has the disadvantage of joint and unlimited liability. Although differences between the CV/SC and other entities have been reduced considerably with the 'Program-law' of July 1991, the CV/SC still requires less formalities than an NV or BVBA. A CV/SC by way of participation is one where the partners have equal voting rights, 50 per cent of the profits are shared equally and 50 per cent according to contribution, and the fact that it is an CV/SC must be clearly stated to the public. If not, any party concerned can ask the courts for the dissolution of the company. A CV/SC by way of participation has a minimum capital of BEF250,000, which must be fully subscribed and paid up.

13.2 Partnerships

13.2.1 Vennootschap onder firma *(VOF)*/société en nom collectif *(SNC)*

This is in effect a general partnership established by a contract between two or more individuals to carry out a commercial activity under a corporate name. The agreement must be incorporated in a special deed, registered with the register of commerce and excerpts must be published in the Official Gazette. If the partnership fails to file for publication, it will be unenforceable against third parties and prevented from starting any court proceedings. A copy of the agreement must also be provided for every party with an identifiable interest. The partnership will be given a separate legal personality but has no specific capital requirements. Partners are held jointly and severally liable for the liabilities and debts of the VOF/SNC, without limit, and will be responsible for managing the partnership themselves.

13.2.2 Gewone commanditaire vennootschap *(GCV)*/société en commandite simple *(SCS)*

The limited partnership also has separate legal personality. It is the equivalent of the general partnership except that there will be general partners (*commandites*) with joint and several unlimited liability, as well as one or more partners, whose liability is limited to the amount of their capital contribution, who are simply investors, (*commanditairen/commanditaires*) and who must refrain from involving themselves in the management of the partnership. Incorporation follows the procedure for the general partnership.

13.2.3 Commanditaire vennootschap op aandelen *(CVA)*/société en commandite par actions *(SCA)*

The CVA/SCA is a form of limited partnership with shares which consists of partners who are jointly and severally liable, without limit, and shareholders whose liability is limited to their capital subscription.

13.2.4 Tijdelijke vereniging/association momentanée

The *tijdelijke vereniging/association momentanée* is a temporary partnership which controls the operation of one or more trading activities without using a corporate name. This is often used for joint ventures, eg for public activities, such as the temporary partnership set up for some urgent charitable purpose. The creation of the temporary partnership requires no special incorporation and the partners are jointly and severally liable.

13.2.5 Vereniging in deelneming/association en participation

The *vereniging in deelneming/association en participation* is a partnership agreement whereby one or more persons join together in order to carry out one or more businesses. This partnership does not have separate legal personality and is occasionally referred to as a 'secret' partnership because its existence does not have to be made known to third parties. Such a partnership can, for example, be used by a group of banks in order to share investment risks.

13.3 Other types of business association

13.3.1 The principal forms of business entity are set out in 13.1 and 13.2.

13.3.2 The concept of the trust used in common law systems does not exist in Belgian law. However, the Anglo-American trust is recognised as a legal entity to a limited extent.

13.3.3 A mechanism which is sometimes used but which suffers from a number of fiscal and legal uncertainties is the Dutch administration office (*het Nederlands administratiekantoor*) by which shareholders transfer their stock to a foundation (*stichting administratiekantoor*). In return they receive certificates with certain economic rights attached.

13.3.4 The foreign company undertaking business in Belgium may need to set up a branch operation (*bijkantoor/succursale*), see 14.3.

14 INTERNATIONAL

14.1 Restrictions or consents required for inward investment

There are generally no restrictions on foreign ownership of property or investment in property or the introduction of funds for this purpose.

14.2 Exchange controls

There are no material exchange control restrictions on the introduction or transfer of funds overseas.

14.3 Restrictions and registrations on carrying on a business

There are no special restrictions on foreign entities or companies doing business on the Belgian property market as long as they comply with Belgian company law. Any investor seeking to begin commercial activities in Belgium must decide whether to open a branch, to incorporate a subsidiary under one of the corporate forms, to use a representative office or to start as a sole trader. The decision will depend on the activities he undertakes, the legal obligations he is prepared to take on, the cost he is prepared to pay, the length of time he will be using the vehicle and the desired taxation consequences. A branch of a foreign corporation (*bijkantoor succursale*), which carries out commercial activities, is subject to the same legal requirements as those applicable to Belgian corporations. Depending upon the activities which the branch undertakes, prior authorisation may or may not be required from the Belgian authorities. Branches do not have a separate legal personality, but form a single entity with the parent company. They are established by filing a true copy of the articles of incorporation and a certificate of the resolution of the parent company with the register of the commercial court. A branch manager must be appointed as a legal representative of the foreign corporation in Belgium. A translation of the documents must be filed and excerpts published in the Official Gazette in the language of that part of the country in which the branch is to be located. Registration with the register of commerce is required. The foreign corporation setting up a branch must file its financial statements annually with the court of commerce and is required to keep appropriate accounting records. If the activities of the office in Belgium are merely concerned with providing information and canvassing for clients, then the office can be classed as a mere representative office and will not need to use any of the structures described. There need be no registration, publication or accounting formalities, as there would for a normal commercial branch. Often, however, third parties will not be keen to do business with such an office due to its lack of legal status and recognition.

14.4 Repatriation of income and proceeds of property trading and development

There are no consents or restraints involved in the repatriation of investment income and proceeds subject to the deduction of withholding tax where appropriate.

14.5 Withholding taxes

Interest and other payments resulting from investment in Belgian property by non-residents may be subject to withholding tax (see 11.1.4).

14.6 Double taxation relief

Belgium has signed double taxation treaties with a number of countries. One of the main principles common to most treaties is that income from property is taxed only by the country in which such property is located.

CHAPTER 3

Denmark

C Bennetsen

Partner, Gorrissen Federspiel Kierkegaard, Copenhagen

CONTENTS

1 OWNERSHIP OF LAND 71
2 OTHER INTERESTS IN LAND 74
3 TITLE TO LAND 77
4 TRANSACTIONS IN LAND 78
5 LEASES AND OTHER RIGHTS OF OCCUPATION 81
6 FINANCE AND INVESTMENT SOURCES 83
7 FORMS OF SECURITY 86
8 PLANNING AND BUILDING REGULATION 88
9 ENVIRONMENTAL MATTERS 91
10 DEVELOPMENT 94
11 TAXES 97
12 GRANTS AND INCENTIVES 100
13 COMPANIES AND BUSINESS ENTITIES 100
14 INTERNATIONAL 102

CHAPTER 3

Denmark

1 OWNERSHIP OF LAND

There are two legal systems for real property, the general regime in Denmark and simplified adaptations which apply in the Faroe Islands and Greenland. This chapter deals only with the general regime. Property law has been codified, the principal statute being the Land Registry Act 1927, although certain parts are supplemented by court decisions. The principal form of land ownership is absolute ownership. Many businesses lease their property, but this is not a form of land ownership and does not create a right in or against the land itself (a right in rem). As with other Scandinavian jurisdictions, the distinction between rights in rem and rights in personam is of little relevance, and ownership as well as occupation are both enforceable against all third parties. Absolute ownership and leases are the two main vehicles for owning or using land.

1.1 Types of tenure

1.1.1 Freehold or absolute ownership

Absolute ownership (*ejendomsret*) implies the right to own, occupy and dispose of the land and any buildings on the land, subject to any general public regulation in force. Anything fixed to the land or the buildings is considered a fixture and part of the property. Under the Land Registry Act, the property includes cables, heating installations, and household appliances incorporated into the building. For business property, unless agreed otherwise, trade fixtures and equipment, machinery and technical equipment of any kind are included (although number-plated vehicles are not). With respect to agricultural land, livestock, fertiliser, growing crops, tractors and machines used on the property are also included. It is possible for land and buildings to be owned separately where the third party builds on the land leased to him and owns the building for the duration of the right (see 2.1.3). However, it is far more common for leases to be granted over the land together with the right to use existing buildings on the land. Absolute ownership generally carries with it the right to the soil below and the air above the land, although there are legislative provisions enabling public authorities to restrict the use of air space over 25 metres above the ground. Absolute ownership also carries the right to mines and minerals, but extraction requires a licence which may be difficult to obtain.

1.1.2 Leasehold

Long leases in the Anglo-American tradition, for a premium or capital payment, do not exist. Leases, or tenancies, are mere contractual arrangements and do not grant an interest in the land, but will confer the exclusive right to use and occupy the property. There are strict restrictions regarding the ability of a landlord to terminate an agreement unless the contract expressly states it is a short-term tenancy. Similarly, a tenancy is not generally transferable unless expressly provided for in the contract (see section 5 for more detail).

1.1.3 Joint ownership

Joint ownership creates shared rights exercised jointly, and each owner will have a joint right to the entire property unless otherwise agreed. It is wise for joint owners to enter into an agreement regulating the right to exercise ownership. Joint ownership of land may only be conferred for a 30-year period, whereas the joint ownership of a building may be for an indefinite term. In the event of a sale by a joint owner, the remaining owners will not have a legal right of pre-emption, unless otherwise agreed. In practice, the remaining joint owners may often be the only prospective buyers willing to pay an acceptable price. Any one of the joint owners may demand a dissolution of the joint ownership.

1.1.4 Condominia

1.1.4.1 The Condominium Act (*Ejerlejlighedsloven*), which applies to all types of property, applies where there are both individually owned units and jointly owned common areas in the building. The condominium will be formally regulated by the articles of association of the condominium owners' association. The law will impose a mandatory standard set of articles of association where the condominium owners do not adopt their own. Condominium owners vote and decide matters in accordance with their share of the property, and each condominium is registered separately in the land registry. Since 1976, a specific permit has been required to subdivide existing residential properties into condominia, which is rarely granted, therefore in practice new condominia only come into existence when new buildings are built.

1.1.4.2 A widespread and similar arrangement is regulated under the Cooperative Housing Association Act which imposes strict controls on the transfer of shares in cooperative housing associations and specific incorporation procedures and rules. Members of some smaller associations may be granted favourable tax treatment for interest on their share of the finance for the association's purchase of the property. The sale of residential property to partnerships is restricted.

1.1.5 Lesser rights

See 2.1 where lesser rights are commented on in more detail.

1.2 Legal and beneficial ownership

The use of trusts has been statute-barred since 1919. There are no effective legal mechanisms for a person to own property on behalf of another, although see 2.8.

1.3 Restrictions on ownership and dealing

1.3.1 Those resident in Denmark may freely acquire property. Minors and the legally incapacitated may own land under certain circumstances through legal guardians. A limited company or association may only acquire property if its articles of association provide for such ownership. Additional restrictions apply to 'summer houses', ie houses intended for recreational purposes during the summer or at weekends located in specific areas and subject to specific zoning regulations.

1.3.2 Agricultural land holdings exceeding 30 hectares may only be acquired by adult EU member state citizens who do not already own other agricultural land in Denmark or abroad, and who possess the prescribed agricultural training (see also 5.3.3). They must take up residence within six months of purchase and farm the land. It is possible to purchase agricultural property through a limited company in which a person possessing the requisite qualifications must have a minimum 10 per cent shareholding. There are other restrictions on the ownership of land by foreign persons and entities and these are referred to in section 14. There are some legislative restrictions to protect the public interest and they include planning regulations, rights of access, preservation of natural beauty and compulsory purchase. Other restrictions protect private interests such as the laws pertaining to neighbours.

1.3.3 Land exceeding 6,000 square metres located in an urban zone (see further section 8 for zoning and planning regulations) may not be sold without first being offered to the local municipality. The municipality may either purchase at the price and on the terms offered by the seller within six weeks, or suggest alternative terms. If the owner is not willing to accept the municipality's proposed terms, he may request the Road Expropriation Appraisal Committee to value the property and the municipality to acquire the property at the price it sets. If the municipality does not exercise its right of pre-emption, the owner is free to sell the property for the next eight months. For private rights of pre-emption see 2.4. Disposals of land by public authorities must be properly authorised; the property must be offered to the general public and cannot be transferred by a private sale agreement. There are no legal restrictions on the disposal of land by charities, subject to their articles of association and the terms of any bequest.

1.4 Adverse possession or acquisitive prescription

It is possible to obtain full ownership by adverse possession or prescription or use this to provide a defence to claims by the rightful owner, or to create a servitude by prescription (see 2.1.1 and 2.1.2). To acquire positive title to land, the occupation must be in good faith and for a continuous 20-year period or the possessor must have exercised owner's rights over the property without the owner's permission.

2 OTHER INTERESTS IN LAND

This section deals with those private and public interests in property that do not give a full ownership right to a property. The most common are servitudes, mortgages, conditional deeds and public property charges.

2.1 Servitudes or easements, usufruct, building and dwelling rights

2.1.1 Servitudes or easements

A distinction is generally made between positive and negative servitudes (*servitutter*) and a special category of public servitudes. A positive servitude is a limited right over one piece of land (the servient tenement) in favour of another piece of land (the dominant tenement) which may include the right to cross the property, eg by the use of a road or path. For negative servitudes, see 2.2. The right generally attaches to the land rather than a specific owner at any one time. Servitudes may be created by agreement, which need not be in writing, or by 20 years' usage. In practice, all servitudes are in writing and registered, as registration is the only way they may be enforced against third parties in good faith and against creditors. A servitude may be granted in perpetuity provided a restricted right has been granted. If the right granted is a right of full and exclusive use over the land, the duration of the servitude may not exceed 30 years; if the beneficiary wishes the right to be secured for more than 30 years, it will be necessary to parcel out the property. However, it may not always be possible to do so under the relevant planning regulations. A number of servitudes still exist from the period prior to 1990, when the maximum duration was 10 years. The right may be in favour of a specific person (including his successors for one generation only) or an owner of specific property and his successors. Therefore beneficiaries need not always have an interest in adjoining land. Transfer of ownership of the property will automatically transfer the benefit of the servitude. For the right to hunt or collect fruits to be acquired by long usage, the right must have been exercised for a full generation, so no one living in the area can remember the right not having existed. Public authorities have the power to grant public servitudes over private property under zoning and planning legislation without the servitude amounting to expropriation.

2.1.2 Usufruct

The terms 'usufruct' and 'profits à prendre' are unknown. Rights to obtain certain supplies from the property such as water, or the right to use the property for grazing, collecting firewood or hunting do exist, but are deemed to be servitudes (see 2.1.1).

2.1.3 Building and dwelling rights

It is possible for the ownership of land and buildings to be separate. The land may be leased by the owner to a tenant who will then erect a building which will belong to him and not the owner. This type of arrangement is rare (as land and buildings over it are usually leased together), but is used by port authorities who will lease land upon which tenants will construct warehouses and the like. The building may be registered as a building on a leased plot of land to provide protection against third parties, but registration is not a prerequisite to validity. The lease of the land itself will usually provide for the removal of the buildings and structures upon expiry of the lease, so the ownership of the building will effectively be temporary. The duration of the lease will depend on the agreement, and there may be contractual restrictions on transfer (eg requiring the payment of a sum upon each transfer).

2.2 Restrictions on use and other restrictions

A negative servitude grants the beneficiary the right to secure the status quo over the subject property, eg restricting the location and height of buildings, or the use the property may be put to. When registered, successors in title will be bound for the duration of the servitude, which may be indefinite. Only a beneficiary may enforce the right but he need not be an owner of other land. A negative servitude may only be removed by agreement (see 2.1.1). Private property charges obliging the owner of land to pay a set annual fee, or supply a set quantity of eg gravel or wood, are barred under statute. Planning and other public law restrictions are commented on at section 8.

2.3 Private mortgages, privileges and charges

A lender can secure monetary liabilities on the borrower's property by three different types of mortgage:

(a) an ordinary mortgage on land (*pantebrev i fast ejendom*);
(b) an indemnity mortgage (*skadesløsbrev*); or
(c) an owner's mortgage (*ejerpantebrev*).

(See further section 7.) The bailiff courts may create charging orders to secure judgments obtained in the civil courts.

2.4 Contracts and options

In principle, any contract for the sale of land can be a preliminary contract granting a beneficiary an interest in the land. The wording of the contract will determine whether the contract is a conditional deed, a right of pre-emption or even a lesser right. If the beneficiary wishes to protect himself against third parties in good faith and against creditors, the right may be registered over the property either as a conditional deed (see 3.2.2) or as a servitude. Therefore, a potential buyer may secure the right to purchase the property at a specific or defined time in the future, at a pre-determined or market-related price. The seller will not wish the deed to be executed until the buyer has made a cash-down payment and has obtained the necessary financing as there is no seller's lien.

2.5 Public or municipal charges

A number of acts grant priority to sums owed to public authorities over other debts of a property owner, to recover payment of taxes, insurance premiums and for the supply of public utilities to the property. These are first priority charges against the property, overriding any private mortgages or other charges registered against the property before the debts accrued. However, first in the order of priority are municipal property taxes and fire insurance premiums to government-approved fire insurance companies. These are not recorded in a register, although the relevant public authority will usually be willing to assist potential buyers and others with details of any outstanding charges over the property. Tax authorities may also impose a charge by the intervention of the tax bailiffs. The owner of a residential property eligible for a retirement pension may postpone the payment of municipal property taxes until sale or death in return for a charge against the property.

2.6 Other interests

A condominium owners' association may secure its claim against individual condominium owners for the association's service charges by registering the articles of association or the potential debt as a mortgage against the property. Note should be made of the public rights of access to beaches and forests.

2.7 Liabilities attaching to land

Liabilities attaching to property are based on negligence, usually in cases involving injury or damage to passers-by, whether as a result of inadequate maintenance or a failure to clear dirt or ice in breach of pavement and road regulations. Case law stipulates that the duty of care expected in such instances is relatively high. The owner may be liable for damage caused to adjoining land by negligent or unreasonable use. Similarly, occupiers may have a claim against the owner of the land also based on negligence. For building works that affect neighbouring properties, liability may be strict if an assessment of the reasonable alternatives indicates that the owner could have chosen less damaging methods for the building works or if it is generally considered reasonable for him to bear the risk of damage. Environmental damage is dealt with in section 9. Employees will generally be protected by the provisions of the Working Environment Act. Fiscal liability attaches to land in the form of municipal property taxes and fire insurance premiums to government-approved fire insurance companies. Comment is made on tax in section 11.

2.8 Legal and equitable interest

It is possible for a person to hold land on behalf of another, but as it is very difficult for a beneficial owner to enforce his interest against third parties, such arrangements are not common.

2.9 Protection of interests

The protection of all types of interests, be they ownership interests or more limited interests in land, is achieved by registration (see section 3). Most interests cannot be enforced against the land and subsequent buyers, third parties in good faith and creditors (the latter whether in good faith or not), unless they are protected by some form of registration. However, some limited rights enjoy protection without registration such as the right to use and occupy, mainly applicable to agricultural land which is not regulated by landlord and tenant regulations.

2.10 Priority of interests

Priority of interests in land depends entirely upon the date of registration rather than the date of creation of the interest and there are provisions for the possibility of more recent rights extinguishing older rights, if the older rights have not been registered. However, public and municipal charges override this principle, so that irrespective of being created later in time, they will take priority over existing registered interests. Rights to use and occupy (see 2.9), which do not require registration, are another exception.

3 TITLE TO LAND

3.1 Proof of title

The beneficiary of any right, including ownership or some lesser right, may choose whether or not to register it in the land register. Therefore, registration is not a prerequisite to validity as any right would still be valid between the parties. Registration secures the right of the beneficiary against any third party who would be able to extinguish the rights under the rules of the Land Registry Act on the basis that new rights extinguish older, unregistered rights. Virtually all land in Denmark, with the exception of a few coastal areas, is covered by the land registry. The land registers are also used by the tax authorities for valuation purposes and serve as a basis for assessment of municipal property taxes. The registers are open for public inspection, and transcripts are available.

3.2 Land registers

A local land registry is administered by the local court in all of the 83 local court districts.

3.2.1 Plans

The *Cadastre Directorate* is responsible for the subdivision of the entire country into mapped-out plots which are the basis for registration of any rights against the land and the boundaries are definitive. Searches are by reference to plot numbers and generally each municipality will keep a register where addresses make reference to the relevant plot number.

3.2.2 *Content*

Rights against properties are divided into three categories in the registers: ownership rights (*ejendomsret*); mortgages (*pantehaeftelser*); and servitudes (*servitutter*). There is only one category of ownership, full ownership, which may be entered. The notion of conditional ownership is recognised, but only subject to the condition of full payment of the purchase price. These conditional deeds may be registered in the category of ownership rights. In order for a document to be registered it must establish, create, alter or extinguish a right against specific property.

3.2.3 *Errors*

The registers are conclusive. The government will be strictly liable for any errors that occur, usually in the form of compensation rather than rectification. However, the registers can be rectified where this will not affect any other party.

3.3 Passing of title

For most purposes title will pass when the contract is signed or at the date the contract indicates it should pass. However, protection against third parties will only be enjoyed from the time the document is filed at the land registry. Documents to be registered must be stamped by the municipal property tax authorities which will certify that there are no outstanding property taxes; unstamped documents will not be accepted for registration. Registration will be backdated to the date of application. There is no specific time limit within which registration must occur. Non-registration will simply render the right unenforceable against third parties and enable later registered rights to take priority over it.

4 TRANSACTIONS IN LAND

The most common transactions in land are the sale and purchase of absolute ownership rights, the creation of mortgages, and servitudes.

4.1 Procedures

The transfer of ownership normally falls into two stages. The first is generally relatively swift, whilst the second, dealing with documentation and securing of finance, may take longer. A completion time of one to two months is not unusual. Based on the offer for sale prepared by a state-authorised estate agent (see 4.5), a sales contract will be drawn up during the first stage based on one of the two or three standard forms normally used. The contract will specify the form of finance which is normally established by the seller and subject to the approval of the financial institutions in the light of the buyer's status. This contract will govern the relationship between the parties. Investigation of title is straightforward and a transcript of the registration of the specific property will provide all the requisite information. A physical survey of the property is often undertaken. Environmental issues are only generally investigated where the transaction involves an industrial estate or if there are specific concerns. The parties are contractually bound once an unconditional sale agreement has been signed. The subsequent deed of title will only reiterate the agreement and is usually prepared by the buyer's lawyer. Until the buyer is in possession of the signed deed of title, he cannot make an application for registration. In certain urban zones the public right of pre-emption may be enforced by the municipal authority (see 1.3). The conditional deed may be used to secure protection against creditors and other third parties or against any 'double sale' that may have occurred, provided the contract is only subject to payment of the outstanding purchase price (see 3.2.2). The second stage of the transfer of ownership entails finalising finance arrangements, preparing a deed on the basis of the initial contract which is then stamped by the municipal tax authorities (see 3.3), and application to, and registration in, the land register. There is no need for notarisation. As mentioned in section 3, registration is voluntary, but is almost always complied with.

4.2 Contract terms

4.2.1 The seller is under a legal obligation to provide the buyer with any relevant information of which he has knowledge. He will normally give a number of warranties regarding the physical condition of the property, eg freedom from physical and hidden defects to the seller's knowledge or compliance with the relevant planning or zoning and building regulations. The seller will usually be required to provide an energy consumption certificate. Normally, under the standard terms of a sale contract, the purchase price will not be released to the seller until the buyer has had his ownership registered. So ownership will not normally be the subject of a warranty. A deposit will generally be paid when the initial contract is signed. Risk will pass at the time of the 'take-over date' or transfer of the property (when the keys are handed over and physical possession will pass). Insurance will remain the seller's responsibility until the date of transfer, although risk in relation to fire will pass from the date of the initial contract. The seller owes a duty to maintain the property in the same condition between the date of contract and the date of transfer.

4.2.2 Generally the parties are entitled to contract out of warranties, although consumer protection legislation will apply in the case of residential property. Material breaches of warranty will give the buyer the right to choose between repudiation, compensatory damages and a reduction in the purchase price. The general time limit for an action for breach of warranty is 20 years, although specific rules apply to residential property. If a survey has been undertaken and insurance cover has been purchased for any faults not disclosed by the report, the buyer may not bring any further claim. If the survey is defective, claims must be made within five years from the date of transfer or, if earlier, six years from the date of the report.

4.2.3 In the event of delay, the contract will generally contain provisions dealing with the payment of interest pending completion. The concept of forfeiting the deposit is not known. Non-completion is not expressly provided for, but is considered a breach of contract which may give rise to compensatory damages or repudiation, depending on the circumstances.

4.3 Formalities

Although there is no legal requirement for the transfer of ownership to be in writing, in practice it always will be. Whilst the first contract may be informal, the document used to register the transfer of ownership to the property must be a deed, which is then stamped by the municipal tax authorities (see 3.3) ensuring the transfer of the obligation to pay property taxes to the local municipality to the new owner. The parties can agree to other terms and conditions orally or in other documents, provided there is evidence that all the terms form part of the total contractual relationship between the parties. However, it is very common for a contract between parties to be based on a preprinted form. Notarisation is not required. The registration of leases, particularly commercial leases, is recommended.

4.4 Fees, costs and taxes

4.4.1 The seller pays the estate agent's commission and usually bears the expense of establishing the mortgage finance, although this trend is changing. A seller does not usually arrange a lawyer but if he does, he must bear his fees. The buyer pays the fees of the only lawyer likely to be involved. Estate agents' commission varies – for residential property, the fee will normally range from 2.5–4 per cent of the sale price, depending on whether advertising costs are included. For commercial property, the fees will be subject to negotiation and will vary more. Joint agents are usually only appointed on larger commercial transactions. It is uncommon for prospective buyers to instruct an agent but his fees would be subject to negotiation. Commercial landlords normally pay their agent 10–15 per cent of the first year's rent, subject to negotiation. Fees are only usually paid on a successful transaction.

4.4.2 Lawyers may charge on a time basis, or charge a set fee, which will vary according to the value of the property but is commonly between 0.4 and 1 per cent plus. Lawyers will often not charge if initial negotiations are unsuccessful, and a transaction will probably complete once the initial contract is signed.

4.4.3 Stamp duty is charged at 1.2 per cent of the sale price. This is reduced to 0.6 per cent if the property has been used as a principal residence by the seller or will be used as such by the buyer. Lease contracts attract stamp duty, normally payable by the tenant, of one per cent of the highest annual rent, or total rent if the lease is for less than 12 months.

4.4.4 A land registry fee of DKK700 is charged for each document that is submitted for registration.

4.4.5 Transaction costs vary from one sale or lease to another.

4.4.6 All estate agents' and lawyers' fees (except those for any second mortgage) attract value added tax (VAT) of 25 per cent.

4.5 Professionals' roles

The majority of property sales are conducted through state-authorised estate agents ('real estate brokers'), who must have completed the specified courses and examinations. It is possible to operate as an estate agent without being a 'real estate broker', but only for commercial property. Exceptions also apply to lawyers who are members of the Danish Bar Association, and to certain banking, mortgage credit institutions and insurance companies. Estate agents usually represent sellers and are assisted by banking institutions and mortgage credit institutions who put together the financing package offered to the buyer. Lawyers normally represent buyers, and prepare the documentation to be filed with the land registry. Notaries are not involved. In the case of residential property, the survey is commissioned by the seller and the professional conducting the survey, who will be an architect or an engineer, must also be a licensed property surveyor. Buyers can commission surveys for all other types of property and the professionals involved need not be licensed.

5 LEASES AND OTHER RIGHTS OF OCCUPATION

All tenancies, of which there is only one type, are contractual and do not grant an interest in land. Tenancies are generally granted for a periodical rent and not for a premium or capital sum. Although they may be for a fixed term lasting a few months or one to two years at most, they are usually granted for an indefinite period subject to termination on three months' to a year's notice, depending on the reason for termination (see 5.3). A distinction is drawn between residential and commercial property.

5.1 Rent and other terms

For commercial property, freedom of contract prevails in principle, and rent for commercial property reflects market levels. An amended version of the statutory standard form contract will often be used by the parties. A mechanism exists for rent review by the local courts, although the parties may have agreed an automatic rent increase of a fixed percentage or linked to the cost of living index, and the landlord may increase the rent to reflect increases in property tax rates. The statutory standard form contract is mandatory for residential leases, and significant restrictions are imposed on rent (see 5.3.1). Rent may be reviewed downwards as well as upwards. Rent is generally payable monthly and in advance, although quarterly payments are increasingly used both for residential and commercial leases. Turnover rents are generally confined to the retail sector. The assignment of a non-residential tenancy is a statutory right, unless the landlord has material objections, such as insufficient information about the tenant's financial status or commercial activities. These provisions may be excluded by contract, although this is subject to the application of the Commercial Property Rent Adjustment Act (see further 5.3). Assignments between spouses are generally permitted. The landlord will usually be responsible for external repairs, and the tenant for internal repairs. The tenant may undertake external repairs in a commercial lease. It is possible to contract out of the repair obligations. The tenant cannot alter the property without authorisation. The landlord will insure the building and will commonly require a deposit of three to six months' rent. Tenancies may only be terminated by the landlord under exceptional circumstances, eg upon material breach by the tenant or fire, and there are statutory restrictions on such a right (see also 5.3).

5.2 Privity of contract and estate

The landlord and tenant will remain personally liable for the obligations under the lease agreement even if they cease to be the landlord and the tenant. The landlord's obligations will be registered against the property as a charge and will rank ahead of other registered rights such as servitudes or mortgages.

5.3 Rent control and security of tenure

5.3.1 Commercial rents are subject to the Rent Act and Commercial Property Rent Adjustment Act. The landlord and tenant may request the property court to increase or decrease the rent but not in the first four years of the lease, nor within four years of the last adjustment. The parties may choose to extend the four-year period by a further eight years, ie to 12 years. A precondition for this is that the tenant will have the right to assign the rights under the lease without acting as surety for the new tenant and to re-enter into the lease if the landlord wishes to terminate the lease with the new tenant, due to a default on the part of the new tenant. This right to renew is a general right under the Rent Act, although the parties may agree to contract out of it. The adjustment will take place over a four-year period, with a quarter of the adjustment coming into force every year. Under the Rent Act and the Temporary Regulation of Residential Property Act both the landlord and the tenant of residential leases may request an adjustment of rent to reflect the 'value' of the property, which is often unrelated to market terms and invariably lower than that on the free market. In addition the Rent Act imposes a very strict cost-based fixing of rent on residential property. A significant exception is made for property let for commercial purposes on 31 December 1991 but now let for residential purposes.

5.3.2 The rules relating to termination and security of tenure apply to both residential and commercial properties. A landlord may not generally terminate a tenancy or make it for a limited time, subject to narrow exceptions. Fixed-length tenancies will only be upheld if the period is usually no more than five years, and if the terms and the length of the lease are considered reasonable, taking into consideration the general circumstances of the parties. Tenancies (except short ones) do not stipulate the length of the lease although the landlord may agree not to terminate the lease for a period and the tenant not to use his normal right to terminate with three months' notice. If the tenancy is not for a fixed period, it may only be terminated by the landlord under exceptional circumstances, eg where the landlord wishes to use the property himself (although a commercial landlord must not use the premises to set up business in competition with the tenant), where he wishes to demolish or carry out major renovation works, or where the tenant's behaviour is unreasonable (eg interfering with the quiet enjoyment of fellow tenants). Under these specified circumstances, the landlord may terminate on three months' notice (or one year's notice when recovering the premises for his own use). This will be subject to a general requirement of reasonableness as between landlord and tenant. Compensation will include relocation expenses and any expected loss of turnover.

5.3.3 In respect of agricultural properties, the Minister of Agriculture may grant a buyer permission to acquire agricultural land without requiring the buyer himself to fulfil the conditions of the Agriculture Act (see 1.3.2), where the buyer has already entered into a conditional lease agreement with a tenant who himself does satisfy those conditions. An agricultural lease may not be for more than 30 years.

5.4 Other legislative restrictions

Under the Temporary Regulation of Residential Properties Act certain property previously used for residential purposes must continue to be used for the same purpose and the Act proscribes any conversion to use as a summer residence or for commercial purposes. The prior use as residential property can be checked in the central persons register where all persons resident in Denmark must register an address. The local municipality has the power to prosecute and also to let the property in the name of the landlord to persons within the municipality seeking a residence. These rules do not apply to new buildings not previously used for residential purposes although planning regulations may impose similar restrictions on the owner. The rules apply automatically to municipalities where rent control rules apply. Other municipalities have a discretion whether the rules should apply or not.

5.5 Method of measurement

Government Order No 311, 1983 sets out the rules calculating the area for residences and commercial premises.

6 FINANCE AND INVESTMENT SOURCES

The property market is financed largely by real credit institution loans which raise funds by the issue of mortgage-backed bonds. The majority of the market is loan finance, but a number of leasing arrangements exist, often tax driven. Real credit institutions may only finance immoveable property and a few ancillary activities. Real credit institutions have the sole right to issue mortgage-backed bonds.

6.1 Loan finance

There are currently six real credit institutions (akin to building societies in the United Kingdom) whose lending is strictly regulated by the Real Credit Institutions Act. The system has been refined to a point where it is only possible for other finance institutions to compete with the real credit institutions in very exceptional cases. Banks do not generally provide loan finance for the acquisition of property, although there are two important exceptions. The first is in relation to large commercial properties where banks may often compete with real credit institutions for loans by offering favourable corporate rates. The second exception is where banks provide second loans for the purchase of residential property behind the real credit institutions (see further 6.3). Real credit institutions may only lend a percentage of the value of the security (generally 60 per cent for commercial, 70 per cent for agricultural, 80 per cent for residential and 91 per cent for social housing). They will also examine the creditworthiness and the expected cash-flow of the borrower. The maturity period for the loan may be up to 30 years. The average length of a loan ranges between 20 and 30 years, with a notable preference by borrowers in recent years for the 30-year loan. Repayment will be amortised as bullet payments and balloons are not used for property finance. Loans are generally standard and will not be tailored for the particular investment or project. However, more flexible real credit products have been introduced recently with an increasing number of different maturity periods, interest fixing periods and interest fixing methods. Real credit institutions may also grant loans on so-called 'index terms'. This means that the principal is linked to the cost of living index and will be adjusted twice yearly. Therefore the interest will be substantially lower than on a straight mortgage. When interest rates are not on index terms, they will generally be fixed as a reflection of the fixed interest on the underlying bond giving the sale price of the bond, ie above or below par. The new finance vehicles allow interest to be fixed for shorter periods and at variable rates. The duration of the underlying bond and the shape of the product are just two of the aspects regulated by statute.

6.2 Investment or equity finance

Equity capital is still largely provided by private investors although institutional investors, and pension funds in particular, took advantage of the preferential tax treatment of new buildings, until this was abolished. Some property companies are quoted on the stock exchange. Unit trusts are not generally used as finance vehicles. It is doubtful whether the stock exchange would accept a single asset company, ie based on one major property, even though such a property could be the subject of a collective investment scheme. It should be mentioned that these collective investment schemes have been created in recent years mainly as partnerships and limited partnerships for tax-related reasons, granting investors the direct benefit on personal income of any tax depreciation.

6.3 Mezzanine or mixed funding

The real credit institution will take the first security. The remainder of the finance is normally divided between (a) a second mortgage set up by the seller often through a specialised second mortgage company, and (b) a cash payment. For residential properties, the split is commonly 80 per cent provided by real credit institutions, 14 per cent by second mortgages, and six per cent paid by means of a cash payment, which could be lent as tertiary finance by banks. The financing of commercial properties varies considerably as compensation for the lesser security. The mezzanine lender will generally only look for a higher rate of interest.

6.4 Sale and lease-back

Some companies and individuals prefer to free funds from property investments and rent their property. The sale and lease-back transaction, whereby the property is sold to an investor for a capital sum and then leased from the investor to the seller for an annual return, is a fairly commonly used device, and frequently tax driven in partnership or limited partnership structures. Typical investors in such schemes will be smaller or limited partnerships and institutional investors largely dominated by pension funds.

6.5 Tax leasing

The investments of partnerships and limited partnerships are tax driven and may take the form of a strict lease, a sale and lease-back transaction, or a turn-key lease whereby a property is built to the specifications of the tenant. Recent changes in tax legislation have reduced the importance of partnerships and limited partnerships as property investors as depreciation no longer applies to the asset if there are more than 10 partners.

6.6 Other types of property finance

Unit trusts are not common. Any public tender of securities must be carried out in accordance with the Danish Securities Act which implements the EU Directive regulating the position regarding prospectuses. It is possible to enter into hire-purchase or lease-purchase transactions, but these are not widespread due to the restrictions in the Rent Act (see section 5). Businesses generally tend to decide whether they want to be owners or tenants and remain either one or the other.

6.7 Institutional investment

Institutional investors largely dominated by pension funds comprise the other large group of investors. The incentive for pension funds to make property investments is that, on certain conditions and quotas, they are granted an exemption from the provisions for taxation of real interest. Insurance companies and other institutions set the investment criteria especially in respect of larger offices and high value residential property. The institutions usually invest directly in property.

6.8 Other investors

Smaller partnerships or limited partnerships invest in the property market although recent changes in taxation legislation have reduced the importance of partnerships (see 6.5). The tax driven partnership focuses primarily on retail leases as they have the highest tax depreciation rate, but also on industrial property as this is the only other type of property where depreciation is permitted. No tax depreciation is allowed on office buildings or residential property.

7 FORMS OF SECURITY

Because of their importance, this section focuses on the types of mortgages granted by the real credit institutions (see 6.1) and the category of property securing the loan. Real credit institutions always require security and there is no emphasis on relationship banking. By using objective criteria, they concentrate primarily on security, and then look at the finances and cash-flow of the borrower. Bank managers are not permitted to hold board memberships, although in some instances, banks will appoint lawyers or others to represent them on supervisory (rather than management) boards. The mortgage security will represent joint and several security for the bondholders for the repayment of the entire debt under the bond issue. The amount that a real credit institution can lend against each property is calculated as a percentage of the cash value of the property (see 6.1). The loans granted by the real credit institutions are for fixed purposes. Working capital is generally provided by commercial banks. Security in the form of mortgages or other security will be required by the commercial banks on asset finance, although a more flexible view may be taken on overdrafts and working capital.

7.1 Mortgages

7.1.1 Real credit institutions borrow against a bond issue and mortgages then secure the funds generated. Borrowers are personally liable for the mortgage debt which also attaches to the property. The Real Credit Institutions Act prescribes an amortisation profile and the form of the mortgage to be used. Real credit institutions only grant mortgage loans in accordance with the prescribed form. Mortgages require registration to ensure protection against third parties; in practice the loan will not be paid out under the mortgage unless registration has taken place. Mortgages granted by real credit institutions are always for a fixed sum. It is possible to issue a so-called 'indemnity mortgage' (see further 7.1.2) which secures the mortgagee up to the amount of the indemnity. The mortgage must specify the exact property as there may be more than one property charged by the same mortgage. Private mortgages, often the second mortgage, also have to follow a specific form. These may be issued by any type of borrower, in favour of any type of lender, eg private banks, private investors and sellers of properties, other than real credit institutions. The main difference between this private form, and that of real credit institutions, is that under a private mortgage the mortgagee cannot prevent the transfer of ownership although an extraordinary instalment of five per cent may be demanded (if this has been agreed to in the documentation) to reduce the debt more quickly. By way of contrast, real credit institutions will conduct a full review of a potential buyer's finances and will only grant the transfer of the loan to the buyer if this does not affect the standing of the loan. The new owner will then acquire the right of ownership and occupation of the property. A land registry fee of DKK700 is charged for each mortgage.

7.1.2 Private mortgagees have the choice between two other forms of mortgage, namely the indemnity mortgage (*skadesloespantebrev*) and the owner's mortgage (*ejerpantebrev*). The indemnity mortgage stipulates that the mortgagor will indemnify the mortgagee up to a set amount; the amount of the mortgage will consequently be fixed according to the amount due under the underlying secured loan at the time when the indemnity mortgage is enforced (subject to the maximum amount specified). The owner's mortgage is an unusual creation. The mortgagor issues a mortgage to himself. The mortgagor will then go to a lender and transfer his rights to the mortgage to the lender. The advantage is flexibility, as the owner's mortgage may be transferred successively to different lenders and received back by the mortgagor without the necessity of issuing a new mortgage and further stamp duty.

7.1.3 On default, a lender will have initial recourse to a bailiff court for an execution levy (enforcement order) over the property. Following the execution levy, he may return to the court and request the property be sold by public auction under the supervision of the court, with the auction prospectus usually being prepared by the lender's lawyer. The notion of foreclosure and direct sale is unknown, although it is both commercial practice and legally acceptable for the lender to be given power of attorney to sell the property either at the best price obtainable or within a certain price range. All enforcement of security will be undertaken through the court. The lender may take possession and take the income, which is of particular relevance to agricultural and rented properties with a substantial continuous cash flow. Convertible mortgages are not used, and separate pre-emption rights are employed instead. The lender has a duty to ensure that the breach is a material one entitling him to terminate the agreement or to enforce. If the borrower is dissatisfied with the highest bid obtained for the property at auction, he may request a second auction (provided he gives security for the additional costs involved).

7.2 Floating and other charges

The notion of floating and other charges is not known in Denmark. The only other types of security available are the three types of mortgage mentioned in 7.1. It is not possible to charge unspecified future assets but it is possible to mortgage a specific asset which is not yet owned; but protection against third parties will not be obtained until ownership has been acquired and registration completed.

7.3 Performance bonds and guarantees

It is not very common for real credit institution loans to be backed by guarantees from third parties, eg by the borrower's bank. However, guarantees are sometimes issued in specific cases particularly where finance is obtained through banks or other channels, eg small finance houses or private investors; a guarantee may then be issued for the borrowed amount or for a part of it. Guarantees may be issued either as surety (*simpel garanti*) or by the guarantor as a primary obligation of the borrower (*selvskyldnerkaution*). No formalities are required in connection with the issue of a guarantee other than to specify the type of guarantee, the subject-matter and the signature of a person acting on behalf of the guarantor. What is known as the bond elsewhere would probably be considered a guarantee under Danish law.

7.4 Credit insurance

Credit insurance plays no material role in the property market in Denmark.

8 PLANNING AND BUILDING REGULATION

The development and use of land and buildings are under the control of various levels of authority as described in the Planning Consolidated Act 1993 (the 'Planning Act'). The Building Act regulates the actual construction of buildings.

8.1 Planning authorities

The Minister for the Environment, who acts under the control of Parliament (*Folketinget*), is responsible for establishing planning policy for the entire country and for conducting the necessary surveys in order to ensure compliance. Locally, decisions are taken by local government at two levels: the counties, of which there are 15 (including the municipalities which are part of the capital) and the individual municipalities, of which there are 275. As local officials are controlled by the elected councils, the planning procedure is more of a political process.

8.2 Zoning and development plans

8.2.1 The planning system is hierarchical. The Minister for the Environment prepares a national plan setting out the general planning strategy for the whole country and he may call upon local authorities to prepare plans detailing zoning and land use in specific instances (eg military installations, electricity installations and refugee camps) and to provide information. On a local level, the counties prepare a framework plan, setting out the main uses for areas within the county; the detailed planning is left to the municipalities which are under a duty to prepare a plan. Most properties are now subject to plans prepared and adopted by the specific local municipality. The county plan must split the county into the three types of areas as outlined under the Planning Act, namely agricultural, urban and summer house areas, and designate which areas should be designated for retail purposes as well as the maximum size of retail units, which has been a controversial issue in recent years. The county also takes decisions regarding larger developments which will have an environmental impact (see also section 9) and other resources. Each municipality must prepare a municipal plan which must contain a more specific subdivision of the general division prepared at county level. In addition to this, the municipality may also prepare local plans for areas within the municipality. The county plan must not conflict with the national plan and the municipal plan must likewise not conflict with the county plan. At the local level, zones are very specifically designated and tightly controlled. All areas are designated, although some areas may be subject to less detailed regulation, eg where a municipal or local plan has not been prepared for the area. In these areas, where proposed development is deemed unsuitable, the municipality has the power to freeze all development pending the preparation of a local plan. All plan proposals are subject to a public hearing. After publicising a proposed plan, no material changes may be made to properties affected by the plan.

8.2.2 A local plan for a section of the municipality must be prepared before major subdivision construction work or demolition is undertaken or if it is necessary to implement the parts of the municipality plan. The municipality must prepare a local plan as soon as possible, which in practice has been deemed to be within one year, if, eg the owner of a property wishes to subdivide the property and the subdivision is in accordance with the municipality plan. Therefore a private landowner may indirectly instigate the zoning process. Whether a project is of a magnitude that requires a local plan is decided on a case-by-case basis and considerations will include the extent to which the proposed development will affect the surroundings. Plans must be revised every four years. If a person legally affected by a plan wishes to contest it, an action to have the plan set aside must be filed within six months of adoption of the plan. An administrative appeal is possible in some instances and must be made within four weeks of notification of the decision. If development conforms with the contents of the local plan, permission will normally be granted, provided the project complies with the relevant building codes as well (see further 8.4) and certain development is automatically permitted (see 8.3) without the need to obtain a permit. The request for use not permitted by the plan will require a new local plan. The municipality may grant limited dispensations provided they do not go to the main purpose of the plan, generally on issues such as density, siting and appearance.

8.3 Planning control and procedures

If building work is over a certain size as defined in the Building Act (see 8.4), an application for a building permit must be submitted to the local municipality which will grant or deny the building permission. A building permit (*byggetilladelse*) will almost always be required for alterations of some substance. Only development falling below the Building Act threshold will be allowed (provided it complies with the local plan) without the need to apply for a building permit (see 8.2.2). Permits will be required for engineering works, demolition, change of use and mining. In the event of doubt it is advisable to apply for a permit as the municipality may then inform the applicant that no permit is required or grant or refuse the permit. An applicant is under an obligation to report any building works not covered by the permit to the municipality, which then has two weeks within which to object.

8.3.1 The building permit (*byggetilladelse*) is issued by the local municipality. Fees may be payable and may be fixed by each municipality on the basis of the actual cost of processing the permit. There is no public consultation for building permits; public enquiry is confined to the local plan procedure (see 8.2). A permit application must contain full details of the proposed development.

8.3.2 A building permit application may take from a few weeks to several years. There is no real remedy available for delay, although it is possible to file an acknowledgement suit against the municipality arguing that the permit should be issued, or to file a complaint with the Parliamentary Ombudsman. The municipality will be liable for damages in the event of unreasonable delay. Administrative appeals are only available in limited cases (buildings close to the dividing line between properties, prohibition orders on further construction and decisions regarding securing unused property). The appeal should be made to the local state representative (*Statsamfret*). No further appeal is possible. Building permits are generally made conditional upon the applicant complying with the building regulations applicable to the specific type of property. It is not possible to challenge a building permit but the municipality will be liable in damages if the permit is subsequently determined not to be well founded on the Building Act or any existing plans.

8.3.3 The building permit application will normally be made by the owner or his representatives. A prospective buyer may also file an application, although the municipality would require a statement of consent from the current owner before dealing with the application. A building permit is valid for one year. A repeat application may be made immediately but is unlikely to be decided differently as decisions are largely based on objective criteria. There is no obligation to complete construction once it has started.

8.3.4 The municipality acting as enforcement authority may require an immediate halt to any construction works not in accordance with the Building Act. If the works have been partly or fully completed, a rectification order may be issued and the municipality may request a court order for payment of weekly fines pending rectification. Where rectification is not carried out, the municipality may execute rectification works itself at the owner's expense. A breach of the Building Act provisions is both a civil and criminal matter. Fines can be appealed against.

8.4 Building standards, control and supervision

In addition to complying with the local plan, the municipality plan, the county plan and the national plan, anyone wishing to build must also comply with the construction regulations under the Building Act. The regulations deal with construction and the siting and height of buildings and the Act authorises the issue of building codes which are legally binding. There are two building codes, the Building Code 1995, which is generally applicable, and the slightly less stringent Building Code 1985 which applies to smaller buildings and family houses. The building permit will make it a condition that the relevant building regulations are complied with.

8.5 Protection of buildings of special interest

The Minister of the Environment may issue preservation orders for buildings of architectural, cultural or historical value. These are usually over 100 years old, but they include more recent buildings of outstanding value and all buildings constructed prior to 1536. A building subject to an order must be kept in reasonable condition, with a water-tight roof and walls. Any building work or demolition must be authorised by the Minister of the Environment. If an owner wishes to demolish a building and permission is denied, he may request the state to expropriate the building at market value. Decisions regarding preservation orders on land (as opposed to buildings) are made by a preservation council. Such an order may contain specific orders as to the use of the land covered by the order and for the expropriation of the property. The Forestry Act requires forests to be maintained as forests, which requires felled timber to be replanted.

8.6 Expropriation or compulsory purchase and compensation

Land may only be expropriated if it is in the public interest. As a result expropriation procedures may only be initiated by public entities, and under statute. Compensation, which is calculated by the expropriation commission, must be at full market level, and will usually be fairly rapid provided an agreement as to the appropriate level of compensation is reached. Compensation awards will carry interest at five per cent above the official discount rate of the Danish Central Bank from the date of the decision. It is possible to bring the matter before the courts, with a right of appeal from the first decision, and from the court of second instance to the supreme court.

9 ENVIRONMENTAL MATTERS

9.0.1 The Environmental Protection Act 1973 ('the EPA') regulates air, water, soil and subsoil pollution and the prevention of vibration and noise, and aims to reduce the use and waste of raw materials and other resources, and to promote the use of cleaner technology. It also regulates the production and transportation of dangerous substances. The EPA is mainly administered by local and regional councils, although as the EPA is a framework Act, much of the ministers' powers have been delegated to the National Agency for Environmental Protection (*Miljoestyrelsen*) which has issued a number of guidelines. Licensing requirements are based on the type of business conducted and not in accordance with the type of environmental risk that the activity in question might cause. The powers of the regional environmental authorities allow them to prohibit the polluting activity, order remediation, or execute remediation itself at the cost of the polluting party.

9.0.2 The 'polluter pays' principle applies and the basis for liability will normally be negligence. In practice, other parties such as occupiers, owners, lenders or others will not be faced with a direct claim. However, an owner may be faced with substantial restrictions on the use of the property based on clean-up orders issued under the EPA. Violation of the EPA may result in fines and, if the violation is wilful or caused by gross negligence, imprisonment of up to two years. The EPA places owners and users of land under the obligation to notify the environmental authorities immediately of any incidents of pollution of the soil. The Environmental Damages Act 1994 ('the EDA') imposes strict liability for environmental damage caused by certain undertakings (listed in the EDA) commonly considered to pose a major pollution risk. The limitation period under the EDA is 30 years instead of the normal 20-year period. However, any claimant must file his claim within five years of becoming aware of his right of action.

9.0.3 Certain industrial activities which could cause potential damage to the environment require a licence from the authorities. Once a licence has been granted, there will be an eight-year period during which an order or prohibition regarding any pollution resulting from the business activities may only be issued if new information is obtained on the harmful effects of the pollution in question, and the pollution causes environmental damage which could not be foreseen when the licence was granted, or the pollution otherwise considerably exceeds the conditions upon which the licence was initially granted. After the eight-year period, the licence-granting authority may change the conditions for renewing the licence. Undertakings not covered by the licensing requirements may be ordered by the authorities to take measures to reduce any pollution resulting from activities causing insanitary conditions or waste generation. Orders for the use of clean technology may also be issued. As an alternative to directions for the reduction of pollution, a total prohibition may also be issued or the authorities may order measures to be taken at the expense of a polluting party after the expiry of a specified time limit. Decisions of regional and local authorities may be appealed to the National Agency for Environmental Protection. Decisions by the agency may be subject to further appeal to the environmental appeal board. Violation of the EPA may result in fines and, if the violation is wilful or caused by gross negligence, imprisonment of up to two years.

9.1 Protection against atmospheric and noise pollution

9.1.1 The EPA regulates atmospheric pollution and its prevention as well as nuisances resulting from vibration and noise. The Minister of the Environment has the power to set specific standards for particular types of emission, such as noise, carbon dioxide and dust. Enforcement and monitoring are undertaken at regional level.

9.1.2 Noise regulations are issued in the form of government orders under the EPA and cover individual types of business or machinery and set noise levels and provide for the testing of certain equipment. Similar rules apply to motor vehicles. Substantial fines, and imprisonment in serious cases, may be imposed (see also 9.0.2).

9.2 Water pollution

The EPA regulates water pollution and its prevention. The county authority will set and enforce local regulations for various water resources, be they ground water, streams, rivers, lakes or coastlines, within the general framework prepared by the national agency. The EPA requires each municipal council to prepare a plan for the disposal of waste water which must be in accordance with the Minister of the Environment's government order on waste water (see also 9.0.1).

9.3 Waste storage and disposal

The Minister of the Environment has the power to issue government orders dealing with waste storage and disposal. The municipalities have a duty to receive waste and must retain control of the collection and disposal of waste, although they may use subcontractors. (For powers of enforcement, see 9.0.1.) Specific regulations also exist dealing with oil tanks and the handling and disposal of oil and chemical wastes by commercial undertakings.

9.4 Contaminated land

If there is suspicion that land is contaminated, a buyer may instigate an environmental audit. Where no examination is carried out, the general rules of contract law will apply to decide whether the seller should have notified the buyer. If the regional environmental agency is aware of potential contamination, it may register a declaration against the land which will be revealed by a simple search in the land registry. The regional environmental authority has no power to require a landowner to clean up contamination. The remediation will be carried out by the authorities which will seek compensation from the polluter. The owner may undertake the remediation himself at his own expense, and seek to recover this from the previous owner and/or polluter. The purpose of registration is merely to put potential buyers on notice, and subsequent enquiries and audits may lead to de-registration if the threat of contamination proves unfounded. Public funds, raised by general taxes, are allocated to pay for decontamination and remediation.

9.5 Environmental impact assessments

A government order implements the EU legislation regarding environmental assessment. An application for the type of development or infrastructure project listed in the government order must be filed with the Minister for Traffic who will make an independent assessment which is distinct from the procedure to obtain a building permit or to modify the local municipal plan (see 8.2).

10 DEVELOPMENT

10.1 Development projects, structures and vehicles

It is quite common for businesses to build their own premises. Developers still operate but are reluctant to build without first having leased the property or found an institutional investor. Development on a speculative basis has yet to return. In the residential market, pension funds are the main investors owing to certain tax incentives, and often undertake the development themselves usually providing all the finance. The housing market is presently recovering. The development project may include a developer and an institutional investor such as a pension fund where the completed development is to be leased. Otherwise the developer will own the land and undertake the project management, obtaining the project finance from a commercial bank. After completion, the final tranche of finance may be provided by a real credit institution, which may also provide the project finance loan. The developer provides the equity which may be limited depending on the arrangement with any investor and the end user. It is common to set up public limited liability companies for each project or group of projects.

10.2 Building contracts and appointment of professionals

10.2.1 Typical forms of building contract

Building contracts will normally be undertaken for a fixed price. There are two types. Either the contract is entered into with the principal contractor who is responsible for the work of his subcontractors, or individual contracts are entered into with each contractor for the specific type of work to be undertaken. In the latter case, there are no subcontractors and responsibility is assumed individually. The design is usually undertaken independently by an architect.

10.2.2 Common terms

The standard form of contract AB 92 (see 10.2.3) enables the contractor to submit his invoice on a monthly basis for work completed and to receive payment 15 working days from receipt of the invoice. Frequently, however, payment is made by reference to different stages in construction. Under AB 92 the contractor may provide security through a bank or a guarantee insurance company. The security amounts to 15 per cent of the contract price until the construction has been delivered and 10 per cent of the contract price thereafter.

One year after delivery the security will be reduced to two per cent which will remain outstanding for five years from the date of delivery. Extensions of time are also found in AB 92, and are granted if the owner changes the work or causes delay, and in the case of force majeure or other matters outside the contractor's control. The contractor is liable for delays and liquidated damages are normally fixed. Under AB 92, the owner may request changes to the works provided that the adjusted price can be kept to within 15 per cent of the total price of the works, and within 100 per cent of the cost of the individual item. Delivery will take place when the owner and the builder have agreed on a protocol of delivery. The protocol will contain any observations the owner may have in relation to the works and any admissions or denials by the builder in reply. AB 92 contains rules on termination of a building contract, which may include material delays with serious consequences to the owner. Repudiation will also ensue automatically in the event of a suspension of payments, and insolvency.

10.2.3 Standard form of contracts

It is rare for major building contracts to be entered into without using the AB 92 standard contract containing General Conditions for the Provision of Works and Supplies within Building and Engineering, although the parties commonly vary the standard terms on a number of points. For contracts with one principal contractor a special version of the AB 92, called the ABT 93, is now gaining widespread use.

10.2.4 Appointment of the professional team

In respect of services provided by an architect and a consulting engineer, it is becoming increasingly common for the parties to refer to ABR 89, which contains the general conditions for consulting services, but the use of this contract is not yet widespread except in relation to major construction projects. It contains no specific provisions on the personnel to be engaged and, although agreements as to price are at the discretion of the parties, most are on a fixed price basis.

10.3 Those involved and their roles

The owner of the land normally employs his own professional team direct. The architect, appointed by the owner, frequently acts as project manager. Independent project managers are not employed in practice. Several quotes for construction work are normally sought, and the Tenders Act may apply. The parties in the construction process are usually the builders, whether they are general builders or a number of individual specialised builders, a civil engineer responsible for structural and technical issues and an architect responsible for design and coordination. The process is largely consensual and based on meetings between the parties.

10.4 Defects and remedies

10.4.1 Remedies of employer in respect of defects in design and materials

The party responsible for any defect will be liable in negligence for the cost of putting this right. Generally, the owner/employer will not have a direct claim against the subcontractors but will have to bring an action against the main contractor (although the concept of 'leaping recourse' has been accepted in certain circumstances).

10.4.2 Remedies of subsequent owners/occupiers other than the contractual employer

Only subsequent owners will be entitled to remedies, and occupiers and financiers will not. Subsequent owners will have to rely mainly on a claim against the seller. However, it should be noted that the concept of 'leaping recourse' has been accepted in certain specific cases. As the usual claim will be against the seller, it will be brought under the contract for sale transferring the property. The action may be based either on misrepresentation, or on hidden defects the seller should have been aware of, and for which he is liable. As there are no statutory provisions regulating these remedies, general liability under contract will apply. AB 92 sets a five-year defects period from the time of delivery and a guarantee will secure compliance (see 10.2.2). If a defect is found, the contractor will be required to remedy it if it is within the five-year remediation period. If the defect is one of design or has been caused by the negligence of another contractor, insurance cover may be operative when the other party is joined under the claim.

10.5 Defects insurance

Almost all professional participants in the construction industry market have liability insurance but a more general defects insurance is not common.

10.6 Copyright

The architect owns and retains copyright to the drawings and the owners automatically have a licence to use the drawings and design after construction is completed.

10.7 Fees

A distinction must be made between projects with one principal contractor, where the architect's fees are normally included, and other types of projects where the professional fees are obviously higher as they include both fees for an architect and an engineer and are therefore at a level of five to six per cent. If an actual manager, often a lawyer, is undertaking the project and financing the management, the fees increase to a level of seven to eight per cent.

10.8 Taxes

All construction is subject to VAT at a rate of 25 per cent which is the only tax payable as a direct consequence of construction costs (see 11.8 for more detail on VAT).

11 TAXES

11.1 Corporation tax

Danish tax jurisdiction excludes Greenland and the Faroe Islands. Companies are resident in Denmark if they are incorporated in Denmark. Resident companies pay corporation tax on worldwide income and capital gains (subject to double taxation relief). Corporation tax is also payable on most income earned in Denmark by a non-resident company.

11.1.1 Tax rates

The Danish corporate tax year ends on 31 March. Corporation tax is charged at 34 per cent. Companies can choose either to pay the tax in two instalments, on 1 March and 1 November, or to have 11.75 per cent added to the amount due if payment is not made until after the tax year, resulting in an effective corporate tax rate of 38 per cent.

11.1.2 Computation and administration

In calculating profits, companies can deduct expenses incurred necessarily or exclusively in obtaining a profit, including fees, commissions, interest, salaries and other normal overheads. Trading losses may be carried forward for up to five years, subject to the continuity of share ownership. Carry-back is not permitted. Items such as entertaining and business gifts are not deductible. Tax assessment is dealt with by the Customs and Taxation Agency. However, the initial calculation and review have been delegated to the municipal tax authorities of each of the 275 municipalities. An appeal system exists through the Customs and Taxation Agency or the administrative tax court. An array of anti-avoidance provisions have been incorporated into almost all tax laws and the tax authorities look carefully into the substance of a transaction rather than at its form.

11.1.3 Depreciation and capital allowances

Tax depreciation plays an important role. Industrial and certain other buildings may be depreciated by using the straight line method. Buildings used for manufacturing industries and retail purposes are allowed a write-off of six per cent per annum until the total depreciation is 60 per cent and thereafter two per cent annually until 100 per cent is depreciated. Cinemas, hotels, restaurants, are depreciated at four per cent until 40 per cent is depreciated and thereafter at one per cent annually until 100 per cent is depreciated. Very significantly, office buildings and car parks may not be depreciated. Plant, machinery and ships may be depreciated on a declining balance basis at 30 per cent. Immediate 100 per cent depreciation is allowed for equipment worth less than DKK8,700 as well as for computer software. Capital allowances accumulated by depreciation may be recaptured from any consideration at the time of sale. All costs generally incurred to generate profit are deductible. This also applies to expenses incurred in relation to land if the land or property is used for business purposes. There are no special geographical tax areas as the enterprise zones have now lapsed (see section 12).

11.1.4 Withholding tax

The Tax at Source Act requires the payer to withhold 25 per cent of dividends paid on shares to a resident or a non-resident. This is subject to a number of exemptions or provisions allowing the shareholder to recapture the withholding tax. This follows from the EU Directive 90/435, providing that the payment of dividends from a subsidiary to a parent company holding more than 25 per cent of the share capital in the subsidiary, both being resident within member states, is exempt from withholding tax. A number of double taxation treaties reduce or eliminate the withholding taxes. Special rules will apply if the payee of Danish royalties has a permanent place of business in Denmark but otherwise no withholding tax will apply.

11.2 Taxes on development value

There are no taxes relating to the increase in value of land due to rezoning other than general capital gains taxation.

11.3 Capital gains

Capital gains on land are taxed at the full corporate taxation rate if the sale occurs within the first three years where the tax payer does not deal in property. After three years' ownership, part of the capital gain is taxed on a decreasing basis until the minimum taxable level is reached after more than eight years' ownership, at which time 70 per cent of the capital gains are taxed and certain deductions are available for maintenance costs and inflation. For resident individuals, special exemptions apply to residential properties below a certain size. Roll-over relief can be applied for provided a seller purchases other property within the same income year. Roll-over will only be available for another property.

11.4 Taxes on owner of property

A land tax applying to the public valuation of each piece of land (but not the buildings over it) is in force. This will be imposed upon the owner of the property, although this may be recovered from the tenant (see 11.5). This grants the local municipality the right to levy an annual property tax ranging between 0.6 per cent and 2.4 per cent, and the counties a further one per cent tax on the land value. Exempted are government property, charitable institutions, and buildings subject to preservation orders. The municipality may charge a further tax on the value of office, retail, hotel, manufacturing, workshop or similar buildings of up to one per cent of their value.

11.5 Taxes on occupier

There are no taxes on the occupier of a property. However, the Rent Act provides that rent may be varied upwards and must be varied downwards in relation to any increase or decrease in property tax.

11.6 Taxes on land transfer

A stamp duty of 1.2 per cent is payable on the transfer price of any property. If the public valuation of the property is higher than the transfer price, the stamp duty is charged on the valuation. For residential properties, a preferential rate of 0.6 per cent applies. No transfer tax is payable on the transfer of shares of a property holding company. Share transfer tax of 0.5 per cent is levied instead. In partnerships, however, the transfer stamp duty will be payable upon the transfer of a share in the partnership, as the partner will be considered the direct owner of the property for tax purposes. The transferor and the transferee are jointly liable.

11.7 Wealth tax

No wealth tax applies to companies and wealth tax has been abolished with effect from 1998.

11.8 Value added tax (VAT)

Value added tax (VAT) on goods and services is 25 per cent. Any business with a turnover exceeding DKK20,000 annually must register for VAT purposes. The owner may choose to register a property for VAT purposes but only if the property is to be leased for commercial and business use, by those who are themselves VAT registered. It will then be possible to reclaim all VAT paid on construction and maintenance costs but VAT must be charged on the tenants' rent. If property is registered for VAT purposes and is subsequently sold to a non-VAT registered owner or its use changes to a non-VAT type use (ie residential or non-profit making) the VAT initially deducted must be paid back. The obligation to repay the deducted VAT will decrease in a straight line over a 10-year period. The Tax and Customs Directorate calculates and collects the VAT through regional offices. VAT is collected on goods and services supplied on a quarterly basis and collected one month and 10 days later. All construction is subject to VAT at 25 per cent (see 10.8). VAT is payable on the services of all professionals, including lawyers, architects and real estate brokers at the normal VAT rate (see 4.4).

11.9 Local and other taxes

No taxes other than the ones above apply.

12 GRANTS AND INCENTIVES

Denmark is one of the EU member states allocating the smallest amount per capita towards business and investment incentives. The rules dealing with such incentives are found in the Business Incentives Act 1993.

12.1 Subsidies, grants and loans

The Business Incentives Act lists 10 activities in which the government can assist businesses with non-returnable amounts, capital participation in companies, loans, development contracts and project guarantees. These include high risk development projects; exploitation of public sector know-how; new businesses initiatives; business structure initiatives; internationalisation initiatives; export promotion; development, collection and reworking of technical and other know-how; regional and local business promotion; and business development in underdeveloped areas. Public subsidies are kept at a very low level.

12.2 Tax allowances and reliefs

Provisions were in force for a reduction in property taxes in special enterprise zones, but these enterprise zones no longer exist.

12.3 Other public schemes and incentives

The enterprise zone scheme has not been renewed and there are no longer any enterprise zones in existence.

13 COMPANIES AND BUSINESS ENTITIES

A distinction is made between companies with limited liability and partnerships where some or all of the partners are fully liable.

13.1 Limited and unlimited companies

Companies are created with a simple memorandum of creation in the form of minutes of a constituting general meeting. No consents are required but registration with the commerce and companies agency is required. Limited companies have limited liability; other forms of corporate entity such as limited partnerships, joint ownership shipping companies and unlimited partnerships exist and have different liability structures. The main difference between a public and a private limited company is that a public limited company is required to have a minimum paid up share capital of DKK500,000 whereas a private limited company must have a minimum paid up capital of DKK200,000.

Other differences include the management structure where public limited companies require a two-tier management structure with a supervisory board and a management board. There is a minimum requirement of three supervisory board members in a public limited company. Private limited companies with a capital of less than DKK300,000, which is the large majority of private limited companies, may decide not to elect a supervisory board. A public limited company may have different share classes with different voting ratios, own up to 10 per cent of its own shares and be subject to a 0.5 per cent tax upon transfer of shares, whereas such rules do not apply to private limited companies. The Corporate Taxation Act provides for separate taxation of limited companies. A company is an entirely separate legal person for all purposes from its shareholders.

13.2 Partnerships

13.2.1 General partnerships (*interessentskaber*) arise where all the partners are fully and jointly and severally liable, and limited partnerships (*kommanditselskaber*) where one or more of the partners will be general partners fully liable for all the debts of the partnership, and some will be limited partners liable only for a specified limited amount of partnership debts. Partnerships are used for businesses where it is common to operate in partnership or where tax transparency requires this. Each of the partners will be taxed on an individual basis on their share of the profits. There is no statutory regulation of partnerships. Partnerships are created by a formation meeting where a set of articles of association or a partnership agreement is adopted. This will be the basis for the partnership. The rules for partnerships are generally based on case law. Limited partnerships and partnerships consisting only of partners with limited liability are obliged to register with the commerce and companies agency.

13.2.2 Limited partnerships have been popular for the last 10–15 years for more passive investments where the investor wishes to limit his responsibility to his share. The general partner with unlimited liability will usually be a private limited company with a minimum capital, the shares of which are owned proportionally by the limited partners and the partner with unlimited liability must have the management responsibility for the partnership. This is deemed sufficient to fulfil the requirement that one partner assumes unlimited liability. Each partner will be jointly and severally liable up to the maximum agreed. The articles of association should detail the decision-making procedure but otherwise unanimity will be required.

13.3 Other types of business association

13.3.1 Cooperative societies with limited liability and non-profit making associations are only subject to fragmented statutory regulation complemented by case law. Cooperative societies with limited liability may be established in a less formal way but nevertheless have to be registered with the commerce and companies agency. No specific capital requirements apply. Non-profit making associations are considered separate legal entities with limited liability for their assets, provided that they have been firmly established and have adopted a set of articles of association. The Corporate Taxation Act provides for separate taxation of cooperative societies whereas non-profit associations are generally tax free.

13.3.2 Joint ventures are generally operated either through a limited liability company or as a partnership on the basis of a shareholders' or partnership agreement, possibly supplemented by a joint venture agreement.

14 INTERNATIONAL

14.1 Restrictions on inward investment

There are no restrictions on the introduction of funds into Denmark for the purchase of property. However, there are rules restricting non-resident individuals and entities buying property in Denmark. Citizens of other EU or EEA member states and companies or associations registered in other EU or EEA member states may acquire land in Denmark, provided that:

(a) the property shall serve as a year-round residence for the buyer, and
(b) the buyer is subject to the rules in the EU or EEA treaties on free movement for workers and providers of services, or will use the property for business purposes covered by the rules on free movement.

In all other instances, foreign citizens or foreign companies or associations must apply to the Ministry of Justice for permission to acquire property in Denmark. This will generally be granted if the foreign citizen intends to, and has been permitted to, take up permanent residence in Denmark or has previously been resident for a period exceeding five years or if the company or association establishes a branch in Denmark. If a foreign entity sets up a subsidiary in Denmark, it will no longer be considered a foreign entity but will be deemed a resident company, the shares of which happen to be owned by a foreign entity. Therefore, purchasing subsidiaries will not require permission provided the rules for the acquisition of, eg residential properties or summer houses by corporate entities, are complied with (see further 1.3.1). The permit may be time-limited.

14.2 Exchange controls

There are no exchange controls limiting the transfer of funds in and out of Denmark but for statistical reasons all payments exceeding DKK60,000 must be reported to the Danish Central Bank.

14.3 Restrictions and registrations on carrying on a business

A foreign entity wishing to carry on business in Denmark must set up a branch (see 14.1 in relation to subsidiaries). This is a simple formality for companies incorporated within the EU. Companies incorporated in countries outside the EU may set up a branch in Denmark if this has been agreed through a bilateral or multilateral international agreement or if, according to the assessment of the Minister for Trade and Industry, Danish companies are granted similar rights in the specific countries or if the Minister for Trade and Industry grants permission for the establishment of such a branch.

14.4 Repatriation of income and the proceeds of property trading and development

Proceeds may be freely repatriated subject, however, to any tax laws.

14.5 Withholding taxes

Withholding taxes only apply to dividends and in some instances to royalties and even then may be subject to double taxation relief (see 11.1.4).

14.6 Double taxation relief

Relief from double taxation is granted in a number of double taxation treaties entered into by Denmark with almost all European countries and a number of other countries.

CHAPTER 4

England and Wales

D A Hurndall

Solicitor, MA (Oxon), FRSA

CONTENTS

1 OWNERSHIP OF LAND 107
2 OTHER INTERESTS IN LAND 110
3 TITLE TO LAND 113
4 TRANSACTIONS IN LAND 114
5 LEASES AND OTHER RIGHTS OF OCCUPATION 116
6 FINANCE AND INVESTMENT SOURCES 118
7 FORMS OF SECURITY 121
8 PLANNING AND BUILDING REGULATION 123
9 ENVIRONMENTAL MATTERS 126
10 DEVELOPMENT 128
11 TAXES 132
12 GRANTS AND INCENTIVES 135
13 COMPANIES AND BUSINESS ENTITIES 138
14 INTERNATIONAL 140

CHAPTER 4

England and Wales

1 OWNERSHIP OF LAND

In the United Kingdom, there are separate legal systems in England and Wales, Northern Ireland and Scotland. This chapter deals with England (which will be treated as including Wales). Other chapters deal with Scotland and Northern Ireland and indicate the differences in those jurisdictions. England does not have a codified system of law and its sources of law comprise Acts of Parliament, local byelaws, delegated legislation made under statutory powers and the common law (case law deriving from the decisions of the higher courts). The principal statutes relating to property law are the Law of Property Act 1925, the Trustee Act 1925 and the Land Registration Act 1925. They divide real property into 'land' (or property) itself, which can be either freehold or leasehold, and interests in land, 'legal' and 'equitable'. These interests are either rights in rem, ie rights to the thing itself enforceable against all the world, or capable of being enforced as such. For rights in personam, see 1.1.4.

1.1 Types of tenure

The two types of land, or 'estates' in land as they are called, are freehold and leasehold.

1.1.1 Freehold

Freehold ownership is akin to absolute ownership. It carries with it a right to own, occupy and dispose of the land and any buildings on the land. There is no distinction between land and buildings as there is in many jurisdictions. Ownership of both remains with the freeholder even where the tenant puts up the buildings and is granted a long lease say of 99 years or more. The tenant will, however, have exclusive right to use and occupation. Anything which is fixed or annexed to the land or buildings is termed a fixture and is treated as part of the land. The freehold carries with it the right to the soil below and the air space above, but certain minerals such as coal are excluded.

1.1.2 Leasehold

A lease (or tenancy) will be used to grant a right to occupy or take the profits from land or buildings for a fixed term, commonly of up to 999 years, or by way of periodic tenancy, eg on a recurring monthly or yearly basis until determined by notice. There is no limit on the length of the lease. It is unusual but technically possible to grant a lease to last for an individual's lifetime. The lease is peculiar to the common law systems. Civil law jurisdictions use other vehicles such as usufruct, building rights and rental contracts to serve a similar purpose. The lease is used where something less than absolute ownership is intended, such as a right to occupy land for a limited period, or a right to occupy only part of a building on set terms, where in other countries they might use a condominium. The lease will grant the owner of the lease the exclusive right to use and occupy the property and can be fully transferable. It will usually be granted either for a premium (or capital sum), in the case of longer leases, or for a monthly, quarterly or other periodic rent, or a combination of both. Due to the high value of land many businesses do not wish to tie up their capital in land ownership and will therefore lease their premises. Leases are dealt with more fully in section 5.

1.1.3 Joint ownership and condominia

1.1.3.1 As soon as more than one person owns land, he will automatically become a 'trustee' with the other legal owners of the land and hold the property on trust. Until 1997 the 'trustees' were treated as the legal or nominal owners of the land itself and the interests of the true, or beneficial, owners were transferred to the proceeds of sale or income. This distinction has been substantially reduced by the Trusts of Land and Appointment of Trustees Act 1996. The beneficiaries' rights will not be against the land but against the trustees. Third parties can however continue to deal with the trustees and need not generally concern themselves with the rights of the beneficiaries. The trustees are given wide powers to deal with the land, and subject to the terms of the trust or any agreement between the beneficial owners, decide how the land is to be used by the beneficiaries. They will not have to sell unless the trust so provides or the court orders sale. Where the owners, or trustees, hold for themselves and not for other beneficiaries they will do so either as joint tenants or tenants in common. Joint tenants' ownership is entirely merged and joint and the land passes to the survivor on death. Tenants in common have a separate and divided share in the proceeds of the land. There can be no more than four legal owners, or trustees, of land as distinct from beneficiaries. Further comment on the trust is made in section 2.

1.1.3.2 English law does not recognise any form of condominium, co-ownership or family ownership. A system of commonhold has been under consideration with a view to providing for some element of co-ownership to overcome the problems of freehold law which does not provide for enforcement of positive obligations eg for repair or provision of services between adjoining freeholders. The proposals are supported by the two main parties and will pass into law in the not too distant future. For the present the lease (or tenancy), or less often the rentcharge, is commonly used. Equally, unincorporated associations, cooperatives and collectives are not recognised under English law and so cannot own land.

1.1.4 Lesser rights

Lesser rights than freehold or leasehold ownership are termed interests in land, legal or equitable. These will be interests in the land of others and enforceable in rem. They will include easements, such as rights of way or drainage, restrictive covenants, rentcharges and mortgages. Comment is made on these in section 2. Rights less in turn than these, which will be personal and not enforceable in rem, only in personam, ie only between the parties themselves, will include temporary licences, eg to store goods. Any right of exclusive possession for a known period of time will, since the House of Lords' decision in *Street v Mountford* in 1985, usually be treated as a tenancy, attracting security of tenure (see section 5) and be enforceable in rem. Lesser rights of occupation, eg to share facilities in a business centre, will be contractual licences enforceable in personam, ie only between the contracting parties.

1.2 The role of the trust and the distinction between legal and beneficial ownership

The trust is an unusual product of the common law system. It comes about where owners of land (or other assets) are treated as holding these for others, the beneficiaries, either as a result of an express declaration of trust, where the settlor transfers the property to a trustee with directions as to how it is to be dealt with, or by operation of law, where the courts have held that justice requires the owners to account for the property to others. It is a vehicle of great flexibility and beneficiaries can have a variety of interests in the income and capital, present or future, and for different periods of time, commencing on a number of different events. It is of particular use in the areas of financial provision, for families, pension and investment funds, clubs and community or charity activities. The trustee will be bound to manage and account for the property to the beneficiaries and there is a substantial body of law dealing with the powers and obligations of trustees and their relationship with their beneficiaries. Central to the law of trusts is the rule that the beneficiaries' rights are against the trustees, and that any person dealing with the trustees can ignore the beneficiaries and their interests, so long as he deals correctly with the trustees themselves, in particular that he ensures on a purchase of land that he gets a receipt from at least two trustees.

1.3 Restrictions on ownership and dealing

There are few restrictions on the ownership of land, although a minor may not own land except through trustees; a company may only hold land if empowered to do so by its memorandum and articles of association; and restrictions, or terms, may be imposed on a body by its constitution or statute. Restrictions apply to those suffering from mental incapacity. Adverse rights may be imposed to protect the public interest, eg in respect of matters such as planning, rights of access, conservation, and compulsory purchase. There are, however, no general municipal rights of pre-emption as in some other countries. Certain specific statutory restrictions exist upon the disposal of land by bodies such as local authorities, charities and certain trustees, but otherwise land is freely disposable. Since 1987 the tenants of a building which contains residential flats have a right of pre-emption on a sale of the building.

1.4 Adverse possession or acquisitive prescription

Unlike most civil law countries, there is no concept of acquisitive prescription creating title after a period of occupation but there is an equivalent in that anyone who has occupied land for over 12 years has a defence to any claim for possession under the Limitation Act 1980 by reason of adverse possession, so long as his occupation has been open and free from objection. There is no requirement for good faith.

2 OTHER INTERESTS IN LAND

Interests over another's land enforceable in rem, ie against all comers to the land, will be either legal or equitable (see 2.8); legal interests essentially comprise either easements and profits à prendre or mortgages and rentcharges. The former will be enforceable without any need for registration or notice, while the latter will normally need to be protected by some form of registration. This will be at the land registry or land charges department depending on whether the land is registered or not (see 3.1). All other than legal interests, such as restrictive covenants and contracts for the sale or grant of a legal estate or interest, are equitable interests and will require some form of registration. Where registration is required, a buyer, ie someone who pays for the land, will generally take free from the interest if it has not been registered.

2.1 Servitudes or easements, usufruct, building and dwelling rights

2.1.1 Servitudes or easements

The English equivalent to the servitude is the easement or profit à prendre. An easement is a right over land (the servient tenement) in favour of other land (the dominant tenement). Easements include the right to run services such as drains and cables, rights of access, car parking rights, and rights of light and support. Profits à prendre are rights to take produce from another's land such as rights to fish, to take game or to take minerals. Unlike easements they do not require the owner of the profit to own adjoining or other land. Both can be acquired by deed or long usage (20 to 40 years) and do not need registration.

2.1.2 Usufruct

English law does not recognise the civil law concept of a 'usufruct' or the right to use or enjoy the produce of another party's land. The nearest equivalent is the long lease, which may be made determinable on death to make it similar to the usufruct for life.

2.1.3 Building or dwelling rights

The nearest equivalent to the building right used in some countries is a building lease, ie a long lease under which the tenant agrees to erect a building. This will belong to the freeholder but be occupied by the tenant under the lease until its expiry.

2.2 Restrictions on use and other restrictions

Freeholders may enter into restrictions on the use of their land, to protect the amenities and value of other land, and, subject to certain conditions, these restrictions will be enforceable by and between successive owners. These rights can only be removed by agreement or, eg if obsolete, by application to the Lands Tribunal. Public law restrictions under planning and other legislation are commented on in section 8. It is not possible to impose positive obligations so as to bind freehold successors in title, eg to contribute to the cost of repairs of common services. This can only be done by way of leases or rentcharges (see 2.6). It is for this reason that the concept of commonhold may be introduced.

2.3 Private mortgages and charges

Monetary liabilities can be secured on land in a number of ways. Private mortgages can be either legal or equitable mortgages. These are described more fully in section 7. The courts can make charging orders to secure judgment debts. Other private rights in the nature of security include liens, such as the seller's lien for any unpaid purchase price on the sale of a property, which automatically attaches to the property if the seller is not paid in full. Civil law privileges are not used in English law, though certain debts may be treated as preferential over others.

2.4 Contracts and options

Between contract and completion of the sale the buyer has an 'estate contract' giving him an interest in the land. This will happen not only where there is an unconditional contract for sale, but also where there is an option or right of pre-emption. There are no municipal or other automatic rights of pre-emption as elsewhere except as mentioned at 1.3.

2.5 Public or municipal charges

Certain public liabilities, such as the liability to meet the cost of highway improvements, drainage work, the repair of dangerous buildings, and other administrative matters such as planning restrictions, consents and enforcement orders, compulsory purchase orders, highway schemes, tree preservation, conservation, and smoke control orders, and the listing of protected buildings may be registered with the local authority as local land charges. Failure to register will not prevent these binding a buyer but they will give him a right to compensation. Taxes are not a charge on property, with very limited exceptions.

2.6 Other interests

The principal remaining interest in land is the rentcharge, which gives a right to periodic payments secured on property. Since the Rentcharges Act 1977 these can normally only be imposed to secure the enforcement of covenants, or the meeting of the cost of common facilities or services, eg on an industrial or residential estate. In the absence of any condominium system in England, this is one of the few ways a landowner can enter into a positive obligation which will bind successors. There are no general rights of public access over private land, although the present government is proposing that there will be.

2.7 Liabilities attaching to land

Liabilities arising out of land may attach either to the owner or occupier, or both, eg for injury or damage to visitors or their goods under the Occupier's Liability Acts, in nuisance for the unreasonable use of land to the prejudice of an adjoining owner, for dangerous escapes under the doctrine of *Rylands v Fletcher*, or for negligent injury or damage to passers-by and their goods. There are also statutory liabilities for the repair of dangerous structures, for preserving buildings listed as being of historic or architectural interest, and for the health and safety of employees. Finally, there are fiscal liabilities, which attach to land in the form of business rates or council tax, according to whether the premises are business or residential premises. General comments on tax are made in section 11.

2.8 Legal and equitable interests

As explained at 1.1 interests in land are legal or equitable, the latter being creations of the courts of equity, like the trust, which were set up to reduce the injustices of the older, more rigid, common law courts, commonly where there was some defect in the strict form of a transaction. So, for example, a legal mortgage or legal easement is one which has been formally and correctly granted as a deed, and registered, where necessary, and an equitable mortgage or easement arises where the parties have not completed the transaction or there is some defect in the formalities. The main difference used to be that legal interests were enforceable against all the world but equitable were only enforceable against a buyer if he had notice. The distinction has been eroded and enforceability against third parties will now depend largely on whether registration is required and has taken place. Equitable interests, however, still generally require a greater degree of registration to achieve enforceability.

2.9 Protection of interests

As explained above most interests cannot be enforced against the land and subsequent buyers, unless protected. The type of protection or registration required will depend on the type of interest and whether the land is registered or unregistered land (see section 3). Interests which require no protection include legal easements and the rights of those in 'actual occupation' of the land. Where the land is registered, these and a few other interests are termed 'overriding' interests and need no entry on the land registers; all others are termed 'minor' interests and require the entry of either a notice, caution, restriction or inhibition. A mortgage can be protected either by being fully registered with its own separate certificate, like a freehold or leasehold, in which case it will be a legal mortgage, or by having a lesser entry entered on the charges register of the land affected. Unless fully registered, the mortgagee, as a mere equitable mortgagee, will enjoy fewer benefits and will not be able to sell the property or appoint a receiver. In the case of unregistered land, interests requiring registration are classified as different types of land charge and entered at the land charges department.

2.10 Priority of interests

Priority between interests in land will depend generally on the date of registration, not the date of creation of the interest. The principal exceptions are: first, where registration is not necessary, such as in the case of a legal easement, and the date of creation will be the determining date; or secondly, between equitable interests where the first in time prevails. It is also generally true that a greater interest will take priority over a lesser, so a legal will take priority over an equitable interest.

3 TITLE TO LAND

3.1 Proof of title

Title is established either by registration at HM Land Registry, if the land is registered, or by production of the deeds of title showing an ownership of at least 15 years, if the land is unregistered. Since 1990, the whole of England and Wales has been an area of compulsory registration and now every transfer of freehold land or the grant or transfer of a lease with more than 21 years to run will require registration and the land (or lease) will be given a land certificate and title number. Shorter leases will be overriding interests (see 2.9) and will not need an entry on the register. Interests which are not overriding interests will be minor interests requiring protection on the charges register (see 3.2.2). Failing such protection they will be void against a buyer of the land. The registers have been open for inspection by the public since 1990. Disposals of unregistered land will become increasingly rare. Searches will be made against the land where it is registered and otherwise against the seller.

3.2 HM Land Registry and the land register

The land registers are kept by HM Land Registry (who also administer the land charges department). The register of local land charges is kept by the local authority.

3.2.1 Plans

HM Land Registry uses plans only for identification purposes; the boundaries are not definitive.

3.2.2 Content

The registers are divided into three: a 'property register' describing the property, whether it is freehold or leasehold, and any rights such as easements enjoyed over other property; a 'proprietorship register' giving the name of the owner and grade of his title; and a 'charges register' showing any adverse charges or entries. An owner can be registered with different grades of title – 'absolute', 'good leasehold', 'qualified' or 'possessory' – depending on how satisfied the land registry is with the title shown to them. These categories can be up-graded. For example, where someone is registered with possessory title because they have established they have been in possession for a period of time, their title can be subsequently up-graded to absolute after 12 or 15 years.

3.2.3 Errors

The registers are conclusive, but in certain circumstances rectification and/or compensation may be awarded.

3.3 Passing of title

Title of unregistered land passes on conveyance. For registered land, title passes in stages, the buyer only acquiring formal or legal title once registered at HM Land Registry, although registration will then be backdated to the date of application. If not lodged with the land registry within two months, a transfer is technically void.

4 TRANSACTIONS IN LAND

The most common transactions are sale and purchase, lease, and mortgage.

4.1 Procedure

A sale or lease usually takes place in two stages, commonly of two to four weeks each. First, the parties negotiate the contract and carry out preliminary searches and enquiries as to the property and its title, including searches of the local authority. The buyer will undertake any survey, and any environmental audit, and negotiate his finance at this stage. Until the written contract is entered into either party can withdraw, unlike in many continental countries, where the parties will be committed at an earlier stage. At the point of contract risk will pass, but the seller will become responsible to the buyer to protect the property in certain ways. Title and usually possession will not pass until completion. Prior to completion the buyer will carry out his last searches, eg at the companies registry to establish that no charges or winding-up orders have been lodged. The buyer can protect his position against third parties by various means such as entry at the land registry, or a land charge, or by a search at the registry which will give him priority over third parties for a period of up to 30 days. Notarisation is not required, the purchase being negotiated between the parties' solicitors, with the buyer's solicitor being responsible for lodging the transfer with the land registry following completion.

4.2 Contract terms

4.2.1 The seller will give certain warranties as to title in the transfer, but few warranties in the contract, and it is for the buyer to satisfy himself as to the absence of title and physical defects on the principle of caveat emptor. The parties may introduce other provisions such as a term making the sale conditional upon planning consent if this has been negotiated. The contract will usually provide for a deposit of 10 per cent, to be payable on contract, and stipulate a default rate of interest to be payable by the buyer if there is a delay in completion. It will also stipulate a date for completion.

4.2.2 If either party defaults, the other can apply for an order compelling performance or treat the contract as repudiated. The seller can charge interest and/or forfeit the deposit in the event of delay or failure to complete.

4.3 Formalities

The Law of Property (Miscellaneous Provisions) Act 1989 requires that a contract for sale of land be in writing and signed on behalf of both parties in order to be enforceable. It must contain all material terms agreed between the parties. A lease of more than three years must be by deed. Notarisation is not a requirement of English law.

4.4 Fees, costs and taxes

4.4.1 On a sale, the seller will pay the agent's commission and each party will pay his own solicitors' fees. The buyer will pay the stamp duty and any land registry fees. The agent's commission will vary between one to three per cent of the sale price and if the buyer instructs an agent to find the property, he will usually pay him a commission of 0.5 to 1 per cent. In the case of a lease, the letting agent's commission will be based on 10–15 per cent of the first year's rent. Commission is payable only if the transaction takes place. Lower fees will be paid where there is a sole rather than a joint agency.

4.4.2 While solicitors' fees are commonly charged on a time basis, they are often a percentage of between 0.25 and 1 per cent of the value. There are statutory guidelines as to the amount that should be charged.

4.4.3 Stamp duty is not payable on mortgages, but is payable at one per cent of the purchase price if over £60,000, one and a half per cent if over £250,000 and two per cent if over £500,000. In the case of leases, it is charged also on a percentage of the rent of between 1 and 24 per cent depending on the length of the lease.

4.4.4 Land registry fees will be assessed on value up to a maximum figure of £1,800 for transactions of over £5,000,000.

4.4.5 Transaction costs are generally lower than elsewhere in Europe, a buyer rarely having to pay more than 4 per cent on purchase, although this is in part compensated for by high property values.

4.4.6 In the case of commercial property which has either been built since

1988 or where the seller has elected to charge this, value added tax (VAT), currently at a rate of 17.5 per cent, will be charged on the property. VAT will always be charged on professional fees related to land.

4.5 Professionals' roles

The marketing and sale of land are usually conducted by estate agents. Although many may be members of professional bodies such as the Royal Institution of Chartered Surveyors, many are unqualified and estate agency has therefore become subject to increasing statutory control. Each party will be represented by his own solicitor. There is, though, no role for a notary as there is on the Continent.

5 LEASES AND OTHER RIGHTS OF OCCUPATION

Rights of occupation in England almost invariably take the form of a lease (or tenancy). They will either be for a fixed period or periodic, eg terminable on a month's or year's notice. A fixed-term lease will vary in length, the longer leases being generally of 99 or 125 years, and granted for a capital sum reserving only a nominal rent. Leases of up to 35 years in length are often granted at an open market rent. Offices are commonly let for periods of between three years, in the case of small office suites, and 25 years for larger lettings. Residential accommodation is let for periods of generally up to five years. Agricultural land is let by the year. Other commercial buildings will be let for periods of up to 35 years. Good quality accommodation let by institutions used to be let almost invariably for 25 years but with the recession the average length of leases has been reduced to 10–15 years, or the lease will include a break clause for the tenant to determine the lease in the tenth or fifteenth year. These institutional leases granted on strict terms have played a central part in the UK investment market for many years. The investment value of property will commonly be assessed by reference to its yield, ie the return on cost of the property. In the case of some prime properties this has historically been as low as 3.5 per cent.

Since the House of Lords' decision in the case of *Street v Mountford*, anyone who has exclusive possession of property will usually be treated by the courts as having a tenancy, which will result in his having greater security of tenure than when he has a licence. A licence will only arise, for example, where there is a sharing of occupation as in the provision of serviced office accommodation.

5.1 Rent and other terms

Most present-day market rent leases contain upward only rent reviews by which the rent is increased to the current open market rent usually every five years. Arrangements may be made for linking increases to the retail price index or for fixed increases. Retail premises are sometimes let at a rent based on turnover. Rents are usually payable in advance and there are no statutory or standard form leases in common use. The terms of the lease may be heavily negotiated particularly on high value premises. The tenant will be subject to restrictions on alteration, assignment and sub-letting, and will usually be left with full responsibility for the cost of repair and insurance. However, the landlord will usually undertake the insurance himself and recover the premium from the tenant. In the event of default by the tenant or on insolvency, a market rent lease will allow the landlord to forfeit and take back the lease. There is no statutory or legal restriction on such a right. It is common for leases to be guaranteed or covered by other rental security where the tenant's credit is inadequate (see 7.3).

5.2 Privity of contract and estate

5.2.1 A peculiarity of English property law is that the original parties to a lease remain liable to each other for the duration of the lease under the doctrine of privity of contract, regardless of any assignment of the other's interest. Tenants taking an assignment of the lease are usually expected to take on a similar liability to the landlord by way of novation. This can lead to injustice where a tenant is sued by the landlord for the non-payment of rent by a subsequent tenant long after the original tenant has parted with the lease.

5.2.2 Significant changes to the doctrine have been introduced by the Landlord and Tenant (Covenants) Act 1995 for tenants of almost all leases granted after 1 January 1996 and these limit the liability of the tenant to its period of ownership or, at the most, until the first subsequent assignment. Tenants of leases granted prior to 1 January 1996 are unaffected by these changes.

5.3 Rent control and security of tenure

For agricultural land, the previous protections available to the tenant were substantially reduced by the Agricultural Tenancies Act 1995. Under this, the parties are able to agree the length of the lease without rights of renewal or any prescribed minimum term and to negotiate rent freely. However, existing tenancies under the Agricultural Holdings Act 1986 will continue to restrict the agricultural landlord's ability to obtain possession until the existing tenancy, and with it the right to renew, expires. In the case of residential property, the old law prior to the Housing Act 1988 made it almost impossible for residential landlords to obtain possession of houses and flats once they had been let and restricted the rent to a level considerably below that payable on the open market. Regulated tenancies under the old law remain protected, but since 1988 it has been possible to grant tenancies with limited security of tenure, and a greater freedom for the parties to negotiate their own rents. Since 1997 nearly all new residential lettings by private landlords will be assured shorthold tenancies where there is no security of tenure. Lettings of business premises are subject to the Landlord and Tenant Act 1954 which provides a tenant with the right to stay on after the end of a business tenancy and/or to apply for a new lease of up to 14 years, subject to payment of the market rent. The landlord can recover possession only on grounds relating to a default or for certain other limited purposes (eg where the landlord wishes to occupy himself or redevelop the property). Where there is no default the landlord has to pay compensation approximately equal to one or two times the rental value of the premises.

5.4 Other legislative restrictions

Both agricultural and residential premises are subject to specific legislative controls on the terms which the parties can agree, so that, for example, the landlord of residential premises let for a term of less than seven years is responsible for the structure and for certain of the equipment. These provisions are mandatory. Otherwise there are few regulations which affect lettings and it is generally for the tenant to satisfy himself as to the suitability of the property for his purposes and to ensure the landlord undertakes any obligations he considers appropriate.

5.5 Method of measurement

Rents are usually calculated by reference to the net internal or net lettable area excluding common areas such as lavatories and staircases. The gross external area is generally only of relevance when calculating the size of a new building for other purposes.

6 FINANCE AND INVESTMENT SOURCES

The United Kingdom has a sophisticated finance and investment market. The principal forms of finance continue to take the form of loan, investment or equity capital.

6.1 Loan finance

The traditional sources of loan finance are high street, investment and merchant banks and more recently building societies. Companies may borrow money from their shareholders and issue them with loan stock or preference shares. The loan stock may itself be convertible into shares. More complex instruments and types of commercial paper have evolved, such as zero coupon and deep discount bonds. These will give the holder limited income but entitle him to repayment of a substantially higher sum on maturity than that invested, possibly linked to an increase in income as the property income improves. These may be marketed privately amongst a narrow range of investors or floated on the stock exchange. The merchant banks will tend to coordinate larger project loans and the high street banks and building societies provide retail and commercial loans for specific investments or particular commercial concerns. Loans are usually provided for a fixed term, for up to three years in the case of development finance, and for five to 10 years in the case of investment finance. Repayment of capital will either be at the end of the term, ie a 'bullet' repayment, be made in stages possibly with periodic escalations, or provide for amortisation. Interest will based either on the bank's own base rate or be charged by reference to the cost of funds, eg if the bank borrows on the inter-bank market. In this case it will also charge a margin, commonly between 0.5 to 3 per cent over cost. The parties are generally free to negotiate their own terms without statutory restriction and interest is usually paid gross and not just if the bank is based in the United Kingdom. There are no statutory restrictions on the rate of interest or terms for commercial loans. Security is usually provided for property loans (see section 7). The willingness of banks to lend depends on recent experience, general market sentiment and the weight of unlent funds. Larger loans may be syndicated and on occasion, with a strong borrower, may be left unsecured.

6.2 Investment or equity finance

The small company will be funded by its private shareholders who may be individuals or other companies or institutions. Quoted companies raise their investment funds on the UK and other stock exchanges but securitisation of individual investment properties remains problematic. There is continued pressure to relax regulations to enable these to be more readily traded. Unit trusts, investing in a wide range of properties, are also common and these issue units, not unlike shares, which are not traded but bought back by the unit trust and resold. There are other devices for single asset investment, such as PINCS, but these are complex and have not found favour.

6.3 Mezzanine or mixed funding

Prime lenders will usually have a maximum which they are prepared to lend of between 60–80 per cent of a property's value. Lending above this figure carries a higher risk and this will usually only be provided by mezzanine financiers who will take either a higher interest return or a share in the value of the property itself. Some prime lenders may provide both prime and mezzanine finance.

6.4 Sale and lease-back

A common form of finance, particularly for companies who wish to release capital by the sale of their assets, is the sale and lease-back. Under this arrangement, the company will sell an existing or new building to an investor such as an institution and take a lease-back at a market rent. The combination of the property and the income guaranteed by the seller will provide an attractive investment package. This arrangement has greater attraction in the United Kingdom than elsewhere because of the prevailing high property costs.

6.5 Tax leasing

To encourage investment in plant and machinery and certain buildings, eg in areas in need of regeneration, the government allows the cost of such investments to be deducted from taxable income and profits by way of tax allowance. These schemes were less attractive in the early 1990s with lower allowances and tax rates, but it was still not uncommon for a tax payer to put up a building, take the benefit of the allowances, and lease the building to a user who would pay a reduced rent to take account, in part, of the allowances. The latter part of the decade may see changes with a new government. The user may well have an option to buy the building once the allowances have been stripped out.

6.6 Other types of property finance

While investment in single asset companies is still difficult, there are vehicles such as investment trusts and property unit trusts which buy a number of investment properties and raise cash through a stock exchange listing or by direct investment in the case of unit trusts. As elsewhere in Europe, the raising of money by subscription by the public through collective investment schemes is closely regulated. The use of hire and lease purchase schemes is rare.

6.7 Institutional investment

6.7.1 The proportion of property in institutional and pension fund portfolios fluctuates. Having been as high as 20 per cent, there has been a move towards more indirect investment through shareholdings in property companies, but institutions have historically played a dominant role in the property market as a major source of funds for development and investment properties. They will usually look for prime locations and buildings with a secure income from a tenant with a sound credit rating. Institutions set the standards in the market eg by imposing the 25-year full repairing and insuring lease with five yearly, upward only rent reviews. With the weakening in the market in the early 1990s, institutional standards have been eroded, and many leases are now for shorter terms of 10 or 15 years or include tenant's break clauses. With this erosion the institutions' appetite for new and speculative development was also reduced, but this may well change again with a change in market sentiment. The doctrine of privity of contract (see 5.2) has been part of the institutional appeal as it effectively gave the landlord the benefit of a guarantee from each successive tenant for the duration of the lease. While the effect of this has been diluted by the Landlord and Tenant (Covenants) Act 1995, it still retains some relevance.

6.7.2 The institutions do not usually invest in the residential market because of management problems, the transient nature of the tenants, and the complexity of rent control and security of tenure legislation. Residential property remains a largely secondary form of investment. Institutions tend to invest only in commercial buildings, and to a lesser extent, agricultural land. Although the recession resulted in an increase in yields on investment property during the early 1990s, they have started to decrease again and remain steady on prime property. There are a number of specialist investment markets such as those for ground rents, ie the freehold reversions to long residential leases.

6.8 Investors other than institutions

Other investors include investment trusts listed on the Stock Exchange; unit trusts; property investment and development companies (listed and unlisted); family trusts, and the private investor. Investors in the better quality property will conform to institutional standards as far as possible in terms of tenant, location, quality of construction, and documentation. Smaller property companies or family trusts often buy secondary and tertiary properties such as older retail parades, blocks of flats and mixed industrial dwellings. Property continues to be an attractive area for investment because, despite recent falls, values on a long-term basis are considered to be likely to hold up and provide both security and a degree of inflation proofing.

7 FORMS OF SECURITY

Relationship banking, where the bank becomes closely involved with and establishes a long-term relationship with its customer, having a director on the board, is not as common in the United Kingdom as elsewhere. This is in part due to the lack of a supervisory directorship under company law. Banks tend, particularly when lending on property investments as such, to insist on full security and to have their loans covered by assets with a value of at least 125 per cent of the loan. Overdrafts or general purpose loans to companies of good standing will often be provided without security where they represent a small proportion of the borrower's overall indebtedness. Non-recourse loans, ie those secured solely by the asset without personal liability on the part of the borrower, have been highly unusual since the end of the 1980s property boom. Property being a cyclical business, banks' willingness to lend will itself depend on the stage of the cycle, their tendency being to follow rather than anticipate this.

7.1 Mortgages

A mortgage will either be a legal mortgage by way of deed, registered at the land registry, or protected by a land charge in the case of unregistered land, or an equitable mortgage as where the mortgagor deposits the title deeds accompanied by a written agreement for mortgage by way of security with the lender. In either case, in addition to registration at the land registry, a mortgage by a company will need to be registered at the companies registry within 21 days to be enforceable even between the original parties. Although mortgages are rights in rem, they will usually not be enforceable against third parties unless protected by the appropriate registration. In the case of equitable mortgages, this will involve the entry of a notice or caution at the land registry for registered land or a land charge in the case of unregistered land. Although the mortgagor retains title to and use of the property, the legal mortgagee has a number of rights, eg to take possession, sell or let the property, or appoint a receiver, who may sell on behalf of the bank but with less risk to it. The mortgage will be enforceable once there is a default, though the mortgagee may have to wait for up to three months in certain events. The law gives considerable freedom to the mortgagee who is not required to sell the property by public auction or to enforce through the courts, unless he is only an equitable mortgagee. The mortgagor is less well protected under English law than under many systems. Although the mortgagee is obliged on sale to take reasonable steps to obtain the best price it is very difficult to show breach on the part of the mortgagee. The mortgagee may also foreclose, ie have the property vested in him, or apply to the court for an order for sale, but these remedies have disadvantages and are rarely used. A receiver will usually have similar powers as the mortgagee and the advantage of appointing a receiver is principally that the duties imposed by law on the mortgagee, who takes possession of the property and uses his powers to enforce his mortgage, are avoided, if the bank acts through a receiver, the receiver technically remaining the agent of the company until it goes into liquidation. For the priority of mortgages, see 2.10. It is possible for a mortgage to secure a variable or unspecified sum and even an equity interest in the property, ie to create a convertible mortgage, though this requires careful drafting.

7.2 Floating and other charges

7.2.1 Where the borrower is a company it may widen the legal mortgage, by means of a mortgage debenture, to incorporate fixed charges over other assets such as properties to be acquired in the future, as well as book debts. The debenture will also include a floating charge over all other assets which will not attach until default. Debentures have become increasingly common, particularly since the Insolvency Act 1986. Their principal advantage arises because, since the Act, once an administrator has been appointed, no enforcement action can be taken against the company or its assets. The best way to avoid administration is the appointment by the debenture holder of an administrative receiver. A debenture will need to be registered at the companies registry and to the extent it incorporates a fixed charge, whether by way of a legal or equitable mortgage over land, will need similar protection by registration as any other mortgage.

7.2.2 A judgment creditor may apply for a charging order which will give him similar rights to a mortgagee although he will have to enforce through the courts.

7.3 Performance bonds and guarantees

Where either the credit of the borrower or the adequacy of the other security are in doubt, it is common to obtain a personal guarantee from a third party who will be called upon to repay the loan and any interest should there be a default by the borrower. Guarantees have a place in other property transactions such as leases, where the guarantor may not only be obliged to make good any non-payment of rent, but also make good other lease defaults and, in an extreme situation, may be called upon to take up a new lease on the insolvency of the original tenant. The guarantee is a flexible arrangement and only actual losses will be made good. There are no particular formalities required although there are a number of complications which make it necessary to take particular care over their drafting. An older form of security is the bond, which consists of a simple promise to pay a fixed sum of money upon the default of another party. This is an arrangement which is quite common where a specific task has to be undertaken, such as the construction of a road, and another party wishes to know that there will be sufficient money to complete the task if the contractor or developer defaults. This type of bond is usually arranged through insurance companies.

7.4 Insurance

In certain cases, credit risk can be insured against but this is a difficult area and it is frequently where it is most needed that it will be most difficult to obtain.

8 PLANNING AND BUILDING REGULATION

The development and use of land and buildings are subject to control under various town and country planning statutes, the principal being the Town and Country Planning Act 1990.

8.1 Planning authorities

Ultimate control of all matters relating to town and country planning rests with the Secretary of State for the Environment. On a local level, decisions on policy and enforcement are taken by the local planning authority for the area; this may be the county council for certain matters but is usually the district or borough council. In both cases ultimate decisions are taken by elected representatives and can be influenced by political considerations.

8.2 Zoning and development plans

Local authorities are obliged to prepare strategic planning policies, known as development plans, for their areas at two levels: county councils must prepare a structure plan setting out the authority's general policies and proposals in respect of the development and use of land in their county, and the district or borough council must prepare a local plan showing the authority's detailed policies and proposals for the development and use of land in the local district or borough. Together they form the development plan. As a general rule, the local plan must be in conformity with the structure plan. However, in the case of a conflict, the local plan usually prevails (and must do so if both plans were created by the same local authority). In metropolitan areas the structure and local plans are combined to form a single or unitary development plan. The development plan has assumed great importance because the 1990 Act provides that, when determining a planning application, the planning authority should make its decision in accordance with the development plan unless material considerations indicate otherwise. Subject to this the planning authority retains discretion and control, eg on matters of siting, density and appearance. There is considerable public discussion on the content of the development plan before it is finally adopted.

8.3 Planning control and procedures

Planning permission is required for all 'development', which includes any building, engineering, mining or similar operation and any material change in use. The 1990 Act goes into some detail about what does and does not constitute development; eg, improvements which do not materially affect the external appearance of the building are not development. Similarly, if a property is used for a purpose within any class of use specified in the Town and Country Planning (Use Classes) Order 1987, it is considered not to constitute development if it is used for any other purpose in the same class. Specific types of development are also expressly permitted. There are additional controls on advertisements on land. In case of doubt as to whether there is development requiring consent, it is possible to apply to the local planning authority for a certificate of lawfulness for any proposed or existing activity.

8.3.1 If planning permission is required, an application must be made to the local planning authority together with the appropriate fee. It may be a detailed application giving full details of the proposal or an outline application. The applicant does not need to have an interest in the land, but if he does not the owner must be notified of the application. The authority can refuse to determine an application if, within the previous two years, a similar application has been made and refused on appeal.

8.3.2 If the local planning authority does not make a decision within eight weeks, the applicant may treat this as a deemed refusal and appeal. In practice, this time limit is rarely met. The local planning authority can grant the permission unconditionally, subject to conditions, or refuse the application. If conditions are granted or the application is refused the local authority must give full reasons. These will assist the applicant in deciding whether or not to appeal to the Secretary of State. An appeal must be made, in writing, within six months. The majority of appeals can now be heard and determined by an inspector appointed by the Secretary of State. Appeals are dealt with either by holding a public enquiry, a private hearing, or by using the written representation procedure (the most common). Once the Secretary of State's decision has been made, it can only be challenged within six weeks by a 'person aggrieved' on a point of law in the High Court. A person aggrieved is defined widely enough to include anybody who can show a sufficient interest. It has included bodies such as Save Britain's Heritage and local interest groups. Public enquiries can be lengthy and on major and controversial matters decisions can take more than a year.

8.3.3 A full planning permission must be acted on within five years. An outline planning permission is followed by an application to have the remaining details or 'reserved matters' approved; this must be made within three years and the development must be begun within five years of the grant of the outline permission, or within two years of the approval of reserved matters, whichever is the later. Planning permission attaches to the land and is not personal to the applicant unless this is made a condition of the permission.

8.3.4 There are time limits for enforcement in the event of any breach, so no enforcement action can be taken after four years where the breach consists of building or other operations or a change to use as a single dwelling house, and in the case of any other breach no action can be taken after 10 years from the date of the breach. If no enforcement action can be taken then the use becomes lawful. The main means of enforcement is the issue of an enforcement notice by the local planning authority, which is subject to appeal to the Secretary of State. Failure to comply can result in an unlimited fine. Other means of enforcement include: a planning contravention notice which can be served to elicit a response within 21 days from a developer to encourage discussion prior to any enforcement notice; a breach of condition notice (against which there is no appeal) which can be issued if a condition in a planning permission is breached; and a stop notice which can be served if the local planning authority considers it necessary to put an end to specific activity, before expiry of the period for compliance with the relevant enforcement notice.

8.4 Building standards, control and supervision

In addition to obtaining planning permission, which is a matter of policy, a developer must obtain approval under the Building Regulations 1985, which is a statutory and mandatory code of construction standards. The regulations deal with the design and construction of buildings and the provision of services, fittings and equipment. Plans for the proposed work must be deposited with the local authority for approval prior to building work being undertaken. The building regulations also contain powers for the local authority to inspect and test work and take samples. Building controls are administered by different officers from planning matters and are the subject of a separate application.

8.5 Compulsory purchase and compensation

A public utility or government body may by notice acquire land or an interest in land for a range of public purposes, from the laying of cables to major road projects or town centre shopping developments. A compulsory purchase order will then be made and, subject to objection and if appropriate a public enquiry, this will be confirmed by central government and will result in the land being acquired at a compensation figure equal to the open market value at the time possession is taken. While a private developer cannot initiate any compulsory purchase, it is common for public bodies to undertake projects with the private sector and to agree to be responsible for obtaining the necessary compulsory purchase orders. Because of the English tradition for private rights to be respected and for full public consultation and enquiry, it can on occasion take a long time for major projects to come to fruition.

8.6 Protection of buildings of special interest

The Secretary of State may include any building in a list of buildings of special historic or architectural interest. Once listed it is an offence to alter or demolish the building without listed building consent. Areas of architectural or historic interest may be designated conservation areas and similar but lesser controls apply to all buildings, and trees, within such areas. Trees can themselves be made the subject of separate tree preservation orders.

9 ENVIRONMENTAL MATTERS

Environmental issues have become increasingly important in recent years. Common law liabilities for pollution have existed for many years and are based on nuisance, the case of *Rylands v Fletcher* and negligence. As a result of recent case law there is now little difference between *Rylands v Fletcher* and the law of nuisance which imposes liability for any unreasonable interference with another's reasonable use of his own property. In addition, however, statutory control has been introduced in a number of important areas including soil, ground and water contamination, air pollution and noise pollution. The relevant statutes are the Environmental Protection Act 1990, the Water Act 1989, the Water Resources Act 1991 and the Environment Act 1995. The Environment Act centralises responsibility for environmental control in the Environment Agency which shares its duties with the local authorities. The Environmental Protection Act provides for the local authority to be responsible for dealing with any statutory nuisance and it may serve an abatement notice where appropriate. The local authority may abate the nuisance itself if the notice is not complied with and recover its reasonable costs in doing so. Environmental law is the subject of increasing harmonisation as a result of EU directives.

9.1 Protection against atmospheric and noise pollution

An air quality management system has been introduced which sets certain standards for atmospheric pollution as well as for emissions of smoke, dust and grit. Local authorities are to carry out regular assessments of air quality, with a view to targeting areas for action. They are the enforcement bodies and are responsible for regulation and control of atmospheric emissions from a variety of industrial processes and mobile plant. Regulations establish a licensing procedure and liability is strict subject to defined statutory defences. In the case of smoke pollution liability attaches to the occupier, but otherwise to the polluter and only if he cannot be found to the owner or occupier. Local authorities are also the bodies responsible for control of noise pollution.

9.2 Water pollution

The legislation establishes and passes environmental control to the Environment Agency for all inland and coastal waters. The Agency is responsible for the establishment of water quality objectives. The discharge of trade and sewage effluent can only be undertaken with a discharge consent from the Agency. There are a range of offences allocating principal liability to the polluter but leaving the owner and occupier liable in certain circumstances. The Agency has a number of powers to carry out preventive action, investigate incidents and carry out remedial work at the reasonable cost of those who have caused or knowingly permitted the pollution. Except in an emergency, it is necessary for the Agency first to serve a works notice 'that any poisonous, noxious or polluting matter or any solid waste matter is likely to enter or to be or have been present in any controlled waters'. They can remedy the situation and recover expenses reasonably incurred from the person who caused or knowingly permitted the pollution.

9.3 Waste storage and disposal

The legislation is intended to secure that waste is properly managed, that the production of waste is minimised, that waste is recycled and that all management functions in relation to waste disposal collection and storage are transferred to a single body, the Environment Agency. There is now also a landfill tax imposed on the dumping of waste. The Environmental Protection Act 1990 creates criminal offences for the deposit, keeping, disposal and treatment of waste, except pursuant to a licence. A duty of a care is imposed on any person who imports, produces, keeps, treats or disposes of waste to prevent any contravention of the Act. Additionally, a notice can be served on the occupier to remove waste deposited in contravention. The Agency can deal with the waste itself, if the notice is not complied with, but is not obliged to do so. It can reclaim the costs from the person responsible and in some cases from the owner or occupier of the land.

9.4 Contaminated land

The government had intended to introduce local registers of any land that had been put to a contaminative use but abandoned its proposals in the face of strong opposition from landowners and developers. As part of a new move to ensure the clean up of contaminated land the Environment Act has set up a framework which is now being implemented. This includes a local register of remediation notices. The local authorities are made responsible for identifying and securing the cleaning up of contaminated land under the guidance of the Agency. They are to serve remediation notices in respect of such land, and if these are not complied with, they can undertake the work and recover the reasonable cost from the polluter and failing this from the present owner or occupier, although not from a mortgagee who is not in possession, nor from an insolvency practitioner, unless he is in some way responsible for the contamination. The remediation requirements must be reasonable taking into account their cost and the seriousness of the problem. They are likely to be less stringent where the recipient is not the person responsible for the contamination. There is no central fund for the cost of decontamination measures as there is, for example, in the United States.

9.5 Environmental impact assessments

It will always be wise for a buyer to enquire as to nearby landfill sites, previous contaminative uses, whether the land has been used as landfill or for waste disposal, particularly in the absence of any contamination registers. As a result of EU directives, however, it is mandatory to carry out an environmental impact assessment when a construction or infrastructure project falls into one of two categories specified in the 1988 and 1995 planning regulations. The first are specifically listed. The second are those which may have a significant effect on the environment. At present this requirement is being interpreted fairly narrowly by the courts but this may change. It is not unusual for an environmental impact assessment to be made a condition of planning consent.

10 DEVELOPMENT

10.1 Development projects, structures and vehicles

10.1.1 The simplest development project will typically involve the purchase of a site by an owner/occupier and the construction of the premises he requires by his own contractor. He may, however, approach a developer to arrange both site purchase and construction. The developer may, alternatively, find a site and once he has identified an occupier build out the development to an agreed design. He may equally put up the buildings entirely speculatively to his own design in the anticipation that he will find a buyer and/or occupier and retain the property for his own investment or sell it on having taken his profit. Where he has not secured the end user and investor, and particularly where the development is conditional on planning consent, the developer may reduce his risk either by entering into an option or conditional contract with the landowner, or by 'forward selling' the development to an investing institution. In this case, the institution will acquire the site at an early stage, finance the development and leave the developer, the management, construction and letting, for a fee or profit share based on the rentals achieved and the end cost of the project.

10.1.2 Although contracting companies did set up their own property development companies during the 1980s largely to create work for their contracting arms, by the mid-1990s all but the residential builders had retreated from development activities and gone back to concentrate on their core construction businesses. On the more complex schemes, there may be a number of parties who provide different skills using a number of different joint venture vehicles, one partner providing the development and property skills, another the financial and taxation expertise, and others providing the finance itself. Some developments are funded by the lending banks on straight commercial loans and others will have a mixture of equity and loan finance provided by external investors in addition to their own equity. On more substantial developments, each building may be put into a separate company with a management company responsible for the overall development. Each company may then be sold to an investor such as an institution or investment or unit trust. Speculative development was rare in the early 1990s although it has resumed again on a lesser scale.

10.2 Building contracts and appointments of professionals

10.2.1 Typical forms of building contract

The traditional contract, where the entire building will be designed by the employer and his professional team, and tenders will be invited from contractors, has the benefit of a greater certainty as to price but suffers from other disadvantages; the principal disadvantage being delay in that no work can start until all aspects of the scheme have been designed and tendered for. This has led to increasing use of the design and build contract, where the contractor takes over the entire project including its design, and the management contract, where the contractor is brought in at an early stage to advise on and organise the sub-contract packages for a fee, but takes no responsibility for the work itself. While this makes for speed and flexibility, the disadvantage of both is that there is no certainty as to price or completion date, and the manager merely provides budget or estimate figures at the outset.

10.2.2 Common terms

The traditional contract will provide for a start and finish date and stipulate that the contractor is paid the value of the work undertaken each month, although payments are also made sometimes by reference to various stages in the project. The contractor will usually be entitled to determine the contract if he is not paid any monthly or stage payment and the employer will be entitled to determine for a number of reasons including the suspension of work by the contractor. If the work is not completed by the contractual practical completion date, liquidated damages are paid weekly unless the contractor is entitled to an extension because the delay is due to force majeure, ie some factor outside his control. Contractors rarely give an absolute guarantee as to cost or time without a corresponding increase in price to cover the additional risk. Retentions and a maintenance period will be provided for (see 10.4) to secure the making good of defects. The Housing Grants Construction and Regeneration Act 1996 has introduced a number of standard requirements, eg as to stage payments, the mechanisms and dates for payment and the right to suspend performance for non-payment, in an attempt to make the system fairer.

10.2.3 Standard form of contracts

The most common form of building contract used throughout the industry is the JCT Building Contract (1980 Edition) of which there are a number of different versions according to the size and type of project. Nearly all building contracts not including a design role for the contractor are supervised by an architect or other professional, engaged by the employer, but also responsible to both parties to certify completion, variations and extensions of time. The complexity of this form of contract and the adversarial nature of traditional contracting roles, as well as the fragmentation of responsibilities under the standard form contracts, have arguably increased the likelihood of dispute and come under some criticism.

10.2.4 Appointment of the professional team

Just as the builder will have his contract, the members of the professional team will have their own letters of appointment. These usually specify the personnel who will be employed on the project, the fees for each stage of the project and the hourly rates for any additional work. The Royal Institute of British Architects and the Royal Institution of Chartered Surveyors have prepared standard form letters of appointment which are favourable to the professionals concerned, but are increasingly adopted.

10.3 Those involved and their roles

10.3.1 One of the failings of the British construction process is the division of responsibilities between so many parties. This can lead to complexity and difficulty in determining responsibility for defects in the works or their design, but it does give the employer the comfort that he is being advised by professionals who are independent of the contractor. Conventionally, the owner of the land may employ his own professional team and contractor direct, or use a project manager or developer, who will undertake the wider role of finding the site and taking overall responsibility for the project, its location, cost and execution. The owner or developer will then appoint an architect who will be responsible for the overall design of the building. Other professionals will be involved, including a quantity surveyor who will assess the amount of labour and materials required for each part of the project; a mechanical and electrical engineer, who will be responsible for the various systems such as lifts, heating and air conditioning; and a structural engineer who will advise on matters such as floor loadings and structural strength. Their different roles indicate the variety of functions that can arise. The contractor will execute the project to the design which has been submitted to him, having usually first quoted by way of competitive tender with other contractors. The architect will supervise the works on behalf of the employer and issue instructions and variation orders as appropriate, certifying payments due, extensions of time, practical and final completion.

10.3.2 The contractor will take principal responsibility for the building works, unless he has only a management role. As there is no contractual relationship between the subcontractor and the employer in the case of all but management contracts, it is common to negotiate warranties from the subcontractors and also from the suppliers of materials and plant direct with the employer.

10.3.3 Where the contractor has a design responsibility, the only professional representing the employer during the contract will be responsible essentially only for monitoring the cost and making limited decisions on the employer's behalf. In practice the initial brief for the contractor will still often be prepared by an architect engaged by the employer.

10.3.4 The system remains largely adversarial and there are pressures for alternative approaches such as placing the entire project, both design and execution, in the hands of a contractor and leaving him with overall responsibility.

10.4 Defects and remedies

10.4.1 Remedies of employer in respect of defects in design or materials

The contract will provide for a defects and maintenance period, commonly of six months for structural works and 12 months for mechanical and electrical works, during which time the contractor will maintain the building and put right any defects which have arisen. From each monthly payment there will be a retention, commonly of five per cent, and when the building is certified as practically complete, with a snagging list of minor defects which need to be attended to during the defects and maintenance period, the full contract price will normally be released to the contractor, less half of the retention, which will in turn be released at the end of the defects period upon the issue of a certificate of making good defects.

10.4.2 Remedies of subsequent owners/occupiers other than the contractual employer

A subsequent owner or occupier of a building, other than the direct contractual employer, is unable to recover the cost of remedying defects in a building from the original professional team as there is no right to this except by contract. Accordingly, it is commonly arranged with the professional team and the contractor that they will provide collateral warranties with subsequent owners, occupiers and financiers, acknowledging a direct contractual liability to those parties, similar to that owed to the original employer.

10.5 Defects insurance

Collateral warranties create a number of problems as it is often difficult to establish who will be liable for any particular defect and it is possible that the professional concerned will not have the funds, or adequate insurance, to meet the claim. Defects insurance has therefore been developed in different forms and the Continental decennial system has been used on occasion. None of these systems, however, provide cover for the full cost of remedying defects in a way which is entirely satisfactory and further types of insurance are being devised. In the case of house building there is a specialist scheme, secured by the National House Builders Council, to cover private buyers against major defects for a period of up to 10 years.

10.6 Copyright

The copyright in the design of the building will remain that of the design team and licences to use the design drawings will need to be negotiated by building owners, tenants, and possibly funders.

10.7 Fees

The total professional fees for a project will generally vary from between 7.5 to 8 per cent of the total cost of large projects to 15 per cent for smaller projects, where a single professional, usually an architect or building surveyor, will be employed.

10.8 Taxes

The tax which is most relevant to the construction process is value added tax (VAT) and all commercial construction is subject to VAT at the UK standard rate of 17.5 per cent. New residential construction is zero-rated as is construction of charitable premises and the provision of residential accommodation for the disabled.

11 TAXES

11.1 Corporation tax

Any company which is resident in the United Kingdom for tax purposes is liable to pay corporation tax on its worldwide profits (including capital gains, see 11.3), subject to relief under any double taxation treaty with the country where its profits originate, whether or not those profits are remitted (or sent) to the United Kingdom. Companies incorporated in the United Kingdom are treated as resident in the UK, as are companies whose central management or control is in the United Kingdom. Management and control is usually decided by reference to where board meetings take place. Non-resident companies are taxed on the profits of any trade carried on by a branch in the United Kingdom and on chargeable gains on the disposal of trading assets.

11.1.1 Tax rates

The rate of corporation tax is 31 per cent and 21 per cent for small companies, ie those whose profits do not exceed £300,000 per annum.

11.1.2 Computation and administration

In calculating its profits, a company can deduct expenses of a revenue or recurring nature (rather than a capital nature) which are wholly and exclusively incurred for the purposes of the trade of the company. This would extend to fees, commissions and loan interest as well as the usual deductions such as salaries and normal overheads. The rules relating to deduction of interest are complex but, essentially, any interest payable to a UK bank or branch is deductible as is any other interest which is exclusively charged to income. The tax payable by individuals on income, capital gains and inheritance tax is dealt with by the Inland Revenue, as is the calculation of corporation tax. The system is one of assessment based upon returns of information provided by the tax payer. Assessments are issued and, if unsatisfactory to the tax payer, may be appealed against. The appeal is initially to the General Commissioners of the Inland Revenue and then through Special Commissioners to the High Court on matters of law. Each tax has a different payment date and interest is charged at a rate published from time to time by HM Treasury. Corporation tax is payable generally within nine months of an accounting period. While it is open to a tax payer to arrange its affairs in such a way as to minimise tax, tax avoidance, any unlawful non-payment, or evasion, of tax is a criminal offence. Shemes whose only function is tax avoidance may be set aside.

11.1.3 Capital allowances

Expenditure on the construction of industrial buildings, certain hotels, and on plant and machinery as well as certain other buildings and assets is allowed as a deductible expense or capital allowance against profits. This is usually on the basis of 25 per cent of the expenditure being allowed as a writing-down allowance in the case of plant and machinery each year (declining balance basis); the allowance for industrial buildings is four per cent per annum (on a straight line basis). The allowances are taken back upon sale or in certain other circumstances by crediting the sale proceeds or value to the profits of the company. Special and higher allowances in the year of purchase (up to 100 per cent) apply to certain categories of building, eg commercial buildings in enterprise zones (see 12.4). The cost of the land is excluded from the allowance. Post 1996 acquired assets with a useful life of 25 years or more may be depreciated on a straight line basis at six per cent per annum

11.1.4 Withholding tax

Where a UK resident makes certain income payments to a non-UK resident, the UK resident must deduct tax from such payments. Income subject to such withholding includes interest on loans capable of lasting a year or more and rental on land and buildings (but not equipment). It does not extend to dividends although there are arrangements by which a company making distributions has to account for tax in advance which can subsequently be recovered by way of offsets against its UK corporation tax liability. The withholding tax rate for interest is 20 per cent and for royalties 23 per cent.

11.2 Taxes on development value

At various times, there have been taxes on the increase in value of land attributable to the issue of planning permission or any increase in value over and above the existing use value due to development potential, but the last of these, development land tax, was abolished several years ago.

11.3 Taxes on capital gains

Until recently, trading profits and profits realised on gains in the value of investments or capital assets of a company were taxed at different rates, but now there are no significant differences in the rates of corporate taxation for capital gains, though the rules for calculating these are slightly different. Tax is payable on the increase in the price realised over the cost of purchase increased in line with inflation. Overseas residents do not pay tax on capital gains on property investments in the United Kingdom.

11.4 Taxes on owner of property

The only taxes on the corporate ownership of property are those described above in respect of a company's profits. Individuals may be subject to inheritance tax when passing property by way of gift (or inheritance on death), but there are no other specific taxes on ownership of property.

11.5 Taxes on occupier

The occupier of a business property will pay the uniform business rate, which is a set levy representing a percentage of the rateable value of the premises. This is collected by central government and distributed to local councils for the provision of local services. Land and buildings are intended to be revalued every five years and the first valuation took place in 1989. The uniform business rate for the year 1996/97 is 45.8p in the pound for every pound of rateable value. This will go up each year in line with inflation. The rateable value is intended to be the rental value of the property and is set by the district valuer. Where the property is empty no rate is charged for the first three months and after this it is subject to 50 per cent of the usual rate and certain types of property are exempt, including agricultural land and buildings. Charitable organisations are entitled to 80 per cent relief but this can be extended by a discretionary 20 per cent making 100 per cent relief possible.

Residential premises are subject to council tax which is paid by the occupier, and if there is no occupier, by the owner. Unlike the uniform business rate, council tax is set by the local authority. A property will be placed in one of eight bands according to value. The highest level of tax charged by an authority for the highest band presently exceeds £1,600 a year.

11.6 Taxes on land transfer

Apart from inheritance tax referred to above, the only direct tax on the transfer of land is stamp duty. This is charged on the price paid at one per cent and is paid by the buyer. If the property is £250,000 or more in value the duty increases to one and a half per cent and if it is £500,000 or more to two per cent. There is an exemption for properties worth less than £60,000. Gifts of land do not attract stamp duty, neither do transfers between group companies.

11.7 Wealth taxes

There are no taxes on the wealth of individuals or companies.

11.8 Value added tax (VAT)

11.8.1 Any business providing goods or services with a total value in excess of £48,000 a year has to register with HM Customs & Excise and charge VAT on the value of those supplies at a standard rate of 17.5 per cent. Some supplies are, however, zero-rated, and others are exempt. The business accounts to Customs for the tax it collects but is allowed to deduct or offset the VAT that it has paid on supplies which it has, itself, recovered. Where the amount of tax payable by a taxable person is greater than the amount he recovers on his taxable supplies in any accounting period, usually one or three months, he can recover this amount from HM Customs & Excise. Tax is calculated on sums invoiced not received. The purpose of this tax is to charge only the value added by any taxable person in the chain of supply of goods or services so that the VAT charged is suffered in full only by the ultimate non-business or VAT-exempt consumer. At the end of each VAT accounting period, the taxable person must account to Customs for the excess of output tax (tax chargeable to customers), over input tax (tax payable on supplies received). VAT is administered by HM Customs & Excise and appeals are made to a special VAT Tribunal. Appeals on points of law can be taken to the High Court.

11.8.2 The sale or lease of land and buildings is generally exempt (though dwellings are zero-rated). The construction and sale of new non-residential buildings are standard-rated (ie taxable at 17.5 per cent). It is open to a tax payer to elect to waive exemption, ie to charge VAT on disposals to those who make wholly or largely taxable supplies in their own business. Certain surrenders and dealings with holiday homes are standard rated. See also 10.8.

11.9 Local and other taxes

Apart from the uniform business rate and council tax referred to in 11.5, there are no other local taxes or taxes of general application.

12 GRANTS AND INCENTIVES

There are a large number of central and local government grants and other forms of financial aid available for companies and businesses, often those located in areas of economic need. The Department of Trade and Industry (DTI) in England, and the Welsh Office Industry Department, are the main providers of government support for commerce and industry. The collective measures of the DTI are known as the 'Enterprise Initiative'. The Department of the Environment also oversees urban regeneration, through its urban development corporations; and the Rural Development Commission oversees the measures available in designated rural areas. The Invest In Britain Bureau is another useful source of information providing advice on most schemes.

12.1 English Partnerships

The English Partnerships are government-sponsored regional agencies which allocate resources from the central English Partnerships' Investment Fund. This fund replaced three former grant schemes: the derelict land grant, the city grant and the English Estates. English Partnerships aims to support otherwise unprofitable urban regeneration and investment projects in areas of need. The fund provides resources to facilitate projects which either provide jobs, create new industrial or commercial floor space, re-activate disused land or provide property for employment or housing. Assistance is in the form of:

(a) advice and help (with site clearing and acquisition, environmental issues, market and project assessments, etc);
(b) joint venture finance (sharing profits and losses with companies re-employing assets or property);
(c) rental guarantees;
(d) loans and guarantees (where there is no other suitable lender); or
(e) occasional direct development (where proactive private sector initiatives are unlikely).

The assistance is discretionary and varies according to the type of scheme.

12.2 Regional enterprise grants

Regional enterprise grants are discretionary grants, controlled by the DTI, for investment or innovation projects. Investment grants are available to small companies located in 'assisted areas' (development areas or intermediate areas) with less than 25 employees. Innovation grants are available to small companies in the same areas with less than 50 employees. Investment grants cover up to 15 per cent of the cost of fixed assets (including plant, machinery, buildings, site vehicles, land purchase and site preparation) costing a maximum of £15,000, whenever the need for the grant can be shown. Innovation grants cover 50 per cent of eligible costs, without the need to prove the need for the grant.

12.3 Regional selective assistance

The DTI offers 'regional selective assistance', mainly for manufacturing, construction or mining activities in 'assisted areas' (development or intermediate areas), to any size of company. These discretionary grants cover the minimum amount required to make the project feasible, and are based on the employment possibilities and the one off capital costs (in the first three years). The majority of funding, however, must still be provided by the company or private sector sources.

12.4 Enterprise zones

Enterprise zones, controlled by the Department of the Environment, are areas of economic need offering financial and administrative assistance for 10 years, to encourage private sector activity. The zones provide:

(a) relief against corporation tax for the capital cost of new industrial and commercial buildings;
(b) exemption from rates on such property; and
(c) exemption or mitigation of planning restrictions.

The most well known of the zones was the London Docklands Isle of Dogs enterprise zone which expired in 1992, but which enabled the Canary Wharf development to take place. No new zones are being declared and many have already expired.

12.5 Enterprise Investment Scheme

The Enterprise Investment Scheme has replaced the former Business Expansion Scheme. It provides tax relief for investments by individuals resident in the United Kingdom in respect of capital subscriptions for shares in certain trading companies subject to certain conditions and criteria.

12.6 Assistance from the European Union

Further types of assistance are available from the European Union.

12.6.1 European Investment Bank loans

European Investment Bank loans support regional development and EU objectives by providing loans for investment in fixed assets for industry, services to industry, hotels and tourism or general infrastructure. Investment projects based in any EU country are primarily eligible for the loan (even if controlled by a non-European company or investor). Although the loans tend to reflect usual commercial terms, they do not include arrangement fees or other general expenses. Larger investment projects (over £20 million) receive direct loans, whereas small to medium projects (with a maximum of 500 employees and £50 million fixed assets) receive loan support for loans of at least £30,000 over four years and employment creation loan support for loans of at least £15,000 over five years.

12.6.2 ECSC loans

European Coal and Steel Community (ECSC) loans are available in steel and coal 'closure areas' designated by the European Commission. The loans are usually for eight years and cover up to half the fixed capital costs, for the creation of new industrial opportunities and jobs.

12.6.3 RECHAR

RECHAR is a similar project of the European Structural Funds Initiative aimed at economic regeneration of old mining areas and for the provision of new jobs. However, the assistance can take the form of either a loan or a grant.

13 COMPANIES AND BUSINESS ENTITIES

13.1 Limited and unlimited companies

13.1.1 A company is either unlimited or more commonly limited by shares. Companies limited by guarantee are possible but rare. Ceitain professions are not allowed to have limited liability, such as lawyers and accountants, but are entitled to incorporate themselves into an unlimited company, the members of which will have unlimited liability for its debts but will otherwise have the benefits of incorporation. Members of companies limited by shares will have no liability for the debts of the company beyond the amount which they have to subscribe for their shares, though the directors may be liable for fraudulent or wrongful trading under the provisions of the Companies Act 1985; there is no distinction between an executive or supervisory director. Incorporation is a simple and speedy process requiring no government consents. Only one director and a minimum of two shareholders, with one share of one pound each, are needed to incorporate any of the three types of private company. A single shareholder can now incorporate a private company limited by shares or by guarantee, but never an unlimited company. Shares can be issued unpaid or part paid and for a consideration other than cash.

13.1.2 If a company limited by shares is not a public limited company, it will be a private limited company. In order to be a public limited company, there are a number of conditions which have to be met, such as the requirement that the company has a minimum share capital of £50,000, of which 25 per cent must have been paid up. The shares must be paid for in cash, unless the value of any non-cash contribution is valued by an external examiner. Public companies also have a number of advantages, including the right to issue shares to the public. A public company may also be listed or quoted in the London Stock Exchange subject to a number of further conditions.

13.1.3 The company is a separate legal person from its shareholders and directors, has its own assets and liabilities, and is taxed separately and under different rules. What it may and may not do will be set out in its memorandum and articles of association or charter.

13.2 Partnerships

13.2.1 The most common way to carry on a business is as partners. A partnership exists where two or more persons carry on business in common, with a view to profits, and their relationship is regulated by the Partnership Act 1890. There is no distinction, as elsewhere, between civil and commercial partnerships and the partnership does not have a separate persona from its individual members; this means that each partner pays his own tax on his share of the profits. There is no need for a formal partnership agreement and each member of the partnership is liable for all the debts of the partners and will usually negotiate an indemnity from the other partners. Clubs and societies are not partnerships within the meaning of the Partnership Act as they are not generally conducted to make a profit. It is not necessary to register partnerships. Decisions have to be unanimous unless all partners agree otherwise.

13.2.2 A limited partnership can be set up under which certain partners have general liability (the general partners) and the other partners may have their liability limited to a fixed financial contribution to the partnership. The general partner is usually a company whose liability is unlimited to the outside world, but whose members have only a limited liability under usual company law principles. The limited partners have no right to take part in the management of the business or to bind the business. A limited partnership must, however, be registered in accordance with the Limited Partnerships Act 1907 and will be deemed to be a general partnership unless so registered. The advantage to the limited partners is that they can set up a company as the general partner and leave themselves with limited liability while having the advantages, such as separate tax treatment, of partnership.

13.3 Other types of business association

Companies and partnerships being the principal forms of association recognised by law, other unincorporated associations have no legal recognition. Note should however be made of the position of trusts and joint ventures.

13.3.1 The trust is described at 1.2. It is a simpler vehicle than the company, and in certain circumstances can be tax transparent, ie leave the beneficial owner with the tax liability for the property as though he were the true owner, rather than merely a shareholder in a company. This creates a form of ownership somewhere between full ownership and the limited or diluted ownership that the individual would have if he merely had shares in the company which owned the property. As a result of its flexibility, the concept of the trust has become commonly used in English speaking countries as a way of providing for multiple ownership of assets for example in relation to the unit trust, a vehicle which has spawned its own industry.

13.3.2 The joint venture is not a recognised legal entity and there is no body of law relating to it. The principal document in any joint venture arrangement is, therefore, the joint venture agreement, negotiated between the parties. Various vehicles may be used to form a property joint venture, including trusts, limited partnerships, equity sharing leases, and joint venture companies. In the case of the latter, their relationship is governed by either the joint venture agreement or by a shareholders' agreement. The joint venture arrangements will provide, in particular, for the financial contributions of each party, the division of profits, the duration of the joint venture, the restrictions and pre-emption terms on the disposal of any parties' interest in the venture, and for the termination and winding up of the joint venture. There are no particular fiscal regulations for the taxation of joint ventures and the tax treatment will depend on the vehicle used. If a joint venture company is used, the company will bear corporation tax and the joint venture parties will bear tax on the dividends and distributions of the company in the usual way: this is not entirely satisfactory and other approaches, such as partnerships, are frequently used to avoid this double charge to tax.

14 INTERNATIONAL

14.1 Restrictions on or consents required for inward investment

There are no restrictions on the introduction of funds into the United Kingdom for the purchase of property or on the ownership of UK property by foreign entities, with certain very limited exceptions when trade embargoes are imposed on specific countries.

14.2 Exchange controls

The United Kingdom used to have exchange controls limiting the repatriation or transfer of funds out of the United Kingdom but there are no controls or restrictions at present.

14.3 Restrictions and registrations on carrying on a business

There is no restriction on a foreign entity or company carrying on business in the United Kingdom, with certain limited exceptions, although a company which has a place of business in the United Kingdom does need to register itself at the companies registry; this is a simple formality.

14.4 Repatriation of income and proceeds of property trading and development

There are no consents or restraints involved in the repatriation of income and proceeds subject to the deduction of withholding tax (see 11.1.4).

14.5 Withholding taxes

Withholding taxes have been referred to at 11.1.4 and interest and rental payments may be subject to these.

14.6 Double taxation relief

The United Kingdom has separate double taxation treaties with a number of countries.

CHAPTER 5

Finland

Kaj Swanljung **Susanne Mattsson**

Roschier-Holmberg & Waselius, Helsinki

CONTENTS

1 OWNERSHIP OF LAND 143
2 OTHER INTERESTS IN LAND 146
3 TITLE TO LAND 149
4 TRANSACTIONS IN LAND 150
5 LEASES 155
6 FINANCE AND INVESTMENT SOURCES 158
7 FORMS OF SECURITY 160
8 PLANNING AND BUILDING REGULATION 162
9 ENVIRONMENTAL MATTERS 164
10 DEVELOPMENT 166
11 TAXES 169
12 GRANTS AND INCENTIVES 173
13 COMPANIES AND BUSINESS ENTITIES 173
14 INTERNATIONAL 175

CHAPTER 5

Finland

1 OWNERSHIP OF LAND

Finnish property law, as well as the Finnish legal system as a whole, has its roots in the old Swedish-Finnish legal tradition on the one hand, and in German law on the other. Over the last few years much of the legislation relating to property law has been revised, the most important revision being the new Land Law Code 1995, which came into force on 1 January 1997. In the Finnish legal system, the rights related to property are usually divided into ownership (see 1.1–1.4) and limited property rights (see section 2) such as servitudes, other rights of use and mortgages, and leases (see section 5).

1.1 Types of tenure

1.1.1 Freehold or absolute ownership

Ownership carries with it a right to own, occupy and dispose of land unless these rights of the owner have been limited by statute, contract or by customary law. Anything which is fixed or annexed to the land and which permanently serves the purposes of the property is termed a fixture and is treated as part of the property. However, there is not necessarily a link between ownership of the land upon which a building is constructed and the ownership of the building itself (see further 2.1.3). Minerals are considered part of the land and belong as such in principle to the landowner, although the right to utilise the deposit may be divided between the landowner and the finder.

1.1.2 Leasehold

Leases or tenancies are contractual relationships. Long leases in the Anglo-American tradition, granted at a premium or for capital payments, are not used in practice, although it is possible for a landowner to grant a right to build over his land to a third party, in which case the grantee of the building right will own the building for the term of the right (see 2.1.3). The owner of land or a building can grant the right to occupy the land or the building to another party by entering into a lease agreement with that party. The statutory provisions applicable to the lease agreement will vary depending on whether the lease is a land lease, a residential or a commercial tenancy. As the provisions concerning the various types of lease are different it is important to distinguish between them (see section 5). It is not unusual for companies to lease the buildings and/or land used for their business. The lease agreement will usually give the tenant an exclusive right to use and occupy the leased premises for a specified term or until terminated by notice. The right to use the leased property will be restricted and governed by the lease agreement and the relevant Tenancy Act. Leases are dealt with more fully in section 5.

1.1.3 Joint ownership

With a few exceptions, joint ownership of land is regulated by the Joint Ownership Act 1985. Each joint owner is deemed to own an equal share in the land, unless otherwise agreed, without exclusive ownership of a specific and identifiable area of the land. Each joint owner may freely enjoy the use of the land in so far as his actions do not encroach upon the benefits and rights of the other owners. Usually every joint owner has the right to dispose of his own share independently. Pre-emption rights for the other joint owners may, however, be established by agreement. A joint owner also has the right to divide the share owned by him from the rest of the property. If this is not possible (eg due to restrictions on plot size) or would lead to a depreciation of the price of the property or would cause disproportionately high expenses, the local court has the power to order the whole property to be sold at the request of any of the joint owners. An agreement between the owners concerning the right to use certain areas of the land or certain buildings can be registered in the register of mortgages and will then be binding not only between the parties but also against a third party.

1.1.4 Condominia

The condominium system is not commonly used in Finland. Private ownership of multiple-unit buildings is generally by companies limited by shares under the Housing Companies Act 1991. Shareholding in a housing company normally gives the shareholder the right to use and dispose of a specified flat in the building owned by the company as well as access to the common areas in the building. The relationship between the shareholders in the housing company is regulated by the Housing Companies Act 1991 and the articles of association of the company.

1.1.5 Lesser rights

Lesser rights of ownership are dealt with in more detail in section 2.

1.2 Legal and beneficial ownership

There is no concept similar to the beneficial interest and trust in land that exists under common law jurisdictions.

1.3 Restrictions on ownership and dealing

1.3.1 There are few restrictions on the ownership of land in Finland. Foreign residents and foreign companies and associations need only seek permission from the authorities for the acquisition of leisure property (ie property designated for recreational use, mainly holiday homes) and for property specifically designated for national defence (see section 14 where the restrictions on foreign ownership are dealt with more fully). In addition to the restrictions on foreign ownership, there are some limitations on the rights of banks and religious communities to own land. In the administrative district of the Aland Islands, land can only be owned by the Islands' residents, or by those having a close connection with the Islands (eg by marriage to a resident). There are some legislative restrictions on the extent of the rights of a landowner, which are mainly aimed at protecting the public interest and include planning regulations, rights of access, preservation of natural beauty and compulsory purchase. There are also some restrictions protecting private interests, such as the laws of nuisance.

1.3.2 There are certain specific restrictions upon the disposal of land by bodies such as housing corporations where the decision-making procedure is more strictly regulated and all shareholders have to agree on the sale of land. Otherwise land is freely disposable by corporations subject to any restrictions which may be contained in the articles of association of the corporation.

1.3.3 Although there are no limitations on a minor or a person lacking legal capacity from owning land, he or she will be subject to restrictions when wishing to dispose of it. The disposal must be undertaken by the guardians on behalf of the minor or the person lacking legal capacity. A court order is needed for the sale of land, while the purchase of land is to be approved by the local guardianship board. Parents, who are statutory guardians of their child, need not seek permission to purchase land on a dependent child's behalf.

1.3.4 Under the Pre-emption Act 1977 a municipality may have a right of pre-emption in a property transaction and be entitled to purchase the land at the purchase price agreed upon between the seller and the original buyer. However, the right may only be exercised if the land is to be used for community construction and for recreational use and protection purposes (eg streets, parks and areas of historical or environmental interest, although this limitation does not apply in the cities of Helsinki, Espoo, Vantaa and Kauniainen). In practice however the municipalities seldom exercise this right.

1.3.5 The sale of agricultural and forested land exceeding 30,000 m^2 is restricted by the Right to Acquire Agricultural and Forestry Land Act 1978 which may impose a requirement to obtain a permit to dispose of the land. The aim is to prevent forests and land used for agricultural purposes being sold for non-agricultural use. The Act is not applicable to land that is used for, or has been specifically designated for, another purpose, or which is covered by a town plan. The disposal of land by the state and the municipalities is restricted by statutory provisions.

1.4 Acquisitive prescription and adverse possession

Under the old Land Law Code 1734, a person who had occupied land in good faith without interruption for so long that it had become impossible to certify how his forefathers or the previous owner had acquired the land could be deemed the owner of the land. The Land Law Code 1995 does not include any provisions concerning acquisitive prescription, although rights based on acquisitive prescription which can be deemed to have been created before it entered into force on 1 January 1997 will be recognised also in the future. Acquisitive prescription is of little importance today.

2 OTHER INTERESTS IN LAND

There are various interests in land which confer a right less than ownership. The most common are servitudes, other rights of use and mortgages. For leases, see section 5.

2.1 Servitudes or easements, usufruct, building and dwelling rights

2.1.1 Servitudes or easements

A servitude can be defined as a right over land in favour of other land. Although servitudes are generally permanent, it is, under certain circumstances, possible to establish servitudes in force for only a defined period. A servitude is established in official procedures conducted by an authorised official and two elected representatives appointed by the municipal council and is a right in rem, enforceable by and between successive owners. Servitudes are generally based on an agreement between the landowners, although it is under certain circumstances possible to establish servitudes against the will of a landowner. Servitudes include road servitudes which secure access to land by using or building a road on land belonging to a different owner and rights to run services such as drains and cables.

2.1.2 Usufruct

The right of usufruct does not exist as such under Finnish law but comparable rights permit the owner to grant such rights freely (eg timber felling rights and rights to take minerals) in respect of a third party either under contract or by way of informal agreement. These rights are therefore personal and do not bind successors in title unless there is a special reason, eg the new owner was aware of the right when he purchased the land or the right has been secured by registration.

2.1.3 Building and dwelling rights

The right to construct a building on a plot of land owned by another is usually granted under a land lease agreement governed by the Land Lease Act 1966 where the tenant is given the right (or obligation) to erect buildings on the leased land. The buildings erected by the tenant become the property of the tenant. Upon termination of the lease agreement, the owner of the property will generally have either the right or obligation to purchase the building from the lessee, unless otherwise agreed. The lessee can build on land used for business or industrial purposes provided that he is not forbidden to do so under the lease agreement. The lessor will, however, have the right to purchase the buildings at market value from the lessee at the end of the lease period unless otherwise agreed. If the lessor elects not to purchase the buildings, the lessee has to remove them. The terms on which these leases are granted are dealt with in more detail in section 5. The limitations on the right of construction will be determined not only by the lease agreement but also by the planning authority decisions concerning the land. Rights of residence are usually granted by way of a lease agreement (see section 5). Rights of residence are sometimes also established in connection with property transactions where, eg the seller of land is left with a right to use and occupy a certain part of the land for a certain period or for the rest of his lifetime. Such a right can under certain conditions be protected by registration.

2.2 Restrictions on use and other restrictions

Landowners may by way of contract agree to enter into restrictions on the use of one piece of land to protect the amenities and value of another piece of land. Those restrictions cannot be protected by registration and are as a rule not enforceable by and between successive owners. Restriction on use by way of contract is not very commonly used in Finland and many of the matters that might otherwise be the object of such an agreement are dealt with by way of planning regulations. Restrictions under planning and other legislation are commented on in section 8.

2.3 Private mortgages and charges

Monetary liabilities can be secured on land by way of mortgage. The creation of mortgage rights requires registration of the mortgage with the local court. Specific comment is made on mortgages in section 7.

2.4 Contracts and options

A notarised contract in writing for the sale of land (a pre-contract) is binding between the parties and creates an enforceable right for each to demand completion. The seller will remain the owner of the land until the final purchase contract has been entered into and he can still exercise certain rights of ownership, eg establish mortgage and other rights in the land. If the seller sells the land to a third party in breach of the pre-contract, the pre-contract buyer does not have a right over the land and can only claim damages from the seller.

2.5 Public or municipal charges

Various public law liabilities may be secured over property such as the cost of carrying out land surveys and the repayment of certain loans and grants. Under the Land Law Code 1995, public charges have to be registered in the register of mortgages. Unless a public law liability is registered within one year of its creation, the charge will cease to exist and the liability can only be collected from the person who is personally liable for the debt. Charges created before the Land Law Code came into force on 1 January 1997 must be registered by 1 January 2000.

2.6 Other interests

The owner's right to use and to restrict the use of his land has traditionally been limited by public access rights. Public access rights grant the public the right to use land owned by someone else for recreational purposes which do not cause inconvenience to the owner. The right of access is limited to walking, skiing and cycling. Certain private areas actively used by the owner such as courtyards, gardens and land used for agricultural purposes are excluded. In addition, there is a public right to use watercourses. Fishing and gaming rights are usually confined to the owner, although a recent change in the legislation grants the public limited fishing rights for recreational purposes.

2.7 Liabilities attaching to land

A landowner may be made liable for the unreasonable use of his land to the detriment of adjoining owners under the Neighbourhood Act 1920. Specific comment on restrictions imposed by environmental legislation is made in section 9. Further statutory restrictions can be found in the legislation on planning, building, public health and preservation of buildings and areas of special historic interest. Infringements against these may lead to liability. Comment on planning and building regulations is made in section 8. Finally, there are fiscal liabilities, the most important of which attach to the land in the form of real estate tax in accordance with the Land Tax Act 1992 (see section 11).

2.8 Legal and equitable interests

There is no concept similar to the trust or equitable interest of common law jurisdictions.

2.9 Protection of rights and interests

Servitudes established by authority decision or in conjunction with land division procedures are, as a rule, enforceable between successive owners. Existing servitudes over a certain plot of land can be checked in the land register. Lease agreements, usufruct and other comparable rights and interests, with some exceptions, cannot be enforced against subsequent bona fide owners, unless protected by registration in the mortgage register. Under the Land Law Code 1995 most rights of any practical or economical importance can be secured by registration. However, an unregistered land lease agreement can, under certain circumstances, be binding on a subsequent owner if the tenant is in occupation when the land is sold.

2.10 Priority of interests

Priority between registered interests (such as mortgages) in land will depend generally on the date of the application for registration, not the date of creation, with the oldest in time being given priority. The principal exceptions are registered public law liabilities which take priority over other interests.

3 TITLE TO LAND

3.1 Proof of title

Land is divided into 'units'. A unit may be owned by a single owner or in shares by several owners. A specified area, a 'parcel', of the unit can also be owned by a separate owner. A transfer of ownership of a unit of land, a share of a unit or a parcel obliges the new owner to register his ownership. The application for registration must be filed with the local district court within six months from the date of the purchase agreement or other transfer document; however, when ownership is transferred by inheritance, divorce or as a result of an authority decision, the six months' registration period is calculated differently. Although title to the land will pass to the new owner independently of registration (see 3.3), the registration of ownership will provide protection for both the registered owner and other parties who have relied on the registered information. Where the same land has been transferred to two different parties, a later buyer in good faith will be given the title to the land if he files his application for registration prior to the other buyer. A buyer can acquire title even if the seller was not the rightful owner, provided the seller was registered as the owner of the land at the time of sale, and the buyer did not know (and had no reason to know) that the seller was not the rightful owner. The rightful owner has a right to compensation from the state for damage suffered as a result. A rightful owner may also lose his right to the land to a registered owner in good faith who has possessed the land as registered owner for a period of at least ten years. Both the land register and the register of land ownership and mortgages (see 3.2) are open to inspection by the public.

3.2 Land registers

The land register deals with the registration of land and water into units. Every unit of land registered in the land register has its own number for identification. The land register is kept by the local surveying authorities or the municipal real estate engineer, depending on the type of land. The register of ownership and mortgages, which is based on the same division into units as the land register, is kept by the Ministry of Justice. The district courts act as registration authorities. Both the land register and the register of ownership and mortgages are now computer-based.

3.2.1 Plans

Land register plans are used to show the location of units, whilst the definitive boundaries are shown by plans based on the formal division of the units.

3.2.2 Content

The land register includes information about the area of the unit, rights over land granted in favour of another unit and rights over the land in common use. The register of land ownership and mortgages includes information about ownership of land, registered rights over the land and mortgages, as well as information about attachments and seizures concerning the land and any insolvency proceedings against the landowner.

3.2.3 Errors

A decision concerning registration of ownership and mortgages can be appealed against in the Court of Appeal. Written errors in the register of land ownership and mortgages can, however, usually be corrected on the initiative of the district courts. Decisions that are manifestly incorrect may also be corrected at the district courts' initiative under certain circumstances provided everyone who suffers the loss of a right approves the correction. Individuals who have suffered the loss of a right in reliance upon information contained in the register of land ownership and mortgages may, under the Land Law Code 1995, under certain circumstances, have the right to compensation from the state regardless of whether the state has acted negligently or not. The state is also strictly liable for damage created by written errors. The state may be liable for negligence for other types of damage arising from errors in the register of ownership and mortgages, under the Tort Act 1974. There is also provision for rectification and compensation in relation to errors in the land register.

3.3 Passing of title

Title to the land will pass at the time agreed between the parties in a valid purchase agreement. The passing of title is not dependent upon the registration of ownership (see 3.1). It is in fact possible for a buyer to sell the land without the first transfer being registered. Title will often pass when the agreement is signed, but it is quite common for the parties to agree to separate possession and title, so that possession passes when the agreement is signed, with title passing once the purchase price has been paid. Although the passing of title is not dependent on the registration of title, it is not possible for an owner to register a mortgage of the land before the transfer has been registered.

4 TRANSACTIONS IN LAND

The most common transactions in land are the sale and purchase of property, the creation and transfer of leases (see section 5) and the creation of mortgage rights to secure a loan or other liability (see section 7).

4.1 Procedures

4.1.1 The first stage in the purchase of land is the negotiation of the main terms of the contract, during which the buyer will normally undertake a thorough examination of the land and buildings. A private person buying residential property may simply choose to ask a builder to examine the state of the buildings, while a larger company buying industrial property may prefer to undertake a thorough survey to include any environmental risks connected with the property (see further 9.4). However, under the Land Law Code 1995, the seller has a wide obligation to inform the buyer of matters related to the land and buildings that may be of relevance to the buyer (see 4.2). When the parties have reached agreement on the terms of the transaction, a purchase agreement will be signed. It is not unusual for a deposit to be paid by the buyer prior to the signing of the actual purchase agreement. If the parties decide to enter into the actual purchase agreement at a later date, they may wish to enter into a pre-contract which must fulfill the same formal requirements as the actual contract in order to be binding on the parties (see 4.3). The time involved in completing a purchase of land will vary greatly, although the transaction could, at least in theory, be completed in a day. Following completion, the buyer of a unit or a parcel will pay the transfer tax and apply to register the transfer in the register of land ownership and mortgages.

4.1.2 A pre-contract fulfilling the formal requirements described in 4.3 is binding between the parties and creates an enforceable right entitling each party to claim completion of the purchase agreement. An informal agreement concerning the purchase of land or the payment of a deposit does not constitute an obligation to complete the transaction, although the party refusing to complete the transaction has to reimburse the other party's reasonable expenses for the preparation of the transaction, and the deposit has to be repaid (less any expenses payable by the party to whom the deposit is to be returned).

4.2 Contract terms

4.2.1 A land purchase agreement would typically include terms relating to the transfer of ownership and possession, the payment of the purchase price, security given by the buyer, mortgages, responsibility for taxes, the condition of the property and specification of any moveables sold together with the land. Land purchase agreements are generally quite short in comparison with English or American agreements and it may be necessary for a foreign investor to consider the rights and obligations of the buyer and the seller under the Land Law Code 1995.

4.2.2 The contract provides the basis for determining whether there is a physical defect in the property. Under the Land Law Code a physical defect exists not only if the property does not fulfil the requirements of the contract but also if the seller has given the buyer wrongful or misleading information about the area of the land, the condition or structure of the buildings or about any other attribute of the property and the information is regarded as having influenced the transaction. A physical defect can also, under certain circumstances, exist if the seller has failed to inform the buyer or failed to correct a buyer's erroneous impression concerning matters of importance in relation to the quality of the property. If there is a considerable discrepancy between the standard of the property sold and what can be expected under the relevant circumstances from a property of that type due to a hidden defect, the Land Law Code will also imply a physical defect. The buyer cannot make any claims in respect of a physical defect of which he can be regarded as having been aware when he entered into the contract, or that could have been detected by an examination of the property. There is generally no obligation on the buyer to check the information provided by the seller or to extend his examination to such matters as require technical or otherwise extraordinary measures.

4.2.3 The seller has a wide obligation to investigate and to inform the buyer of matters relating to the right to use and occupy the property. Under the Land Law Code 1995 a defect is deemed to exist if the seller has given the buyer wrongful or misleading information about a plan, building prohibition, restriction on transfer or other comparable authority decision and the information can be regarded as having affected the transaction. The seller is not only responsible for wrongful or misleading information, he also has a positive obligation to inform the buyer of any existing authority decisions and he cannot validly claim that he was unaware of any such decision. The seller must also correct any erroneous impression on the part of the buyer concerning matters that may prevent the buyer from using or occupying the property as intended. A defect can also be regarded as existing on certain other grounds, eg that a parcel or share of a unit of property cannot be formed into an independent unit. The buyer cannot make a claim in respect of a defect as to the right to use and occupy the property of which he can be regarded as having have been aware.

4.2.4 The seller has a further obligation to investigate and to inform the buyer of matters regarding the ownership of the property and the rights relating to it. A legal defect is regarded as existing if, eg, the buyer risks losing the ownership of the property to a third party who can be considered the rightful owner of the property. A legal defect will be implied if the seller has given the buyer wrongful or misleading information or failed to inform the buyer of matters relating to registration of ownership, mortgage rights or tenancy agreements which can be considered to have affected the transaction. A legal defect will also exist if the buyer cannot register ownership due to uncertainty regarding the seller's ownership of the property.

4.2.5 If there is a defect in the property, the buyer has a right to a price reduction, or if the defect is fundamental, a right to cancel the agreement. With the exception of hidden physical defects, the buyer also usually has a right to damages. The buyer can lose his right to claim for the defect if he fails to inform the seller of the defect and to make his claim within a reasonable time from the detection of the defect or from the time that the defect should have been detected by the buyer. The seller must be informed of a physical defect within five years from the transfer of possession of the property.

4.2.6 Whether there is a defect in the property is determined by the condition of the property when the contract was entered into. After the contract has been entered into the seller has a duty of care in relation to the property while it remains in his possession. Unless otherwise agreed between the parties, the risk will pass when the purchase agreement is signed. It is therefore in the interest of the buyer to insure the property as soon as the purchase agreement has been entered into. Under the Insurance Act 1994 insurance will, however, as a rule, remain in force for the benefit of the new owner for a period of 14 days after the transfer of ownership. If the seller breaches his duty of care, uses the property in a way he is not authorised to do or otherwise negligently causes damage to the property, the buyer has a right to a reduction of the price or, if considerable damage has been caused, to cancel the agreement. The buyer also has a right to damages. If the seller does not deliver the possession of the property to the buyer at the agreed time, the buyer has the right to demand completion of the contract or, if the delay is considerable, the right to cancel the agreement. The buyer again has the right to damages. If the buyer does not pay the purchase price at the agreed time, the seller can demand completion and damages. If there is a considerable delay in paying the purchase price, the seller can cancel the contract and demand damages where the transfer of ownership is connected to the payment of the purchase price under the purchase agreement. Unless agreed otherwise between the parties, the seller has a right to interest on the delayed payment at the rate set annually by the Bank of Finland. This is currently 11 per cent.

4.2.7 It is possible for the parties to contract out of the rights and obligations discussed under 4.2.2–4.2.6 except where a professional in the property business sells land to a private buyer for residential purposes. The Land Law Code 1995 also protects the rights of private buyers of residential property in other ways.

4.2.8 Unless otherwise agreed between the parties, title is transferred and possession is delivered to the buyer when the contract is entered into. The parties may agree upon both dissolving or suspensive clauses with a maximum duration of five years. An example of a dissolving clause is one where the buyer has the right to cancel the contract if he is not granted permission to build on the land by a certain date. An example of a suspensive clause is a condition by which ownership is not transferred until the purchase price has been paid. A clause giving the seller the right to redeem the land from the buyer or a clause obliging the buyer to give the seller a right of first refusal will not be binding. The parties are free to agree the arrangements for payment of the purchase price, but it is not uncommon for title to be withheld until the purchase price has been fully paid.

4.3 Formalities

4.3.1 An agreement for the transfer of land must be in writing, signed by both parties and witnessed by a notary. The buyer, the seller and the notary must all be present at the completion of the contract. The parties may be represented by agents but will have to provide written authorisation specifying the agent and the object of the transfer. The contract must state the parties' intention to transfer ownership and specifically identify the land, the parties to the transaction and the purchase price. A failure to follow the formal requirements will result in the transfer being void. The formal requirements are the same for the transfer of both registered units and parcels, and apply whether the agreement is a sale or a gift. It is the duty of the notary to check that the formal requirements are fulfilled. A defect in the form of the contract is cured if the conveyance has been registered in the register of ownership and mortgages. Dissolving and suspensive clauses are not valid unless included in the formal contract. Other terms can be agreed upon without any formal requirements, eg orally or in a separate document. The parties will be contractually bound once a valid contract has been signed.

4.3.2 Land lease agreements must be in writing and all terms of the agreement must be included in the written agreement in order to be valid. A lease agreement concerning land used for business purposes may, however, be entered into orally if it is entered into for a maximum period of two years or is to be in force for an indefinite period. Tenancy agreements can be entered into either orally or in writing, with the exception that an agreement for a fixed period must be made in writing.

4.4 Fees, costs and taxes

4.4.1 On the sale of land, the seller will usually agree to pay all taxes and other charges until an agreed date, eg the date of completion, whereupon the buyer assumes responsibility. Agents' commission will usually vary between four and five per cent of the sale price. However for land used for commercial purposes, agents' commission will vary between one and five per cent. Agents from smaller companies may charge less. The commission will usually only be payable if the transaction takes place. Each party will usually bear its own agents' and lawyers' fees.

4.4.2 If lawyers are used in connection with the transaction, their fees will usually be based on a time charge basis and calculated at an hourly rate. The fees would normally be charged irrespective of whether the transaction is successful or not. The notary fee is charged at a flat rate of FIM200 per agreement.

4.4.3 Transfer tax at a rate of four per cent is charged on the purchase price. The transfer tax is normally payable by the buyer.

4.4.4 The land registry fee for registration in the register of ownership is FIM310, irrespective of the value of the land or consideration.

4.4.5 Agents' and solicitors' fees attract value added tax (VAT), currently at a rate of 22 per cent. VAT is not charged on sales and lettings of land and buildings.

4.5 Professionals' roles

The marketing and sale of land are usually conducted by estate agents, who are subject to statutory control under the Estate Agency Decree 1993 setting down minimum requirements for estate agents' qualifications. Lawyers are sometimes, although by no means always, used in connection with land transactions. Depending on the type of property in question and the parties involved, a surveyor or a similar professional may be used by the buyer in connection with the investigation of the property. The notary (who acts as official witness at the signing of the purchase contracts) checks the identity of the parties and whether the contract fulfils the requirements of the Land Law Code 1995 before signing the contract. The duties of a notary also include informing the relevant local authorities and the district court about the conveyance of land he has been professionally involved with. The actual application for registration of land will, however, be made by the buyer.

5 LEASES

The lease of land is a contractual relationship. The statutory provisions applicable will vary with the type of property leased. Where the main object of the lease is land (including possible buildings), the lease agreement will be governed by the Land Lease Act 1966. Where the main object of the lease is a building or a part of a building used for residential purposes, the lease will be governed by the Residential Tenancy Act 1995, and where the main object of the lease is a building or a part of a building used for business purposes, the lease agreement will be governed by the Business Tenancy Act 1995. Leases can be either of fixed length or for an indefinite period subject to termination on notice. It is not unusual, especially in the case of business tenancies, for the parties to agree to an initial fixed term, such as five years, after which time the agreement will remain in force for an indefinite period subject to termination by either party. The length of the lease period will vary according to the needs of the parties and the type of property used. Generally, land lease agreements are entered into for longer periods than business or residential tenancies. A lease agreement concerning land for residence can be entered into for a fixed period only and may not exceed 100 years. (If the lessee intends to build on the land, the lease period may not be shorter than 30 years.) A lease agreement for land to be used for business or industrial purposes can be entered into for an indefinite period or for a fixed period that may not exceed 100 years.

5.1 Rent and other terms

5.1.1 The parties to a lease agreement are, with some exceptions, free to negotiate the rent. Tenancy agreements may contain an arrangement for linking rents to an index. However, this is subject to the condition that the agreement is in force until determined by notice, or for fixed length of a minimum of three years. Land leases can only generally contain index clauses if they have been entered into for a fixed period of not less than 10 years with limited rights for the landlord to terminate the agreement (for limitations on this right see 5.3). The rent is usually payable in advance at regular intervals. The rent for business and residential premises is most often payable monthly, while the rent for land is often paid annually. The non-payment of rent is generally sufficient ground for termination of the tenancy or land lease agreement. The rights and obligations of the landlord and tenant under different types of tenancy agreement are regulated in detail by statute. It is therefore not always necessary for the parties to enter into a very detailed agreement, unless they specifically want to contract out of specific statutory provisions, and tenancy agreements are often relatively short. It is not uncommon for tenancy agreements for business and residential premises to be in a short standard form which generally includes provisions concerning the rent and the procedures for review, the length of the leasing period and the payment of a rent deposit. Depending on the needs of the parties, other matters may also be agreed upon. Rent deposits or other types of security are often required from the tenant. Land lease agreements are equally often quite short, although lease agreements for land for business purposes often require more detailed regulation of the rights and obligations of the parties and land lease agreements will often regulate the right of the tenant to erect buildings on the land and to otherwise use and alter the property. Another provision commonly included is the right of the tenant to transfer the lease agreement to a third party, as this will enable the tenant to use the leasing right and the buildings owned by the tenant on the property as security by way of mortgage. The landlord would usually insure the building while the landlord would insure its own machinery and equipment, although it is not uncommon that the parties agree that the lessee also insures the building.

5.1.2 A land lease agreement for land to be used for permanent residence, business or industrial purposes may be transferred by the tenant to a third party without consent unless this right has been restricted in the lease agreement. Under the Land Law Code 1995, a lease agreement which is transferable without the consent of the landlord must be registered in the register of mortgages if the tenant owns buildings or structures on the land or if he has the right to erect buildings or structures. A tenancy agreement may not be transferred to a third party by the tenant without the consent of the landlord, unless otherwise agreed between the parties. In land leases the tenant is responsible for the maintenance of the leased property, unless otherwise agreed between the parties. In tenancies it is the obligation of the landlord to keep the leased premises in such condition as can reasonably be expected under the circumstances (such as the age of the building) unless otherwise agreed between the parties.

5.2 Privity of contract and estate

There is no concept of privity of contract and estate as under English law.

5.3 Rent control and security of tenure

5.3.1 Lease agreements are generally not subject to rent control although Finnish law does provide for a general principle of fairness, according to which any provision in an agreement, including one concerning rent, considered not to be in accordance with good practice or considered to be otherwise unreasonable, may be altered or terminated without compensation. Under the Residential Tenancy Act 1995, the rent may be adjusted if it is substantially higher than the market rent for comparable premises in the area in question without an acceptable reason for the higher rent.

5.3.2 A land lease agreement in force for an indefinite period may be terminated by either party provided notice is given. A fixed period land lease agreement will terminate at the end of the fixed period without notice. Under the Land Lease Act 1966, a fixed period land lease may only be terminated before it has run its natural course upon specific limited grounds. In addition to the landlord's right to terminate for certain types of default, such as non-payment of rent, neglect of maintenance or putting the land to an otherwise than agreed use, the statutory provisions also permit termination of the lease where there is a significant diminution in the tenant's ability to use the land due to circumstances beyond the control of either party or where an assignment is made by the tenant to a third party contrary to the provisions of the Land Lease Act 1966 or to those contained in the land lease agreement itself. When leasing land for business or industrial purposes it is generally possible to contract out of the limitations on termination.

5.3.3 A fixed period tenancy agreement terminates without notice at the end of the lease period. Tenancy agreements concerning business premises which are in force for an indefinite period can be terminated by notice to the other party in writing stating the grounds for the termination. Unless otherwise specified in the tenancy agreement, the notice period is three months when notice is given by the landlord and one month when given by the tenant. A court may, at the request of the tenant, deem a termination invalid if the ground for termination is an adjustment of the rent and the intended adjustment can be regarded as unreasonable or if the termination will otherwise be regarded as unreasonable and there is no acceptable ground for termination. If the landlord terminates the tenancy agreement on grounds that cannot be regarded as good leasing practice (although not unreasonable) the landlord may have to pay damages to the tenant for costs and loss of goodwill and clientele. Tenancy agreements concerning residential premises in force for an indefinite period may also be terminated in the same manner as tenancy agreements concerning business premises. When notice is given by the landlord, the notice period is three months during the first year of the lease and six months thereafter. The tenant need only give one month's notice. A provision to prolong the notice period of the tenant or shorten the notice period of the landlord is invalid. The notice periods in tenancies are calculated from the end of the month when the notice was given unless otherwise provided in the agreement.

5.4 Other legislative restrictions

Both the Residential Tenancy Act 1995 and the Business Tenancy Act 1995 contain mandatory provisions (relating to, amongst other things, the termination of the agreement) for the protection of the tenant which it is not possible to contract out of. Both Acts further contain provisions permitting the adjustment or leaving out of provisions which are unreasonable or against good leasing practice. (See 4.3 for the formalities to be observed when entering into a lease agreement.)

5.5 Method of measurement

Buildings are generally measured and rents are usually expressed by reference to the net internal area which usually excludes lavatories and staircases and certain common areas. The gross external area is generally only of relevance when calculating the size of a new building and does not generally feature in the calculation of rents.

6 FINANCE AND INVESTMENT SOURCES

Finance is essentially provided in the form of loans. The traditional sources of loan finance are the deposit banks, mortgage banks, finance companies and credit card companies. The financial sector also includes investment companies, mutual funds, securities companies, insurance institutions and state and social security funds.

6.1 Loan finance

6.1.1 The most important sources of loan finance are the deposit banks which extend loans to resident as well as foreign-owned enterprises and individuals. By comparison with other countries, these banks provide a large proportion of the total finance since over half of the credit granted by finance and credit institutions comes from the deposit banks. The deposit banks are divided into three groups: commercial banks, cooperative banks and savings banks. All deposit banks provide short, medium and long-term loans. Private individuals account for approximately half of domestic credits, companies one third and others, mainly financial institutions and local authorities, the remaining share. Mortgage banks, which are subsidiaries of the deposit banks, supplement the deposit banks' services, by granting residential loans to individuals and housing companies as well as by providing services to the corporate sector. About half of their outstanding loans go to the corporate sector, with emphasis on property activities and industry. The mortgage banks acquire their funds from Finnish and international capital markets and they will normally provide long-term loans, eg from 10 to 20 years.

6.1.2 Practically all bank loans currently granted by Finnish banks carry market interest rates, the interest rate normally being linked to the official Finnish Helibor rate or the prime rate of the particular bank or, for loans in foreign currencies, to the Libor. Helibor loans come with fixed loan periods, generally of three or six months. Repayments of capital and interest payments generally take place at the end of the interest period, unless the interest period exceeds six months. Early prepayment on an interest rollover date is normally allowed without penalty. The banks' prime rates are determined by the individual banks based on the official short and long-term market rates and future expectations. Prime rates may be more stable but, by contrast, are generally higher than on Helibor loans. Long-term fixed interest rate loans are sometimes granted but the increased risk for the bank is usually reflected in the higher interest rate. The demand for fixed interest loans depends largely on future expectations in the financial markets. Short-term loans with fixed interest rates can be obtained more easily. Larger bank loans often come with flexible repayment arrangements. The most common repayment structures, however, are even instalments and bullet repayments, where the principal of the loan is paid back in full at the end of the loan period.

6.1.3 The general willingness of banks to lend depends on their recent experiences in the market, general market sentiment and the weight of unlent funds they hold. Since the recession created difficulties for debtors to service their loans, the banks have increased their requirements for the value and type of security as well as the creditworthiness of the borrower. For the corporate sector, banks have started to rely on a careful cash flow analysis of companies instead of collateral. A company with a healthy cash flow may be granted a loan with less collateral if the prospects of the company are good. Requirements for bank loans also depend to some extent on the legal form of the company, its size and its future expectations. In smaller limited liability companies, an absolute guarantee or a lawful suretyship is often required from the company's owners, normally in addition to other collateral. One means of avoiding this can sometimes be the use of public guarantees. These guarantees are granted by both KERA and the Finnish Guarantee Board. A guarantee from either may also reduce the total costs of financing as the lender's risk decreases.

6.2 Investment or equity finance

The sources of equity or investment finance are varied. A small company will be funded by its private shareholders who may be individuals or other companies or institutions. There are also about 20 professional capital investors in Finland which are either publicly financed, private, regional or tied to a major enterprise or bank. These capital investors provide fixed-term equity ranked investment, in minority holdings in unquoted small and medium-size enterprises, by subscribing shares, convertible bonds or warrant bonds. However, taken as a whole, the venture capital industry is in its infancy in Finland. Quoted companies raise their investment funds on the Helsinki and other Stock Exchanges. In addition to the Helsinki Stock Exchange, public trading in securities also takes place on the OTC-list and the Broker's list. Many Finnish companies have in recent years benefited from the general growth in the capital markets by launching sizeable issues of securities, many of them abroad. Various devices have been used to raise money on the markets for the purpose of investment including convertible bonds and warrant bonds. Three new means to obtain corporate finance, namely preference shares, subscription warrants and capital loans, have been regulated in a recent amendment to the Companies Act 1978 since 1 September 1997.

6.3 Mezzanine or mixed funding

Finnish companies have not been able to issue warrants without a link to bonds (subscription warrants) or preference shares because of the lack of relevant legislation. This applies to capital loans as well, even though they have been used for years without legislative support. The amendments to the Companies Act 1978 concerning new financing devices (see 6.2) increase the possibilities to use mezzanine funding in Finnish corporate financing.

6.4 Sale and lease-back

The sale and lease-back of land is mainly used in transactions inside a group of companies for tax purposes. A parent company may sell land to its subsidiary and lease it back and then be able to deduct the leasing expenses in taxation (see further 6.5). It should be noted that a repurchase option, under which the vendor (and lessee) of the property has the option to buy the property back after the leasing period, is void under the Land Law Code 1995.

6.5 Tax leasing

Tax leasing, also known as partner leasing, is used to some extent in groups of companies. The usual way of doing this is for a parent company to purchase certain equipment, eg machinery under an instalment plan, and then lease the equipment to a subsidiary. The parent company is thereby allowed to take depreciation of the asset for tax purposes as well as to benefit from any tax incentives attached to the new investment.

6.6 Other types of property finance

A construction company may carry out a construction project by establishing a separate housing or real estate company which purchases the land and enters into a building contract with the construction company. The construction project is then, at least in part, financed by selling shares in the housing or real estate company to the future residents. The control of the company will usually remain with the construction company until the building is finished.

6.7 Institutional investment

Investment portfolios of insurance companies and pension funds will generally include land and property.

6.8 Investors other than institutions

Other property investors include foundations, which are independent legal entities founded to support a specific charitable purpose. The foundations generally obtain their financing by making low-risk investments. The government has proposed to enact legislation on real estate funds to create a secure and sufficiently regulated means for investing in property, which could increase the attractiveness of investing in Finnish property. The real estate funds would be listed limited liability companies with a minimum share capital of FIM 20 million. In comparison with the limited liability companies, the proposed real estate funds would be subject to stricter disclosure requirements with respect to, inter alia, share capital, investment policies, risk management, profit distribution and corporate management. As opposed to other listed companies subject to the provisions of the Securities Markets Act, a real estate fund would be required to have its real estate investment policy approved. The legislation is expected to come into force on 1 January 1998.

7 FORMS OF SECURITY

See 6.1.3 for a summary of the banks' willingness to lend and security requirements.

7.1 Mortgages

7.1.1 The legislation concerning mortgages was amended with the introduction of the Land Law Code 1995. Under the Land Law Code 1995 a mortgage may be registered against a unit of land, a fixed share of a unit or a parcel of land. The mortgagor's title to the land must be registered. In addition, a mortgage may be registered against a lease agreement, when the lease is transferable without the prior consent of the landowner and the tenant owns buildings or has the right to build on the land (see section 5). The owner (or tenant) has the sole right to register and establish a mortgage. When establishing the mortgage, a special mortgage note will be given to the mortgagor. The mortgage right to the land is created when the note is delivered to the creditor, who will then have a lien over the land as security for his claim on the debtor. The mortgagor retains the title and full use of the property. Stamp duty is payable at the rate of 1.5 per cent on registration.

7.1.2 To enforce his right, the creditor cannot take possession of the property in satisfaction of the debt, but he may apply to the court for the sale of the property by public auction. A public auction of property is a complex procedure during which the priority of mortgages and other obligations and rights attached to the property will be examined (for priority see 2.10).

7.2 Floating and other charges

The floating charge over company assets is available to all businesses that are registered in the trade register held by the National Board of Patents and Registration. A company may, despite a registered floating charge, freely use and sell its business property in the ordinary course of business and, correspondingly, new assets automatically become a part of the floating charge property. It is also possible to register mortgages over vessels, aircraft and certain types of vehicles and to enter into pledges over moveables.

7.3 Performance bonds and guarantees

The guarantee is commonly used in Finland as supplementary security in property and other financing. If not agreed otherwise, a guarantee is considered to be a secondary obligation, ie repayment can be demanded from the guarantor only after the debtor has been proved to be without means. This type of guarantee is called a legal suretyship. In practice, most guarantees are absolute suretyship, ie the guarantor is responsible for the debtor's obligations as if it were his own debt.

7.4 Credit insurance

Insurance against credit risk is available from the major Finnish insurance companies.

8 PLANNING AND BUILDING REGULATION

The development and use of land and buildings in Finland are principally subject to the controls of the Building Act 1958, which provides two main methods of regulation: plans and building permits.

8.1 Planning authorities

Ultimate control of all matters relating to town and country planning and building operations rests with the Ministry of Environment. In practice most decisions are taken by the local authorities for the area. As the decision-making body will usually consist of elected representatives, planning is to a certain extent influenced by political considerations.

8.2 Development plans

8.2.1 Local authorities are obliged to prepare the necessary strategic development plans for their area. The master plan sets out the local authority's general policies and proposals in respect of the development and use of land in their municipality, whilst the regional plan, which is prepared by several local authorities acting jointly, sets out the combined authorities' general policies and proposals in respect of the use of land covering those local authorities' areas. The town plan and the building plan show the authority's detailed policies and proposals for the development and use of land in the town or rural area in question. A shore plan may be prepared by property and land owners setting out detailed policies and proposals for the development and use of holiday homes and use of land in seaside or lakeshore areas not covered by a town plan or building plan. The shore plan must be approved by the local authorities.

8.2.2 Only one type of plan can be in force in an area at any one time. When a detailed plan enters into force, the general plan becomes redundant. The various plans have assumed great importance because urban development is generally not permitted in an area where there is no town or building plan in existence. As existing plans often contain restrictions on land use, eg the right to build on the land, it is advisable for buyers of land to check the plans and the building regulations in force in the relevant area. Under the Land Law Code 1995 the seller is also under the duty to inform the buyer of any restrictions in force (see 4.2).

8.3 Planning control and procedures

Building permits are required for all 'building work', which includes the construction of new buildings, extensions to new and alterations to existing buildings, as well as any substantial change in the use of a building. The construction of light structures such as platforms or canopies or minor installations such as statues or masts do not require a building permit, but may still require permission from the local authorities.

8.3.1 If a building permit is required, an application must be made to the local building committee before building work is commenced. It will usually be a detailed application giving details of the proposal and submitting the drawings and plans to the committee.

8.3.2 The principle of good administration requires that the decision of the building committee is reached in a reasonable time. The building committee may attach conditions to the permits granted. The committee's decision may be appealed to the county administrative court.

8.3.3 A building permit must usually be acted on within three years, and the construction work must be completed within five years.

8.3.4 Construction work in breach of the provisions of the Building Act, or other related regulations, will entitle the local authority to interrupt the work. Other means of enforcement include an order from the local authority obliging the developer/owner to neutralise or alter the effects of work done, or to restore the building to its previous state under the threat of a penalty. There are no time limits for enforcement, although in practice, enforcement action is seldom taken when a substantial amount of time has passed since the breach occurred.

8.4 Building standards, control and supervision

In addition to obtaining a building permit, the building must also comply with the applicable building regulations. The building regulations have, in addition to the Building Act 1958, also been supplemented by other laws and regulations, including the Building Decree 1959, government decisions, ministerial decisions, local building codes and detailed plans. The regulations deal with the design and construction of buildings and the provision of services, fittings and equipment. The local authority may undertake inspections of the work during construction, and is required to make a final inspection of any new building upon completion.

8.5 Protection of buildings of special interest

Buildings of cultural or historical significance are protected in town and building plans as well as by preservation decisions under the Building Protection Act 1985. Areas of architectural interest and prehistoric relics are protected under the Protection of Antiquities Act 1963. A landowner whose rights are restricted by a protection order may be entitled to compensation from the state or the local authorities.

8.6 Compulsory purchase and compensation

The expropriation of property for the purpose of public works is mainly regulated by the Expropriation Act 1977. Expropriation is subject to permission granted by the Council of State or, in certain cases, by the county administration or the Ministry of the Environment, and may not be undertaken if the purpose of the measure can be effectively achieved in some other way. Expropriation may be made either on the general grounds of common needs or on the basis of specific grounds found in other legislation, such as the Building Act, which permits expropriation in order to enable infrastructure or development projects to take place. The owner of the expropriated property is, as a rule, entitled to full compensation. Other legislation includes the Pre-emption Act 1977 and the Right to Acquire Agricultural and Forestry Land Act 1978 that may entitle the authorities to expropriate land. The owner is usually entitled to compensation.

9 ENVIRONMENTAL MATTERS

As has been the case throughout Europe in the last few years, there has been an increased awareness of environmental issues. Earlier legislation has been amended to correspond to both the increased demand for environmental protection and the legislation of the EU. Statutory control extends to matters including soil, ground and water contamination, air pollution and noise pollution. Recent statutory provisions which have an impact upon property dealing are contained in the Environmental Impact Assessment Act 1994 and the Environmental Damages Act effective from June 1995 ('the 1995 Act') although there are several other enactments, including the Environmental Procedures Act 1991, the Waste Management Act 1993, the Air Pollution Control Act 1982, the Water Act 1961, the Noise Abatement Act 1987, the Land Resources Act 1981, the Building Act 1958, the Neighbourhood Act 1920 and the Public Health Act 1994, which contain measures concerning environmental protection. A breach of the provisions of the environmental legislation will often incur criminal sanctions, usually a fine. Companies and other legal entities may also, under certain circumstances, be made to pay fines for actions taken by employees or other persons acting on their behalf. The relevant authorities usually have a right to order the person or company in breach to undertake certain action or to abstain from certain behaviour. They may threaten to impose financial penalties or insist that the activity in question be discontinued or undertake the necessary remedial measures at the expense of the party in breach. The 1995 Act provides for the liability on the basis of 'polluter pays' principles for environmental damage which includes water, soil and air contamination, noise, smell, and vibration pollution as well as other similar disturbances. The Act does not apply to damage regulated in other Acts. Liability under the 1995 Act is strict, ie irrespective of negligence or intent, and the imposition of liability under the 1995 Act only requires that it is probable that the nuisance emanated from the potentially responsible party's activity. Under the 1995 Act, the web of liability extends to the current and previous operators of the activity causing the environmental damage as well as the buyers of the activity where the buyer was aware of the damage or the threat of it. The acquisition of a polluting activity does not attach liability unless the new owners continue the polluting activity and upon acquiring the activity knew or should have known of the pollution (or threat of this). The party suffering damage has to tolerate disturbance held to be reasonable.

9.1 Protection against atmospheric and noise pollution

9.1.1 The Air Pollution Control Act 1982 regulates the pollution of air. Prevention of air pollution is supervised by a requirement for the polluter to apply for a permit under the Environmental Procedures Act 1991. The limitations imposed upon the polluter are to a great extent based on the general recommendations and regulations provided by the Council of State.

9.1.2 According to the Noise Abatement Act 1987 a producer of noise (ie any sound that is detrimental to health or significantly reduces enjoyment of one's property or work efficiency) has an obligation to provide for noise abatement to a reasonable extent. This principle is in practice implemented through the general recommendations and regulations for internal and external maximum permitted noise levels provided by the Council of State on the basis of the Act. The prevention of noise in individual cases is regulated on the basis of permits granted under the Public Health Act 1994 and the Neighbourhood Act 1920 in accordance with the procedures provided for in the Environmental Procedures Act 1991, although the supervision of temporary noise is based on a notification procedure. The Environmental Procedures Act 1991 combines various key permits, notifications and plans affecting the environment and health (under the Neighbourhood Act 1920, the Public Health Act 1994, the Air Pollution Control Act 1982 and the Waste Management Act 1993) into a single simplified procedure for obtaining an environmental permit, processed by the local authority.

9.2 Water pollution

The Water Act 1961 regulates the pollution of water and prohibits the closing off of waters and the alteration of water (eg the alteration of the water level). It provides a legal mechanism for issuing discharge permits for any activities in breach of the prohibitions against pollution of water from the water court, a specially constituted tribunal, and imposes strict liability for activities conducted under the permits. Activities not authorised under the Water Act 1961 or subject to a discharge permit are, as a general rule, subject to the liability provisions of the Environmental Damages Act 1995. All industrial plants and other plants specified in the Water Pollution Control Notification Decree 1962 are placed under the obligation to notify the authorities of any potentially polluting activities in advance. This, however, does not remove the necessity for a pollution permit, and the water court may assess the need for anti-pollution measures differently from the authority which received notification.

9.3 Waste storage and disposal

The Waste Management Act 1993 creates a general obligation to prevent the production of waste and establishes offences for the deposit, keeping and disposal and treatment of waste in breach of legislation. A duty is imposed on the owner or occupier of land to provide for the proper collection of waste produced on the land. The producer of the waste (if he is not the owner or occupier of the land) is placed under an obligation to deliver the waste to a space assigned by the owner or occupier of the land. As a general rule, the relevant local authority has an obligation to arrange transportation for the subsequent disposal of the waste. The local authorities have the power to order where the waste has to be delivered for arranged transportation. The occupier, or in some cases the owner, has a secondary obligation to collect and dispose of waste, should the producer fail to do so.

9.4 Contaminated land

The Waste Management Act 1993 further provides a general prohibition against the contamination of land. Although the primary obligation to clean up contaminated land remains with the contaminator, the occupier of the land may under certain circumstances be liable to clean up the land. However, a buyer of contaminated land is not liable to clean up the land, unless he was or should have been aware of the contamination when he purchased the land. The seller (or landlord) of land has an obligation to inform the new occupier of the type of activities conducted on the land, of contaminated areas and of waste and substances that may cause contamination. In major transactions relating to the purchase of plants or other industrial areas it is not uncommon for an environmental due diligence investigation to be undertaken by the buyer.

9.5 Environmental impact assessment

The Environmental Impact Assessment Act 1994 imposes the obligation to make an assessment of the environmental consequences where permission is being sought for certain types of specifically designated projects; these include the construction of paper plants, harbours and motorways.

10 DEVELOPMENT

10.1 Development projects, structures and vehicles

A building project is often a complicated, long-term procedure involving many different parties. The owner of land is generally faced with two different alternatives for the development of his land. He can either use his own organisation for the development, or approach a contractor who will perform the work for consideration. The former is mainly used by the state, the municipalities and larger industrial companies. More than half of all building projects for new buildings are carried out under contract.

10.2 Building contracts and the appointment of professionals

10.2.1 Typical forms of building contract

The four most typical forms of building contracts used are the total contract, the shared contract, the partial contract and the turn-key contract. In a total contract the developer enters into a contract covering the entire project with one contractor. The contractor will often hire subcontractors to perform parts of the project. The contractor will usually be responsible to the developer for the performance of the subcontractors. In a shared contract the developer chooses several contractors who will then perform different parts of the project. The developer will coordinate the work of the different contractors working simultaneously on the building site, so that the activities of one contractor will not encroach upon those of the other contractors any more than necessary. Where the developer performs some of the work himself, the contract becomes a partial contract. In total, shared and partial building contracts, the construction plans will usually be the responsibility of the developer but in a turn-key project the contractor is in charge of both the plans and the coordination of the project. In a shared contract the developer runs the risk of responsibility for the damage the different contractors cause each other (eg when the delay of one contractor causes delay and loss for the other contractors) as the contractor suffering damage is generally in a contractual relationship only with the developer and not with the other contractors. The developer can then try to get compensation from the contractor that actually caused the damage.

10.2.2 Common terms

10.2.2.1 Building contracts provide for alternative ways to remunerate the contractor for his services. In a fixed price contract the contractor undertakes to perform the work defined in the contract for a price which has been decided in advance. In a unit price contract the work will be divided into easily separated units and the contractor will get a fixed price for each unit performed. This form of payment is usually used when the amount of work to be performed is difficult to estimate in advance. Under an invoice contract, the contractor will undertake to achieve a predetermined result for a remuneration based on actual costs with a profit margin. The total price for the building contract is not defined and the work performed is invoiced by the contractor at agreed intervals. If the building is certified as practically completed with a list of minor defects which need to be attended to during the defects liability period (see 10.4), the developer will usually have the right to retain part of the contract price to be released to the contractor when the defects are made good.

10.2.2.2 The contract will usually include a date for completion of the work. This can be extended by agreement and on the occurrence of force majeure such as a strike or extreme weather conditions. In the event of delay the developer will generally under the agreement have the right to a certain penalty (such as 0.25 per cent per week of the total price calculated on a maximum of 15 weeks). The developer can terminate the contract for cause, eg if it is obvious that the work will not be finished in time, it becomes evident that the work of the contractor will not conform with the contract or the contractor goes into bankruptcy. The contractor can usually terminate the contract if, eg the developer does not fulfil his duties to pay for the work performed, prohibits the fulfilment of the work, or goes into bankruptcy. The contract may under certain circumstances be terminated by either party on the basis of force majeure.

10.2.3 Standard form of contracts

The various building industry associations representing both developers, contractors and other parties involved in the building industry have developed a selection of standard form contracts and general contract conditions (the most important being perhaps the General Contract Conditions YSE 1983 which are being amended). The standard form contracts and general contract conditions are widely used in the building industry.

10.2.4 Appointment of the professional team

See 10.2.3.

10.3 Those involved and their roles

The contractor's arrangements will depend on the size of the building project and the tasks undertaken by the contractor. With the exception of turn-key contracts, it is usually the developer's responsibility to appoint the architect and other professionals (such as electrical, structural and services professionals) for the design of the building. It is not unusual for competitive tendering to take place to select contractors, with the most cost-efficient quote being chosen. The work performed by the contractor is supervised by a representative of the developer. In larger building projects, the developer's representative is often aided by supervisors specialising in different areas of construction work. The supervisors may not usually undertake the same kind of work as the contractor without his prior approval.

10.4 Defects and remedies

10.4.1 The contract will commonly provide for a one year defects liability period, during which time the contractor is under the obligation to put right any defects which have arisen. After the defects liability period has elapsed, the contractor will usually only be liable to repair defects caused by intent or gross negligence on his part.

10.4.2 Although the recovery of costs for remedying defects is generally confined to the contractual parties, the Land Law Code 1995 also provides the right for a consumer purchasing residential property to recover costs directly from the original professional team.

10.5 Defects insurance

The concept of defects insurance is comparatively new but the major insurance companies are currently preparing for the introduction of defects insurance to be used in conjunction with building contracts. Under the present system the contractor is usually under the obligation to give security (eg in the form of a bank guarantee) for the fulfilment of his obligations under the building contract. The security is generally ten per cent of the building contract price during construction and two per cent during the defects liability period.

10.6 Copyright

It is necessary for the developer or contractor to obtain from the design team the right to use the plans, drawings, computer programs and other material subject to copyright created by the designers. The developer or contractor is usually only given the right of use for the purpose(s) specified in the contract.

10.7 Fees

The total professional fees for a project will generally vary between six and twelve per cent depending on the size and complexity of the project.

10.8 Taxes

The tax which is most relevant to construction is value added tax (VAT) and all commercial development is subject to VAT at the standard rate of 22 per cent. This will also apply to professional fees on all construction.

11 TAXES

11.1 Corporation tax

Resident companies are taxed on their worldwide income, whereas non-resident companies are taxed only on income obtained in Finland. There are no provisions under tax legislation concerning the residence of companies, but companies incorporated in Finland are treated as resident in Finland, as are companies whose central management or control is in Finland. Management and control is usually assessed by reference to where the board meetings take place. Double taxation treaties usually contain provisions concerning residence for tax purposes. Under the double taxation treaties, a company's tax burden is usually alleviated either by the tax credit method or the exemption method depending on the country in question as well as the type of the income. The former method means that foreign withholding tax on dividends, royalties or interest is set against Finnish taxes charged on repatriated income. The latter method means that the foreign income in question is not taxed in Finland. All business income of a resident company, including dividends, interest, royalties as well as capital gains, is charged to national income tax.

11.1.1 Tax rates

The rate of corporation tax is 28 per cent which is equal to the capital income tax rate of individuals.

11.1.2 Computation and administration

Under the 1992 tax reform, the concept of business income was defined broadly. Business expenses are generally deductible provided they are incurred in order to acquire or maintain taxable income. Therefore, deductible expenses include fees, commissions and loan interest as well as the usual deductions such as salaries and normal overheads. The tax is levied on the net income after these deductions have been made. Companies and partnerships are allowed a loss carryover period of 10 years. The losses may only be set against future profits and cannot be carried back. Foreign currency losses are deductible in the year during which the rate has changed. The foreign currency loss may also be capitalised and written off at the latest in the year when the loss is realised. The calculation of deductions may be challenged under the 'arm's-length' doctrine where payments have been made to non-resident group companies. No detailed regulations concerning the application of the doctrine exist. However, the supreme administrative court has on several occasions held that it is up to the relevant company to prove sufficient grounds for deduction of expenses. While it is open to the tax payer to arrange his affairs in such a way as to minimise tax, tax avoidance, any unlawful non-payment or evasion of tax is a criminal offence.

11.1.3 Depreciation and capital allowances

Plant, machinery and equipment as well as buildings are depreciated under the declining-balance method. The depreciable basis is the acquisition cost of the asset, which is decreased by depreciation and the sale of the asset. Plant, machinery and equipment are depreciated at an annual rate of 0 per cent to 30 per cent while the maximum annual depreciation rate is seven per cent for industrial buildings and four per cent for other buildings. Fixed asset, such as railways, bridges and dams, are depreciated in accordance with an estimated plan based on the anticipated lifespan of the particular asset. However, no depreciation of land or shares is allowed. Intangible rights are amortised on a straight-line basis during 10 years, or if the useful lifespan of the asset is proven shorter, during that period. Certain investments in machinery and industrial buildings that are made in development areas in northern and eastern Finland are allowed a depreciation rate which is 50 per cent higher than in other areas.

11.1.4 Withholding tax

No withholding tax is levied on dividends, interest or royalties paid to resident companies. Dividends paid to non-resident shareholders are subject to a withholding tax of 28 per cent unless alleviated by a double taxation treaty. Dividends payable to associated companies in the EU are not subject to withholding tax. This does not, however, apply to dividends that are paid to a shareholder in the United Kingdom if they are entitled to a Finnish imputation credit. No withholding tax is levied on interest paid to non-resident companies or individuals. Royalties paid to a non-resident company or individual are subject to a withholding tax of 28 per cent unless alleviated by a double taxation treaty. In double taxation treaties the withholding tax for royalties is typically five or ten per cent.

11.2 Taxes on development value

There are two different levies with different objectives relating to development value of property. First, land not used productively in city areas in southern Finland and which is zoned for housing can have a payment levied on the land in order to force the owner to use the land for housing. This system was in use during 1989–1993 when there was a great demand for residential housing land. The payments are not charged at present and the system is expected to be abolished. Secondly, the Council of State has the power to impose a construction tax should it be necessary to control the growth of the construction industry. The tax does not, however, apply to residential housing construction. The construction tax is not presently in use.

11.3 Taxes on capital gains

Capital gains including trading profits and profits realised on gains in the value of investment shares are fully taxed as ordinary corporate income at a flat rate of 28 per cent.

11.4 Taxes on owner of land

The owner of land is subject to an annual land tax calculated on the basis of the value of the property and payable to the local authority where the property is located. A charge is also levied on the value of the buildings situated on the land. If the buildings belong to someone other than the owner of the land upon which the building is erected, the owner of the building will be subject to the tax on the buildings. The tax is payable by the person or company that owns the property at the beginning of the calendar year. The local authority has a limited discretion to decide the annual rate at which the tax is imposed. At present the land tax rate can vary between 0.2 per cent and 0.8 per cent. The tax on residential buildings is somewhat lower. The municipalities are not liable to pay tax on their own land located in their own area. Forests and farms, castles, monasteries, graveyards as well as land used for military purposes are exempt.

11.5 Taxes on occupier

A tenant is not liable under statute to pay land tax for the property he occupies but the parties under the tenancy or lease agreement are free to agree otherwise in the tenancy.

11.6 Taxes on land transfer

Transfer tax is charged on the purchase price at a rate of four per cent. The transfer tax is also payable on the transfer of buildings and the transfer of certain land lease agreements, and at a rate of 1.6 per cent on the transfer of shares not listed on the stock exchange. Stamp duty at a rate of 1.5 per cent is payable on the mortgage capital when the mortgage is registered.

11.7 Wealth taxes

Resident limited liability companies are not subject to wealth tax. However, companies not resident in Finland are subject to net wealth tax, currently charged at a rate of one per cent on the net assets of their permanent establishment in Finland. Individuals resident in Finland are subject to wealth tax if their taxable wealth exceeds FIM1,100,000.

11.8 Value added tax

Any business providing goods and services with a total value in excess of FIM50,000 per annum has to register with the county tax office and charge value added tax (VAT) on the value of sales at a rate of 22 per cent. A lower rate of 12 per cent is applicable to some commodities such as medicine and books. A rate of six per cent is applicable to personal transportation, accommodation and entrance fees to museums and theatres. In principle, the tax covers all goods and services with only a few exceptions that are zero rated, such as health care, social welfare, education and financial and insurance services as well as the sale and lease of land, buildings and apartments. Services in relation to the lease of property, such as waste disposal and the sale of electricity, gas, heat or water, are also tax-exempt. Full VAT is however charged on commercial development. Businesses not subject to VAT may choose to register for it in order to receive credit for VAT paid for inputs. Businesses subject to VAT must calculate and report their sales and VAT payable on a monthly basis.

11.9 Local and other taxes

A municipal income tax is paid to the municipalities at rates from 15 to 21 per cent, depending on the municipality in which the taxpayer has his domicile. The tax rates are set each year by the municipalities. A church tax is levied on the members of the national churches and the church tax rate is commonly imposed at rate of one to two per cent. Corporate taxable income is not subject to municipal income tax or church tax. Excise taxes are payable to the state on the sale of fuel, electricity, mineral oils, alcohol and alcoholic beverages as well as tobacco, sweets and soft drinks. The excise taxes are of great importance since they represent over 20 per cent of the total of state taxes collected.

12 GRANTS AND INCENTIVES

12.1 Subsidies, grants and loans

There are a large number of incentives available to companies and businesses in Finland. Incentives are given to Finnish and foreign companies on equal terms. The support may consist of cash grants, loans, tax benefits, investments in equity, guarantees and employee training. Since Finland became a member of the EU, companies have had access to structural funds through nationally agreed programmes. Most areas in northern and central Finland have been classified as development or structural adjustment regions. The Regional Development Fund of Finland (*KERA*) finances and supports companies in development regions by granting long and short-term loans and guarantees on terms that are usually more lenient than ordinary market terms. The start fund of KERA is a venture capital company providing financing for high technology industries. The Ministry of Trade and Industry and its regional business service offices also provide several grants and incentives, including regional investment aid, aid for small businesses and development aid for small and medium-size companies. The amount of aid granted will range from 15–50 per cent of the costs depending on the type of company involved, the intended investment and the state of development in the region in question. The Technology Development Centre (*TEKES*) provides grants and loans to reduce the risks involved in developing new and innovative products. The grants may cover up to 50 per cent of the costs of salaries, machinery and raw materials and loans amounting to a maximum of 60 per cent of the costs involved may be granted. For applied research and development, grants can cover up to 25 per cent of the costs. The Finnish Guarantee Board grants venture capital guarantees. The maximum compensation for loss of investment is 50 per cent.

12.2 Tax allowances and reliefs

In some areas classified as development areas companies are entitled to a raised depreciation on certain investments (see also 11.1.3).

13 COMPANIES AND BUSINESS ENTITIES

With certain exceptions, the method of carrying out a trade or business in Finland may be freely chosen. Presently, the law recognises the following forms of doing business: sole practitioners, general partnerships, limited partnerships, limited liability companies and cooperatives. Most foreign companies establish a corporate presence in Finland by incorporating a limited liability company and generally this is by far the most popular form of doing business in Finland.

13.1 Limited and unlimited companies

13.1.1 Unlimited companies are not used. To form a limited liability company several formalities must be followed. First, a memorandum of association must be drawn up and signed by the person or persons forming the company. This memorandum of incorporation must include the articles of association of the company being formed, the offer and subscription of the company's shares and the date of the constitutive shareholders' meeting, during which the articles of association are approved and the board of directors and auditors are appointed. The actual incorporation of the limited liability company occurs through its registration in the national trade register. An amendment to the Companies Act 1978 has, since 1 September 1997, introduced public limited liability companies and private limited liability companies. Only a public limited company may have securities offered to the general public and only these securities may be subject to public trading. The minimum share capital of a public limited company is to be at least FIM500,000. The amendment will raise the minimum share capital requirement for private limited liability companies from FIM15,000 to FIM50,000. Unless the company's share capital is less than FIM500,000, the board of directors must comprise at least three members. At least one-half of the board members and the managing director must be domiciled in an EEA member state unless the Ministry of Trade and Industry grants an exemption.

13.1.2 A shareholder of a limited liability company will not be subject to personal liability for the debts and obligations of the company. However, a shareholder may be liable to compensate the company, or another shareholder or any other person for any damage which he has caused deliberately or by gross negligence by violating the Companies Act or the articles of association. The managing director and members of the board must act in the best interests of the company and in accordance with both the articles of association and the Companies Act. They are liable to compensate the company for all damages caused deliberately or through negligence by them in their respective positions. The same applies to damage caused to shareholders or third parties by breaching the provisions of the articles of association or the Companies Act.

13.1.3 The recent amendment of the Companies Act also affects the provisions concerning mergers and liquidation of companies and the payment of share capital, and introduces provisions concerning division of companies, capital loans and preference shares.

13.2 Partnerships

Limited and general partnerships are normally only used for small businesses. The partners of both general and limited partnerships may be individuals or legal entities. A general partnership is a partnership with a minimum of two partners engaged in business with a view to profit on the basis of the partnership agreement. The partners are jointly and severally liable to third parties for the liabilities of the partnership. A limited partnership can be set up with a minimum of two partners under which certain partners have general liability (the general partner(s)) and the other partners (the silent partner(s)) may have their liability limited to a fixed financial contribution to the partnership. The silent partners have neither managerial power nor a right to represent the company. A limited partnership must be registered in accordance with the Partnerships Act 1988. Partnerships are not considered to be independent taxable entities. Therefore, the income of a partnership is computed as company income, but is allocated to the owners and taxed partly as their earned income and partly as capital income.

13.3 Other types of business association

13.3.1 Cooperative societies

A cooperative is a trading society the purpose of which is to carry on business operations in order to support the finance or trade of its members by having the members use the services of the society. The number of members and amount of capital are not determined in advance, and the members are not personally liable for the debts of the cooperative.

13.3.2 Joint ventures

There is no body of law relating to joint ventures. The statutory framework, therefore, consists of general contract law on the one hand and corporate law on the other. The most common vehicle for a joint venture with foreign partner(s) is a limited liability company which will be regulated either by the joint venture agreement (negotiated between the parties) or by a shareholder agreement. It is common for the shareholding partners of a joint venture company to agree that rules other than those prescribed under statute shall be applicable between themselves and in relation to the joint venture company. Often, many of the provisions of a joint venture agreement are such that they could not be included in the articles of association of the company because they would not comply with the Companies Act 1978 and therefore would not be valid under company law. However, they will be valid between the parties of the joint venture agreement in contract.

14 INTERNATIONAL

14.1 Restrictions or consents required for inward investment

14.1.1 Most restrictions on foreign investment have been abolished in recent years. The restrictions on foreign ownership of shares in Finnish limited liability companies were abolished on 1 January 1993. Shares in Finnish companies can, in principle, be acquired by foreign investors without the approval of the authorities. However, the Act on the Control of Foreigners' Acquisition of Finnish Companies of 1992 (the 'Control Act') provides a degree of governmental control for purposes of protecting essential national interests. Apart from the acquisition of companies in the defence industry, the Control Act is not applicable to foreign investors from EEA and OECD member states.

14.1.2 The purchase of land is regulated by the Act on the Control of Foreigners' Acquisition of Land 1992 (the 'Land Control Act'). Foreign residents, foreign companies and Finnish foreign-controlled entities only need clearance from the authorities for the acquisition of land acquired for recreational use and land in national defence sensitive areas. Clearance is given by county government. Clearance for the purchase of land intended for recreational use can be only refused on the basis of specific reasons listed in the Land Control Act, eg the development of land would cause considerable harm to nature conservation. The purchase of land in national defence sensitive areas will only be authorised under special circumstances.

14.2 Exchange controls

Foreign exchange transactions made through a duly authorised Finnish bank need only be notified to the Bank of Finland for statistical purposes.

14.3 Restrictions and registrations on carrying on a business

With certain very limited exceptions, there are no restrictions on a foreign-controlled company carrying on business in Finland. Such an entity will usually be regarded as a domestic company. A foreign company wishing to carry on trade in Finland on a regular basis needs to register a branch office in Finland. Companies coming from outside the EEA will need to obtain clearance from the Ministry of Trade and Industry before registration.

14.4 Repatriation of income and proceeds of property trading and development

There are no consents or restraints involved in the repatriation of income and proceeds subject to the deduction of withholding tax (see 11.1.4).

14.5 Withholding taxes

Withholding taxes are described at 11.1.4.

14.6 Double taxation relief

Finland has separate double taxation treaties with a number of countries.

CHAPTER 6

France

Maître Philippe Dubois

Partner, Jeantet & Associés, Paris

CONTENTS

1 OWNERSHIP OF LAND 179
2 OTHER INTERESTS IN LAND 181
3 TITLE TO LAND 184
4 TRANSACTIONS IN LAND 185
5 LEASES AND OTHER RIGHTS OF OCCUPATION 188
6 FINANCE AND INVESTMENT SOURCES 191
7 FORMS OF SECURITY 193
8 PLANNING AND BUILDING REGULATION 194
9 ENVIRONMENTAL MATTERS 198
10 DEVELOPMENT 201
11 TAXES 204
12 GRANTS AND INCENTIVES 207
13 COMPANIES AND BUSINESS ENTITIES 208
14 INTERNATIONAL 209

CHAPTER 6

France

1 OWNERSHIP OF LAND

France has a codified system of law, the Napoleonic Code, otherwise known as the *Code Civil*, the provisions of which regulate property law. The law distinguishes between rights in rem and rights in personam, and the distinction between personal property (*biens meubles*) and real property or immoveables (*biens immeubles*) to which different rules and procedures apply. Rights in rem are more important in relation to the ownership of land and this section deals with the law of real property otherwise referred to as land. The principal form of land tenure is freehold or absolute ownership; leasehold is not a recognised form of land ownership.

1.1 Types of tenure

1.1.1 Freehold or absolute ownership

Under the *Code*, absolute ownership (*propriété)* carries with it a virtual 'monopoly' over the property. It grants the right to own, occupy and dispose of the land and any buildings on the land, provided this is not incompatible with any legislation or third party rights of ownership, as well as any objects placed on the land by the owner for the purpose of using the land, eg grazing animals. Absolute ownership carries with it the right to the soil below and the air space above, but there are exceptions imposed in the public interest, eg for overhead electricity cables, and for mines, with minerals and water below the surface generally excluded. Mineral deposits belong to the state and can only be worked with a state concession. It is possible to own the buildings and even parts of a building separately from the land.

1.1.2 Leasehold

The principal form of tenure remains absolute ownership. Long leases granted at a premium or for a single payment in advance in the Anglo-American tradition are not customary. Shorter leases take the form of tenancy agreements (*bails*) which are personal and contractual in nature only. While these are rights in personam and not registrable, they will bind most buyers, eg if they are entered at the fiscal registry, are notarised, or the tenant is in occupation. They can only be transferred if the contract specifically permits this, although residential tenancies may pass to dependants living with a deceased holder of the tenancy at the date of death. The nearest equivalent to the long lease used for building purposes, is the building right (*bail à construction*), granted for a term ranging between 18 and 99 years. Under this, the tenant undertakes to erect buildings which will revert to the landlord at the end of the agreement (see further 2.1.3). Tenancies and the terms on which they are granted are dealt with more fully in section 5.

1.1.3 Joint ownership

Where property is owned by two or more persons, they are in an undivided state (*indivision*). They will each be owners of shares in the property and there will be no material division of the property into separate parts. Each joint owner may encumber the land in proportion to his share or dispose of his share without the consent of his co-owners, although they may have rights of pre-emption in the other shares.

1.1.4 Condominia

Condominium (*co-propriété*) ownership occurs when a building, or group of buildings, not confined to residential buildings, is divided into privately owned units, *lots*, and common areas over which the owners will all have rights of ownership. The rights over the common parts combined with the right of absolute ownership of the individual units are not separately disposable, and together constitute a parcel of rights making up the condominium ownership. There is a statutory duty on condominium owners to establish internal regulations to administer the management of the building and the rights and duties of the parties. The overall management of the building is in the hands of all the individual owners, who together form a syndicate which is a legal entity of its own. Decisions are taken at general meetings of the syndicate. A managing agent will deal with day-to-day management and there is usually an executive committee composed of a number of the owners. There are limited rights of pre-emption in certain circumstances.

1.1.5 Lesser rights

Other rights of use or occupation falling short of full ownership are dealt with in section 2.

1.2 Legal and beneficial ownership

The distinction between legal and beneficial ownership, as found in common law jurisdictions, does not exist. There is a very rarely used device, the *déclaration de commande*, which entitles a purchase to take place in the name of another but the identity of the true owner has to be disclosed within a fixed period of time. There are proposals to introduce a concept of a *fiducie* similar to the trust and other vehicles used in Luxembourg and Switzerland, although these remain at a preliminary stage.

1.3 Restrictions on ownership and dealing

1.3.1 There are few limitations on the ownership of land, although there are some legislative restrictions on the extent of the rights of a landowner, which aim mainly to protect the public interest and include zoning regulations, rights of access, and rights of expropriation. Minors can own land but can only act through their legal guardians or by judicial order. There are special rules for charities and trade unions. Whether a company can deal with land depends on its constitution. There are also restrictions designed to protect private interests, such as the laws regulating the rights and obligations of adjoining landowners.

1.3.2 In urban areas the municipality has a right of pre-emption on the sale of property in zones the municipal authority (*mairie*) has designated. Exceptions include some buildings less than 10 years old and some sales upon liquidation. Prior to the sale, if the property is in a designated zone, the seller must declare his intention to sell to the municipal authority. A failure to do so will render the sale void. The relevant municipality has several options: it may waive its right expressly, or by implication, if it fails to respond within two months; it may exercise its right on the same conditions as those of the initially envisaged sale, in which case the seller is under the obligation to sell to the municipal authority at that price; or the municipality may offer a different price, which the seller is not obliged to accept.

1.3.3 The tenant of agricultural land has pre-emption rights on the sale of the land let. Residential tenants also have a right to buy rather than renew at the end of their current tenancy, where the owner states he wishes to sell with vacant possession.

1.4 Acquisitive prescription and adverse possession

Title may be acquired by acquisitive prescription (*usucapion)* as long as this is continuous, public and unequivocal. The relevant periods are 10 or 20 years depending on how close the true owner resides. If any of these qualities is missing title can still be acquired but the relevant period is 30 years. Good faith is always necessary.

2 OTHER INTERESTS IN LAND

There are various interests in land, which confer rights less than absolute ownership. These may be public or private and include servitudes, usufruct, *bails à construction*, mortgages and options. While most will require notarisation and registration to bind third parties, they will remain valid between the original parties without notarisation and registration.

2.1 Servitudes or easements, usufruct, building and dwelling rights

2.1.1 Servitudes or easements

A servitude is a right over land in favour of other land. Servitudes include rights of access, rights of light and air and car parking rights. Servitudes are rights in rem but must be notarised and registered (see section 3) in order to be enforceable against third parties. Administrative servitudes, which include the right to run services such as electric cables, are imposed by public bodies and may entitle the owner to compensation (for expropriation of land, see 8.6). Otherwise servitudes may be created in three different ways: by law, by contract or by prescription. A legal servitude is imposed by operation of law and violation may lead to enforcement by anyone who can show specific damage. A contractual servitude is created by agreement between the parties. A servitude will arise by prescription where there has been 30 years' exercise in a manner which is continuous, uninterrupted and apparent. Unlike the position in some countries, it is possible to create negative servitudes where it is intended to agree to a restriction on the use of neighbouring land. A servitude may be extinguished by 30 years' non-use, where it no longer serves a purpose, or when the burdened and benefited land are merged.

2.1.2 Usufruct

Usufruct (*usufruit*) is the right to use and enjoy property belonging to another for a limited period of time provided the nature and use of the land are not altered. It can be granted for life or any fixed period. However, it cannot survive the death of the original usufructuary. The usufruct is not transferable by way of succession but it may be transferred during the lifetime of the grantee. It will be terminated by 30 years' non-use, by neglecting the upkeep of the property or by abusing the right. It is a right in rem but must be notarised and registered to be enforceable against third parties. Usufruct is not common and is generally only used in family arrangements.

2.1.3 Building rights and dwelling rights

2.1.3.1 The surface right (*droit de superficie*) is a right to the surface and airspace. It is a right in rem not limited in time, a right in perpetuity, and allows for the erection of buildings. However, once the building is erected, the building will then be owned absolutely by the holder of the surface right either alone or with others by way of condominium ownership and the surface right will fall away. The right has to be notarised and registered to be enforceable against third parties. The more common interest is the building right (*bail à construction*). Unlike other tenancies, it is a right in rem, requiring notarisation and registration. It is akin to a building lease. It must have a duration ranging between 18 and 99 years, and the agreement will provide for the tenant to erect buildings which will revert to the landlord at the end of the term without compensation, except where this is provided for. There may sometimes be a provision enabling the tenant to acquire ownership when the building right comes to an end (for the provisions governing contractual tenancy agreements, see section 5).

2.1.3.2 While residential tenants under a tenancy have a certain security of tenure (see section 5) there is no formal long-term dwelling right in common use as found in some countries. The nearest comparable right is the *droit d'habitation et d'usage*. Like the usufruct, it is a registrable right but it is seldom used, and only then for family and domestic purposes.

2.2 Restrictions on use and other restrictions

Landowners may agree to enter into restrictions on the use of a piece of land to protect the amenities and value of another piece of land. These will take the form of negative servitudes (see 2.1.1) and can be enforceable by and between successive owners. It is possible to impose positive obligations on land so as to bind successive absolute owners, eg to contribute to the cost of repair of common walls or fences separating adjoining properties. Public law restrictions under planning and other legislation are commented on in section 8.

2.3 Mortgages and privileges

The *Code Civil* recognises certain debts as privileges, a type of preferred debt. They are creatures of the law and not of the parties. If registered within two months they will take priority over all other debts including those protected by registered mortgages. The holders of privileges will have first call on the proceeds of the assets to which the privileges attach. General privileges attach to all property of the debtor, real or personal, and protect public dues such as taxes, certain employee claims and court costs. Special privileges attach generally to the assets to which the debts relate. Special privileges include the seller's lien for unpaid sale proceeds, the lien for money lent for the purpose of purchase, builders' and architects' liens. In the case of conflict between privileges, general take priority over special. If not secured as a privilege, a loan or other liability can be secured by mortgage (*hypothèque*). Further comment is made on mortgages in section 7.

2.4 Contracts and options

Options (*promesses de vente*) and agreements for sale (*compromis de vente*) are not interests in land and are dealt with more fully in section 4. Pre-emption rights are dealt with in section 4 and at 1.3.

2.5 Public and municipal charges

Most debts to the municipality, whether for payment of the cost of any repairs required by law or repayment of grants, will be personal to the owner and will not attach to the property. Taxes and other charges may be protected as privileges if registered (see 2.3). Other public or administrative law matters affecting the property will bind buyers whether or not registered and there is no central source or registry maintained by the municipality to record these. Enquiry therefore has to be made on purchase by the notary or buyer. The notary will ensure a buyer is issued with a special certificate (*certificat d'urbanisme*) dealing with the relevant planning issues.

2.6 Other interests

There are no other interests in land of significance and no general public rights of access other than rights such as the right of passage along the seashore, and hunting and shooting rights (*droits du chasse*) enjoyed as a matter of law over certain land by specified bodies or groups.

2.7 Liabilities attaching to land

Liabilities arising out of land and from any defects will attach to the owner and not the occupier; it will be for the owner to obtain any indemnity he requires under the tenancy, or in some other way. An owner may be liable in some situations for injury or damage to third parties or their goods without proof of negligence. Taxes are dealt with in section 11, but these and many public liabilities will take the form of privileges and will be payable by the owner out of the proceeds when he comes to sell.

2.8 Legal and equitable interests

The distinction recognised in common law countries, as between legal and beneficial ownership does not exist under the *Code Civil.*

2.9 Protection of interests

For an interest to be enforceable against the property, ie against third parties, it must usually be protected by registration. The interest or contract will, however, normally be valid and enforceable between the parties without registration.

2.10 Priority of interests

Priority between interests in land and, indeed, between dealings in land will depend generally on the date of registration.

3 TITLE TO LAND

3.1 Proof of title

Registration at the registry of mortgages and deeds (*bureau des hypothèques*), will be evidence of ownership, but the buyer will establish ownership, or title, through investigation by the notary, who will undertake the necessary searches and examine the deeds registered at the registry before satisfying himself that the party entering into the transaction has the necessary title and capacity. The purpose of registration is not usually to render the transaction valid between the contracting parties, but to ensure that it is enforceable against third parties. The grant of nearly all interests in rem, and even of privileges, will require registration to ensure these bind all those who deal with the land. While the registers are open to the public, searches are usually carried out by a notary.

3.2 Registration

The registrar (*conservateur des hypothèques*) is in charge of the registry of mortgages and deeds.

3.2.1 Plans

There are two separate but connected registers. The first is the cadastral register (*cadastre*), the country wide register maintained in each district (*commune*). This register establishes a system for valuing land for the charging of a tax on land ownership (see further 11.4). While this is therefore primarily a fiscal register, it sets out the land in plots or cadastral units and each unit or lot is given a plot number. The plans maintained by the cadastral register are not intended to be definitive, but are the only plans contained in any register, and it is the plot numbers they allocate which are then used by the second registry, the *bureau des hypothèques*, to identify land and to operate its registers. There is at least one registry in each *département*.

3.2.2 Content

The registrar of mortgages and deeds keeps two principal registers: one has the name of the owner of the land and the other contains a record of the deeds and dealings with the land under that plot number.

3.2.3 Errors

The registers are not intended to be a guarantee of title and if an error is claimed, the question arises as to whether the notary has failed to examine the registers or some other aspect of the title correctly, or whether there has been a mistake on the part of the registrar. The error may be corrected without loss to any party, but where this is not possible, a further question arises as to whether the registry or the notary should compensate the claimant.

3.3 Passing of title

Title effectively passes between the parties at the time of the agreement to purchase (*compromis de vente*). The subsequent transfer (*contrat de vente*), which is the notarial act or deed perfecting the transaction, is necessary to enable it to be registered and to be effective against third parties. Between the parties themselves, however, ownership may be said to have passed once there is an enforceable contract, even if money is outstanding and the seller retains possession.

4 TRANSACTIONS IN LAND

The most common transactions in land are the sale and purchase of land and the creation of mortgages. This section concentrates on the former.

4.1 Procedures on sale

There are two stages in the purchase.

4.1.1 The first is the entry of the parties into a preliminary agreement to purchase. Once this is entered into, the parties will be contractually bound, at an earlier stage than is common, for example, in England. The agreement will usually be conditional on matters such as the obtainment of a loan in a specified amount, investigation of title by the notary, notification to the municipality if the property lies in an area designated as subject to municipal pre-emption rights (see 1.3.2) and any other agreed matters, such as the obtainment of any planning consent. As a usual condition, the notary public will arrange for the procurement of a town planning certificate (*certificat d'urbanisme*) during this period, to ensure that the property can be used in accordance with planning law. While the preliminary agreement does not create an interest in land as such, the ownership of the property as between the parties can be said to pass at this stage. Third parties will not, however, be bound and the property could be sold again to another buyer, who will take free of the first sale, if this is not perfected by notarised deed, and registered.

4.1.2 Instead of entering into a bilateral preliminary agreement, the seller may grant the buyer a unilateral right or option to purchase (*promesse de vente*) for a maximum duration of six months. This binds the seller but leaves the buyer the option whether to proceed with the purchase; it is subject to certain additional formalities such as registration at the tax office.

4.1.3 It is the contract of sale by notarial deed (*contrat de vente*), which can be described as the formal transfer comprising the second stage of the sale. The drawing up of the deed, notarisation and subsequent registration at the *bureau des hypothèques*, along with the payment of all taxes and registration fees will be attended to by the notary public, acting on behalf of both parties, or by two notaries, where both parties choose to be separately represented. Without this, the agreement, while it may bind the original parties, may not bind third parties. Although the preliminary agreement is often entered into by the parties without the involvement of a notary and need not be notarised or even made in writing, the buyer may choose to have it executed by notarial deed for greater protection pending the execution of the contract. Alternatively, where the matter is straightforward or urgent, the parties may decide to dispense with the intermediate preliminary agreement altogether, and go straight to the *contrat*, or notarial deed, and registration at the registry of mortgages and deeds. Priority between transactions will depend on the date of receipt by the registry.

4.2 Contract terms

4.2.1 The preliminary agreement (either in the form of a *compromis* or *promesse de vente*) will contain conditions precedent concerning the investigation of the property before the sale (see 4.1.1). It will also contain warranties as to title, servitudes, encumbrances and vacant possession and stipulate the payment of a deposit, commonly 10 per cent of the purchase price (it cannot exceed 5 per cent in the case of development land). The deposit will be forfeited to the seller if the transaction does not complete, ie if the buyer's notary does not execute the contract and/or pay the balance of the price. The preliminary contract will specify the timetable for the transaction and the date the parties are to attend for the *acte de vente*. The French Insurance Code provides that fire cover passes automatically, but it is for the preliminary agreement to state whether this is to be at the preliminary or final stage of the sale agreement. The buyer may rescind the agreement where there is a change in the property but the seller owes no fiduciary or similar duties in respect of the property between the preliminary and final agreement.

4.2.2 The contract may deal with apparent defects and may make the sale conditional on a survey, but there is an implied warranty that the property is free from latent defects. It is not possible to exclude liability for this in certain situations, even where the seller is not aware of them, eg where the seller is in the property or construction business. Claims have to be brought within a very short time of discovery of any defect, but the guarantee can otherwise last for 30 years.

4.2.3 On default, the defaulting party may be summoned to attend the notary's office but he cannot readily be compelled to complete the transaction. However, the buyer may apply for a judicial order, which can be registered instead of the *acte de vente,* to complete his title. There may be provisions in the preliminary agreement to deal with compensation on default.

4.3 Formalities

The *acte de vente* has to be notarised, stamped and registered. The preliminary agreements (*compromis* and *promesse de vente*) do not have to be notarised and can be oral, although this is neither common nor desirable. Tenancies of over 12 years will also require notarisation. Residential tenancy agreements must be in writing.

4.4 Fees, costs and taxes

4.4.1 On the sale of land the seller will pay the selling agent's commission. The buyer will be responsible for the payment of notarial fees and the stamp duties and registration fees. Where the notary acts as a selling agent his commission will be considered part of the notary fees and will be paid by the buyer. The agent's commission will vary according to the agent, the type of the property and the strength of the market. Fees commonly range from one to five per cent of the sale price. The commission will only be paid if the transaction completes. For tenancy registration taxes see 11.6.

4.4.2 The choice of notary is usually made by the seller although the buyer is entitled to appoint his own notary without incurring extra cost, as the two notaries will then share the statutory fee. The notary jointly incurs liability for taxes, registration fees and various other related charges with those who execute documents before him. Consequently, the notary will obtain payment on account prior to completion, in order to cover fees, taxes and other disbursements connected with the transaction. The notary's own fees are governed by a complex statutory tariff being 0.825 per cent on urban sales. As it is difficult to calculate accurately the total amount of disbursements until a considerable time after completion, it is customary for notaries to slightly over-estimate their requirements in this respect.

4.4.3 The buyer usually pays either value added tax (VAT) currently charged on new or renovated buildings at 20.6 per cent (see 11.8), or will pay registration tax (*droit d'enregistrement*) at rates generally between 9 and 15 per cent. Lower rates are payable for some property, in particular residential property.

4.4.4 A recording, or land registration fee, is charged by the registry of mortgages and deeds at approximately 0.1 per cent of the transfer price as well as a land publicity tax (*tax de publicité foncière*) of 0.615 per cent. (See also section 11 where taxes are dealt with in more detail.)

4.4.5 With overall costs starting at around 10 per cent, purchase costs in France are high.

4.4.6 Notarial fees are subject to VAT at a rate of 20.6 per cent.

4.5 Professionals' roles

The marketing and sale of land is usually conducted by estate agents who are subject to statutory control. Anyone not in possession of the requisite accreditation is precluded from negotiating a sale of land on behalf of an owner. The certification will only be granted when an application is made to the local *préfecture* on the basis of appropriate professional qualifications. The notary is a lawyer with seven years' training, and a public official, independent of the parties. He will draw up the contract, witness the signatures, collect and pay out the purchase price and all fees and taxes, and deal with all necessary formalities, notifications, eg the prior declaration to the local authority where there is a right of pre-emption, and all registrations. The parties will very rarely employ any other lawyer to negotiate a property transaction.

5 LEASES AND OTHER RIGHTS OF OCCUPATION

The concept of leasehold does not exist in France which instead uses the tenancy agreement, a personal agreement between the parties by which one allows another the use of a thing, be it moveable or immoveable, and commonly translated as a lease (*bail*). Different types of building are subject to different regulations and terms. The building right is different from other tenancies in a number of respects, eg its purpose, length and the fact that it is a right in rem, and it is described at 2.1.3.1.

5.1 Rent and other terms

5.1.1 Residential premises

Residential tenancies are governed by a 1989 Law known as the *Mermaz* Law unless the building was built prior to 1948 in which case it may still be subject to the Law of 1948. Under the 1989 Law, the tenancy agreement must be in writing and state the duration, rent, the method of rent review, the amount of the deposit and the use of the property. It must also attach a schedule of conditions (*état des lieux*). The landlord must hand over the property in good repair and free from hidden defects and maintain it in a state fit for its contractual purpose, although he may impose certain obligations on the tenant. The landlord must accept renovation and alteration so long as it does not constitute a transformation of the premises. The tenant must respect the use of the premises, cause no damage and pay for agreed repairs. He must insure the premises and is not allowed to assign or sublet unless this has been agreed by the landlord. Where the landlord is an individual the minimum duration of the tenancy, with certain exceptions, must be three years; otherwise it must be six. In practice six years is the length adopted on most lettings. The tenant may terminate the tenancy agreement on three months' notice, or one month's notice in the event of unemployment or certain other events, on or before the expiry of the tenancy. The landlord may reserve the right to terminate on certain statutory grounds, such as non-payment of rent or abandonment of the premises, although the tenant has the right to apply to the court for extensions of time in cases of non-payment. There are rights of pre-emption where the landlord wishes to sell the building with vacant possession at the end of the tenancy or where the landlord is selling the building in which the tenant has his permanent residence. At the expiry of the tenancy the tenant will have a right to renew the tenancy for a further period equal to the previous one unless there has been serious default or where, eg, the landlord or a member of his family wishes to move there. The landlord must either charge VAT or a tenancy registration tax, usually in the region of 2.5 per cent of the rental value or rent charged, whichever is higher. Landlord and tenant are jointly liable for the tenancy registration tax (see further 11.6 and 11.8). The rent that may be charged on a first letting in a new building is unrestricted but thereafter the rent on each renewal or subsequent letting can only be increased to the open market rent, and if this increase is greater than 10 per cent, it has to be staggered. In the interim, however, the rent can be raised each year by the increase in the government construction index.

5.1.2 Commercial premises

Tenancy agreements for retail, industrial and commercial, but not professional, premises are deemed to be commercial. Commercial tenancy agreements are governed by a decree of 1953 and are required to be not less than nine years in length, and to be notarised if over 12 years in length. Nine years is therefore the most common tenancy term. The tenant is entitled to break the lease every three years and the rent can be increased to the open market rent at similar intervals but not by more than the increase in the cost of construction index in certain cases. At the expiry of the nine years the tenant has a right to renew at market rent, unless the tenant is in substantial default or the landlord pays suitable compensation for disruption. The compensation will be assessed by the court in each particular case. In the case of offices where alternative premises are in ready supply, the compensation will not be much greater than the relocation costs, but where location and goodwill are important, as in the case of retail lettings, the amount awarded can be substantial. Otherwise the parties are generally free to agree the terms of the tenancy. A rent increase on the renewal of a lease may be capped, but this does not apply to office premises or to tenancies exceeding nine years' duration. The decree specifies the extent to which the tenant may be allowed to alter the premises, assign and/or sublet.

The maintenance and repair of the building are not covered by the decree but by the *Code Civil* and the provisions are not mandatory. In practice, tenancies often provide that the tenant bears all the costs of repairs, whether structural or not, particularly where the entire building is let to a single tenant. In the event of default on the part of the tenant or on his becoming insolvent, the landlord may forfeit and take back the lease. Rent is payable every three months, in advance, and the payment of a deposit, or increasingly the provision of a bank guarantee, for three months' rent is customary. Where the tenant wishes to change the use of the premises he must follow the procedure set out in the decree. A temporary right of occupation is a concept used to avoid the security of tenure and rent control protections available to tenants, and which carries none of the statutory protections available on other lettings. It must, however, be for a maximum period of two years. There are variations on the rules described, particularly for retail premises.

5.1.3 Professional premises

Premises used by certain professionals must be let for a term of six years but are not otherwise subject to statutory controls and there are no automatic rights of renewal.

5.2 Privity of contract

The doctrine of privity of contract known in common law jurisdictions is not recognised in the Code Civil.

5.3 Rent control and security of tenure

Different provisions exist for different types of tenancy. For ease of reference these have been divided according to property type and dealt with in 5.1.

5.4 Other legislative restrictions

These are dealt with at 5.1.

5.5 Method of measurement

The method of measuring floor areas for letting purposes is effectively by reference to the net internal or net lettable area. In the case of the sale of new flats it is compulsory that the floor area is measured and stated in the way prescribed by law.

6 FINANCE AND INVESTMENT SOURCES

The principal methods of financing the acquisition of commercial property are by way of a long-term loan, by lease purchase and by direct equity investment by funding institutions.

6.1 Loan finance

Commercial loan finance is generally obtained from the high street banks and merchant banks. Loan finance may also be obtained from property development banks which are subject to special legislation and granted privileged fiscal status. They are specialist property lenders whose sole function is to deal with finance leasing operations (see 6.6) and property development and investment. There are other less regulated forms of leasing companies who are able to offer more flexible loan structures. Conventional loan finance, as provided by the clearing or merchant banks, will usually be for a fixed term of 10 to 15 years in the case of investment loans or conventional commercial or personal loans, and two years for development and construction loans. Interest rates are generally variable and may be linked to inter-bank rates with a margin. Interest is often paid monthly. The loan to value ratio where the loan is secured will vary, but has commonly been up to 80 per cent. Companies may borrow from their shareholders but these loans enjoy no particular preference over the shares themselves. Short-term loans particularly for development purposes may have no provision for repayment of capital during the loan, the principal being repaid in one lump sum at the end of the term. Longer term loans may be on the basis of amortisation or fixed repayments. For the different types of security see section 7. Certain loans cannot be redeemed within the first seven years, and where this is the case the building may be sold subject to, and with the benefit of, the loan.

6.2 Investment or equity finance

While property companies may often be set up by private investors there is no body of property investment and trading companies quoted on the stock exchange and it is not common for companies to raise property finance on the stock exchange.

6.3 Mezzanine or mixed funding

A bank or prime lender will usually take the first security and lend between 70–80 per cent of the value of the property. If any further loan is made, it will naturally carry a higher risk and there are lenders who will provide the next

10 per cent of the finance and take a return by way of a higher interest rate or other return.

6.4 Sale and lease-back

The device of a sale and lease-back, where a company buys a site and erects a building which it then sells to an investor, or where it simply sells an existing building to an investor to raise cash, taking a lease-back of the property from the investor for its own occupation at a market rent, is a device which is used but not on a regular basis.

6.5 Tax leasing

Tax leasing does not play a major part in financing of property.

6.6 Other types of property finance

One of the most common financing procedures is lease or hire purchase by which the occupier makes regular payments to give the 'lessor' an income and defray purchase costs and the occupier has an option to buy the property after a 10 to 15 year period. Hire purchase is arranged through the property development banks.

6.7 Institutional investment

Institutions and insurance companies are major investors in the property market. Banks not only lend on property but also take an atypically active investment role. The institution will usually be looking for a prime location, a first-class building and secure income from a company with a sound credit rating.

6.8 Investors other than institutions

Other investors include trading and development companies, specialist property investors (including a sizeable proportion from overseas), foundations and the private investor. One of the major investors in the market is the banking industry. Although the quoted property company is not a feature of the investment market, there is one vehicle used to make investments by smaller, private groups of investors (*société civile de placement immobilier*). Their shares are difficult to market because the shares can only be sold privately and in a recessionary market this difficulty is even more pronounced.

7 FORMS OF SECURITY

7.1 Mortgages

There are three types of mortgage: a legal mortgage (*hypothèque légale*) which arises by operation of law or statute, eg in favour of a spouse, the state or the *département*, or a minor over the land of a guardian or administrator; a judicial mortgage (*hypothèque judiciaire*) which may be granted by the court to a judgment creditor; and the most common, a contractual mortgage (*hypothèque conventionelle*) created under contract which can only be entered into by the owner of the property. The contractual mortgage is a right in rem. It must be notarised to be valid and must detail the property which is to be secured. It must be registered at the registry of mortgages and deeds (see 3.2) to be enforceable against third parties. The validity of the contractual mortgage is dependent upon the debt secured being defined. If the debt is dependent upon a contingency or is undetermined, the mortgage may state an estimated sum. On registration a land publicity tax is payable at a rate of 0.6 per cent on the amount of the mortgage, along with a fee to the registrar of 0.05 per cent of the security. The notarial fees will be payable at a rate of 0.55 per cent, in addition to VAT at the rate of 20.6 per cent in most cases (subject to the amount of the debt). The mortgagee has a number of rights to take possession, sell or let the property, or appoint a receiver. He may also foreclose or apply to the court for an order for sale at which only members of the bar may bid on behalf of their clients. For the priority of mortgages see 2.10. To avoid the costs of a formal mortgage, the parties may enter into a mortgage agreement. This will have to be notarised, but does not have to be registered to be enforceable between the parties; while it remains unregistered, it will not bind third parties. Upon registration it operates as a full charge.

7.2 Debenture

There is no concept of a floating charge or general charge over assets. If a number of assets are to be charged these must be individually specified and in the case of land, they must be the subject of a mortgage or, in the case of other assets, of a pledge (*nantissement*).

7.3 Bonds and guarantees

Due to the cost of mortgages, use is often made of guarantees. The banks have pooled resources to set up specialist guarantee companies. Their services include a guarantee for a fee which can be repaid in part at the end of the term of the guarantee, where no call has been made during the term. Guarantees take the form of *garanties* or *cautionnements*. The former will be a primary obligation independent of the sum guaranteed. This is commonly used in international, banking and trade relationships. The latter is an obligation to pay where another has first made default and the guarantor (*caution*) will have the same defences as the debtor. The *cautionnement* is more frequently used in property and leasing transactions and loans than the *garantie*. In many cases the *cautionnement* will itself be supported by a mortgage (*caution hypothècaire*), over an asset of the guarantor, eg where a company director guarantees the loans to a company and puts up security in support of the guarantee. Bonds are not in regular use.

7.4 Insurance

While credit insurance exists it is rarely used and greater use is made of guarantees.

8 PLANNING AND BUILDING REGULATION

The development and use of land and buildings are regulated largely by the planning code (*code de l'urbanisme*) and the construction and housing codes (*codes de la construction et de l'habitation*).

8.1 Planning authorities

There is no central planning authority although the Ministry of Planning and Land Use plays a central role in matters such as the designation of motorways, conservation areas and certain other strategic land use issues. The principal planning authority for all purposes is the municipality within each commune. Central, regional and even departmental bodies have no significant planning role. It is useful to remember that power is divided to a large extent between the municipality and central government. Central government and each of its ministries having representatives in each *département*, the representatives of the individual ministries in each *département* being under the supervision of the chief administrator (*préfet*) who is the overall representative of central government.

8.2 Development plans

The planning code sets out a framework of national and local regulations governing land use and development. The national regulations apply throughout the country (*réglement national d'urbanisme, RNU*) and include rules on construction siting and servicing, layout and measurements as well as appearance. Supplementary legislation exists at national level and includes town and country planning laws, which are in turn clarified by directives. Other directives focus on the preservation and enhancement of landscapes. A second set of more specific national regulations only apply to certain parts of the country, eg regulations concerning areas of natural beauty or conservation. The areas targeted by these regulations are subject to preservation measures, and where appropriate, reinstatement or enhancement of all or part of a group of buildings or area of land. Local regulations are set out in planning documents and only apply to the particular area in question. These documents are intended to strike a balance by, on the one hand, imposing criteria to restrict the development of land, preserve agricultural activity, protect forests, prevent foreseeable natural damage and technological hazards, whilst ensuring on the other that there is sufficient land for housing development as well as economic and other activity in the public interest. The plan (*schéma directeurs d'aménagement et d'urbanisme, SDAU*) prepared by the Ministry of Planning and Land Use sets out general policy guidelines but no specific planning policies or land use designations. There is no central or national land use or development plan for the country, region or *département*. Within each commune the municipality prepares a land use plan (*plan d'occupation du sol, POS*) setting out detailed policies, proposals and zoning for the development and use of land within the commune. Land is usually zoned at a general level either as existing urban use (*zone urbaine*), land not to be built on (*zone verte*) or designated for future development. Within this zoning there will be more detailed provision of a more specific nature. Smaller communes may ask for the *département* to prepare the POSs. The POS have assumed greater importance because when determining a planning application, permission has to be granted if the proposed development complies with the use permitted in the particular zone. Conversely, the application will be refused if the proposed development contravenes it. This means that there is little scope for discretion on the part of the municipality once the POS has been established, except on matters of detail and interpretation. The only way to deviate from the POS is to get the POS itself amended. There is considerable public consultation before the POS is adopted.

8.3 Planning control and planning procedures

A building permit (*permis de construire*) is required not only when a new building is erected; it is also required in respect of works on existing buildings if the effect would alter the exterior aspect of the building, increase its size or change its use, where the declaration procedure (see below) is not applicable. However, a permit is not required for engineering works as such. Mining activities are covered by a separate permit procedure. Certain types of development are not regulated by the standard building permit procedure, but require a declaration prior to commencement of the works. Such development includes military constructions, restoration works, reconstruction or repair of buildings of special historic or architectural interest (see 8.5), installations of technical plants, eg for gas distribution, and certain alteration works. A town planning certificate can, and usually will be obtained by a buyer before purchase (see 4.1). This will give complete information about the possible uses of the land and any planning restrictions. It is sometimes thought that this type of certificate is unnecessary when an application is made for a building permit, as the latter will set out all the applicable conditions upon which the building may be erected and restrictions to which it will be subject. However, the town planning certificate will give the applicant some idea of the plans envisaged by the municipality for the area in which the property is situated, and thus avoid an application for unsuitable development being made in a zone where such use is not permitted.

8.3.1 If a building permit is required, an application must be made to the municipal authority giving full details of the proposal. The application will need to be made by the landowner but there is no restriction on repeat applications being made where the initial application is refused, and the owner can authorise another to make the application in his name, eg where an option to purchase has been entered into. The application has to be in an official form and include a location map, site plan and elevations. It has to be prepared by a registered architect or someone of equivalent relevant competence.

8.3.2 When the application is lodged, the municipal authority will state the time within which it will make its decision (usually two months for applications for residential buildings although this is extendable to three for commercial developments). The permit may be granted conditionally or unconditionally, and may include a contribution to any public development involved, although the free transfer of land required, eg for the widening of a highway, may not exceed 10 per cent of the surface area of the development site. If the authority considers it will need a longer time period than that initially estimated to determine the application for the permit, eg because the application is incomplete, a letter to that effect will be sent to the applicant. If no response is received from the authority within the designated time limit, and the period is not extended, the applicant is entitled to the building permit by default; this has the same validity as an expressly granted building permit, although it should be noted that a default permit is rarely put into effect as it may well be opposed by the municipal authority and entail litigation. An appeal against a refusal may be lodged with the administrative tribunal. As the POS is the determining consideration, the appeal will usually need to be based on the failure of the municipality to grant permission where the POS indicates this should have been granted. The appeal will not therefore be decided on political or discretionary grounds. Any third party objecting to the grant of a permit is entitled to bring an action before the administrative tribunal within two months of publication of the local authority decision. In the absence of objections within this two-month period, the permit becomes definitive. By way of contrast with other jurisdictions, the municipality will not take objections into account, or even seek these, before the grant of permission, but leave these to be lodged after the event and during this two-month period. For this reason it is advisable to obtain a certificate from the municipality stating that a copy of the permit has been displayed continuously during the period and that no third-party action has been initiated. Objections can be made by those with a legitimate interest, such as neighbours and special interest groups.

8.3.3 A building permit must be acted on within two years, and construction must not be interrupted for more than 12 months, or it will lapse. It is insufficient simply to provide the foundations. Development must have started and be seen to continue within the time limit. It is common though to have the permit renewed for an additional year and this is done by stamping the original, provided the application to renew is made at least two months before the expiry of the permit, and planning policy and any circumstances surrounding the initial grant of the permit have not altered significantly. The building permit runs with the land and the owner of the land is automatically entitled to the benefit of the building permit, although a buyer will need to apply for the transfer of the permit. This is a formality in the usual course of events, although four conditions will have to be complied with: the permit must be valid; the parties must agree to it; the administration must authorise the transfer; and the responsibility for development has to be transferred from the previous holder of the permit to the new holder. Once the development has commenced it has to be completed. Breach of planning law is a criminal offence.

8.3.4 The grant of a permit does not override other private rights, such as servitudes and rights of light, and consents in respect of these will have to be negotiated separately. Where there is a breach of planning control the municipality can take enforcement action and if appropriate demolish or reinstate the premises; the mayor is empowered to carry out any necessary enforcement measures, eg seizure of building materials, to ensure immediate compliance with a judicial decision or court order. The municipal authority has a number of inspection rights and the planning code imposes obligations on both the supervising architect and the municipal authority to issue compliance certificates following completion of the work. Criminal proceedings and civil enforcement action in respect of breaches of planning control need to be brought within fixed time limits, generally three years.

8.4 Building standards, control and supervision

Save in respect of certain buildings, such as private residential developments, those within the public sector, and buildings over a certain height, there are few regulations or controls operated by the municipal authority or much scope for it to supervise or check the standard of work, unlike the position in other jurisdictions. There is however a body of legislation covering technical standards. As the building industry is run largely by registered professionals and builders, the assumption is that they will secure compliance and the principal responsibility for compliance therefore lies with them. The insurance industry also maintains a supervisory role in practice because of the obligation to secure decennial insurance (see section 10) and they will often insist on inspection and a monitoring of standards by an independent entity (*bureau de contrôle*).

8.5 Protection of buildings of special interest

The Minister for Culture designates certain buildings as being of special historic or architectural interest under the Law of 1913. Certain works on buildings of special historic interest will be regulated exclusively by the Law of 1913, although in other cases the mainstream planning and zoning regulations will apply. The latter combine authorisations under both sets of legislation as the mainstream permit will be issued in lieu of the special permit required under the Law of 1913, usually with the agreement of the authorities responsible for the implementation of the Law of 1913. A third situation arises where the mainstream planning regulations may require special permits for works to be carried out on protected ancient monuments; these may be located in certain protected 'architectural heritage zones'. Where the standard construction permit does not apply, these works are subject to special authorisation granted by the competent planning body after approval has been obtained from a special body (*L'Architecte des Bâtiments de France*). There are some obligations imposed on owners of buildings included on the list of designated monuments, eg the cessation of certain industrial or commercial activity which imposes a serious risk to the building, such as a fire hazard. In the event of automatic listing subsequent to a designation by the Minister for Culture, the owner may ask for special subsidies if the inclusion on the list has given rise to the imposition of servitudes or some other obligation, or a change of use or circumstances which gives rise to immediate, material and specific loss or damage.

8.6 Compulsory purchase and compensation

For the construction of infrastructure facilities, and other public projects, any land needed may be expropriated by compulsory purchase or by the creation of compulsory servitudes over the land concerned (see 2.1.1 on the creation of administrative servitudes). Although the situation is improving, compensation rates remain low in spite of the intention that they should reflect the market value of the land expropriated at the time of the compulsory transfer order. Compensation is assessed by a judge who will make an assessment of the expropriated assets and an appraisal of their value. The formal assessment is made at the time of the compulsory transfer order, and will include an evaluation of the property and any rights over it. Expropriation powers can only be exercised by public bodies and where a private developer wishes to develop land in collaboration with a public body it is the public body which will acquire the land. It may then possibly enter into some form of construction joint venture with the developer by setting up a public-private sector joint venture company (*société d'économie mixte*), although in practice, private sector involvement is limited. In an area pre-designated by the municipality as a ZAC (*zone d'aménagement concerté*), it may set aside land for development with the private sector; it will then select a private company to undertake the development. The designation of a ZAC is independent from the expropriation procedure; the creation of a ZAC does not involve an obligation or a right to expropriate the land. Where development is to be carried out by a private developer, there is no reason in principle why the purchase of the land should be undertaken compulsorily. However, in practice the local authority may exceptionally have to resort to expropriation to settle particular difficulties related to land control which would otherwise preclude the entire development of the zone.

9 ENVIRONMENTAL MATTERS

As has been the case throughout Europe, there has been an increased awareness of environmental issues in France, although liability for certain types of pollution has existed for many years. Environmental liability exists in tort, in nuisance, under civil law statutes and criminal legislation. Liability in tort or negligence generally arises only where it can first be shown that there has been a breach of the criminal law applicable to the environment. It is a general principle of law that an individual who can show damage can recover compensation where this is due to a criminal act. Strict liability may arise in a number of situations where damage is shown to have been caused by toxic gas, polluted matter or water within the 'custody' of another. Custody arises where someone has the 'use, control and direction of' the thing or substance in question. Strict liability will also attach to oil spillages from tankers and the operators of nuclear reactors. Liability for nuisance or disturbance to neighbours arises when a disturbance exceeds normally accepted standards whether in relation to noise, odours or pollution. The courts will apply a relatively subjective approach to each situation. The relevant provisions of the *Code Civil* have been in existence for many years. Companies have been capable of criminal prosecution as well as their officers since 1994. To comply with obligations at EU level, legislation has been introduced to protect the environment in a number of important areas and regulation extends to matters including soil, ground and water contamination, air and noise pollution. Environmental protection and its legal framework are the responsibility of the Minister of the Environment and his local representatives at regional or departmental level. Subject to the principle of liability attaching generally to the person who has custody, the principle of polluter pays applies in France as elsewhere. It is often necessary, however, for the owner of property to pay damages in the first instance as the person with custody, and then bring an action against the person who caused the pollution to recover those damages.

9.1 Protection against atmospheric and noise pollution

The general provisions relating to air pollution control are set out in the Air Act 1996. While this sets general standards, it leaves local regulation, monitoring, licensing and enforcement to the *préfet*. This law provides that a building must be constructed and used in such a manner as to avoid atmospheric pollution in the area so as to prevent discomfort and risk to the public, risk to agricultural production and damage to monuments of historical or cultural significance. Parties will often invoke liability under the *Code Civil* for damages in nuisance or neighbourhood law (*troubles de voisinage*). Breach is established where the nuisance exceeds a level which is considered acceptable in the locality, thus granting the courts a significant measure of discretion in applying this subjective standard. Further liability may be established on the basis of the Code Civil's provisions governing strict liability in tort, although the burden of establishing causation will depend on the plaintiff being able to demonstrate not only that the damage suffered was caused by the polluting matter but also that the defendant had control over it.

9.2 Water pollution

Under EU legislation which has been transposed into national law, any activity causing matter to enter and alter the quality of controlled or sea water requires authorisation from the licensing authority. Licensing and enforcement are the responsibility of the water agency for each region, the regions for this purpose being the principal river basins. Where breaches of provisions are committed by an individual, liability will be criminal and will only attach to the polluter and fines and/or imprisonment may be imposed; however, where the breach is committed by a corporate entity, a variety of penalties may be imposed including fines as well as a five-year shut down of the industrial plant which caused the pollution, close supervision of industrial activity for a five-year period, and widespread media publicity of the breach. It may also have adverse stock exchange consequences.

9.3 Waste storage and disposal

The municipality is principally responsible for domestic waste and the laws dealing with industrial waste, its treatment, storage and disposal and licensing issues are generally a matter for the *préfecture*. Other ministries including agriculture, health and the interior will also be involved in the administration of waste disposal, and their different roles are coordinated by an interministerial commission. Radioactive waste is regulated by the national agency (*ANDRA*).

9.4 Contaminated land

There is little in law which enables government to enter private land and remove contamination as a preventive measure in the absence of escapes or specific damage to others, and the law in this area is somewhat less advanced than legislation in some other countries. There are no contaminated land registers. The exception to this is in respect of asbestos, where there are extensive clean-up duties and powers and strict liability attaches. There are also a number of criminal and administrative sanctions under the law regulating classified installations which are a class of industrial plants which require special operating licences (*permis d'exploitation*).

9.5 Environmental impact assessments

Before making a commitment to purchase property it is important to make appropriate environmental searches and enquiries but in the absence of government registers this is a matter largely of private enquiry. The obtainment of a town planning certificate (see 4.1.1) may be a condition precedent to the sale. The Law of 1976 covers classified plants and manufacturing facilities which may have an impact on the environment, and aims to protect various habitats against the potential effects these facilities may have. The protection of 'nature and the environment' and the conservation of special sites and monuments are also included in the legislation. Two types of facility are defined in the Law of 1976. Those which are likely to involve serious dangers or detrimental effects for the environment must obtain prior authorisation, while a simple declaration will suffice for those facilities which only entail circumscribed effects. The application for authorisation will entail an environmental impact assessment, a public enquiry and widespread consultation with various public authorities. The authorisation includes conditions to ensure risks to the environment are minimised to the greatest extent possible. The facility for which the authorisation was obtained must be fully operational within three months, or the authorisation will lapse.

10 DEVELOPMENT

10.1 Development projects, structures and vehicles

The simplest form of development project will involve the purchase of a site by an owner/occupier, and the construction by the buyer of premises he requires using his own builder. Although the construction industry is a major employer and includes large construction companies capable of handling international projects who moved into development in the 1980s, they do not now generally act as developers in the domestic market. The insurance companies and banks take a much more active role often through subsidiaries. Frequently, however, they will act through independent developers (*promoteurs*) paying them in a number of different ways, whether by fixed fees or by performance-related fees or profit share. There is a recognised standard development contract (*le contrat de promotion immobilière d'ouvrage*), but this is seldom used because it imposes a number of particularly onerous obligations on the developer. Various adaptations of this are often used instead. A simpler variant more akin to the project management agreement is the *contrat de maîtrise d'ouvrage*. Joint venture companies as such between financiers and developers are not common and partnerships are not recognised in France (see 13.2). There are also two specific types of development agreement, the *vente d'immeuble construire* and more commonly, the *vente en l'état futuré d'achèvement (VEFA)*, involving the construction and sale of a building by a developer to a purchasing investor or owner/occupier. To the extent these are transactions in land they will need to be notarised unlike the ordinary building contract. Many developments are undertaken entirely speculatively by developers who will buy and let or sell on the land using a mixture of loan and equity finance. On more complex projects, a number of parties will typically be involved, each providing different skills.

10.2 Building contracts and appointment of professionals

10.2.1 Typical forms of building contract

While single building contracts are becoming more frequent, the building industry is structured on the basis of individual trades each entering into a contract (*marché de travaux*) with the building owner or developer. This contract will often include the design aspects for that element of the works. The trade contractors or the main contractor stipulate before entering into a contract that they have sufficient information from the client and the design team to carry out the project. The most common contract is the fixed or lump sum contract (*marché forfait*) although contracts without fixed quantities are also used (*calculé en fonction metrée*) assessed by a qualified professional (*métreur vérificateur*) (see further 10.3.1). There are various published and also government indices for calculating the cost of fluctuations where these apply and also for calculating the price on contracts without fixed quantities. The work will almost invariably be put out to competitive tender, this method of award being known as *l'appel d'offres*. The invitation to tender (see 10.3.2) will not generally provide detailed construction drawings as the design and method of construction are often left to the individual contractors. The employer will have a coordinator (*maître d'ouvrage*) who will oversee and coordinate the contracts and the project. The coordinator may be the architect, an engineer, one of the lead subcontractors, or a specialist design bureau. Sometimes the developer will enter into a closer supervisory role as part of his contract and take on this coordination as part of his function. The employer, or developer, generally then contracts directly with the various trade contractors. Turn-key design and build contracts are also sometimes used. As the design undertaken by the architect does not extend to detailed construction drawings, the contractors undertake a considerable amount of design work. For a turn-key design and build project, the contractors will readily accept unqualified responsibility for the design and construction.

10.2.2 Contract terms

The contract will have provision for payments, usually on a monthly basis, to be assessed on the work done and verified by the contract administrator, usually the architect with the aid of a cost consultant (see 10.3.1), who will also assist on variations. A five per cent retention is normal although the contractor can insist on replacing it with a bank guarantee. Delays will be compensated for by fixed daily rates or by a percentage per day of the contract sum. This will be around 10 per cent in the case of residential development and possibly higher for commercial construction. Force majeure extensions, principally for bad weather, are allowed. Upon handover and completion as certified by the architect (*réception des travaux*), defects and outstanding works will be agreed as well as a timetable for these to be remedied.

10.2.3 Standard form of contracts

There is a recognised standard development contract (*contrat de promotion immobilière*), but this is seldom used because it imposes a number of particularly onerous obligations on the developer. (See 10.1 for typical forms of contract used.) On major projects, the building contract is usually drafted specifically for the project as there is no commonly adopted standard form of building contract. There is a standard form contract available, though not ordinarily used, known as *le cahier des clauses administratives particulières (CCAP)*. Minor projects however may adopt a standard document (AFNOR PO3.001).

10.2.4 Appointment of the professional team

Each member of the professional team will have his own contract. Standard forms are typically used where these are produced by the relevant professional bodies.

10.3 Those involved and their roles

10.3.1 Reputable contractors are members of the *Fédération Nationale du Bâtiment* and national registers are maintained of all such contractors, divided into different trades. These will give a number of details about the contractor. Owing to the legal status of the employer in many building contracts, the employer often takes a far more active role in the administration of projects than might otherwise be the case and may appoint an agent to act on his behalf. On small and medium-sized projects, the client will often appoint a lead consultant rather than make individual appointments for architecture, structure and so on. The lead consultant will usually be an architect for building projects and an engineer for civil engineering projects. Architects do not usually prepare detailed working drawings and these will be for the contract and subcontract teams. The role of the independent quality control consultant (*bureau de contrôle*) required by most decennial insurers has been mentioned at 8.4. The *bureau de contrôle* will be paid for by the employer and will be responsible for the quality of the design and the execution of the structure, facades, weatherproofing and technical services, and the contractor is under an obligation to comply with the requirements of the control office at no extra cost to the employer. Design at a technical level is often also left to specialist design bureaux. This is partly due to the segmentation of the industry into contract and subcontract teams who will have overall responsibility for all the work within their contract package including its design. Cost control, which is the responsibility of the quantity surveyor elsewhere, is split commonly between the expert who will look at budgets (*économiste de la construction*) and the expert who will deal with quantities (*métreur verificateur*). There are a multiplicity of different professionals involved in construction, particularly in the engineering sector and they are most easily referred to by their principal representative bodies and their acronyms: OPQIBI, Syntec, and CICF.

10.3.2 The tender for a construction project will be based on specifications and drawings. The procedure is flexible, and the tenders are not confined to those who have been invited to bid; in the case of public sector works, the contract has to be advertised and usually there is an obligation to accept the lowest bid. Some degree of negotiation will often follow before the contract is awarded. On site, supervision of the construction works is not always the responsibility of the design architect as it will frequently be the role of a separately appointed architect, or will be included amongst the duties of the contract coordinator.

10.4 Defects and remedies

10.4.1 Remedies of employer in respect of defects in design and materials

On handover, or *reception des travaux*, as certified by the architect, defects and outstanding works will be agreed as well as a timetable for these to be remedied. Failing this the period for the remedying of defects can typically be one year. The remedies available in respect of defects are available to both the employer and subsequent owners, and are described in 10.4.2.

10.4.2 Remedies of subsequent owners/occupiers other than the contractual employer

The *Code Civil* imposes an obligation on all contractors and professionals to compensate the owner and subsequent owners for minor defects appearing within two years (*responsabilité garantie biennale*). Major defects such as structural defects or those which affect fitness for purpose, eg services such as lifts and electrical services, are guaranteed for up to 10 years (*garantie décennale*). A lesser obligation attaches to the contractors alone to make good defects appearing within one year as described above (*garantie de parfait achèvement*). These obligations are mandatory and run from the date of the *réception des travaux*.

10.5 Defects insurance

The owner is obliged to insure the decennial liability of the builder referred to in 10.4.2 as is the builder himself. If a claim is made, the owner's insurers are obliged to make payment within three months and are then entitled to make a claim against the builder's insurers. This insurance obligation will be mentioned in the building permit.

10.6 Copyright

Copyright generally vests in the architect or other designer.

10.7 Fees

Because of the multiplicity of roles and professionals involved and the fact that much of the design will be left to contractors, it is difficult to place a figure on the professional fees that will be charged, but it is unlikely that these will be less than 10 per cent of the building costs.

10.8 Taxes

In the case of the *marché de travaux* (see 10.2.1) all building costs attract VAT at 20.6 per cent. However in the case of the *vente d'immeuble construire* (*VEFA*), the sale will be subject in part to VAT and in part to the registration tax (see 11.6).

11 TAXES

11.1 Corporation tax

Any company resident in France for tax purposes will be liable to pay corporation tax on its worldwide profits, subject to relief under any double taxation treaty with the country where the profits originate. This will include its capital gains, though these will be charged to tax at a lower rate. A company is treated as tax resident if it has its management in France. Tax transparency applies to those companies where the shareholders are liable for the debts of the company (*sociétés civiles de vente* and *sociétés en nom collectif*) (see further 13.1) and will be subject to tax on their share of the income of the company.

11.1.1 Tax rates

The rate of corporation tax is 33 per cent. Tax on capital gains is generally paid at 19 per cent. There are certain areas (*zones franches*) such as urban areas and the island of Corsica, where investment is to be encouraged, where no corporation tax is charged.

11.1.2 Computation and administration

In calculating its profits, a company can deduct expenses (including loan interest) of a revenue or recurring nature incurred for the purposes of the business of the company. This extends to any registration tax payable on the transfer of all property except new or recently renovated buildings (see 11.6 and 11.8). Tax is not payable on certain profits reinvested in the company and, up to certain limits, a company will not pay tax on income paid to a parent company. The tax system is administered by the Finance Ministry. Appeals on direct taxation issues go to an administrative tribunal and indirect taxes are dealt with in the civil tribunal. While it is open to the tax payer to arrange its affairs in such a way as to minimise tax, tax avoidance, any unlawful payment or evasion of tax, is a criminal offence. Artificial transactions, the sole purpose of which is to avoid tax, will be ineffective for tax purposes.

11.1.3 Capital allowances

Expenditure on the construction of certain buildings and the purchase of certain assets can be depreciated on the straight line method. Land itself is treated as a non-wasting asset and is therefore not depreciable. The period of depreciation will vary according to the asset from two to three years for assets such as cars, to 20 years for buildings such as offices.

11.1.4 Withholding tax

Withholding tax is charged on dividends at 25 per cent and on interest at 15 per cent. However interest is not charged to withholding tax on certain loans to non-residents and all withholding tax is subject to the terms of any international double taxation treaty.

11.2 Taxes on development value

There are no taxes on the development value of land or the value arising from its being designated as a development zone.

11.3 Taxes on capital gains

As mentioned at 11.1.1 the rate of corporation tax applicable to capital gains is 19 per cent.

11.4 Taxes on owner of property

11.4.1 The valuation of land forms the basis for land publicity tax (*taxe de publicité foncière* – see also 4.4) which is an annual tax on the ownership of all land. It is payable by the owner of the land. The state values the land and assesses its rental value, and subsequently charges tax on this value; the rate is commonly between 5 and 10 per cent. This will be divided between the *commune*, *département*, and central government.

11.4.2 There is tax of three per cent on the value of property owned by certain companies although this rarely applies in practice.

11.5 Taxes on occupier

Residential occupiers pay a residential dwelling tax calculated in a similar fashion to the land publicity tax (see 11.4), but applied to residential rather than commercial property. There are deductions for the number of dependants in residence. The occupier of a business property will pay a business licence tax, which will be based on a percentage of a figure assessed by reference to the area of the premises, the salaries of staff and the turnover of the business.

11.6 Taxes on land transfer

Direct taxes on the transfer of land include land publicity tax levied at 0.615 per cent and registration tax or VAT. Registration tax is levied at a rate of approximately 9 to 15 per cent, according to the type of property. If the building attracts VAT (see 11.8 where VAT is dealt with more fully), principally where it is new or renovated, this will be paid instead, at a rate of 20.6 per cent and no registration tax will be paid. Registration taxes may not be recovered except as an expense against corporation tax. There will be a tenancy registration tax of 2.5 per cent on certain tenancy agreements, such as those for a fixed term of over 12 years. This will not be charged as well as VAT.

11.7 Wealth tax

Wealth tax is levied on all of an individual's assets worldwide above a figure of around five million francs, subject to certain exceptions and reductions applicable to assets such as forests. The rate varies between 0.5 per cent and 2.5 per cent annually.

11.8 Value added tax

Value added tax (VAT) is a tax on the cost of goods and services, the principle being that the tax paid to a supplier is deducted from the tax that a taxable business charges on its own onward supplies to its own customers. The business will then account to government for the difference or the tax on the value it has added. Land and buildings are exempt. Construction attracts full VAT at 20.6 per cent whatever the type of building and will then be charged on any new building or renovated building. The purchase of a new or recently renovated building or land where the buyer is committed to build within the following four years is subject to VAT at 20.6 per cent. VAT applies to the first sale of a building which takes place during the first five years following completion. Any subsequent sale, even during the five-year period following completion, ceases to be liable to VAT. For a renovated building to be liable to VAT, the renovation must be substantial and may include significant internal modifications or an increase in the size of the building. No VAT is payable on a tenancy of land (unless the landlord so elects) or unfurnished buildings, but VAT will be payable on the letting of furnished buildings and parking. The landlord may only elect in certain circumstances and not where the building is residential and unfurnished. Where there is no VAT, registration tax may be payable, see 11.6.

11.9 Local and other taxes

Certain foreign investors are subject to a tax of three per cent on the value of their buildings. This tax will be subject to any double taxation treaties that may apply.

12 GRANTS AND INCENTIVES

12.1 Subsidies, grants and loans

There are extensive loans and subsidies available and the information on these is available from a number of different sources.

12.2 Tax allowances and reliefs

There are certain areas (*zones entreprises*) such as urban areas and the island of Corsica, where investment is to be encouraged, where no corporation tax is charged, provided the commercial enterprises benefiting from this arrangement comply with certain conditions. Companies benefiting from fiscal advantages in these areas will not be able to avail themselves of additional state aids which would otherwise be available.

12.3 Other public schemes and incentives

See 12.2.

13 COMPANIES AND BUSINESS ENTITIES

13.1 Limited and unlimited companies

The most important forms of commercial companies are the *société anonyme* (*SA*), the *société à responsabilité limitée* (*SARL*), the *entreprise unipersonelle responsabilité limitée* (*EURL*) and the *société en nom collectif* (*SNC*). Where the activity in question is considered to be civil rather than commercial, the *société civile* (*SCiv*) may be used (see 13.1.3). The shareholders of the *SA*, the *SARL* and the *EURL* companies enjoy limited liability for the debts of the company up to the amount of their share capital, whereas the participants in an *SNC* and *SCiv* do not. The latter are a type of mechanism permitting professionals or others to combine and establish a legal entity which will enable them to invest and undertake business together but without the protection or disadvantages of full incorporation with limited liability. Members of these companies will therefore enjoy tax transparency akin to the partners in a partnership in some other countries. Both are used in a property context and are attractive vehicles for small groups of investors. Lawyers and accountants are subject to close regulation and lawyers cannot, for example, issue capital to non-lawyers.

13.1.1 The *SARL* will have a minimum share capital of FF50,000 and the *SA*, FF250,000 francs, or 1.5 million francs if it wishes to invite the public to subscribe. There is a minimum number of two shareholders for the *SARL* and other companies, and seven for the *SA*. By definition the *EURL* has only one member. As for directors, each must have one manager (*gérant*) save that the *SA* must have three directors of whom one will be the *président*. For a public company to be listed or quoted on the Paris Stock Exchange, it must comply with a number of further requirements.

13.1.2 Subject to the possible tax transparency and liability of shareholders in the case of the *SNC* and *SCiv*, the company will have separate legal identity and members will enjoy protection from claims against the company. Notarisation is not necessary, no stamp duty or tax is chargeable, and there are no government consents required for the formation of the company although there are requirements as to advertising or notification, and there are further formalities regarding the holdings in a property investment or holding company, eg limited notarisation.

13.1.3 The *société civile immobilière*, regulated under the *Code Civil*, is a non-profit making civil entity or partnership whose purpose is to manage and rent property, by acquiring property directly or by constructing buildings which are then rented. The property may also be redistributed to shareholders or third parties. The partners in a *société civile immobilière* will have unlimited liability for the company's debts.

13.2 Partnerships

Because of the availability of the *SNC* and *SCiv* there is less need for the concept of partnership and no legal framework exists for this structure. Where two or more people trade together the law will generally impose a form of quasi-incorporation on them as though they had intended to incorporate but failed to do (*société crée de fait* or *société en participation*). For the same reason there is no provision for limited partnership.

13.3 Other types of business association

It is possible to set up unincorporated associations under the Law of 1901 for non-profit making purposes, such as clubs and societies, and these will have legal recognition. There are no other forms of legal entity of significance. While joint ventures exist they do not have separate existence and rarely take the form of companies.

14 INTERNATIONAL

14.1 Restrictions on inward investment

There are no restrictions on the introduction of funds into France for the purchase of property or on the ownership of French property by foreign entities.

14.2 Exchange control

There are no restrictions limiting the repatriation or transfer of funds out of France.

14.3 Restrictions and registrations on carrying on a business

There is no restriction on a foreign entity or company carrying on business in France.

14.4 Repatriation of income and proceeds of property trading and development

There are no consents or restraints on the repatriation of income and proceeds subject only to the deduction of withholding tax.

14.5 Withholding tax

Withholding taxes have been referred to at 11.1.4.

14.6 Double taxation relief

France has separate double taxation treaties with a number of countries.

CHAPTER 7

Germany

Gleiss Lutz Hootz Hirsch

Written by: Gerhard Wegen, Stefan Lingemann (property), Wolfgang Spoerr (planning and environment), Edgar Joussen (construction), Dirk Wasmann (corporate law), Eckhart Schweyer and Christopher Kuner

CONTENTS

1 OWNERSHIP OF LAND 213
2 OTHER INTERESTS IN LAND 215
3 TITLE TO LAND 219
4 TRANSACTIONS IN LAND 220
5 LEASES AND OTHER RIGHTS OF OCCUPATION 223
6 FINANCE AND INVESTMENT SOURCES 226
7 FORMS OF SECURITY 229
8 PLANNING AND BUILDING REGULATION 230
9 ENVIRONMENTAL MATTERS 234
10 DEVELOPMENT 237
11 TAXES 240
12 GRANTS AND INCENTIVES 243
13 COMPANIES AND BUSINESS ENTITIES 244
14 INTERNATIONAL 247

CHAPTER 7

Germany

1 OWNERSHIP OF LAND

As a civil law country, Germany has a codified system of law and its sources of law comprise the Civil Code (*Bürgerliches Gesetzbuch*, *BGB*) and various statutes, known as codes, and delegated legislation. By way of contrast with common law jurisdictions, there is no doctrine of precedent, although in practice frequent references are made to decisions deriving from the higher courts. The principal statutes relating to property law are the *BGB* and the Land Register Act (*Grundbuchordnung*, *GBO*) which deals with the formal entries and registrations in the land register, without which property rights cannot be acquired or enforced. Ownership of land involves an important distinction between moveables and immoveables and attaches less significance to the difference between rights in rem and rights in personam. The principal form of tenure or land ownership is absolute ownership, which creates a right in or against the land itself (a right in rem).

1.1 Types of ownership

1.1.1 Freehold or absolute ownership

Absolute ownership (*Eigentum*) carries with it a right to own, occupy and dispose of the land, and is the most common form of legal ownership. Buildings and anything which is fixed or annexed to the land or buildings are treated as part of the land. In exceptional cases the building may be owned by someone other than the landowner, eg where the landowner has granted a hereditable lease over the building (see 2.1.3). Absolute ownership carries with it not only the right over the surface but also to the soil below and the air above the land. Although the same legal system now generally applies throughout unified Germany, the provisions regulating absolute ownership of land located in the former East German states are complex and it is advisable to seek specialist advice in this regard.

1.1.2 Leasehold

There are legal vehicles akin to the long lease in the Anglo-American tradition, granted at a premium or for capital payment in advance and these are considered at 2.1.3. However the most common type of lease is contractual and may be granted for a fixed term or periodically and will require the payment of rent. The terms on which contractual leases or tenancies are granted are dealt with more fully in section 5.

1.1.3 Joint ownership

Joint ownership of land (*Miteigentum*) arises where land is owned jointly by two or more people. Unless specified otherwise, a right owned jointly by two or more is held in *Bruchteilsgemeinschaft*. This is a form of common ownership where each of the parties owns a specified and (in the absence of evidence to the contrary) equal undivided share in the property and its fruits, and bears a corresponding share of the charges over the property. Each joint owner may dispose of his share as he chooses, but the jointly owned property may only be disposed of by all the parties acting jointly. Each party may demand dissolution of the *Bruchteilsgemeinschaft* at any time and enforce this by foreclosure. For the transfer of a tenant's interest in the joint ownership to be effective, the transfer will have to be notarised by a notary and then entered into the local land registry. As this is cumbersome, a partnership under the Civil Code (*BGB-Gesellschaft*) is usually formed, since the partnership interests can then be transferred informally. However, a share owned by a joint owner can be transferred by way of succession under inheritance laws, whereas a share in the *BGB-Gesellschaft* cannot, unless the *BGB-Gesellschaft* provides otherwise.

1.1.4 Condominia

Condominium ownership (*Wohnungseigentumsgesetz*) is the absolute right of ownership over a self-contained unit of a building. Each owner retains absolute rights of ownership over individual self-contained units of the building whilst owning the common parts jointly and proportionally with the other owners. To create a condominium, the owner of the property makes, or the joint owners agree upon, a declaration of partition (*Teilungserklärung*) which is made to the local land register in the appropriate county court. The land registry subsequently sets up the residential land register (*Wohnungsgrundbuch*). The approval of the local building authorities (see section 8) is also required. The relationship between condominium owners is governed by the Condominium Act (*Wohnungseigentumsgesetz, WEG*), and the declaration of partition (*Teilungserklärung*) as well as by resolutions of the condominium ownership association (*Wohnungseitümergemeinschaft*). Condominia may also exist in relation to commercial premises (*Teileigentum*).

1.1.5 Lesser rights

A wide variety of lesser rights of ownership exists which may be interests in land or mere contractual rights. Further comment is made on these at 2.1.

1.2 Legal and beneficial ownership

Beneficial ownership (*Wirtschaftliches Eigentum*) plays a less significant part in regulating property rights than legal ownership in the form of absolute ownership. In the case of a joint venture, a company may be founded which will be registered as the legal owner of the property. The parties will then become the beneficial owners without becoming legal co-owners. In addition, there is the option of establishing beneficial ownership by an agreement to create a legal trust (*Treuhand*). This is particularly useful where one of the beneficial owners does not wish to be disclosed.

1.3 Restrictions on land ownership and dealing

1.3.1 There are some legislative restrictions on the extent of the rights of a landowner, which aim principally to protect the public interest and include rights of access and compulsory purchase, and planning and building controls, and on which specific comment is made in sections 8 and 9.

1.3.2 There are certain specific restrictions upon the disposal of land giving third parties legal rights of first refusal (*Vorkaufsrecht*) when land is sold. These may be registered interests (see 2.4). However, statutory rights of first refusal are the most important. A number of rights of first refusal have been introduced by statute over the years in favour of the authorities for the purpose of urban planning, and nature and wildlife preservation. A foreign investor, unfamiliar with the current planning status applicable to the piece of land he intends to acquire, should be aware of the existence of such statutory rights of first refusal (which are not always entered in the land register) and of the possibility of these being exercised by the various authorities.

1.4 Acquisitive prescription or adverse possession

Title can become vested in a person who is not actually the owner of the land if he is registered as the owner for at least 30 years and has actual possession of the land. As a result, rights are only very rarely acquired by acquisitive prescription.

2 OTHER INTERESTS IN LAND

There are lesser rights and interests to that of absolute ownership. These may be public or private. Certain interests do not require registration to be enforceable between successors in title.

2.1 Servitudes or easements, usufruct, building and dwelling rights

2.1.1 Servitudes or easements

The holder of a servitude may use the servient tenement for certain (limited) purposes (eg a right of way), or certain activities may be restricted over the servient tenement (eg certain types of construction, or certain types of use). Alternatively, rights which would otherwise attach to the servient tenement may be waived (eg the right to object to emissions, eg noise). Examples of servitudes include rights of way, wayleaves for electricity pylons or oil pipelines, and restrictive building covenants. Real servitudes (*Grunddienstbarkeiten*) come into force by agreement and subsequent entry in the land register. They are charged in favour of a plot of land (the dominant tenement) and they run with that land, over another plot of land (the servient tenement) and are rights in rem and are normally granted in perpetuity. The limited personal servitude (*beschränkt persönliche Dienstbarkeiten*), by way of contrast with the real servitude, is a right exercisable by a specific owner but which does not run with the land. Limited personal servitudes create a right which is only bestowed upon certain individuals and expires upon the death of the individual in question (a right in personam).

2.1.2 Usufruct

Usufruct (*Nießbrauch*) is comparable to the life estate in common law countries, and may be granted to an individual. The usufruct, which may be granted for life or for a certain limited term, is a right incapable of being transferred. It entitles the usufructuary to reap the fruits of (or to use) the property or right belonging to another. It is created by agreement and must be registered to be valid. The beneficiary of the right has the right of possession although he has no permission to alter the nature or use of the land or to transform existing buildings, unless there is specific agreement authorising him to do so. There is the further obligation to maintain the condition of the land, which will include maintenance of any buildings. Usufruct may be terminated by mutual agreement, or since it may not be transferred by way of succession, upon the death of the usufructuary. If the usufructuary is a company, it may be terminated upon its dissolution.

2.1.3 Building rights

A hereditable building right (*Erbbaurecht*) grants the holder the exclusive right to build, use and occupy the property and are fully transferable. This is similar to the concept of the building lease found in common law countries, with the important distinction that the holder of a hereditable building right will actually own the building for the duration of the right. Hereditable building rights are regulated by the Decree on Hereditable Building Rights (*Erbbaurechts-verordnung, ErbbauVO*). The right is usually granted for a rent payable annually, which may be index linked, rather than for a premium (or capital sum). A building right is normally granted for a fixed period, often 99 years. The right is treated as if it were an independent plot of land and can be charged with land charges or mortgages. It must be registered in the land register to be valid. Upon termination of the hereditable building right, the building erected by the beneficiary becomes the property of the owner of the land who will have to compensate the holder.

2.1.4 Dwelling rights

Dwelling rights (*Dauerwohnrecht*) can be granted for the lifetime of the holder or for a fixed period. They have no maximum duration, may be transferred and may bind successors in title although they will normally be rights in personam.

2.2 Restrictions on use and other restrictions

Freeholders may agree to enter into restrictions on the use of one parcel of land, to protect the amenities and value of another parcel of land. Subject to certain conditions, these restrictions are enforceable by and between successive owners provided they have been registered. These rights are freely negotiated between adjoining owners, and are in the nature of servitudes commented on at 2.1.1. Public law restrictions under planning and other legislation are commented on in section 8.

2.3 Mortgages and privileges

Monetary liabilities can be secured on land in a number of ways. The procedure and regulations governing the creation and enforcement of mortgages are commented on in section 7. The law allows for two forms of right which perform approximately the same function as a mortgage in common law. These are mortgages (*Hypotheken*) and land charges (*Grundschulden*), both of which require registration. Privileges as such and as known in a number of civil law jurisdictions do not exist though there are preferential debts which can take priority even over registered mortgages, particularly of a public law or fiscal nature. These can also include wages such as those of agricultural workers.

2.4 Contracts and options

2.4.1 When an owner of land contracts to sell the land, but the sale has not yet been completed, the buyer has a contract giving him an interest in the land. Restrictions on the disposal of land where third parties may have legal rights of first refusal can be entered in the land register, but only in certain cases. These rights must be notarised to be valid. This type of right of first refusal is of practical importance with regard to long-term tenancies of business premises in order to secure the tenant's chance to buy the building which he occupies if and when the landlord wishes to sell it. Without an entry in the land register, the rights will not bind third parties. This also applies to contract options.

2.4.2 The right of first refusal (*dingliche Vorkaufsrechte*) may be entered in the land register. This right can be granted to the owner of another parcel of land. It can also be granted for particular types of sale or for any sale. The right must be exercised within two months of notification of the conclusion of a sale and purchase contract with a third party, unless the contract of the right of first refusal provides otherwise. If exercised, the holder of the right automatically becomes the purchasing party under the sale and purchase contract negotiated with the third party. As a consequence, the holder of the right may enforce the transfer of the contract against the buyer, who may otherwise be liable for any damages incurred as a result of the right of first refusal.

2.5 Public and municipal charges

There are financial charges imposed to protect the rights of government and public bodies or public law matters, eg to recover payment for statutory works such as highway improvements, drainage construction, cleaning or repairing unsanitary/dangerous buildings. Other specific planning or administrative restrictions and charges also exist. These may be registered. The repayment of government grants and tax liabilities may be secured on the property but this is rare.

2.6 Other interests

There are no interests in land worthy of note other than those mentioned in this section.

2.7 Liabilities attaching to land

Liability may arise under public building law (*Baugesetzbuch, BauGB*), the law relating to monuments (*Denkmalschutzgesetz*), the law protecting natural resources (*Naturschutzgesetz*) and development charges pursuant to local charges law (*Kommunalabgabengesetz*). Liability may also be incurred under other public law provisions, such as those relating to environmental law (see section 9). There are fiscal liabilities which attach to the land. General comments on tax are made in section 11.

2.8 Legal and beneficial interests

The concept of beneficial ownership does exist under the general principles of civil law (but see 1.2 and in particular the *Treuhand*).

2.9 Protection of interests

Interests in land do not necessarily have to be registered to be enforceable against the land and subsequent buyers. Some private interests in land, such as restrictions, can be, but do not have to be, entered in the land register to be enforceable, however, if they are granted on a purely contractual basis without an entry in the land register, they will not bind third parties. Therefore, if an interest can be entered in the land register and is to bind third parties, it should be registered. On the other hand, all contractual tenancies do bind successors in title although not entered in the land register. Many interests in land under the former East German legal system were not entered in the land register, although such interests are protected by the transition regulations. As a result, the East German land register is a less reliable source of information in relation to rights over land.

2.10 Priority of interests

Priority between registered interests in land will depend generally on the date of registration, not the date of creation of an interest. The principal exception to this is where a priority notice has been entered where final entry is delayed (see 4.1.3).

3 TITLE TO LAND

3.1 Proof of title

Title to land can only be established by registration in the land register (*Grundbuch*). Only in exceptional cases can there be land ownership without an entry in the register, eg in the case of succession. Every new transfer on sale of freehold land and the transfer and creation of servitudes, mortgages, hereditable building rights, registrable rights of first refusal (see 2.4) require registration if third parties are to be bound. The land registers are not open for inspection by the public and anyone making a private enquiry must show a legitimate interest.

3.2 The land registry and the land register

The land register is maintained by the local land registry which forms a division of the local county court (*Amtsgericht*).

3.2.1 Plans

The land registers include references to the topographical land survey, taxation registers and the size of the land. Actual plans are not included in the land register and only identification numbers are referred to.

3.2.2 Content

Every plot of land in a local court's district is entered in the land register and has its own folio (*Grundbuchblatt*). The register is subdivided into three sections. Details of the owner of the particular parcel of land are entered in section one. The various forms of private law encumbrances, such as servitudes, rights of first refusal, and usufruct are entered in section two. Mortgages and land charges are listed in section three. There is no gradation between types of ownership.

3.2.3 Errors

There is a presumption of accuracy in favour of the land register in order to protect those who act in reliance upon it. The person registered as the owner is presumed to be the owner, and the bona fide buyer for value who acts in reliance upon the register will have the title transferred to him unless he has notice that the registration is defective. A party acquiring an interest in land which has been entered in the local land register may acquire the interest even if the existing registered party who granted the interest is not the rightful owner. Therefore lack of rightful title will not prevent the transfer of title by a registered owner; even a non-existing encumbrance which is registered might be acquired in this way. Only in specific cases may the land registry correct errors by right of office. In most cases, the correction of errors requires the consent of the person affected by correction. If he refuses to approve a correction, then the person requesting the correction has the option of bringing an action against the uncooperative party.

3.3 Passing of title

Change of ownership requires a sales contract, an agreement as to the transfer of title as well as an entry of the transfer of title in the appropriate land register (see 4.1). Title passes as soon as the transfer of title is entered in the land register, although a system of priority notices exists to protect the buyer until the actual change of title is completed (see 4.1.3).

4 TRANSACTIONS IN LAND

The most common transactions in land are the sale and purchase of the freehold, the grant and assignment of a hereditable building right, and the creation of mortgages and servitudes.

4.1 Procedures

4.1.1 German law distinguishes between the contractual obligation and the real transaction, ie the passing of title following the performance of the contractual obligation. The distinction between the contract and its fulfilment by transfer of title is called the 'principle of abstraction' and is an important principle of property law. Therefore the prerequisites for the valid acquisition of a plot of land are (a) a sales contract, (b) an agreement on the transfer of title (*Auflassungsvormerkung*), and (c) an entry of the transfer in the land register.

4.1.2 A sale takes place in various stages. The first stage will consist of the negotiation of the contract. As the transfer of title cannot take effect without an entry in the land register, the land register is taken to reflect the current legal status of a piece of land so that title investigation is unnecessary. For the same reason, there is a presumption of accuracy in favour of the land register in order to protect those who act in reliance upon it (see 3.2.3). Once the buyer decides that he wishes to acquire the property and has successfully negotiated the contract, he may register a priority notice, the second stage. This usually takes place when an application is made to register the transfer of title in the land register.

4.1.3 The entry of the priority notice is expedited by the land registry. It protects the buyer against all later entries in the register until the actual change of title procedure is completed. However, a priority notice only takes effect between the parties. At this stage the buyer cannot be certain of acquiring title to the property concerned because a public authority may exercise its statutory right of first refusal (see 1.3.2) or because the purchase permission, which has to be granted by the local authority under certain circumstances, may still be pending. Once the buyer is satisfied that the sale agreement will not be interfered with, he enters into the third and final stage. The sale contract, the agreement on transfer of title and application for registration must all be notarised (see 4.3) and this will usually take place when an application is made to register the transfer of title in the land register. In many cases, the passing on of the purchase price by the notary is subject to the transfer of title being fully secured. A certificate confirming that all the requisite charges on the transaction have been paid (see 4.4.3), along with confirmation by the local authorities that they are not entitled to a right of first refusal, is a prerequisite for registration of the transfer of title in the land register.

4.2 Contract terms

4.2.1 The contract will usually contain two types of statutory warranty, the warranty of title (*Rechtsmängelgewährleistung*) and the warranty of quality (*Sachmängelgewährleistung*). Both can be modified by agreement to expand or restrict the obligation, as they are not mandatory. Under the statutory warranty of title, the seller is bound to transfer good title to the property to the buyer unencumbered by any third-party private rights and free of any charges, even where these charges are known to the buyer, unless the seller restricts his obligation. The warranty does not extend to public law encumbrances not subject to registration in the land register. With regard to the warranty of quality, the seller warrants that the property is free of defects regarding the normal or contractually proposed use of the land; the warranty includes physical or structural defects, and the buyer is not under the duty to check for himself. In addition to this, the seller can give a guarantee that the land has specific qualities (*zugesicherte Eigenschaften*). The statutory period of limitation within which to make a claim for breach of warranty is one year after the buyer takes over the land. Time starts to run from the completion of the change of title procedure.

4.2.2 Where a breach of warranty occurs, the buyer is entitled to demand the cancellation of the purchase agreement (*Wandlung*) or a reduction of the purchase price (*Minderung*). The seller can also incur liability for damages if he makes misrepresentations as to quality (*zugesicherte Eigenschaft*) about the property as well as for intentional concealment of a defect. Claims for breaches of warranty as to quality take precedence over other breach of warranty claims. Therefore it is common practice for representations as to quality to form a major contractual extension of the warranties.

4.2.3 The contract usually provides for the payment of a deposit, which will vary from one transaction to another. This may be forfeited to the seller if the transaction does not complete and specific contracts may also make provision for the payment of interest should there be a delay in completion. The payment of a deposit may also, in some cases, ensure repayment in case of warranty claims. These provisions are usually regarded as sufficient to safeguard both buyer and seller against default.

4.3 Formalities

The sale requires a contract, an agreement on the transfer of the title as well as an entry in the land register (see 4.1.1); the contract and the agreement to transfer land and the application for registration must all be fully notarised. All contracts where one party binds himself to transfer ownership of immoveable property require notarial form, and this includes a gift of land or the grant of an option. On the other hand, the creation, extinction or transfer of all other titles can be entered into by mutual agreement. However, notarisation is recommended, as a notarised agreement is irrevocable. Where the sale and purchase contract is not in the required notarial form, the acquisition becomes valid in spite of such lack of form, providing the transfer of title is entered in the land register and the parties still agree on the purchase at the time the entry in the land register takes place. However, as the contract for sale will not comply with the requisite formalities, if some of the terms on which the parties agreed have not been included correctly in the notarial instrument, the contract may be void for lack of formality.

4.4 Fees, costs and taxes

4.4.1 On a sale of land, or the grant of a building right, the buyer will pay fees, costs and taxes, and the seller will bear the cost of freeing the property from encumbrances, although the contract may provide otherwise. However, both parties remain jointly and severally liable for the costs of the land registry, the notary and the tax authorities. The agents' fees are mutually agreed in advance and are generally based on a certain percentage of the value of the land, commonly between three and six per cent for sale transactions, although these are subject to negotiation. Agents' fees in the case of lettings vary from one region to another, and in any event may not exceed two months' rent. On sales they are often paid by the buyer, although there are regional variations. Their fees are negotiated on a contingency basis and only become due in the event that the transaction takes place.

4.4.2 The fees of the notary are fixed by statute and are based on the value of each of the agreements contained in the contract. Notaries' fees are usually less expensive than those charged by lawyers with regard to sale transactions. It is possible to reduce the cost of notarisation by including the contract of sale, the agreement on transfer of title and the application for the transfer of title in one single document. Generally, lawyers' fees are based on statute (*Bundesrechtsanwaltsgebührordnung, BRAGO*) and depend on the value of the agreement to be concluded. However, in many cases special fees for negotiations are agreed based on considerations including the time involved and the complexity of the matter. Alternatively, a fixed fee for the entire agreement can be agreed. The notary's fees are around 1 to 1.5 per cent. The legal fees will depend on the value of the transaction and whether the lawyer takes part in the negotiations. For transactions worth over DM1 million, the legal fees will commonly be around 0.3 per cent, although the figure will be double if the lawyer is involved in the negotiation.

4.4.3 All transactions involving land are subject to a land transfer tax (*Grunderwerbssteuer*), which is levied on the agreed consideration (*Bemessungs-*

grundlage) at a rate of two per cent. The recording notary is obliged to submit copies of all the agreements that may be subject to land transfer tax to the tax authorities. When the tax is paid, the tax authorities issue a clearance certificate (*Unbedenklichkeitsbescheinigung*) to the notary. This certificate, along with confirmation by the local authorities that they are not entitled to a right of first refusal, is a prerequisite for registration of the transfer of title in the land register.

4.4.4 The land registry fees are fixed by statute and are charged according to the value of the land.

4.4.5 Overall transaction costs are between five and six per cent, although the costs will be higher where an agent is involved.

4.4.6 Value added tax (VAT) is charged both on the transaction and on the professional fees, at 15 per cent, but whether or not it is charged at all will depend on the residence of both the seller and buyer.

4.5 Professionals' roles

Various professionals may become involved in the search for land. Real estate agents and estate brokers may be engaged. Neither are members of a recognised official public body, although more reputable estate brokers are members of the German Real Estate Brokers' Association, which is a private body. Charges vary from one individual broker to another. Where an unsurveyed plot or where only a part of the plot is to be sold, surveyors must be engaged, as only surveyed plots of land can be entered in the land register. It is usual that a mandate be given to a lawyer for the sales negotiations and the drafting of the contracts. Finally, the notary plays a crucial role as the various stages for the acquisition and transfer of land require notarial form.

5 LEASES AND OTHER RIGHTS OF OCCUPATION

The right of permanent dwelling and hereditable building rights (see 2.1.3) are akin to common law leasehold tenure. However, it is much more common for land and buildings to be leased on a contractual basis (*Miete*) either for a fixed period or for unlimited duration. There are statutory provisions which affect the expiry of the tenancy agreement and these are dealt with in more detail at 5.3. The length of the tenancy will normally depend on the purpose of the letting. Residential tenancies are generally concluded for an indefinite period, but in specific cases may be for a limited period of three to five years. Commercial tenancies are concluded for periods of up to 25 or 30 years though terms of five or ten years are common. There is no legal fixed limit preventing a tenancy from being concluded for more than 30 years. However, agreements concluded for over 30 years will automatically be deemed to be of indefinite duration and can be terminated by law at any time after that time, so in practice it is not advisable to grant tenancies for more than 30 years.

5.1 Rent and other terms

The rent of premises to be used for commercial purposes may be freely negotiated. Residential tenancies may be concluded either as fixed tenancies or as graduated tenancies with increases which are agreed upon in advance; see further 5.3 where indexing is also dealt with. Due to a shortage of residential housing in German cities, negotiations by the tenant to substantially alter the usual standard terms of the contract in urban centres is unusual. Maintenance and repairs are borne by the landlord unless the damage is caused by the tenant, although it is common for day-to-day expenses to be passed on to the tenant. However, in the case of residential tenancies, there are strict limits on the maximum amount which can be imposed upon the tenant. It is the duty of the landlord to insure the premises, but this duty is often transferred to the tenant by contract. Certain breaches of the tenancy agreement entitle the landlord to forfeit and take back the lease. These breaches include a use of the tenanted property which violates the tenancy agreement, failure to make rental payments for more than two months, and serious breaches of the lease contract. It is common for a deposit (*Kaution*) of several months' rent to be left as security with the landlord until the termination of the tenancy for all types of rental agreement.

5.2 Privity of contract and estate

After the tenant has moved in, a transfer of ownership of the rented property to a new landlord has no effect on the contractual tenancy arrangement. The new owner simply becomes a party to the tenancy agreement by replacing the previous landlord. Therefore, the principle of privity of contract does not apply with regard to the landlord's legal successor. However, the transfer of the tenant's contractual rights requires the consent of the landlord.

5.3 Rent control and security of tenure

5.3.1 The rent of a residential tenancy may in areas of housing shortage not exceed the prevailing market rate by over 20 per cent; the local rent control authorities have a tendency to sometimes apply unrealistically low 'market rents'. Subsequent increases in rent are permissible but only if the prevailing market rent of the tenancy is higher than the contractual rent. There are no rent controls for commercial tenancies and the parties are free to negotiate the rent at the time the agreement is entered into. For commercial premises the parties may review the rent during the term, although the agreement itself will generally regulate what the parties may and may not do, eg rents under contracts for a fixed period with a fixed rent may not be raised. The parties may increase the rent more often than annually if this is provided for in the agreement. Rent adjustment clauses can be linked to the cost of living index but only with approval of the central bank for the respective federal state (*Landeszentralbank*) and index-linked rents included in tenancy agreements without approval are invalid. Approval is more likely if the change can be upwards and downwards. Approval is not required for clauses which contain a variable rent based on the tenant's sales or an equalisation clause adjusting the rent to comparable rents for comparable premises in similar locations. The parties are therefore not limited to the inclusion of increases linked to the cost of living index and agreements to adjust the rents to current market levels are being used increasingly.

5.3.2 Legislative restrictions on the parties' freedom to agree the length of a tenancy and its terms vary according to the type of tenancy. It will only be possible to terminate an indefinite residential tenancy if the landlord can show that he has a legitimate reason (eg he needs the premises to live in). In reality, the courts have taken a firm line in the past and, as a result, the landlord will now often have to pay the tenant compensation if the tenant is to vacate the premises. Private landlords availing themselves of government subsidies for construction will be under even stricter regulation. Different legislation regulates residential tenancies in the former East Germany unless the premises were built after 1990. There are no similar restrictions with regard to commercial tenancy agreements and there is no security of tenure for commercial tenants. Commercial tenancies of 25–30 years may provide for an automatic extension if no notice of termination is given. Renewal and option clauses are often inserted in short-term tenancy agreements. Agreements concluded without a fixed term may be terminated within a statutory notice period ranging between three and twelve months. This notice period depends, among other things, on the length of the tenancy. Fixed period tenancy agreements often provide for an automatic extension of the agreement at the end of the term; provided neither party terminates the agreement, the notice period is usually the same as the statutory period. Where there is no provision for extension, no notice need be given to terminate the contract as it will then terminate automatically. However, if both parties remain parties to the tenancy agreement after the rental period has expired, the contract is prolonged for an indefinite period and may be terminated by either party by serving notice within the statutory period.

5.4 Other legislative restrictions

There are no important legislative restrictions other than those discussed above.

5.5 Method of measurement

The measurement of rented premises is regulated by a DIN standard, which does not, however, have the force of law. There are four different standards. Where the size of the buildings is an important issue in the negotiations, the parties should specify which standard has been selected for measurement. It is more helpful to refer to the particular standard used rather than to use generic 'gross' or 'net' figures, although it may be pointed out that measurements will generally include everything in the self-contained unit, eg lavatories but not staircases.

6 FINANCE AND INVESTMENT SOURCES

Germany has a very sophisticated banking system which plays a vital part in financing investment in the property market.

6.1 Loan finance

Banking institutions are the main source of loan finance in Germany. Several different types of bank exist.

6.1.1 There are several 'universal banks' in Germany providing a full range of banking and other financial services without the traditional separation between commercial and investment banking found in the US and UK. Among the commercial banks, there are the big three private branch banks with a nationwide network, the regional state banks (*Landesbanken*) which are closer to the savings banks described at 6.1.2, branches of foreign banks, and private banks which all extend a significant amount of short-term finance and to a lesser extent will involve themselves with long-term property finance.

6.1.2 The savings banks (*Sparkassen*) place special emphasis on property lending. A savings bank is restricted to extending loans, which are for the most part long term, to those located within the region where the bank is incorporated. Credit associations (*Kreditgenossenschaften*) are cooperatives offering loans to both members and non-members. They serve mainly small businesses, although their central institution, the *Deutsche Genossenschaftsbank* (DG Bank), provides long-term finance to international investors. The mortgage banks (*Realkreditinstitute* or *Hypothekenbanken*) extend long-term loans to local authorities and other public institutions as well as financing commercial and residential property. The building societies (*Bausparkassen*) which are mutual societies also finance property transactions, principally for residential investors. Other sources of finance include insurance companies and pension funds, which are a major source of long-term funds.

6.1.3 Conventional loan finance, as provided by mortgage banks, savings banks and commercial banks, will be granted for any term up to 30 years, although interest rates are rarely fixed for more than five to ten years. At the end of this time the interest rate will be renegotiated and if not acceptable to the borrower the loan will be terminated. Most loans are on a sinking-fund or amortised basis (*annuitätdarlehen*). This means there will be fixed payments throughout, which initially will be largely of interest but include larger instalments of capital as the amount of the loan reduces. There is no ability to increase the amount of repayment on the principal or repay the entire amount of the loan before it matures, and borrowers will be liable to damages if they do so. Nevertheless, other provisions may be agreed to. Irrespective of the term of the loan, the interest rate payable may be flexible or fixed. Savings banks normally grant mortgage loans with flexible interest rates which may be changed by the bank at short notice. Mortgage banks usually offer flexible rates or rates which are fixed for terms of five or ten years or longer and which can be adjusted at the end of that period. Mortgage banks will rarely lend more than 60 per cent of a property's value and have less flexible criteria than the commercial banks. There are no regulations as to maximum or minimum interest rates or charges which may be set by the banks. This means that the terms and conditions of loans can be freely negotiated and this field of banking is highly competitive. Loans financing the acquisition of property are usually secured (see section 7 for types of security) and are never made on an entirely non-recourse basis though single-asset companies may be set up as the borrowers. Banks have a close relationship with their borrowers, commonly having a member on the board, and their decision to lend will usually depend more on their relationship with their customers or assessment of their business than on the value of the security. Commercial banks will often lend more than mortgage banks and will either charge a higher rate of interest, or by reason of their relationship with their customer, maintain the same rate. They generally lend no more than 80 per cent of value.

6.2 Investment or equity finance

The stock market in Germany has been relatively underdeveloped, as a result of the traditionally close ties between many companies and their banks. This has meant it is particularly unusual for property companies to be listed. To rectify this, new laws and regulations have been passed recently and include guidelines requiring greater disclosure of company information and prohibitions against insider trading. Subsequent to these reforms, the level of stock market activity in Germany is expected to increase. As a corollary of the traditional organisation of the German money markets, the number of private investment opportunities, such as mutual funds and other investment funds, has traditionally been limited by the conservative stance of investors and by over-restrictive regulation. Deregulation measures have already been introduced and further restrictions are expected to be lifted in the near future.

6.3 Mezzanine or mixed funding

Mezzanine funding is common for the commercial banks due to the low level of funding by the mortgage banks who limit loans to 60 per cent of value. The commercial banks will provide the next tranche of borrowing either because of their strong relationship with the borrower or in exchange for an increased rate of interest. The banks will rarely take a share in the equity or value of the property.

6.4 Sale and lease-back

Companies wishing to realise their assets in order to release capital, or who wish to finance a new project, are increasingly resorting to sale and lease-back arrangements. The company negotiates the sale of the property to an investor, which will then grant the company a lease-back, enabling the investor to obtain an income from the property. Such arrangements require notarisation. The arrangement is not as popular as elsewhere.

6.5 Tax leasing

Tax incentives are at the heart of many investments particularly in areas such as Eastern Germany where the government has introduced high rates of tax deduction and depreciation. As individuals have more favourable tax treatment, it is common for investment funds to be made up of individuals, who may take on personal liability to increase the gearing of the fund, ie its ability to borrow and invest in tax subsidised property investments, eg shopping centres and offices, which are then let to business tenants. Tax leasing will be more popular where investment attracts above average rates of depreciation. In some cases, investments can be fully depreciated over 10 years, and up to 40 per cent can be allowed in the first year.

6.6 Other types of property finance

6.6.1 There are various other forms of property finance available to investors in Germany. Investors often make a loan to a property holding company (*Objektgesellschaft*), which makes the actual investment in the property. The holding company then deducts the interest paid on the loan from the rental income of the property. There are also closed-end property funds in the form of limited partnerships, which make use of imputed losses/deductions to reduce the tax charge. Open-end property funds are structured in such a way that management companies manage a separate fund of assets comprising both the cash contributed by the investors and the investments made by an investment company. Recent deregulation now enables an investment company to establish a special fund for a single or small group of investors. This type of funding has reduced the supervisory role of the banking authorities and is quite common. Investment in single-asset vehicles is also possible though these will not be listed on the stock exchange.

6.6.2 There are also financial leasing arrangements (*Leasingverträge*), for commercial and residential property investments, under which the lessor temporarily assigns the property to the lessee, and the lessor is relieved of the risks and liabilities connected with possible damage to the property. This type of arrangement is similar to a lease purchase agreement, and often includes an option to purchase. It is not necessarily tax driven, though it may have tax benefits, and should not be confused with the tax lease used in other countries.

6.7 Institutional investment

The institutions play a major part in property investment, but do not set the market standards in quite the same way as elsewhere. The life insurance companies, for example, will not only invest but lend on property. The institutions generally invest only in first class commercial property and not in residential or agricultural land.

6.8 Investors other than institutions

While there are no listed or other investment trusts as such, the banks and others operate investment schemes which offer units to the public which are not traded but bought in and sold by the operators of the scheme. Private investors are common and it should be remembered that no capital gains tax is chargeable on private property investments so long as the tax payer is not in the business of dealing in property.

7 FORMS OF SECURITY

Relationship banking is common, largely because the banks play a major part in industry as lenders, shareholders and as operators of proxies and powers of attorney for shareholders. It is not uncommon for bankers to be represented on the board particularly of the more major companies. Nevertheless most loans other than overdraft and working capital facilities are usually secured by mortgages, guarantees, or charges over moveables such as stock in trade.

7.1 Mortgages

7.1.1 There are two types of property securities in Germany, mortgages (*Hypotheken*) and land charges (*Grundschulden*). Mortgage loans are granted primarily by mortgage banks and savings banks but also by the commercial banks. The difference between a mortgage and a land charge is largely historical as different regions used one or the other and in a federal Germany both are now available. However, a mortgage may be validly created only as security for a specific obligation. The legal fate of the mortgage is connected to, and strictly dependent on, the fate of the obligation or claim itself and is therefore referred to as collateral (*akzessorisch*). Once that debt has been paid the mortgage falls away. The land charge, on the other hand, may be created independently of a specific claim or obligation and no personal liability on the part of the borrower arises unless a promissory note is issued. The land charge will survive repayment of the loan and it can be used again for another loan or by another creditor to whom it has been assigned. Often though a promissory note will be included in the land charge agreement. Although the mortgage is an important form of security, a land charge is often used by banks as it is independent from any secured debt, is more flexible and grants a higher level of security. As the land charge exists independently of the actual claim until the land charge is transferred back to the owner, this allows the continued use of a land charge as collateral even after the loan has been repaid by the borrower. This versatility has made land charges, which may be registered in the land register or incorporated into a deed, quite popular. If the land charge is also to be discharged this must be made clear when the loan is repaid.

7.1.2 Both contingent and future liabilities can be secured though unspecified sums are less easy to secure by mortgages than by land charges. It is customary to specify the actual amount lent rather than a maximum amount but for interest it is more usual to give a maximum rate creating the flexibility to charge a variable rate of interest. Priority for up to three years' interest over subsequent mortgage principal and interest is guaranteed, but after this the principal sum secured by a later mortgage may well take priority. It should be remembered that certain preferential debts (see 2.3) take priority even over registered mortgages. A judgment debt can be turned into a land charge by order of the court. The mortgage or land charge does not give the lender any direct rights over the property but various remedies can be obtained under the administration of the court. The court may order compulsory administration and this will ensure the income from the property is made available to the creditor or he can require a sale of the property by the court by public auction.

7.1.3 While both mortgages and land charges need to be registered, assignment can take the form of a registered transfer or an unregistered transfer of the mortgage, or land charge, certificate. No stamp duty or tax is charged on either type of security but notarial and registration costs of around one per cent are normal.

7.2 Floating and other charges

There is no concept of a floating, or general, charge or debenture. Each category of asset such as land, moveables and shares has to be separately secured by its own type of charge.

7.3 Performance bonds and guarantees

Guarantees are a common form of security. They do not need to be in writing but almost invariably are. Fixed bonds exist but are not a common form of security.

7.4 Credit insurance

While available, the insurance of another's obligations is sometimes difficult to obtain, particularly where it is most needed, and it does not play a major role as a form of security in property investments.

8 PLANNING AND BUILDING REGULATION

The most significant statutory provisions on the development and use of land are found in the Building Code (*Bauordnung*) of each state (*Land*) and in the Federal Planning Act (*Baugesetzbuch*). There is a very rigid distinction between zoning (planning) law regulations which are federal in nature, and permit regulations which are regulations issued by the state.

8.1 Planning authorities

Building controls are regulated by local authorities (building supervision authorities) which form part of the local administration, called the municipality (*Stadtverwaltung*) in urban areas and the *Landratsamt* in rural areas. The municipality is responsible for zoning plans in all areas. Permit decisions are taken by civil servants, whilst zoning plans are adopted by the local council which consists of elected representatives (*Gemeinderat*). The preparation of zoning plans is usually heavily influenced by local political considerations, although decisions whether or not to issue a permit are not. The building permit will include both the planning permission (which is not a political decision since matters of policy are decided at zoning plan level) and the building regulation approval (see 8.3 and 8.4).

8.2 Development plans

8.2.1 Development (land use) planning is a three-tier system consisting of centralised regional or state planning (*Regional und Landesplanung*), local preliminary (strategic) development plans and zoning plans. The lower level plans have to conform to higher level plans. Centralised regional or state planning exists in all the federal states but is organised differently. Regional or state development plans are the main source of guidance for municipalities from a higher source. As a general rule, regional and state development plans are only binding on lower level planning decisions of the administration, but not on private citizens and companies, and they do not affect permit decisions. The local authority is required to establish a preliminary development plan (*Flächennutzungsplan*) setting out the local authority's general policies in respect of the development and use of land covering the entire local authority area. Although preliminary development plans give a fairly reliable overview of the local authority's policies, they do not have the force of statute and do not give rise to legal expectations.

8.2.2 The more detailed 'zoning' plans (*Bebauungsplan*) are issued on the basis of the preliminary development plan. Zoning plans have the status of local bye-laws and may be appealed against in the superior administrative court (*Oberverwaltungsgericht*). They are binding on all parties, and will affect permit decisions. Where a zoning plan exists, the building permit must be granted if the project corresponds to the zoning plan and complies with the applicable building regulations. The applicant has a legally enforceable right to a permit where the proposal conforms with the plan; the only way the administration may take away this right is by initiating zoning plan proceedings (see 8.2.3). If a developer is able to demonstrate sufficient reason, minor exemptions may be granted from the zoning plan in particular cases. Where no zoning plan exists to regulate land use in a particular area, development which generally conforms to its surroundings will be permitted. Conformity is judged in terms of appearance and use. Where the proposed development does not conform to its surroundings, the decision will be negative. Outside existing settlements, development is not allowed if no zoning plan provides authorisation for it. There are a few exceptions, eg for agricultural developments.

8.2.3 To facilitate the grant of a permit which may not be issued under the existing land use or zoning plan, private investors may ask for a zoning plan to be issued or for an existing plan to be altered. The local authority is under no obligation to issue such a plan but if it does give the matter consideration, it will hold a public enquiry. Usually private developers can only make a successful zoning application for a major project if the local authority wants the specific development. The municipality is completely free to issue the requested zoning plan or not. It also has almost complete discretion regarding the contents of the plan, and will only be bound by regional or state development plans and the local preliminary development plan. The plan is only subject to legal control by the superior (state) authority of the *Land.* No administration fees are charged for the actual zoning plan application. However, the cost of drawing up these plans (including architect's fees and expert reports, eg concerning transport and environmental matters) is considerable and often paid for by the private developer. The distribution of costs, including development costs (eg road building, water and sewerage) is often agreed in 'planning contracts' concluded between the municipality and the developer. As the right is confined to making an application for a zoning plan, and does not extend to having the enquiry held or the plan adopted, there is no right of appeal if the municipality exercises its discretion to reject a zoning plan proposal, or if it refuses to issue or change a zoning plan.

8.2.4 There are also other restrictions on land use which may prevent private development proposals. These restrictions arise in respect of water protection zones (see 9.2), riverside areas, nature protection regulations (even in urban areas), urban reconstruction areas (*Sanierungsgebiete*), urban development areas (*Entwicklungsgebiete*) and buildings of special interest (see 8.5). In large towns, residential use must not be changed to other uses. Exemptions are difficult to obtain and must be applied for in addition to the building permit application for the change of use.

8.3 Planning control and procedures

Building permits (*Baugenehmigung*) or notifications are required for most types of development, including building, substantial alterations, demolition and material changes of use. However, minor construction, such as garden fences or small garden huts, will not require a permit. Mining activities and some types of industrial plant are subject to the requirement of a different type of permit. The building permit will include both the planning permission and the building regulation approval (see 8.4).

8.3.1 If a building permit is required, an application must be made to the local building permit authority. There is a fee payable by law upon issue of the permit. The applicant must have an interest in the land and it is common for the building authority to ask for the owner's written consent. The application for the permit needs to be detailed and will be prepared by an architect. Where there are a number of contentious issues to be resolved before a full application can be made, a preliminary building permit (*Bauvorbescheid*) may be applied for. For smaller projects, most states have replaced the building permit procedure by a notification procedure, although the applicable regulations in individual states vary considerably. The notification has to be as detailed, if not more so, than a permit application. If the building supervision authority considers there is a breach of the zoning or building regulations, it may issue a prohibition order within a prescribed period. If no prohibition order is issued within the prescribed period, construction may begin.

8.3.2 The building permit application has to be decided within three months where it relates to an 'ordinary' case, ie one not involving extremely complex issues. Since it is not actually possible to change or issue a zoning plan within a three-month period, the municipality may impose a development freeze for up to four years if it wishes to oppose a project which conforms to the existing zoning plan or its surroundings. In this way, the building permit application may be held in abeyance. If a building permission is refused, an appeals procedure exists. The same applies for conditions imposed which are unacceptable to the applicant.

8.3.3 The building permit attaches to the land and will be valid for an unlimited period of time, if construction begins within three years. Land use may be restricted or changed by altering the zoning plan, which has the effect of withdrawing an existing right to build, where no building permit has been issued. Compensation may be available where an existing permit had been issued in accordance with a zoning plan of less than seven years' standing, or where the owner of the property has incurred expenditure in detrimental reliance on the plan's validity.

8.3.4 Construction without a building permit or notification is a regulatory offence punishable by monetary fines. The same is true for changes to existing or approved buildings made without permission. This may lead to a prohibition order against the new use by the competent authority. The prohibition order may sometimes be supplemented by a compulsory demolition order or an order for reversion to the former use. The order is issued by the building supervision authority. There is a right of appeal against the building supervision authority's decision. The appeal has to be filed within a month. There is no time limit for enforcement in the event of a breach.

8.4 Building standards, control and supervision

Building standards are imposed when the building supervision authority considers the application for a building permit. Numerous technical standards must be complied with in the construction process, but they seldom lead to legal disputes. After completion of construction a final building inspection may (and in some cases must) be carried out by the building supervision authorities, which enables the local authority to monitor compliance.

8.5 Protection of buildings of special interest

Protection for buildings of special interest (usually of historic or architectural interest) is governed by state law. The regulations vary considerably from one state to another. In some states, buildings meeting the protection criteria are protected by law; in other states, protection is contingent upon protection orders or the entry of the building in a statutory list. In most states, such lists do exist, but they are not conclusive. Some buildings may be protected although they are not listed. A special consent is required from the protection authority for alteration and demolition; it will depend on the state and the circumstances of the case whether the special consent is included in the building permit. Obligations may be imposed to keep the buildings in good repair. All obligations to protect and preserve are limited by the principle of proportionality, and obligations which are not commensurate with the revenues from the building may not be imposed.

8.6 Expropriation or compulsory purchase, and compensation

Land may be expropriated only for public interest infrastructure or development projects. In principle, expropriation procedures may only be initiated by the government and public utilities. Compensation is based on market value and no premium is payable.

9 ENVIRONMENTAL MATTERS

Few areas of law in Germany over the last two decades have grown as fast or become as complex as that of environmental law. Among the principal reasons for such growth are the scarcity of environmental resources requiring a high degree of regulation in a densely populated country as well as heightened public awareness of the effects of pollution. Pollution control has an increasingly direct impact on the costs of any company basing its manufacturing operations in Germany. In addition, a buyer's liability for potentially contaminated land has become an important concern in the context of property transactions. The enforcement authority has broad powers to remedy pollution. It may issue clean-up or stop orders against the polluter, but also against the landowner, and in many cases also against the occupier. As a general rule, enforcement authorities will choose the party most suited to remedy the pollution of those potentially liable, which may or may not be the actual polluter.

9.1 Protection against atmospheric and noise pollution

9.1.1 The Pollution Control Act (*Bundes-Immissionsschutzgesetz*) regulates air and noise pollution. The statute provides for a two-tier system to regulate industrial plants: (a) those subject to administrative permits, and (b) those for which no pollution control permits are required. Industrial plant and large agricultural projects may require a permit under the Act; where a permit has been issued under the Act, there is no additional requirement to obtain a building permit under general planning law. The procedure for obtaining the permit according to the Act is complex, but where the substantive requirements are fulfilled, the competent authority must issue the permit. Maximum levels of pollution are set by detailed statutory regulations and conditions attached to permits. Noise from stationary sources is subject to the same legal rules as air pollution. The limit for noise depends on the zoning law status of the site and is regulated by statutory instrument.

9.1.2 A significant statutory restriction on the right of adjoining landowners to seek redress from a neighbouring source of pollution, is the requirement to tolerate emissions from neighbouring land to the extent that the use of the owner's land is not substantially affected. Even significant nuisances have to be tolerated if they conform to local custom and if prevention would be unreasonably expensive.

9.2 Water pollution

Protection against water pollution is regulated by the federal Water Act (*Wasserhaushaltsgesetz*) supplemented by detailed provisions in the water laws (*Wassergesetze*) enacted by each state (*Land*). These statutes regulate both rivers and ground water and the prevention of water pollution. The protection of ground water may be important, particularly if the land lies within a ground water protection zone (*Wasserschutzgebiet*). These zones are designated by statutory instrument; within such a zone, there may be severe restrictions on land use. The legal framework for 'direct' sewage disposal (into rivers) differs considerably from the regulations governing 'indirect' (ie via the public sewage system) disposal. In all states, direct disposal always requires a permit, whereas in most cases indirect disposal is not subject to any licensing procedure.

9.3 Waste storage and disposal

Waste storage and disposal were regulated in the federal Refuse Disposal Act (*Abfallgesetz*), which has now been replaced by the Integrated Economy Act 1996 (*Kreislaufwirtschaftsgesetz*), and the corresponding state statutes (*Abfallgesetze*). The Refuse Disposal Act is not normally relevant for private development of land. The local authorities are under an obligation to dispose of household waste but not commercial waste, and there are general duties to recycle waste. Specific permits are required for storage, disposal and treatment of waste, and specific duties are imposed upon those dealing with waste. Breaches often lead to criminal proceedings.

9.4 Contaminated land

9.4.1 Companies may be liable to pay very considerable clean-up costs in connection with soil contamination ordered by local authorities under public nuisance law. This type of liability may occur as a result of illegal dumping of hazardous waste, spills or leakage of hazardous substances such as oil, or may arise as a result of activity from contaminated industrial premises or landfill sites, even though the contamination may have been caused many years before. The local authority has the discretion to order the person responsible for the contamination, or the owner of the contaminated site, to clean up the site. If the clean-up must be carried out immediately in order to be effective, the authorities may proceed themselves and recover the full clean-up cost from the person responsible or the site owner, although as a general rule, the owner is responsible for the necessary clean-up measures, even if he can prove that he was not personally responsible for the pollution. In a few states, funds are available to pay for decontamination in specific, narrowly defined cases.

9.4.2 In the context of liability for clean-ups, potentially contaminated sites should be of concern to buyers. Although recent case law has established that contaminated soil triggering liability for clean-up is within the scope of the seller's warranties implied under statute, the buyer's remedies (repudiation of contract or reduction of the purchase price) are subject to a statutory period of limitation of one year after the transaction and the pollution may only become apparent much later. Prior to the acquisition, the buyer should investigate the history of the site. The enquiries undertaken will depend on circumstances and the former land use as well as information and warranties provided by the seller. Enquiries may include interviews with the competent administrative authorities about their site audits. The buyer should attempt to seek express warranties from the seller that no soil contamination has occurred. The seller is under an obligation to disclose any information regarding contamination if the buyer specifically asks him to do so. If no warranties can be obtained, the statutory period of limitation should at least be extended by agreement. Warranties do not affect the liability of the buyer as owner of the site but enable the buyer to repudiate the agreement or to obtain damages. Contamination registers are not yet regulated at federal level, but federal legislation is to be introduced soon. In most states, local authorities have begun to maintain registers listing contaminated land. These registers are quite reliable for cases of major contamination but are not conclusive.

9.5 Environmental impact assessments

Environmental impact assessments have been routinely established in the past as part of the planning and permission process (*Planfeststellungsverfahren*) for a number of projects such as hydroelectric power plants or waste disposal facilities. More commercial projects now require more specific and costly environmental impact assessments on the basis of the Environmental Impact Assessments Law 1990 (*Gesetz über die Umweltverträglichkeitsprüfung*), implementing EC Directive 85/33, intended to give the assessment more importance within the planning process. A specific, formal environmental assessment is required for major projects if a local development plan is issued (see section 8). The law implementing the directive follows the directive closely. Projects not requiring an impact assessment under the directive and the implementing legislation are in fact examined equally carefully.

10 DEVELOPMENT

10.1 Development projects, structures and vehicles

Private development projects usually involve construction by the owner of the property. Even professional developers often obtain title to the land. Larger projects usually involve a number of partners. Development is frequently financed by the developer's own funds, but loan finance granted by banks or equity finance is also used. Industrial development is more often financed by the developer's own funds, whereas commercial (retail) and other developments are often financed by equity raised from third parties. In the case of larger projects requiring zoning plans (see 8.2), it has become increasingly common for the local authority and the private landowner/developer involved to conclude contracts with each other. Generally, the construction project is the sole responsibility of the private partner, whereas the development of the land and public planning procedures are the joint responsibility of both parties. These contracts serve to give the local authority a share in the development profits, although this practice is illegal in most cases. Development without an identified end-user or occupier used to be common, but has become less so in recent years.

10.2 Building contracts

10.2.1 Typical forms of building contract

The two most typical forms of building contract used are the general contractor agreement and the individual contract with a building contractor or tradesman which is very common. They can be fixed in price or allow for variation in price. Under a general contractor agreement, the contractor performing the work is under the general obligation to construct and complete the building. He then brings in the necessary subcontractors. Each subcontractor is responsible for the work he undertakes. The full responsibility for construction remains with the main contractor. Sometimes, the contractor also assumes responsibility for the design. In the case of individual contracts, the developer awards the various contracts directly. Every contractor is responsible for his own work and the developer assumes responsibility for the whole construction.

10.2.2 Common terms

For larger building contracts, it is usual to agree that payments will be based on the progress of construction of the building. Only in exceptional cases do other arrangements for payment exist, eg on a monthly basis. Under the contract, five to ten per cent of the total amount to be paid is normally retained from interim and final payments to secure completion and making good of defects. Most contracts set a date for completion of the work. This date may be extended only on the grounds of force majeure, official strikes, reasons caused by the principal/building owner, or exceptionally bad weather. Most contracts contain a penalty clause which imposes fines on the subcontractor or his staff, eg to the amount of one per cent of the fixed price per week for the delay in the event of the subcontractor's failure to meet the deadline.

However, the penalty clause will only be valid if a maximum ceiling of fines (up to 10 per cent of the total price of the contract) has previously been agreed upon. An employer can vary the original design or works if so agreed in the contract. The builder, often represented by the architect, certifies completion. For important buildings, there is often a technical completion inspection before the final contractual completion inspection. The builder may terminate the contract at any time, but the employer is only entitled to do so for important reasons (*wichtiger Grund*), eg for default.

10.2.3 Standard form of contracts

Building contracts are regulated by the Civil Code. The contracting parties may expressly agree to incorporate the statutory compilation of legal rules governing building contracts (*VOB*) into the contract. If the parties do not incorporate the *VOB*, only the general provisions of the Civil Code (*BGB*) apply. No common form of building contract exists.

10.2.4 Appointment of the professional team

Professional advisers, eg architects, mechanical and electrical, civil and structural engineers, building or quantity surveyors often propose standard terms for their contracts. Most of these standard terms are prepared by their own professional associations. These terms favour the professional advisers rather than the builders. The contracts normally specify the personnel to be engaged and a fixed or percentage price for the job, or an hourly rate on a time charge basis. The compensation mostly depends on the building costs and fees as governed in a statutory fee schedule (*HOAI*, see 10.7).

10.3 Those involved and their roles

10.3.1 The owner generally assumes the role of the developer. Where there is a developer, he develops the property and then immediately resells it to an investor. Often the property is sold before it has been developed. It is unusual to involve a special project manager in addition to the developer.

10.3.2 Other professionals taking part in a development project include the various tradesmen (electricians, plumbers, carpenters, and the like) and employees of the construction companies who will usually only perform the basic construction work. Various additional jobs are then distributed to the specialist subcontractors. The architect, appointed by the developer, plays an important role in building projects. He not only draws up the building plans, but also deals with the building permit application, to the extent that this is not taken care of by a lawyer, frequently awards the building contracts, and supervises and coordinates the construction activities. Although the architect does not take responsibility for the entire range of subsidiary activity, he will often find himself liable for all defects. Normally in a general contract there is no contractual relationship between the subcontractor and the employer. Technical engineers are generally brought in to undertake and complete the technical work and to plan installations, such as heating and electrical systems. In most cases, there is one individual who is principally responsible for design and construction. The responsibilities are only fragmented for bigger buildings, where special architects are responsible for the internal architecture.

10.4 Defects and remedies

10.4.1 Remedies of employer in respect of defects in design and materials

There is a statutory warranty period of five years for structural defects. In contracts governed by the *VOB* (see 10.2.3), this period is reduced to two years for most parts of the building; for other parts, eg electronic installations, the period will extend for a maximum of one year. In respect of defects in design, workmanship and materials, the employer's most effective remedy is to retain the fees. Generally, the employer only has a direct remedy against his contractor and not against subcontractors and suppliers.

10.4.2 Remedies of subsequent owners/occupiers other than the contractual employer

Where newly developed land is sold, the buyer can rely on warranties with respect to visible or latent construction defects. Subsequent owners and occupiers only have direct remedies against the person with whom they contracted, but not against the developer, unless the first buyer assigned his own remedies against the developer to the subsequent owner. Often such assignments of remedies are found in contracts between subsequent owners and financiers. There is a direct contract or warranty between all such parties. Clauses excluding warranties for new construction and an exclusion of warranties as to defects fraudulently concealed are void under the General Terms of Business Law (*AGBG*). The limitation period for warranty claims for newly developed property is five years or, under certain circumstances, two years after takeover. Warranties for undeveloped property and for land that is not newly developed are subject to a statutory limitation period of one year after purchase. Again, these can only be enforced against the contractor/seller.

10.5 Defects insurance

The principal's legal warranty enables him to bring an action against the contractor for any defects in the building work. The contractor can produce bank guarantees to secure remedy of these defects but only where this is expressly agreed in the contract. Insurance in respect of defects in workmanship and materials is unusual. Only architects and engineers regularly take out insurance against defects they are liable for, and such insurance includes the cost of remedying the defects. There are various limitations which will depend on building costs. However, general terms (*Allgemeine Haftpflicht-Bedingungen, AHB*) exclude payments in many cases. Nevertheless, even such insurance does not affect the employer's right to claim against architects for defects.

10.6 Copyright

The copyright in the design of the building will remain that of the architect and will be protected by copyright law. Subsequent changes to major building projects may often only be made with the architect's approval, which can be costly.

10.7 Fees

The architects' and engineers' fees are governed by a statutory fee schedule (*HOAI*). A certain amount of flexibility is permitted when negotiating fees, but these may not go above or below the parameters set down in the statutory schedule. If the architect is working with the principal on a number of projects over a period of time, it is common practice in some cases to negotiate lower fees. However, contracts which purport to set such fees in advance are invalid. The architect can request the minimum *HOAI* fee, even if he has previously agreed on a lower fee. In general, the fees as determined by the *HOAI* represent a percentage of the value of the building work. Overall professional fees are between 10 and 15 per cent.

10.8 Taxes

Services provided by architects and building contractors are subject to value added tax (VAT), at the German present standard rate of 15 per cent. VAT may only be reclaimed if the property is let for the purposes of tax turnover.

11 TAXES

11.1 Corporation tax

In Germany, any resident corporation is subject to German corporate income tax with respect to its worldwide income unless a tax treaty exempts particular items of income from German taxation. A corporation qualifies as a resident if it maintains either its statutory seat as defined in the articles of association or its actual principal place of business within Germany. A foreign corporation will be treated as resident in Germany if it transfers its principal place of business to Germany. A non-resident company is subject to limited corporate tax liability (see 11.1.1).

11.1.1 Tax rates

The rate of corporation tax for the financial year (which may or may not be identical with the calendar year depending on the local tax authority) is calculated at a rate of 45 per cent on retained earnings and 30 per cent on distributed profits regardless of the size of the company and the amount of taxable profit. Corporations with limited tax liability are subject to a rate of

42 per cent. There is a local trade income tax (described at 11.9) which is deductible for corporation tax purposes.

11.1.2 Computation and administration

In calculating its profits, a company can generally deduct all expenses incurred for the purposes of the trade of the company irrespective of whether they are necessary, appropriate, customary or useful. However, in the case of related parties such expenses will be very closely scrutinised by the tax authorities as to whether they meet arm's length standards. In addition, certain expenditure (such as organisational expenses incurred in connection with the organisation and its incorporation) is only deductible if, according to the articles of association, such expenses have to be borne by the corporation. Other expenses (such as income tax, wealth taxes, fines and half of the remuneration paid to members of the supervisory board) are specifically disallowed, and expenses such as business gifts are only deductible up to a certain amount. The tax assessment is carried out by the local tax authorities (*Finanzamt*). The assessment system is based upon information in the tax returns provided by the tax payer. If the tax payer does not agree with the tax assessment, there is a right of objection to the local tax authority provided this is done within a month of issuance of the tax assessment notice. If the local tax authority dismisses the tax payer's objections, he has a right of appeal to the relevant tax court (*Finanzgericht*) and to the federal tax court (*Bundesfinanzhof*). While it is open to a tax payer to arrange his affairs in such a way as to minimise tax, tax avoidance, any unlawful non-payment or evasion of tax is a criminal offence.

11.1.3 Depreciation and capital allowances

Depreciation allowances may be claimed for tax purposes but only if the same or higher depreciation allowances are used for financial reporting purposes. On the other hand, tax law restricts the options available to the corporation under generally recognised accounting principles where such rules would permit the corporation to understate its profits and thus to reduce its taxable income. Acquisition and construction costs are capitalised and written-off over the expected lifetime of the investment. Therefore the depreciation rate and period depends on the type of property. Land is not depreciable. Financing, maintenance and administration costs are immediately deductible items. Depreciation for improvements to land is calculated according to the purchase and construction cost of the building. Buildings may generally be depreciated at a fixed rate of two per cent over a period of 50 years. Higher rates apply to different categories of building, with factories having the highest general rate of 10 per cent for the first four years after construction. The Development Area Law (*Fördergebietsgesetz*) makes special allowances for the depreciation of immoveable assets of up to 50 per cent if certain preconditions are met (see 12.2).

11.1.4 Withholding tax

Under certain circumstances, withholding taxes may be levied on the commercial profits of non-residents not permanently established in Germany. There is a 25 per cent withholding tax on certain types of interest income, which is, however, generally waived under most tax treaties. Dividends are subject to 25 per cent withholding tax, although this is also usually waived under the provisions of double taxation treaties. There is no withholding tax on income from rented property.

11.2 Taxes on development value

There are no taxes on development value.

11.3 Taxes on capital gains

If the property sold is a business investment, profits realised on sale are treated as current profits subject to tax levied on ordinary income. Under certain circumstances, a roll-over provision exists, ie taxation of a capital gain may be deferred by transferring the hidden reserves disclosed to a substitute asset. If property is privately held, profits realised on sale are not subject to income tax, unless the sale qualifies as a speculative transaction. A transaction is deemed to be speculative where the period between the acquisition and the sale of the property is less than two years. In addition a land owner is subject to trade tax if the income from the property forms part of his business income. There is no indexation relief.

11.4 Taxes on owner of property

Individuals and corporations are subject to inheritance tax when passing or receiving property by way of gift or inheritance on death. The tax rates vary between 5 and 50 per cent. Land tax (*Grundsteuer*) is a recurring tax levied by local authorities on all land in their district, whether or not it is developed. The basis of assessment is the net tax worth (*Einheitswert*) and not the market value. The value is then multiplied by a factor fixed by the local authorities, which varies between 0.5 per cent and 1.4 per cent. Land tax is a deductible item when determining the net income for corporation tax purposes.

11.5 Taxes on occupier

There are no taxes on the occupier or tenant of a parcel of land, but there are municipal charges imposed on occupiers of property, eg for the provision of amenities in the area such as refuse collection.

11.6 Taxes on land transfer

Property transactions are subject to a land transfer tax at a rate of 3.5 per cent. The basis of assessment is usually the stated purchase price. The acquisition of all of the shares in a company owning land is also subject to the land transfer tax. The basis of assessment in this case is 12.5 times the annual rent for the property. As a general rule, the tax worth is much lower than the fair market value.

11.7 Wealth taxes

Since 1997 wealth tax has been abolished.

11.8 Value added tax

In general, all businesses providing goods or services including construction generating turnover in excess of a certain value are required to register with the local tax authorities and charge value added tax (VAT) to customers on the value of those supplies at a rate of 15 per cent. This is a uniform rate. A lower rate of seven per cent applies to businesses providing certain goods like agricultural products, books and newspapers. Some supplies are exempt from VAT. Businesses are accountable to the local tax authority, who administer VAT, for the tax they collect but are allowed to deduct from this amount the VAT paid on supplies received. They must account to the local tax authorities at the end of each VAT accounting period, usually being the tenth day of each calendar month. For rights of appeal, see 11.1.2. In principle, both the letting and the sale of property are exempt from VAT. A landlord has the option of waiving the VAT exemption, if the property is not residential and is let to another business for business purposes.

11.9 Local and other taxes

The land tax levied by the local authorities on all land in their district is described at 11.4. Municipalities charge trade income tax on business income at a rate varying between 11 and 20 per cent. This is deducted for corporation tax purposes.

12 GRANTS AND INCENTIVES

12.1 Subsidies, grants and loans

A large number of federal, state and local governmental grants and other types of financial aid are available to companies, businesses and individuals. They are granted on the basis of the fulfilment of substantive requirements laid down in the particular subsidy programme, the availability of public funds and the degree of economic need. Most subsidies are granted on a discretionary basis. Subsidies are granted not only by federal, state and local administration, but also by other authorities such as the Bank Institute for Reconstruction Activities (*Kreditanstalt für Wiederaufbau*)

12.1.1 Economically, the *Gesetz über die Gemeinschaftsaufgabe* is the most important subsidy programme. Its aim is the promotion of less developed areas (mainly, but not exclusively, located in East Germany). The subsidies are usually granted in the form of direct financial assistance. The maximum assistance lies between 10 and 35 per cent of the eligible costs of the investment and is dependent upon the type and the geographic area of investment. Only investment in assets (including property) is subsidised, and the owner must use these assets for commercial purposes. Commercial properties to be let to third parties are not eligible under the subsidy programme.

12.1.2 In most states, subsidies are also available for the renovation of buildings of historical interest.

12.1.3 Other subsidy programmes are designed to encourage technology, research and development, export oriented activities, small and medium-sized enterprises and environmental investments.

12.2 Tax allowances and reliefs

Certain types of immoveable assets in Eastern Germany qualify for tax allowances for special depreciation pursuant to the Development Area Law (*Fördergebietsgesetz*). The depreciation covers up to 40 per cent of the acquisition costs and may be claimed for the year in which the acquisition was made. Tax allowances for special depreciation are also granted for the renovation of buildings of special interest and, to a lesser degree, of residential accommodation. The rules are frequently changed.

12.3 Other public schemes and incentives

Residential property is subsidised by differing programmes from state to state. There are no other public schemes and incentives worthy of note.

13 COMPANIES AND BUSINESS ENTITIES

13.1 Limited companies and stock corporations

There are two types of companies: the private limited liability company (*Gesellschaft mit beschränkter Haftung*, *GmbH*) and the public limited liability company (*Aktiengesellschaft*, *AG*). The liabilities towards the creditors are limited to the company's assets. The shareholders' own assets may not be exempt from the creditors' attachment in some very strictly defined cases. However, at least one shareholder is personally liable for the partnership limited by shares (*Kommanditgesellschaft aufAktien*), a special type of German public limited company. The *GmbH* is the most widely used corporate entity in Germany, and allows a business to be conducted with the benefit of limited liability, without a complex corporate structure, as with an *AG*. It is the most convenient type of company for a business requiring a small amount of capital and relatively few shareholders. Its articles of association (there is no distinction from the memorandum in German law) must be adopted by a resolution recorded before a notary and filed for registration with the commercial register which is open to public inspection. The overwhelming majority of German subsidiaries of foreign corporations are *GmbHs*; the flexibility of the *GmbH* ensures that its statutes can be more specifically tailored to the shareholders' requirements.

13.1.1 Public limited liability companies (*AGs*) have to comply with a number of conditions. The minimum share capital is DM100,000, 25 per cent of which must be paid up. Share certificates must have a nominal value of at least DM5. The shares are negotiable securities which may be admitted to stock exchange listing and trading on one or all of the eight German stock exchanges. The Stock Exchange Act (*Börsengesetz*) and the Admission to the Stock Exchange Decree (*Börsenzulassungsverordnung*) set out the stock exchange admission requirements (in particular as to size and duration of the minimum share issue price).

13.1.2 Once the company is registered, it becomes a separate legal person from its shareholders and directors. Therefore the company disposes of its own income, which is taxed as income of the corporation and not of the shareholders. German company law does not recognise the ultra vires doctrine, so that once a *GmbH* or *AG* is registered, it has the same legal powers as any natural person. This explains why a German company's articles can do without lengthy objects clauses; a brief general description of its intended activities will be sufficient.

13.2 Partnerships

There are four main types of partnerships: the civil law partnership (*BGB Gesellschaft*), the general partnership (*Offene Handelsgesellschaft*), the limited partnership (*Kommanditgesellschaft*), and the silent partnership (*Stille Gesellschaft*). In addition, there is the special limited partnership (*GmbH & Co KG*). This is of considerable importance.

13.2.1 Civil law partnership

The civil law partnership is the basic model for partnership. It may be set up for any common legal purpose pursued jointly by the partners, except for commercial purposes. No formal incorporation procedure is necessary and there is no requirement to pay mandatory capital or any other monetary contribution. It is used to set up professional firms, building and construction partnerships, and by banks syndicating loans. The partners are free to determine whether voting requires unanimity, or whether the partners represent the partnership individually or jointly. There are no company name and no registration requirements. All partners are jointly and severally liable to third parties when they act jointly. A partnership is dissolved upon achievement of the common purpose. It is also dissolved upon notice of resignation of a partner, or by the bankruptcy or death of a partner, unless the partnership agreement provides otherwise, or if the other partners decide to continue.

13.2.2 Commercial partnerships

13.2.2.1 The law recognises two types of commercial partnerships: the general partnership and the limited partnership. The general partnership (*OHG*) consists of two or more general partners with unlimited liability agreeing to carry on a commercial undertaking for profit under a common firm name. Although the *OHG* is not a legal person, it acts under a firm name, may acquire property, and may sue and be sued before the courts. The *OHG* must also be registered in the commercial register. Title to the assets of the partnership vests in the partners jointly. Unless the partnership agreement provides otherwise, the *OHG* is dissolved upon expiry of a specific term, by decision of the partners, or by bankruptcy or death of a partner. All income from the *OHG* is taxed as personal income of the partners.

13.2.2.2 The second type of commercial partnership is the limited partnership (*KG*) with at least one general partner (*Komplementär*) and at least one partner (*Kommanditist*) who is liable only to the amount of his agreed contribution. The *KG* carries on business under a firm name and the rules governing general partners apply, with the exception of a number of specific provisions regarding the limited partner. Thus, the *KG* is not a legal person, but may, under its firm name, acquire property and sue and be sued before the courts. The name of the partnership, the names of the partners, and the amount of the contribution of each limited partner must be entered in the commercial register.

13.2.2.3 The special limited partnership (*GmbH & Co KG*) is not a specific partnership form, but a limited partnership where the general partner is a limited liability company (*GmbH*), limiting the general partner's liability. Tax law favours the *GmbH & Co KG*. The majority of limited partnerships are structured as *GmbH & Co KG*s.

13.2.3 Silent partnerships

In a silent partnership (*Stille Gesellschaft*), a person participates in the business carried on by another by making a financial or in kind contribution to the partnership, but title to all assets will be vested in the active partner. Therefore, only the active partner conducts the business in his own name, has rights and incurs liabilities with regard to third parties. Silent partnerships need not be disclosed and are effectively a legal arrangement combining elements of a loan with those of a commercial partnership. The undisclosed partner has no right to management, but certain control and inspection rights are granted. He shares in both profits and losses of the business, although his risk is limited to the amount of his contribution. However, the partnership agreement may limit or even exclude the undisclosed partner's liability to share the losses.

13.3 Other types of business associations

There are other legal entities which are used in specific fields of commercial activity, such as mining companies, mutual insurance companies, cooperatives, and building loan associations. Note should be made in particular of the position of joint ventures.

13.3.1 Joint ventures

Joint ventures between foreign and German companies are quite common. The joint venture will usually consist of two companies forming a joint venture enterprise for the purpose of carrying on a particular business activity. There are no specific German legal provisions dealing with joint ventures, although the normal rules governing partnerships and companies must be followed. Normally, the joint venture agreement provides for the financial contributions of each party, the division of profits, the duration of the joint venture, and the reasons for the termination and winding up of the joint venture.

14 INTERNATIONAL

14.1 Restrictions or consents required for inward investment

There are no direct restraints on investments by foreign entities in Germany although there are certain special provisions regarding companies in the service industry (such as banks) and regarding employment and restrictions on immigration. Although restrictions may theoretically be imposed on foreign entities on the purchase of land, ships, companies, securities, and other property under the Foreign Trade Act, such restrictions are actually of no practical relevance, and are hardly ever imposed.

14.2 Exchange controls

The German currency is freely convertible into other currencies, although certain reporting requirements may be imposed (see 14.4).

14.3 Restrictions and registrations on carrying on business

To all intents and purposes there are no restrictions imposed upon foreign entities carrying on business in Germany. Both foreign and German business entities must comply with normal legal requirements for carrying on business, such as registration with the tax authorities.

14.4 Repatriation of income and proceeds of property trading and development

There are practically no restraints on repatriation of income and proceeds abroad. There are, however, reporting requirements for all sales and liquidations of foreign-controlled companies and for the re-transfer of credit to foreigners, if the amounts exceed DM20,000 in any calendar year. In addition to this, the establishment or acquisition of a company, branch office, or any other business operated by non-residents, or the capitalisation of such a business, must be reported if it exceeds DM20,000 in any calendar year. For countries within the EU, all restrictions on the transfer of capital have been abolished.

14.5 Withholding taxes

Withholding taxes have been referred to at 11.1.4 and there are no withholding taxes on income from rented properties.

14.6 Double taxation relief

Germany has double taxation treaties with a large number of countries, including all EU member states and the United States.

CHAPTER 8

Greece

S Karaiskakis, C Metaxotou, I Anastassopoulou, A Anghelakos, A Katsiavou, M Sergakis, H Hristakou

Partners, Vgenopoulos & Partners, Athens

CONTENTS

1 OWNERSHIP OF LAND 251
2 OTHER INTERESTS IN LAND 253
3 TITLE TO LAND 256
4 TRANSACTIONS IN LAND 257
5 LEASES AND OCCUPATIONAL RIGHTS 260
6 FINANCE AND INVESTMENT SOURCES 263
7 FORMS OF SECURITY 265
8 PLANNING AND BUILDING REGULATION 267
9 ENVIRONMENTAL MATTERS 270
10 DEVELOPMENT 273
11 TAXES 277
12 GRANTS AND INCENTIVES 280
13 COMPANIES AND BUSINESS ENTITIES 281
14 INTERNATIONAL 283

CHAPTER 8

Greece

1 OWNERSHIP OF LAND

Property law is principally regulated by the Greek Civil Code which, with roots in Roman-Byzantine law, has been influenced by the Napoleonic Code, and is based on the distinction between moveables and immoveables. A principle of major importance in property law is the 'numerus clausus' principle, under which the number and content of real rights are strictly limited. Under the Civil Code, the only real rights are ownership; personal and predial servitudes; pledge and mortgage. These rights are the only ones recognised by law, they cannot be altered or added to. Greek legislation does not provide a definition of ownership. Nevertheless it is possible to determine the nature of ownership from the Civil Code provisions on the concepts of real rights and powers of ownership.

1.1 Types of ownership

1.1.1 Absolute ownership

Ownership (*kyriotita*) establishes direct, absolute and unconditional control over land. The owner is entitled to dispose of the land as he wishes and to prevent others from carrying out any act in relation to it, as long as the rights of third parties and the provisions of law are not infringed. Any thing which cannot be separated from the land without either causing a material change in use or causing damage, forms part of the land. This means that buildings (generally) or mineral substances will not be the subject of separate rights, although a permit is required for mining. However, anything attached to the ground or to a building, which is not intended to become a component of the land and is merely intended to serve a temporary purpose, can be the subject of a separate real right. An owner may not hinder a third party from performing an act above or under the soil, provided that it is not detrimental to the owner's interests.

1.1.2 Leasehold

There is no concept of limited or leasehold ownership as recognised in common law jurisdictions. Leases, or tenancy agreements, are regulated by contractual arrangements, and therefore grant mere rights in personam, not an interest in land. The landlord gives the tenant the (usually exclusive) use of property for a specific period of time in exchange for a consideration (the rent), payable by the tenant. Lease agreements are usually fully transferable provided that there is consent. For further information, see section 5.

1.1.3 Joint ownership

Joint ownership (*synkiorita*) exists when two or more persons enjoy ownership over property held in common, in indivisible equal parts. Joint ownership may arise by voluntary agreement or implication of law, eg in the event of intestacy. The joint property can be severed either by common consent (if the property can be physically divided) or, in case of a disagreement, by way of a court decision. However, a joint owner may freely transfer or encumber his right and the remaining joint owners do not have a legal right of pre-emption. Each of the joint owners has the right to use the property, to the extent that it does not impede the common use by the remaining owners, and to take necessary maintenance measures without the consent of the remaining owners.

1.1.4 Condominia and timeshares

1.1.4.1 Condominia are usually governed by a combination of provisions on horizontal and vertical ownership. Horizontal ownership (*orizontia idioktisia*) is a separate category of ownership and is established contractually by notarial deed. It provides the owner with an exclusive right over a floor or part of it, such as an apartment or an office, and allows joint ownership over the soil upon which the building has been erected. This includes joint ownership and rights of use of the common parts such as halls, car parks, access ways, lifts and staircases. Vertical ownership (*katheti idioktisia*), also established contractually by notarial deed, gives joint ownership over the common parts such as open surfaces whilst the owner retains separate ownership of his own building. Condominia rules are considered predial servitudes (see 2.1.1) and are concluded by notarial deed. They often prohibit changes in the main structure of the buildings, but may also impose restrictions on the use of the properties to preserve their character (eg residential or commercial). In cases where no agreement exists between the joint owners in horizontal or vertical properties, the rights and obligations are implied by law. Expenses are apportioned in accordance with the value of the separately owned property.

1.1.4.2 Under a time-share agreement the grantee is granted the use of an apartment or room and any relevant services, in a tourist resort for a specific annual period during the term of the agreement which can vary between 5 and 60 years. The grantee is obliged to pay the agreed price in a lump sum, in addition to annual fees (for the maintenance of the resort and the services rendered). The agreement is concluded by notarial deed which must be registered at the land register of the area where the resort is situated.

1.2 Legal and beneficial ownership

The law does not recognise the division between legal title and beneficial enjoyment.

1.3 Restrictions on ownership and dealing

1.3.1 The constitution places property 'under the protection of the state' and therefore property rights may be suspended, if necessary, for reasons of 'public benefit', eg the restriction on the enjoyment of private forests or property near national frontiers (see 14.1); the public authorities' right to expropriate or confiscate property (see 8.6); and the imposition of various planning restrictions (see section 8). Ownership may also be restricted by certain provisions of private law such as neighbourhood restrictions, where the legislation intervenes to secure the peaceful co-existence of adjoining owners, eg the owner of land must tolerate the emission of smoke, heat or noise from a neighbouring immoveable, as long as the use of his property is not substantially impeded or the emissions are widespread. (For restrictions on acquisition of ownership by non-residents, see 14.1.) Ownership may also be restricted by rights of third parties, eg by predial and personal servitudes (see 2.1). Such charges on the land should be regarded as restrictions on the use of the land, since such servitudes do not confer rights of separate or concurrent ownership.

1.3.2 There are various restrictions on the disposal of land which depend either on the nature of the land itself or on the transferor or transferee. Transfers of agricultural land in excess of 250,000 square metres to a single owner are not permitted unless permission is granted by the Ministry of Agriculture. Furthermore, no transfer of part of the land is allowed unless a building permit is capable of being granted over the part sold as well as the remaining part. The state, municipal authorities, charities, monasteries and various public legal entities may only take part in land and property transactions under specific statutory procedures. Tax legislation restricts the disposal of property if specific income tax certificates have not been issued and attached to the notarial deed. There are public pre-emption rights for forest land of over 50,000 square metres. For private rights of pre-emption, see 2.4.

1.4 Adverse possession or acquisitive prescription

Under acquisitive prescription, a person who is in possession of land acquires ownership after 10 years if he is in possession with lawful title and in good faith; or after 20 years, if he is in bad faith.

2 OTHER INTERESTS IN LAND

There are interests creating rights less than absolute ownership or possession. These include predial servitudes such as rights of way or rights of light, and personal servitudes, such as usufruct and rights of habitation. These rights are private and are all fairly common.

2.1 Servitudes or easements, usufruct, building and dwelling rights

2.1.1 Servitudes or easements

Servitudes (*doulies*) are interests in land conferring a right over land (the servient tenement) in favour either of other land (the dominant tenement) or in favour of a specific person(s). They are established by notarial contract, will or acquisitive prescription (see 1.4) and require registration in order to be valid. Predial servitudes over land grant a benefit in favour of other land. The owner of the servient tenement either accepts some use of his property by the owner of the dominant tenement or abstains from certain activities which he would otherwise be entitled to perform. Examples include rights of way and drainage; timber and grazing rights might fall into this category, although they are more usually contractual rights. Like ownership, they can be lost by continuous non-use for a period of 20 years.

2.1.2 Usufruct

The usufruct is categorised as a personal servitude as it is imposed over land in favour of a particular person and not in favour of other land. A usufruct is a real right allowing the usufructuary to make full use of land belonging to another and take all the benefits as if he were the owner, while remaining under an obligation to preserve its substance and to restore the land to its original state at the end of the usufruct. It is a right of limited duration. There is theoretically no maximum in the duration of a usufruct and periods ranging from 10 to 30 years are common as are those lasting for the lifetime of the usufructuary. The bare owner of the property subject to the usufruct has no physical enjoyment of the property; however he has the right to transfer or mortgage it (at a lesser value than if he had full use of the property). Usufruct is created by contract, will, acquisitive prescription or court decision and binds third parties. If usufruct is created by will, contract or court decision, it must be registered. Subject to other agreement usufruct is not transferable, but in any event it may not be transferred for a period exceeding the period of the initial usufruct.

2.1.3 Building and dwelling rights

The habitation right is a personal servitude granting the beneficiary the exclusive real right to use as his residence a building or apartment belonging to another. The beneficiary is akin to a tenant or life tenant. The general provisions governing usufruct apply to habitation. Habitation is a right granted with or without consideration.

2.2 Restrictions on use and other restrictions

Restrictions on the use of land can be entered into between two or more owners, eg flats in the same building (horizontal ownership), or buildings on the same land (vertical ownership). These restrictions will be enforceable by and between successive owners. These rights are in effect a category of predial servitude over the property affected and can be removed by agreement. Like all servitudes they do not have a set maximum duration. In order to be valid such agreements must be made by notarial deed and must be registered. Predial servitudes are commented on in detail at 2.1.1. Public law restrictions under planning and other legislation are commented on in section 8.

2.3 Private mortgages and charges

Monetary liabilities can be secured on land in a number of ways. A private mortgage is a real right of security established over another's property with the purpose of securing a monetary obligation. Mortgages can be either legal, judicial or conventional, ie brought about by the law, by the decision of a court or by the will of a private party. See section 7 where mortgages are dealt with in more detail. A consensual mortgage granted by the buyer to the seller is an agreement that a mortgage will attach to the land for the unpaid purchase price. See also 2.5 for the creation of public charges over land to secure debts.

2.4 Contracts and options

The law recognises both binding preliminary contracts and options. In a preliminary contract, which in the case of land must be created by way of notarial deed, the parties undertake the obligation to enter into a final purchase and sale contract in the future. Although the preliminary contract is not registered, the buyer may apply for a court order obliging the seller to sell the property. Under an option, one party may enforce the final agreement to purchase by way of a unilateral declaration contained in a notarial deed addressed to the other party, and registered in the land register, without the need for any involvement by the courts. So a lease agreement which must be in the form of a notarial deed may provide that during the term of the tenancy the tenant may purchase the tenanted property by way of a sole unilateral declaration by the tenant to the landlord/owner.

2.5 Public or municipal charges

There are a number of financial charges imposed on land to protect the rights of municipal authorities and to recover payment for municipal services such as public lighting and cleaning. The state has the right to create a mortgage or attachment over property of those who owe taxes, levies, or duties according to the provisions of the code of collection of public revenues. See further section 11.

2.6 Liabilities attaching to land

There are various liabilities imposed by specific provisions of the Civil Code on the owner or usufructuary of land for damage caused to third parties as a result of the collapse or negligent repair of a building (see 8.5 for the obligations imposed upon owners of listed buildings). Liability resulting from taxation is dealt with in section 11. The Civil Code also provides for liability in nuisance for unreasonable use of one's land to the prejudice of an adjoining owner or neighbour and for emissions of smoke, soot, vibrations and excessive noise which may prejudice another's enjoyment of his land.

2.7 Legal and beneficial interests

The Civil Code does not recognise a distinction between legal and beneficial interests.

2.8 Protection of interests

Ownership can be protected in various ways. Some interests in land are registered (eg interests deriving from contractual acquisition or ownership or other real rights); but there are rights which can be enforced without being registered, eg the rights of acquisitive prescription.

2.9 Priority of interests

Priority of registrable interests in land depends upon the date of their registration. However, there are interests such as acquisitive prescription which do not require registration, in which the date of the acquisition of the interest will determine priority. The date of registration of a mortgage determines priority. Mortgages registered on the same day are satisfied on a pro rata basis.

3 TITLE TO LAND

3.1 Proof of title

The only way to establish title to land is by registration in the land register combined with an inspection which will usually cover the previous 20 years. It is necessary to notarise and register the agreement in order to create, transfer or cancel any real right over land. In general, leases longer than nine years must also be drawn up as a notarial deed and registered to be valid against third parties. Non-registration will prevent the transfer of ownership and the creation or extinction of any real right taking effect. Registers are open to the public.

3.2 Land registers

Land registers are under the supervision of the Ministry of Justice and district land register archives and files are kept locally. There are two types of land registrars: salaried and non-salaried. The state pays a fixed salary to the former, and the latter's fees are a specific percentage of the registration fees.

3.2.1 Plans

The land registers are organised on the basis of an alphabetical list of property owners, although there are a few specific areas where it is possible to search by reference to the land itself. Plans for the identification of property are rare as the land is simply described in the register; proof of ownership in some cases is therefore indirect and often difficult to find.

3.2.2 Content

The land registers contain the name of the owner and his predecessors, the extent and description of the property registered in his name and the existence of any mortgage, prenotations of a mortgage, pending litigation or other encumbrances in favour of third parties registered against the property. Both absolute ownership (see 1.1.1) and the bare ownership (see 2.1.2) are entered on the land register. The bare ownership may be upgraded to absolute ownership when the bare owner acquires the usufruct.

3.2.3 Errors

In case of errors or omissions by salaried land registrars, the state and the employee are jointly liable for compensation. In the case of errors or omissions by non-salaried land registrars, only the non-salaried person is responsible for payment of compensation. Apart from court decisions, the registers constitute the ultimate proof of the existence of ownership or any other real rights or encumbrances over land.

3.3 Passing of title

In case of a contractual transfer of property, in addition to the agreement between the parties, title to land passes upon registration of the notarial deed or other form of legal title in the land register. Registration also confers priority rights over the property. There is no specific time limit within which registration must occur. However, in case a contract is submitted to the land register for registration one year after its conclusion, the competent tax authorities will be requested to re-evaluate the relevant property, prior to the registration of the contract, for registration fees to be calculated. See 2.4 for the protection of a preliminary contract prior to registration. The registration is back-dated to the date of filing of the application.

4 TRANSACTIONS IN LAND

The most common methods of acquiring ownership by contract are sale and purchase, gift and exchange.

4.1 Procedures

A sale, transfer by way of gift or exchange of property takes place by agreement. Upon completion of negotiations, and as soon as the contracting parties agree the transfer of the property, they either sign a preliminary (promissory) contract or proceed with completion immediately. The preliminary contract does not require registration (see 2.4) and creates an obligation to transfer the land for consideration enforceable by court order in the event of a failure to complete. Enquiries will usually take place after negotiation. These will extend to investigations of title in the relevant land register and even if the transferor is the registered owner of the property, a 20-year search must be made to reassure the buyer that in spite of any eventual defects of the seller or his predecessor's title, the 20-year period of possession would (with the exception of public land) have led to acquisitive prescription of the property acquired. Other enquiries will depend on the nature and location of the property; these may include searches with authorities such as the Ministry of Environment, Regional Planning and Public Works, the Municipalities National Tourist Organisation, and the Special Fund for the Implementation of Urban Master Plans. When purchasing a separate property unit in a block of flats, it is advisable to enquire as to the deeds establishing horizontal ownership and setting out the rules of joint ownership. A survey is usually undertaken and finance, if any, is often arranged at this stage as well. The contract is read aloud by the notary public and then signed by the contracting parties, their attorneys and the notary public. The application for the registration is processed by the buyer. Upon registration, the transferee receives a certificate of registration; a certificate that no lien or encumbrance has been registered upon the property, or if such charges exist, their details; and a certificate that no third party has filed any action, claiming that the property should be recognised as his, or relevant details if such an action has been filed.

4.2 Contract terms

4.2.1 The seller does not need to expressly provide warranties since he is, by law, liable to the buyer for any legal and physical defects in the property sold and transferred unless expressly exempted in the contract. However, warranties and representations as to various characteristics of the property are usually found in deeds of sale. Depending on the specific case, the remedies for breach of warranty may be:

(a) the right to terminate the contract when the property and the purchase price must be returned;
(b) the right to a lower purchase price;
(c) in case of fault on the seller's part, the right to compensation for non-performance of the contract.

The time limit on warranty claims with regard to immoveables is two years from delivery.

4.2.2 The final deed of sale or exchange usually gives the names of the parties, a detailed description of the property, an outline of the history of the property's title, and, if applicable, the terms of payment. Although there is a requirement for a deposit, this can be agreed between the parties in the preliminary rather than the definitive contract. It is a matter of agreement whether the deposit will be forfeited or refunded if the sale does not proceed. If the deposit is paid as earnest money, ie as official proof of intention to purchase (*arravonas*), this is deemed to have been paid to cover any loss resulting from non-performance. If the person who paid the deposit is responsible for the failure, the holder is entitled to retain it. If the holder is responsible for the non-performance, he is bound to pay back double the amount of the deposit received. The purchase price is paid either in cash or in one or more instalments. Various methods for securing the payment are used, including the condition precedent clause stating that title in the property will pass back to the transferor in the event of default, or an agreement that a mortgage will attach to the land for the unpaid purchase price. The usual contractual penalties for delay or default are liquidated damages and default interest. The risk passes to the buyer upon the delivery of the property to the buyer or from registration in the land registry, whichever occurs first. The law does not specifically provide for the buyer to insure the property, nor does it happen in practice.

4.3 Formalities

Any contract concerning the creation, transfer or termination of real rights must be executed in the form of a notarial deed and registered at the land register in the district where the property is situated, otherwise the contract does not have legal effect. The document is signed in the presence of a notary public stating the nature of the transfer. The law provides that a lawyer must represent the contracting parties when the final deed is signed if the value of the property, as estimated by the tax authorities, exceeds GRD5,000,000 in the Athens and Piraeus area and GRD750,000 in any other area. As soon as the final contract of sale, donation or exchange of the property is executed, registration must take place in the competent district. Preliminary contracts are not registered at the land register. Tenancy agreements of over nine years need to be notarised and registered to provide protection to the tenant against third parties after the nine-year period.

4.4 Fees, costs and taxes

4.4.1 On the transfer of property the transferee has to pay the registration duties, the fees of the notary public, the lawyer, half of the estate agent's fees if applicable, and any tax on the property transfer. Estate agents' fees are approximately two per cent of the value of the property, for each party, although these can be lower or even excluded. Agents' fees are only payable in the event of a successful transaction, unless otherwise agreed.

4.4.2 Notary publics' fees are charged at approximately 1.2 per cent of the value of the property on a sale or exchange. Lawyers' minimum fees are charged at 1.5 per cent of the transaction out of which an amount calculated at 1 per cent for the first GRD5,000,000 and at 0.5 per cent for the balance of the value of the property is provisionally deposited with the local bar association and 65 per cent of this amount is refunded to the lawyer who was present at the signing of the contract; the remaining 35 per cent is retained by the bar association. Further lawyers' fees may be agreed on a time charge basis or for a fixed amount or a percentage of the value or consideration.

4.4.3 Land transfer tax of 9 to 13 per cent is payable (see 11.6) and approximately GRD1,500 is charged for stamp duty. Stamp duty is paid on all transactions in land on issue of the land registry certificate and additionally on the issue of notarial deeds. The amount of stamp duty depends on the number of certificates required and on the number of pages of the relevant notarial deed.

4.4.4 Land registry fees are calculated at 0.45 per cent of the value of the property in case of sale or purchase and exchange, plus GRD1,000 for each of the certificates issued by the land register (see 4.4.3).

4.4.5 The total transaction costs including taxation and agents' fees approach approximately 17 to 20 per cent of the contract price of the property and similar rates will apply to lettings as to sales.

4.4.6 Lawyers' fees are exempt from VAT but agents' fees attract VAT at 18 per cent charged on all types of property and transaction.

4.5 Professionals' roles

Estate agents are commonly used in property transactions for the sale or lease of land. They are members of a professional body, the Estate Agents Association. A survey may be conducted by the estate agent upon the buyer's instructions. Lawyers do not take part in the negotiations, especially with regard to the purchase price, unless expressly instructed. The role of the buyer's lawyer is more important than the seller's since the former conducts a search regarding the legal status of the property. Seller and buyer are separately represented by lawyers, but there is usually only one notary public who draws up the contract and as representative of the state ensures the procedure for the closing of the transaction is carried out in accordance with the law.

5 LEASES AND OCCUPATIONAL RIGHTS

Common law style leaseholds do not exist but contractual tenancy agreements do and are usually granted at full market rent and regulated by the Civil Code. Whereas generally the Code allows for freedom of contract, special laws have been introduced to cover other forms of tenancy contract which contain mandatory provisions to provide protection for the parties involved. The two main types of tenancy agreement are those for office or business premises and those for residential accommodation. The length of tenancy agreements vary according to the type of lease. For minimum durations and security of tenure see 5.3.

5.1 Rent and other terms

5.1.1 Under statute, some tenancy agreements must be in writing, of a mandatory minimum duration and concluded in accordance with specific procedural rules (eg public tenders). These include land owned by, or leased to, the state and/or public legal entities, municipalities and monasteries. There are specific provisions for other premises such as private forests, quarries and mines. All other tenancy agreements are usually, but not always, in writing. Regardless of the type of tenancy, the contracting parties are generally free to agree on rent and the rate of rent review which may be altered by negotiation. Break clauses can be agreed at the outset or in writing during the term of the tenancy. Responsibility for alterations and repairs can be freely agreed as can insurance, renewal, and extension. Tenancy agreements are freely assignable and transferable to third parties although any such assignment requires the consent of the landlord. The arrangements as to subletting vary according to the type of lease. In the event of default of payment the landlord has a pledge over all the tenant's moveable assets in the let premises. In addition to eviction, the landlord may generally also obtain a payment order against the tenant or apply for seizure or arrest of the tenant's property in case of urgency or imminent danger.

5.1.2 Tenancies of professional accommodation (used for the premises of professional practitioners) are also treated as commercial tenancies. Unless expressly agreed the tenant has no right to sublet the property; if the parties have not provided for rent review at the outset, the law provides for a rental increase to an amount not lower than six per cent of the value of the property, as determined by the current valuation lists established by the Ministry of Finance, two years from the day of the commencement of the agreement. Thereafter, a further increase may be effected annually, amounting to 75 per cent of the cost of living index as determined by the Bank of Greece for the preceding 12 months. Rent is usually paid on a monthly basis. A deposit is paid generally of two months' rent. If the parties wish to add a break clause after conclusion of the tenancy agreement, a subsequent private document of a certified date is required, rather than a notarial deed.

5.1.3 Residential tenancies used to be strictly regulated by mandatory statutory provisions which stipulated a compulsory fixed term and fixed rents, although the market is being liberalised. Residential tenancies which are no longer covered by mandatory provisions include property:

(a) of more than 120 square metres in surface;
(b) of a value exceeding GRD30,000,000 according to the valuation lists established by the Ministry of Finance;
(c) recently constructed;
(d) listed or characterised as historical buildings; or
(e) acquired mainly or wholly with foreign exchange.

Unless contractually excluded, subletting of residential premises is permissible. If the parties wish to include a break clause after the contract has been entered into, this subsequent agreement must take the form of a notarial deed.

5.1.4 Special obligations to keep the land productive are imposed upon the agricultural tenant. In an agricultural tenancy the parties may agree that the rent will consist of a percentage of the produce. Otherwise the provisions are largely the same as those for other types of lease.

5.2 Privity of contract and estate

From the moment landlord and tenant cease to be contractually bound, they are no longer liable on the obligations of the tenancy although they will remain liable for claims which arose while the contract was in force.

5.3 Length of tenancy and security of tenure

The minimum term for regulated residential tenancies was recently set at three years and the tenants may extend for a further year. The minimum duration of tenancies for premises used for professional accommodation will be determined by the specific use for which they are leased, regardless of what the parties may otherwise agree, some such as law offices having a three-year minimum with right to extend for a year. Other professional offices and commercial properties are let for a minimum of nine years. Agricultural tenancies must be for a minimum of four years. There are generally no formalities to be complied with in order to extend the agreement. A residential tenant may terminate the agreement upon expiry of the contract; if he wishes to terminate before the end of the term and there are no provisions to the contrary, he may be liable for the payment of rent until the expiry of the contract. After the expiry of the tenancy agreement, the landlord can reclaim possession for any reason. The nine-year period for commercial premises may be extended unilaterally by the tenant for another three years. Although leases for some professional accommodation provide the tenant with the right to occupy for a period of nine years and even to extend the occupation, the tenant has the right to terminate the lease after two years, regardless of its contractual duration, by giving the landlord six months' notice and by paying a break fee amounting to four months' rent. Upon expiry of the contractual period, the landlord may reclaim possession of the property either for reconstruction purposes or for his own business or office use. The landlord is also given the right to terminate the agreement early in order to use the premises himself or for reconstruction of the property but may not reclaim possession of commercial premises before three years of the lease have elapsed. In the case of leases of land, the landlord may disregard the contractual duration and in general claim the land for purpose of construction one year after the commencement of the lease.

5.4 Other legislative restrictions

The Civil Code provides for the tenant to pay the landlord the necessary expenses for maintenance, the obligation of tenant to compensate the landlord for wear and tear and alterations going beyond those often agreed. These provisions will be implied although they can generally be excluded.

5.5 Method of measurement

There are no specific guidelines on measurement although reference is generally made to net internal areas on lettings. Measurement of horizontal or vertical property does not usually include common areas yet includes auxiliary rooms such as lavatories and kitchens. When whole buildings are being sold, let or measured all spaces, individual, common, principal and auxiliary, are included on a gross internal basis.

6 FINANCE AND INVESTMENT SOURCES

The property market in Greece, unlike that of other European countries, is primarily based on individual (private) investment. Finance is mainly provided in the form of loans, although another common method of construction finance is the system known as *antiparochi* (see 6.6.1). As a result of the large proportion of new commercial investors, long-term borrowing is more usual than short term.

6.1 Loan finance

Credit institutions (banks are called credit institutions) grant loans on the basis of the creditworthiness of their customers and the security they are given. Mortgage banks have expanded their activities from private residential finance to all types of business activities. The cooperative credit societies usually extend loans to their members for working capital and/or investment purposes. There are also two specific credit institutions, the Postal Savings Bank and the Consignment and Loans Fund, both fully owned by the state, which grant housing loans exclusively to employees in the public sector, subject to strict conditions and requirements. Finance provided by the banks, if for a fixed term, is normally for a term of between 5 to 15 years, and is usually amortised. The interest rate may be floating, fixed or a combination of both. These arrangements tend to apply to all property sectors as well as to all lenders. The interest rate is based either on the bank's own base rate or ATHIBOR (Athens Inter-Bank Offered Rate) to which a margin of two per cent to four per cent and contributions to the state (one per cent on the monthly outstanding balance of the loans which every credit institution has to contribute to the Bank of Greece) are added. The floating interest rate is quoted for three to 12 months interest periods and there is no minimum interest rate for any type of finance.

6.2 Investment or equity finance

Companies are funded by their shareholders, who may be individuals, other companies or institutions. Listed companies may obtain their investment funds on the Athens Stock Exchange. Equity finance and increases of share capital are subject to a one per cent tax, while loans by shareholders are subject to stamp duty at 2.4 per cent. Equity finance is therefore less costly and more popular.

6.3 Mezzanine or mixed funding

The credit institutions (banks) usually finance up to 100 per cent of the official tax values of the relevant properties, as defined by the Ministry of Finance, which are adjusted on a two year basis. However, the relevant market prices (on the basis of a willing buyer and a willing seller) usually exceed the official prices by at least 20 per cent. Financing may reach up to 100 per cent of the official value of the property or the value of the project, with gradual draw-down of the loan, according to the progress of work.

6.4 Sale and lease-back

A property used for commercial purposes may be either owned or leased. Only a small percentage of businesses own their own property due to the high cost of purchasing commercial buildings. Acquisition of commercial property by financial leasing is now allowed (see 6.6.2). However, sale and lease-back is not allowed for the purchase of land.

6.5 Tax leasing

Under Greek law the relevant tax benefits when leasing property apply to the tenant and other schemes or vehicles are not recognised.

6.6 Other types of property finance

6.6.1 The *antiparochi* form of construction finance is peculiar to Greece. The parties (the owner of a development site and a building contractor) agree that the contractor will erect a building on the owner's land, and in exchange the contractor will receive part of the new building (eg some of the apartments or offices or shops) while the remainder will belong to the landowner. The contractor will either acquire ownership of the parts concerned or will direct the owner to sell them to third parties, while the purchase price is collected by the contractor. In this way, the owner of the land does not need funds to erect the building, and the contractor does not need funds to purchase the land (although he may need other finance for construction). The owner and the contractor pool their resources and indirectly finance each other. This method of financing construction has been used extensively, especially since the Second World War, and a considerable number of buildings in Athens and other large cities have been built in this way.

6.6.2 Financial leasing has recently been extended from financing of moveables to commercial buildings, but not to land or buildings intended to be used for residential accommodation. The minimum term of the contract is 10 years and the contract is also registered with the land registry of the area of the leased property. Under the financial leasing agreement the tenant acquires the property at the time full repayment is made under the lease contract. At the outset the property is fully funded and purchased by the landlord. Clarification is pending with regard to the tax aspects as initially no transactions had been recorded.

6.7 Institutional investment

A duly licensed Greek insurance company is required to invest its investment funds in deposits, state bonds and other security papers strictly stipulated by law. It may however invest in land provided it is free of liens or encumbrances; located in a city of more than 15,000 inhabitants; constructed pursuant to a duly issued building permit; and the purchase price in the notarial deed does not exceed 30 per cent of the official tax value. Greek pension funds also own land although they must obtain prior governmental approval before purchase and credit institutions may freely invest in land.

6.8 Other investors

Other investors include private individuals and companies. Investment and unit trusts or publicly quoted single-asset companies are not recognised.

7 FORMS OF SECURITY

Credit institutions grant loans on the basis of creditworthiness and security, both being of equivalent value. Security is a prerequisite for property financing provided to individuals for residential purposes. Banks will usually wish to have their loans covered by assets having a value of more than 120 per cent of the amount of the loan. Financing to individuals for housing purposes is always secured by a prenotation of mortgage over the acquired property. Credit institutions provide finance in local or foreign currency for every activity or purpose, eg overdraft, revolving facilities, long-term loans, facilities for working capital purposes, single-asset company finance, investment or construction finance and syndicated loans. Finance to prime customers or enterprises in these circumstances is usually partially secured for 10–20 per cent of the outstanding or it may be fully unsecured, since the credit decision of the lenders focuses on previous servicing of loans/facilities, the borrower's financial statements, a history of continuous profits and its anticipated turnover/income.

7.1 Mortgages and prenotation of mortgages

7.1.1 Real security rights are the pledge and the mortgage. A 'prenotation of mortgage', which is very common, is in fact a conditional mortgage. A mortgage is registered by virtue of a notarial deed (the mortgage deed) or pursuant to a final and irrevocable court judgment. The prenotation of mortgage is registered by virtue of a court judgment which may be entered with consent. A mortgage may be registered over land and ships, aircraft and other assets but the prenotation of mortgage may only be registered over land. The claim secured by a mortgage ranks ahead of other non-priority claims in the event of public auction. The claim secured by a prenotation of mortgage will have a priority ranking only when the prenotation is converted into a mortgage. Once such a conversion is made, the priority of the secured claim takes retroactive effect, from the date the prenotation was registered. It is possible to obtain one mortgage and/or one prenotation of mortgage over more than one property, provided that the properties are owned by one debtor and the security is in favour of a single creditor. It is possible to create a mortgage for a conditional or a future obligation. The mortgage must be for (or up to) a specific sum together with interest. The possession and ownership of the immoveable remain with its owner and are not transferred to the creditor. For the priority of mortgages, see 2.10. The fees for the registration of mortgages amount to approximately seven per cent of the amount to be secured (stamp duty, lawyers' and notaries' fees and registration fees) or four per cent where the loan is by a bank operating in Greece. The fees for the registration of a prenotation of mortgage are significantly lower, amounting to 0.75 per cent of the amount to be secured, representing the fees and expenses of the registrar of mortgages.

7.1.2 A notarial mortgage deed grants an executory title and in the event of default the mortgagee can commence foreclosure proceedings on the basis of his mortgage, whilst the debtor has the right to oppose these. A creditor having only a prenotation of mortgage cannot immediately commence foreclosure proceedings, but must first obtain an enforceable court judgment. As soon as the creditor obtains an executory copy of the mortgage or a final and irrevocable judgment for the conversion of the prenotation into a mortgage (in case of default of the obligor), he can instruct a court bailiff to seize the property and a date for the public auction is fixed. If a third party starts auction proceedings before the mortgagee, the latter must announce his claim within 15 days of the day of the auction to the notary public conducting the auction. The notary public is responsible for the distribution of the auction proceeds between all notified creditors, according to their ranking. Any challenge will be settled by the courts.

7.2 Floating and other charges

A pledge may be taken over moveables but no floating or other charges over immoveable property are recognised.

7.3 Performance bonds and guarantees

7.3.1 Borrowing by a legal entity or by an individual may be secured by a corporate or personal guarantee, if the lender agrees. A guarantee is usually requested by the lender if the guarantor is in possession of assets (such as bank deposits, commercial papers and land) and no real security (mortgage or prenotation of mortgage) is granted by the debtor. A guarantee must be in writing to be enforceable. It is not necessary to notify the principal debtor. However, according to the Civil Code, the guarantor is entitled to refuse payment until the creditor has attempted but failed to secure a compulsory attachment against the principal debtor's property, unless the guarantor waives this right in writing. Borrowing by an individual or a company may be secured by a guarantee called a 'performance guarantee' issued by a bank. However, this creates double costs, ie commission for the bank performance guarantee and security and interest on the borrowing. It is therefore not attractive.

7.3.2 The issue of a commercial bond for a fixed sum is not generally allowed, although bonds may be issued under certain strict statutory provisions, in which case the bond may be offered to any third party, including credit institutions, institutional investors as well as individual or private investors. In the event that the bond is secured by a mortgage over property, the approval of the capital market committee is required.

7.4 Credit insurance

Credit insurance is not common and lenders do not generally require this.

8 PLANNING AND BUILDING REGULATION

The 1975 constitution places responsibility on the state for the protection of the physical and cultural environment. Town and country planning and development are regulated mainly by the provisions of the General Building Code 1985 (GBC). Due to economic constraints and the high construction standards imposed by law, illegal activity in contravention of the GBC is common. The Greek planning system has been criticised for uncertainty and over-centralisation, and requires more coherent development control. Public participation in planning is negligible and the local planning authorities' role is often merely to legalise existing illegal and unauthorised development although a much stricter control is exercised over antiquities.

8.1 Planning authorities

The Ministry of Environment, Regional Planning and Public Works is responsible for various aspects of urban and regional planning and ultimate control over all matters relating to town and country planning. The district planning authorities are responsible for planning control at a local level and the GBC also provides for planning and architectural control committees. Planning issues are decided mainly on a legal and factual basis, although political criteria are often taken into consideration.

8.2 Zoning or development plans

The basic law regarding planning provides for regional plans by presidential decree and under these general master plans and finally the 'city plan'. The city plan sets out the specific terms for construction (eg permitted size and plot ratios), land designated for public use (streets, squares, schools, churches), land for private development, and permitted land use. It relates to both planning control and building control as technical standards of buildings may also be included. The city plan forms part of the general master plan, which itself determines the zoning of one or more municipalities or communities. Each municipality or community is developed in accordance with its own city plan. The GBC does not itself decide land use zones at any level, only criteria and policies. Regional zones may be issued by presidential decrees, subsequent to the proposal of the relevant municipality or community and of the Ministry. Municipalities and communities propose a city plan, in which zones are specified. The Ministry and/or the municipalities or communities prepare the general master plan. Individuals and/or legal entities cannot apply for zoning alone, but they may apply for a city plan, in which zoning is included, provided that their properties have a minimum surface area of 50,000 square metres, are not already included in a city plan and are located outside built-up areas. Once zoning has been implemented, any building which conforms with that use will be permitted, provided that its design, siting, density and appearance are approved by the competent local planning authority. Not all parts of the country fall within a zone and they are regulated separately. Any use not in conformity with the plan is prohibited. The municipality or the local urban planning authority office have no discretion to override zoning and zoning can only be modified by amendment of the city plan, the general master plan or, as regards zones at a regional level, through new presidential decrees.

8.3 Planning control and procedures

Development control is exercised by the issue of building permits under the GBC and no development is lawful unless one has been obtained. A permit is required for construction, demolition (in which case it is called a demolition permit) and for almost any change of use, although minor alterations such as painting are exempt. Following the issuance of a building permit, alterations regarding the form, design and appearance of a building are allowed upon the issuance of an amended building permit by the competent local urban planning authority office. In case of doubt, any interested party may apply to the municipality or community for the issuance of a certificate regarding the land use. Any interested party, who wishes to be informed whether the building to be erected would comply with the relevant legal provisions, may file an application with the local urban planning authority office accompanied by the building's architectural plans and request the conduct of a preliminary control prior to the issuance of a building permit. However, it should be noted that the authorities are under no obligation to carry out the preliminary control. If the control is carried out the plans are officially approved. Additional planning control exists for listed buildings (see 8.5).

8.3.1 The local urban planning authority office considers the application for a building permit (*adeia oikodomis*). Fees are paid by the applicant prior to the issuance of a building permit, which take into account such considerations as value, dimensions and volume of the proposed development. Only an owner may apply for a building permit, and the application must be fully detailed.

8.3.2 A decision by the local urban planning authority office whether to grant a building permit is usually taken within two to three months, although sometimes it may take longer. If no decision is issued within this period, the applicant may address himself first to the head of the local urban planning authority office and then to the competent prefect. The building permit is an administrative act and so any refusal of permission can be appealed against before the competent administrative court on the basis of objective or legal grounds. An appeal must be filed with the Council of State within 60 days of the decision by the local urban planning authority office to refuse the application. The building permit will usually provide that the applicant must comply with various conditions which may, eg relate to the permitted dimensions of the building. Aggrieved third parties such as neighbours with a legal interest may challenge a successful application by filing an appeal with the Council of State. They must prove that the permit has been issued in breach of the law (eg it does not comply with the provisions of the GBC or the city plan) and that this causes them damage.

8.3.3 A building permit must be implemented within an initial period of four years or be subject to review. The building permit benefits the land and is transferred with it. The applicant refused a building permit may file a repeat application once he fulfils the conditions which he failed to meet previously (eg the plans submitted did not comply with the GBC). The permit may be renewed indefinitely upon payment of renewal fees, where the main structure of the building has been completed upon the expiry of the four-year period. Otherwise, the permit may be renewed for another four years upon payment of renewal fees. If the main frame of the building has not been completed upon the expiry of the eight-year period, the initial building permit is cancelled and a new one has to be issued with repayment of fees and a re-examination of the building plans. The exterior of buildings must be completed within six years from the date of the initial building permit. In practice, the fines payable are often not collected due to lack of enforcement by the municipalities or communities.

8.3.4 The strict requirement for a building permit is enforced by the competent local urban planning authority office and the local police authorities. In the event of construction without a permit or in breach of the terms of the building permit, the owner of the building and the builder may face fines and/or criminal charges and the unauthorised construction may be demolished. Buildings may be designated as unauthorised following inspection by the local urban planning authority, and objection may be filed by the owner within 10 days of the inspection on the ground that the construction complies with the building permit and is lawful. Enforcement cannot be carried out until a decision is issued by the authority. The owner may also file an appeal together with an application for the stay of enforcement proceedings before the Council of State. When the local urban planning authority office discovers any illegal construction, it must impose an immediate halt. Owners of unauthorised buildings under construction or already constructed (ie without a building permit or in breach of the terms of the building permit) have the right to file an application with the local urban planning authority office for the issue of a retrospective building permit within two months of inspection. In this case severe fines are payable at the same time as the ordinary fees for the issuance of the building permit. Enforcement cannot be carried out during these two months. No time limit exists within which enforcement must take place.

8.4 Building standards, control and supervision

Building standards are also regulated by the GBC. A building permit must show that the building complies with the GBC provisions, therefore compliance with building standards is checked by examination of the construction plans at the time the application for the permit is made. A breach of construction standards will render the relevant construction unlawful, and the owner of the building and the constructor may face fines, criminal charges and demolition; for this and provisions concerning appeal see also 8.3.4.

8.5 Protection of buildings of special interest

Owners of buildings designated by the Ministry for their historic or architectural interest are obliged to repair or reconstruct them as necessary and, if they refuse to do so, the state, the municipality or the community concerned may carry out the repair or reconstruction at the owner's expense. Lists of such buildings are kept locally. Demolition of these buildings is prohibited. Alterations, such as repairs, of the same buildings may only be carried out with a permit from the local urban planning authority office and the recommendations of the regional committee of architectural control. The control and protection of antiquities are taken very seriously.

8.6 Compulsory purchase and expropriation and compensation

The state, the municipalities and communities may expropriate private property upon payment of compensation if it is required in the public interest. The administrative act of expropriation is published jointly by the competent minister and the Minister of Finance in the Government Gazette. Compensation is fixed according to the value of the property on the basis of the current market price of neighbouring properties in recent notarial deeds and as estimated by the local tax authorities at the time the act of expropriation is published. Procedures are generally time-consuming and cumbersome. Confiscation by administrative act is an alternative in the event of extraordinary and imminent public need. Redistribution of land may also be effected by administrative act for the purpose of improvement of agricultural exploitation or for urban development.

9 ENVIRONMENTAL MATTERS

A Law of 1986 was passed to protect the environment and prevent pollution. The relevant legislation deals primarily with the polluter and provides sanctions. The polluter's liability in most cases is considered an 'objective' liability, ie it does not depend on his intent to commit the offence. In case of breach of any of the provisions, imprisonment of between three months to two years is provided for actual pollution or failure to obtain prior authorisation. Any infringement by a legal entity may result in a penalty being imposed on its directors or managers. Under civil law, there is strict liability unless the specific polluting act is attributable to a third party acting with intent, or to force majeure. The polluter will be liable for damages, and penalties may be imposed for amounts up to GRD100,000,000. Anyone with a special interest, which may include a resident of the respective area, is entitled to file an action against a polluter. Activities of a type or extent likely to cause serious harm to the environment (category A) must be authorised by the Ministry of the Environment and must comply with any conditions laid down. The licence for schemes in this first category is granted jointly by the Ministry of Environment, Town Planning and Public Works and other competent ministries, whose authority may be transferred to the prefect. The applicant must file a report regarding the environmental impact of the project. Also a pre-authorisation must be granted for the project by the competent central or regional town planning office of the ministry. Pre-authorisation is not compulsory when the project is in an industrial zone. The licence for projects not posing a serious threat to the environment (category B) is granted by the prefect and no environmental impact study is required. The applicant is required to fill in a questionnaire and submit certain documents evidencing the compliance with the provisions for the protection of the environment. In certain cases pre-authorisation may be requested. The licence for activities which pose a significant but minor threat to the environment (category C) is granted either by the mayor or the president of the community. The applicant is requested to submit documentation evidencing compliance with the provisions for the protection of the environment. If no response is given within the requisite time limits (60 days for category A, 40 days for categories B and C) approval of the scheme can be presumed.

9.1 Protection against atmospheric and noise pollution

9.1.1 The standards regarding the emissions of substances which pollute the atmosphere are defined by a common decision of the Ministry of the Environment and other competent ministries. The Ministry may conduct controls in order to ascertain the compliance of the parties concerned with the provisions of the law. Enforcement is carried out by the competent central or regional agency and the environment quality control divisions, formed by the prefect. Special sanitary regulations provide for the reduction of the damaging effects of smog, domestic and industrial fumes, obliging the owners or occupiers to install filters or smog collection devices.

9.1.2 Ministerial decisions set maximum emission levels for engines and lay down noise control provisions regarding the construction and operation of highways, traffic noise and maximum noise pollution levels.

9.2 Water pollution

The Ministry of the Environment is in charge of water content analysis and the required composition of water for various uses is stated in a ministerial decision of 1986, which implements the relevant EU Directive. A licensing procedure must be followed for the discharge of harmful substances. Any breach of these standards will incur civil or criminal penalties. Various other acts and decisions regulate the discharge of chemical substances into water, the protection of ground water from discharge of harmful substances, the protection of water from liquid waste and oil pollution. These offer numerous preventive measures and provide administrative, civil and penal consequences in case of breach of their provisions. With regard to oil pollution, there have been instances where the intentional polluter has been held liable for damages.

9.3 Waste storage and disposal

Prior authorisation is to be obtained for disposal or transportation of toxic, noxious, solid or dangerous waste. In consultation with other ministries, the Ministry of the Environment designates the competent authorities in charge of waste management planning as well as the terms and procedure for enforcement. The local authorities are responsible for the management of solid waste, except when this cannot be disposed of together with domestic waste. In this case those who caused its creation are responsible for its management. The prefect is in control of compliance.

9.4 Contaminated land

Transfers of interests in land do not usually include making enquiries, eg of nearby land-fill sites, whether the site was used for waste disposal or whether it was infilled or reclaimed, or whether dangerous materials were used in the construction of any buildings. A contamination register must be kept recording where solid waste is disposed of. The prefect supervises all industries and companies producing, possessing or disposing of toxic waste and the management of toxic and dangerous waste at national level is undertaken by the Ministry of the Environment in consultation with the other relevant ministries and the Central Union of Greek Municipalities and Communities. At regional level, management may be undertaken by the ministries' regional offices.

9.5 Environmental impact assessments

An environmental impact assessment may be required before certain industrial activity, eg construction works and other installations which might cause pollution or have a negative impact upon the environment, will be permitted. Different provisions apply with regard to the pre-authorisation and licensing requirements; depending on the category of activity and the competent authority, the applicant is required to undertake the assessment or complete a questionnaire before the licence will be granted.

10 DEVELOPMENT

10.1 Development projects, structures and vehicles

In its simplest form, the owner or the buyer of the site entrusts a builder with the construction of a building. With larger projects, more parties are involved including financial advisers, technical advisers and consultants. In the last few years, many more substantial projects have been undertaken, although small-scale development still takes place. These larger projects usually involve development sites in new commercial areas, on the outskirts of major cities, such as Athens. In larger projects, development is mostly carried out over private land; this requires considerable investment funds, usually granted by credit and financial institutions, either as straightforward lenders or through their participation in the vehicle or consortium which undertakes the construction. In addition to the contractor a combination of different joint ventures or merged technical companies and their subsidiaries may be involved, as well as banks and other companies who will undertake the role of financial advisers and brokers. The owner may participate in the group constructing the building, availing himself of the profits from the construction and exploitation of the building, either directly or by way of *antiparochi* (see 6.6.1). The end user or an institution will rarely undertake a development project, since these parties prefer to purchase partially completed or completed buildings at a higher price, without taking on the development risks. An investor or a speculative developer, however, often undertakes construction because he accepts the associated risks from the outset for a corresponding profit.

10.2 Building contracts and appointment of professionals

10.2.1 Typical forms of building contract

Building contracts are usually defined by the method of payment; this can be by way of fixed price or an estimate of the cost of construction (most commonly used), or by account, using the real cost of construction as a basis, to which the agreed constructor's fee consisting of a percentage of the resulting cost is added. Finally, the *antiparochi*, a special form of payment, may be used (see 6.6.1). A clause in the contract may allow for re-evaluation of certain prices if increases exceed certain limits. The contractor is fully responsible to the employer for the construction. The subcontractors are responsible to the contractor who is considered their employer, and rarely to the employer/owner of the project, unless they enter into a direct contract with him. The contractor will be liable to the employer for the eventual deficiencies in the designs (architectural, technical, and studies/plans), unless the employer appoints the designer himself, in which case the designer is responsible to the employer. Management contracts are quite commonly used in larger projects where it is necessary to find specialised subcontractors.

10.2.2 Common terms

When the contract is entered into, the employer usually makes the payment of a deposit (unless the form of payment is that of *antiparochi*); the project is paid for by reference to different agreed stages in the construction. A percentage of the fee, which rarely exceeds 5 to 10 per cent of the total cost, may upon agreement be paid subsequently, ie after the completion of the work and provided no serious defects appear. A deadline is usually set for final completion. In certain circumstances there are two dates, the first to complete and deliver the main project and the second to complete and deliver the secondary spaces, common areas and gardens. The contracts do not allow for any extension of these dates, unless incidents of force majeure occur, usually defined in the contract. In the event of late completion where there is no force majeure, the contracts provide for liquidated damages. The contractor cannot modify the plans and the specified works unless he has reserved the right in the contract. After the practical completion of the project, the final completion of the project will be confirmed by a civil engineer acting on behalf of the contractor and the employer will be notified in writing. Almost all construction contracts provide for a protocol of delivery and acceptance giving the opportunity for the employer to refuse delivery with grounds stated or accept delivery and reserve his rights. This provides the contractor with the right to demand the balance of his fees. The approval of the project by the employer usually signifies the final completion of the project and comprises the release of the contractor from any responsibility for deficiencies in the project. The exception is where the deficiencies could not be detected by regular inspection or were intentionally hidden. The Civil Code only provides a right to terminate in favour of the employer. A delay in commencing or progressing with the work, or the discovery of serious deficiencies and defects gives the employer the right to terminate the agreement. Termination by the contractor is not provided for in the Civil Code and the general provisions of the Civil Code and the specific clauses of the contract will be enforced against the employer.

10.2.3 Standard form of contracts

There is no official standard form of construction agreement, although the Athens Bar Association has been working on a draft proposal. Nevertheless, in practice standard contracts are employed and contractors often submit a contract based on a type widely used in the industry.

10.2.4 Appointment of the professional team

In small projects the appointment of professionals is done using short contracts or orally; in larger projects, more detailed contracts are concluded with architects, electrical engineers and the remaining advisers. In these the areas of specialty are defined as well as the conditions of employment and fees, usually fixed as a percentage of the estimate for the project; however, there may often be an agreement to the effect that a fixed price will be paid for a specific task.

10.3 Those involved and their roles

In a building contract, the contractor selects and directs his personnel and arranges for the supply of all necessary raw materials, without excluding the possibility of the employer selecting a civil engineer and/or an architect to draw up the studies, plans or designs for the contractor to execute. It is not unusual for the employer to appoint an engineer to supervise the works. This engineer acts as an independent professional and not as a *prostithis* (auxiliary person) and may be liable for defects. The appointment of a project manager or developer is rare and depends on the size of the project and on the need to coordinate the works. The role of developer has only recently been introduced in Greece; he may usually find the sites and offer the project to the owners, construction companies and to financial organisations. The architects may be appointed by the owner of the land, the developer or the employer. Engineers are responsible for the conduct of the relevant studies and drawings to be submitted to the urban planning authority for the issue of a licence. Whilst architects may only carry out architectural designs and supervise these, civil engineers are entitled to prepare the designs and structural studies. Other technicians, such as electrical and mechanical engineers, will study and install the electrical and other systems, eg lifts, central heating and air-conditioning. Unlike in public projects, the contractor in private works is usually selected without prior tender. This does not prevent the employer, where suitable, from entering into consecutive contacts with subcontractors (direct appointment).

10.4 Defects and remedies

10.4.1 Remedies of employer in respect of defects in design and materials

The employer has a direct claim and right to bring a civil action against the contractor in respect of defects in the design and the construction of the project. The employer is entitled, by insisting on the contract's performance, to request the contractor to remedy the defects, if this is feasible, and to this end he may set a reasonable time limit, after the expiry of which he is entitled to remedy such defects himself at the contractor's expense. In the case of minor defects, the employer is entitled to demand a reduction of the contractor's fees. In case of substantial defects, the employer is entitled to rescind the contract and, if the defects are the contractor's fault, to demand full compensation. The employer does not have a direct claim against the subcontractors, the suppliers of the contractor and the technicians, unless agreed otherwise or if any of these persons has conducted an unlawful act. The surveying engineer, when appointed by the employer, is jointly liable with the contractor for defects.

10.4.2 Remedies of subsequent owners/occupiers other than the contractual employer

In respect of defects, subsequent owners and occupiers do not have any remedies against the initial contractor. However, they are entitled to claim against the former owner/seller for a reduction of the sale price, remedy of the defects or even the rescission of the contract, or alternatively for damages. The grounds of the civil action are the seller's warranties under the Civil

Code. Further, the seller/employer is entitled to file a civil action against the contractor on the basis of this warranty liability. The claim is time-barred after 10 years from completion. Claims under sale contracts are subject to a three-year time limit, although certain contracts may provide for a longer period. Construction contracts often stipulate expressly that the contractor shall be liable for defects which occur within one year of completion. With regard to the various elements of the building (eg lifts and central heating) the warranty period may be longer.

10.5 Defects insurance

Insurance of defects is uncommon. Only recently, and usually in projects where foreign construction firms participate, has insurance been requested. Where it does exist, it is usually limited to remedying defects, since insurance companies hesitate to insure consequential losses which cannot be easily determined. The main disadvantages of defect insurance are that it is very difficult to secure the full cost and premiums are very high.

10.6 Copyright

The architectural designs or drawings constitute intellectual property of their authors; however, they may be used commercially in other building contracts, provided all parties consent.

10.7 Fees

The architects' professional fees are calculated by the urban planning authority on the basis of a mathematical formula provided by the Technical Chamber of Greece. The engineer may require a fixed price equal to a percentage of the construction cost for the supervision of the work. If the project is very expensive, the percentage may be reduced, although in practice for some projects there is demand for well-known professionals, whose fees are substantial. The fees stipulated by law are deposited with a bank in the name of the beneficiary, whilst any other fees are usually paid in stages, according to the progress of the works.

10.8 Taxes

The construction and the transfer of new buildings are not exempt from value added tax (VAT) but are subject to a grace period of exemption. See further 11.8.

11 TAXES

11.1 Corporation tax

Greek companies are taxed on their income at a flat rate applying to the total net profit before distribution. There is no general capital gains tax in Greece other than on transfers of parts and shares in unlisted companies. However, specific gains such as the realised appreciation of fixed assets are considered to constitute income and are taxed as such. The transfer of goodwill, as well as the transfer of other intangible rights, are also taxed at 30 per cent and treated as income. Gains arising from the disposal of fixed assets as well as unrealised gains including those resulting from asset revaluation (to the extent that they are reflected in the company books) are treated as income arising from commercial activities and are subject to income tax. Both resident and non-resident companies are taxable in Greece. Resident corporations are subject to income tax on their worldwide annual income, unless otherwise provided by double tax treaties. Non-resident companies are taxed on income deriving from a Greek source (eg income from rentals), as well as on income deriving from a permanent establishment in Greece. Residence is primarily determined by the place of registration, but also by the principal place of business or place of control.

11.1.1 Tax rates

Tax rates for local corporations and other legal entities with registered shares are currently 35 per cent, whilst resident companies with bearer shares not listed on the Athens Stock Exchange and foreign companies are taxed at 40 per cent.

11.1.2 Computation and administration

A company's taxable profits and gains are assessed by deducting expenses from gross income. Income may be reduced by depreciation and expenses considered to be productive, ie related to the company's activity. Furthermore specific expenses, eg donations to approved organisations, interest (except interest and penalties payable on account of late payment of taxes), taxes (except income and property taxes), royalties and other similar expenses, repairs and maintenance expenses of leased property are tax deductible. The competent authorities for the calculation and collection of taxes are the district financial authorities (*DOY*). The taxpayers have a right of appeal against the tax assessment which is heard by the administrative courts of first instance. There is a right of appeal to the Administrative Court of Appeal and the Supreme Administrative Court. In parallel with legal proceedings, alternative tax settlement procedures are also provided.

11.1.3 Depreciation and capital allowances

Depreciation for tax purposes applies to fixed as well as intangible assets such as goodwill, rights and licences. Initial establishment or preliminary expenses for the acquisition of land may be written off in equal instalments over a five-year period. Extensions and improvements to tenanted property are also amortised over a period of five years or the term of the lease agreement, if less. Fixed assets valued up to GRD200,000 can be written off in the year acquired and put into operation. The applicable depreciation rates are 8 per cent for factories, 10–15 per cent for machinery and equipment, 12 per cent for passenger vehicles, 20 per cent for computers and trucks and 30 per cent for hotel furniture. For fiscal years ending after December 1992 depreciation is optional. Depreciation is calculated by the straight-line method, except for depreciation of new manufacturing machinery and equipment acquired from 1 January 1993 which is to be calculated on reducing rates once the Ministry of Finance has issued a circular on the matter.

11.1.4 Withholding tax

The system of tax withholding aims to impose taxation at source. Companies are subject to withholding or reporting obligations for the payment of, for example, salaries, fees, and rental of equipment to foreign companies. The withholding tax rate on interest income depends on the nature of the recipient and the category of income but varies between 15 and 35 per cent. Service fees and royalties, eg paid to foreign enterprises without a permanent establishment in Greece, are subject to a withholding tax of 20 per cent (10 per cent for motion pictures and television films). Gross revenues of foreign construction companies undertaking the construction of technical projects in Greece are subject to withholding taxes ranging from 3.5 per cent to 8.75 per cent depending on the nature of contract. Many double tax treaties provide for reduced or for zero rates of such taxes on interest and/or royalties.

11.2 Taxes on development value

The owner of land situated out of a building zone is subject to two kinds of contributions to the municipal authorities in the event that the land becomes part of a zoning plan to cover infrastructure work undertaken by the authorities. The first is a contribution of the actual land (which can amount to 60 per cent of the surface area) to be used for the creation of streets, squares and other places of public use and the second is a financial contribution called the zoning tax, which is a municipal tax collected by the state and which ranges from 1 per cent to 25 per cent calculated on the value of the land after the contribution of the actual surface area of the land has been made.

11.3 Capital gains

The law relating to capital gains realised on the sale of property has recently changed. When company property is transferred at a profit, the gain is considered to be ordinary income and will not be taxed separately.

11.4 Taxes on owner of property

An owner of property pays municipal taxes (*TAP*) which may vary from 0.025 per cent to 0.035 per cent of the value of the property. Since 1997 a new tax applies to property of over GRD 60 million (with higher limits for married couples increasing with each child). The tax starts at 0.3 per cent and increases to 0.8 per cent for property with a value of GRD 350 million or more.

11.5 Taxes on occupier

Currently the only taxes on the occupier (for which the owner is jointly liable) are municipal cleaning and lighting charges which are annually readjusted by the competent municipal authorities and are proportional to the size and use of the property.

11.6 Taxes on land transfer

11.6.1 The buyer of land is subject to transfer tax on the value of the property (as determined by the Ministry of Finance), or the contractual purchase price, whichever is higher. For properties situated in cities where there is a public fire authority, the rate of tax is 11 per cent (if the value is less than GRD4,000,000) and 13 per cent (for properties with a value exceeding GRD4,000,000). For properties situated in other areas, the tax rates are 9 per cent and 11 per cent respectively. However, any private buyer who does not own any other property in Greece is not required to pay tax up to a certain value, provided he purchases his first property with the intention to use it as his place of private residence; but the property must not be sold for at least five years. The law also provides for a further benefit according to which the buyer is required not to pay tax on his residence for a second period, subject to certain conditions. A foreign company is subject to the same transfer tax as an individual, irrespective of nationality or residence.

11.6.2 Certain individuals (Greek nationals who have been working abroad for at least six years; Greek nationals employed in the merchant marine for at least six years; or persons of Greek origin having lived abroad for at least six years) who buy property with foreign currency, and can produce receipts ('pink slips') from the bank confirming which foreign currency has been converted, are required to pay only half of the transfer tax. The pink slips have to be issued in the name of the buyer and cover the value of the property. By express provision of a Law of 1995, no property tax is owed upon transfer of land from a leasing company to a tenant (see 6.6.2) on or prior to expiry of the lease. The transfer of shares of a resident corporation is generally exempt from tax, except for companies whose main activity is the ownership and exploitation of property, or companies whose assets consist of 60 per cent or more of civil property. The shares must be registered and the transfer is effected by notarial deed and is subject to a five per cent transfer tax. The tax payable on an exchange of property is calculated at 50 per cent of the rates applying to a sale and purchase, provided that the properties exchanged are of the same value. Any excess in value will be taxed at the normal sale and purchase rate. Inheritance and gift tax apply to individuals at rates between 5 and 65 per cent depending on value and the relationship of the parties.

11.7 Wealth taxes

No wealth taxes are levied.

11.8 Value added tax

Businesses providing goods or services over a certain value have to charge value added tax (VAT) on the value of those supplies. VAT is charged at varying rates ranging from 8 per cent to 18 per cent. Although there are no zero-rated goods or supplies, there are certain categories which are VAT exempt such as the transfer of property, educational and medical services, the collection of property rentals, ship supplies and legal services. However, although the construction and transfer of new buildings are not exempt, they are still covered by a grace period of exemption. In order to charge VAT businesses have to be specifically registered. The competent authorities for the calculation and collection of VAT are the district financial authorities (*DOY*).

11.9 Local taxes

There are no other local taxes.

12 GRANTS AND INCENTIVES

12.1 Subsidies, grants and loans

12.1.1 There are a number of investment areas and industrial estates which provide significant incentives for 'productive' investment projects. The investment areas and industrial estates must be within five specific regions termed A, B, C, D and Thrace. The regional incentive packages currently consist of investment grants, interest rate subsidies, increased depreciation allowances and tax allowances. These schemes are discretionary and all awards will vary according to location, sector and project type. Before establishing an industrial presence in an investment zone, it is necessary to provide information including technical and financial data, construction reports, and a copy of the application and feasibility study for regional incentive benefits. The minimum award for standard activities will be 15 per cent of all expenditure up to a maximum of 50 per cent. Certain special activities, however, will receive a maximum of 55 per cent; these include environmental protection, energy saving and research and development.

12.1.2 The interest rate subsidy for bank loans is proportionally equal to the percentage of the grant which has been awarded; so, if the grant represents 30 per cent of the value of the investment, 30 per cent of the interest from investment bank loans is subsidised. All forms of subsidy, grant or loan are available from the Ministry of National Economy on the basis of this general framework. The aid is advanced in instalments after verification of compliance with certain conditions.

12.2 Tax allowances and reliefs

Increased depreciation allowance may be allowed as an automatic tax concession for certain expenditure. The normal rate of depreciation will be increased by 20–150 per cent, depending on the region in which the investment is being made. Unlike investment grants, tax concessions and increased depreciation allowances can be used without any approval by any governmental authority. The tax concession consists of an allowance against corporation tax liability of up to 60 per cent of the investment costs in regions A, B and C, up to a ceiling of 90 per cent for investments in region D and up to 100 per cent in Thrace.

12.3 Other public schemes and incentives

Other industrial estate incentives exist which include tax exemption for any legal acts connected with the industrial estate except VAT, reduced notary transfer fees and other administrative costs, and reduced expenses for loans.

13 COMPANIES AND BUSINESS ENTITIES

Various legal forms of companies or business entities are used, the most common being the corporation or société anonyme (*anonimos eteria*).

13.1 Limited and unlimited companies

13.1.1 The corporation (*anonimos eteria*) is the most sophisticated corporate entity. It is created by articles of incorporation (describing the corporation's duration and objects and including many compulsory provisions of law) in the form of a notarial deed executed by at least two incorporators, who may be resident or non-resident individuals or corporate entities. There is a minimum capital requirement of GRD10,000,000 which must be deposited with a bank in Greece upon incorporation. The capital is divided into bearer or registered shares with a par value of at least GRD1,000 each. Capital increases or decreases require a resolution of the general meeting of the shareholders and amendment of the articles of incorporation. The general meeting of shareholders is the supreme body of the corporation and decides specific important issues, and elects the board of directors (with at least three members) and approves the annual financial statements.

13.1.2 The limited liability company (*EPE*) is the most common corporate form for small-size businesses and family enterprises. Its creation is also based on articles of incorporation in the form of a notarial deed (also including numerous compulsory provisions). The *EPE* can include any business purposes permitted under national law and these must be described in the articles of incorporation. The *EPE* requires a capital of at least GRD3,000,000, divided into corporate participations (shares) of a par value of at least GRD10,000 each or a multiple of this amount. Previously an *EPE* required at least two members; however, a single member *EPE* is now possible provided specific conditions are met. The transfer of corporate participations, as well as capital increases or decreases or any other amendment of the articles of incorporation, require prior resolution of the members' meeting which is the supreme body of the *EPE* and also a notarial deed. At least one or more administrator(s) organise and represent the *EPE* and their powers are very wide. The *EPE* is an entirely separate entity from its members whose liability is limited.

13.1.3 The requirements for establishing a branch of a foreign company in Greece are dealt with in 14.3.

13.2 Partnerships

The general partnership (*OE*), unlike the corporation and the *EPE*, leaves partners with unlimited, joint and several personal liability for debts towards third parties. A partnership can only be created by a written private deed, including, amongst other matters, the full name of the partnership and of the partners, the partnership's objects, and the partners' share in profits. This is filed with the clerk of the court of first instance. The capital is divided into corporate participations, which may not be transferred without unanimous consent of all the partners, who are responsible for management and can represent and bind the partnership in relation to third parties. The limited partnership (*EE*) is very similar to the general partnership. However, one or more partners may be limited and not general partners, and therefore liable only up to the amount of their contribution to the partnership capital, provided they do not participate in the management of the partnership, their names do not appear in the corporate name and they do not represent the partnership when dealing with third parties. Partnerships are used for small-size businesses. They are a separate person from the partners for all legal purposes. The partnership is taxed on its profits and there is no withholding tax on dividends. Partners are not subject to taxation on dividends received. The procedure and requirements for the creation of a limited partnership are the same as for a general one.

13.3 Other types of business association

The joint venture is formed by means of an agreement among individuals or legal entities in order to carry out a specific business project. This must be described in the agreement and upon completion of the project, the joint venture is dissolved. The major provisions for the operation of a joint venture are the same as those for a general partnership and the liability of the members is unlimited. Except as specifically provided in law, a joint venture is not traditionally seen as a legal entity. Joint ventures are subject to taxation at the usual rate of 35 per cent.

14 INTERNATIONAL

14.1 Restrictions or consents required for inward investment

There are no restrictions on the acquisition of property by non-residents, with the exception of acquisition of mining rights or of property in border areas of significance to national security. Although EU nationals have the same rights as residents to purchase property in border areas they must first obtain a permit from a committee in each prefecture. Those intending to purchase such property should be professionally or commercially established in Greece and prove residence. The purpose of purchase must be for use by the applicant for his business or residence (permission is not granted for purchase of property for recreational or speculative purposes). EU legal entities may also acquire property in the border areas, provided it is to be used for business purposes. Non-EU nationals additionally require a decision from the Ministry of National Defence and sometimes the Ministry of Agriculture. Violation of these restrictions renders the purchase null and void.

14.2 Exchange controls

There are no restrictions on the introduction of funds into Greece for the purchase of property or on the ownership of property by foreign entities in Greece. Restrictions and consents required for conversion into overseas currencies have practically been abolished; the only remaining restriction imposed concerns local residents and the conversion of local currency into foreign currency and holding of foreign currency accounts. Central Bank restrictions no longer apply and any credit institution operating in Greece is allowed to undertake property finance, provided it is entitled to do so under its articles of incorporation.

14.3 Restrictions and registrations on carrying on a business

There is no restriction on a foreign entity carrying on business in Greece. However, if a foreign corporate wishes to establish a branch office it must show that its share capital is equivalent to the minimum share capital of its Greek counterpart (ie 10 million GRD for a société anonyme). Before the branch is established, a representative (Greek or foreign) residing in Greece must be granted power of attorney to act on behalf of the foreign company. The approval of the Ministry of Commerce is published in the Greek Government Gazette. Any change in the board of directors of the foreign company must be notified to the authorities and possible liabilities of the branch office extend to the foreign company itself. A foreign company may establish an offshore branch office in Greece, often called an 'L.89 Office', in order to promote and coordinate its international business activities (but not to carry out any business activities and transactions within Greece). An application must be made to the Ministry of National Economy, with the corporate documentation of the foreign company and a bank guarantee for US$50,000 for full compliance with the relevant legislation. A ministerial decision will then approve the establishment and the foreign company must appoint a representative in Greece (a Greek or foreign national). The foreign company must import annually, and convert into drachmae, an amount covering all the expenses of the offshore branch office of at least US$50,000. The office is fully tax exempt.

14.4 Repatriation of income and proceeds of property trading and development

There are no restraints involved in the repatriation of income and of proceeds by a non-resident beneficiary of property, subject to his compliance with income tax obligations.

14.5 Withholding taxes

There is no withholding tax on income arising from property, regardless of whether a company has a permanent establishment in Greece. See 11.1.4 for withholding taxes generally.

14.6 Double taxation relief

Numerous double taxation treaties include tax credit provisions to avoid double taxation.

CHAPTER 9

Italy

F Ago

Partner, Chiomenti Studio Legale, Rome

CONTENTS

1 OWNERSHIP OF LAND 287
2 OTHER INTERESTS IN LAND 290
3 TITLE TO LAND 293
4 TRANSACTIONS IN LAND 294
5 LEASES AND OTHER RIGHTS OF OCCUPATION 297
6 FINANCE AND INVESTMENT SOURCES 299
7 FORMS OF SECURITY 302
8 PLANNING AND BUILDING REGULATION 304
9 ENVIRONMENTAL MATTERS 308
10 DEVELOPMENT 310
11 TAXES 313
12 GRANTS AND INCENTIVES 316
13 COMPANIES AND BUSINESS ENTITIES 316
14 INTERNATIONAL 320

CHAPTER 9

Italy

1 OWNERSHIP OF LAND

The Italian legal system demonstrates strong Roman law influences and consequently the rules relating to property transactions are often quite different from those under common law systems. The distinction between moveables and immoveables is of fundamental importance to property law. Immoveables include rights over the land itself, but also over trees, buildings, rivers and anything that is annexed to the plot of land; moveables are everything else which do not fall into this category (such as intellectual property rights and machinery). Property rights are real rights and therefore give absolute ownership.

The Civil Code mainly regulates the law of immoveable property rather than moveable property, and also transactions between individuals, rather than activities concerning state-owned land such as expropriation (for which separate regulations exist).

1.1 Types of tenure

1.1.1 Absolute ownership

The Civil Code provides for a number of different types of tenure for private land, the most important of which is absolute ownership (*diritto di proprietà*). Under the Civil Code, the owner has the right to use, enjoy and dispose of his property as he wishes, subject to a few legislative exceptions (see 1.3).

The right of property ownership is perpetual and cannot be lost following non-use for any period of time. Ownership of land extends to the air space above the land and to everything else above it, which serves the land or is used for its adornment on a permanent basis. Ownership of the land also extends to everything below it, except for minerals, archaeological remains, water sources and others, for which special laws apply. The landowner may not, however, object to activities of third parties which are at such a depth below, or height above, the land surface that the owner cannot demonstrate an interest in their prevention. The law regulates the ways in which ownership can be acquired and these include occupation, accession, union, acquisitive prescription, contractual rights and succession (these concepts are discussed later).

It is possible to separate ownership of the land itself and ownership of improvements made to the land (eg buildings erected), and for the owner to grant lesser rights which will further limit his absolute ownership; see section 2.

1.1.2 Leasehold

There is no leasehold (*locazione*) as found in common law jurisdictions. Section 5 gives further details, but broadly speaking a form of lease or tenancy exists where the landlord grants a right less than absolute ownership (the right to enjoy the property) to the tenant for a certain period of time in return for some form of consideration or rent. The tenant will be entitled to enjoy exclusive possession and quiet enjoyment of the premises for the duration of the agreement. The tenancy is only a contractual arrangement. One important principle of Italian law governing leases is that they must all be registered with the tax office. The provisions (other than for short lets) are especially favourable to the tenant. Periodic tenancies are only common for seasonal purposes, for example holiday lets.

1.1.3 Joint ownership

1.1.3.1 In the case of co-ownership (*comunione*), the co-owners each have a separate share in the property, which need not be equal, and each share in the benefits and costs of the property according to the value of their share. If one shareholder forfeits his rights, his share will be divided amongst the remaining co-owners according to their respective shares. Each individual co-owner has personal rights to lease his share; pass it on to another; use the whole property provided that he does not alter its economic use or infringe upon the rights of the other co-owners; or to share in the expenses and benefits and proceeds of the property according to his individual share. However, some decisions, regarding the ordinary administration of the common property, must be taken by simple majority vote. If the act goes beyond the ordinary administration of the property it must be resolved by a vote of co-owners whose shares represent at least two-thirds in aggregate value of the property. This will be the case for certain structural and aesthetic changes or for mortgages to secure money for reconstruction or improvement. Finally, there are also some decisions which can only be made unanimously, such as to dispose of the property or to grant third-party rights over it.

1.1.3.2 Multi-ownership (or 'time share') has developed gradually but was not originally regulated by the law. Each co-owner agrees to purchase a part of the building for a certain period of time each year, and to share the use of the whole property with the other co-owners. The rights and liabilities of the co-owners are usually laid down by the seller of the building.

1.1.4 Condominia

Condominia occur when the flats in one building are owned by different owners who will each be a co-owner of the common parts (such as the lifts, staircases and entrance halls). Unless otherwise agreed, all expenses relating to the common areas of a condominium are payable by the owners in proportion to the value of their property, unless the use benefits a single owner or group of owners more than the others. Condominia are managed by general meeting of the participating owners. If there are more than four co-owners, the co-owners must appoint an administrator and, if there are more than 10 co-owners, they must establish further regulations to govern their relationship. Meetings are only considered to be valid when all members are invited and co-owners holding at least a two-thirds share in value and representing two-thirds in number are present. Certain resolutions, such as the nomination of administrators and the reconstruction or repair of parts of the building, always require a majority vote, ie representing at least one-half of the ownership of the condominium.

1.1.5 Lesser rights

It is possible to create lesser rights of use or occupation. The rules governing these vary. For further details, see section 2. Such rights include servitudes, usufructs, building leases, surface rights and mortgages.

1.2 Legal and beneficial ownership

There is no concept similar to the beneficial interest and trust of land as elsewhere.

1.3 Restrictions on ownership and dealing

1.3.1 There are some legislative restrictions on the rights of landowners. These aim mainly to protect the public interest, and include planning regulations, rights of reasonable and necessary access from adjoining land and protection of areas of natural beauty. There are also, however, restrictions which aim to protect private interests and these include the laws of nuisance protecting neighbouring land, and the obligation not to act in a way that will merely serve to cause harm to others. A property owned by a minor must be administered by the parents or legal guardian. Similar provisions are applicable in the case of an incapacitated person. The law does not impose any limits on a company's ability to buy and sell property within the scope of the company's articles of association. It remains unclear whether private associations which have not been officially recognised by the state, unincorporated associations, have the capacity to own land.

1.3.2 Certain parties have pre-emption rights on the sale of land. In the case of agricultural land, for example, any person who actually cultivates the land (eg the tenant farmer) must be notified of any pending sale contract terms, including the price, and be given a pre-emption right to acquire the land on the same terms. If there is no tenant farmer on the land to be sold, the pre-emption right passes to tenant farmers on adjoining land.

All public property is regulated separately. Some property may never be sold to private individuals or bodies, eg the seashore, rivers, state-owned roads and railways.

Other types of public land may be sold to a private body or individual but the form of public usage must be preserved, eg state archives and libraries. Also, the state has a pre-emption right on the sale of property of recognised artistic or historic value.

1.4 Acquisitive prescription

Property rights can be acquired by continuous occupation for a period of 20 years. The occupier must have treated the property as if he was the rightful owner and have occupied it without the use of force and without the permission of the lawful owner. The term can be reduced to ten years if the property is acquired in good faith from a person who was not the lawful owner, and the purported right was registered.

2 OTHER INTERESTS IN LAND

There are a number of interests less than full ownership which only grant an interest in another's land.

2.1 Servitudes or easements, usufruct, building and dwelling rights

2.1.1 Servitudes or easements

A servitude is a right over one piece of land (the servient tenement) in favour of another piece of land (the dominant tenement). The right is intended to give some objective benefit (whether present or future) to the dominant tenement. Usually, the servitude will be created by contract, but in exceptional circumstances it may be created by law (eg, if land would otherwise have no access to a public highway or the right is required to create passage for water or electrical wires); although a legal right then exists, the servitude will have to be formally created by contract, with the consent of the servient owner, failing which an application to the courts will need to be made. Servitudes may also be created by acquisitive prescription (*usucapione*) if the right has been exercised in a continuous, non-disputed way for 20 years or more. In certain cases, compensation is payable to the owner of the servient plot for any damage caused as a result of the servitude. The holder of the servitude is obliged to exercise his rights so as to keep damage and inconvenience to the servient tenement to a minimum. Unless otherwise specified by law or contract, the owner of the dominant tenement must bear all expenses relating to the maintenance of the servitude (unless its existence also creates benefits for the servient tenement, in which case expenses are shared proportionately). The holder of the servitude may propose a change in the location of the servitude if it would benefit him without prejudicing the owner of the servient plot. The beneficiary may apply to court to have his right enforced. Servitudes will expire either by passage of time (because the dominant owner does not exercise his rights for over 20 years – 'defeasance'); because the owner of the dominant tenement also becomes the owner of the servient tenement, or because the rights have become impossible to exercise or have lost their benefit and 20 years have passed. The most common forms of servitudes are rights of access, rights of drainage, rights of light and air, and rights of wall support.

2.1.2 Usufruct

A usufruct is usually granted contractually by the owner of the burdened property. Usufructs may not continue beyond the lifetime of the grantee. It is hypothetically possible that the usufruct is granted to one person for the lifetime of another, and that the usufruct will expire with the death of the grantee. If given to a legal entity, usufructs may not exceed 30 years. The usufruct gives the holder the right to use, occupy, enjoy and receive the profits from the property of another provided that he does not alter the previous nature or use of the land (*rispetto della destinazione economica*). The landowner retains 'bare ownership'. The usufruct may generally be assigned, but cannot exceed the life of the assignor, unless the agreement states otherwise. However, unless the bare owner is notified of the transfer, the original grantee remains jointly liable. During the period of the usufruct, ordinary expenses (for administration and general maintenance) are payable by the grantee, whilst the costs of extraordinary repairs are payable by the bare owner. On surrender, the grantee will have to pay the cost of any damage he has caused. Additionally, he has a right to compensation (equal to the lower of the expense incurred in connection with the improvement and the increase in value to the property) for improvements. Usufructs expire on death of the grantee, due to non-use for 20 years, when the bare ownership and the usufruct right belong to the same owner, if the property is destroyed, and if the grantee abuses his position and fails to take adequate care of the property.

2.1.3 Building and dwelling rights

For surface rights akin to the building rights of other countries, see 2.6.1.

2.2 Restrictions on use and other restrictions

See section 2.1.

2.3 Private mortgages and charges

A mortgage entitles the beneficiary to the right to force a compulsory sale of the burdened estate (even where the mortgaged property has been sold to a third party) and the right of priority on the proceeds of such compulsory sale to the extent of the mortgage. For further details on the mortgage, and on orders securing judgment debts and public liabilities, see 7.1. The Civil Code lists categories of preferential debts, or privileges, which will all rank ahead of unsecured creditors (these are described more fully at 7.3.2). It is not possible to create liens over real property or land.

2.4 Contracts and options

2.4.1 A preliminary contract is an agreement which binds the parties to enter into a definitive contract at a later date. It can be enforced in court by an order for specific performance. It is most commonly used for the sale of a building still under construction. The terms of the future contract for sale must be clearly set out in the preliminary contract so that, at the time of the contract for sale, there is no need for further negotiation and the preliminary contract must satisfy the formal requirements applicable to the contract for sale (see section 4). If the preliminary contract does not fulfil these requirements it will be void. In the event that the preliminary contract is breached, the other party has a right to specific performance and to damages. As a general rule, the rights of action last for 10 years.

2.4.2 The term 'option' means an irrevocable offer to which one party remains bound for a certain time. The contract is only concluded if the other party exercises the option by accepting the offer.

2.5 Public or municipal charges

Public liabilities in the nature of taxes on a property and its owner are dealt with in section 11. Other liabilities are dealt with at 2.7. In addition there are various duties and charges of a local or municipal nature.

2.6 Other interests

2.6.1 The surface right (*diritto di superficie*) is granted by the landowner to allow the beneficiary to build on the land and become the full owner of the buildings. The landowner will retain title to the land. When the surface right expires the owner of the land becomes owner of the structure. The landowner need not pay any compensation to the beneficiary, unless the contract provides otherwise.

2.6.2 The old right of *enfiteusi* is rarely used as it was more appropriate for feudal social systems. The *enfiteusi* is a property right with a related payment obligation. The holder does not become owner of the land, but has the same rights of the owner over the fruits and any other profits of the land. He is obliged to improve the land and, periodically, to compensate the owner either by payment of a sum of money or a fixed amount of natural products. An *enfiteusi* may be granted for an unlimited or fixed period of not less than 20 years. If the parties fail to specify a term, it is assumed to last indefinitely. It is a typical right in rem and it is not transferable.

2.7 Liabilities attaching to land

Various liabilities may attach to the owner, both private and public, such as the law of nuisance, health and safety regulations (see section 9), and the requirement of planning consent (see section 8). Landowners are liable for damage as a result of collapse of any part of a building, unless it is proved that the damage was not caused by failure of the owner to maintain the building or a defect in the construction. Landowners are also liable even if the third party entered without consent, unless the owner took all suitable steps to prevent entry. The landowner may be liable for both criminal and civil penalties. This will also apply when employees of the landowner suffer damage, eg as a result of negligence, recklessness, lack of skill or infringement of any legal provision or regulation.

2.8 Legal and equitable interests

Legal and beneficial interests are not recognised in Italian law.

2.9 Protection of interests

The law generally requires registration of interests in land, such as mortgages and servitudes, as well as transactions in it. There are, however, interests which do not result from the Registrar of Real Property (eg *usi civici, privilegi fiscali*), and leases not exceeding nine years. For further details, see 3.1. In the case of a conflict, priority depends upon date of first registration even in the case of court judgments.

3 TITLE TO LAND

3.1 Proof of title

Various types of contract must be registered with the Registrar of Real Property (*Pubblici Registri Immobiliari*) in order to bind third parties:

(a) contracts transferring ownership;
(b) contracts creating, transferring or modifying usufructs, surface rights or *enfiteusi*;
(c) contracts creating or modifying servitudes;
(d) contracts creating or extinguishing rights to use or inhabit land;
(e) preliminary contracts;
(f) lease contracts of more than nine years;
(g) contracts creating companies, consortia or associations which confer property rights; and
(h) court judgments which create, transfer or modify any of such rights.

3.2 Land registry

3.2.1 Plans

The Italian Land Register (*Registri Immobiliari*) is normally indexed by the names of individual landowners, rather than individual plots of land. If the owner is unknown, a potential buyer will be able to consult the *Registri*

Catastali to check whether the owner is registered there, and then to check against the name in the land register (which should be more up-to-date). Construction plans are filed in the *Registri Catastali.* These are registers kept for tax purposes rather than to prove ownership. These registers are not definitive although they are usually referred to in contracts for the transfer of land to describe coordinates of the property being transferred. There are, however, a few of the Northern Italian provinces where land is indexed according to plots (these territories are generally those from the old Austro-Hungarian empire). In this case plans are definitive.

3.2.2 Content

Registration is in the name of the individual landowner. The registrar will, therefore, enter the transfer in favour of the buyer and against the seller. Any search will need to be made against the name of the landowner. Registration only serves to notify the public as to the state of the property and any encumbrances on it, and cannot create good title where the claimant did not possess title before. Generally the registries are organised by the *Provincia* or district and they are named *Conservatorie dei Registri Immobiliari.*

3.2.3 Errors

The Ministry of Finance is liable for any damages flowing from errors in the information in the land register. It is possible to register only court judgments, public deeds or private deeds with certification of signature. These deeds can be registered only by filing a certificated copy of court judgments and public deeds and the original of the private deeds. Any omissions or errors in the application information do not make the registration void, unless they result in uncertainty regarding the persons, property or legal relationship between the parties.

3.3 Passing of title

There is no date after which failure to have the transfer registered makes it void, but in case of conflict, priority is established by the date of registration.

4 TRANSACTIONS IN LAND

4.1 Procedures

The seller usually only enters negotiations for sale after his estate agent has found a potential buyer. At this early stage, soon after first viewing, the prudent buyer will have started the process of searches and arrangements for a survey. During negotiations, both parties remain under a duty of good faith, must inform the other of any information regarding the essential terms of the transaction and maintain confidentiality. Once negotiations have been completed, the seller will require a deposit, which the buyer will usually be able to deduct from the final sale price. All this can occur without binding contracts having been signed. Therefore, legal advice is recommended at the time the deposit is paid. It is also usually advisable for the buyer to research the seller's financial position because if a seller becomes insolvent before, or within one or two years after, completion, the property will have to be surrendered to the creditors (with only very limited defences for a bona fide buyer). To obtain further protection, the buyer may request a bank guarantee from the seller and register the transaction with the land registry. When the parties enter into a preliminary contract for sale (see 2.4), it must be in written form. This is followed by the definitive sale contract which is generally signed before a notary public, who is commonly appointed by the buyer, and then duly registered with the Registrar of Real Property in order to bind third parties. During the sale, the seller is obliged to deliver the purchased property to the buyer, transfer ownership or other relevant rights, pay damages to the buyer if he loses the right of ownership to a third party with a legitimate claim to the property and indemnify the buyer against defects in the property which render it unfit for its intended purpose or substantially diminish its value. The buyer is obliged to pay the purchase price in the manner set out in the contract. After the survey, the buyer will usually appoint a notary public who will check the title of the seller and any encumbrances at the land registry. If the buyer fails to complete, he will usually forfeit his deposit (subject to agreement between the parties). The seller who fails to complete commonly has to pay the buyer twice the amount of the deposit, unless the buyer wishes to enforce the contract.

4.2 Contract terms

The sale contract usually contains the following:

(a) the address and a description of the property, including an indication of the boundaries;
(b) a description of the common parts if a condominium;
(c) a reference to its registration in the appropriate *registro catastale*;
(d) a chain of title showing ownership for the last 20 years;
(e) declarations by the seller that the property has been declared to the tax authorities, that building permits and fitness for habitation certificates have been granted for any buildings and that all buildings comply with the relevant regulations and legislation, that all taxes and condominium charges due to that date have been paid, and that the property belongs to him alone, eg it is not held in automatic co-ownership due to marriage;
(f) a guarantee by the seller that he has and is transferring valid title;
(g) the price and the means for payment;
(h) an indication of any intention of the seller to forego his right to an implied legal mortgage (if the price is not immediately and totally paid);
(i) the date upon which possession will pass; and
(j) the division of expenses between the parties.

The agreement will usually also state whether the deposit is to be viewed as a part payment and subtracted from the final sale price, and is to be forfeited on failure to complete by the buyer. It may also detail the seller's financial position and potential liability on failure to complete (see 4.1).

4.3 Formalities

The only formality required is that the purchase of the property must be by way of legalised private document *(scrittura privata autenticata*) or public deed (*atto pubblico*) and registered in order to bind third parties. Transfer of title between the parties occurs when the contract is executed, unless otherwise specified in the contract. A recent enactment permits the registration of the preliminary contract in order to protect the buyer only if it has been drawn up as a public deed or a private writing with verified signature.

4.4 Fees, costs and taxes

4.4.1 The seller will pay for the negotiation of the contract and his share of any agency fees. The agent is entitled to a commission (usually two to three per cent of the contract price from each party) if the contract is concluded as a result of his services and he has a right to be indemnified for costs, even if the sale is not concluded. Agents' commissions vary in Italy on a local basis. It is customary for the buyer to pay the notary and notary fees are based on the value of the contract. Although the registration charges are payable by both parties to the tax authority, the buyer usually also pays the registration charges and transfer taxes.

4.4.2 Legal costs are usually restricted to notary fees as other lawyers tend to have little involvement. Notary fees typically consists of:

- lire 8,600,000 for contracts of 5 billion lire;
- lire 7,400,000 for contracts of 2 billion lire;
- lire 6,100,000 for contracts of 1 billion lire;
- lire 5,100,000 for contracts of 500,000,000 lire;
- lire 3,400,000 for contracts of 100,000,000 lire;
- lire 2,500,000 for contracts of 40,000,000 lire;
- lire 1,950,000 for contracts of 10,000,000 lire.

Notarial fees for leases are always half of those listed.

4.4.3 A transfer of land acquired from an individual is subject to a registration tax of eight per cent of the cadastral value declared by the parties. Property bought from an entrepreneur investing in property or a company, however, is subject to value added tax (VAT) at 19 per cent (see 11.6 and 11.8).

4.4.4 A further three per cent registration and cadastral charges will be levied on the property's cadastral value.

4.4.5 All agents' fees currently attract VAT at a rate of 19 per cent.

4.5 Professionals' roles

Marketing of land is usually undertaken by estate agents, who must be enrolled in their professional registry at the competent chamber of commerce. A surveyor is normally engaged by the buyer. The survey can be very important and may affect the price or even the occurrence of any transaction. Lawyers are not usually involved unless the transaction is large or particularly complicated. A notary is required by law to be involved at the most important stages of the transaction. It is advisable to go to the notary before signing the preliminary contract. He may help with advice on the wider legal and taxation aspects, eg family law implications, rights and charges over the property, inheritance and gift tax, and so forth. He will usually organise the title search on behalf of the buyer, conduct a search for registered mortgages or other charges, check on the building's conformity with the relevant planning permission and whether the property has been declared to the tax authorities. If the property is owned by a company, he will also check whether the company is in danger of being declared insolvent.

5 LEASES AND OTHER RIGHTS OF OCCUPATION

The Civil Code relating to lease agreements proved inadequate for viable dealings in the modern property market and further temporary provisions have been enacted. The Civil Code will now only apply if there are no other applicable regulations. Currently, however, the lessor still does not make the profit he would have hoped when selling whilst a tenancy agreement is still in operation. In addition, the lessee benefits from extensive protection, implied into every category of lease, and is often able to obtain long tenancies at low prices. A lease is a right less than absolute ownership granted for a certain period of time in return for some consideration or rent. Leases are usually written but this is only obligatory if the lease exceeds nine years. All leases must be filed with the tax office for registration within 20 days.

5.1 Rent and other terms

Law 392 of 1978 sets a law of fair rent (*equo canone*) for urban leases. Different rules apply to buildings used for residential and commercial purposes. Another form of lease, the *affitto*, is dealt with at 5.1.3. The contract often provides for subletting but it is otherwise prohibited in principle.

5.1.1 If not specifically agreed to the contrary, the terms of this law are implied into every lease of urban dwelling or residential premises, giving lessees a wide range of protection. The rent must be at the rates specified in the law (*equo canone*) for the various types of building, multiplying the number of square metres by the indexes fixed. The lease may provide for rent review at a rate of no more than 75 per cent of the change in the retail price index over the preceding year. This provision does not, however, apply to temporary leases, eg second homes, or to leases for new buildings entered into after 1992. According to Law 333 of 1992 the parties may contract out of these rental provisions if the lessor waives the right to terminate the lease at its first date of expiration. The provisions concerning minimum duration and renewal are dealt with at 5.3.

5.1.2 As a general rule, there is no regulation of rent for commercial buildings and the parties are free to negotiate, although the rent cannot then be changed for three years. It is increasingly common for the rent to represent a percentage of the income of the business. Nevertheless, again, once the rent has been set, the lessor may not increase it beyond 75 per cent of the retail price index. The provisions for minimum duration and renewal are dealt with at 5.3.

5.1.3 The *affitto* is a lease of productive moveable or immoveable property. The lessee has to manage the property with regard to its economic destination and in the general interest of production. He is entitled to the benefits or other advantages deriving from the property. The lessor is bound to deliver the productive property with all its accessories and appurtenances in a condition suitable for the use and production intended. The right to quiet enjoyment is limited as the lessor may enter at any time to establish whether or not the property is being used correctly. Subletting or assignment is again not permitted without prior approval.

5.1.4 The lessor's main obligations are to deliver the property in a state of good repair, and ensure that the lessee has quiet enjoyment. All lessors must carry out all necessary repairs and restoration to allow the premises to be used in the manner for which they were let, and protect the lessee from interference by third parties. The lessee must use the property for the agreed purpose, take due care that he returns it in the same state, and pay the rent when due. He must carry out all minor repairs and generally may not sublet or assign without consent. For commercial leases, consent is not required if the lessee sublets or assigns the business too. The lessee is also responsible for any loss or deterioration to the property (other than normal wear and tear) during the term of the lease, even if caused by fire, unless it is proven that the lessee was not at fault. If the property is damaged by fire but insured by the owner, the lessee remains liable for the difference between the insurance coverage and the total loss. These general rules can apply to any kind of lease. For urban residential property the Law of 1978 now gives the lessee the right to withdraw on six months' notice, only if provided in the contract. The lessee can also withdraw just giving six months' notice for certain serious reasons. The contract can be cancelled for breach by the lessee (non-payment of the rent).

In case of expropriation performance becomes impossible and the contract is automatically terminated.

5.2 Privity of contract and estate

Italian law does not have any concept equivalent to the doctrine of privity of contract.

5.3 Rent control and security of tenure

5.3.1 All leases of urban residential property must be of at least four years and will be automatically renewed, unless either party notifies the other, at least six months before the end of the term, that he does not wish to renew.

5.3.2 Leases of commercial premises also have a minimum duration, but of six years (nine years for hotels), and they are automatically renewed for a further similar period, unless either party notifies the other at least 12 months

(18 months for hotels) before the end of the term, that he does not wish to renew. The lessor cannot refuse renewal at the end of the first period, unless he needs the premises for his own use, or for restoration or demolition. The lessor must pay compensation for loss of goodwill (equal to 18 months' rent) on any termination other than the lessee's notice, breach of contract or bankruptcy. The amount of indemnity will be twice this if the new lessee of the premises engages in the same form of business and if the new lease commences within a year from the termination of the previous one. The lessee always has a right of pre-emption over any sale of the property. These principles are mandatory and cannot be varied or omitted by agreement. No lease agreement (neither residential nor commercial) can exceed 30 years.

5.3.3 Generally, if no renewal is available, and if the lessor wishes to terminate the lease, he must send notice to the lessee within a specified time (six months for a private dwelling and 12 for commercial premises). The lessor will always be entitled to terminate the lease of commercial premises, if he requires the premises for his own commercial activity or has to demolish the property in order to rebuild or restore it, or if he has been ordered to make some improvements by the local authority.

5.4 Other legislative restrictions

Any property must satisfy regulations, eg as to health and safety, protection of the environment, and planning control.

5.5 Method of measurement

The method of measurement adopted for letting purposes is based on the gross internal area, ie the whole of the internal floor area including common areas measured from the internal face of the walls.

6 FINANCE AND INVESTMENT SOURCES

The most important and commonly used method for financing property investment is loan finance, provided by the large number of banking institutions. The finance lease is also a common means to raise finance for the acquisition of property. Straight equity finance has not yet become an important source although real estate funds and the newly established pension funds might in the future play an important role.

6.1 Loan finance

6.1.1 Different sectors of the credit industry are still regulated by different laws and there are special laws regarding loans for specific purposes (such as industrial, commercial, agricultural, construction, general construction or public works). Loan finance is offered by banks of national interest, public charter banks, commercial banks, credit cooperatives and savings banks. The special banks of national interest are joint stock companies quoted on the stock exchange. The public charter banks consist of six government-controlled institutions, whilst the commercial banks are usually privately owned. The credit cooperatives and savings banks are generally regionally based but have expanded nationally and, except for the savings banks, internationally, and are increasingly commercially orientated. They offer the same range of services as the commercial banks and represent an important source of funding for local government and specialised medium and longer term funding. The regional institutions play a large role in granting the state subsidised loans which are available for regional or industrial investment projects of important national interest.

6.1.2 The main types of loan are the term bank loan, the overdraft, the credit line with the bank and, for the individual who is a professional or carries out a commercial activity, a particular form of credit is available to be used for the acquisition of goods and services not related to the business.

6.1.3 With the implementation of the Second Banking Directive (646/89/EEC) and the new Banking Law of 1993 the distinction between ordinary (short-term) banks and special credit (medium-term) institutions as set out in the old Banking Act of 1936 has been removed and now all credit institutions are authorised to provide all types of credit services. Banking and finance activities are subject to the control and supervision of the Bank of Italy.

6.1.4 The most common type of contract used in property transactions is the *mutuo,* ie a loan agreement in which the delivery of money occurs simultaneously with, and is an essential part of, the agreement. Special provisions are contained in the Banking Law relating to property or mortgage financing (*credito fondiario*). Property financing consists in the granting of medium or long-term loans (mainly in the form of *mutui*) secured by a mortgage on property. The Bank of Italy has determined that the maximum amount of such financing should be 80 per cent of the commercial value of the mortgaged property or of the cost of the works to be undertaken on such property; such percentage may be increased to 100 per cent when additional security (such as a bank or insurance guarantee or a pledge of state bonds) is also provided.

6.1.5 Property financing most commonly provides for a term ranging from seven to ten years and for a repayment schedule of fixed and equal instalments with decreasing interest and increasing capital elements. The interest rates, which are mainly variable based on the banks' prime rate or on other market parameters, are becoming more frequently fixed (also in view of the stabilisation of interest rates and inflation in Italy). Indexed rates are also not uncommon.

6.1.6 Property finance is normally granted by banks to their own clients but in recent years this has been marketed through networks so that banks have increasingly granted property finance to new clients with whom they have had no prior relationship.

6.1.7 Syndication of real estate financing is not particularly common unless in connection with major transactions for corporate clients.

6.2 Investment or equity finance

Investment or equity finance by companies is not common and there are no specialised investors providing this form of financing in Italy. However, there seems to have been more interest in the real estate sector (developments, large department stores, leisure parks, etc) attracting foreign investors in Italy. Following the example of foreign investors it may be expected that Italian corporate investors will also increasingly look at this sector.

6.3 Mezzanine or mixed funding

Mezzanine or mixed financing has been made available in Italy only in connection with buy-out transactions or project finance. It has not been substantially adopted for property or development.

6.4 Sale and lease-back

It is not uncommon for businesses who occupy their own properties to realise capital by sale and lease-back for an annual return.

The technique of selling the property with a lease-back in the form of a financial lease, with the option for the lessee to buy back the property at the end of the lease, has been progressively abandoned in view of its legal uncertainty. It has been seen as violating a basic rule of Italian law which prohibits the creditor from taking all the property given as a guarantee upon the default of the debtor (*patto commissorio*).

6.5 Tax leasing

Tax leasing is not a major source or vehicle for finance other than for specific types of finance dedicated to cooperative housing schemes and made available through cooperative societies.

6.6 Other types of property finance

There are no other major property finance schemes.

6.7 Institutional investment

Traditionally, insurance companies and state pension and insurance entities have invested heavily in the property market in view of mandatory rules which limited their investment choices. Such rules have now been relaxed and such entities are now trying to disinvest from property and concentrate either on their core business or other more profitable businesses or investments.

Legislation for real estate funds has been enacted in recent years but such funds have not yet become important players in the real estate market.

7 FORMS OF SECURITY

7.1 Mortgages

7.1.1 A mortgage is the most complete right of security, and can be created by agreement, by virtue of law or following a judgment. Mortgages arise by law in various circumstances: in favour of a seller to guarantee the obligations of the buyer under the sale contract; in favour of co-heirs, partners and other joint owners to guarantee the payment of any balance in connection with the property; and in favour of the state under the Criminal Code. Mortgages may otherwise be validly created by unilateral declaration of the mortgagor, and must be created by public deed or private written agreement but never by will. Mortgages may be granted in respect of property that is not yet owned or property in course of construction, but may not be registered until ownership is acquired or construction has reached a stage where the building can be adequately described. Mortgages over jointly owned property affect only the portion which would be distributed if the ownership were divided.

7.1.2 Mortgage is a right in rem that attaches to the property and follows the property when transferred and it cannot be assigned. Improvements, usufruct, surface rights, and *enfiteusi* may all be mortgaged. In order for a mortgage to bind third parties and to ensure the creditor's priority, it must be registered with the local Registrar of Real Property (*Conservatoria dei Registri Immobiliari*). If the property is registered in the wrong registry, the registration is ineffective. When applying for registration, the applicant must show proof of title, and if the mortgage is by private deed, the signature of the mortgagor must be authenticated. At first, the mortgage is registered in the name of the creditor with an indication of the issuer, the date of issue and the series, number and value of the instruments used. Registration must specify the property (or property right) to which the mortgage attaches, and the sum secured. Registration provides creditors with priority in relation to the property. Omissions or errors in the documents or request for registration which do not render uncertain the identity of creditor, debtor or the owner of the property or of the mortgage, or the amount of the debt, do not affect the mortgage and may be corrected at the request and expense of the interested party. Registrations of mortgages are valid for 20 years and are renewable before the end of the term without loss of priority. The registration costs must initially be paid by the party requesting the registration, but unless the parties have agreed otherwise, will be borne by the debtor. The party requesting the registration is required to pay the tax (*imposta ipotecaria*). However, all interested parties registered are jointly liable for the payment of the registration tax. Mortgages take priority from date of registration even in respect of a conditional debt or obligations which arise from an existing relationship. If more than one request for registration is filed at the same time, the mortgages are given equal priority. The creditors' rights will then be determined on a pro rata basis in relation to the size of each loan.

7.1.3 The legal mortgagee has a number of rights, including the right to force a compulsory sale and to take monies from the proceeds to settle his debt. The rest of the monies will then be left to subsequent creditors. Compulsory sale can only proceed once the mortgagee has obtained a final judgment from the court. If a secured bank loan is in default, the bank does not need to obtain such judgment, as the *mutuo* contract is sufficient evidence of the debt. (*Mutuo* is a contract by which one party delivers to another a certain quantity of money or of other fungible things, and the other undertakes to return an equal amount of the same kind and quality.) Even if another creditor requests the sale, the proceeds will still be divided according to priority of the creditors. Servitudes, usufructs and rights to use and inhabit which are established after registration of a mortgage are not enforceable against the mortgagee and expire on any forced sale. The holders of such rights then have a claim on the proceeds and will rank above creditors whose mortgages were registered after the establishment of the rights. A mortgage may also be enforced against a third-party acquirer of the property, who must take action against the debtor to protect his interest. A mortgage will be terminated by destruction of the property.

7.2 Floating and other charges

There is no concept of a floating charge over the debtor's assets in Italy.

7.3 Bonds and guarantees

7.3.1 Under a personal guarantee, the guarantor assumes a personal obligation to pay the creditor in the event of the debtor's default. The guarantee can apply to conditional or future obligations, but for the latter the maximum amount guaranteed should be stated. The guarantee can never attach to a sum greater than that owed by the debtor. The guarantor will be jointly and severally liable with the principal debtor, except where the parties have agreed that the guarantee will not be called on before judgment is levied against the principal debtor.

7.3.2 The Civil Code lists categories of preferential creditors who will all rank ahead of unsecured creditors, and as between themselves the order is established by law and is not affected by the time at which they became creditors. Most privileges are held by the state or other public bodies eg the state's general privilege over all the debtor's personal property for the payment of state and local income tax by all legal persons. A privilege may be either general (applying to all the debtor's goods and chattels) or special (applying to specific goods or land). A general privilege does not give the creditor a right to the specific goods but simply confers priority on the debt. If the goods are then passed to a bona fide third party, the creditor will no longer have a claim over them. A special privilege does confer a real right and will override third-party rights created after the privilege arose, unless the object of the privilege is a chattel and not land, and the buyer was acting in good faith. Under certain circumstances, the privilege may have conditions attached. A special privilege over land will rank even before a mortgage.

7.4 Credit insurance

Performance of contractual obligations can be insured also by personal guarantees created by third parties (*fideiussione*).

8 PLANNING AND BUILDING REGULATION

The Republican Constitution in the 1970s granted the regional authorities the power to pass their own statutes regarding planning and building regulation. Gradually, more and more powers have been transferred to the individual regions. Nevertheless, each regional law must conform to general principles established by state framework legislation and must not conflict with state interests or the interests of other regions. The Law of 1985 acknowledged the great many infringements of the regulations that had gone before, and gave all previous infringing buildings an immunity from prosecution, but then tightened up the rules and penalties for all building works to follow.

8.1 Planning authorities

There is a planning authority in each region whose decisions may not contravene the general principles provided by state laws and governmental acts, issued by the Cabinet, as proposed by the Ministry of Public Works. The town council lays down the general town plan or *piano regolatore generale*. This is voted on by the council, approved by the region and covers land use, development areas, public areas and areas of historic, environmental or scenic importance for the whole borough. It is then left to the regions to implement further detailed regulations. Town planning is also carried out by town councils individually or jointly, who are the principal planning authorities.

8.2 Development plans

As stated previously, each region is responsible for implementing its own detailed policies, and therefore attention must be paid to the individual rules of the area. The general town plan scheme, devised by the town council, is supposed to cover the whole borough territory but in reality areas exist for which no provision has been made. In such an area, no permission is required and it is merely necessary to comply with general building regulations and legal standards. The general town plan scheme:

(a) details the main existing and future communication lines;
(b) divides the area into zones (such as expansion areas, industrial zones, agricultural zones, service regions, or historical centres) with each zone having its own characteristics and restrictions;
(c) defines public spaces, schools, sports grounds, airports etc;
(d) contains restrictions on building for historic, aesthetic or environmental reasons; and
(e) outlines plans for the building of economic 'popular' housing, that to be constructed by business enterprises, co-operatives or independent bodies.

There are plans for the south of Italy, particularly aimed at industrial development, for areas of natural beauty and for military zones. Town councils also draw up plans for reconstruction work and for land which is to be used for industry, commerce and artisans.

Once the general town plan has been created, the town council is then responsible for creating further 'implementation plans'. The most important is the detailed plan which implements the general town plan and lays down the regulation for each plot of land. The general town plan may also be implemented by way of general building schemes, which are produced by private individuals or undertakings and must be approved by the town council. These provide for the construction of residential or industrial buildings. The producer of the scheme must contract with the council to bear the whole cost of essential services (eg roads) and part of the cost of providing secondary services (eg schools).

Following the general principles set out by each region, the town councils lay down three to five year implementation plans which play a fundamental role within the planning system. Each region must also enact at least one landscape safeguard plan and check the environmental impact of all building in these areas. The town council will also create a council house plan giving them the authority to take possession of land designated for the construction of council housing.

8.3 Planning controls and procedures

In general, all building activity including construction of new buildings, extension or modification of existing buildings, or transformation of any land, and extensive maintenance, restoration or demolition works, must be authorised by a special permit called a concession (*concessione*), which may include conditions. A concession will be granted when the land has been designated as suitable for development and the applicant has paid the fees and fulfilled the correct procedure. Occasionally, if land is included in a development area, the owner has to build or risk expropriation.

8.3.1 Planning applications are made to the mayor and must include: details of the land and proof of title; a project plan signed by a registered architect, surveyor or engineer; a map from the Register of Real Property; and any additional information requested. The application will then be assessed, and, if the concession is to be granted, a fee will be set and the applicant notified. The fee will be based on the town planning charge, the cost of the original town planning in the area for which there will be a local tariff, and the building charge, based on building cost as assessed by the council and not exceeding

10 per cent. The authorities may request alterations to the plan before recommending that the mayor grant the concession. The office which grants the permission may also attach conditions, eg as to the appearance of the building or alignment with existing structures. However, all such conditions must be justified by a legal provision or regulation. Different types of permit are required for different types of construction work. Some types of work do not require a concession but merely a simple authorisation, for which there will be no charge. Such work includes: extraordinary maintenance work including structural changes or construction of hygienic and technical facilities, provided that such work does not alter the overall volume and surface area and there is no change of use; restoration; open air storage; demolition; construction of disabled facilities and work to reduce energy consumption. Ordinary maintenance work, such as redecoration, does not require any kind of authorisation. Works carried on inside the building which do not change its outward appearance in any way, and do not change its use, are also not subject to a concession, eg movement of internal walls; however, a notice must be given to the mayor accompanied by an expert's report.

8.3.2 The borough authority is under a duty to acquire all the documents (authorisations) necessary for the building concession, within 60 days of application. If, within 90 days the mayor does not respond, the application is considered accepted. A denial of the concession must be justified by the mayor and this may be challenged before the regional administrative tribunal (*Tribunale Amministrativo Regionale*). A negative tribunal judgment is appealable before the national court (*Consiglio di Stato*).

8.3.3 The concession attaches to the land rather than the individual and an application can be made by anyone with an interest in the property. Work must usually be started within a year from it being granted and must be finished within three years, unless there are reasons beyond the control of the developer or due to the nature of the work.

8.3.4 In the face of widespread disregard for building consents and the construction of many illegal houses and other buildings, especially in particular regions, the government has enacted a series of decrees (since the early 1980s) allowing for the ratification of illegal building work on payment of a penalty and an administrative fine based on the cost of providing utilities. When this is unavailable, the penalties for infringement will depend upon the circumstances surrounding the infringement (eg if any neighbour has suffered damage) and the particular regulation infringed. It is possible for the authorities, or for any neighbour adversely affected, to demand demolition of property built in contravention of a regulation which requires a specific distance between buildings. Otherwise the sanction will not be demolition, but a fine or possibly imprisonment. Imprisonment and heavy fines will be imposed for serious infringements such as disregarding the need for permission in areas of environmental or architectural value, or continuing to build when the project has been halted by the authorities. In addition, any transfer of property or a real right in property will be void if a building licence was not granted and construction began after the passing of the Law of 1985. The seller of a property must indicate the details of any building licence in the contract or in a separate contract, and failure to do so will make the contract invalid.

8.4 Building standards, control and supervision

Each regional authority will have its own mandatory building regulations and standards. The government is attempting to increase the stringency of these codes to achieve consistency with EU standards. In certain relatively rare circumstances, the materials and procedures may also require authorisation. Regulations include both local and state health regulations relating to water, light, ventilation, heat etc. Certain regulations relate to specific types of development. Factories emitting smoke, steam, water or any other pollutant dangerous to the health of the population, are listed in a decree and divided into two groups, the more dangerous of which may not be built near residential property. A notice must be given before the commencement of such activities and there are criminal sanctions for failure to comply. Fire regulations differ for different types of building. The mayor also carries out checks on the conformity of the building with the plans, the permit and health regulations. The mayor acts in conjunction with the building commission and will grant a 'fitness for habitation' certificate, which certifies the health and safety of the building and its fitness for habitation, after the works have been completed. There are several special laws relating to building standards which refer to the minimisation of damage caused by earthquakes, particularly in listed seismic areas. Anyone carrying out building operations in such areas must give notice to the mayor and to the relevant technical seismic office. Anyone carrying out building work must contribute to the cost of providing the land with utilities such as gas, electricity, and roads, according to the actual cost of providing such utilities and the cost of the development.

The owner of a building or other construction is liable for damage to third parties from any collapse, unless he proves that such damage was not caused by defective maintenance, or by a defect in construction. There is a right to require demolition of dangerous buildings.

8.5 Protection of buildings of special interest

It is provided that buildings of special interest cannot be altered without the authorisation of the competent authority. Owners are also bound to notify all transfer deeds and on sale the state may exercise a right of pre-emption.

8.6 Compulsory purchase or expropriation and compensation

The town council is entitled to dispossess landowners where this is necessary to build economic 'popular' houses or industrial installations. The Civil Code states that no one can be deprived of his property unless such dispossession is in the public interest. Dispossessed landowners are entitled to fair compensation, which must be substantial. To calculate this it is important to consider the destination of the property.

9 ENVIRONMENTAL MATTERS

The 'Merli' Law of 1976 which governed the waterways and the 'Galasso' Law which protected their natural beauty were the first statutes concerning environmental issues. Currently, there are over 400 laws controlling environmental protection, education and research, pollution control and repair of environmental damage. More recently, a large amount of legislation has been passed as a result of EU Directives. Legislation on environmental matters is passed at state, regional and local levels and generally the emphasis is moving from sanctions towards prevention.

9.1 Protection against atmospheric and noise pollution

9.1.1 Environmental protection against atmospheric and noise pollution is planned on a three-yearly basis. The minister proposes a strategy and a budget after consultation with local bodies and the parliamentary commission, which is then approved by the CIPE (the Interministerial Economy Planning Committee, a body chaired by Italian Prime Minister and composed of 14 ministers; its main function is national economic policy). Every year the minister gives a progress report. Laws of 1934, 1966 and 1988 regulate air pollution wherever there is a danger to human health, a modification of the ecosystem, or a risk to the legitimate activities in the area. The rules do not, however, apply to national defence areas, aircraft, vehicles or ships (all of which are regulated by different legislation). The competent authority of the area is entitled to examine levels of air pollution either by evaluating the quality of the air or by examining any potential risk presented by sources of emission. Any person intending to set up an industrial plant which may produce a risk of air pollution must notify the authorities immediately by formal application for a permit, submitting all technological and production information. A failure to notify will lead to criminal liability and can result in heavy fines or imprisonment. All such factories must be situated away from heavily populated centres. The EU principle of the polluter pays has led to the introduction of ecological taxes, eg on the emission of gases and the production of polymers, as well as to regional and local regulation of the draining into the soil of, eg residual liquids from farming or non-biodegradable effluents from industry.

9.1.2 Two types of noise pollution are recognised: those from stationary or moving sources. Individual landowners cannot prevent the emission of smoke, heat, noise from the land of a neighbour unless they exceed normal toleration levels having regard to the condition of the sites. Collective applicants, such as associations for protection of the environment, can go before the court to notify events which damage the environment. The judge must balance the interests of the property in need of protection against the needs of industrial production. Generally, noise pollution is considered to be a matter of civil liability, much as nuisance, and therefore lesser remedies are available – an injunction or perhaps compensation in the most serious cases.

9.2 Water pollution

The main source of law on water pollution is the 'Merli' Law enforced by the Ministry for the Environment. The 'Merli' Law laid down regulations concerning acceptable limits for, and authorisation of, dumping into any waterways (including sewers), a plan for public aqueducts, sewerage and water purification, a plan for the general improvement of national waters and for the systematic qualitative and quantitative surveying of water sources. Water is considered to have been polluted if it can no longer be used for its original purpose. It is necessary to make an application for an authorisation to carry out any discharge or emission and such permission will only be granted if the drainage is within the official limits. Illegal drainage is strictly prohibited and can lead to criminal penalties of a minimum of two months' imprisonment or a fine of between 500,000 and 10,000,000 lire. The Ministry for the Environment instigates charges for all public services for the collection, removal, discharge and purification of water discharged from factories. Special regulations exist concerning the discharge of pollutants into coastal waters, which are particularly important for tourism.

9.3 Waste storage and disposal

The government became increasingly concerned by the lack of suitable landfill sites and the consequences of factory and domestic waste. Several emergency measures were enacted. A Presidential Decree of 1982 now regulates collection, disposal and storage of both ordinary waste substances and specific classified toxic substances. This waste can be urban (eg from domestic use or common use from civil buildings, or left in public streets), special (eg products from industry, agriculture, service industry etc) or toxic and hazardous. It is possible to give waste substances to authorised plants or landfill sites for storage or destruction but a fee will be charged for this service. A charge is always made for refuse collection and for sewage and purification services. The Ministry of the Environment created a registry of waste in 1989 whereby all producers and disposers of special, industrial or toxic waste must notify the authorities and are easily identifiable. The penalty for infringement of the regulations depends upon the type of waste which has been treated incorrectly, but there will be criminal liability. Disposal of ordinary urban waste is liable to lesser fines of up to 1,000,000 lire but incorrect disposal of special waste will incur fines of between 200,000 and 5,000,000 lire. If the infringer is not in possession of a licence, a heavier fine will probably be accompanied by imprisonment.

9.4 Contaminated land

The provision of information and registers on contamination is still at an early stage.

9.5 Environmental impact assessments

Environmental impact assessments aim to prevent conduct which will be harmful to the environment or the economy. The relevant EC Directive has been implemented so as to require certain projects to be the subject of environmental impact assessment, in particular public and private projects involving various industrial processes, crude oil refineries, gas installations, power stations, waste storage and disposal sites, dams or transport facilities. The enterprise intending to carry out such a project must submit a plan to the Ministry of the Environment, the Minister of Cultural and Environmental Goods and to the regional authority. If the body causes any environmental damage (ie if the environment is entirely or partly damaged, altered, deteriorated or destroyed) it must indemnify the state for the cost of the damage. The cost will be assessed by a judge.

10 DEVELOPMENT

10.1 Development projects, structures and vehicles

Construction work is carried out either by private companies, usually financed by bank loans, or cooperative companies, who then distribute the property amongst the members; or under the *appalto* system where an entity wishing to begin some construction work offers it out to tender rather than undertaking it itself. Public authorities carry out various forms of development including economic 'popular' housing, or public use projects. Popular housing is often undertaken by cooperatives with funding from the state, whereas buildings for public use are generally put out to tender.

10.2 Building contracts

10.2.1 Typical forms of building contract

For private sector construction, the contracts are governed by the Civil Code. The most common contract is the *appalto* which is a contract by which a party undertakes to perform a piece of work or render services, organising the necessary means and operating at his own risk, in return for compensation in money. A special type of *appalto,* the *appalto a regia*, can be used, however, when the building contractor provides materials and workers, but has to take instructions from the developer who has the exclusive management of the project. If the construction began under any type of *appalto*, subcontracting is not permitted unless expressly authorised by the developer, and the building contractor may not alter the plans unless authorised in writing. However, the developer may alter the project plans without the need to enter into a new contract provided that any modifications do not result in a significant alteration to the nature of the work, the quantity of each type of work, or alteration to the total value of the contract by more than one-sixth. The Civil Code does not expressly provide for alterations which reduce the cost of the project but it is deemed that the developer may order them. However, in this case, the building contractor has the right to reimbursement of expenses already borne and those made necessary as a result of the alteration itself. The developer is entitled to supervise the project at his own expense (usually through a chosen professional, the director of works). If unforeseen events during construction cause the cost of the materials or labour to increase or decrease by more than 10 per cent of the contract price, the contractor or developer can require a review of the price. If they do not reach agreement, either may ask the courts to fix a new price. If further unforeseen problems arise during the course of the contract, such as geological, drainage or other difficulties, which make the contractor's task significantly more difficult, he will be entitled to an equitable fee to cover the extra work. The developer has the right to inspect the building once the works are finished and, unless otherwise provided in the contract, need only pay the contractor once he gives final approval of the completion of the work. If he purposely withholds approval to avoid paying, the works are considered accepted. It is common to include a penalty clause to cover late completion. Alternatively, payment may be made at the completion of individual stages. In this case, the director of works issues the building contractor a certificate proving that the works have reached a specific stage.

10.2.2 Collateral warranties and contracts of employment

The building contractor is responsible for all defects in the work unless the developer has accepted the work and the defects were known to him, or were detectable, provided the defects were not passed over in silence by the contractor in bad faith. The developer has to serve notice of any defects within 60 days of discovery and must take legal action within two years from delivery of the building. The developer may ask the building contractor to make good any defects or for a proportionate reduction in price. If the defects are serious and the building is unfit for its purpose, the developer may ask for rescission of the contract, restitution of any monies paid and damages for loss. According to the general principles of contractual liability, damages are limited to the foreseeable loss except in the case of the building contractor's fraud (*dolus malus*). If, within ten years of the end of building work, the construction collapses in whole or in part, or is in a state of imminent collapse or is suffering from serious defects due to subsidence or poor construction, the building contractor is liable to the developer and any subsequent buyer, provided that he is notified of such problems within one year of discovery. Subsequent legal action must be taken within one year of such notice. The developer may withdraw from the contract, despite the fact that work has begun, but must indemnify the building contractor for expenses, work done and loss of profit. Those who work for the building contractor may take action against the developer for payment of debts owed to them by the contractor, up to the amount owed by the developer to the building contractor. There are special rules for employees and public authorities on public sector developments

The individual labour contract, between the building contractor and his employees, cannot derogate *in peius* from the provisions contained in the collective labour contracts drawn up by the respective professional associations.

10.2.3 Special laws govern projects and contracts with public bodies who often use the *appalto pubblico* to regulate their building projects which gives them special rights and privileges. The law requires certain formalities to create such a contract. Once the project has been planned by the authority or a private professional engaged by the authority, the authority passes a resolution and puts the building work out to tender. The procedure governing competitive tendering is regulated by law. Occasionally, however, the contractor will be chosen privately. A contract will then be finalised and checked to see that it is in accordance with the law. In order to enter into a building contract with the public authority (local or state) the building contractor must be registered in the relevant category of the national roll of building contractors, which verifies that he has satisfied various technical and moral requirements (eg absence of criminal record and pending suits). The public authority has the power to oversee the work, by setting up an office for the direction of the works chaired by the director of works. The director of works will be responsible for accepting materials, for seeing that the project adheres to the correct timetable for completion, for deciding the amount which the contractor will be paid according to the quality and amount of the work completed. The public authority appoints technicians (from one to three) to carry out the final tests at the end of the work. The building contractor may not assign or subcontract, without consent. The public authority may, within limits (up to 20 per cent of the contractual price), vary the work and the building contractor is obliged to comply, without any right to indemnity. The public authority may terminate the contract at any time for reasons of public interest, provided that it pays the contractor for work done, the expense of materials purchased and 10 per cent of the value of works not yet completed. Frequently, the contract will contain an arbitration clause for the settlement of disputes. There are special laws by which the *appalto* procedure need not be followed so giving the private party more powers, eg as to the planning, direction of the works, the right to expropriate the relevant land and the power to enter into *appalti* with other contractors, ie to step into the role of the public authority. Mostly these are private companies with state participation. This system is used, eg, to build railways and highways.

10.3 Those involved and their roles

In a public development project, the director of works oversees and inspects the works under the guidance of the chief public engineer. As explained at 10.2 the role of the public authority can be transferred to a private entity.

10.4 Defects insurance

In public developments the building contractor has by law to provide an insurance policy to indemnify the public authority against any risk arising out of execution of the works from any cause, apart from those deriving from errors in the project or by force majeure. The policy must also cover civil liability for damages to third parties during the execution of the works, up to the date of the final test certificate.

10.5 Copyright

Copyright law covers design, architectural plans and engineering projects, provided that they offer an original solution to technical problems.

10.6 Fees

For a new building the professionals' fees might be approximately eight per cent of the total cost, but this will depend on the circumstances.

10.7 Taxes

Value added tax is charged on construction and related services at 19 per cent.

11 TAXES

Arguably, a comprehensive reform of the taxation system is required. Each year, the budget sets out amendments to the law which can be difficult to follow and often succeed merely in worsening the problems in the system.

11.1 Corporation tax

All companies, public and private bodies and associations 'fiscally resident in Italy' (ie incorporated in Italy) are subject to corporation tax on their worldwide income and capital gains, subject to relief under any double taxation treaty with the country concerned. Partnerships do not have to pay corporation tax and their taxation is based upon the individual liabilities of the partners. Non-resident companies (including foreign partnerships) are only subject to corporation tax on their income earned within Italy when they have a permanent establishment there.

Both resident and non-resident companies (including partnerships) are subject to local income tax, *ILOR* (*imposta locale sui redditi*) on Italian source income, and income will be considered to have been earned in Italy for this purpose unless it can be attributed to a permanent establishment with separate management and accounts. The amount of *ILOR* paid cannot be deducted from the *IRPEG* and therefore adds to the total corporation income tax.

11.1.1 Tax rates

The general rate of corporation tax on income for the financial year 1997 was 37 per cent which applies to resident and non-resident companies. The *ILOR* is charged in proportion to the amount of income earned at the rate of 16.2 per cent. The amount of *ILOR* paid cannot be deducted from the amount of *IRPEG* and therefore the total effective rate of corporate income tax is 53.2 per cent.

11.1.2 Computation and assessment

The taxable amount to be taken into account when calculating corporation tax liability is usually the overall income deriving from net profits shown in the organisation's profit and loss account for the relevant tax year. There is, however, some adjustment to allow for exempt profits, non-deductible expenses, special deductions and losses brought forward. This is assessed by the competent tax office and late payment can result in penalties and interest at six per cent. Exempt profits include interest on government bonds (unless issued after 30 September 1986) and income that has been subject to Italian withholding tax at source. Deductible expenses include all expenditures and charges which relate to the production of taxable income and have properly been allocated to the tax period.

11.1.3 Capital allowances

Generally, all assets of the organisation, whether tangible or intangible, apart from land, may be the subject of a continuous decrease in their value. It is possible to deduct this amount accordingly and depreciation will be on a straight line basis. The depreciation will be at rates laid down by the Ministry of Finance and will be calculated on the purchase price or cost of manufacture. It is also possible to include incidental costs in the depreciation, such as customs duties, transport expenses etc.

11.1.4 Withholding tax

When an Italian resident pays income to a non-resident, he must deduct tax from the payments. Income subject to withholding tax includes interest on loans and royalties. Withholding tax is charged at 32.4 per cent on dividends, 12.5 per cent (for Government bonds), 15 per cent (for all types of loans on interest other than bonds), or 30 per cent (for other bonds and interest paid by banks) and 21 per cent on royalties from patents, know-how etc. This will be subject to any relevant tax treaty provisions and exemptions.

11.2 Taxes on development value

There is no specific tax on the development value of land. However, the increase in value arising from any planning or other consent may be liable to income or other taxes such as registration or inheritance tax as appropriate.

11.3 Taxes on capital gains

Capital gains are regarded as ordinary income and are therefore subject to ordinary corporate income tax and local income tax (other than the special regime which applies to the sale of shares of an SPA, quotas of an SRL (see 13.1) or bonds that are held for at least three years). Most capital gains can be spread over five years when certain conditions are met.

11.4 Taxes on owner of property

See 11.9.

11.5 Taxes on occupier

See 11.9.

11.6 Taxes on land transfer

A transfer of land is subject to a registration tax of eight per cent plus three per cent registration and cadastral charges, making a total of 11 per cent for property acquired from an individual. Property bought from an entrepreneur or a company, however, is subject to value added tax at 19 per cent plus three per cent registration and cadastral charges.

11.7 Wealth taxes

There is no wealth tax.

11.8 Value added tax

Value added tax (VAT) is applied at the rate of 19 per cent on the sale price of the property. This rate is reduced to four per cent, 10 per cent, or 13 per cent, for particular goods (such as agricultural products, agronomic goods, fish, milk and dairy products etc). The rate for certain luxury goods is 38 per cent. Transactions carried out in Italy by non-resident entities which have a permanent establishment in Italy are also subject to VAT. Any sales of national or nationalised property located in Italy are considered to be performed in Italy. Certain transactions are exempt (eg credit and financing transactions, insurance transactions, foreign currency transactions, and transactions concerning shares and bonds). VAT is based on the principle of compulsory recourse so that each commercial agent is bound to pay the government, on a monthly or three-monthly basis, any VAT collected after deducting any VAT paid on his transactions. If the payment is late it will be subject to an additional fine. Various steps are included in the process of VAT payments, eg the performer of the service or seller of the goods must issue an invoice (indicating date of transaction, the entity's identification number for VAT purposes, a description of the goods or services, the sum charged excluding the tax envisaged, and the applicable rate) and the entities must keep and maintain a book with a list of all invoices issued and purchases made. Between 1 February and 15 March every year, every taxpayer must file a VAT return stating the transactions performed, as well as the amount of VAT collected and the amount of VAT paid. By 5 March of every year any amount due in addition to the amount paid on a monthly or trimestral basis must be paid. If the return is not accurate, the entity will be subject to investigation. If errors or fraud are suspected, the entity will be subject to prosecution and large fines and other penalties. Any entities setting up a business or constituting a permanent establishment must within 30 days notify the Ministry of Finance who will issue a VAT code number which must be stated on all invoices issued and returns submitted. Various transactions are exempt from VAT such as the renting or leasing of property, banking, insurance operations, supply of hospital services, and schools. In addition, all exports are non-taxable and any tax paid will be refunded.

11.9 Local and other taxes

The owner of the property or a usufruct or right of use is liable to ICI (*imposta comunale sugli immobili*) even if non-resident. This is a municipal tax on the notional income or cadastral value of of the property at a rate of 0.4 to 0.7 per cent per annum.

12 GRANTS AND INCENTIVES

There are a number of different forms of aid which the public authorities will give to approved investment projects, including unconditional capital subsidies, loans at reduced rates, and tax relief schemes.

12.1 Occasionally public bodies offer land to developers in order to promote construction of industrial sites and factories. This practice has been made easier by the new laws on economic development and various national industrial parks have been created in certain areas across the country. The government will negotiate with the developer on the size and location of the land which he will be given. All such agreements are generally regulated by way of a 30-year renewable superficial right deed. These parks are well constructed to provide all necessary facilities and amenities. If the developer does not receive an offer of land within a national industrial park, he may still receive land in one of those parks controlled by the regional authorities or, occasionally, by private entities. The government will often offer help to a potential developer to find suitable land. In exceptional cases, the government itself will undertake construction of industrial buildings and will then sell or lease them at a later date.

13 COMPANIES AND BUSINESS ENTITIES

Property investment in Italy is carried out by various forms of business entity, most commonly individuals, companies and investment funds.

13.1 Limited and unlimited companies

13.1.1 The joint stock company (*società per azioni,* SpA) is frequently used in property development. The capital is divided into equal shares and the objectives and capacity of the company are laid down from the outset. The Civil Code states that an SpA must have a minimum share capital of 200 million lire of which a minimum of three-tenths must be fully paid up. Incorporation must be by way of public act, drawn up by a notary public or other authorised official, and containing various items of information, eg the personal details of the shareholders and promoters and number of shares each holds, the corporate name and address of the registered office, the purpose for which the company has been incorporated, the amount of capital which is paid up, the value and number of shares, the rules for apportionment of profits and the number of directors and their powers. Following registration (within 30 days), the articles of incorporation will be inspected by the court in order to verify that all legal requirements have been complied with. Provided that the incorporation is approved by the court, any contracts entered into by the directors on behalf of the company before registration will become enforceable against the company. Otherwise the directors themselves will be held liable for such contracts. At the time of incorporation there must be more than one member of the company. After the company is registered all the shares may be transferred to one person or legal entity, but in this case the corporate veil can be lifted to make a sole shareholder liable without limitation. Generally, however, the liability of shareholders is limited to their contribution (in cash or in kind) to the share capital of the company. The company will have a separate legal personality and when naming the company its status as an SpA must be evidenced in the choice of name, but the identity of the shareholders need not be. It is not necessary to receive prior approval for the choice of name, although it must be altered if it is found to be similar to that of a company already operating. A clear duration must be set for the life of the SpA.

13.1.2 The limited liability company (*società a responsabilità limitata, Srl*) is similar to the joint stock company but the Civil Code envisaged that it would be used for small to medium-sized businesses. Today, however, there are actually many Srls which are large businesses, but who seek to incorporate as an Srl to avoid the onerous requirements of the SpA. The same rules apply for an Srl as for an SpA regarding capital, although an Srl need only have a minimum capital of 20 million lire, three-tenths of which must be paid up, unless the company is to perform certain activities (such as banks, insurance companies etc) where higher minimum capital requirements are laid down by special laws. Limited liability companies cannot issue shares but rather are divided into quotas (which the articles of association can prevent from being transferred). Quotas, unlike shares, can be of different value but must be more than 1,000 lire each. The liability of each member is limited to his quota. Incorporation is achieved in the same way as for the SpA, by public act drawn up by a notary public, and containing the same information. Unlike the SpA, however, it is possible to incorporate an Srl with merely one founding shareholder. Most of the other rules are the same, eg regarding name, enforceability of contracts concluded before incorporation, separate legal personality and duration. A number of SpA provisions cannot be applied to Srl, eg an Srl cannot issue bonds and its quotas cannot be listed on the stock exchange.

13.2.1 Unlimited partnerships (*società di persone*) create unlimited joint and several liability between the partners. In addition, each partner is jointly and severally entitled to engage in management of the partnership. Such a partnership cannot be transferred without the consent of the other partners. If one of the partners dies, the others will settle his share with his heirs, unless they decide to dissolve the partnership or to continue it with the heirs. There are three kinds of partnership: non-commercial, general and limited partnerships.

13.2.2 Non-commercial partnerships (*società semplic*) are those not formed to carry out a commercial enterprise (eg they can carry out agricultural activities). There are no formalities involved. However, when the contract (written, oral or presumed) provides for contributions of property or real rights or other contributions in kind which can only be transferred with formalities, these must be respected when creating the partnership. Each partner will be entitled to manage the partnership, and has the right to object to an intended act of another partner provided he does so in advance. The contract of partnership may, however, provide for joint management by more than one partner and then partnership transactions must be approved by all managing partners (unless the transaction is urgently necessary in order to avoid damage to the partnership).

13.2.3 If the partnership is formed with commercial purposes in mind, it will be either a general partnership (*società in nome collettivo*) or a limited partnership (*società in accomandita semplice*). The regulations for non-commercial partnerships will apply to general partnerships, unless otherwise provided for by the law. There are no minimum capital requirements for a general partnership and the capital is merely the sum of goods contributed by the partners. Partners will be jointly and severally liable for the obligations of the general partnership. The memorandum of association must be in writing and either in the form of a public act or verified by a notary public. It must contain the personal details of the partners, the name of the partnership and an indication that it is operating as such, the registered address, the purpose for which the partnership has been incorporated, the names of the managing partners, the contributions of each partner, the rules for sharing profits and losses, and the duration. The memorandum of association and any other material fact concerning the partnership must be filed with the Company Registrar, or else that information may not be relied upon against third parties, and failure to do so means that the general partnership will be considered to be an 'irregular partnership' (*società irregolare*) and subject to all the provisions of a non-commercial partnership as to relationships with third parties.

Limited partnerships differ from general partnerships because the partners are divided into two classes, general partners (*soci accomandatari*) and limited partners (*soci accomandanti*). General partners will have the same rights and obligations as under a general partnership, but limited partners are unable to manage the partnership. The rights and obligations of a limited partner in this form of business entity must be distinguished from those of a partner in a partnership limited by shares (see 13.2.4). The partnership limited by shares is a capital based company whereas the limited partnership is not, and the same rules as apply to the general partnership largely apply. Again, if the limited partnership is not registered, it will be considered to be an irregular limited partnership, although the limited partners will still only be liable to the extent of their personal contribution.

13.2.4 Partnerships limited by shares (*società in accomandita per azioni*, Sapa) are joint stock companies where general, acting, partners (*accomandatari*) have unlimited joint and several liability, and limited partners (*accomandanti*) have liability limited to their capital contributions. The rules regulating joint stock companies will also apply to partnerships limited by shares, so long as they are compatible. This type of company used to be extremely rare but was recently adopted by some of the largest family-held companies as a 'super-holding' company to protect the family position against takeover. The acting partners of the company are automatically directors whose mandate cannot be revoked. The capital is divided into shares. The name of the partnership must include the name of at least one of the general partners and must indicate that the company is a partnership limited by shares. The partnership will come to an end in accordance with the normal rules of company dissolution, but also when all the directors forfeit office, unless they are replaced within six months. The board of auditors will appoint provisional directors to manage the company, pending the selection of new, permanent directors. The provisions for SpAs are generally applicable to a Sapa, eg as to incorporation, registration, and contractual liability before registration. The partnership is a separate legal entity.

13.3 Other types of business association

13.3.1 Investment funds or *Fondi comuni d'investimento immobiliari* are run by companies limited by shares, authorised to perform such activities by the Treasury Ministry, and controlled by the Bank of Italy. The minimum value of the property owned by a fund is 100 billion lire and they must be set up as 'close ended funds' (unlike investment funds investing in securities) so that the number of shares in the funds may not vary. An investor may only withdraw from the fund if he can sell his share on the market.

13.3.2 Cooperative companies are non-profit making organisations and can be formed either as limited companies, or as unlimited companies, in which case the members have unlimited joint and several liability for the company's obligations on bankruptcy. Liability on bankruptcy may be limited either to the capital contributions or to a multiple of the members' individual contributions as set out in the memorandum of association.

13.3.3 Joint ventures as such do not exist unless the joint venture takes the form of a company, a consortium or temporary association of businesses (eg where more than one company combines together to compete for public works contracts or other activities contemplated by special laws). The Civil Code describes such consortia as the contract by which two or more businesses plan, in common, to organise or carry out phases of their businesses together. If the contract is not made in writing, it will be void. If the duration of the contract is not stated, a ten-year period is implied by law. Decisions are made on a simple majority basis, unless the contract provides differently. The consortium contract will come to an end either at the end of the stipulated time, when its objective has been achieved or can no longer be achieved, on the unanimous decision of the parties, when the governing authorities declare it dissolved, or in any other circumstances provided for in the contract.

14 INTERNATIONAL

14.1 Restrictions on inward investment

Foreign investment in Italy is defined as either investment carried out by overseas residents in Italy with foreign capital, or investment by Italian residents overseas. The Decree of 1990 replaced the post-war restrictions on inward investment with a totally free investment regime, although there is still some monitoring. Credit institutions must keep internal records of their transfers of monies or securities to or from abroad for five years, whenever such transfers are worth more than 20 million lire, and are carried out by individuals, non-commercial parties or other entities listed by law (mainly companies). Certain records must be sent periodically to the tax authorities and all business carried out as a financial intermediary must be reported by 31 March for the preceding year.

14.2 Exchange controls

Apart from the monitoring obligations referred to in 14.1, there are no longer any exchange controls applicable to the repatriation or transfer of funds out of Italy.

14.3 Restrictions and registrations on carrying on a business

There are no restrictions on foreign entities carrying on a business in Italy. However, the memorandum and articles of association of a company must be deposited at the commercial section of the court.

14.4 Repatriation of income and proceeds of property trading and development

There are no consents or restraints involved in the repatriation of income and proceeds of property trading and development, subject to the deduction of withholding tax.

14.5 Withholding taxes

The effect of withholding taxes is explained at 11.1.4.

14.6 Double taxation relief

Italy has entered into treaties with a number of countries to mitigate double taxation and each treaty needs to be read separately.

CHAPTER 10

Luxembourg

A Schmitt

Partner, Bonn & Schmitt, Luxembourg

CONTENTS

1 OWNERSHIP OF LAND 323
2 OTHER INTERESTS IN LAND 325
3 TITLE TO LAND 329
4 TRANSACTIONS IN LAND 331
5 LEASES AND OCCUPATIONAL RIGHTS 333
6 FINANCE 336
7 SECURITY 338
8 PLANNING AND BUILDING REGULATION 340
9 ENVIRONMENTAL MATTERS 343
10 DEVELOPMENT 345
11 TAXES 348
12 GRANTS AND INCENTIVES 352
13 COMPANIES AND BUSINESS ENTITIES 353
14 INTERNATIONAL 356

CHAPTER 10

Luxembourg

1 OWNERSHIP OF LAND

Luxembourg property law is based on the provisions of the Civil Code (particularly Book II, Articles 516–710) and its subsequent amendments. Hence many concepts and techniques bear a strong similarity to those of other civil law countries such as France or Belgium. In addition to the Napoleonic Code, however, Roman law has also been a strong influence on the law of real and moveable property. Unlike common law jurisdictions, there is no dichotomy between freehold and leasehold, and freehold is the only recognised form of tenure. The only binding sources of property law are the Civil Code and any additional laws and regulations. There is no rule of binding precedent, but court decisions (especially those emanating from the *Cour de Cassation*) have a strong persuasive authority.

1.1 Types of tenure

1.1.1 Freehold or absolute ownership

Freehold ownership grants an interest in land which is akin to absolute ownership. There are, however, various degrees of freehold ownership within the traditional definition of the right of property as defined by the Civil Code. In theory the right is absolute, yet case law has severely restricted the purportedly unlimited use of one's property. Within these limits, freehold ownership entails the right to own, occupy, and dispose of the land and its fixtures. Any buildings on the land are in principle the property of the landowner. However, it is possible to separate the ownership of land and buildings and to create a right of property over the buildings and the surface (*droit de superficie*) in favour of another person (see further 2.1.3). Freehold ownership carries with it the right to the soil below and the air above the land and the freehold owner may exploit mines found on his property, or sell the right to third parties. The right over property is one of the few rights in rem as opposed to rights in personam.

1.1.2 Leasehold

Leasehold (*louage de choses*) is not considered to be a form of tenure, but is merely regulated by way of rights in personam between the landlord and tenant, and is referred to as a contractual tenancy as the rights are found under the law of contract. These contractual rights do not grant rights in rem over the land in the way that freehold ownership or usufruct does; the tenant only has a right in personam against the landlord, who is obliged under the tenancy agreement to ensure the use and occupation of the land by the tenant. Tenancies are in principle transferable, and subleases are possible, except where contracts or special statutes provide otherwise (see further section 5). There is, however, a rare type of leasehold which can be regarded as a form of tenure since it grants a right in rem, namely the heritable lease (see 2.1.3.3).

1.1.3 Joint ownership

It is possible to create joint ownership (*indivision*) whereby an estate (or any other immoveable chattel) may be jointly owned. Each owner is entitled to an undivided share in the whole property, and cannot identify any part of the property which belongs exclusively to him. Joint ownership may be imposed by law in certain specific cases, such as in the case of a shared wall (*mur mitoyen*) between adjoining properties. It may arise as a result of succession (by intestacy or by will), eg when property is left to more than one person, or before the rights of the heirs have been settled, or it may be a voluntary arrangement enforceable under contract. The joint owners cannot freely dispose of their share, but require the agreement of the other owners. However, a joint owner may validly mortgage his share in the common property. He may use and draw profits from his share as long as he does not interfere with the rights of the other joint owners. Where a joint owner wishes to dispose of his share, the other joint owners have a legal right of pre-emption. Furthermore, each joint owner is lawfully entitled to dissolve the joint ownership scheme, if necessary by court order.

1.1.4 Condominia

In the case of condominium ownership (*co-propriété*) there is an important distinction between common parts and private units. Whilst the private units are individually owned, the common parts are subject to joint ownership, every owner of a private part having a certain share in the common property. The condominium owners are free to dispose of their share in the condominium ownership scheme, as well as to mortgage it. Whereas private units may be transferred freely with or without the common parts belonging to them, an owner may not dispose of the common parts on his own. There is no legal right of pre-emption over the sale of individual units, and contractual pre-emption clauses have been annulled by the courts. There is no right to dissolve the condominium arrangement as it is a compulsory legal scheme applying to any property occupied by two or more owners and the scheme is not limited to residential property. Condominium regulations monitoring the use of the property must be drawn up. The condominium is managed by a *syndic* (a representative of the co-owners) taking day-to-day decisions and by the assembly of the joint owners, which is the supreme organ of the condominium ownership scheme.

1.1.5 Lesser rights

The Civil Code provides for lesser rights of occupation such as the dwelling right and the right of use (see 2.1.3).

1.2 Legal and beneficial ownership

The concept of the trust and the distinction between legal and beneficial ownership is not used in civil property law. Luxembourg has recently adopted legislation which introduced the *contrat de fiducie*. This is a very limited use of the concept of the trust, which is confined to banking operations. Under such a fiduciary contract, a person (*fiduciant*) transfers title over certain assets to another person (*fiduciaire*), who must be a credit institution in the sense of Luxembourg law, but the right of property of the *fiduciaire* is limited by the instructions given by the *fiduciant* on the use of the property, laid down in the contract between the parties. This concept is rarely used in property transactions.

1.3 Restrictions on ownership and dealing

1.3.1 There are few restrictions on the ownership of land. Even minors or those suffering from mental incapacity are entitled to own land, provided that their parents or guardians carry out all acts requiring full legal capacity on their behalf. Companies and associations are entitled to own land if they have full legal personality. Various legislative restrictions exist, eg those aiming to protect the public interest such as planning regulations and environmental law. Private interests are also protected by the general principles of abuse of rights and the law of nuisance. Certain entities are subject to restrictions on ownership of land: investment funds may only own land which is necessary for their principal activity. There are exceptions for so-called property funds. There are no restrictions on the ownership of land by foreign entities.

1.3.2 There are no general legal restrictions on the disposal of land, except for contractual pre-emption rights (see 2.4), and in certain situations, public pre-emption rights.

1.4 Adverse possession and acquisitive prescription

It is possible to acquire title by mere possession over a period of time by acquisitive prescription (*usucapion*). Occupation of a continuous, public, unequivocal and peaceful nature must normally have lasted for 30 years in order to acquire good title, although this may be lowered to 20 or 10 years if possession is in good faith. Property may also be acquired by accession, ie an increase in existing land by an act of nature, which might include plants growing in the soil, minerals discovered underground and alluvial deposits.

2 OTHER INTERESTS IN LAND

There are various interests in land which grant rights less than absolute ownership or possession.

2.1 Servitudes or easements, usufruct, building and dwelling rights

2.1.1 Servitudes or easements

The Civil Code defines a servitude as a charge imposed on one piece of land for the use and the benefit of another, which must be owned by a different person. Servitudes may be established by law, by agreement between two owners of adjoining plots of land, or by prolonged, peaceful, public and continuous use of 30 years. The most common examples are a right of way (*droit de passage*), a right to a view (*droit de vue*) and shared rights over a party wall (*mur mitoyen*). Servitudes by agreement will be extinguished by 30 years' non-use and must be notarised and registered in order to bind third parties. Servitudes created otherwise than by agreement, which create a right in rem, remain perpetually attached to the servient tenement and bind successors in title to either piece of land, unless otherwise stipulated by mutual agreement. Servitudes established by law are enforceable against third parties without any further formalities. Servitudes created by prolonged use are also enforceable against third parties without registration. The buyer of the land will be held bound even by an unpublished contractual servitude if he has knowledge of it, which explains the custom of disclosing servitudes in the purchase deed. Although still important in many rural areas, the use of servitudes has rapidly declined in urban areas.

2.1.2 Usufruct

The holder of a usufruct (*usufruit*), the usufructuary, is entitled to the actual and exclusive enjoyment and use of the land and the resultant profits, with the obligation not to alter the nature of the land. The rights will be created either by operation of law (for instance the usufruct over the family home of the surviving spouse) or by voluntary creation (contract, donation or will), in which case the agreement will have to be notarised. This right reverts to the title holder of the land on the death of the usufructuary (unless the parties have provided contractually for a lesser period). The usufruct is a right in rem, thus binding third parties (if it is validly registered). The usufruct is transferable and the transferee will succeed to the same rights and obligations, and the usufruct will continue to end at the death of the first holder (unless a different period is agreed).

2.1.3 Building and dwelling rights

2.1.3.1 The holder of a surface right (*droit de superficie*) may build upon land belonging to another person, and the buildings will be the property of the holder, and not that of the landowner, for the duration of the period of the surface right. The surface right may be created either by operation of law (for instance in the case of certain types of long-term leases) or by contract, for consideration or not. It is a right in rem and may be granted perpetually, for the lifetime of the holder or for a limited period of time. As for all transactions over land, the contract granting it must be notarised and registered to be enforceable against third parties. Where the right is not granted in perpetuity, ownership of the buildings will revert to the landowner, who will in principle be liable to pay compensation to the holder, subject to the terms of the agreement. Where the surface right arises by implication of law, no compensation will generally be due. During the term of the surface right, the holder of the right may freely demolish or alter the buildings provided he does not interfere with the right of ownership over the underlying land.

2.1.3.2 The dwelling right or the right of use (*droit d'usage et d'habitation*), akin to a dwelling right, grants a person (and his family) a right to occupy a building for residential purposes. It is a right in rem. Generally, the rules of the creation, registration, enforceability and termination of the usufruct are equally applicable. However, the right is not transferable, nor may it be leased (except where the contract provides otherwise).

2.1.3.3 The heritable lease (*bail emphythéotique*) is a long-term lease (minimum 27, maximum 99 years) which must be registered and confers a right of enjoyment and use for the tenant, who is under the duty to improve or enhance the material conditions of the leased property. The tenant may exercise all rights of property attached to the leased property, but he may do nothing which diminishes its value. Any buildings constructed without an obligation to do so may be destroyed at the end of the lease and compensation will be payable to the landlord if the property is damaged by the demolition. Otherwise the property of all buildings erected by the tenant will be transferred to the landlord upon termination of the lease. The lease may be transferred unless the contract provides otherwise.

2.2 Restrictions on use and other restrictions

Restrictions on use of land again derive from planning restrictions (see section 8) or from environmental legislation (see section 9). Freeholders may grant servitudes restricting the use of their land (see 2.1.1). Such rights will be enforceable by and between successive owners provided they have been registered. It is only possible to impose obligations on the use of land, not on a person. Thus an obligation to contribute to the cost of repairs or common services cannot be considered as a servitude, as it is an obligation in personam rather than in rem. However, such arrangements are specifically provided for in the case of condominium ownership (see 1.1.4).

2.3 Private mortgages and charges

Mortgages (*hypothèques*) may be created by operation of law, by the courts (a temporary measure in order to secure judgment debts) or by contract. These are commented on in full in section 7. The Civil Code provides for a certain number of charges (*privilèges sur immeubles*) which are a form of preferential debt including the seller's lien for the unpaid purchase price on sale of a property, the lien of the lender of the money having paid the purchase price, and several other less important liens. These liens must be registered in order to be enforceable against third parties. Tax liens (*privilège occultes*) do not need to be registered. A privilege is in reality a lien securing a debt on specific assets of the debtor for the payment of a debt, without actually stripping the debtor of the asset. The lien is secured on all the debtor's assets, all his personal property or on specific real or personal property. The type of lien which will be granted is determined by law according to the nature of the debt. Parties do not consent to liens nor do the courts have the power to create liens, ie they simply arise automatically in certain situations. The seller's lien secures the debt as determined by the price of the property sold. It is the property itself which is earmarked for the lien, giving the seller a privileged access to the proceeds of the property's sale. The lien affecting land, unlike one over personal property, will continue to exist even if the property comes into another party's possession, provided the original deed of sale has been transcribed in the mortgage registry with the indication of the amount of the secured debt. As a rule, the lien takes priority over the mortgage, even if the mortgage is created prior to the lien, but there are some exceptions. For instance, a mortgage, created over a property prior to its sale, will always take priority over the lien of the seller of the property, since the sale itself concerned a mortgaged item. Special liens affecting specific properties generally take priority over general liens affecting all assets or all personal properties of the debtor. The lien generally is extinguished with the debt it secured but may be extinguished independently of the secured debt, as in the case of a waiver by the creditor, a merger of the rights of the debtor and creditor, and under the statutes of limitation.

2.4 Contracts and options

Contracts for the sale of land and promises to sell land are binding, even though completion (by registration in the central mortgage registry) has not yet occurred. They do not however grant the beneficiary a real interest in the land and any remedy against the seller will only result in damages. A landowner may grant a potential buyer a contractual pre-emption right to be exercised if the landowner decides to sell his property. No general right of pre-emption exists save possibly for tenants who have been in possession for over 18 years and farm tenants.

2.5 Public or municipal charges

Local authorities do not secure the payment of local tax by securing charges over land. There are, however, a certain number of charges in favour of public or semi-public bodies for the recovery of payments for statutory works, such as for irrigation and drainage carried out by semi-public associations, and for the recovery of certain payments made by social security agencies, in favour of customs authorities. All these liens are generally registered in the same way as private liens; this is to be contrasted with liens in favour of the state (as opposed to local) tax authorities for the recovery of taxes (*privilèges occultes*), which do not require registration.

2.6 Other interests

There are no other interests in land other than those mentioned.

2.7 Liabilities attaching to land

There are specific statutory liabilities depending on the nature of the premises and the land. In addition, there is strict liability for damage caused by personal property (whether moveable or not). This liability in tort is imposed by the Civil Code and has been heavily extended and modified by case law. Liability is generally strict and also provides compensation for injuries and damages suffered by visitors and their goods, as well as by passers-by and their goods. Liability for nuisance created by the unreasonable use of one's land to the prejudice of an adjoining owner, or of another 'neighbour', is based on the concept of abuse of right (*abus de droit*). Strict liability also applies to damage caused by the collapse of buildings due to faulty construction or repair. Property is subject to local tax (*impôt foncier*), see further 11.4. There is an obligation to keep listed buildings in a proper state of repair. If it is not met, the public authorities may intervene and carry out the repairs themselves, at their own expense (and to a certain extent with the contribution of the private owners).

2.8 Legal and beneficial interests

There is no distinction between legal and beneficial interests in land.

2.9 Protection of rights and interests

All transactions creating or transferring an interest (in rem) in land must be registered in order to be enforceable against third parties. Obligations in personam, relating to land, do not need to be registered, with the exception of certain long-term leases, such as the heritable lease (*bail emphythéotique*) (see 2.1.3.3).

2.10 Priority of interests

The conflict between two beneficiaries of an interest in land will be resolved according to the priority of registration rather than the date of creation of their interest, except where the first-registered beneficiary has acted in bad faith, ie knowing that the same interest had been created before the creation of his own interest. In such cases, the creation date will prevail. This rule only applies in the case of a conflict between holders of conflicting interests acquired from the same grantor/seller of which one must have been effectively registered.

3 TITLE TO LAND

3.1 Proof of title

3.1.1 As is the case for all civil law countries, a system of registration has been introduced which covers all land. Proof of title can be obtained either from the land registry at the keeper of mortgages' office (*bureau de conservation des hypothèques*) or from the original notarial conveyancing deeds which are kept at the notary's office. Registration is required for all transactions creating or transferring interests in land in order to make them enforceable against third parties (with certain exceptions for state and public entities). It is not required to make the contract valid between the parties. The registers are open to the public.

3.1.2 Investigation of title may not be undertaken directly, but will have to be investigated by reference to the files listing the transactions and kept by the *bureau des hypothèques*. The registry is not of land or title but of deeds or transactions. The continuity of title is guaranteed by the application of the principle of relative effect of the registration, ie a transaction may only be validly registered if the person transferring the interest in land did himself hold this land on the basis of a validly registered title.

3.2 Land registry

Whereas the documentation showing actual title (including any encumbrances) is kept by the keeper of mortgages, the plans of the property concerned are found at the cadastral office (*administration du cadastre*).

3.2.1 Plans

Plans are for identification purposes and to establish boundaries between the different plots. It is possible to search both by reference to a plot number and by reference to the land. There is no actual land-based registry.

3.2.2 Content

As explained the register as kept by the *bureau des hypothèques* is a register of deeds not title.

3.2.3 Errors

The registers may be rectified in case of errors. However, the holder of the title must not bear the consequences of any errors and the entries in the register are conclusive (except in case of mortgages). The keeper of mortgages will be liable for any losses arising from his error and his liability must be covered by a bank guarantee.

3.3 Passing of title

Title passes between parties at the time of the contract according to the general principles of civil law. In practice, transfer of title is often suspended until the date of notarisation. There is no general time limit for registration in the case of transfer of property. The transfer of title becomes enforceable against third parties from the date of registration.

4 TRANSACTIONS IN LAND

The most common transactions in land are sale of land and private mortgages.

4.1 Procedures

A *compromis de vente* (ie a preliminary contract which may include certain conditions precedent which need to be realised if the sale is to complete) generally precedes the conclusion of the contract before a notary. At this first stage, the parties will decide upon the general terms (price and interest in question) of the contract and this agreement will become binding between the parties. The agreement for sale will not, however, be enforceable against third parties at this stage. Title will be investigated by the notary prior to notarisation, and he will bear responsibility for the accuracy of the search. Finance and all preliminaries will be arranged prior to notarisation. After notarisation has taken place, registration will be carried out by the notary himself. Between the signing of the *compromis* and notarisation, the buyer is only protected by the existence of an obligation in personam binding the seller, whose liability will be contractual. There is no procedure allowing prior notice to be given to the registry.

4.2 Contract terms

4.2.1 Under present law, the seller gives two warranties. The first warranty ensures quiet enjoyment of the property (*garantie d'éviction*) and the second ensures freedom from inherent defects (*garantie des vices cachés*). The guarantee of quiet enjoyment may be expressly excluded by the parties. The seller (unless he is a professional of the same sector) may exclude the warranty of freedom from inherent defects, but this exclusion will not cover any apparent defects discovered within one month after commencement of occupation. If a relevant hidden defect is subsequently discovered, and if the seller was not a professional or was unaware of the defects, he will only be liable for reimbursement of the sale price and any costs incurred by the sale. The buyer can elect to apply for damages in lieu of refund of the purchase price if the seller was aware of the defects or if he was a professional. The buyer must notify the seller of the defect within a 'short period of time' (undefined), and start proceedings within a year of notification. If the price paid was very low, the seller may, within two years of completion and after registration of the sale, rescind the contract, subject to certain stringent conditions.

4.2.2 Parties may freely determine price and manner of payment. Only forfeiture clauses for non-payment are illegal. Rescission of the contract can only occur by mutual agreement or by court order. The payment of the purchase price or the balance is secured on the land by the entry of a seller's lien (*privilège du vendeur*) by the keeper of mortgages. Therefore, property retention clauses (clauses allowing the transfer of property, which normally takes place at the date the parties agree on price and object, to be delayed until full payment of the sale price) are uncommon.

4.2.3 Transactions in land (other than the creation and enforcement of leases) are under the sole control of the notaries public. They will search the title for encumbrances under a strict professional duty (*obligation de résultat*) to inform their clients of their discoveries and to carry out their wishes. Risk passes as soon as the notarised conveyancing deed (*acte authentique*) has been signed by the parties and the notary himself. In principle the property will be insured by the holder of title at any given moment, but a preparatory contract may provide otherwise for the negotiation period. Parties may also decide that certain deposits are paid, for instance in exchange for a promise not to negotiate with another party. The contract will generally mention existing tenancies, management arrangements and/or liabilities, although this is not a requirement for such liabilities to pass on to the successor in the land, where liability will pass in any event by operation of law.

4.3 Formalities

Transfers of all property interests by contract must be made by notarial deed (and either an authenticated deed or a private signed deed may be used) and registered in the mortgage registry to be effective against all parties. The notarial deed itself must be in writing, and signed by the parties and the notary himself. The contract for sale of land is however a valid contract between the parties even if it is not drawn up by formal contract or even in writing. The notary deed is only required for evidentiary purposes and for registration. Any gift of land (*donation*) requires written notarial evidence. A contract for the sale of land for development use needs to be an *acte authentique* ie a notarial deed, containing certain compulsory information. Leases do not need to be registered but this may provide greater protection.

4.4 Fees, costs and taxes

4.4.1 On a sale of land (or the grant of a tenancy), the seller or landlord will pay the agent's commission commonly of around three per cent. The buyer will pay the notarial fees, stamp duty and land registry fees.

4.4.2 Notary fees depend on the amount of the transaction and are determined by reference to a schedule of charges varying from 0.5 per cent to 2 per cent for transactions of less than LUF400,000.

4.4.3 Transfers of property are subject to registration duty (*droit d'enregistrement)* fixed at six per cent of the purchase price (or market value if higher) with a three per cent surcharge where the property is located within Luxembourg-City or Esch/Alzette. The tax applies to sales, resales, sales by auction, assignments and all other civil deeds and court orders transferring title for consideration. Registered lease contracts are subject to a duty of 0.6 per cent on total lease payments (see 11.6).

4.4.4 Land registry fees in the form of a transcription duty are charged at one per cent of the purchase price.

4.4.5 Overall costs are comparable to most European countries and are in the region of 16 per cent of the whole.

4.4.6 Value added tax (VAT) will not be charged on any transactions subject to registration duty. Solicitors' and agents' fees attract VAT currently at a rate of 12 per cent.

4.5 Professionals' roles

The marketing of land and buildings for their sale or lease is generally undertaken by estate agents. They are members of a professional body and as such subject to certain regulations for the conduct of their profession. There is no organised profession of surveyors in Luxembourg. The activity of examining the property prior to the sale is generally carried out by independent experts (including architects and agents) commissioned by one of the parties (generally every expert acts for one of the parties). Lawyers intervene during the negotiations, but their involvement depends on the parties' decision. Generally, there is only one notary acting for both parties in the transaction, who will notarise the agreement which the parties have already expressed in their *compromis*.

5 LEASES AND OCCUPATIONAL RIGHTS

Leases or tenancies are not considered to be rights in rem but grant mere personal contractual rights between the landlord and tenant. Residential tenancies are regulated by the Civil Code and by the 1955 Law. Industrial, commercial and agricultural tenancies are not subject to the compulsory regime of the 1955 Law. Industrial and commercial leases are subject to the general rules of the Civil Code, as well as certain specific regulations concerning protection of the tenant's rights in case of sale of property, or termination of the contract. Agricultural tenancies are regulated by a specific regime. Tenancies may be for a fixed term (which may be renewable) or for an indeterminate period of time. In practice, tenancies are often granted on a so-called '3-6-9 scheme', ie renewable every three years. The length of notice is determined by local custom, but generally, notice periods will be of one or two months, except where the tenancy agreement provides otherwise. For registration and taxes see 4.3 and 4.4.3.

5.1 Rent and other terms

5.1.1 Obligations of the landlord and the tenant are determined by the Civil Code and are therefore applicable to all types of leases. The landlord will essentially have three obligations. He must deliver the object of the tenancy (including all accessories). Furthermore, he must proceed to do all repairs to the premises. Whilst by law he must carry out most major repair work, the parties' contract often imposes most repair obligations on the tenant. Finally, he must guarantee the peaceful use of the property to the tenant, although he does not guarantee the tenant against any acts by third parties. In principle, all leases may be sublet, except where the agreement provides otherwise (which is generally the case). In case of a sublease, the main tenant remains entirely responsible towards the landlord for all obligations under the lease agreement. The main landlord has no obligations whatsoever towards the subtenant. Assigning the lease is possible (except where the agreement provides otherwise). If all formalities are respected (especially notification of the assignment to the landlord), the assignee will validly take over all rights from the assignor. However, existing debts and obligations may not be assigned, except where the landlord agrees.

5.1.2 Residential tenancies

As a general rule, the parties are free to negotiate the terms and conditions of the rental agreement, subject to certain compulsory rules regarding rent control and certain landlord and tenant liabilities. In residential leases, statutory maximum rents are determined according to complex procedures depending on the age of the building, the number of rooms, its comfort and value. There is a prohibition on the indexation of residential rent. Modern (post-1944) buildings are limited to a rent of five per cent of capital investment. Every municipality has a rents commission: a body composed of members of the municipal authorities, representatives of landlords and tenants. This commission may, upon application of either party, determine the rent applicable to the premises, according to the legally determined standards. This system only applies to residential leases. It is permitted for the parties to agree a fixed sum, which may not exceed three months' rent, as reimbursable security for payment of the rent or any possible damage to the premises rented. Rent is generally payable in advance every month. Rents may only be reviewed three full years following the prior determination of the rent. Such review may be in an upwards or downwards direction. Costs and charges will generally be borne by the tenant. He will pay a monthly advance, and at the end of the year, landlord and tenant will determine the real charges and adjust their accounts.

5.1.3 Industrial and commercial tenancies

There is no specific legislation dealing with leases of business premises. As a result, the parties have contractual freedom, particularly as regards the determination of the amount of the rent, and the renewal of the lease. It may be a certain percentage of the turnover, it may be linked to the evolution of an official price index (which is prohibited in residential leases), or it may be paid annually or quarterly. It is common for the parties to agree 'key money', ie a fixed sum which is payable when the keys are handed to the tenant and which grants the right to enter the premises. Rights and obligations of the parties will generally be the same as those provided for in the Civil Code (see 5.1.1). Tenancy agreements cannot prevent commercial tenants from subletting the property when disposing of their business, provided that the new tenant intends to carry on the same form of business from the premises. Any clause attempting to prevent such a sublease will be void. The landlord under a commercial lease will be responsible for the external repairs to the property, insuring the building and payment of any property tax. The tenant will retain responsibility for all other issues in relation to the building, eg internal maintenance and taxation.

5.1.4 Agricultural leases

Agricultural farm leases, whether for a complete farm, or only for a parcel of land, do not have to follow any particular provisions relating to the determination of rent. At the end of each three-year period, the landlord and the tenant may request the revision of the farm rent (although the revision may not be based on indexation, notwithstanding any contract provisions). If the parties have not agreed on the criteria regulating the revision of the rent, it will be carried out in accordance with the value of the agricultural output of the property rented.

5.2 Privity of contract and estate

In principle, for all three types of leases, the rights and obligations of the lease agreement are only transferred in the event of a sale of the premises if the lease is in notarised form or if it has been registered.

5.3 Rent control and security of tenure

5.3.1 Residential tenancies

A residential lease will be automatically renewed at the end of the term, except where the landlord can claim any one of the following termination causes: a personal need for the premises (for himself or members of his close family), the violation of major obligations under the lease agreement by the tenant or other serious and legitimate reasons. Termination (which is only possible in contracts for an indeterminate period of time and for one of the causes mentioned above) must be preceded by sufficient notice.

5.3.2 Commercial and industrial tenancies

The Civil Code regulates renewal of commercial and industrial tenancies and provides that any commercial tenant who has been in business for more than three years, either himself or through his heirs or successors, has a preferential right to renew the contract which takes priority over any third party's right to become the new tenant. However, eviction may be justified in a limited number of cases, such as the existence of serious grievances, personal need of the landlord or a member of his family, total transformation or reconstruction, or abandoning commercial leases in the premises. The preferential right of renewal expires after 15 years of tenancy.

5.4 Other legislative restrictions

Municipalities may also intervene on the basis of the preservation of public health to close down premises unfit for human habitation. Statutes give the right to municipal authorities to force landlords to refurbish unfit buildings, or to expropriate them if work is not carried out after a certain period of time.

5.5 Methods of measurement

Standards of measurement exist in the profession on the basis of common practice. However, they have never been officially recognised and have no legal value (except those standards used for the determination of rent in residential leases).

6 FINANCE

There is a wide variety of financing sources from which the investor may choose. Among the most common are loans granted by commercial banks. The most important property market is that of Luxembourg-City, whose significance continues to grow, largely driven by its requirements as both a European city and as a financial centre. Areas of increasing relevance within the market are the investment funds, private banking and the reinsurance sector.

6.1 Loan finance

Loans are granted by a variety of institutions: merchant banks, investment banks, cooperative societies, building societies and savings banks. The latter three specialise in private residential property investment. Large projects are generally financed by investment or merchant banks, the sector being dominated by a few Luxembourg and large foreign banks. Although Luxembourg has a very large number of banks, most of them specialise in private banking and financing projects in their home countries rather than in Luxembourg. Most banks are privately owned. State-owned banks in Luxembourg include the *Banque et Caisse D'Epargne de l'Etat* and the *SNCI* (see section 12). Conventional loans will generally be for a fixed term and provide for payment of periodic fixed interest and staged repayment of the capital. However, parties are free to adopt different terms, especially in complex, commercial transactions including variable interest rates and bullet repayments. If a loan is for an indefinite period of time, imperative rules of civil law allow all parties to terminate it unilaterally by giving reasonable notice, except where issues of lender liability are concerned. Loans will be secured, except where there is a special relationship with the borrower. There is an important market for syndicated loans in Luxembourg, but most of them are granted for projects abroad. Companies may borrow money from their shareholders within the limits imposed by tax law regarding concealed distributions and under-capitalisation. These shareholders will obtain no preferential treatment by simply granting a loan to their company. Other methods of financing for companies are *prêts participatifs* and other types of subordinated debt, convertible bonds and fiduciary bond issues (ie a bond issue by a bank with the single purpose of financing a loan granted to a particular company).

6.2 Investment or equity finance

Sources of investment and equity finance are numerous due to the great variety of expertise existing in one of the world's largest financial centres. Small companies will generally rely on equity and debt financing from their shareholders, as well as conventional loans. Larger companies will use more complex methods of financing such as listing on the stock exchange (although few Luxembourg companies are publicly traded), bond finance and convertible stock to name a few. Due to tax advantages for individuals, investment is also carried out to a large extent by investment funds dedicated to participate in the capital of Luxembourg-resident and fully taxable companies, which fulfil the role of institutional investors.

6.3 Mezzanine or mixed funding

The exact structures of funding for large projects are generally not disclosed by the parties. Nor is there a pre-set structure of mixed funding which would be used on a regular basis. The parties prefer to negotiate their financing structures case-by-case, using a mixture of debt and equity financing where required.

6.4 Sale and lease-back

In the past, sale and lease-back as well as property leasing structures (*crédit-bail immobilier*) have been rare, due to the fact that, for the purpose of registration tax, the tax authorities regarded sale and lease-back as two independent taxable operations. Starting in 1997, a new tax regime for this type of operation has been introduced. Eligible transactions will be spared registration tax at the initial stage of the contract, and will only be taxable if at the end of the contract the tenant acquires the property. The total acquisition price (including the part of the rent representative of the sale price) will be retroactively taxed. This regime is subject to a certain number of conditions: the 'landlord' (*crédit-bailleur)* must be a professional of the sector. The property must be used by the 'tenant' for professional purposes. The contract must be concluded for a limited duration corresponding to the duration for the write-off of the property for tax purposes. The contract must provide for a choice between the following outcomes: restitution of the property, renewing of the contract or acquisition of the property at the conditions laid down in the contract. The lease part of the contract must be made subject to value added tax (VAT).

6.5 Tax leasing

There are no known structures allowing the transfer of tax advantages for the benefit of another party. Investment incentives through tax measures or other government initiatives are discussed in section 12.

6.6 Other types of property finance

Accommodation-savings contracts (*contrats d'épargne-logement*) are a popular method of property finance for private investors and residential property, especially due to their tax advantages. Those contracts are limited to government approved accommodation-savings institutes (*caisses d'épargne-logement*). They involve the making of savings by the depositor up to a certain figure which then entitles the depositor to a loan of a further sum to provide a pre-agreed total.

6.7 Institutional investors

A considerable proportion of property investment is carried out by the investment funds or the insurance and reinsurance companies doing business in Luxembourg. Among the other institutional investors, some banks, especially those from Luxembourg and neighbouring countries, also invest in office development plans. Investment in residential premises is less popular with the institutional investors because the Law of 1955 restricts the freedom to determine the rent, while the same limitation does not apply to the office sector, nor to industrial estates (see section 5 for details).

6.8 Investors other than institutions

Apart from the institutions, there are private investors; and many projects are carried out by development and construction companies often belonging to the same group. They operate generally under the same terms as institutional investors. They are very active in the residential property markets (especially housing projects), while larger investors tend to focus on office buildings.

7 SECURITY

In rare cases, banks might grant loans on the basis of the general creditworthiness of a company or a group of companies. In most cases, however, they will require security of some kind.

7.1 Mortgages

7.1.1 The Civil Code states that a mortgage (*hypothèque*) is a right over immoveable property which guarantees the execution of an obligation. A mortgage is indivisible and attaches to the entire property. It is a right in rem and will continue to bind the land even if the property is transferred, thus enabling the mortgagee to trace the mortgaged property into the hands of third party buyers. A mortgage must be either a legal, judicial or conventional mortgage. Legal mortgages result from operation of law (eg in favour of minors on the assets of their guardians, and in favour of public authorities). Those provided for under civil law are not as relevant as those provided for under tax law. Judicial mortgages are used to enforce judgments, not arbitration awards, unless the latter have been enforced. The beneficiary of such a mortgage will proceed with its registration. Conventional mortgages result from agreement between the parties and depend on the form of the contract.

7.1.2 In order for a contractual mortgage to be valid, it must be created by way of a properly registered notarial deed drawn up by a notary public, who is the only person entitled to register the mortgage with the keeper of mortgages. The exact sum secured, and the nature and location of each element of the mortgaged property must be stated in the deed. It will be the notary's duty to check the property title in order to establish all encumbrances which may affect an estate. All mortgages, be they legal, judicial or conventional, rank in order of their registration at the mortgage registry and registration is vital in order for the right in rem to bind third parties (see 2.10). Only certain fiscal debts may be secured by legal mortgage without registration. Registration usually secures a mortgage for a period of 10 years, although renewal is possible. Once the mortgage is created, the owner retains the full right of disposal and use. However, if he sells the mortgaged object, the new owner will be expected to redeem the mortgage and to receive a 'clean' property.

7.1.3 The mortgage may be executed through a seizure by the mortgagee or any other creditor. The seizure of land is subject to complex regulations which are intended to guarantee the rights of the debtor. The seizure is subject to retrospective control by the court. As a result, the property will be sold at an auction, and at this stage the mortgagee will exercise his privilege by receiving preferential payment of the proceeds of sale. Alternatively, the mortgagee may stipulate in the mortgage agreement that he may appropriate the property in payment of the debt: in this case the procedure is more straightforward. A receiver will intervene in case of insolvency proceedings or bankruptcy. Under these circumstances, the receiver will proceed with the sale of the property and distribute the proceeds according to the legal priority of the creditors. Otherwise, a receiver will rarely intervene, except where there are numerous creditors with conflicting charges over the property and they decide to appoint a receiver to arbitrate their claims.

7.2 Floating and other charges

Under certain circumstances, it is possible to create a floating charge over a business as a going concern (*gage sur fonds de commerce*) in favour of certain bank and credit institutions approved by the government. It must be registered within 15 days to be effective. Privileges (or liens) are dealt with in 2.3. Pledges over a business and its goodwill or over securities are available but not strictly relevant to property security. Chattel mortgages are generally not available.

7.3 Bonds and guarantees

Collateral may also be provided through a personal obligation taken by a third party. Classically, such guarantee takes the form of a *cautionnement*, an obligation which is dependent on the validity of the underlying obligation. Generally, the banks require the guarantor to be jointly and severally liable with the main debtor. A second type of guarantee secures payment upon first demand or upon simple allegation of default. They are often given by banks in exchange for security provided by the debtor to the bank, such as a pledged deposit. Alternatively, the parties may agree over a guarantee deposit which the creditor may appropriate in the event of default. Such guarantees and deposits (both by the tenant and by third parties) may also be used in the case of leases (see 5.1.1). In the case of a *cautionnement*, the guarantor will only have to pay those debts and make good those losses which validly exist against the main debtor and/or which have been recognised by the courts.

7.4 Credit insurance

Credit insurance (apart from export insurance provided by public bodies) is generally not used except for major transactions. Conditions will vary from case to case.

8 PLANNING AND BUILDING REGULATION

The regulation of development and use of land are essentially based on two laws: a 1937 Law dealing with planning and development in major towns, and a 1974 Law on national planning.

8.1 Planning authorities

Planning policy is carried out both on the national and local level. Most municipalities have adopted a land use plan in conformity with the 1937 Law. These plans are all subject to ultimate approval by the Minister of the Interior. The application and enforcement of the plans are carried out by elected local representatives at the local level. These decisions are subject to review by the administrative courts.

8.2 Development plans

Local land use plans will distinguish between residential, agricultural and commercial areas within the territory open for construction. In these areas, buildings are only authorised if they are compatible with the area's rules, ie only residential buildings may be erected in residential areas. In accordance with legislation regulating environmental protection, buildings erected for the purpose of residence, trade, industry or sport are only authorised if they fall within the territorial ambit of a national or local land use plan, or, in absence of such plan, if they are in the immediate vicinity of five permanently occupied dwellings. Apart from these zones, remaining areas are referred to as 'green zones', where no construction is authorised, except with special authorisation of the Minister of the Environment. This authorisation will be granted if the construction's appearance conforms with the aesthetic and environmental requirements of the surroundings and does not jeopardise natural resources or the environment generally. These decisions are subject to full judicial review. Under certain circumstances, the zones may be modified: this is generally subject to public discussion, and to control by the administrative judge. Even if the purpose of construction conforms to the plans, the municipal authorities will still retain a certain amount of control through the building permit.

8.3 Planning control and procedures

The activities which require authorisation are laid down in the local land use plans: generally, such activities are new construction, alterations and renovations. Permission is generally not required for internal alterations which do not alter the external appearance of the building. In case of doubt, it is advisable to contact the local authorities and to obtain a statement regarding the necessity, or otherwise, of an authorisation. A further permission is required where the building has an opening on a public street (*permission de voirie*).

8.3.1 The application for a building permit (*permis de construire*) will be made to the municipality and specifically to the mayor (*bourgmestre*); it will generally include full details of the proposal.

8.3.2 There is no general time limit for the consideration of an application for a building permit by the municipal authorities. However, according to general administrative law, if the authority remains silent for more than three months, there is a deemed rejection of the application; the applicant may then apply for judicial review by the administrative courts, as in the case of an express refusal. The permit may be granted unconditionally, but generally the mayor will give a conditional authorisation. The municipality must give reasons for its decisions. The applicant may appeal to the administrative courts, which may annul the decision of the mayor and thus force him to reconsider the application. Third parties who can show a legitimate interest (such as neighbours) may appeal. Actions by collective interest groups are generally rejected, except if a specific law grants them the right to act, such as in environmental cases.

8.3.3 There is no general time limit for the use of a building permit. However, the mayor will often require construction to start within a certain time, especially if the permit is granted within the framework of a general development plan. In such cases, the building permit will be lost if the condition regarding commencement of development is not fulfilled. The building permit attaches to the applicant, not to the land. In case of sale of the land, the permit will lapse.

8.3.4 Infringements of planning control are punished by criminal sanctions provided for by the Laws of 1937 and 1974, ie a fine up to LUF500,000 and imprisonment from eight days to three months. The court may also order the demolition of the executed works and the restoration of the site, at the expense of the contravener, and generally at the demand of the municipalities or the state. Public authorities have a right of action to claim such remedies, and may even claim compensation for the damage suffered by the community.

8.4 Building standards, control and supervision

Every municipality must now have building regulations (*règlement des bâtisses*) which will determine the character of constructions and will provide measures for the conservation of sites and monuments from an aesthetic point of view. In addition to the separate building permit, all construction must meet with the provisions of the building regulations of the relevant municipality. These regulations are concerned with issues of solidity of the constructions, sanitary equipment, and the development within the municipality as a whole. They are also concerned with the density of constructions, as well as aesthetic questions such as form, appearance and location of the building. The application for a building permit will have to show that the project complies with all these regulations. Any modifications of the plans at a later stage have also to be approved by the local authorities. The technical services of the municipality may at any moment inspect the premises and order changes to the construction in order to ensure compliance with the building regulations. The mayor has the power to suspend construction in case of serious violations of the regulations. All decisions of the mayor are subject to judicial review. The sanctions referred to in 8.3.4 apply also to the violation of building regulations.

8.5 Protection of buildings of special interest

The building regulations will also define monuments of artistic, historic or archaeological value and zones of special significance designated by the land use plans. New constructions, extensions, posters and other advertising facilities within such areas will be authorised only if they do not harm the beauty of the site. A list of these buildings is kept by the Ministry of Culture. The Minister is the competent authority to authorise all modifications, extensions, etc. He may also require the owner to repair the listed buildings, or proceed to order the repairs himself, if the buildings are at serious risk due to their state of repair. The state will have to bear a certain part of the repair costs.

8.6 Compulsory purchase or expropriation and compensation

Expropriation may only be carried out by order of a judge, which provides guarantees to the owners. Expropriation proceedings may be initiated by the state, by municipalities, by public bodies and by private persons, if they invoke a public interest. The courts may only order expropriation if there is a formal decision either by statute (if the state initiates the expropriation) or by regulatory act (in all cases) which determines that the expropriation is carried out in the public interest. Judicial review of such acts should be allowed from 1997, in the framework of the administrative law reform. As a matter of principle, the expropriated owner is entitled to just and prior compensation for his land. Compensation is determined by the judge.

9 ENVIRONMENTAL MATTERS

The general Environmental Protection Law of 1982 aims to preserve the general environmental character and diversity and to protect natural resources. Every facility, activity or manufacturing process is subject to licensing requirements if it is a potential source of nuisance or may be harmful to the safety, health or well-being of the general public, the neighbourhood, employees or the environment. The authority (central or local governmental) responsible for granting the licence will depend on the classification of the installation according to the degree of risk involved. A 1990 statute establishes three categories of facilities depending on the potential risk to the environment. Only licensing of category one facilities is subject to a public discussion held in the installation's local community, during which all objections will be heard (*enquête commodo et incommodo*), while category two and three installations are subject to a less complex licensing mechanism. The applicant must supply information on the proposed facility, the intended manufacturing process, all possible sources of pollution and their harmful effects on the environment, as well as approximate data on the measures proposed to prevent or reduce these. The licence will specify the requirements to ensure environmental protection (including compliance with all special legislation) and these requirements can be made subject to conditions, at the outset or subsequently. At various stages, citizens may present their claims and objections, and within 40 days of the notification of approval, any affected party, ie who can claim a personal and direct interest, may appeal. Associations for the protection of the environment have been approved by ministerial order to defend the collective interests of affected individuals. It should be noted that there is a requirement on foreign investors to obtain a business permit, certifying compatibility with environmental protection legislation (see further section 14 detailing issues for foreign investors).

9.1 Protection against atmospheric and noise pollution

9.1.1 Protection and improvement of air quality are subject to a 1976 Law and a number of regulations applying the principles to various sectors, prohibiting certain production methods, requiring certain measures to prevent pollution or the creation of pollution-free zones. Violation of these regulations amounts to a criminal offence subject to criminal penalties (including fines and imprisonment, closing of the business, confiscation and loss of business licence). Appointed state agents (including police) have very wide powers of investigation for the purpose of determining the person responsible for pollution. Furthermore, there are several measuring stations analysing the quality of the air dispersed over the territory. The general rules of civil liability and the laws of nuisance apply. The polluter will commonly be held liable and liability of the owner or lender of the facilities is not automatic: they must have themselves been negligent. In addition, the competent minister may take urgent provisional measures prohibiting the use of polluting equipment, which are subject to appeal. The rules apply both to vehicles and to stationary sources of noise.

9.1.2 Noise pollution is regulated by a 1976 Law, which also provides for a certain number of regulations to be adopted to prevent such pollution. The rules regarding investigation, provisional measures and penalties are similar to the law regulating atmospheric pollution.

9.2 Water pollution

Water pollution is subject to a 1993 Law regarding the protection and the management of water resources and subsequent regulations. This law prohibits any form of pollution of water and contains an authorisation procedure for use of water other than from the public network, and for any disposal of dirty water or other substances into the water. Discharges in breach of authorisations or of the law and regulations are subject to criminal sanctions. Civil liability is subject to the general rules referred to in 9.1.1. A national inventory of water quality has been set up, as well as a national plan for the management of aquatic resources. Special protection rules apply to certain areas providing drinking water to the public network.

9.3 Waste storage and disposal

Waste storage and disposal are subject to a 1994 Law. The Law introduces the principle that the polluter must bear the costs of the waste disposal and storage (including infrastructure costs). Local authorities must ensure that waste produced within the confines of their territorial ambit is properly stored and disposed of. However, this does not apply to industrial waste. The law introduces a new regime of strict liability for any damage caused by waste. The victim will no longer have to prove any fault on behalf of the polluter and any other person responsible for the damage. Any waste disposal undertaking as well as any installation or machinery used for such purposes is subject to prior authorisation by the Minister of the Environment. Special rules apply to the disposal of hazardous waste. Offences under these regulations are subject to criminal penalties and may give rise to civil liability (see above). Furthermore, the courts may order the restoration of the area polluted by illegal waste disposal to its previous state, at the polluter's expense.

9.4 Contaminated land

In case of a transfer of interest in land, it will be up to the interested parties to research any prior pollution of the land. Such investigations have been facilitated by a 1992 Law providing for the freedom of access to information concerning environmental matters and an obligation to cooperate which is binding upon all public authorities. The central authority monitoring and supervising the pollution and cleaning up is the *Administration de l'Environnement*. There is no dedicated fund for the decontamination of land, and any liabilities are dealt with on the basis of general civil law.

9.5 Environmental impact assessments

All major industrial undertakings bearing high pollution risks are required to carry out an environmental impact assessment, while less dangerous undertakings may be required to carry out such an assessment because of the nature of their activity, their characteristics and their location. The assessments are carried out by professionals who are specifically authorised by the competent minister to carry out this type of analysis. The information to be gathered and the measurements to be taken are in conformity with the EU requirements.

10 DEVELOPMENT

10.1 Development projects, structures and vehicles

There are many different development schemes in Luxembourg. Large projects are generally built on the basis of a group of contracts concluded between the builder and the different contractors. Residential property may also adopt this form of development, but often developers will enter into urbanisation projects with local authorities and sell a completed building to the private investor. Common development structures generally take no particular form, but remain an informal agreement based on contracts between the different parties. Sometimes the cooperation between developers or contractors becomes so close that the agreement takes the form of a temporary association under the unofficial form of a *société par participation* or of a more organised *groupement d'intérêt économique*.

10.2 Building contracts and appointment

10.2.1 Typical forms of building contract

The most common form of building contract is the traditional building contract (*contrat d'entreprise*) either between the investor as employer and the developer or between the employer and each of the individual contractors. The situation whereby an owner/occupier enters into an agreement with a contractor to build premises according to a specified design is regulated by the traditional builder's contract. This contract, regulated by the Civil Code, allows the investor to use one or more contractors to construct the building. There may be only one contractor, often a developer, who will then be in charge of the construction, and who will usually subcontract certain parts of the job to other craftsmen. The contractor will manage the subcontractors, this service being part of the overall price. In most cases, he will retain full responsibility for the execution of the contract. The subcontractors are liable both to him and to the employer. On the other hand, the employer may also, often with the help of an architect, contract himself with the different professionals, in which case a separate contractual relationship exists with each one of them. The remaining type of contractual arrangement used in development projects is the contract for the construction of future housing (*vente d'immeubles à construire*), which is a sale contract, where the developer provides a complete service. The developer will sell the land, build the premises to the specifications of the employer and deliver it in a completed state and will be responsible for all defects, even those resulting from the work of his subcontractors. The regime of the *vente d'immeubles à construire* will apply to all contracts whereby one person, who will conduct the operations, undertakes to build a residential or mixed building for periodic payments prior to completion. The purpose of the law is the protection of private or semi-private investors, therefore professional development undertaken on behalf of clients within the industry is excluded. The law imposes an obligation on the developer to deliver a bank guarantee to the investor for the completion of the project. Often, large projects are pre-financed, and the different buildings are sold at different stages of completion.

10.2.2 Common terms

The *contrat d'entreprise* (either between the employer and the developer or between the employer and each of the individual contractors) provides for start and finish dates, but these dates are generally expressed to be estimated rather than definite dates. The contract may be for a lump sum, which excludes any additional payments in principle (except for changes agreed upon by the investor or additional work imposed by reasons independent from either party). Payments will generally be made to the main contractor, who will make his own arrangements with the subcontractors. If the investor contracts individually with all parties, he will pay each of them separately. The investor may decide to terminate the contract at any point, but he will have to pay the price of the work already carried out. He may be liable for any loss caused by such termination, but the contractor will have to prove his negligence or fault in the termination of the contract, and the compensation will never be the full price payable on completion. Alternatively, the contract may have no set price, and the parties may agree on the stages upon which payment will become due as the project progresses. The subcontractors, if they have been approved by the developer, are in a contractual relationship with him, and they have a right to direct payment by the developer, even though their contract has actually been concluded with the lead contractor. Under a *vente d'immeubles à construire* payment is periodic and will only generally be made upon proof of progress; the different stages and related payments must be defined in the contract. The developer/seller's main obligation is to deliver the building to the specifications agreed.

10.2.3 Standard form of contracts

There is no statutory standard form of contract, except for those elements imposed by the law on construction.

10.3 Those involved and their roles

There is no organised profession of surveyors in Luxembourg as such. Experts may intervene on the parties' request to analyse the project and assist in the planning and construction. Architects may be involved either to coordinate the construction project of the investor, or at the request of the developer, depending on which type of contract is chosen (see 10.2.1). They are generally chosen by the investor on an informal tender basis, except where the rules of public procurement apply.

10.4 Defects and remedies

10.4.1 Remedies of employer in respect of defects in design and materials

Under the *contrat d'entreprise*, the contractors are directly liable for any defects which come to light after the completion of the building. Apparent defects discovered at the time of completion have to be repaired immediately. Liability for hidden defects is of a contractual nature. It lapses 10 years after completion of the building for major defects, such as watertightness, and after two years for minor defects. These limitations apply to all those who have either a direct contract with the investor, or those (like the subcontractors) who are put in the same legal situation. All other persons are merely liable in tort, without time limitations. In the case of the *vente d'immeubles à construire*, the general principle of liability of the seller for the hidden defects of goods applies, but certain specific rules have been adopted. Thus, the seller will only be discharged for apparent defects one month after the buyer has acquired the building. For hidden defects, the 10 year and two year guarantee has been applied, but with the additional requirement that the buyer must file the claim within a short period of discovering the defect.

10.4.2 Remedies of subsequent owners/occupiers other than the contractual employer

The guarantee and remedies mentioned in 10.4.1 are transferred with the building and land, and the subsequent owners may exercise them in exactly the same way as the initial owner. All other parties who suffer damage due to defects, such as third parties or secured creditors, will have an action in tort against the contractor or the architect if they can prove fault, causation and loss, under the general rules of civil law liability. Contractual warranties are rare in residential property, but in larger projects the parties may provide for penalty payments. Under these circumstances, persons other than the initial parties may claim damages on the basis of these clauses, only if they are valid successors to the contracts (generally on the basis of a valid assignment).

10.5 Defects insurance

Defects insurance is not compulsory for developers. However, in practice, many professionals are insured. For contracts for the construction of future houses, the law requires the seller to provide a completion guarantee (*garantie d'achèvement*), typically in the form of a bank guarantee, to protect buyers against the risk of insolvency of the seller or the developer. However, this guarantee does not include the cost of remedying defects or consequential loss.

10.6 Copyright

Copyright law protects all literary and artistic creations. Non-residents are treated in the same way as Luxembourg citizens. The copyright in the design of the building falls within the category of literary or artistic creation, insofar as it has a certain originality and is the product of creation rather than reproduction of existing concepts. All rights belong to the author of the creation, but he may dispose of those rights. Whilst the protection of plans, models and designs is recognised, the degree of protection of the building itself, as a realisation of the architect's concept, is debatable.

10.7 Fees

Fees will generally be borne by the investor, except in the case of *vente d'immeubles à construire*, where they will be paid by the developer, but will be part of the overall price of the project.

10.8 Taxes

Construction is subject to value added tax (VAT) at a rate of 15 per cent. Private investors may obtain a reimbursement of the VAT paid for the construction at a rate of 12 per cent.

11 TAXES

11.1 Corporation tax

Corporate income tax (*impôt sur le revenu des collectivités*) is payable on the worldwide income of resident companies (including capital gains) subject to relief under any double taxation treaty with the country from which the profits originate and on the Luxembourg source income of non-resident companies. A company is considered to be resident if its statutory seat or principal establishment or management is in Luxembourg. While the initial test for residence is the statutory seat, it may be shown that the decision-making centre of the company is situated in a different location, such as the location of the board meetings.

11.1.1 Tax rates

Corporate income tax rates are progressive, from 20 per cent to 33 per cent. For income exceeding LUF1,312,000 per annum, the rate applicable is 33 per cent plus a tax surcharge for unemployment contribution. In addition, all business activities are subject to municipal business tax, which is deductible for corporate income tax purposes. From 1997 onwards the tax rate is progressively reduced to 32 per cent in 1997, 31 per cent in 1998 and 30 per cent in 1999. The total effective rate, including municipal business tax and solidarity surcharge, will be 39.24 per cent for 1997 and ultimately 37.45 per cent in 1999.

11.1.2 Computation and administration

Taxable profits are based on profits disclosed in the annual accounts approved by shareholders, adjusted for non-deductible items, such as directors' fees, corporate income tax and net worth tax. The profit is established by deducting from the revenue all expenses which are exclusively incurred for the purposes of the trade of the company, as well as write-offs of the company's assets and provisions. Tax on gains from certain fixed assets (investments in land and other permanent investments) which have been held for at least five years may be deferred by reinvestment in eligible assets. Foreign income, unless exempted by treaty provisions, is fully taxable in the hands of domestic corporations. Credit may be claimed for foreign taxes paid, limited to the amount of Luxembourg tax on the foreign income. Excess foreign tax which does not qualify for tax credit is deductible from taxable income. The companies calculate themselves the taxes on the declared profit. Tax assessments are then carried out by the *administration des contributions.* They also deal with the collection of the tax. It is possible to appeal against such assessments to the new *tribunal fiscal*, subject to control by the *cour administrative d'appel.* Special mention should be made though of the tax treatment of holding companies described at 11.9.

11.1.3 Capital allowances

As mentioned in 11.1.2, a company may write off, ie deduct from its profits, the depreciation of its permanent assets, including the buildings (but not undeveloped land) on its balance sheet. The time period for depreciation is determined by the tax authorities on the basis of regulations and practice, and varies according to the prospective length of service of the asset. For instance, an industrial building will be written off in 25 years, ie four per cent per year of the balance sheet value. Undeveloped land may not be written off. Special regimes exist generally allowing for a quicker depreciation such as for research and development or for assets used to further environmental protection.

11.1.4 Withholding tax

Withholding taxes apply to dividends and interest paid on profit-related bonds at a rate of 25 per cent and royalty payments at a rate of 10 or 12 per cent depending on the type of licence. However, no withholding tax is levied if the dividend income is distributed by a 1929 holding company (ie a company with corporate objects restricted to holding and managing participations). Reduced rates (generally 15 per cent) are available under the various treaties for the avoidance of double taxation concluded by Luxembourg if the payee is a company resident in another treaty country. Under the EC Parent-Subsidiary Directive 1990, dividends from a Luxembourg subsidiary of a company in another EC member state are exempt from withholding tax if the parent has owned a minimum of 25 per cent of the shares of the Luxembourg subsidiary for two years. There is no general withholding tax on Luxembourg sourced revenues. There is no withholding tax on interest payments generally.

11.2 Taxes on development value

Taxes will only be due on the increase in value of property due to be developed, when the asset is sold or otherwise transferred (eg mergers and transfers) or when the accounting value of the asset is readapted. There are special provisions for the taxation of such profits (*plus-values*).

11.3 Taxes on capital gains

Capital gains are treated as income. Capital gains from the disposal of a domestic or foreign shareholding are exempt if the shareholding is at least 25 per cent or if the acquisition cost was at least LUF250 million and the holding was owned for 12 months preceding the year of disposal. Dividends received from a domestic or foreign shareholding are exempt if the shareholding is at least 10 per cent or the acquisition cost was at least LUF50 million and has been owned for 12 months preceding the year of receipt. To qualify for the dividend or capital gain exemption, the subsidiary must be subject to an income tax similar to Luxembourg income tax.

11.4 Taxes on owner of property

Property tax (*impôt foncier*) is a municipal tax levied on immoveable property. The use made of the premises is irrelevant for the application of taxation. However, the use determines the rate, which varies between 0.7 per cent and 1 per cent of the value of the premises as established by the tax administration. The municipal business tax is also levied for the benefit of the local authorities. Inheritance tax is payable by all heirs of a Luxembourg resident on the value of all worldwide assets with the exception of land and certain moveable assets located abroad. Inheritance tax will also be payable on inheritance of land located in Luxembourg, where the last residence of the deceased was abroad. Immediate successors in title are exempt from taxes. Tax rates for other heirs vary according to the degree of kinship between 2.5 per cent and 15 per cent, with possible surplus tax depending on the value of the inheritance.

11.5 Taxes on occupier

There are no taxes on the occupier of property.

11.6 Taxes on land transfer

Transfers of property are subject to a registration duty (*droit d'enregistrement*) fixed at six per cent of the purchase price indicated in the registered contract (or market value if higher), plus a three per cent surcharge for property located in Luxembourg-City or Esch/Alzette, as well as a one per cent transcription duty. This applies to sale by auction, sales, resales, assignments and all other civil deeds and orders of the court transferring title to property for a consideration. Registered lease contracts are subject to a duty of 0.6 per cent on total lease payments. The duties are paid on behalf of the parties by the notary at the time of registration of the deeds. A reduced rate of 1.2 per cent applies to property sold in case of bankruptcy proceedings, and under certain conditions for public housing. If the buyer declares to the notary public upon signature of the deed that he purchases with the intention to resell, the registration duty is 7.2 per cent; the buyer will obtain a reimbursement of six per cent if he resells within five years.

11.7 Wealth taxes

Luxembourg residents are subject to an unlimited tax obligation concerning their assets. The tax applies both to natural persons and to legal entities. The rate is 0.5 per cent of the estimated value of the assets. The further municipal tax levied on a company's assets has been abolished.

11.8 Value added tax

Value added tax (VAT) is charged by suppliers of goods and services to their customers. Apart from the VAT issues already mentioned, eg on solicitors' and agents' fees and construction work, it is possible to charge VAT on a transfer of land where both parties are VAT-taxable persons, in order to allow the buyer to deduct the VAT paid. While leases are also generally exempt from VAT, and subject to registration tax in case of registration, it is also possible to opt for VAT taxation of a lease between two VAT taxpayers. According to a general principle of Luxembourg tax law, no registration or transfer duties will be levied where VAT is applied. The taxes are calculated by the tax payers every month on their VAT declaration. Tax assessment is carried out by the *Administration de l'Enregistrement et des Domaines*. The tax payer may lodge an appeal against such assessment before the civil courts.

11.9 Other tax issues

Holding companies and investment funds benefit from extremely favourable tax treatment.

11.9.1 Their tax base is the value of the shares not their income. Upon incorporation, a registration tax of one per cent on holding companies' statutory capital must be paid. During its lifetime, the only tax which will be levied is the annual subscription duty of 0.2 per cent on the current value of securities issued. There are no other taxes. No taxes on profits or withholding taxes on distributed profits or interest apply. For holding companies with statutory capital of at least LUF1 billion, or an equivalent thereof in foreign currencies, special rules of taxation may apply if the company so elects. Holding companies are however excluded from all double tax treaties concluded by Luxembourg.

11.9.2 Investment funds (*sicavs* or *sicafs*, see 13.3.3) pay a single capital contribution tax of LUF50,000 and then an annual 0.02 per cent subscription duty on the net asset value of their portfolio. This is reducing to 0.01 per cent in 1998. They pay no other tax on capital or income.

11.9.3 The tax on creation of companies should also be noted. A one per cent capital contribution tax is charged on assets brought in as capital on incorporation or on any increase of a company's share capital. The tax is based on fair market value if assets other than cash are contributed. The establishment of a branch in Luxembourg by a company not having its registered office or centre of effective management in an EC member state is also subject to this tax. Tax is levied on the value of the net assets of the branch. For the purpose of assessing the one per cent duty in the case of a share capital expressed in a foreign currency, the notary converts the share capital into LUF at the average exchange rate prevailing at the date of incorporation. The tax administration then levies the duty on that amount.

12 GRANTS AND INCENTIVES

The government provides several types of financial assistance to those planning to construct or buy a house or flat which will be the applicant's main dwelling provided it is to be located within the Grand-Duchy of Luxembourg. This assistance may take the form of state guarantees for loans, capital grants such as saving, construction or acquisition subsidies, reduced interest rates on loans, and various tax advantages, for instance for certain savings schemes. There are a variety of investment incentives for industrial and commercial undertakings. These are based on direct or indirect aid or through tax incentives, as well as the intervention of the *Société Nationale de Crédit à l'Investissement* (*SNCI*), which is the designated public body providing investment incentives. Finally, the incentives programmes of the EU are also available to Luxembourg investors. There are specific schemes for the development of certain industrial areas, which may take the form of any of the aids mentioned in this section.

12.1 Subsidies, grants and loans

The state may provide investors with guarantees for loans (which generally already benefit from a reduced interest rate) of up to 50 per cent of the expenses to be covered by the loan, where the applicant has already taken considerable measures to provide collateral himself. The state will also provide aid in the form of subsidies in favour of investment programmes, restructuring of undertakings or research and development programmes. Both the state and the *SNCI* provide loans at reduced interest for investment programmes. If an applicant benefits from one of these grants or subsidies, then he may also benefit from a state contribution to the cost of the architect and technical advisers, as well as for feasibility studies, generally in the form of a subsidy granted retrospectively. Other aid is available, eg for feasibility studies, preparatory analysis and technical assistance.

12.2 Tax allowances and reliefs

12.2.1 There are a certain number of tax incentives for commercial undertakings. The Tax Code provides for the deduction at a specific rate for certain types of permanent investments which are made in the Luxembourg establishment of a tax payer. However, land is excluded from these except where the investment is for refurbishment. The Minister of Finance may also grant tax exemptions in individual cases for inward investment for a maximum period of 10 years.

12.2.2 Interest grants available for commercial and industrial undertakings may reduce the market rates by up to four per cent, and up to six per cent in the case of research and development programmes.

12.3 Other public schemes and incentives

12.3.1 A Law passed in 1993, which represents one of the cornerstones of the state incentive scheme, provides for a specific aid to property-related investment. In order to draw industrial activities to Luxembourg, local and state authorities may buy plots of land, rearrange and develop them with the aim of creating industrial areas. These plots may then be leased, exchanged or sold at attractive prices to undertakings representing a major interest in terms of investment and employment. There are further specific programmes in support of certain sectors, eg tourism and agriculture.

12.3.2 The *SNCI*, regulated under a 1977 Law, has a specific programme of incentives, which generally take the form of long or medium-term loans (15 to 10 years), with reduced interest rates, to finance a company's infrastructure (including real estate). The *SNCI* may also provide aid in the form of a contribution to the company's share capital.

13 COMPANIES AND BUSINESS ENTITIES

Luxembourg commercial companies are governed by a Law of 1915, as amended.

13.1 Limited and unlimited companies

13.1.1 In unlimited companies, the members are liable for all the corporate debts. Such liability will be joint and several if the company's business is of a commercial nature. These companies arise where there is a close personal relationship between the members. They are generally small or medium-sized family companies.

13.1.2 The private limited liability company (*société à responsabilité limitée*) traditionally requires a minimum of two members and the maximum number is restricted to 40. It is now possible, however, to create a small or medium-sized limited liability company which is formed by one member only; either at the time of incorporation or when all the shares fall into the hands of one member. Private limited liability companies are run by one or several managers (*gérants*), who need not be members. Meetings in general assembly of all members are only required if there are more than 25 members, otherwise any resolution may be submitted to them for decision by post and their vote may be expressed in writing. Members' liability is limited to the amount of their investment. Capital of this type of company must be at least LUF500,000. Shares must be subscribed and paid for in full. This type of company does not issue registered or bearer shares, but only participation certificates the transfer of which is subject to strict regulations. Limited liability companies require a notarial deed for creation. Limited liability companies are considered to be legal entities with separate existence from their members.

13.1.3 The public limited company (*société anonyme*), the most popular form of business entity amongst foreign investors, must have two or more shareholders and must be incorporated by way of notarial deed. There is no maximum number of shareholders. There must be a minimum share capital of LUF1,250,000 divided into shares, which are freely transferable unless the corporate charter includes restrictions. Shares will be in registered or in bearer form. Capital must be fully subscribed, but only 25 per cent needs to be paid up at the time of incorporation. Contributions that are not in cash must be valued by an external qualified auditor. Liability of shareholders is limited to the amount of their investment. The company is governed by a board of directors, consisting of at least three members.

13.2 Partnerships

A partnership is considered to be civil if its purpose is not commercial. Since buying property for sale or lease and extracting produce from the soil are not considered acts of trade, mining and property companies may be civil partnerships unless they adopt a commercial form. Civil partnerships are considered to be separate judicial entities from their members. Partnerships are commercial if their intended purpose is to undertake trade, or, even though their activity is civil, they have adopted one of six forms of partnerships or companies which are deemed commercial by law. General and limited partnerships must have two or more partners. There are no restrictions as to nationality of partners or as to their residence.

13.2.1 In a limited partnership (*société en commandite*), there will be certain partners who have general liability (the general partners) and other partners who have their liability limited to a fixed financial contribution to the partnership. The general partners are in sole control of the management of the partnership and their liability will be unlimited once they have taken an active part in the management. Silent partners may not take part in the management of a limited partnership and their liability is limited to the amount of capital they have contributed to the partnership.

13.2.2 In a general partnership (*société en nom collectif*), if there is no term otherwise in the charter, every partner represents and can bind the partnership, but decisions require the consent of all partners. The charter often appoints one or more managers. In a general partnership, partners are fully and personally liable. General partnerships have no separate existence under tax laws, and tax is levied upon individual partners according to their respective share in income. For all legal purposes other than tax, general partnerships are seen as private legal entities.

13.2.3 Limited partnerships by shares (*sociétés en commandite par actions*) are a combination of a joint stock company and partnership. While the shareholders have a liability limited to their contributions, some partners have an unlimited liability for the company's debts. The company or partnership is managed by one or more members of this second group of partners. They are separate legal entities for legal purposes. For tax purposes, they are treated as a limited partnership, with certain adjustments for the jointly and severally liable partners for the benefits they receive as shareholders. A notarial deed is compulsory for the incorporation of the company. The management and organisation of this type of company generally follow the rules relating to the joint stock company.

13.3 Other types of business association

13.3.1 In a cooperative society, partners have unlimited liability, unless the charter provides otherwise (which it generally does). Partners are free to agree its management structure.

13.3.2 Holding companies must have as their object the holding of investments and participations in other Luxembourg or foreign companies, and management and development of such participations. Holding companies may not carry on any industrial or trading activity of their own. They may not have any establishment open to the public. They are subject to the general rules of corporate law, but have particularly favourable tax status (see 11.9).

13.3.3 *Sicavs* (*sociétés à capital variable*) and *sicafs* (*sociétés à capital fixe*) are exclusively devoted to performing the role of collective investment funds. In addition to a specific 1988 Law on collective investment, these fund companies are regulated by general corporate law. Although there is no restriction on the nationality of these companies, they must have their central management and keep share registers in Luxembourg. All investment funds are subject to prior approval of the *Institut Monétaire Luxembourgeois*, as well as certain reporting requirements. *Sicavs* are companies with variable share capital, varying with the redemption and issue of shares. *Sicafs* have a fixed share capital. In both instances, the minimum capital required is LUF50 million or its equivalent in foreign currency. Besides the forms of *sicav* or *sicaf*, a collective investment fund may also choose the form *fonds commun de placement* (*FCP*), ie unit trust or mutual fund. *FCP*s are undivided co-proprietorships of assets made up and managed to spread risk on behalf of unit holders who are liable only up to the amount invested by them. Their rights and obligations, and investment rules, are all determined by the *FCP*'s management regulations. These funds have no legal personality themselves and therefore need to rely on a management company to do business. The same rules regarding regulation and taxation apply to these funds as apply to *sicavs* or *sicafs*.

13.3.4 The economic interest group (EIG) and the European economic interest group (EEIG) both aim to facilitate or develop the economic activities of their members and to improve or increase the results of these activities, and can have no other purpose. Both have legal personality and their members are fully and personally liable. There are no essential differences between the EIG and the EEIG. Members of EEIG must however originate from at least two EU member states.

14 INTERNATIONAL

14.1 Restrictions or consents required for inward investment

There are no restrictions on the import of capital to Luxembourg by foreign entities, nor are there any restrictions on the ownership of local property by foreign entities.

14.2 Exchange controls

Luxembourg is a member of the *Union Economique Belgo-Luxembourgeoise (UEBL)*. Therefore all exchange controls are handled by a common body, the *Institut Belgo-Luxembourgeois du Change (IBLC)*. However, there are, apart from some exceptional cases, no exchange controls operating at the moment.

14.3 Restrictions and registrations on carrying on a business

Luxembourg favours foreign investment, and formalities concerning foreign investments are very limited. In principle, every company wanting to establish itself in Luxembourg needs prior authorisation delivered by the competent minister (depending on the particular economic sector concerned), as well as a business permit, certifying compatibility with environmental protection legislation. None of these requirements apply to holding companies.

14.4 Repatriation of income and proceeds of property trading and development

There are no consents or restraints involved in the repatriation of income and proceeds subject to the deduction of withholding tax.

14.5 Withholding taxes

These taxes have been referred to at 11.1.4.

14.6 Double taxation relief

Luxembourg has separate double taxation treaties with a number of countries.

CHAPTER 11

The Netherlands

Cornelis Slangen **Evert Wiggers**

Partners, Trenité van Doorne, Amsterdam

CONTENTS

1 OWNERSHIP OF LAND 359
2 OTHER INTERESTS IN LAND 361
3 TITLE TO LAND 364
4 TRANSACTIONS IN LAND 365
5 LEASES AND OTHER RIGHTS OF OCCUPATION 368
6 FINANCE AND INVESTMENT SOURCES 371
7 FORMS OF SECURITY 374
8 PLANNING AND BUILDING REGULATION 377
9 ENVIRONMENTAL MATTERS 380
10 DEVELOPMENT 382
11 TAXES 385
12 GRANTS AND INCENTIVES 389
13 COMPANIES AND BUSINESS ENTITIES 390
14 INTERNATIONAL 392

CHAPTER 11

The Netherlands

1 OWNERSHIP OF LAND

The Civil Code regulates the law on ownership of, and other rights and obligations with respect to, land and other real property (*onroerende zaken*) such as buildings and structures over land. There are also numerous acts of parliament and other administrative regulations on property matters. This chapter deals exclusively with land and other real property. The principal forms of right or interest in land or other property are ownership and long-term leasehold (*erfpacht*) which create a right in or against the land itself.

1.1 Types of tenure

1.1.1 Ownership

Ownership *(eigendom)* is the most comprehensive right in land. It carries with it the exclusive right to own, occupy and dispose of the land, provided this does not conflict with third-party rights and/or the statutory restrictions or provisions of unwritten law. Any building or structure on the land will be treated as part of the land unless the right over it has been granted to someone other than the absolute owner (see 2.3). Absolute ownership also carries with it the right to the soil below and the air space above, and this includes certain minerals, although others may be excluded.

1.1.2 Long-term leasehold

Long-term leasehold (*erfpacht*) over land is the exclusive right to use and occupy the land for a fixed or indefinite period. In principle, the right may be transferred but this might be made subject to the prior approval of the owner under the deed by which the right is created. The local authorities (eg Amsterdam, Rotterdam and The Hague) and public corporations are the main grantors of long-term leasehold tenure. A long-term lease will be created in the same way as other lesser rights in land (see section 2) and the relevant provisions of the Civil Code will regulate the rights and obligations of the parties. In most cases, the deed creating the long-term leasehold will stipulate the payment by the tenant of an annual ground rent (*canon*); in certain cases, the parties may agree to single payment of a lump sum instead. Other commonly used leases are contractual and the terms on which leases or tenancies are granted are dealt with more fully in section 5.

1.1.3 Co-ownership

Where property is acquired by two or more persons, they will each be owners of equal shares in the property and there will be no division of the property into separate parts. Each co-owner/participant may transfer or encumber his share over the joint property; unless otherwise agreed between the parties, he will not require the prior consent of the other owners.

1.1.4 Condominia

The owner, or the long-term leaseholder with the permission of the owner, is entitled to divide the land and/or the buildings erected over it, into two or more condominium rights (*appartementsrechten*). The condominium right comprises the exclusive right to use and occupy a specifically designated part of the property (as described in the notarial deed of division) and the right to use the common areas of the property.

1.1.5 Lesser rights

The various rights to use and enjoy land not amounting to rights of absolute ownership or long-term leasehold are dealt with in section 2.

1.2 The role of the trust and the distinction between legal and beneficial ownership

A beneficial interest in land may be created by means of a contract where the holder of a right in rem in respect of land or other property (eg the owner or the long-term leaseholder) sells or otherwise disposes of the beneficial or economic interest in the property. It does not constitute a right in rem. The buyer or beneficiary is entitled to all benefits or proceeds from the property against payment of the purchase price. In order to safeguard his interest, the beneficiary is advised to obtain a mortgage over the property as security for the seller's obligation to transfer title. This type of interest was frequently created to avoid property transfer tax (*overdrachtsbelasting*) but since 31 March 1995 property transfer tax has been levied upon the creation of a beneficial interest.

1.3 Restrictions on ownership and dealing

1.3.1 There are few restrictions on the ownership of land although there are some legislative restrictions on the extent of the rights of a landowner, which mainly aim to protect the public interest and include planning regulations, rights of access, preservation of monuments and compulsory purchase. There are further restrictions arising from unwritten law aiming to protect private interests such as neighbours' rights permitting the use of land only to the extent where this does not encroach upon the enjoyment and use of adjoining landowners. A minor or a person suffering from mental impairment is not legally prevented from becoming an owner of property or a beneficiary of a right in rem, provided the requisite approval of the parent or trustees is obtained; a failure to do so will render the transaction voidable. Companies and/or other legal entities are only restricted from owning property if such a restriction is expressly provided in the articles of incorporation.

1.3.2 There are no generally applicable provisions, statutory or otherwise, upon the disposal of land by the owner.

1.4 Adverse possession and acquisitive prescription

Title to registered property may be acquired by 10 years of uninterrupted possession in good faith; there is a presumption of good faith unless there is conclusive proof to the contrary. A further form of acquisitive prescription, akin to adverse possession, is provided for under the Civil Code, where a person possessing land or other property as owner but without title or any right to the property, will acquire legal title to the property when a 20-year limitation period has elapsed. In the latter case, there is no requirement of good faith on the possessor's part.

2 OTHER INTERESTS IN LAND

There are various public or private interests which do not confer a right of ownership over the property itself but a right over or connected with the property of another. The most common are servitudes, qualitative obligations and mortgages.

2.1 Servitudes or easements, usufruct, building and dwelling rights

2.1.1 Servitudes

A servitude or easement (*erfdienstbaarheid*) is a right in rem over land (the servient tenement) in favour of other land (the dominant tenement) consisting of an obligation to submit to, or to abstain from, certain activities. The servitude runs with the land and may not be disposed of separately. The servitude is created by notarial deed between the owners, and will require registration (see section 3 for registration generally). A servitude may also arise as a result of acquisitive prescription after 10 years' exercise of the right in good faith, and 20 years' non-use will terminate the servitude.

2.1.2 Usufruct

A right of usufruct (*vruchtgebruik*) is the right to use and take the profits of land or property belonging to another. The right may be over the land itself or over other rights in rem to property, such as the long-term leasehold (see 1.1.2) or building and planting rights (see 2.1.3). Usufruct is tied to the life of the person in whom it is vested, where the beneficiary of the right is an individual, and will terminate automatically after 30 years where the beneficiary is a legal entity. It is created in the same way as a servitude (see 2.1.1).

2.1.3 Building and dwelling rights

Building and planting rights (*opstalrecht*) are rights in rem to own buildings or what has been erected over or planted upon land of another. The right to a building on land may be granted as an independent right in rem, but is usually granted in conjunction with the right to use land under a tenancy agreement, or together with a long-term leasehold over the land. Building and planting rights, like all rights in rem, are created by notarial deed and registration. They may be granted for either a fixed or indefinite period and are transferable unless the deed requires the prior approval of the property owner. The ownership of the building will revert to the landowner upon termination and no compensation will be payable unless agreed.

2.2 Restrictions on use and other restrictions

Restrictions or qualitative obligations (*kwalitatieve verplichtingen*) may be created in respect of property where an agreement entered into between a person and the owner or long-term leaseholder of property places an obligation upon the latter, which will pass to successors in title, to suffer certain conduct or to abstain from certain acts over that property. To render such a qualitative obligation binding upon and enforceable against successors in title, it must be in a notarial deed and registered. Another form of restriction on owners of property may be created on a transfer, by perpetual covenant (*kettingbedingen*), where the owner or long-term leaseholder may impose a positive or negative undertaking upon the transferee, together with the obligation on the transferee to impose such an undertaking on any subsequent buyer of the land, failing which the transferee will forfeit a penalty payment to the transferor. Public law restrictions under planning and other legislation are commented on in section 8 and public pre-emption rights at 4.1.2.

2.3 Private mortgages, privileges and charges

Monetary liabilities can be secured by a mortgage (*hypotheek*) on land or other property, whether the title to the land consists of ownership, long-term leasehold, building and planting rights, condominium rights or usufruct. The mortgage right is a right in rem and is dealt with in section 7. This section does not deal with the law regulating pledges. A contractor who has carried out work in connection with the land or buildings has a lien (*rentierecht*) by operation of law on such land or buildings until the sum agreed under the contract has been paid in full, provided the contractor remains in control of the building site.

2.4 Contracts and options

Sale and purchase agreements and option agreements with respect to land or other property cannot be registered in the land register and therefore cannot in principle create any title or interest in favour of the buyer or beneficiary under the option. Registration of sale and purchase agreements and option agreements is possible under the Municipal Pre-emptive Rights Act (*Wet voorkeursrecht gemeenten*) as amended in 1996 and offers protection against a municipal pre-emptive right created later, but has no effect as against third parties.

2.5 Public or municipal charges

Financial charges may not be imposed on property by public bodies to recover payment for grants or for statutory works.

2.6 Other interests

Where land is left unfenced, any person has a right of access over it provided the exercise of the right does not prejudice the owner, or cause damage to the property. The right does not extend to property where a prohibition on entry by members of the public without the owner's consent has been clearly indicated.

2.7 Liabilities attaching to land

As a general rule, the possessor (the owner in most cases) of any building or structure on land will be strictly liable for any damage or loss caused by a defect in the property. In the case of a long-term leasehold right, the leaseholder and not the owner will be accountable. In principle, liability is not dependent upon finding fault. Most municipal authorities will inspect the state of buildings, and issue a notice to the owner to carry out any necessary repairs. Non-compliance may result in a fine, and repairs may also be carried out by the public authority at the owner's expense. More detailed comment on planning and building regulation is made in section 8. Liability may also arise under the provisions regulating the law between neighbours for the unreasonable use of one's land to the prejudice of an adjoining owner. Third-party insurance cover is usually taken out by private individuals and corporate entities against the consequences of strict liability. Finally, there are fiscal liabilities which attach to land in the form of tax, such as local taxes which are apportioned between owner and occupier. General comments are made on tax in section 11.

2.8 Legal and equitable interests

There are no other rights in rem other than those referred to in sections 1 and 2 where the economic or beneficial interest is also dealt with (see 1.2).

2.9 Protection of rights and interests

In general, the rights and other interests set out in sections 1 and 2 in respect of land and property are only valid and enforceable against third parties if they have been properly created or acquired by means of a notarial deed and subsequent registration in the land register. An exception is made for the lien created in favour of the contractor (see 2.3) and for rights and interests acquired by acquisitive prescription (see 1.4), which should be expressly invoked against any party opposing such a right or interest. Rights and interests acquired by prescription may be registered in the land register.

2.10 Priority of interests

Priority between rights and interests in respect of property will generally depend upon the date and time the notarial deed is submitted to the land register for registration. An exception can be made in respect of mortgages where the mortgagee's written consent is obtained.

3 TITLE TO LAND

3.1 Proof of title

Registration of property is regulated by the Civil Code and the Land Register Act (*Kadasterwet*). Title to land and other property (including ownership, long-term leasehold and other rights in rem described in sections 1 and 2) is established by registration of the notarial deed by which such a title is transferred or created. Title may also be acquired by prescription (see 1.4) or by succession upon inheritance. Registration will constitute prima facie evidence of title, although an interested person may render proof to the contrary, eg where the legal facts registered are proved to be incorrect, or the formalities required in connection with the conveyance by notarial deed have not been complied with or where it can be established that the transferor or grantor did not intend to convey the title or interest, the transfer agreement will be nullified.

3.2 Land registers

The land register is kept locally. The registers are open to the public.

3.2.1 Plans

All land is covered by the registration system under the Land Register Act, and for the purposes of identification and registration, land is divided into municipalities. The land pertaining to each municipality is subdivided into sections which are further divided into plots (each bearing a plot number). The measurements of each plot are taken by the land registry officials and are binding, except where there is proof to the contrary in the case of manifest error. The notarial deed transferring or creating title to land or other property must contain an adequate description of the relevant land or property by reference to the particulars (ie municipality, section, plot number, and where available, measurements) as shown in the land register. Where there are discrepancies between the description in the notarial deed and that contained in the land register, the latter will prevail.

3.2.2 Content

The land register is, for administrative purposes, divided into several sub-registers in which different rights in rem over land or other property are registered. Ownership, leasehold title, building and planting rights, rights of usufruct and servitudes are recorded in a different register from that in which mortgages and attachments on property are recorded. The land register will contain details of all legal transactions which affect the title to the land and copies of any relevant notarial deeds or writs of attachment can be obtained.

3.2.3 Errors

Where it is established that an error has been made in the land register, there are provisions for rectification of the registers under certain circumstances.

3.3 Passing of title

Title to land or other property will not pass when the sale and purchase agreement is executed, nor upon the execution of the notarial deed providing the transfer of title or the creation of the relevant right in rem. Title will only pass upon registration of the notarial deed in the land register. Possession will normally pass upon the execution of the notarial deed (unless otherwise agreed between the parties). The date of registration of the notarial deed is the date on which it is submitted for registration in the land register. It is the responsibility of the notary involved to arrange for the immediate submission of the notarial deed for registration, although there is no statutory time limit.

4 TRANSACTIONS IN LAND

The most common transactions in land are the sale and purchase of ownership and the grant and assignment of rights such as long-term leasehold interests, and building and planting rights, and the creation of servitudes (see 2.1.1), qualitative obligations and mortgages.

4.1 Procedure

4.1.1 The purchase and conveyance of land take place in two stages, the first being the negotiation and conclusion of a sale and purchase agreement, and the second the execution of the notarial deed providing for the transfer of title. The deed will be executed at the time agreed between the parties pursuant to the sale and purchase agreement. Prior to entering into a purchase agreement, a non-professional buyer may first wish to negotiate the mortgage loan with the bank and, if appropriate, investigate whether he qualifies for a national or municipal subsidy or mortgage loan guarantee.

4.1.2 Professional buyers will usually have a technical survey undertaken of the buildings and the land, as well as an environmental survey (see further 9.4). The notary will make enquiries on the buyer's behalf regarding title to the property, with searches undertaken in the land register regarding existing mortgages, servitudes and other encumbrances over the property. In addition, the notary should investigate whether the local authorities possess a right of pre-emption over certain transactions in land and may only execute a notarial deed if he is satisfied that such pre-emption rights will not be exercised. If satisfied, the buyer will enter into the sale and purchase agreement, which will place the parties under a binding obligation to transfer and accept legal title. It is not possible to protect the sale and purchase agreement at this point by an entry in the land register. However, parliament is currently considering a proposal for new legislation, permitting this. The registration would be valid for six months and would create priority over any subsequent sale and purchase agreement. The sale and purchase agreement will sometimes contain 'conditions subsequent' which must be fulfilled during the intervening period, if the transaction is to be completed. These may relate to the finalisation of any financial arrangements, the obtaining of a guarantee from the municipal authority or of the residence licence required by certain local authorities. The second stage to complete the transaction requires the execution of a notarial deed (see 3.3) which must be recorded in the public land register. The transfer of title will only take effect upon registration, when the documents required for registration are submitted.

4.2 Contract terms

4.2.1 In principle the parties are free to incorporate the terms of their choice in drawing up the contract of sale. In practice, a standard contract is used for most transactions between non-professional parties, eg the standard form drafted jointly by the Royal Homeowners' Association (*Vereniging Eigen Huis*), the Consumers' Association (*Consumentenbond*) and the Dutch Estate Agents' Association (*Nederlandse Vereniging van Makelaars*), or in Amsterdam, the standard form of the Royal Civil Law Notaries' Organisation (*Koninklijke Notariële Beroepsorganisatie*). These standard forms do not contain many warranties given by the seller, except as to the full and unencumbered title to the property and the absence of mortgages, attachments and servitudes other than registered servitudes. Professional parties may negotiate more extensive warranties as to, eg the technical state and condition of the property, the absence of pollution, compliance with laws and regulations (in particular zoning regulations) and guaranteed rental income.

4.2.2 The contract will often stipulate from the buyer a bank guarantee or the payment of a deposit to be held in escrow by the notary charged with the preparation of the conveyance deed. The bank guarantee or deposit is in most cases for the equivalent of 10 per cent of the purchase price, corresponding to a penalty usually imposed upon the buyer upon default and rescission by the seller. Alternatively, if the seller does not rescind the agreement, the buyer may be required to pay default interest at the statutory rate (or some other rate agreed between the parties). Possession will usually be given upon completion, ie when the notarial deed is executed, when risk will also usually pass and so the buyer will insure from that date. It is normal for the professional buyer to satisfy himself as to whether there are any physical defects to the property, and it is common to undertake a thorough survey before the finalisation of the transaction. Pending completion, the seller must take certain basic steps to protect the property.

4.2.3 If either party defaults, the other party may apply to the courts for an order for specific performance compelling the defaulting party to complete, or alternatively, the other party may rescind the agreement. The buyer may forfeit the penalty secured by the bank guarantee or the deposit, if he defaults and fails to complete, and may be liable to the seller in excess of the penalty.

4.3 Formalities

All transfers of ownership and other interests in rem in respect of land or property require the execution of a notarial deed, by a civil law notary (*notaris*) appointed by the Crown. The legal basis for the transfer (such as the underlying sale and purchase or other contract) must be mentioned in the notarial deed, but the terms of the agreement do not have to be repeated. It is common for the parties to the notarial deed to be represented under a power of attorney. The notarisation must be followed by registration in the appropriate land register (see section 3).

4.4 Fees, costs and taxes

4.4.1 On a sale of land or the transfer of an interest in land, the fees and costs of the notary and the taxes incurred will usually be payable by the buyer. If an agent has been commissioned by either one of the parties, he will pay the agent's commission which will vary according to the type and value of the property and the strength of the market and is generally negotiable at between one and two per cent and on a contingency basis payable only if the transaction completes. The buyer will pay value added tax (VAT) on the purchase price (see further 4.4.6 and 11.8) where newly developed property is transferred and the property transfer tax (see 4.4.3) is then not applicable in most cases.

4.4.2 There is no fixed statutory scale governing notarial fees, but the Royal Civil Law Notaries' Organisation (*Koninklijke Notariële Beroepsorganisatie*) prescribes the fees and costs its members may charge which consist of a certain percentage of the value of a completed transaction (based mostly on the purchase price), from 1 per cent for transactions with a value of NLG 100,000 to 0.2 per cent concerning transactions with a value in excess of NLG 20 million. If the transaction fails to complete, the notary will charge on a time charge basis at the commonly applied hourly rate. If any of the parties retain the services of a lawyer (*advocaat*) he will charge on a time charge basis and the hourly rate (if not previously agreed) will depend on the value and the complexity of the transaction.

4.4.3 The notary and the buyer are jointly and severally liable for the payment of a six per cent property transfer tax levied on the purchase price. The notary will ensure the buyer pays the transfer tax due (together with the purchase price) to him prior to the execution of the notarial deed. An exemption applies to the acquisition of a building plot or other property for development use and newly developed land, as these types of transfer will be subject to VAT (see 4.4.6).

4.4.4 The registration of the notarial deed in the land register will require the payment of registration fees payable to the land register (payable by the notary usually on the buyer's behalf). The actual amount will depend on the number of plots involved in the transaction, ranging between NLG 133 for each existing plot and NLG 705 for each unmeasured plot.

4.4.5 On the basis of widely available information, it would appear that property values (excluding commercial property in city centres) are lower than those in the United Kingdom, France and West Germany.

4.4.6 VAT is levied at a rate of 17.5 per cent.

4.5 Professionals' roles

4.5.1 The marketing and sale of land are usually conducted by estate agents who are often members of a national organisation with its own written general terms and conditions. There is no obligation to engage the services of an estate agent to negotiate the agreement and the price, although where one is instructed, it will be incumbent upon him to draw certain matters to the attention of the buyer, such as (visible) defects in the property and whether his client qualifies for a government grant in relation to financing arrangements (see 4.1). Surveyors may also represent the buyer in undertaking a survey of the property.

4.5.2 The notary will check the legal capacity of the parties and undertake the title searches on the buyer's behalf (see 4.1). In exceptional cases, eg if the seller agrees to transfer the property at no cost to the buyer, the seller may instruct the notary, although this will not relieve the notary from his responsibilities and duty of care vis-à-vis the buyer. As the purchase price and other amounts due from the buyer will be paid to the notary prior to the execution of the notarial deed in virtually all cases, the principal responsibilities of the notary will be to:

(a) ensure free and unencumbered title will be conveyed to the buyer and the seller will receive the purchase price;
(b) pay off and cancel the mortgages over the property;
(c) procure the immediate execution of the relevant notarial mortgage deed if the purchase price is funded by a financial institution with a (first ranking) right of mortgage; and
(d) register both the notarial deed of transfer and the mortgage deed in the land register.

A notary failing to discharge these responsibilities may be liable for any loss and should therefore take out professional liability cover.

5 LEASES AND OTHER RIGHTS OF OCCUPATION

The Civil Code describes a lease or tenancy as a contractual agreement whereby the landlord grants the right of use and occupation for a fixed or indefinite term. The contractual tenancy grants only a right in personam to the tenant as distinct from the long-term leaseholder who will be granted a right in rem (see 1.1.2). The Civil Code distinguishes between residential premises, which are usually let for an indefinite period, and retail premises which will usually be let for an initial five-year term, which will be renewed by operation of law for another five years unless terminated by the tenant. Other commercial premises, eg industrial or office, regulated under the Landlord and Tenant Act (*Huurwet*), are generally also granted for a term of five years, with an option for the tenant to renew for a further five years (see further 5.3). Agricultural tenancies are regulated by the Agricultural Land Lease Act

(*Pachtwet*), granting the tenant an initial six or twelve-year term with an option to extend the tenancy agreement for an additional six years. The value of property will, for investment purposes, generally be assessed by reference to yield, ie the rental return on the price paid for investment in the property. Yields vary between 5.5 and 7.5 per cent for residential property, between 7 and 10 per cent for industrial and office premises and between 7.5 and 10 per cent for retail business premises. Generally speaking, there is no shortage of lettable commercial property and as a result, rentals are not yet in line with the rest of the European Union (such as London and Paris), although rents for commercial property in prime locations are increasing.

5.1 Rent and other terms

5.1.1 With the exception of residential and agricultural rents which are regulated by a rent control system (see further 5.3) the parties are free to negotiate rent and other terms, subject to the restrictions dealt with in 5.3. Commercial tenancy agreements usually provide for open market rent reviews at five-year intervals, as well as annual indexation against the cost of living. Notwithstanding any provision to the contrary in the tenancy agreement of retail premises, the landlord and the tenant may both seek a rent review every five years and failing agreement, each of the parties may file an application with the court to determine the new rent. Rent reviews may be upwards as well as downwards. Rents by reference to turnover are seldom used and rent will generally be payable in advance, quarterly or monthly.

5.1.2 Except where otherwise agreed, the tenant will not be allowed to assign or surrender or to sublet or allow a third party to use the tenanted premises. For all property, the landlord is responsible for external and structural maintenance and repairs, repairs to fixtures and other equipment installed by the landlord (eg air-conditioning, central heating and lifts), floors, ceilings and the like. The tenant is responsible for the internal day-to-day maintenance of the premises. The landlord will usually carry out internal repairs to the common parts of a property used by more than one tenant and recover the cost from the tenants in proportion to the floor areas rented, in the same way as for supplies of gas, electricity, water and other utilities. Unless otherwise agreed, the tenant may not make alterations to the premises and if such alterations are carried out without the landlord's consent, the landlord may require that they are reversed upon expiry of the tenancy agreement. The landlord will insure the property and usually charge the premium paid to the tenant. The tenancy agreement will almost always provide for a number of events which will terminate the tenancy, and these will include, eg a material breach or default by the tenant, bankruptcy or moratorium of payment granted to the tenant. The Council for Real Property (*Raad voor Onroerende Zaken*), a private organisation of institutional investors and associations of real estate agents, has developed a standard form tenancy agreement for commercial property, although there is no obligation on the parties to adopt it. Security in the form of a cash deposit or bank guarantee for an amount equivalent to three months' rent and service charges plus VAT, is commonly required by the landlord.

5.2 Privity of contract and estate

The rights and obligations of a landlord pass to a new landlord upon transfer of title. The tenancy agreement remains in force and the new owner takes over from his predecessor. Generally, the landlord and tenant will no longer be liable under the tenancy once they have ceased to be the landlord or tenant. The tenant of retail premises may request in the event of transfer of the tenant's business at the premises that the buyer should substitute the tenant and assume all the rights and obligations under the tenancy. If the landlord refuses the tenant may apply to the courts. In the event of such a substitution, the new tenant becomes liable for existing obligations of the previous tenant. The original tenant is no longer liable once he has assigned the tenancy and substituted the third party.

5.3 Rent control and security of tenure

5.3.1 There are different types of rent control for agricultural land, and for residential property, regulated by the Residential Property Rent Control Act (*Huurprijzenwet Woonruimte*) which only allows increases in rent by a certain percentage set by it in accordance with what is deemed to be reasonable. An indirect form of rent control applies to retail property in the form of a compulsory market rent review. Otherwise, the parties are free to negotiate rent and any increase. Except where a residential tenancy is deemed by its nature to be a short tenancy (which will seldom apply other than in the case of holiday lets), the residential tenants are strongly protected against termination of both indefinite and fixed-term agreements, as the landlord must give notice of termination by writ served by a bailiff or registered letter with confirmed receipt. The notice must state one of the exhaustive reasons listed in the Civil Code and inform the tenant of the requirement to notify the landlord in writing within six weeks whether or not he agrees to termination. If the tenant does not agree to termination, the tenancy will remain in force by law until such a date as the court shall determine, following the application by the landlord for the termination of the tenancy and the eviction of the tenant. An eviction order will only be granted in exceptional circumstances as provided in the Civil Code.

5.3.2 Tenants of retail property are granted considerable protection under the Civil Code, unless the tenancy is entered into for a period shorter than two years, in which case the tenancy will automatically terminate upon the expiry of the term. Retail tenancies will usually be granted for five years, unless a longer term is provided for in the agreement. Tenancies for a period longer than two years and shorter than five years will be deemed to have been entered into for a five-year period. Tenancies entered into for a period longer than five years, but shorter than 10 years are automatically extended to a 10-year term, unless the tenant terminates the agreement at the agreed expiry date by notice in accordance with the terms of the agreement. The tenant or the landlord may give one year's notice at the end of the term of the tenancy agreement which must be by bailiff's writ or registered letter. Unless notice of termination is given in compliance with the statutory requirements, the tenancy for a five-year period is automatically extended for a further five years. Where the landlord has given notice, it will only be valid on material breach or default by the tenant, or if the landlord urgently requires the premises for his own personal use. If the tenant does not agree to termination, the landlord should seek termination by court order. If the tenancy has run for the full statutory term of 10 years, the landlord's grounds for termination are less restricted.

5.3.3 All other business premises, including offices and industrial buildings, are generally granted for a term of five years with an option for renewal for a further five years. There are no statutory provisions overriding the terms of the agreement and the tenant has only limited security of tenure. Following expiry of the term, the tenant's obligation to vacate the premises is suspended for two months during which the tenant may apply to the courts to extend the term for a one-year period; the application for extension may be repeated twice. The courts will be inclined to allow the application if the tenant can show that his continued occupation of the premises should prevail over the reasonable interest of the landlord.

5.3.4 Agricultural tenancies are not regulated by the Civil Code but by the Agricultural Land Lease Act (*Pachtwet*). Agricultural tenancies must be for a fixed term, which is 12 years for a farm and six years for separate plots of land.

5.4 Other legislative restrictions

The terms of an agricultural tenancy agreement are subject to the approval of the Agricultural Land Chamber (an official public institution) which will examine whether the terms comply with the provisions of the Agricultural Land Lease Act. If amendments are not feasible in the event of non-compliance, the agreement will be void. Agricultural tenancies will invariably be recorded in writing. Oral agricultural tenancies may not be terminated by the landlord and there are very restrictive grounds for termination of agricultural tenancies. Other than in respect of rent and security of tenure (see 5.3), there are no legislative restrictions, eg to regulate the repairing obligations of the residential landlord.

5.5 Methods of measurement

The Dutch Normalisation Institute in Delft (*Nederlands Normalisatie Instituut*) has developed a standard method of measuring either the gross or net lettable floor area of office and industrial as well as retail premises. Gross floor area includes common areas, lobbies, lavatories and other areas not specifically used for the conduct of the tenant's business, while net floor area will be limited to the space used for the conduct of the tenant's business.

6 FINANCE AND INVESTMENT SOURCES

6.1 Loan finance

6.1.1 The most commonly used method for financing residential property is the loan facility secured by a mortgage. Certain lenders, especially those linked with an insurance company, have developed sophisticated financial products (comprising a loan and life insurance) in order to achieve the maximum tax deductibility of interest payable by the borrower under the loan. These loans are usually for a 20 to 30 year period with full repayment upon expiry of the term. The remainder of this section deals principally with finance for commercial property.

6.1.2 The principal property lenders are the commercial or merchant banks, mortgage banks (specialising in property finance), savings banks (*spaarbanken*) and insurance companies through wholly owned subsidiaries with a banking licence. Foreign banks such as German mortgage banks are becoming increasingly active. With some exceptions, the banks are privately owned and certain large banks are quoted on the stock exchange. The mortgage banks and large commercial and merchant banks tend to specialise in property finance as do certain leasing companies (owned by the banks). The banks are supervised by the Dutch Central Bank. Where the loan finance is provided for the purchase or refinancing of property, the lender will be primarily concerned with the value of the security (in the form of a mortgage and a pledge of rentals if the property is let). If a mortgage over property is intended to secure a credit facility to the borrower for general business purposes, the lender will equally be concerned with the creditworthiness of the borrower. Representatives of banks (in most cases a board member or senior officer) may sometimes be supervisory directors of important clients, but rarely in the case of property investment. Non-recourse lending is not unusual, although the non-recourse aspects may not be explicitly provided for in the loan documentation, and will be the consequence of lending to a special purpose property company with no other assets than the real property. Such financing may be backed up by a parental guarantee, depending on the lettability of the property, the term of the lease and the creditworthiness of the tenant.

6.1.3 The term of the loan normally varies between five and 10 years, depending on the financial standing of the borrower and the term of any lease generating the cash flow for interest payments and repayments. Repayments will generally be by instalments, payable quarterly or annually during the term of the loan, followed by a bullet repayment at the end of the term. The calculation of the repayment instalments depends on agreement and may vary from fixed and equal instalments to annuities. Loans are flexible and tailored for the particular investment as are interest rates, which may be referable to the Amsterdam Interbank Offered Rate or the bank's cost of funds, increased by a margin. With the exception of residential property and lending to private individuals, there are no mandatory regulations on maximising or minimising interest, duration or other aspects of the loan. Shareholders may extend loans to the company investing in property, which will usually be in the form of intercompany loans, subordinated to bank loans. Large property investors, in most cases listed companies, may attract equity financing by issuing commercial paper such as bonds or shares. There is a growing market for syndicated loans involving a number of banks on larger investments (eg government infrastructure projects involving private funding). However, all the banks involved must be party to the security documentation, which complicates matters.

6.2 Investment or equity finance

There is a wide range of methods for equity finance depending upon the form of investment vehicle. If it is a private company with limited liability it will usually be funded by its shareholders by equity (or subordinated) loan, while listed companies raise their funds on the stock markets. Venture capital funds, mostly private companies with limited liability or companies limited by shares, may invest in the vehicle by taking shares or granting (subordinated) loans (see further section 13 on business vehicles). In addition, there are so-called 'closed funds', in which private investors, venture capital funds or institutions participate. The participants form a partnership and the property is held by a separate entity, generally a foundation (*stichting*). Single-asset companies are rarely floated on the stock exchange.

6.3 Mezzanine or mixed funding

A market is developing for mezzanine lending whereby a second lender will provide the additional funds required and whose rights will be subordinated to the rights of the primary lender. The second lender will look for a higher rate of interest and, if appropriate, a 'success fee' or some other form of commission may be agreed between the parties. The maximum percentage provided by a mezzanine lender will be in the region of 20 per cent.

6.4 Sale and lease-back

It has become increasingly common for a company to convert a long-term asset into liquid funds to be used for the conduct of its business, and the banks and their various leasing companies offer a range of sale and lease-back arrangements. These may either be in the form of the financial lease, an operating lease or a mixture; the actual form selected will depend mostly on the tax consequences (on balance or off balance leasing). These arrangements will usually include call and put options. Even under an operating lease, the lessee will normally bear all the risks regarding the property.

6.5 Tax leasing

The benefit accruing to the bank or lessor from the depreciation of property will usually be shared by the bank in the form of a reduction of rent (see further 6.4).

6.6 Other types of property finance

Another form of property finance is the hire purchase arrangement which is similar to financial leasing; the seller/lessor, who may also be the investor, will acquire title to the property and sell the property to the buyer subject to the payment of the purchase price in instalments. This is regulated under the Temporary Hire Purchase (Real Property) Act.

6.7 Institutional investment

Insurance companies, pension funds and large listed property investment funds are the major investors in the Dutch property market. They invest in all sectors of the property market. Depending on their specific investment policies, they may concentrate on industrial/commercial, agricultural or residential property or a combination of these. They will invest either directly, or indirectly through a wholly owned subsidiary. The criteria and preferences set by the large institutions have a significant influence on the market views and policies of other investors.

6.8 Investors other than institutions

Large contracting companies have recently made substantial investments in land expected to be designated by the government as industrial or residential development land. There is a wide range of investors, including private individuals, contractors, investment companies or funds as well as the large institutions.

7 FORMS OF SECURITY

Dutch banks will usually negotiate finance arrangements to obtain adequate security. Where no adequate security is provided, the lending decision will depend on the financial standing of the client. If a relationship already exists, the bank may forego the requirement for additional security, if it takes the view that the existing security is sufficient to cover the additional risks. Group financing will require other means of security than a specific project vehicle. In any event, the banks will require an undertaking to provide adequate security, either on first demand or upon the occurrence of certain events (eg financial ratios not being met). Businesses tend to maintain a principal banking relationship with one of the prime commercial or merchant banks, but it is not uncommon for commercial entities to seek funding for specific purposes, and difficulties may arise from competing demands for security. Security by assignment or transfer of an asset is prohibited under Dutch law. Overdrafts and working capital loans will normally require a pledge of inventory, equipment and accounts receivable. For general purpose finance the bank may also require a mortgage over real property. Single asset finance requires a security interest over the asset and all products and proceeds resulting from it. There is a tendency for the banks to request an increasing amount of security.

7.1 Mortgages

7.1.1 Monetary liabilities can be secured on property by a mortgage (*hypotheek*) and any security interest created on any other goods and assets, tangible or intangible, are defined by law as a right of pledge (*pandrecht*). A mortgage may be created over real property and other registered property (eg ships and aircraft) including the right of ownership, long-term leasehold rights, building rights and usufruct. A mortgage will automatically create a pledge of compensation claims attaching to the secured property, eg under an insurance policy. Under the Civil Code, the mortgage is a right in rem and must be created by a notarial deed signed by the parties and registered in the land register. The deed must detail the mortgaged property and must specify the amount for which it is secured. Where the fixed amount has yet to be established, the deed must state the maximum amount. It is possible to have several properties mortgaged under the same notarial deed. When a mortgage is created it will secure all present and future obligations and liabilities up to the maximum stated amount. It is not possible to create a mortgage over property which may be acquired in the future, as opposed to a pledge on future tangible assets. The maximum amount will include a reservation for interest and costs, usually in the region of 35–40 per cent of the amount due. Until default the mortgagor retains title to the property encumbered by the mortgage and the full use of the property.

7.1.2 On default, the mortgagee may sell the property without a court order, or manage and take possession of the property subject to the approval of the courts (if so stipulated in the mortgage deed) and collect any rents provided these are duly pledged to the lender under the mortgage deed or separately. Sale is the principal means to enforce the mortgage and must be by public auction before a civil notary, unless either party obtains a court order for private sale. The mortgagee has no rights of appropriation, although the lender may bid under a public or private sale. Dutch law does not provide for the appointment of receivers. There are detailed statutory requirements to ensure the maximum price may be realised by public or private sale. At the time of sale the obligations secured should be actual, due and payable; it is questionable whether a bank is entitled to retain the sum which exceeds such secured obligations in order to satisfy contingent liabilities which are not payable at the time of enforcement.

7.2 Floating and other charges

7.2.1 The creation of security over assets other than immoveable or registered property will be effected by means of the pledge. This will be created by agreement (which in respect of tangible assets such as stock and equipment can be oral) provided the assets are physically delivered to the pledgee. As this is usually inconvenient, to be valid, the pledge is usually embodied in a written agreement which must be registered with the tax authorities; the register is not open to public inspection. In respect of tangible assets, the security may be created over (a) assets owned at the date of agreement, and (b) assets which the pledgor will acquire later provided that these are sufficiently determinable under the terms of the agreement. A pledge will have no effect in respect of tangible assets acquired by the pledgor after he has been declared bankrupt or a suspension of payment is granted to him. Intangible assets such as receivables and rights and claims against third parties are pledged under a written agreement either with notification to the third party or with registration with the tax authorities. In the event of suspension of payment or bankruptcy the pledge will not take effect against receivables deemed not to exist at that date, or rent instalments not yet due.

7.2.2 Upon default or other agreed termination, the pledgee is entitled to take possession of the tangible assets and to notify the debtors of the accounts receivable; until notification, the pledgor remains entitled to collect the receivables. There is no automatic lien or other charge for unpaid sale proceeds, but the seller may transfer title with a mortgage or pledge in his favour. Unsecured creditors may attempt to secure payment by an attachment on the registered property or tangible or intangible assets, either prior to judgment following the approval of the courts or afterwards. If the asset is already mortgaged or pledged, the unsecured creditor will rank after the mortgagee or pledgee. As a mortgage is registered in the (public) land register, it will be protected against successors in title; however the pledgee of the tangible asset will not be protected against successors in title in actual possession who were not aware, nor had any reason to be aware, of the pledge, when the asset was acquired. In the case of pledges of receivables, the successor in title is generally not protected against a pledge over the receivable.

7.3 Bonds and guarantees

7.3.1 Where the borrower's creditworthiness and any collateral are not satisfactory a guarantee is quite common. This may vary from an on-demand guarantee, to a simple surety which is more or less a secondary obligation only enforceable on default, and entitling the guarantor to all defences which the principal debtor may have. Normally the guarantee and surety obligation is accessory to the principal guaranteed obligation, so that in the event of unenforceability, invalidity or non-existence, the guarantee is also void or non-existent. For these reasons, a guarantee is sometimes construed as an independent undertaking by the guarantor. Certain financial institutions specialise in putting up guarantees and surety undertakings.

7.3.2 In order to stimulate home ownership (see also 12.1) the local authority may issue a guarantee to the bank for the repayment of a bank loan. Where proceeds from a forced sale are insufficient, the government pays the shortfall to the bank, which therefore runs no risk in lending up to the guaranteed amount. For a local authority guarantee a number of conditions must be fulfilled, eg a NLG315,000 ceiling on the purchase price (which may vary from time to time); it applies only to a first mortgage over the permanent residence of the applicant; and the guarantee must be issued prior to acquisition of title.

7.4 Insurance

In the case of major financing, especially where international cross-border banks are involved, a credit risk insurance is required and the premiums are substantial. Credit risk insurance may also be taken out in connection with national or international trade.

8 PLANNING AND BUILDING REGULATION

The principal statutes regulating the development and use of land and buildings are the Town and Country Planning Act (*Wet op de Ruimtelijke Ordening*, the 'TCPA') and the Housing Act (*Woningwet*, the 'HA').

8.1 Planning authorities

At municipal level, the city council is in charge of local zoning planning and this is subject to the review of the provincial authority (*Gedeputeerde Staten*) (see further 8.2.1). The city council and the provincial authority are elected and their decisions are influenced by political considerations. Decisions on certain essential infrastructure projects and strategic zoning decisions are taken at national level. A new Act enables central government to compel local and provincial authorities to cooperate over the construction of unpopular infrastructure facilities, eg incinerators and motorways. Ultimate control of town and country planning matters rests with the Minister for Housing, Planning and Environment, who may impose binding planning directives upon local or provincial authorities.

8.2 Development plans

8.2.1 Under the TCPA, the local authority (the city council) is obliged to prepare and adopt a local zoning plan which is subject to the approval of the provincial authority. The local zoning plan will set out in detail permitted use and development and should not interfere with the more general regional zoning plan adopted by the provincial authorities, nor with the overall national plans (*structuurschema's*) and strategic zoning decisions (*planologische kernbeslissingen*) at national level.

8.2.2 Construction will only be permitted if in accordance with the development and land use permitted within the particular zone of the plan; where it deviates it will not be granted permission, although new zoning plans do not have retroactive effect. Before a zoning plan is adopted, a public enquiry will take place; the local zoning plan will come into force after approval by the provincial authorities. The regional zoning plan will come into force after adoption by the provincial authorities and is not subject to approval by central government, provided it does not interfere with essential elements of the overall national plans and strategic zoning decisions. The TCPA grants power to the Minister for Housing, Planning and Environment to require the local authority to prepare and adopt a zoning plan where none has been adopted, and to revise an existing zoning plan in specific circumstances. A local zoning plan will have a 10-year life span but will remain in force should this period expire without the adoption of a new plan.

8.3 Planning control and procedure

The HA generally requires a building permit for the construction of a new building or other permanent structure and any alteration or refurbishment to an existing building or other structure. Less extensive building activities are allowed without a building permit, eg the construction of a dormer, or a garden shed, may only require the local authority to be notified prior to commencement of any works.

8.3.1 Permission to build will only be granted if the building activities and use comply with the local zoning plan (see 8.4 for building regulation compliance). If a building permit is required, an application will be made to the local executive (*burgemeester en wethouders*). In principle, this must be accompanied by a soil survey. The applicant does not have to have an interest in the property, eg a contractor or the property developer is under no obligation to notify the owner of the application. The application is published in the local newspaper and any interested party (eg owners and residents in the immediate locality) may express their views orally or in writing. A so-called provisional application may be filed to obtain an indication of the views of the local executive (or officer) but this informal enquiry will have no legal effect. The formal application must be fully detailed, with documents prescribed by the HA and accompanied by the requisite fees relating to the building costs. These may be substantial.

8.3.2 A planning application will normally take between two and six months. If there is no decision within 13 weeks, the permit will be deemed granted by default, unless the city council has extended this by a maximum of a further 13 weeks. The local executive may grant the permit unconditionally or subject to conditions, to safeguard compliance with the zoning and building regulations, or it may refuse the application. If the permit is granted subject to conditions or is refused, the applicant may object to the local executive within six weeks. Any interested third party may also object to the grant of a permit. Where the local executive dismisses an objection, the party concerned may appeal to the administrative chamber of the courts. If the applicant's appeal is accepted, the courts will refer the matter back to the local executive and if the appeal is lodged by an interested party, the courts may cancel the building permit. The parties may lodge a further appeal with the administrative chamber of the Council of State (*Raad van State*). Where an environmental permit is required for a proposed development, the HA provides for the simultaneous application for a building permit and an environmental permit. The building permit application will be suspended until there is reasonable certainty that an environmental permit will be issued (see section 9 for environmental matters).

8.3.3 Generally planning permission will expire if not acted on within two years. The building permit is a right personal to the applicant which may not be transferred, although under most building regulations the holder of the permit may request the local executive to grant the building permit in the name of another interested party.

8.3.4 There are no time limits for enforcement in the event of a breach of planning legislation. Where a breach has occurred, the local executive has the authority to suspend building activities and they may require restoration if the order is not complied with. Penalties may be imposed or the local executive may undertake the remedial work itself at the cost of the defaulting party. The same objection and appeal procedure (described in 8.3.2) applies to challenges against enforcement action by the local executive.

8.4 Building standards, control and supervision

In addition to compliance with the local zoning plan, the building permit will also require the proposed development to be in accordance with the Building Decree (*Bouwbesluit*), passed by central government, and the local building regulations (*Bouwverordening*) issued by the city council. These statutory and mandatory codes of construction standards deal with the design and construction of buildings and the provision of services, fittings and equipment. Plans and specifications for the proposed work must be deposited with the local authority for approval before the permit may be granted. Throughout the building process, the local construction surveyors will inspect the building activities on behalf of the local executive, to ascertain whether they are being performed in accordance with the building permit.

8.5 Protection of buildings of special interest

Under the Listed Buildings Act (*Monumentenwet*), the owner or user of buildings of special historic, architectural, scientific or cultural value may not undertake any external or internal alterations without the prior approval of the local executive. The buildings are listed and registered in the land register. The owner or the long-term leaseholder cannot be obliged to keep listed buildings in a proper state of repair. However, in the case of neglect, an order may be issued by the local executive to carry out such works to any building listed or otherwise, as are required to remedy the neglect. (See 12.1.2 for subsidies for repair of listed buildings and monuments.)

8.6 Expropriation or compulsory purchase and compensation

Under the Expropriation Act (*Onteigeningswet*), central government, the provincial authority, the local authority and the water boards may require the expropriation of land or other property to carry out public works or for the implementation of the appropriate zoning plans. If no agreement is reached regarding compensation, the matter will be referred to the courts. Experts will advise the court on compensation and only in exceptional cases will the court not follow the advice. The legislation prescribes full compensation, including loss of income and loss of capital, as well as other damages such as relocation and reinvestment costs.

9 ENVIRONMENTAL MATTERS

Since the early 1970s the protection of the environment has been an important political issue. On a national level, environmental objectives are set out in the National Environmental Policy Plan (NEPP), reviewed at least every four years. Similar policy plans exist at provincial and municipal level. The Environmental Control Act (the ECA) which is underpinned by the 'polluter pays principle', aims to codify the provisions of environmental law and provide for a uniform licensing procedure. The permit required under the ECA replaces those previously required under the Nuisance Act, the Air Pollution Act, the Noise Control Act, the Waste Act and the Chemical Waste Act. Further important legislation is found in the Surface Water Pollution Act, the Soil Protection Act, the Nuclear Energy Act and the Ground Water Act, to name a few. In addition, the Ministry of Housing, Planning and Environment considers the cooperation of the public and business community to be important resulting in various covenants between the government and industrial organisations, eg concerning recycling of packaging materials and the collection and disposal of batteries and automobile accessories. Breach of environmental legislation will generally constitute a criminal offence and will enable the public authorities to take administrative action, eg to enforce compliance. Failure to comply will incur penalties and compliance at the expense of the defaulting party. In addition, the authorities may seek a court injunction and damages. A third party who can demonstrate that breach has caused, or threatens to cause, damage will have an action in tort and may get an injunction or damages.

9.1 Protection against atmospheric and noise pollution

9.1.1 The ECA and the royal decrees enacted in accordance with it regulate production facilities and other business enterprises to protect the environment from atmospheric, noise, water and soil pollution as well as waste storage and disposal. Production facilities and other business enterprises require a specific environmental permit under the ECA, unless they belong to a category for which a general regulation has been implemented, eg the royal decree for office buildings and shops. If a business enterprise is not capable of complying with the general regulations, it should apply for a special permit. In most cases, the issuing authority is the local executive of the municipality or sometimes the provincial authorities. Where national safety is in issue, the Minister of Housing, Planning and Environment is the competent authority.

9.1.2 Permits must ensure maximum protection for the environment, although cost effectiveness may be taken into account. The applicable rules are set out in the royal decrees, provincial and municipal environmental policy plans, directives of the Ministry of Housing, Planning and Environment and other policy documents. This leaves the competent authority the discretion to decide on the specific requirements it will impose. Any third party may file an objection against a draft permit after it has been made public and it is quite common for private individuals or public interest groups to exercise this right. There is a right of appeal with the Council of State against the issue of the permit for those who filed objections against the draft permit. The ECA places the authorities under the obligation to review and update all licences regularly in accordance with technical and environmental developments.

9.2 Water pollution

The Surface Water Pollution Act (SWPA) provides for specific discharge permits, levies on discharges to surface water and regulations by royal decree to combat and prevent surface water pollution. Often an ECA permit is needed in addition to an SWPA permit. There are regulations for harmonisation of the applications.

9.3 Waste storage and disposal

The permit and other procedures required under the ECA and any royal decree enacted under it (see 9.1) also apply to waste storage and disposal.

9.4 Contaminated land

9.4.1 The aim of the Soil Protection Act (*Wet Bodembescherming*) is to shift the financial burden of clean up from government to the polluters and owners or long-term leaseholders of contaminated land. Under the Act the owner (or holder of a long-term leasehold) is responsible for clean up (there is no need to seek the actual polluter first or for the polluter to be insolvent) unless he can prove he has no legal ties with the polluter, was not otherwise responsible and on acquisition did not know or could not have known of the pollution. In practice it will be difficult to avoid liability and the buyer is expected to carry out a soil survey or require the seller to submit a suitable certificate. Environmental enquiries form an important part of pre-transaction investigations. There is no register of contaminated sites, although clean-up orders will be registered in the land register. In the absence of other means, the authorities may undertake the necessary remediation, and recover the costs from polluter or owner (where liable).

9.4.2 In 1988 the government established the Cleaning Industrial Sites Committee for the development of a clean-up plan for industrial sites. Participation under the scheme is voluntary, although companies refusing to participate will be subject to investigation and clean-up orders under the Act.

9.5 Environmental impact assessments

Where the Ministry of Housing, Planning and Environment determines that a particular activity may have a significant adverse effect on the environment, eg major infrastructure works, the competent authorities are required to undertake an environmental impact assessment (*Milieueffectrapportage*) under the ECA (implementing EC Directive 85/337), prior to any decision on licensing or exempting the activity.

10 DEVELOPMENT

10.1 Development projects, structures and vehicles

The traditional development project typically involves the purchase of a site by the owner or future occupier and the construction under a contracting agreement based on the owner's specification, usually provided by the owner's architect. Alternatively, the contractor takes the initiative, acquires the land, engages an architect to design the building and offers the project to interested third parties. On a housing project, the developer, which may be a subsidiary of, or otherwise affiliated to, the proposed contractor, a bank, an insurance company or a pension or investment fund, will prepare a comprehensive development plan and take an interest in, or an option to acquire, the land. It will not usually proceed with construction unless a certain percentage has already been sold to future residents. On or before the start of building, the buyer will acquire title (which will enable him to obtain a mortgage loan) and pay the value of the land to the developer. The mortgage loan will include the cost of construction and may be secured by a government guarantee (see 7.3.2 and 12.1). The contractor's obligations are usually secured by bank guarantees of between 5 and 10 per cent of the contract sum. Industrial property is developed in accordance with tailor-made plans, prepared with the future occupier's requirements in mind. There are various methods of funding from straightforward secured loans to sale and lease-backs. For office accommodation and shopping centres, the developer (there are a number of specialised development companies) will find the site, prepare a plan and usually find a tenant before it can sell the project to an investor. The level of rent will decide the price by reference to yield to be paid by the investor. There are various ways of financing the development; prime investors will generally require the developer to arrange its own finance, paying only on completion. If the investor funds the project, he will acquire title at the start of building works and pay the consideration in fixed instalments. In addition, the developer may guarantee the rental income for a year or until the premises are fully let to tenants acceptable to the investor at agreed rent levels. The developer may use a special purpose vehicle but the investor will at least require a parental guarantee. In many cases, the investor will acquire the completed project through a separate entity.

10.2 Building contracts and appointment of professionals

10.2.1 Typical forms of building contract

The Civil Code applies to the construction of new property as well as works to existing property at a fixed price. In larger projects, there may be more than one contractor, each liable for a part of the project, which will require detailed coordination agreements. In most cases the agreement is with one contractor who may contract out certain parts of the building project to subcontractors, whilst remaining entirely responsible for their performance. Even if the price is fixed, it will be subject to adjustment for an increase or reduction in the work or wage and price increases. It has become common practice for a contracting company to seek to design the building to increase its profits. If the principal commissions an architect for the design the contractor will not be responsible for design defects. Management contracts with the contractor responsible for overall management of a team of subcontractors for a percentage fee are not common although the market for these is gradually developing.

10.2.2 Common terms

The sum payable to the contractor is usually divided into three parts: first, a down-payment when the building works begin (and/or the land is transferred to the buyer); second, instalments by reference to the progress of the building works; and third, usually between 5 and 10 per cent of the consideration payable upon completion and delivery of the works or, upon expiry of any agreed maintenance period following completion. The contract will usually have a date set for completion which will be extended for material alterations to the specifications, even if a right of extension is not explicitly agreed. The parties usually agree that the principal will be entitled to fixed compensation for delay and in the absence of grounds for an extension. The principal may not claim additional damages, unless expressly agreed. The principal may vary the original design, specification or scope of the works within reasonable limits. The contractor may refuse a reduction or increase in work of over 10 per cent. The contractor may complete and deliver the work to the principal prior to the agreed date. The principal, usually represented by an agent or manager (eg an architect), will be informed of the date of completion and invited to inspect. Minor defects capable of being remedied within a very short period will oblige the principal to accept completion and delivery. For major defects, completion will be postponed and the defects recorded in a written report. In the event of a material default by the principal (eg non-payment of more than one instalment), the contractor may terminate the contract. Generally speaking, the principal is entitled to terminate the contract at any time; however, in the absence of default by the contractor, the principal will be liable to pay the remainder of the contract sum less any cost savings by the contractor.

10.2.3 Standard form of contracts

There is no standard contract but the usual form will be similar: ie a written agreement between the parties, setting out the principal (commercial) terms (eg price, delivery date, permitted variations, instalments and security). A set of standard general terms and conditions such as the Uniform Administrative Conditions (*Uniforme Administratieve Voorwaarden*, the 'UAV') developed by the Ministry of Public Works with investors and contractors will be incorporated.

10.2.4 Appointment of the professional team

Standard regulations have been developed by the professional associations to regulate the relationship between principal and architect and principal and engineer. Architects and engineers are reluctant to enter into an agreement with principal or contractor unless the standard terms apply. The agreement will rarely specify the personnel to be engaged and the consideration payable could vary between a percentage of the contract sum, a fixed amount or an hourly time charge.

10.3 Those involved and their roles

The principal, who may be either the owner or the developer, normally appoints an architect as the lead consultant and to be responsible for design although he will invariably subcontract engineering designs; in the low-lying Netherlands, particular consideration must be given to groundwork and foundations. Although cost and quality control is traditionally within the remit of the architect, the client may appoint an independent cost-control organisation and sometimes a quality controller. Building or quantity surveyors are rarely used. The principal will usually appoint a main contractor, while maintaining control over the mechanical, electrical and other specialist works. The contractor may be selected out of a number who have offered against a specification prepared for the principal; this is common for commercial property. Regulations implementing the EC Public Procurement Directives require government bodies to allow a certain number of contractors to tender if the work is worth ECU5,000,000 or more. The principal is generally responsible for the design, and the engineers and the contractor carry out the work in accordance with the design and specifications. If the owner does not want to accept full responsibility, he may commission a project developer, possibly the contractor, to prepare and undertake responsibility for design and performance of the works.

10.4 Defects and remedies

10.4.1 Remedies of the employer in respect of defects in design and materials

On inspection and acceptance of the works by the principal the contractor's liability will cease, except for:

(a) any specific warranties in respect of parts of the works, eg foundations, roof and technical installations;
(b) hidden defects which were not and could not have been detected by the principal at or before completion; and
(c) major defects in the structure and soundness of the works.

In addition, the principal may in the event of faulty design have recourse against the architect or the engineer. If the principal entered into an agency or management agreement for supervision of design and carrying out of the works, he may have an additional claim against the agent or manager. The principal will not have a direct remedy against subcontractors and suppliers who have entered into an agreement with the contractor.

10.4.2 Remedies of subsequent owners/occupiers other than the contractual employer

The rights of the principal will pass to the subsequent owner by operation of law; however, for the avoidance of doubt, a specific provision to this effect is usually incorporated in the notarial deed of transfer. Occupiers and financiers have no direct remedy against those involved in the work. There are very few Civil Code provisions relating to building contracts, the position being regulated by the agreement. If the agreement includes standard terms (see

10.2.3 and 10.2.4), the time limit for claims will be specifically agreed; for hidden defects this will be five years and for structural defects 10 years. The liability of the architect or engineer is limited in time and amount, in accordance with their standard conditions.

10.5 Defects insurance

The contractor is generally obliged to insure the building work, until completion, or if a maintenance period is agreed to, until the end of this period. Sometimes the principal may require insurance for a longer period or specific warranties. For larger projects, the contractor may be required to take out insolvency insurance.

10.6 Copyright

Copyright in the design of the building vests in the architect or engineer responsible. The beneficiary of the copyright may require the building works to be carried out in accordance with the design and, once completed, object to any material alterations.

10.7 Fees

The total professional fees will generally vary between 20 per cent for large projects and 15 per cent for smaller projects where a single professional, usually an architect, will be employed.

10.8 Taxes

All construction and fees are subject to value added tax, currently at a rate of 17.5 per cent.

11 TAXES

A general distinction can be made between taxes levied by the state and taxes levied by provincial or local authorities. This section deals mainly with state taxes.

11.1 Corporation tax

Corporation tax (*vennootschapsbelasting*) is regulated by the Corporation Tax Act 1969. Any company resident for tax purposes, including foreign-based companies deemed to have a permanent establishment (*vaste inrichting*) for tax purposes, is liable to pay corporation tax on its worldwide profits, regardless of source, subject to relief under any double taxation treaty. Companies incorporated in, or whose head office or place of management is in, the Netherlands are treated as resident. Non-resident companies are taxed on profits of any trade carried on by a branch in the Netherlands, including capital gains on business assets, income from property in the Netherlands, and interest from loans secured on such property.

11.1.1 Tax rates

The rate of corporation tax is 35 per cent but the first NLG100,000 is taxed at 36 per cent.

11.1.2 Computation and administration

Taxable income and deductions include dividends, capital gains and losses, interest, royalties, exchange differences, expenses and items of tax return such as any loss carry-over available. Dividends are normally fully taxable, unless received from 5 per cent or more participations which qualify for full 'participation exemption'. An advance ruling is often sought to find out if this applies. Interest income is taxable as ordinary income and interest expenses are allowable as a deduction against taxable income. However, if a company qualifies for the participation exemption, interest expenses incurred to finance the acquisition and the cost of management are not deductible, unless they serve to generate income taxable in the Netherlands. Expenses are generally deductible with exceptions. Depreciation and interest are deductible expenses. In each state the Inland Revenue is divided into two departments, one for the levy of tax, and the other for collection. Corporation tax is payable upon filing a tax return and subsequent assessment. An appeal against assessment may be made to the tax inspector, usually within six weeks; a further appeal may be made to the courts. Appeal will not by itself entitle a person to defer payment although the tax collector is usually prepared to agree postponement.

11.1.3 Depreciation and capital allowances

Certain expenditure is allowed as a deductible expense against profits through a system allowing depreciation on assets during their respective economic or technical lifetimes. Depreciation on land is not allowed, whilst depreciation on buildings ranges between 2 and 2.5 per cent over a 40 to 50 year period. Depreciation rates on machinery and equipment range between 15 and 20 per cent. Depreciation is usually on a straight line basis, although other schemes such as progressive or degressive depreciation also apply. There are no longer special rates to encourage, or discourage, investment in certain areas as these have been abolished. Costs and tax in connection with the purchase of property such as property transfer tax are often capitalised and depreciated for a period of 40 to 50 years.

11.1.4 Withholding tax

Dividends and other distributions of profits are subject to 25 per cent withholding tax; for non-residents the tax may be reduced by tax treaty. The tax withheld must be paid to the collector of taxes within one month of the dividend becoming due and payable. There is no withholding tax on interest (other than on profit sharing and bonds) or royalties paid by resident companies. The employer should withhold wage tax (and social security premiums) on the gross amount of wages payable to employees.

11.2 Taxes on development value

Other than usual corporation tax there are no specific taxes levied on the increase in value of land, attributable to planning permission or potential changes in use.

11.3 Taxes on capital gains

Capital gains made by businesses assessable to corporation tax are taxable as ordinary income when realised, except where the participation exemption applies (see 11.1.2). In certain cases, taxation may be deferred by roll-overs. A capital loss is normally tax deductible. There are special rules for a participation which qualifies for the participation exemption. In case of a revaluation of the assets including land and property, a revaluation reserve should be formed as well as a reserve for contingent tax liabilities.

11.4 Taxes on owner of property

The ownership of land and property by a company or individual is subject to property tax by each local authority based on the net open market value or on the adjusted replacement value for certain property such as specific technical plants or churches. Each local authority will determine its own rate. Rates vary throughout the country. Whilst the interest on mortgages is fully deductible for individuals in relation to their income tax, the individual owner/occupier of residential property may not deduct any expenses incurred in relation to such property and is required to add a fictitious amount to his annual taxable income, related to the deemed rental value of the property.

11.5 Taxes on occupier

Tenants and other occupiers of land or property, corporate or individual, are also subject to the levy of property tax, although at a different rate. As a result, the owner/occupier of property is taxed in each capacity.

11.6 Taxes on land transfer

11.6.1 The acquisition of legal or beneficial title to land is subject to a six per cent property transfer tax on the consideration or market value of the property if higher, under the Tax on Transactions Act (*Wet op Belastingen van rechtsverkeer*). The tax is payable by the buyer. Where property is acquired within six months of a previous transfer which was subject to transfer tax or value added tax (VAT), the subsequent property transfer tax is on the positive difference between the purchase prices.

11.6.2 There are certain exemptions such as for the qualifying internal reorganisation. A transfer of newly developed and unused property is not subject to property transfer tax but to VAT at 17.5 per cent provided the buyer qualifies for full VAT relief. If the assets of a company consist of more than 70 per cent of property, a sale of the shares is also subject to property transfer tax.

11.7 Wealth taxes

Wealth tax is levied on the net value of the assets less the liabilities of individual persons, taking certain matters into account at 0.8 per cent (1997) and 0.7 per cent (1998).

11.8 Value added tax

Turnover tax or value added tax (VAT) is levied under the Turnover Tax Act on supplies or services in the Netherlands and the import of goods. The rate is currently levied at 17.5 per cent. For a limited number of goods and services, a reduced rate of six per cent applies and related exports rendered are zero rated. The tax is payable on the amount charged. The transfer and letting of property are exempt, with exceptions, eg the transfer of newly developed property before, on, or within two years of first occupation, ie newly constructed property, or where land has been prepared for development; or where the buyer opts for taxation upon transfer of the property. If a property is transferred within 10 years from a purchase subject to VAT, the transferor is liable to repay the VAT in proportion to that deducted or reclaimed on purchase. For this reason, a seller and a buyer will opt for taxation upon a subsequent transfer. This is only permissible if the property is used for the delivery of supplies or services which are all or at least 90 per cent subject to the levy of VAT, or is let under VAT taxable rent to a tenant who supplies services and goods, at least 90 per cent of which are subject to VAT. Both property transfer tax and VAT may be levied on a transfer, although in certain cases, an exemption from property transfer tax may be obtained (see 11.6.2). The letting of property is in principle exempt from VAT. The commercial landlord and tenant may jointly apply to be excluded from the exemption; provided that the tenant uses the property for the delivery of goods or services, of which 90 per cent or more are subject to VAT. As governmental bodies, banks, insurance companies and hospitals, to name a few, do not charge VAT, the letting to any one of these is exempt from VAT.

11.9 Local and other taxes

11.9.1 The local authority may levy a tax for a maximum 30-year period in order to recover a fair part of the cost of providing certain services. A building land tax may be levied for services which improve the land for building purposes.

11.9.2 A local tax (*precario*) is levied on works and structures which overhang or encroach upon public highways or other public property. The protruding works will also require prior authorisation.

11.9.3 Under certain environmental statutes a landowner may be charged with pollution levies.

11.9.4 Under the Water Boards Act (*Waterschapswet*) a water authority may impose a levy for the cost of carrying out its duties and obligations under statute.

12 GRANTS AND INCENTIVES

12.1 Subsidies, grants and loans

12.1.1 The grant of subsidies delegated by the state to local authorities under the Residential Subsidies Decree is intended to stimulate home ownership. Newly built private residential housing is classified as premium housing attracting subsidy if the building costs amount to NLG171,000 or less (in 1997). The subsidy is determined by the income of the buyer and applicable interest rates.

12.1.2 With a view to maintaining and refurbishing monuments and other listed buildings, the state may grant a subsidy up to 80 per cent of the costs of qualifying maintenance or refurbishment.

12.2 Tax allowances and reliefs

Apart from specific tax allowances or reductions, there are no allowances available for smaller companies or specific projects, or to encourage economic growth and employment. EU funds under the relevant EU regulations may be made available to the provincial or local authorities for financing specific projects in areas of economic need.

12.3 Other public schemes and incentives

There are no other public schemes and incentives of significance, other than those already mentioned.

13 COMPANIES AND BUSINESS ENTITIES

13.1 Limited and unlimited companies

The legal forms of business undertaking are the privately owned business (*eenmanszaak*) where the owner assumes full liability, the general partnership (*vennootschap onder firma*), the partnership firm (*maatschap*) which is a qualified form of general partnership, the limited partnership (*commanditaire vennootschap*) and legal entities or legal persons (as opposed to individuals). The most commonly used form of legal entity for conducting business is the limited liability company. Dutch law does not recognise companies with unlimited liability.

13.1.1 There are two types of company with limited liability, the company limited by shares (*naamloze vennootschap, NV*) and the private company with limited liability (*besloten vennootschap, BV*), structured and regulated in a very similar way.

13.1.2 The *BV* is a legal entity whose authorised capital is divided into shares. It may not issue share certificates and the shares are not freely transferable. *BV*s can only have registered shares without share certificates. The shareholder will not be personally liable for company transactions and will not be obliged to contribute to losses in excess of the amount subscribed. Before incorporating a company by executing a notarial deed of incorporation containing the articles of association (*statuten*), a draft deed of incorporation must be submitted to the Ministry of Justice to obtain a declaration of no objection, which enables the Minister to exercise administrative control over the contents of the deed and verify the credentials of the proposed owners and managers. Generally, the deed of incorporation must be executed within three months of the date of the declaration of no objection. An amendment to the articles of association is also subject to the Minister's approval. The articles of association of a *BV* must contain restrictions on issue and transfer of shares, such as rights of pre-emption for shareholders on the issue or transfer of shares and the requirement for prior consent of the general meeting of shareholders to any transfer. The minimum issued and paid-up share capital for a *BV* is NLG40,000 and it must be paid up at incorporation. The Civil Code contains various specific provisions and regulations with regard to the required contents of the deed of incorporation, including the first articles of association.

13.1.3 The *NV*, or company limited by shares, is a legal entity with a minimum issued and paid-up share capital of NLG100,000. The *NV* can issue bearer shares; its articles of association may contain restrictions on the transfer of registered shares but there will be none on bearer shares. A shareholder is not personally liable for transactions of the company, and is not required to contribute to losses above the amount that must be paid up on his share(s). Only *NV*s may also be listed on the Amsterdam stock exchange, and only the bearer shares are capable of being traded on the exchange. For the incorporation procedure see 13.1.2.

13.1.4 The company is a separate legal entity from its shareholders and directors, has its own assets and liabilities, and is taxed separately under different rules. What the company or its 'bodies' (eg the boards of managing directors and supervisory directors (if applicable), and the general meeting) may do will be set out in the notarial deed of incorporation, in the articles and in the Civil Code. Certain Civil Code provisions are mandatory and the deed will be carefully reviewed by the Minister for compliance.

13.2 Partnerships

A partnership is an agreement whereby two or more parties agree to make a joint contribution, carry on business in common, under a common name, with a view to sharing the business's profits. Partnerships do not have legal personality, although they can sue and are capable of being sued. A distinction can be drawn between general partnerships (*vennootschap onder firma*), limited partnerships (*commanditaire vennootschap*) and partnership firms (*maatschappen*), a special form of general partnership, used by the professions, eg lawyers and accountants. The Civil Code contains certain provisions for each partnership. A general partnership is set up by agreement which may be oral, but is usually in writing. The agreement will contain all material terms, eg duration, type of business, distribution of profits, representation of the partnership in relation to third parties and the transfer of a partnership interest by a partner (although this is unusual). Each partner is jointly and severally liable for the obligations and liabilities of the partnership, whether resulting from agreements entered into on behalf of the partnership, or by operation of law. In order to protect the partners vis-à-vis each other, the partnership agreement usually provides for two partners acting jointly to represent the partnership. A general partnership is usually tax transparent; the partners, and not the partnership, will be liable for tax.

13.2.1 A limited partnership is established in the same way. The principal difference is that a limited partnership has managing partners (*beherende vennoten*) and limited partners (*stille vennoten* or *commanditaire vennoten*). Limited partners are not liable for obligations of the partnership in excess of the amount of their contribution, whilst managing partners are jointly and severally liable for all the obligations of the partnership.

13.2.2 There is a distinction between open and closed partnerships of relevance for tax purposes. In a closed partnership all partners must approve the transfer of partnership interests, whereas the interests in an open partnership will be either freely transferable or not subject to all partners' approval. A closed partnership is transparent, as the individual partners will be taxed and not the partnership.

13.3 Other types of business association

Companies and partnerships are the principal forms of association recognised by law although other types should be noted.

13.3.1 Trusts

Dutch law does not provide for the legal concept of the trust as a business association or legal entity although foreign trusts are recognised under the recently ratified Trust Convention.

13.3.2 Associations

An association is a legal entity incorporated by notarial deed with members formed for certain non-commercial activities or common purposes, eg sporting activities, business promotions and charitable purposes. The deed of incorporation containing the articles of association must comply with the Civil Code, although there is no requirement for approval by the Ministry of Justice. The members may not share the profits.

13.3.3 Cooperatives

A cooperative is an association formed by a notarial deed, with the objective of attending to the interests or needs of its members. Its articles must set out those objectives. Where a cooperative engages in a business on behalf of its members it must enter into a contract with them.

13.3.4 Mutual insurance societies

A mutual insurance society is an association created by a notarial deed to enter into insurance contracts with its members or to keep them insured under statutory or other regulations.

13.3.5 Foundations

A foundation is another type of legal entity created by notarial deed to realise an objective stated in its articles with capital allocated for the purpose. It has no members. The objects may not include the distribution of profits or benefits in kind to those who formed the foundation or to members of its constituent bodies or to others unless, in the latter case, for an idealistic, social or charitable purpose.

13.3.6 Joint ventures

A joint venture is an agreement to collaborate which can be freely entered into upon the terms and conditions agreed by the parties.

14 INTERNATIONAL

14.1 Restrictions on inward investment

There are no monetary restrictions on the introduction of funds into the Netherlands for the purchase of property or on the ownership of property in the Netherlands by foreign entities although certain financial transactions have to be reported to the Dutch Central Bank for various purposes, including those of a statistical nature.

14.2 Exchange controls

There are no exchange controls, although there are reporting requirements which enable the Dutch Central Bank to monitor financial transactions. All residents including foreign legal entities domiciled in the Netherlands and Dutch branches of non-resident legal entities must report to the Dutch Central Bank with direct and indirect movement of funds relating to foreign countries.

14.3 Restrictions and registration on carrying on a business

Foreign entities wishing to invest or set up business do not need specific government approval, although they must comply with the rules and regulations generally applicable to companies and business undertakings. If the entity is set up as a branch, there are a number of registration requirements, eg the registration of the branch in the local commercial register of the chamber of commerce. With effect from 1 January 1998 new legislation has come into force to restrain the improper use of entities incorporated and regulated under foreign law but which undertake most of their activity in the Netherlands, and have no actual connection with the country of incorporation. This legislation imposes the obligation to register in the commercial register, to maintain the issued and paid-up capital required of Dutch private companies with limited liability and to comply with Dutch regulations on bookkeeping and accounting. A failure to comply with the latter obligation will make foreign entities and directors as liable for manifest and improper management as Dutch companies.

14.4 Repatriation of income and proceeds of property trading and development

There are no consents or restraints involved in the repatriation of income and proceeds subject to the deduction of withholding tax (see 11.1.4).

14.5 Withholding taxes

Withholding taxes have been referred to at 11.1.4. Interest (other than interest on profit sharing bonds), rents or royalties paid by residents in the Netherlands are not subject to dividend withholding tax, unless deemed to be dividends; where a loan by a parent to its subsidiary is considered to be informal equity by the tax authorities, interest may be considered a dividend.

14.6 Double taxation relief

The Netherlands has separate double taxation treaties with a number of countries.

CHAPTER 12

Northern Ireland

Laurence Mahood

Partner, Elliott Duffy Garrett, Belfast

CONTENTS

1 OWNERSHIP OF LAND 397
2 OTHER INTERESTS IN LAND 399
3 TITLE TO LAND 402
4 TRANSACTIONS IN LAND 403
5 LEASES AND OTHER RIGHTS OF OCCUPATION 405
6 FINANCE AND INVESTMENT SOURCES 409
7 FORMS OF SECURITY 409
8 PLANNING AND BUILDING REGULATION 410
9 ENVIRONMENTAL MATTERS 413
10 DEVELOPMENT 416
11 TAXES 417
12 GRANTS AND INCENTIVES 417
13 COMPANIES AND BUSINESS ENTITIES 419
14 INTERNATIONAL 419

CHAPTER 12

Northern Ireland

1 OWNERSHIP OF LAND

Whilst there are many similarities, there are also many substantive differences between the law and practice of real property in Northern Ireland and that existing in England and Wales and this chapter deals with the major similarities and differences between the two jurisdictions. Like England, Northern Ireland does not have a codified system of law but its sources of law comprise statutes and orders and the common law. The principal English property law statutes (unlike statutes in other areas such as tax) do not apply and Northern Ireland largely has its own legislation relating to property law. Under the doctrine of precedent, decisions of the higher English courts are persuasive authority for Northern Ireland courts and decisions of the House of Lords in England are binding on the courts in Northern Ireland. The principal forms of tenure are, as in England, freehold and leasehold, but with some substantive differences.

1.1 Types of ownership

1.1.1 Freehold

The comments on freehold in the English chapter generally apply equally to Northern Ireland, but absolute freehold ownership is not usual in Northern Ireland. Whilst it is common to find absolute freehold ownership in rural areas, absolute freehold ownership in urban areas is the exception rather than the rule. In the majority of cases, freehold ownership in urban areas would be derived under a deed known as a fee farm grant which is virtually unknown in England. A fee farm grant creates a freehold estate in land, but normally reserves a yearly ground rent to the fee farm grantor (which would generally be a nominal amount and not subject to annual review) and contains various covenants on the part of the fee farm grantee, similar to those found in a long-term lease, such as covenants to insure and to repair. The fee farm grant does not generally contain any restrictions on alienation such as one would normally find in shorter term leases but usually contains certain (though often limited) restrictions on the permitted use of the property (a common example in residential areas being a covenant not to use the property other than as a private dwelling house). The negative and positive covenants contained in a fee farm grant are enforceable against the successors in title of the respective parties because, whilst creating a freehold estate in land, a fee farm grant creates the relationship of landlord and tenant between the parties. Fee farm grants are rarely created today, most having been created in the nineteenth and early twentieth centuries. Sub-fee farm grants have been created out of the original fee farm grant and in turn long leases and subleases created out of the fee farm grants/sub-fee farm grants. The final report of the Land Law

Working Group (1989) made certain recommendations in regard to existing fee farm grants and legislation has been enacted banning future creation of fee farm grants. Recent legislation also entitles, and upon sale requires, most long leasehold residential tenants to buy out their landlord's interest, but any restrictive covenants will remain; there are exceptions, eg for flats.

1.1.2 Leasehold

The comments in the English chapter generally apply equally to Northern Ireland but there is a major difference in the law of privity of contract in leases and this is commented on in more detail in section 5. A further difference between the two jurisdictions is that in Northern Ireland it is possible to create a sublease for the entire unexpired residue of the term of years granted by a lease, whereas in England any purported sublease for the entire unexpired residue of the term granted by the lease acts as an assignment. The above legislation also bans the future creation of long leaseholds

1.1.3 Joint ownership

Unlike in England, when more than one person owns land, there is no automatic trust created. Joint owners of land can hold the legal estate as joint tenants (where one person's estate passes on death automatically to the survivor) or as tenants in common (where each person holds an undivided share in the land and can sell or devise his estate to a third party). There is no restriction on the number of legal owners of land.

1.1.4 Condominia

A system of common hold has also been recommended by the Land Law Working Group but there has not been as yet any statutory enactment of the Group's recommendations.

1.1.5 Lesser rights

The comments in the English chapter generally apply equally to Northern Ireland.

1.2 The role of the trust and the distinction between legal and beneficial ownership

The law is substantially similar to that in England although there are some differences. There is no upper limit on the number of trustees; nevertheless, it is advisable to have a minimum of two, except in the case of a trust corporation acting as trustee.

1.3 Restrictions on ownership and dealing

1.3.1 The law in Northern Ireland is substantially similar to that in England. There are certain specific statutory restrictions upon the disposal of land by bodies such as the Department of the Environment for Northern Ireland, district councils, charities, church bodies and certain trustees. Otherwise land is generally freely disposable subject to any restrictions contained in the constitution of any landowning corporation and any restrictions contained in the title under which the land is held, such as for example in the case of a letting of commercial property at an open market rent where it would invariably be provided that the landlord's consent was required to any dealing with the land by the tenant. Such provisions would normally restrict absolutely any dealing with part only of the property but entitle the tenant to assign or sublet the entirety of the property with the landlord's consent, such consent not to be unreasonably withheld.

1.3.2 Where a lease contains a provision restricting the tenant from dealing with the property 'without the landlord's consent' but with no reasonableness qualification, landlords in Northern Ireland could generally act arbitrarily in deciding whether or not to grant such consent. However, the Business Tenancies (Northern Ireland) Order 1996 provides that leases will be deemed to be subject to a qualification that a landlord is not to unreasonably withhold or delay consent and any issue as to reasonableness can be referred to the lands tribunal for determination. Such implied qualification of reasonableness will not apply though to 'absolute' covenants – a covenant 'not to assign or sublet the property' would not attract the implied reasonableness proviso but a covenant 'not to assign or sublet the property without the landlord's consent' would.

1.4 Adverse possession or acquisitive prescription

The law in Northern Ireland is substantially similar to that in England although regulated by different legislation, the Limitation (Northern Ireland) Order 1989.

2 OTHER INTERESTS IN LAND

The law in relation to these interests is generally similar to that in England but there are differences, for example there are certain different registration systems (see 2.5).

2.1 Servitudes or easements, usufruct, building and dwelling rights

The law in Northern Ireland is generally similar to that in England.

2.2 Restrictions on use and other restrictions

Again, the law on such matters is substantially similar to that in England. Application can be made to the Lands Tribunal for Northern Ireland to modify or wholly or partially extinguish a restriction on the title to the land on the basis that it unreasonably impedes the enjoyment of the land or, if not modified or extinguished, would do so. However, in the case of leasehold property, no application can be made without the consent of the lands tribunal until 21 years of the term of the lease have expired.

2.3 Private mortgages and charges

The law is substantially similar to that in England, although there is no concept of a 'legal' mortgage. In the case of property the title to which is registered in the land registry, the owner of the land would normally grant a charge to the lender; and in the case of unregistered property, the owner would grant a mortgage over the property by way of demise for a specified number of years in the case of freehold unregistered property, or for the residue of the term of the lease less the last few days in the case of leasehold unregistered property.

2.4 Contracts and options

The law in Northern Ireland is substantially similar to that in England.

2.5 Public or municipal charges

The English Local Land Charges Act 1975 does not apply and there are no land charges registers. Instead there is a statutory charges register which is situated at the land registry of Northern Ireland and, under the provisions of the Land Registration Act (Northern Ireland) 1970, certain matters require to be registered in the statutory charges register. Some examples are any prohibition or restriction on the permitted use of land imposed by a local authority, housing orders and conditions in relation to housing grants, resolutions proposing an area as a redevelopment area, notices under the roads legislation and private streets, and notices that a building is listed as being of special architectural or historic interest.

2.6 Other interests

As commented earlier, in Northern Ireland positive obligations in freehold land could be enforced by the use of the fee farm grant although the future creation of these will not be possible. The English rent charges legislation does not apply in Northern Ireland.

2.7 Liabilities attaching to land

The law is substantially similar to that in England, although Northern Ireland has its own statutes dealing with occupier's liability, health and safety at work, factories and fire precautions.

2.8 Legal and equitable interests

There are several interests in land which have been created by the courts of equity (as explained in the English chapter). These include trusts, equitable mortgage by deposit of title deeds with a bank or lender as opposed to registration in the land registry or the registry of deeds, and restrictive covenants where equity ruled that certain covenants would 'run' with the land so as to bind successors in title.

2.9 Protection of interests

Generally, interests will be protected either by registration at the land registry in the case of registered land or at the registry of deeds in the case of unregistered land, and also at the companies registry in relation to a company. In the case of registered title, a charge would be registered against the owner's land certificate and a certificate of charge issued to the chargee. In the case of unregistered property, the mortgage would be registered in the registry of deeds. An agreement for the sale or lease of land can also be registered in the registry of deeds in the case of unregistered property. There is no provision for registering such an agreement in the land registry in the case of a registered title but a priority search in relation to such an agreement can be lodged in the registry which gives protection for a period of 40 days and this can be renewed. Where land is registered, certain interests do not require registration. These include:

(a) death duties and Crown rents;
(b) certain annuities and rent charges;
(c) statutory provisions which prohibit or restrict alienation, assignment, sub-division, or subletting of any land;
(d) express and implied covenants affecting leasehold land;
(e) rights of the public;
(f) easements and profits à prendre;
(g) any lease where the term granted does not exceed 21 years;
(h) rights acquired or in course of being acquired under the Limitation (Northern Ireland) Order 1989 (adverse possession); and
(i) the rights of every person in actual occupation of the land or in receipt of rents and profits thereof unless they fail to disclose their rights when asked.

2.10 Priority of interests

As in England, priority between interests in land will generally depend on the date of registration and not the date of creation of the interests. In the case of registered land, the date of registration of any dealing is the date on which the application is received by the land registry. As commented in 2.9, certain interests affect registered land without the need for registration.

3 TITLE TO LAND

3.1 Proof of title

As in England, title to land can be established either by registration at the land registry where the land is registered (generally a land certificate would be issued) or by the production of the title deeds where the land is unregistered (though ownership for a period of at least 12 years is only required in Northern Ireland as opposed to 15 years in England). The Land Registration Act (Northern Ireland) 1970 envisaged a scheme of creeping compulsory registration of land whereby each county or county borough would, over a period of time, be declared a compulsory registration area with landowners having unregistered titles being obliged to register their title upon sale or grant of a lease for a term exceeding 21 years. Only very recently has this scheme commenced and only in a minor fashion, the first designated area being two small towns and surrounding areas in North Down, Newtownards and Comber. As in England, the land registry is open to the public for inspection upon payment of a fee.

3.2 Land registry

Registered title is administered by the land registry of Northern Ireland. There is no land charges register in Northern Ireland.

3.2.1 Plans

The boundaries shown on the land registry maps are not conclusive. Applications can be made to make boundaries conclusive although this can be a time consuming and expensive process involving all adjoining owners.

3.2.2 Content

There is a single title register for freehold estates and leasehold estates (excluding an estate granted for a term of 21 years or less). There is no separate charges register, for example a charge granted to a bank is registered against the registered owner's land certificate. The categories of ownership are 'absolute', 'good fee farm grant', 'good leasehold', 'qualified' or 'possessory' and there are rules and procedures for applications to be made to upgrade lesser categories of ownership.

3.2.3 Errors

As in England, there are certain provisions for compensation for and/or rectification of errors.

3.3 Passing of title

The comments made in the English chapter generally also apply to Northern Ireland, although there is no time limit in Northern Ireland within which a transfer (by way of outright sale) of registered land is to be lodged in the land registry and the period of time for lodgement of a lease exceeding 21 years is six months, as opposed to two months in England. There are provisions for application to be made to the land registry to register a lease out of time.

4 TRANSACTIONS IN LAND

The most common transactions in land are the sale and purchase of the leasehold or freehold, the grant or assignment of a lease, and the creation of a mortgage in favour of a bank or other lender to secure a loan (but note the position on long leaseholds mentioned at 1.1).

4.1 Procedures

4.1.1 The average timescale for a sale transaction is eight to ten weeks but conveyancing practice differs to that in England. The first stage also comprises the negotiation of a contract, prior to which the buyer's solicitors will carry out an investigation of title, raise enquiries with the seller with regard to the property and the title, make searches at the land registry or in the registry of deeds and in the companies registry if the seller is a company, make application for a certificate of search in the statutory charges register and make standard enquiries of the Department of the Environment, the local authority and the Northern Ireland housing executive (eg regarding planning, building regulations, compulsory purchase and environmental health matters). If the buyer is obtaining a loan to finance the purchase of the property he will make application to a bank or building society and the lending institution will arrange for a survey to be carried out, although this may not be done before the contract is entered into between the parties. Usually, the contract is entered into between two to three weeks of the sale having been agreed in principle. The contract will specify a fixed date for completion but the buyer's obligation to complete would be commonly conditional upon him obtaining, before the completion date, a satisfactory statutory charges search and replies to the property enquiries, and, in residential sales, to the buyer obtaining an offer of finance for not less than a specified amount (and without onerous or unusual clauses) from a lending institution on the security of the property being purchased. Such a condition relating to finance would not, however, be the norm in sales of commercial property.

4.1.2 Prior to the completion date the buyer's solicitors will carry out such further searches and enquiries as are necessary, eg an up-to-date search in the land registry or a search in the companies registry if the seller is a company to ensure that no liquidator or receiver has been appointed. In the case of property the title to which is registered, as commented earlier, the buyer can protect his interest under the contract by lodging a priority search in the land registry which will provide the buyer with a certain period of priority, and which can be renewed. In the case of unregistered title, there is no land charges register in Northern Ireland, but a buyer can register a contract in the registry of deeds, though this is not commonly done, and only provides a degree of protection.

4.1.3 The timescale for the completion of commercial property transactions generally depends to a large extent on the particular nature of the transaction and the bargaining strength of the parties. It is not uncommon that very quick completions are required in large commercial property transactions.

4.2 Contract terms

4.2.1 Subject to the comments in 4.1.1 with regard to contracts being dependent upon certain conditions being satisfied (commonly property enquiries and availability of finance), contract terms are generally similar to those in England although each jurisdiction has its own standard conditions of sale and the latest standard conditions in Northern Ireland place a greater degree of disclosure on the seller.

4.2.2 The parties' rights in relation to default would generally follow those in England.

4.3 Formalities

The English Law of Property (Miscellaneous Provisions) Act 1989 does not apply. A contract for the sale of land need not be in writing but s 2 of the Statute of Frauds (Ireland) 1695 at least requires that there should be written evidence in the form of a 'memorandum or note' of the contract. Whilst there are no statutory provisions as to what such a memorandum or note must contain, common law has prescribed certain requirements for it to be enforceable and these are often referred to as the 'Four Ps'. These are specification of the parties, the property, the price, and any other essential provisions. A memorandum or note of a contract to grant a lease must contain some additional information such as the date of commencement of the lease. All such documents must be signed but the section does not require signature by both parties. It requires only signature by the party to be sued for enforcement of the contract or by that party's lawfully authorised agent. Oral leases can only be for a term of a maximum of one year or yearly tenancies. In certain circumstances, the court may award the specific performance of an agreement which does not comply with the requirements of the Statute of Frauds, if the buyer has incurred expense in reliance upon acts by the seller. Whilst there are certain general principles of this doctrine, each case very much stands or falls on its own facts.

4.4 Fees, costs and taxes

4.4.1 The English practice is generally followed in Northern Ireland and the fees paid to agents are similar. A landlord cannot require the tenant to pay the landlord's agents' commission for negotiating a lease.

4.4.2 Solicitors' conveyancing fees on sale of land are generally similar to those in England, although sometimes slightly higher in Northern Ireland as there are fewer high value transactions. Fees on commercial leases at open market rents are often based on a percentage (approximately five per cent) of the initial annual rent passing. Any stipulation made on the sale of any land (which includes the grant of a lease) to the effect that the buyer is to be liable for the seller's/landlord's solicitors' costs is void in Northern Ireland, whereas in England, depending on negotiating strengths, a landlord can still require a tenant to pay the landlord's legal fees on the grant of a lease.

4.4.3 The stamp duty legislation in Northern Ireland is the same as in England.

4.4.4 The fee to register a deed in the registry of deeds in the case of unregistered title (see 2.9) is currently £14. Land registry fees are, as in England, charged according to the value of the land or consideration. The minimum fee is £25 and the maximum fee for a transaction of over £65,000 is £350.

4.4.5 Transaction costs in Northern Ireland are generally similar to those in England although they can occasionally be slightly higher depending on the nature of the transaction or the title to the property. As commented in 3.1, registered title (land certificate in the land registry) is uncommon in urban areas of Northern Ireland and quite frequently the title to one property can be made up of several lots resulting in substantial time being required to investigate in detail bulky sets of title deeds. A common example of this would be a large building in a city centre which has been constructed on land consisting of several different title lots acquired over a number of years.

4.4.6 The value added tax (VAT) legislation is the same as in England and similarly agents' and solicitors' fees attract VAT, currently at a rate of 17.5 per cent.

4.5 Professionals' roles

The negotiation of sales is usually conducted by estate agents and Northern Ireland has its own branch of the Royal Institution of Chartered Surveyors. Surveyors may also be appointed by a buyer to carry out a survey of the property or engaged by the lending institution to whom the buyer has made application for a loan. Each party will generally be represented by his own solicitor although in certain circumstances one firm of solicitors can represent both parties (but a different individual practitioner would represent each party). There is no role for a notary or similar lawyer as is generally the case on the Continent.

5 LEASES AND OTHER RIGHTS OF OCCUPATION

The comments made in the English chapter generally apply equally to Northern Ireland but there are certain differences. Where a lease is granted for a capital sum reserving only a nominal rent, the term of years granted in Northern Ireland is generally 999 years or 1,000 years, save in the case of commercial premises where the term would commonly be 125 years. The 25-year institutional lease is also very common for good quality commercial property although more frequently now the term of the lease will be 15 or 20 years and may contain a break clause in favour of the tenant, eg at the end of the fifth year or possibly the tenth year. (Note, however, the changes mentioned for long leases at 1.1.)

5.1 Rent and other terms

5.1.1 The comments made in the English chapter in relation to rent reviews and other terms of leases generally apply equally to Northern Ireland. In relation to forfeiture of the lease a tenant has a right to apply to the court for relief against forfeiture and this is a discretionary remedy. Institutional leases in Northern Ireland are very similar to those used in England but there are certain differences.

5.1.2 As a result of terrorist activities, the British Insurance Association in 1977 agreed a standard form of exclusion to insurance policies which, in general terms, states that insurance taken out on property in Northern Ireland will not cover loss or damage resulting from terrorist activities or civil commotion. In the event of such loss or damage a person having an estate or interest in the property can make an application to the Secretary of State for compensation under the provisions of the Criminal Damage (Compensation) (Northern Ireland) Order 1977. Regard will be had to all circumstances, including any failure on the part of the applicant to take reasonable precautions, failure to comply with statutory provisions relating to the safety of the property and any unlawful use of the property or provocative or negligent behaviour of the applicant which contributed directly or indirectly to the loss or increased the chances of it being sustained. The Secretary of State has power to refuse or reduce compensation. The first £200 of any compensation claim has to be borne by the applicant. In addition to claiming compensation for the cost of repairs to a damaged building, applicants can also claim consequential loss and additional bank costs or charges incurred in carrying on business.

5.1.3 The standard insurance exclusion and the criminal damage legislation in Northern Ireland have resulted in various additional provisions being inserted in leases of commercial property. One example is a covenant on the part of the tenant to take all precautions and to comply with all requirements and recommendations of the police and the Northern Ireland Office for the protection and security of the property and to indemnify the landlord against any reduction in compensation resulting from any act, neglect or default of the tenant. Another example is specific covenants to claim compensation in the event of damage by a compensatable act or event and to make up any shortfall in compensation resulting from any act, neglect or default of the tenant. Often tenants under shorter term lettings or in lettings of secondary properties are able to negotiate and avoid such liability and also to ensure that they do not need to continue to pay rent if the property is damaged by a compensatable act (until the damage is repaired). In the latter case, the landlord can include the loss of rent in his claim for compensation, although not for an indefinite period as a landlord must take proper steps to minimise his losses.

5.1.4 In England, where a lease contains a covenant on the part of the tenant that he is not to assign the property without the prior consent of the landlord or carry out improvements to the property without prior consent, the landlord is statutorily barred from unreasonably withholding consent. The Business

Tenancies (Northern Ireland) Order 1996 introduced similar provisions into Northern Ireland for the first time for leases granted after 1 April 1997.

5.2 Privity of contract and estate

The concept of privity of contract also applies in Northern Ireland as in England but there are substantial differences between the two jurisdictions. The law in Northern Ireland in relation to the liability of original parties and their assignments is as follows:

5.2.1 The tenant

5.2.1.1 Where there is no restriction on assignment, the original tenant remains liable even after he has assigned his lease by virtue of the common law doctrine of privity of contract. Hence the necessity for the original tenant to take an indemnity covenant from his assignee in the deed of assignment. Generally, subsequent assignees are only liable in respect of obligations under the lease during the period they are tenants, ie so long as privity of estate exists between them and the landlord: s 14 of the Landlord and Tenant (Amendment) Act 1860 ('Deasy's Act'), which confirmed the common law position. There are three qualifications to this general proposition:

(a) the assignor is not liable for any breaches of the obligations under the lease after he has assigned the lease provided that he has given written notice of the particulars of the assignment to the landlord;
(b) the assignor remains liable for payment of rent up to the end of the quarter in which the date of service of notice of assignment occurs; and
(c) where the assignor indemnified the party who assigned to him (whether the original tenant or an assignee of the tenant's interest) he may be liable on the indemnity and should obtain an indemnity from his assignee.

5.2.1.2 In the event of a restriction on assignment and the landlord's consent being required, where the original tenant or a tenant by assignment assigns his lease with the landlord's consent he is released and discharged from all future liability under the lease. The qualification in relation to payment of rent up to the end of the quarter in which completion of the assignment takes place would still appear to apply and it should also be noted that under Deasy's Act the landlord's consent must be evidenced by him either being a party to the deed of assignment or endorsing his consent in writing on the deed of assignment – a mere licence to assign (signed by the landlord as is the practice in England) is not technically sufficient in Northern Ireland in the absence of the landlord also being joined as a party to the deed of assignment or endorsing his consent in writing on the deed of assignment.

5.2.2 The landlord

The original landlord remains liable even after he has assigned his reversion by virtue of the common law doctrine of privity of contract. Again, as in 5.2.1.1, the landlord on assigning his reversion would generally take an indemnity covenant from his assignee. A subsequent assignee is only liable in respect of obligations under the lease during the period that he is the landlord but he may be liable under an indemnity given to the party who assigned the landlord's interest to him and should obtain an indemnity from the person to whom he assigns that interest. It should be noted that as far as landlords are concerned there is no proviso requiring written notice of the particulars of the assignment of the reversion to be given to the tenant.

5.3 Rent control and security of tenure

5.3.1 Tenancies of agricultural land are extremely rare in Northern Ireland and unlikely to grow in popularity until new legislation is introduced. This is mainly because the old Land Law Acts of the nineteenth century have never been repealed and farmers have been wary of creating agricultural tenancies in case some of the very complex and unclear provisions of the Land Law Acts could give security of tenure to a tenant. Instead, conacre and agistment lettings are generally used. Conacre, sometimes termed the 'eleven month take', is a licence to enter the farmer's land to sow, reap and harvest a crop, and agistment is a similar licence to graze livestock. The licence is seasonal and no landlord and tenant relationship is created.

5.3.2 Certain low value residential tenancies are governed by the Rent (Northern Ireland) Order 1978 which restricts the amount of rent which can be charged and provides security of tenure for the tenant. Tenants of the Northern Ireland housing executive and registered housing associations also have certain rights to security of tenure and there are limitations on the amount of rent which can be charged by the executive or the registered housing association in question. There are also protected shorthold tenancies which are tenancies granted for a term certain of not less than one year and no more than five years. The security of tenure and other provisions of the Landlord and Tenant Act 1954 in England in relation to lettings of business premises are similar to the Northern Ireland provisions which are contained in the Business Tenancies (Northern Ireland) Order 1996. There are, however, certain important differences between the two jurisdictions, one of which being that in Northern Ireland there are no provisions similar to those as exist in England under the 1954 Act entitling the parties to contract out (by agreement) of the security of tenure provisions. Consequently, a tenant of business premises in Northern Ireland is entitled to a renewal of his lease unless the landlord can establish one of the statutory grounds of objection, which are similar to those in England although again with certain differences. If the parties cannot agree the terms of the renewal tenancy they are determined by the Lands Tribunal.

5.4 Other legislative restrictions

As is the case in England, it is generally a matter for a tenant in Northern Ireland to satisfy himself as to the suitability of the property for his purposes and that if appropriate the landlord gives express covenants as to repair and maintenance because at common law few obligations are implied in the lease or tenancy agreement. Whilst Deasy's Act imposes a covenant by the tenant to keep the premises in good and substantial repair and condition, the general rule of common law is that the landlord undertakes no responsibility for the condition of the premises when let or the repair and maintenance of the premises during the term of the lease or tenancy. The one exception is that on a letting of furnished accommodation there may be an implied warranty on the part of the landlord that the premises are fit for human habitation at the commencement of the tenancy. In addition, certain statutory provisions impose minimum standards in respect of housing provided by private landlords and public authorities and a landlord could also incur liability under the law of tort and negligence.

5.5 Method of measurement

The comments made in the English chapter generally apply equally in Northern Ireland.

6 FINANCE AND INVESTMENT SOURCES

The comments contained in the English chapter generally apply equally to Northern Ireland and in recent years there has been a major growth in property dealings in Northern Ireland by English institutions and pension funds. Whilst the terrorist activities which have afflicted the country for so long do occasionally have an adverse effect on property dealings, Northern Ireland is generally regarded as a very attractive area for investment and development. This is evidenced for example by the considerable number of shopping centres in the province which have been constructed and financed in recent years such as the very successful Castlecourt Centre in Belfast and the Foyleside Centre in Londonderry. The differences in Northern Ireland law in relation to privity of contract (see 5.2) have not had any adverse effect on investment in Northern Ireland. There is no real investment in agricultural land in Northern Ireland.

7 FORMS OF SECURITY

The comments contained in the English chapter generally apply equally to Northern Ireland although the specific form of security on property would be a mortgage for unregistered property registered in the registry of deeds or a charge for registered property registered at the land registry. Equitable mortgages also exist in Northern Ireland and, as in England, a mortgage or charge given by a company is required to be registered at the Northern Ireland companies registry within 21 days otherwise it is void as against a liquidator of the company though application may be made to the courts for late registration. Northern Ireland has its own insolvency legislation but this essentially mirrors the English legislation.

8 PLANNING AND BUILDING REGULATION

The development and use of land and buildings are subject to the controls contained in the Planning (Northern Ireland) Order 1991.

8.1 Planning authority

Control of matters relating to planning rests with the Department of the Environment for Northern Ireland and there are no specific local planning authorities. There is, however, consultation with the local district council for the area affected by a planning application.

8.2 Zoning and development plans

The Department of the Environment may at any time make a development plan for any area or alter, repeal or replace a development plan adopted by it for any area. Where the Department proposes to make, alter, repeal or replace a development plan, it is obliged to consult with the district council for the area to which the plan or proposed plan relates. The Department must also take such steps as will, in its opinion, ensure adequate publicity in the appropriate area, and ensure that those persons who may wish to make representations are given the opportunity to do so. The Department is under an obligation to consider any representations made to it within a certain period. Once the plan has been prepared it must be made available for inspection and this fact must be advertised as well as the prescribed period within which any objections may be made. These various procedures can be shortened if, in the opinion of the Department, the proposals are not of significant importance. There will be considerable public discussion on the content of a development plan before it is adopted and the Department may cause a public local enquiry to be held by the Planning Appeals Commission. The Department, however, is not bound by any report of the Planning Appeals Commission and may by order adopt the plan, with or without modifications, or reject it. Following the 1991 Order, the Department must have regard to the development plan and any other material consideration when dealing with applications for planning permission.

8.3 Planning control and procedures

Planning permission is required for all 'development' and this generally has the same meaning as under English planning legislation. As in England, the 1991 Order goes into some detail as to what does or does not constitute development. In case of doubt, an application can be made to the Department of the Environment for a determination as to whether or not the proposal constitutes development. One major difference however is that, unlike the position in England (where planning permission is not required), in Northern Ireland where planning permission is granted for a limited period to change the use of property, a further permission is required to resume the original use of the property. It should also be noted that Northern Ireland has its own 'use classes' legislation, the Planning (Use Classes) Order (Northern Ireland) 1989, although the classifications are similar to those in England.

8.3.1 If planning permission is required, the application is made to the Department together with the appropriate fee. The applicant himself need not have an interest or estate in the property, but he must give notice of the application to all those who do have such an interest or estate. The application can be for outline planning permission, whereby the applicant seeks permission for the proposal in principle, or for full permission in which case the application sets out the proposal in detail. In the case of major planning applications the Department may require a public local enquiry to be held by the Planning Appeals Commission. In such event the Department is obliged to take into account the report of the Planning Appeals Commission but is not bound by it.

8.3.2 The Department can grant the permission with or without conditions or refuse the application. The Department also has the power, having regard to any development plan and to any other material considerations, to revoke or modify any permission granted, to order discontinuance of any use of land, or to impose conditions on a use and to require any buildings or works to be altered or removed. Persons affected are entitled to appear before and be heard by the Planning Appeals Commission. In the event of the Department refusing an application for planning permission or granting it subject to conditions, the applicant may appeal to the Planning Appeals Commission within six months from the date of notification of the decision although the Commission has the discretion to allow an appeal outside this period. Also, if no decision is given within two months, the applicant may treat this as a deemed refusal and appeal to the Planning Appeals Commission, the decision of which is only subject to appeal to the Court of Appeal or judicial review on a point of law.

8.3.3 As in England, unless the permission expressly states that it is personal to the applicant, planning permission attaches to the land. The timescales for implementing planning permissions and obtaining approval of 'reserved matters' following grant of an outline permission are similar to those in England.

8.3.4 There are certain time limits for enforcement of breaches of planning control. In the case of a failure to comply with any condition or limitation relating to mining operations, enforcement action can only be taken within the period of four years from the date on which the failure came to the knowledge of the Department. Where building, engineering, mining or other operations are carried out without planning permission, or there is a failure to comply with any condition or limitation relating to the carrying out of such operations (excluding mining operations) or changing the use of any building to use as a single dwelling house, or failure to comply with a condition which prohibits or has the effect of preventing a change of use of a building to use as a single dwelling house, enforcement action can generally only be taken within the period of four years from the date of the breach. There are no time limits on enforcement for certain breaches of planning control, eg, there is no time limit in the case of a change of use without planning permission from office use to retail use or vice versa, or in respect of a breach of the planning legislation affecting 'listed' buildings (those listed as being of special historic or architectural interest). Enforcement is by means of enforcement notices issued by the Department and an appeal can be made to the Planning Appeals Commission. The Commission is obliged to notify the district council and to take into account any representations. The Commission can quash the enforcement notice, vary its terms or uphold it, and may grant permission for the development to which the enforcement notice relates or discharge any condition or limitation subject to which planning permission was granted. Failure to comply with an enforcement notice can result in a fine. If any steps required to be taken by the enforcement notice are not taken within the time stipulated (other than in the case of discontinuance of a use of land), a person authorised in writing by the Department may enter upon the land and take such steps and recover from the owner expenses reasonably incurred by it. For example, in the case of a building erected without planning permission the Department can enter and demolish it.

8.4 Building standards, control and supervision

8.4.1 When applying for planning permission, the applicant will generally also have to obtain building regulations approval from the district council. As in England, the building regulations legislation in Northern Ireland deals with the design and construction of buildings and the provision of services, fittings and equipment. In the event of a breach of the building regulations the district council for the area may serve a contravention notice on the owner requiring him to pull down or remove the work or, if he elects and the council agrees, to effect such alterations or additions to the work as may be necessary to make the work comply with the requirements of the building regulations. There are different time limits and provisions in relation to the enforcement of breaches of the building regulations. A contravention notice cannot be served after the expiry of 18 months from the date of completion of the work in question but this provision does not affect the right of a district council, the Attorney General or any other person to apply for an injunction for the removal or alteration of any work on the ground that it contravenes any building regulations. Any person aggrieved by a contravention notice served on him has a right of appeal to the Department of the Environment.

8.4.2 Under the Disability Discrimination Act and the Disability Discrimination (Employment) Regulations (NI) 1996 employers have in certain circumstances a duty to make reasonable adjustments to properties if there is a physical feature of that property which causes substantial disadvantage to an employee.

8.5 Compulsory purchase and compensation

There are similar legislative provisions in Northern Ireland to those in England in relation to the powers of the Department of the Environment and government bodies to compulsorily acquire land for a variety of public purposes and for the payment of compensation to affected persons. It is also not uncommon in Northern Ireland for the Department of the Environment to take the requisite steps to compulsorily acquire land required by a developer for a town centre development scheme.

8.6 Protection of buildings of special interest

There is similar legislation in Northern Ireland (contained in the 1991 Planning Order) to that in England in relation to the protection of buildings of special interest, conservation orders and trees, and such matters are the responsibility of the Department of the Environment.

9 ENVIRONMENTAL MATTERS

A combination of increased public awareness, high profile media attention and European intervention has, in recent years, resulted in the increasing importance of environmental issues. Common law liabilities for pollution have in Northern Ireland generally followed those of England and Wales, eg nuisance, the case of *Rylands v Fletcher* and negligence. However, Northern Ireland has for a number of years markedly lagged behind the rest of the United Kingdom in the implementation of environmental legislation, often relying on somewhat antiquated legislation. However, draft legislation is currently being implemented which will redress this imbalance to a large degree. The proposal for a draft Waste and Contaminated Land (Northern Ireland) Order enacts provisions broadly similar to those operative in the remainder of the United Kingdom under the Control of Pollution (Amendment) Act 1989, the Environmental Protection Act 1990 and the Environment Act 1995. The proposal for a draft Industrial Pollution Control (Northern Ireland) Order makes provision for a new system to control pollution from industrial plant processors in Northern Ireland broadly similar to that operating in the rest of the United Kingdom by virtue of Part I of the Environmental Protection Act 1990, as amended by the Environment Act 1995. From 1 April 1996, the Environment and Heritage Service was established as an executive agency within the Department of the Environment. It is the leading body in the implementation of the government's environmental policy in Northern Ireland and principal enforcing authority of environmental protection legislation in Northern Ireland. The regulatory responsibilities of the agency in this area are expected to increase in the future following the introduction of this new legislation.

9.1 Protection against atmospheric and noise pollution

9.1.1 The Clean Air (Northern Ireland) Order 1981 is the principal legislation controlling and monitoring emissions of dark smoke, smoke, dust, grit and fumes from both industrial and domestic sources. It is enforced by Northern Ireland's 26 district councils. Emissions from the most polluting industrial and commercial activities are currently (at the time of writing) regulated by the Alkali & c Works Regulation Act 1906 as amended. This Act requires industries with the greatest potential for air pollution to employ the 'best practicable means' for controlling emissions. The draft Industrial Pollution Control (Northern Ireland) Order creates a three-tier system of industrial pollution control to be administered by two enforcing authorities, namely the Environment and Heritage Service and the district councils. The Order provides the statutory basis for compliance with the EC Air Framework Directive (84/360/EEC) and the proposed Directive on Integrated Pollution Prevention and Control (IPPC) and will bring Northern Ireland standards on industrial pollution control into line with those now governing industrial processes in the rest of the United Kingdom whilst catering for Northern Ireland's unique industrial processes.

9.1.2 The common law remedy of nuisance has generally been regarded as limited as a means to prevent noise pollution. Due to this fact Parliament created a statutory nuisance. This is contained in Part III of the Pollution Control and Local Government (Northern Ireland) Order 1978. For the most part it remains within the remit of local government, and more specifically, the Environmental Health Departments within district councils. The Department of Environment does however deal with appeals from the decisions of councils and has power under the Order to issue and approve codes of practice for minimising noise.

9.2 Water pollution

9.2.1 Under the Water Act (Northern Ireland) 1972 (as amended) the Department of the Environment is responsible for the conservation of water resources in Northern Ireland and for promoting the cleanliness of water in waterways and underground strata (with the advice of the Water Council established under s 4 of the Act). The Act allows for two principal regulatory mechanisms. The first of these is a discharge consent system, which regulates the discharge of trade and sewage effluent and any other polluting matter into such waters. It is an offence to discharge polluting substances without such a consent. The second is the imposition of statutory water quality standards. There is also a general pollution offence which applies when pollution is caused to such waters by the discharge or deposit of polluting matter – whether knowingly or otherwise. It is, however, a defence to proceedings if it can be established that all reasonable care has been exercised to prevent any such discharge. The Act further confers on the Department a wide variety of preventive and administrative powers designed to facilitate the execution of its functions (eg works to remedy or mitigate pollution; the recovery of expenses from the person in default; powers of entry and obtaining and removing samples).

9.2.2 The Water Executive of the Department of the Environment is responsible under the Water and Sewage Services (Northern Ireland) Order 1973 (as amended) for the supply of water throughout Northern Ireland and also the provision and maintenance of sewers and sewage services. Legal proceedings under the Water Act (Northern Ireland) 1972 may only be instituted by the Department of Environment or by, or with the consent of, the Attorney General. Penalties for water pollution offences were recently raised from £2,000 to £20,000. Clean-up costs and compensation for damages may also be imposed.

9.3 Waste storage and disposal

9.3.1 The Environment and Heritage Service within the Department of the Environment will take over the responsibility for the legislative regime for waste management. It is also the body to which district councils submit waste disposal plans and the appellate body for licensing decisions taken by the councils on waste disposal site licences. The 1978 Order referred to is the relevant legislation currently applicable to most waste collection and removal and the licensing and execution of its final disposal. 'Special waste' (eg inflammable substances and substances likely to cause death or serious damage on ingestion, inhalation, skin or eye contact) is dealt with separately under the Pollution Control (Special Waste) Regulations (Northern Ireland) 1981.

9.3.2 District councils are the designated authorities for the collection and disposal of waste and for the licensing of private waste disposal sites and facilities. The Department of the Environment has supervisory jurisdiction. It is an offence to dispose of 'controlled waste' on any land except pursuant to a licence. Examples of controlled waste are scrap metals, effluent or other unwanted surplus substances arising from the application of any process, and any substance or article which requires to be disposed of as being broken, worn out, contaminated or otherwise spoiled. Under the draft Waste and Contaminated Land (Northern Ireland) Order, waste disposal licensing is dealt with by the Department of Environment. The purpose of this legislation is to improve standards in the management and disposal of controlled waste. It also makes provision with respect to land contaminated by pollution. A key element of the new Order is the introduction of a duty of care on all concerned in producing, handling and disposal of waste. This imposes a new level of responsibility for ensuring that waste is not illegally managed. Faced with new environmental liabilities and the possibility of penalties arising from any failure to exercise proper care, companies will need to look more closely at the track record competence of those waste management operators acting on their behalf.

9.3.3 Under the 1978 Act, if controlled waste is deposited on land in contravention of the Act, the district council may serve a notice on the occupier of the land in question requiring him either to remove the waste within a specified period or take specified action to eliminate or reduce the consequences of the deposit. Councils may also take 'emergency' action to remove deposited waste contrary to the Act to prevent danger to public health. Costs in so doing may be recovered from the occupier of the land.

9.4 Contaminated land

Contaminated land is dealt with by the draft Waste and Contaminated Land (Northern Ireland) Order which follows provisions implemented in the remainder of the United Kingdom under the Environment Act 1995. It defines contaminated land as land in such a condition that significant harm is being caused or there is a significant possibility of such harm being caused, or pollution of waterways or underground strata is being, or is likely to be, caused.

Contaminated land will be the responsibility of the district councils, though the Department of the Environment is given responsibility for 'special sites' as defined in the new Order (contaminated land designated as such by the Department). Councils will be required to inspect their district for contaminated land and if such an area is identified the council must notify the Department of the Environment, the owner of the land, the occupier of the land and any other person deemed appropriate. A remediation notice can then be served specifying action to be taken and a time in which to do so. It is an offence not to comply with a remediation notice and the enforcing authorities can carry out remediation themselves if necessary to prevent imminent danger or serious harm or pollution of waterways or underground strata. Costs may be recovered from the polluter and, failing this, from the present owner or occupier. A local register of remediation notices is to be kept by the enforcing authorities.

9.5 Environmental impact assessments

The relevant legislation is the Planning (Assessment of Environmental Effects) Regulations (Northern Ireland) 1989. An environmental assessment is carried out by a state authority on the basis of the environmental information generated by the assessment process (made up of the promoter's (the developer's) environmental statement and additional environmental information contributed by expert state agencies, non-governmental organisations and the general public).

10 DEVELOPMENT

The comments in the English chapter generally apply equally to Northern Ireland in relation to the various types of development project structures and vehicles and the roles, appointments and duties of contractors and professionals. Defects insurance is not common in Northern Ireland but as in England major tenants, buyers and funders of newly constructed properties would normally require collateral warranties to be given to them by the building contractor and the professional team or would negotiate an obligation on the part of the landlord/developer to enforce its rights against the contractor and the professionals in respect of defects, eg for the benefit of the tenants (possibly limited to a period of time and/or subject to the tenants underwriting the costs of legal proceedings). Such warranties or obligations to enforce rights are required by buyers and others, as, not having themselves appointed the contractor or the professionals, they have under the principles of privity of contract generally no right to claim damages on a contract to which they were not a party. There are certain exceptions to this general rule, one of these being to the effect that where the parties to a contract know or envisage that the property may be transferred, an original party to the contract may in certain circumstances be treated in law as having entered into that contract for the benefit of all persons having or acquiring an interest in that property. Notwithstanding this exception, collateral warranties or obligations to enforce rights are and continue to be sought by buyers, tenants and others.

11 TAXES

Generally the tax legislation of the English Parliament also applies equally to Northern Ireland. There is, however, no concept of uniform business rate for commercial properties or council tax for residential properties in Northern Ireland where rates are assessed on properties (both residential and commercial) by the Department of the Environment in association with the district councils. Rates bills in Northern Ireland are made up of two elements – a district rate to meet the cost of local services and a regional rate to cover the costs of services such as education, roads, housing, social services, water and sewerage. The regional rate is uniform throughout Northern Ireland whereas the district rate varies from district to district. In 1996 there was a general revaluation of all non-domestic properties in Northern Ireland for rating purposes. This was the first general revaluation for 20 years, and took effect on 1 April 1997. This revaluation does not result in an increase in revenue but sought to redistribute the burden among the various types and locations of occupiers to reflect current property values. One of the major effects of this revaluation is a shift in the burden of rates onto the retail and office sectors. On average retail rates are up by 30 per cent and office rates up by 15 per cent but this covers a very wide range of increases. For example, prime retail locations generally face an increase of 100–150 per cent. In the office sector the revaluation generally results in a neutral increase for modern city centre offices, but rates for refurbished office buildings and offices converted from dwellings are increasing by up to 50 per cent. The revaluation results in various decreases for certain types of properties, eg warehouses, licensed premises, schools and hospitals. It should be noted however that whilst the revaluation has resulted in significant increases in rates in certain sectors, rates and also commercial rents in Northern Ireland generally remain considerably lower than those for comparable properties in England. In Northern Ireland an owner of residential property can claim relief from payment of rates if the property is vacant but there are no hard and fast rules in Northern Ireland (as there are in England) in relation to claiming relief from rates for commercial premises. Essentially each case is treated on its own merits but the general proposition is that relief can be obtained for a commercial property which can be separately occupied. For example, the owner of a vacant single occupancy building (such as an industrial warehouse or other type of property intended for single as opposed to multiple occupation) can claim relief from rates. On the other hand, to take the example of an office building let in suites to various occupiers, the owner of the building would not be able to claim rate relief for a vacant floor as it has a common access (communal lift or staircases) and is accordingly not capable of separate occupation. Occupiers engaged in manufacturing in Northern Ireland enjoy a unique position within the United Kingdom in that property occupied for manufacturing purposes is exempt from rates.

12 GRANTS AND INCENTIVES

There are a number of substantial types of grants and incentives available in Northern Ireland. As in England further types of assistance are available from the European Union.

12.1 Subsidies, grants and loans

Internationally mobile projects locating in Northern Ireland can apply for cash grants from the Industrial Development Board of up to 50 per cent of the cost of new buildings and machinery and equipment. Grants can also be awarded covering up to 100 per cent of rent costs for up to five years and as commented in section 11, manufacturing properties are not liable to pay any rates. Other incentives available are:

(a) grants towards start-up costs (employment grants related to the number of newly created jobs);
(b) interest relief grants (grants to reduce interest on loans from non-government sources);
(c) company development programmes (up to 50 per cent of total net training and development costs including wage costs, fees and travel);
(d) management incentive grants to attract top quality management, marketing development grants to assist companies in developing a strategic approach to marketing planning and implementation; and
(e) incentives towards research and development programmes.

Government loans may be considered in certain circumstances and can include an interest-free period, and an investment in the share capital of a company may be possible to suit the needs of a particular project. Industrial development grants may be available for viable light and general manufacturing facilities up to 930 square metres in size. Conservation grants are available on a discretionary basis from the Department of the Environment for the development of external features of older buildings in designated conservation areas. The grant is up to 20 per cent of the cost of the external works and is generally not available for modern materials such as PVC windows.

12.2 Tax allowances and reliefs

In addition to industrial de-rating (manufacturing properties paying no rates), depreciation allowances are also available for capital expenditure on machinery and equipment, and construction costs of industrial buildings, including the total value of IDB grant (see 12.1) received (up to 45 per cent), can be written off at a rate of 25 per cent per year on a reducing balance basis for machinery and equipment and four per cent per year on a straight line basis for buildings.

12.3 Other public schemes and incentives

Various types of assistance are available from the International Fund for Ireland including grant aid for investment in new tourism amenities. The fund has an urban development programme aimed at stimulating viable economic activity in the commercial core of towns and villages in Northern Ireland. This programme is aimed at refurbishing property which is in poor or derelict condition and where commercial activity is proposed, and the amount of the grant can be up to £100,000.

13 COMPANIES AND BUSINESS ENTITIES

The comments contained in the English chapter generally apply to Northern Ireland although Northern Ireland has its own company and partnership legislation.

14 INTERNATIONAL

The comments contained in the English chapter generally apply equally to Northern Ireland. A 'foreign' company having a place of business in Northern Ireland must register at the Northern Ireland companies registry and in this context English companies are treated as foreign corporate entities.

CHAPTER 13

Norway

L O Askheim and C Rødsæther

Klikborg Rein, Oslo

CONTENTS

1 OWNERSHIP OF LAND 423
2 OTHER INTERESTS IN LAND 425
3 TITLE TO LAND 428
4 TRANSACTIONS IN LAND 430
5 LEASES AND OTHER RIGHTS OF OCCUPATION 432
6 FINANCE AND OTHER INVESTMENT SOURCES 434
7 FORMS OF SECURITY 436
8 PLANNING AND BUILDING REGULATION 437
9 ENVIRONMENTAL MATTERS 440
10 DEVELOPMENT 443
11 TAXES 446
12 GRANTS AND INCENTIVES 448
13 COMPANIES AND BUSINESS ENTITIES 450
14 INTERNATIONAL 452

CHAPTER 13

Norway

1 OWNERSHIP OF LAND

In Norway there is a single legal system for real property. This chapter deals only with mainland Norway, and therefore excludes Spitzbergen and other Norwegian possessions in the Arctic and Antarctica. Norway does not have a codified system of law; the most important sources of law comprise statutes and precedents, deriving from the decisions of the higher courts such as the Supreme Court (*Høyesterett*). The principal statute relating to property law is the Land Registration Act 1935 (*Tinglysingsloven*). The main form of land ownership is absolute ownership.

1.1 Types of tenure

1.1.1 Absolute ownership

Absolute ownership (*eiendomsrett*) is the prevailing form of ownership of land. It carries with it a right to own, occupy and dispose of the land and any buildings on the land. Anything which is fixed or annexed to the land or buildings is treated as part of the land. However, there is not necessarily a link between ownership of the land upon which a building is constructed and ownership of the building itself. The building may be owned by someone other than the landowner, who might have granted him a lease with a right to build (see 2.1). Even the act of building illegally on land by a third party does not transfer ownership of the building to the landowner. Absolute ownership carries with it the right to the soil below and the airspace above, but these rights do not extend very far. For example, the owner is not protected against tunnelling below his property, provided that the present and foreseeable uses of the property are not adversely affected, or against air traffic over the property. With respect to mines and minerals, ownership only gives exclusive rights to substances such as sand, clay and rock. Valuable minerals such as metal ores may be searched for and developed by anyone, and the owner is only entitled to a royalty of 0.1 per cent of the gross value of the substances produced, as well as compensation for any topside areas used for developing the mine.

1.1.2 Leasehold

The principal form of land tenure is absolute ownership. Long leases granted at a premium or for a single capital payment in advance, in the Anglo-American tradition, are not used in practice, but there is no legal prohibition against these. Long-term or short-term leases at a market rent are, however, commonly used. A lease may be granted where a right less than absolute ownership of a property is intended, where the holder's interest is limited to a period of time, and possibly to a part of the property, for a rent payable at specified intervals. The lease or tenancy will grant the holder of the lease the exclusive right to use and occupy the property and may be fully transferable. It is quite normal for a business to take property on lease and this is not seen as an adverse reflection on its creditworthiness. The terms on which leases are granted and other aspects of leases are dealt with more fully in section 5.

1.1.3 Joint ownership

Land can be owned jointly by several persons and/or companies as co-owners (*sameie*) under the 1965 Co-ownership Act (*Sameieloven*), where the co-owners will own shares in the entire property rather than each owner owning a separate part of it. There are no restrictions on the number of potential co-owners. Where several individuals own property, the rights and obligations related to the property are shared between them proportionately, in accordance with the respective owners' share of the property. The Act contains provisions on the use of the property, how decisions are made, how the property is to be maintained, the share of profits and costs, the right to transfer shares of the property and the winding up of the joint ownership.

1.1.4 Condominia

Under the provisions of an Act of 1983 (*Eierseksjonsloven*), it is possible to divide a building into several parts (*seksjoner*). The parties hold the land and the building as co-owners, although each owner maintains an exclusive right of use of his part of the building. All the co-owners retain rights of access to the common parts such as hallways and gardens.

1.1.5 Lesser rights

It is possible to create lesser rights of exclusive occupation falling short of full ownership. These include building rights and other rights, such as the right to park cars or to have access across land, and are treated as servitudes. Comment is made on these at 2.1 dealing with other interests in land. These other interests do not give a full or exclusive right of use or occupation and also include interests such as mortgages, restrictive covenants and rent charges.

1.2 Legal and beneficial ownership

Norwegian law has not adopted the Anglo-American doctrine of trust. Under some circumstances the true or beneficial owner of the property might not be the same person or entity as the registered owner, eg due to the desire of the true owner to be anonymous, or due to a failure to register a bill of sale evidencing the transfer of ownership (see 3.3). However, such arrangements are rare, and generally discouraged. They are also inherently insecure, as the interest of the true owner may be lost if the registered owner refuses to cooperate, or makes dispositions over the property in favour of third parties acting in good faith (see 2.9 and 2.10). Depending on the circumstances, the interest of the true owner might also be lost against the creditors of the registered owner, particularly in bankruptcy proceedings.

1.3 Restrictions on ownership and dealings

1.3.1 Any person, including minors and those suffering from mental incapacity, or any legal entity (including companies and bodies such as associations and co-operatives) may own land. Most acquisitions of property in Norway are subject to the Concession Act 1974 or the Business Acquisition Act 1994. Under the 1974 Act, all property acquisitions require prior approval from the authorities, unless specific statutory provisions state otherwise. The main exceptions include the acquisition of small residential property (although this is limited to one per buyer per local authority and excludes property located in designated zones in the most popular holiday resorts); land and buildings not exceeding 5,000 square metres; and transactions between members of the same family.

1.3.2 If a transaction requires approval under the 1974 Act, in some circumstances the government, and, more rarely, the local municipality, will have a right of pre-emption (see also 9.4.) The 1994 Business Acquisition Act establishes a notification procedure for the sale of businesses, including corporate entities, over a certain size. Depending on the circumstances, the Ministry of Industry may make enquiries, and may require a licence to be obtained for the acquisition. Both Acts also apply to indirect sales, ie sales of shares in property and/or business owning companies.

1.3.3 In principle land is freely disposable, subject to the restrictions contained in the constitution of any landowning entity, and any other restrictions binding on the owner. The exact limits will have to be verified on an individual basis. Special entities such as charities and local authorities are not generally prevented from disposing of land they own.

1.4 Adverse possession

Title can be acquired by acquisitive prescription (*Hevd*) by continuous occupation for over 20 years in good faith. In practical terms, entire properties are rarely acquired by this method, but minor changes of borders between properties may quite commonly occur in this way.

2 OTHER INTERESTS IN LAND

There are various interests in land which confer rights less than absolute ownership or possession. These may be public or private. The most common of these are positive servitudes (*positive servitutter*), similar to the common law concepts of easements and profits à prendre, and restrictive covenants (*negative servitutter*), mortgages, rent charges (*grunnbyrder*) and options.

2.1 Servitudes, usufruct and building rights

2.1.1 Norwegian law recognises several limited rights to property, eg the right to use or the right to enjoy the produce of land belonging to another.

Such rights will in most cases be transferable and registrable, and if registered, will be enforceable against subsequent owners, (see 2.9 and 2.10). Examples of servitudes include rights of access, the right to run cables and powerlines, and the right to hunt or fish and to fell timber. Servitudes are regulated by the Servitudes Act 1965 (*Servituttloven*). Most servitudes may be granted for an indefinite period of time. Agricultural tenancies (*forpaktning*) are governed by a separate Act of 1965; the tenant is generally entitled to seed and harvest crops, but is obliged to re-deliver the property substantially unchanged.

2.1.2 Building rights are governed by the Building Rights Act 1975 (*Tomtefesteloven*), and are commonly used for residential and recreational property; they enable a third party to construct buildings on land belonging to an absolute owner. The third party will then own the building. The Building Rights Act contains complex provisions about extension of the period, and the disposal of the building at the end of the period. Most such arrangements should be viewed from the owner's side as generating a continuous stream of income rather than a lump sum payment, and from the builder's as a way of financing the land.

2.2 Restrictions on use and other restrictions

Absolute owners may agree to enter into restrictions on the use of one piece of land (*negative servitutter*), to protect the ownership of another piece of land, and, subject to certain conditions, these restrictions will be enforceable by and between successive owners provided they have been registered. These rights are freely negotiated between adjoining owners and can only be removed by agreement, or in extreme cases, by compulsory extinction at the request of the owner, or by local authorities. Public law restrictions under planning and other legislation are commented on in section 8.

2.3 Private mortgages and charges

Monetary liabilities can be secured on land in a number of ways. The procedure and regulations governing the creation of private mortgages are dealt with in section 7. The courts can make charging orders to secure judgment debts. The seller of a property will have an unregistered lien against the buyer for the unpaid purchase price, but this lien will lapse upon the buyer registering the bill of sale (*skjøte*) to be given to him by the seller.

2.4 Contracts and options

When an owner of land contracts to sell the land, but the sale has not yet been completed, the purchase contract will be considered an interest in the land. Similarly, options to purchase and pre-emption rights will also be considered as interests in land. All of these rights may be registered as an interest in the property. They will be enforceable against the owner even if not registered; the main purpose of registration is to secure priority against subsequent buyers, mortgagees or holders of other interests in the property (see 2.9 and 2.10).

2.5 Public and municipal charges

There are a number of financial charges imposed to protect the rights of various government bodies to recover payment for statutory works such as water and drainage charges and waste disposal fees. These are secured by a first charge on the property (*legalpant*) without any requirement for registration.

2.6 Other interests

2.6.1 Rent charges

Rent charges (*grunnbyrder*) grant the right to periodic payments secured on property but are now rarely used. Service charges (*fellesutgifter*), ie payments made for the provision of communal facilities in an apartment block, should be seen as an interest in land, and will outrank mortgages registered by the individual owners. They will also bind any subsequent owner even if not registered.

2.6.2 Public access rights

Where land is not used for development or agricultural purposes, the public has a general right of access which cannot be defeated by the landowner.

2.7 Liabilities attaching to land

Liabilities arising out of land may attach either to the owner or occupier or to both. There may be liability for injury and damage to visitors or their goods under various statutes including the 1961 Neighbours Act (*Naboloven*), or for dangerous escapes in accordance with the no-fault doctrine of strict liability (*ulovfestet objektivt ansvar*); in nuisance for the unreasonable use of land to the prejudice of an adjoining owner and for negligent injury or damage to passers-by and their goods. There are also statutory liabilities for the repair of dangerous structures and for preserving buildings which are listed as being of historic or architectural interest, as well as those to protect employees under statute. Certain public liabilities are automatically secured on a property for the payment of certain charges such as property tax, municipal water and sewage charges.

2.8 Legal and equitable interests

The Anglo-American distinction between legal and equitable interests is not recognised in Norwegian law.

2.9 Protection of interests

Most interests can be enforced against the grantor even if they have not been registered. However, if the interest is not registered, there is no protection against subsequent buyers (including subsequent mortgagees) unless the subsequent buyer knew about the prior right (or should have known about it), or against creditors, whether acting singly or in a bankruptcy. Interests which do not require protection by registration are limited, but include rights acquired through adverse possession (see 1.4), as well as ordinary leases which can be terminated, where the tenant is in possession. The interests which do require protection are protected by the holder of the right by the registration of a document executed by the registered owner giving details of the right created; the procedure is dealt with in more detail in section 3.

2.10 Priority of interests

Priority between interests in land will depend generally on the date of registration, not the date of creation of the interest, although those public liabilities secured on the property without registration will always take priority. The principal exception is that an older, unregistered right will take priority over a more recent registered right if the holder of the more recent right knew (or should have known) about the older right.

3 TITLE TO LAND

3.1 Proof of title

The only way to perfect title to land (with the exception of the greater part of the county of Finnmark, where the land is owned by the government but not covered by the registration system), is by registration at the local land registry office where the property is located. Every new transfer or sale of freehold land will require registration. Leases where the tenant remains in possession and rights acquired by adverse possession do not generally need an entry to protect them (see 2.9). All other interests require some form of protection in the registration book in order to bind subsequent interests created by the registered owner (see 3.2.2). The land registers are open for inspection by the public, and the public may request transcripts (*pantattest*). The data in land registry offices have recently been transferred onto a computer-based system, and a central copy database can be accessed on-line.

3.2 Land registers

In rural areas, the land registry office will be kept by the local court, whereas in most urban areas a separate land registry office exists.

3.2.1 Plans

Every property is identified by the municipality it is located in, and two numbers: *gårdsnummer* or *gnr* and *bruksnummer* or *bnr.* Condominia in a building are identified by *seksjonsnummer* or *snr* in addition to *gnr* and *bnr*. It is important to realise that a property sold as a single property, may actually contain several *gnr* and *bnr*, eg a farm where some of the fields may have separate numbers. When an existing property is subdivided resulting in the creation of separate new freeholds, a special map (*delingsforretning*) must be produced by the local authorities, which will be entered in the records of the properties affected. Most properties will be identified by some form of plan or plans, but the quality is variable, especially in rural areas, where only old text descriptions of borders may be available.

3.2.2 Content

Each land register is divided into two separate registers: a daily journal (*dagboken*), where all documents filed for registration are noted when received, and a registration book (*grunnboken*), which contains all the records of the various properties. Entry in the registration book will be made once the documentation has been checked and found to be in order. For each property a separate record is kept, where a note of the registered owner is made; sections of a building are also given their own individual record sheets and the various charges, mortgages and interests, if any, attaching to the property in question are identified separately. The local land registry may at its discretion decide to create a separate record sheet (with *gnr* and *bnr*) for an interest in land, which serves a useful purpose when an interest has become subject to further secondary interests. If no separate record sheet is made, the interest and any interests carved out of it will be recorded on the same record sheet as the property in question. It is important to recognise that only an abstract of the registered document will be entered in the registration book. To find details of a particular right or transaction, it may be necessary to go to the document itself, which will be kept in a general filing system.

3.2.3 Errors

If it is established that an error has been made in the register, there are provisions for compensation and/or rectification of the registers of title, subject to certain restrictions.

3.3 Passing of title

In the case of all transfers of land, it is necessary for a bill of sale (*skjøte*) in the prescribed form to be filed at the local land registry. The bill must be executed (or approved) by the registered owner, and identify the new owner. The bill serves as confirmation from the seller that the buyer has performed his obligations, such as paying the purchase price, and that the purchase is no longer subject to conditions. (See 4.1 for protection pending registration.) Title will usually be deemed to have passed at the time of filing, even though the registration may be completed at a later date, because most land registry offices have a backlog of up to 14 days.

4 TRANSACTIONS IN LAND

The most common transactions in land are the sale and purchase of a freehold, the grant or assignment of a lease, and the creation of a mortgage to secure a loan or other liability.

4.1 Procedures

4.1.1 It is usual for a sale to go through several stages but the details will vary, and there is no fixed pattern as to the time scale. Typically the process will take between two and six weeks. The first stage will be the negotiation of a contract before which certain preliminary investigations and enquiries will be undertaken. At this stage, the buyer will make enquiries concerning the property and the title, and searches will be made with the local authority to check whether there are any local charges registered against the property and/or whether any local planning restrictions are in force. The seller will usually also have made available sketches, descriptions (*salgsoppgave*) and a report with an assessment of the market value (*takst*) from a surveyor (*takstmann*). During this period the buyer will undertake any survey, investigate environmental issues and ascertain whether there is any risk of expropriation or of the exercise of pre-emption rights (see 9.4), and negotiate any offer of finance. Once the buyer has been satisfied on the above points, he will enter into a binding contract, called the purchase contract.

4.1.2 In many cases, especially in respect of residential property, the property is marketed for sale by an estate agent, who solicits bids. Bids will be binding upon the bidder. After one or more bid rounds (the first usually open, the second possibly closed, where details of the bids are not available to the other bidders), a bid is accepted. A binding contract will then exist, but a purchase contract will be entered into shortly thereafter, containing more details.

4.1.3 The buyer may protect the purchase contract by registering it with the land registry, but this requires the consent of the seller, and is not usually done. The contract will in any event rank after all interests registered before it. There is no need for notarisation of any transaction and in most transactions the whole matter is handled by the parties and/or their estate agents. After the exchange of the purchase price, the bill of sale (*skjøte*) is issued by the seller to the buyer and must be registered at the local land registry (see 3.3).

4.2 Contract terms

4.2.1 Although the Sale of Property Act 1992 (*Avhendingsloven*) now regulates the sale of property, its provisions are not mandatory (except for consumer contracts) and only serve to set out the contract terms. The contract will usually contain few warranties, other than those as to title. The most usual remedies for breach of warranty are price reduction (covering the diminution in value of the property) and damages (which in addition to the reduction in value of the property, could also include other losses). The principle of 'buyer beware' does apply to a certain extent, eg in respect of defects not known to the seller. The contract will usually stipulate the payment of a deposit which in many areas is commonly 10 per cent of the purchase price. If the transaction is not completed due to the buyer's fault, the deposit serves as security for the seller's claim for compensation for his losses, if any. The contract specifies the timetable and the date of completion. It will also commonly specify the arrangements for payment of interest, should there be a delay in completion. Possession will not usually be given until completion. In the period between the signing of the purchase contract and completion, the seller must take steps to protect the property against damage and deterioration. Risk passes on completion, ie on payment of the balance of the purchase price and the issue of the bill of sale. Insurance before completion will be a matter for the seller, and be at his own risk.

4.2.2 If either party defaults, the other party can apply to the courts for an order for specific performance compelling the defaulting party to complete, or it may terminate the contract and claim compensation. If the buyer is in default of his payment obligations, the seller can usually charge interest and, in addition, may claim compensation for any re-sale of the property at a loss.

4.3 Formalities

A contract for sale of land or a lease does not have to be in writing, but both parties have the right to request it to be formalised. As for the creation of lesser rights, the need for a written contract will vary between different types of contract. However, since a written contract is a prerequisite for registration, most interests will be evidenced in writing, and signed by both parties or their agents. If a written contract is drawn up, it should contain all material terms, but a party will not be prevented from presenting evidence about the negotiations or any oral side agreement.

4.4 Fees, costs and taxes

4.4.1 On a sale of land the seller will pay the commission to his agent, and his own legal costs, if any. The buyer will pay his legal costs, stamp duty and the land registry fees. The agent's commission will vary according to the agent, the type and value of the property and the strength of the market. Fees commonly range between one and two per cent of the sale price. Sometimes the buyer will instruct an agent to find him a property, in which case the buyer will also pay the agent a commission, or share the commission owed to the seller's agent. Agents' commissions are negotiated on a contingency basis and will usually be payable if a binding contract is entered into, but are not dependent on the sale being completed. The custom is to use sole agents, and for the agent to receive his commission even where he did not introduce the buyer.

4.4.2 Lawyers are usually not involved in ordinary property transactions. Their fees are based on the usual principles for calculating lawyers' fees, and will thus primarily be based on time used.

4.4.3 Stamp duty is charged at 2.5 per cent of the purchase price, but not in respect of mortgages.

4.4.4 Land registry fees are charged as a flat fee. The fee currently is NOK757 in respect of a bill of sale and NOK1,010 in respect of a mortgage.

4.4.5 It will be seen that transaction costs in Norway are generally lower than many other countries in Europe.

4.4.6 There is no value added tax (VAT) on estate agents' and lawyers' fees at present and currently no VAT on sales or rentals of property.

4.5 Professionals' roles

The negotiation of sales is usually conducted by estate agents. Estate agents are subject to statutory requirements and a licensing regime; the principal Act which applies to them is the Estate Agents Act 1984 (*Eiendomsmeglingsloven*). There is, though, no role for a notary or similar lawyer as there is in some other countries, and the land registry processes the registration of any transfer. Lawyers are not involved in most property transactions, and it is usual to confine the involvement of professionals to a minimum. The seller often engages a surveyor (*takstmann*) who prepares a report of the property and gives his assessment of its market value. This report is annexed to the documents made available to prospective buyers.

5 LEASES AND OTHER RIGHTS OF OCCUPATION

Norwegian law makes no distinction between tenancies and licences. All leases are seen as interests in land, are registrable interests and may be fixed or periodic. Leases of buildings (*husleie*), are governed by the Tenants Act 1939 (*Husleieloven*) which makes an important distinction between leases with a fixed period which will terminate on the expiry date, and leases with no fixed period which entitle the owner to terminate at any time, provided that he has reasonable grounds. There are statutory provisions which affect the expiry of the lease and these are dealt with in more detail at 5.3. There is no distinct market practice as to the period of a lease; it is all a question of the needs of the parties. However, with respect to office leases, it is fairly to usual to have a 5 + 5 or 10 + 10 year structure, with the second period being at the option of the tenant, or only as some sort of 'first right of refusal' on market terms at that point of time.

5.1 Rent and other terms

Most leases (whether commercial or residential) contain rent review provisions by which the rent is increased annually by reference to the consumer price index. Rent reviews are almost invariably in an upwards only direction, ensuring that the income from the premises cannot decrease. Retail premises are sometimes let on a combination of a fixed rent and a percentage of the income (or profit) generated by the retail unit. Rent is generally payable in advance, monthly (in the case of residential leases), quarterly or six monthly (in the case of commercial leases). Common provisions will relate to the extent to which the tenant may be allowed to alter the premises, assign and/or sublet, and will usually leave the tenant responsible for repairs and the cost of insurance. Where the tenant only takes a part of a building, it is common for the landlord to be responsible for the provision of services including the repair of the exterior of the structure and for the tenant to pay a service charge. The landlord will usually retain responsibility for insurance, with no direct contribution from the tenant. While a right to terminate the lease is sometimes agreed, most leases contain no break clauses. In the event of default by the tenant or on his becoming insolvent, nearly every lease will provide for the landlord to be able to terminate the lease and take the property back. There are some statutory restrictions on such a right, as the liquidator may have the right to assume the rights and obligations under the lease. Some landlords request a bank guarantee or deposit for lease payments, but this is a matter for negotiation. By law, any deposit cannot be for more than six months' rent. There is no mandatory lease form, although a number of standardised lease forms do exist. The parties are under no obligation to adopt any of these forms.

5.2 Privity of contract and estate

A lease may, depending on the circumstances, be assigned, in which case the new occupier will be the only party liable to the owner. This will, however, usually require the prior consent of the owner. On the other hand, a tenant may, subject to the approval of the landlord, enter into a sublease, in which case the head tenant is still liable to the landlord.

5.3 Rent control and security of tenure

Housing properties in some cities are subject to rent control, but this only covers pre-1940 apartment buildings. Tenants on leases with no fixed expiry date generally enjoy security of tenure as a lease with no fixed period entitles the owner to terminate at any time, provided that he has reasonable grounds. In practice, however, it is not easy for the owner to convince the courts that reasonable grounds exist and the notice will then be held invalid if the tenant challenges the termination in the courts. There is no minimum notice period which can be used to terminate any type of lease. Apart from the usual default grounds for possession, it will be difficult for the owner to recover leased premises in contravention of the stipulated terms, should he desire, eg to reconstruct or relet the entire building.

5.4 Other legislative restrictions

There are a number of legislative restrictions upon various types of leases and other interests. Many terms of residential leases are mandatory (as well as a number of business lease terms, although the impact is not as great), so the provisions of the Housing Lease Act 1939 cannot, eg, be contracted out of to the tenant's detriment.

5.5 Method of measurement

There are several systems for measuring leased premises. The main difference lies in the handling of exterior and interior walls. The gross internal method is the prevailing method of measurement most commonly used.

6 FINANCE AND OTHER INVESTMENT SOURCES

The Norwegian property market attracts a variety of financing and investment techniques, but the usual procedures are fairly simple. Property in Norway is a major investment but values are not very high by European standards. Finance is essentially provided either in the form of loan, or investment or equity finance.

6.1 Loan finance

The traditional sources of loan finance are the banks, savings banks and insurance companies, and property finance unions and companies. A company may also borrow money from its shareholders, and there are various ways to give them preferential treatment over ordinary shareholders, eg by giving them preference shares which give an earlier right to interest dividends, while allowing the preference shareholders to participate in the capital appreciation of the shares. Conventional loan finance as provided by the main financing institutions is usually for a fixed term, and will either provide for a 'bullet' repayment at the end of the term of the loan, or provide for staged repayments of capital during the term. The usual period for the length of the loan is 20 years. There is no legal maximum, and the issue of length is left to the parties to decide on a commercial basis. Interest will either be fixed, or calculated by reference to the bank's own base rate or the inter-bank market rate plus a margin, commonly between one and two per cent over the cost of the borrowing. There are no legal limitations (either maximum or minimum) on the duration of the interest period or other aspects of property loans. Interest is always paid gross. Such loans are almost invariably secured (see section 7).

6.2 Investment or equity finance

The sources of equity or investment finance are varied. The small company will be funded by its private shareholders who may be individuals or other companies or institutions. Quoted companies raise their investment funds on the Oslo Stock Exchange, or more rarely, on foreign stock exchanges. Various devices have been used to raise money on the markets for the purpose of investment in single properties. The most usual investment technique is to establish a limited partnership (*KS*) or general partnership (*ANS*), which are tax transparent structures, allowing the tax benefits to flow through to the investors.

6.3 Mezzanine or mixed funding

The prime lender will usually take the first security and lend up to, typically, 80 per cent (60 per cent if the prime lender is an insurance company) of the value of the property. If any further loans are made, they will naturally be at a higher risk, and there are lenders who will provide additional finance and take a return by way of a higher interest rate, and possibly a share in the equity in the property or project being financed. Some lenders will provide both prime and mezzanine finance. Primary lenders rarely require a share in the success of the project in order to lend.

6.4 Sale and lease-back

Companies who wish to realise their assets to release capital or who wish to finance a new project may negotiate a sale and lease-back by which they will sell the property to an investor, commonly an institution, which will then grant them a lease-back and obtain an income from the property. This is a common arrangement with new buildings and owner/occupiers who do not wish to take the assets onto their accounts or wish to use their capital for more active purposes in the business.

6.5 Tax leasing

Allowances for deductions against income and corporation tax exist for investment in plant and machinery and for certain commercial buildings. There are no special enterprise zones or other similar areas, but the depreciation allowance is higher in some provincial regions. With reduced tax allowances and reduced tax rates, leasing schemes have become less common, but it is still a usual funding technique for the user of a building to lease it from a tax payer who has tax which it can shelter by use of the allowances, and who will then receive a reduced rent to take into account the tax allowances available to the tax investor.

6.6 Other types of property finance

Property companies exist, which have a number of properties in their portfolio and which raise funds through a listing on the stock exchange. There are restrictions on the extent to which subscriptions can be invited from the public and the way they are advertised, similar to the restrictions which apply throughout the EU to all such collective investment schemes. If privately circulated, however, there is some scope for the raising of private funds for such schemes. Hire purchase is not used in practice. The tenant of a lease will occasionally have an option to purchase the property, or at least a right of pre-emption in the event of sale.

6.7 Institutional investment

Property is an important area for investment in Norway and will represent an important element of many institutional investment portfolios, but the percentage varies. Property is generally seen as a safe and long-term involvement, but offering only modest upside potential. There are no prevailing institutional standards either in investment strategy or in lease terms. The institutional investor will be looking for a good location, a good building and secure income from a company with a sound credit rating. The institutional investors tend to concentrate on the retail, office, industrial and warehousing sectors. Residential property is usually disregarded by major investors. Ownership of agricultural land is more or less reserved for farmers due to the 1974 Concession Act (see 1.3), so there is little outside investment in agricultural land.

6.8 Investors other than institutions

Other investors include property investment and development companies, public and private, and the private investor.

7 FORMS OF SECURITY

When making finance available for property investment, banks and other lenders will usually require both adequate security and that the borrower has the ability to pay interest and instalments from his earnings. Obviously, major companies may borrow on the strength of their creditworthiness, but in such loans the loan proceeds will be for general corporate purposes, and are not restricted to property investment. Borrowers who might arrange an unsecured loan will find it more favourable to offer security, as the interest rate and other terms will improve.

7.1 Mortgages

There is only one type of mortgage (*pantobligasjon*): a mortgage deed which is fully protected by registration at the local land registry. The deed and text must be in a prescribed form. There are no taxes on registration of the mortgage, only a nominal registration fee. The current mortgage registration fee over one property is NOK1,010. The mortgagor retains title to the property, and full use of it. The mortgage will secure the debt identified on it, or more usually, the obligations identified in an unregistered declaration (*pantsettel-*

seserklæring). The obligations secured may be current, future or both. A mortgagee has the right to foreclose by applying to the courts for an order for sale (which will usually be through an estate agent rather than by a forced auction). The mortgagee may request *tvangsbruk,* which enables him to take over the operation of the property (through a third party appointed by the court) and let it. The income can then be set against principal and interest. *Tvangsbruk* is usually an interim solution, followed by a sale. Protection against other creditors, including bankruptcy, and other interest holders is dependent upon registration (see 2.9). As a general rule priority of interests is based on the date of registration, but the parties are free to enter into alternative agreements. The exceptions referred to in 2.10 will also apply.

7.2 Floating and other charges

Norwegian law does not recognise general charges on the company's assets as a whole. Each asset has to be pledged separately, in accordance with the rules applying to the particular asset in question.

7.3 Performance bonds and guarantees

Where either the credit of the borrower or the adequacy of the security is in doubt, it is common to obtain a guarantee from a third party who will be called upon to repay the loan and any interest should there be a default by the borrower. Guarantees have a place in other property transactions such as leases where the guarantor is usually only under an obligation to make good any non-payment of rent. Depending on the terms he may also make good other lease defaults and, in extreme situations, may be called upon to take up a lease itself on the insolvency of the original tenant, but such extended guarantees are rarely seen. Bonds consisting of an unconditional promise to pay a fixed sum of money upon the default of another party in relation to the payment of property are rarely used. A Norwegian peculiarity is its use of the letter of indemnity (*skadesløsbrev*), which, once registered, serves as security for all or some of a party's future obligations towards another.

7.4 Credit insurance

Credit risk insurance is not commercially available for property transactions.

8 PLANNING AND BUILDING REGULATION

The development and use of land and buildings are subject to the controls provided for in the Planning and Building Act 1985, and regulations issued thereunder.

8.1 Planning authorities

Ultimate control of all matters relating to town and country planning rests partly with the Ministry of Environment and partly with the Ministry for Local Government. On a local level, decisions are taken by the local planning authority for the area; this will be the municipality (*kommune*) at the first level and the county (*fylke*) at the second level. In both cases ultimate decisions are taken by elected representatives, but wide powers have been delegated to the administration.

8.2 Development plans

8.2.1 The municipalities have to prepare strategic planning policies evidenced by a zoning plan for the municipality (*kommuneplan*), detailing the various zones and the restrictions applying to them. In addition, the municipality draws up development plans (*reguleringsplan*) for smaller areas. The development plan and the zoning plan will be binding upon owners of land covered by them. The county combines the different plans from the municipalities to form a county plan (*fylkesplan*) for the entire county.

8.2.2 The authorities will also consider suggestions as to development in the area in question and detailed plans presented to them by private parties, who might forward a proposal for a development plan. When a development plan has not yet been made for an area, but it is the authorities' intention to do so, a temporary prohibition against development can be issued. Applications will be considered in the light of the development plan, the zoning plan and other regulations, and will have to be in accordance with the plans unless material considerations indicate otherwise. There is an element of discretion involved on the part of the local authority, where development in compliance with the applicable plans might not necessarily be granted.

8.3 Planning control and procedures

Building permits are required for changes in use of property and for development of land. Under the Planning and Building Act, improvements which do not materially effect the external appearance of the building do not require permission. For minor changes, notification of the planned works must be sent to neighbours and to the planning authorities who may request the builder to submit an application for a building permit, if they have any objections to the planned works, within a specified time limit. If no such request has been received within the time limit, the works can be carried out without a permit.

8.3.1 If a building permit is required, an application must be made to the local planning authority. An application can be detailed, setting out the proposal in full, or confine itself to outline details. The applicant does not need to have an interest in the land, but the owner must be notified of the application. Further, owners and tenants of neighbouring land have to be notified of the planned works and will be given a two week time limit within which to submit any comments on the works planned. The neighbours have to be listed in the application. Important environmental issues must be assessed when a building permit is considered (see 9.4.2). The authority can refuse to determine the application if within the previous two years a similar application has been made and refused on appeal.

8.3.2 The local planning authority is directed to give a decision as soon as possible. In extreme cases of delay, the owner may complain to an *ombudsmann*. The local planning authority can grant the permission unconditionally, subject to conditions (for instance on measures being taken to prevent pollution, see section 9), or refuse the application. If conditions are imposed or the application is refused the local authority must give full reasons. These will assist the applicant in deciding whether or not to appeal to the Ministry of Local Government. Appeals are dealt with by written representation. Once the Ministry's decision has been made, it can only be challenged in the courts on points of law, by a 'person aggrieved'. The term 'person aggrieved' is wide enough to include anybody who can show a sufficient interest in the matter and might include a pressure group.

8.3.3 A building permit must be acted on within three years. If the work carried out under the permit is suspended for more than two years, the permit will lapse. Building permits attach to the land, and are not personal to the applicant unless the permit states otherwise.

8.3.4 If work has been carried out or development has commenced without a building permit or in contravention of one, the planning authority will request the removal of the work or building or the immediate cessation of the activity. In addition, the planning authority has the power to require restoration of the property to its previous condition. There is no limitation period during which the authority must take action. The main means of enforcement is the issue of an enforcement notice by the local planning authority. The notice can be challenged in the courts. Failure to comply with the notice can result in a fine, and if the notice is not challenged or judgment obtained, the authorities can demand that the property be restored to its previous condition, or undertake the cessation of the activity themselves, assisted by the police or by contractors. The builder will be liable for any enforcement costs incurred.

8.4 Building standards, control and supervision

A developer or builder must also comply with certain standards, mostly found in or based on the Planning and Building Act regarding the actual construction and the way the works are carried out. The compliance with the standards will be considered by the local building authority when the application for a building permit is made, and supervised by it during the period the works are carried out. The authorities can inspect and test the work and take samples of, eg the building materials used, to ensure that they comply with the requisite laws and regulations.

8.5 Protection of buildings of special interest

Buildings or land having special architectural or other value can be listed so as to prevent any alterations or development on these, or so as to require additional consents.

8.6 Expropriation or compulsory purchase and compensation

Legislation exists regulating the expropriation of property for the purposes of environmental preservation (see 9.4). There are also provisions for the compulsory purchase of and compensation for land needed to carry out the construction of major infrastructure facilities and other public works. Expropriation procedures may not be initiated by private developers. Under the constitution, compensation for property expropriated is to be at 'full value', but there is legislation providing supplementary rules as to the compensation payable. The general rule provides for compensation to be calculated on the basis of market value, but if the value for the owner is calculated taking into account his use of the property, the rental value will be compensated. Further, if the property is used as the owner's residential or commercial premises, he will be able to claim the costs incurred in order to purchase similar property, if these are greater than the market value. There is no premium over market value. Expropriation procedures are relatively quick.

9 ENVIRONMENTAL MATTERS

Due to the increased awareness of environmental issues over the last couple of decades, environmental law has become a distinct area in its own right, and is no longer incorporated under other heads of law. Recent statutory provisions, which have an impact upon property dealing, introduced to enhance protection of the environment and to complement existing liabilities, are set out in the Protection against Pollution and Waste Disposal Act 1981 (the Pollution Act) and the Planning and Building Act 1985. Under the Planning and Building Act, the local and central authorities have the power to give high priority to environmental matters and ensure the protection of areas targeted as risk areas. Furthermore, building permits can be made conditional on the use of certain technology or materials harmless to the environment, or on the basis that certain measures will be taken to prevent pollution.

The Pollution Act sets out provisions intended to protect the environment against pollution, reduce existing pollution and to promote a better handling of pollution and waste. The central pollution authorities and their local branches are responsible for the implementation of the Act. Anyone planning activity which might lead to pollution in a new area, or planning to alter the industrial use of an existing plant, must notify the pollution authorities, and supply them with an assessment and analysis of the consequences of the proposed activity in order to obtain a special permit authorising the conduct of the business or activity which might lead to pollution. The Pollution Act indicates the conditions to which a permit may be made subject, and these will include clean-up provisions and the recycling of waste. Permits may be limited to a specific period of time. Permits given can be withdrawn, and the conditions for the permit can be changed due to a change of circumstances.

Under the Pollution Act, the polluter is strictly liable for damage due to pollution. The Act is based on the internationally recognised 'polluter pays principle', under which the polluter is liable for all damage and loss connected with or arising from pollution. Generally, the owner of a property will not be liable for an occupier's polluting activities, unless there are separate grounds for liability for the owner, outside the Pollution Act. Breach of environmental legislation is a criminal offence, the penalty being a fine or imprisonment. So far, fines have been imposed in the majority of cases in which legal action has been taken. It should be noted that with respect to restorative actions ordered by the pollution authorities on a polluter's property, the owner will be liable even if the pollution was caused by a previous owner. An alternative method of enforcing the government's environmental policy, and one which may have a significant impact on property investment and development, is the expropriation of property and the use of pre-emption rights. Legislation also exists regulating available concessions for the purchase of certain types of properties. A more controversial approach is to restrict the use of land by issuing rulings or regulations to that effect. In general, the landowner is not entitled to compensation for these restrictions. These regulations enable agricultural land to be kept for agricultural use, open spaces in urban areas may be kept as parks and natural wildlife habitats preserved as national parks. On the other hand, grants and incentives are used to encourage the development of land and properties in an 'environmentally conscious' way and to prevent pollution.

9.1 Protection against atmospheric and noise pollution

Atmospheric and noise pollution is now covered under the Pollution Act although the Neighbours Act is still applicable. The permitted level of emission is determined by the 'emission licence' granted by the pollution authorities. The licensing procedures are fairly simple; the general test the pollution authorities will have to consider is the balance between the benefits of the activities and the consequences of pollution. Liability is determined on the basis of the general principle that the polluter will pay; the owner of the property will generally be liable if he also uses it. Where this is not the case, the owner will not be liable on a 'no-fault' basis, and liability will be imposed on the occupier or the person using the property. The Neighbours Act only protects neighbours, which are somewhat narrowly defined, and they are only protected against unreasonable and unforeseeable levels of pollution. See above for more details of the Pollution Act. The use of 'environmental taxes' on pollutants such as petrol demonstrates the extent to which importance is attributed to environmental policy. The environmental levy varies with the lead content, or in the case of certain polluting industries with the emission of specific gases. Noise is not governed by the pollution legislation.

9.2 Water pollution

Water pollution is dealt with under the provisions of the Pollution Act (see 9.1).

9.3 Waste storage and disposal

9.3.1 Waste storage and disposal are regulated under the Pollution Act, which covers the collection, disposal and storage of all waste, including commercial, industrial as well as toxic waste. The municipality is responsible for the collection and disposal of waste from households. The municipality has to adopt a plan for the reduction and disposal of waste in its area. The plan will set out a list of sources of waste, determine the method of sorting, collecting and recycling this, and estimate the expected income and expenses related to the waste disposal. The cost is covered by charges on residents fixed by the municipality for the collection, transportation, and storage of the waste, and which rates vary from one municipality to another.

9.3.2 Toxic and industrial waste must be brought to a designated waste disposal site in cases where it is not collected by the municipality. If industrial waste can be recycled or otherwise used, the authorities may approve other methods of waste disposal and may attach conditions to the consent. An individual or entity having disposed of waste in a manner inconsistent with the regulations can be given an order for the removal of the waste within a specified time limit and may also have costs awarded against him to enable a third party to recover any costs incurred by the removal of the waste.

9.4 Contaminated land

9.4.1 There are no provisions for contamination registers in Norway nor any statutory proposals to introduce them in the foreseeable future although enquiries relating to environmental matters are to be undertaken both by the developer or builder *and* by the authorities in connection with major development of land, and otherwise if so decided by the authorities.

9.4.2 The extent of the obligations imposed under environmental legislation enabling the authorities to implement environmental policy requires a developer to give careful consideration to the environmental implications before a property is acquired or a development project started. The development plans for the area should be checked carefully, and proper enquiries should be made of nearby land; it is necessary to ascertain whether the site was used for waste disposal, whether the building is located on a landfill site, whether dangerous or prohibited materials were used when the building was constructed and whether there is any risk of expropriation or exercise of pre-emption rights. The developer will also wish to establish whether there are any proposals for expropriation or pre-emption, both of which feature in the government's powers to protect the environment. The seller is under a general obligation to disclose any contamination of the land known to him, or which he ought to have known about. The pollution authorities have general authority to require treatment and/or clean-up activities. The responsibility will initially be borne by the person responsible for the pollution, although the authorities also impose liability upon the owner of the land at the time the pollution occurred, or at the time liability is apportioned.

9.5 Environmental assessments

See above.

10 DEVELOPMENT

10.1 Development projects, structures and vehicles

The simplest development will take the form of a purchase by an owner/occupier of land and the construction of premises he requires. He may, though, employ a developer, or a developer may find the site and build on it for a certain fee, or speculatively, for an owner/occupier. The developer may bring the project to an institution who will acquire the site, finance the development and then let the building or use this itself, and reward the developer by a fee or an interest in the development. The building contractor is not very often involved in these arrangements, although contracting companies during the 1980s did set up their own property development companies to initiate developments to create work for themselves. In more complex schemes, there may be a number of parties who provide different skills, one partner providing the development and property skills, another the financial and taxation expertise, and another providing the finance itself. Some developments are funded by the lending banks on straight commercial loans and others will have a mixture of equity and loan finance provided by external investors in addition to their own equity. The development can be undertaken by a joint venture or a partnership which undertakes such projects generally or which has been established for one particular project. In more substantial developments, each building (or a part of it) may be put into a separate company with a management company responsible for the overall development. Each company may then be sold to an institution or put into an investment company. During the 1980s, many developments were undertaken speculatively, with no committed end users, but this has been rare in the early 1990s. Developments are only undertaken where there is a clearly identified end user or it is certain that end users will be found once the development has been completed. They will then take leases and the investor will be sure of an income flow.

10.2 Building contracts and appointment of professionals

10.2.1 Typical forms of building contract

There are two common forms of building contract: the fixed price contract and the management contract. Few contracts are truly fixed price, as they will usually include a formula for variations in price to reflect difficulties in obtaining labour and/or building materials or time delays. If a number of parties and contractors are involved, a management contract is often used along with a design and management contract, where the contractor is essentially no more than a contract manager who employs a number of subcontractors either in his own name or in the name of the employer. Under NS 3430 (see 10.2.3), the employer may hold the subcontractors directly liable if the claim cannot be made directly against the contractor. The contractor's personal liability will be limited and he will undertake the work for a fee calculated by reference to the total contract price or on a fixed basis. While this makes for speed and flexibility, from the employer's point of view the disadvantage is that there is no certainty as to price or completion and the manager merely provides budget or estimate figures at the outset.

10.2.2 Common terms

The building contract provides for a start and finish date and will conventionally state that the contractor is paid the value of the work undertaken each month, although stage payments are also made sometimes by reference to various stages in the project. The contractor will usually be entitled to determine the contract if he is not paid in accordance with the contract (and the security does not cover the amount due) and the employer will be entitled to determine for a number of reasons, including the suspension of work by the contractor or the initiation of bankruptcy proceedings against him. If the work is not completed by the contractual completion date, liquidated damages are to be paid on a daily basis unless the contractor is entitled to an extension of time due to factors outside his control. The damages are fixed according to a table set out in the contract and are usually limited to 15 per cent of the contract price. Alternatively, the contractor might be entitled to a bonus if the work is completed before the time limit. The contract also contains provisions on variation of price. Depending on the circumstances either or both of the employer and the contractor will have to provide security for their obligations under the contract. The contractor has to provide security, usually through a bank guarantee, equivalent to 15 per cent of the contract price.

10.2.3 Standard form of contracts

The most common form of building contract which is used throughout the industry in Norway is the NS 3430 (Norwegian Standard 3430) setting out general conditions concerning construction and building. This is an 'agreed document', negotiated by trade federations from both sides and is therefore deemed to be fairly balanced. There is little use of architects or quantity surveyors engaged by the employer for the purpose of semi-independent determination of completion, variation and extension of time.

10.2.4 Appointment of the professional team

NS 3430 is used commonly also between the contractor and subcontractors. Other members of the professional team will be employed on the project under separate contracts, depending on the work to be carried out. The Association for Architects has prepared standard contracts which are commonly used for their employment.

10.3 Those involved and their roles

The construction process is segmented with different parties having different responsibilities, which can lead to complexity and difficulty in resolving disputes in relation to responsibility for defects in the works or their design. The structure will to a large degree depend on the project itself. The simplest structure is like a 'turnkey' concept (*totalentreprise*) when the owner only has a single contract with a single contractor, who might use subcontractors. Often the owner employs an architect for the design, and possibly also for supervision during the construction period. There might be a main contractor (*hovedentreprenør*) and several other contractors with separate contracts with the owner (*side-entreprenør*). These might be co-ordinated and/or supervised by the main contractor, or by a separate company. Surveyors and mechanical, electrical or structural engineers are rarely employed.

10.4 Defects and remedies

10.4.1 Remedies of employer in respect of defects in design and materials

The defects period is three years during which the contractor will be obliged to remedy any defects that have arisen. The security is held throughout the period to ensure fulfilment of the contractor's obligations, but will only be three per cent in the first year, two per cent in the second year and one per cent in the third year. In most cases, the employer will not have a direct remedy against subcontractors and suppliers and other members of the professional team, although this may vary in individual cases.

10.4.2 Remedies of subsequent owners/occupiers other than the contractual employer

Norwegian law offers some scope for 'direct action' by a subsequent buyer against a builder, and he may in any event have the claim assigned to him, or have the first owner act on his behalf. As it is unusual for there to be a direct contract or warranty between these parties, this remedy will generally be based on principles of general law.

10.5 Defects insurance

There is no system providing for defects insurance. The owner will have to sue the relevant parties, who might be protected by liability and indemnity insurance.

10.6 Copyright

The copyright in the design of the building will remain that of the architect. No licences will be required by the owners and tenants of the building for the purpose of using the building itself.

10.7 Fees

The total professional fees for a project will vary depending on the circumstances. It is very difficult to give definite figures but they may range between one and three per cent.

10.8 Taxes

The only tax which is relevant to the construction process is value added tax (VAT), and all construction is subject to VAT at the standard rate of 23 per cent.

11 TAXES

11.1 Corporation tax

Any company which is resident in Norway for tax purposes is liable to pay corporation tax on its worldwide profits (including capital gains, see 11.3) subject to relief under any double taxation treaty with the country where its profits originate, and whether or not those profits are remitted to Norway. Companies incorporated in Norway are treated as resident in Norway, as are companies whose central management or control is in Norway. Management and control is usually assessed by reference to where board meetings take place. Non-resident companies are taxed on their Norwegian income only, which will include capital gains and rentals from property located in Norway.

11.1.1 Tax rates

The rate of corporation tax is 28 per cent for all companies. The corporate tax of 28 per cent is levied on the corporation's total net income, including capital gains and income derived from property.

11.1.2 Computation and administration

In calculating its profits, a company can deduct expenses (including operating costs, interest and depreciation) which are incurred for the purposes of the trade of the company. This would extend to fees, commissions and loan interest as well as the usual deductions such as salaries and normal overheads. The tax payable by corporations and individuals on income, including capital gains, is dealt with by the local assessment board, as is the calculation of taxes. The system is one of assessment by the local assessment board based upon tax returns provided by the tax payer. Assessments are issued and, if unsatisfactory to the tax payer, may be appealed against administratively or in the courts. While it is open to the tax payer to arrange his affairs in such a way as to minimise tax, tax evasion and failure to provide relevant information are criminal offences and also subject to a heavy surtax.

11.1.3 Depreciation and capital allowances

Expenditures on fixed assets, eg construction of industrial buildings, hotels, and on plant and machinery as well as certain other buildings and assets must be capitalised and depreciated according to the declining balance method. The assets are usually depreciated at a rate of five per cent whilst office buildings are depreciated at a rate of two per cent. These depreciation rates may be increased to 10 per cent and four per cent respectively for business properties located in the countryside and with a short lifetime. Upon the sale of property there are very few deferral devices available.

11.1.4 Withholding tax

There is no withholding tax on interest payments to a non-Norwegian resident. However, dividend payments from a Norwegian resident company to a non-Norwegian resident are subject to a withholding tax of 25 per cent, unless a tax treaty provides for a lower withholding tax rate.

11.2 Taxes on development value

There are no taxes based on or payable on development value.

11.3 Taxes on capital gains

Any capital gain realised upon sale of property or shares of a company owning property will be included in the corporation's total net income and be subject to a tax rate of 28 per cent. There are no reliefs by way of indexation or revaluation. Capital gains on the sale of property will be taxed in the same way for residents and non-residents.

11.4 Taxes on owner of property

There is a special municipal property tax, 'the municipal tax' on property, which is payable by the owner. The municipality has the discretion to choose whether or not to levy the tax. The tax rates may vary between 0.2 per cent and 0.7 per cent and are levied on the gross taxable value of the property. In general, property tax can only be levied in built-up areas, including industrial land. The only other taxes on the corporate ownership of property are those described above in respect of a company's profits. Individuals may be subject to municipal property tax, wealth tax, the inheritance tax when receiving property by way of gift (or inheritance on death) and income tax on a deemed benefit in respect of living rent-free in a property owned by the occupier, but there are no other specific taxes which affect the owner of property.

11.5 Taxes on occupier

Tenants are not required by law or, in the contracts normally used, to pay or contribute towards the municipal property tax.

11.6 Taxes on land transfer

Upon registration of a transfer of property, the transferee must pay a stamp duty of 2.5 per cent of the property's value. The duty does not apply to the sale of shares in property owning companies and partnerships.

11.7 Wealth taxes

There are local and state taxes on the net wealth of individuals, but there are none on companies. The local tax is one per cent of net wealth worth more than NOK120,000. The state tax is progressive, and the top rate of 0.8 per cent is levied on net wealth in excess of NOK120,000.

11.8 Value added tax

Value added tax (VAT) is levied on sales of goods and certain defined services at a rate of 23 per cent calculated on the sums invoiced. VAT is not currently charged on sales and rentals of property. Some supplies are, however, zero rated, and others are exempt. Any registered person may deduct the VAT it pays on supplies received by it from VAT charged by it on its own deliveries. Where the amount of tax payable by a taxable person is greater than the amount it is entitled to recover on its taxable supplies in any accounting period, the amount can be recovered. In addition to VAT, there is a special investment tax of seven per cent levied on the purchase of most non-circulating assets in a business subject to VAT. The investment tax is part of the VAT system, and is only payable when a refund for incoming VAT is claimed. Value added tax is administered by the county tax office and appeals against decisions are made administratively or to the courts.

11.9 Local taxes and other taxes

Apart from the municipal property tax referred to above, there are no other local taxes nor any taxes of general application.

12 GRANTS AND INCENTIVES

12.1 Subsidies, grants and loans

The main purpose of the Norwegian Industrial and Regional Development Fund (SND) is to promote and extend the profitable, commercial and socioeconomic developments of the Norwegian economy to all parts of the country. The SND also contributes towards product development, the establishment of new enterprises and it assists in the development, modernisation and restructuring of business and industry. There are loans, guarantees, grants and equity investments (venture capital) at its disposal, and in 1993 the total funds allocated for these measures amounted to NOK5.8 billion. Through the special venture capital scheme, the SND may purchase shares in both new and established Norwegian companies.

12.1.1 Nationwide loan schemes

A range of loans are available for investments and are not confined to specific regional investment. Examples include secured loans made for investment in tangible assets, specific limited marketing and product development projects; risk capital loans for investment in buildings, plant and machinery and associated costs by companies with less than 50 employees. Commercial loans can be made for the establishment of new enterprises, expansions, mergers, structural and cooperative measures, utilisation of research and development projects. Product development loans can be granted whereby up to 50 per cent of the loan may be written off if the project proves not to be economically viable. Interest rates vary for the secured loans, according to the security offered. However, risk capital loan interest rates tend to be fixed at 10.5 per cent per annum. In all cases the loan period varies according to the type of loan and investment between 5 and 25 years.

12.1.2 Regional loans

Regional venture capital loans are available for projects in certain designated underdeveloped regions for the expansion, modernisation, restructuring and development of projects and new enterprises. Priority is given to investments in buildings, machinery and associated equipment. Interest rate repayment is currently fixed at 10.5 per cent per annum. The term of the loan for machinery and equipment varies according to the technical and economic life expectancy of the equipment in question and the income it is expected to generate. The term of the loan for commercial buildings may be up to 20 years.

12.1.3 Nationwide grants

These include development grants used mainly for human resources development programmes; individual grants may be made to entrepreneurs of up to NOK200,000, intended to cover the development stage prior to the establishment of a new enterprise. Although the assistance is available in all regions, priority is nevertheless given to the less developed regions, the unemployed and to women. There are also specific grants for the promotion of public sector research and development contracts (OFU).

12.1.4 Regional development grants

Investment grants are available in particular regions for investment in buildings, plant and machinery, but not for reinvestment. Grants may also be made in designated areas to companies for development projects, including pre-project surveys, planning product development, market surveys, company start-ups, training and moving, and to cover interest on regional loans.

12.2 Tax allowances and reliefs

There are no tax incentives or allowances applicable to investments in property.

12.3 Other public schemes and incentives

There are no 'enterprise zones' with specific tax regimes, but certain tax benefits are available in designated provincial areas.

13 COMPANIES AND BUSINESS ENTITIES

The term 'company' is generally used for business entities which are formalised by separate agreements between members, including companies limited by shares and partnerships. All business entities must be registered in the register of business enterprises before they start trading. This registration requirement also extends to branches of non-Norwegian companies if they carry on business in Norway from a fixed place or on a permanent basis.

13.1 Limited and unlimited companies

A company is either unlimited (see the discussion on partnerships at 13.2) or limited by shares. The provisions applying to limited companies are laid down in the Joint Stock Companies Act 1976. For companies limited by shares, the shareholder's liability for the debts and liabilities of the company will not exceed the amount which he has subscribed for his shares. Directors may be liable for fraudulent or wrongful actions under the Joint Stock Companies Act. There is no distinction between an executive and a supervisory director. Executives are not usually members of the board. A private company must have a minimum share capital of NOK50,000, of which at least half must be paid up on registration and the balance within a year.

13.1.1 Most limited companies are private. For public limited companies there are a number of conditions which have to be met for admission on to the main list of the Oslo Stock Exchange such as the requirement that the company has a minimum share capital of NOK10,000,000, of which at least 25 per cent must be distributed amongst members of the general public. The company's business must have been in existence for at least three years. Investigations into the financial position of the company will be undertaken. Foreign companies may apply for listing on the Oslo Stock Exchange, either for a primary listing or for a secondary listing, and a number of non-Norwegian companies have been admitted. Listed companies must observe quite stringent requirements with respect to information relating to the pricing of the shares. Buyers of Norwegian publicly listed shares will be subject to Norwegian insider regulations, will have to disclose share ownership above certain thresholds (starting at 10 per cent) and will have to comply with the relevant tendering regulations.

13.1.2 The company is a separate legal entity, distinct from its shareholders and directors, and has its own assets and liabilities, and is taxed separately and under different regulations. The purpose of the company's business and how it is to be conducted are set out in its articles of association and in the Joint Stock Companies Act.

13.2 Partnerships

A common way for two or more people to carry on a business is as partners. A partnership exists where two or more persons carry on a business in common, with a view to profits, and their relationship is regulated by the Norwegian Partnership Act of 1985. There is no distinction between civil and commercial partnerships. Most partnerships are separate legal entities, with rights and obligations towards public authorities and the courts. The liability of the partners towards third parties will depend on the type of partnership (see 13.2.1 and 13.2.2). Clubs and societies are not partnerships within the meaning of the Partnership Act as they are not generally conducted as businesses intending to make a profit. Some partnerships are internal with a less formal structure and do not deal with third parties.

13.2.1 General partnerships

The most common form of partnership is the general partnership (*ansvarlig selskap, ANS*) which is a separate legal entity from its members with rights and obligations towards public authorities and the courts. This does not, however, apply to tax liabilities; each partner pays his own tax on his share of the profits. A formal partnership agreement has to be entered into, and each member of the partnership is liable for all the debts of the partnership, unless liability for each partner is limited in accordance with his share. If so, the relevant apportionment of liability has to be registered in the register of business enterprises to be effective, and the form of liability has to be indicated in the name of the partnership, by adding *DA* (*delt ansvar*; proportionate liability) after the name of the partnership.

13.2.2 Limited partnerships

To be considered as a limited partnership (*kommandittselskap, KS*) under the Partnership Act, at least one partner must have general (unlimited) liability for the partnership's liabilities and obligations, while the other partners (the limited partners) can limit their liability to a specific amount. In the same way as the general partnership, a formal partnership agreement has to be entered into to set up a limited partnership, setting out the different partners' shares of the capital, liabilities, and provisions on exclusions or release of partners. The limited partnership can have its own board of directors, or the day-to-day management can be carried out by the general partner. The advantage of the limited partnership is that the partners can set up a limited company which will be the general partner and leave themselves with limited liability while having the advantages of a partnership, such as separate tax treatment. The limited partners have the right to take part themselves in the management of the business but they are not able to bind the business. A partnership will be deemed to be a general partnership unless it is specifically registered as a limited partnership.

13.2.3 Silent or internal partnerships

Silent partnerships are not considered to be separate legal entities; one of the members will act in his own name (but on behalf of the parties). He will have unlimited liability for his rights and obligations towards any third parties. Such 'internal' or 'silent' partnerships cannot be registered with the register of business enterprises. By way of contrast with formal partnership agreements, no formal legal requirements need to be met to enter into a silent partnership. The Partnership Act will, however, regulate any issues or disputes which may arise between the silent partners if the matters have not been set out in an agreement.

13.3 Other types of business association

13.3.1 Companies and partnerships are the two principal forms of business entities recognised by law. Other unincorporated associations do not have the same legal recognition.

13.3.2 Joint ventures

Joint venture is not a term of art in Norwegian law and there is no specific body of law relating to joint ventures. The principal document in any joint venture arrangement will be therefore the joint venture agreement which is negotiated between the parties. Various vehicles may be used, including limited partnerships and joint venture companies, and their relationship is governed either by the joint venture agreement, the partnership agreement or by the shareholders' agreement setting out the relationship of the shareholders in a joint venture. The agreement will provide, in particular, for the financial contributions of each party, the division of profits, the duration of the joint venture, the restrictions and pre-emption terms to apply to the disposal of any parties' interest in the venture, and will set out the arrangements for the termination and winding up of the joint venture. There are no particular fiscal regulations for the taxation of joint ventures and the tax treatment will depend on the vehicle used. If, for example, it is a joint venture company (limited company), the company will bear the corporation tax and the joint venture parties will bear tax on the dividends and distributions of the company in the usual way; this is not entirely satisfactory and other approaches, such as partnerships, are frequently used.

14 INTERNATIONAL

14.1 Restrictions or consents required for inward investment

There are no restrictions on the introduction of funds into Norway for the purchase of property or on the ownership of Norwegian property by foreign entities. However, certain notification procedures to customs and other authorities may apply for taxation and statistical purposes and the acquisition may be subject – as are acquisitions by Norwegians – to the Concession Act described in 1.3.

14.2 Exchange controls

No exchange controls or restrictions exist at present.

14.3 Restrictions and registrations on carrying on a business

With certain very limited exceptions there are no general restrictions on a foreign entity or company carrying on business in Norway, although the company has to register with the register of business enterprises (see section 13).

14.4 Repatriation of income and proceeds of property trading and development

There are no consents or restraints involved in the repatriation of income and proceeds subject to the deduction of withholding tax payable on receipt of dividends from Norwegian companies (see 11.1.4). In addition, certain information has to be given to the authorities.

14.5 Withholding tax

This has been referred to in section 11. Interest and rental payments are not subject to withholding tax.

14.6 Double taxation relief

Income derived from and capital gains on sale of property in Norway will generally be subject to Norwegian tax under Norwegian law. Relief from double taxation must be obtained in the investor's home country.

CHAPTER 14

Portugal

Luis Vinhas, Isabel Garcia, Partners **Ana Menéres**

Goncalves Pereira, Vinhas, Castelo Branco e Associados

CONTENTS

1 OWNERSHIP OF LAND 457
2 OTHER INTERESTS IN LAND 460
3 TITLE TO LAND 464
4 TRANSACTIONS IN LAND 466
5 LEASES AND OTHER RIGHTS OF OCCUPATION 469
6 FINANCE AND INVESTMENT SOURCES 472
7 FORMS OF SECURITY 474
8 PLANNING AND BUILDING CONTROLS 476
9 ENVIRONMENTAL MATTERS 479
10 DEVELOPMENT 481
11 TAXES 484
12 GRANTS AND INCENTIVES 487
13 COMPANIES AND BUSINESS ENTITIES 487
14 INTERNATIONAL 489

CHAPTER 14

Portugal

1 OWNERSHIP OF LAND

Portugal has a codified system of law. The relevant code for land is the Portuguese Civil Code of 1966. The principal forms of land ownership are the freehold (*direito de propriedade*), the joint freehold (*direito de compropriedade*) and the condominium or horizontal property ownership (*direito de propriedade horizontal*). There is a traditional preference for holding land under a form of freehold rather than leasehold. This is because leasehold ownership still emphasises the protection of the tenant in spite of progressively introduced legislation intended to lessen this protection as an incentive to landowners to let land, in particular by allowing them to terminate leases exceeding five years with notice. However, leases are very commonly used and tenants still enjoy a number of protections.

1.1 Types of tenure

1.1.1 Freehold or absolute ownership

The holder of the freehold right (*direito de propriedade*) to the land has the absolute and exclusive ownership of the land, which comprises the right to use, enjoy and dispose of land within the limitations set by law. The holder of the freehold interest to the land has the right to the buildings and produce from the land and to moveable assets permanently fixed to any building. There is no separate freehold ownership of the land and the buildings. The land and the building will form one sole urban property (*Prédio Urbano*). However, land and buildings may sometimes be the subject of other ownership rights, eg under a surface right granting a right to build (see 2.1.3) which will bestow absolute ownership of the building on a third party for the duration of the surface right. The freehold right extends in principle to the air above the land and to the soil and subsoil below, except where these are considered to belong in the public domain, eg mineral deposits or archaeological discoveries.

1.1.2 Leasehold

The leasehold (*arrendamento*) as an interest in land in the Anglo-American tradition is not used, although see 2.1.3 describing the use of surface rights which are the nearest equivalent to the long lease. A tenancy or rental agreement is a contractual arrangement by which one party provides the other with the temporary use of a property in return for consideration, which will usually be market rent. Tenancies do not grant the right to dispose of or encumber the property or to collect its produce; in fact, tenancies grant fewer rights than the usufruct or the surface right (see 2.1). Tenancies do not confer rights of ownership or an interest in the land. Although a tenancy will grant the holder the exclusive right to use and occupy the property, the tenant may not transfer the tenancy to a third party without the prior consent of the landlord. Tenancies only grant the right to occupy and use a property for a limited period of time and for the purpose the tenancy was granted. Tenancies may be for a term certain, ie for a fixed period, so that both landlord and tenant may terminate the contract upon expiry of the term without an obligation to renew. Tenancies may not exceed 30 years. See section 5 where the provisions regulating tenancies are dealt with in more detail.

1.1.3 Joint ownership

Joint ownership (*compropriedade*) is recognised but not encouraged. A joint owner is never obliged to remain in joint ownership and can always opt for division of the common property by way of a special judicial procedure. Common property arises when two or more persons have a property right over the same asset. Each joint owner has a right over the entire property and qualitatively this right will be the same for each joint owner, even though his percentage share may be different. Joint owners may act jointly or separately. Whenever they do act jointly, they will be entitled to exercise any of the rights of freehold. When acting separately, they are restricted to certain rights, eg to claim the land from a third party, to use the property, and to sell their share. Each joint owner is entitled to the income from the property and bears the charges of the property in accordance with his share. Upon sale of a share, the remaining joint owners have a legal right of pre-emption (see 1.2.2). If a joint owner is not given notice within which to exercise his right of pre-emption, he is entitled to the part sold provided he files a judicial claim within six months of the date he becomes aware of the price and conditions of sale.

1.1.4 Condominia

1.1.4.1 Condominium ownership, referred to as 'horizontal property' (*propriedade horizontal*), is a form of ownership which requires the building to be composed of independent and autonomous parts (*fracções autónomas*). Each part must be completely independent and must have its own access to the common parts of the building. Each owner is sole owner of his unit and co-owner of the common parts of the building. Horizontal property must be established by a formal act where the autonomous and common parts are identified; this will most commonly be done by notarial deed but it may also take the form of a judicial decision or usucaption (*usucapião*, see 1.4). The courts may enforce horizontal property ownership whenever an owner of a common property files a judicial claim for the purpose and the building in question complies with all the legal requirements necessary to establish horizontal property. By law, certain parts such as the roof, entrance and soil are deemed to be common; others such as lifts and garages are presumed to be common. The title deed may establish that some common areas of the property are subject to the exclusive use of any one of the owners. It is important for each unit to be described thoroughly in the title deed, and the relative value of each unit must also be set out. In case of non-compliance the title deed will be void. Any change must be executed by way of notarial deed, requiring the approval of all the owners. Unlike joint ownership, condominium property owners do not have a pre-emption right on the sale of another owner's unit and the owner of a unit may freely dispose of his unit. The management of the common parts is carried out by the 'owners' assembly', and an administrator appointed by the 'owners assembly' who may be one of the owners or a third party. Where there are more than four condominium owners it is mandatory that the use and maintenance of the common parts is regulated by a specific document, the 'condominium regulations'. These can be included in the title deed. Condominiums may be used for any type of building or for groups of buildings.

1.1.4.2 There has been specific legislation for time sharing (*direito de habitaçào periódica*) since 1981. Time shares grant an interest in land for a short period each year provided the building or sections of a building are situated in an area designated for tourism or recreational purposes, and the sections constitute independent units with access to the common parts of the building, and are owned by one person (individually or collectively). In the absence of any specific provision to the contrary, the time share right lasts for life, and although it is possible to agree a different period, there is a 30-year minimum duration period. A time share must be executed by notarial deed containing details of the building and of the units. The *Direcção-Geral do Turism* (the governmental tourism office) has to approve the time-share arrangement and, subsequently, the deed has to be registered in the local property register (see section 3). The interest holder may live in the unit during the period agreed and use all the installations, equipment and services, the use of which is included in the price, by law or regulation.

1.1.5 Lesser rights

It is possible to create lesser rights of temporary use and occupation of a contractual nature such as the *commodatum* and the *deposit*, which are of relatively minor importance and are not commented on further. Other interests in land are dealt with in section 2.

1.2 Legal and beneficial ownership

There is no equivalent to the English concept of beneficial ownership.

1.3 Restrictions on ownership and dealing

1.3.1 Adults over 18 years of age and validly incorporated companies may freely acquire land. Minors and those persons suffering from mental incapacity, as recognised by a court order, may only purchase property via a legal representative but may hold absolute or qualified title to land if received by way of succession or gift. There are also legislative restrictions on the rights of a landowner, mainly designed to protect the public interest, and these include planning regulations, rights of access, preservation of natural beauty and expropriation (see section 8). There are also legal restrictions on air and noise emissions as well as the deposit of liquid and solid waste (see section 9). There are no restrictions on ownership of land by foreign persons or entities.

1.3.2 Public or private entities may dispose of land provided the legal procedures imposed by their enabling legal provisions are complied with. There are restrictions on the division of land (in certain areas) to prevent the indefinite division of agricultural land into smaller plots which would become economically unviable. If an owner intends to divide his land and use it for agricultural purposes, he can only do so if each portion amounts to the minimum cultivation unit (*unidade de cultura*) applicable in the particular geographical area, which is set by decree (with the minimum cultivation unit ranging from half a hectare to 7.5 hectares). A division of land which fails to comply with the minimum cultivation unit requirement can be declared void by a court decision. The owner of land adjoining a plot of less than the minimum cultivation unit has a legal right of pre-emption. Other automatic rights of pre-emption include those of joint owners, tenants of over a year, and landowners in respect of the sale of building or surface rights. The owner of land the subject of a right of way also has pre-emption rights over the land enjoying the right of way.

1.4 Adverse possession and acquisitive prescription

Title can become vested in the occupier of land by means of acquisitive prescription or usucaption (*usucapião*). Where the occupier acts as owner and is in good faith he will acquire title, provided possession of the land is public, without opposition, and has lasted for a minimum of 10 years since the date of registration of possession. Where the occupier is not in good faith, he will require 15 years' possession from the date of registration. Where there is no registration and the occupier is in good faith, there will be a requirement of 15 years' possession; if there is no registration and the occupier is in bad faith, the period of occupation is increased to 20 years. Usucaption provides a defence to a claim.

2 OTHER INTERESTS IN LAND

Those with absolute ownership over land may create and grant lesser interests in the land to third parties. These include the usufruct, surface rights, dwelling rights and servitudes which are dealt with in this section; mortgages and privileges which are dealt with in section 7 and the time share which is dealt with in 1.1.4.2.

2.1 Easements or servitudes, usufruct and building and dwelling rights

All these rights may be created voluntarily by means of an agreement comprised in a notarial deed or may be created by will. Servitudes, usufruct, surface rights and dwelling rights are rights in rem but all require registration if they are to bind third parties.

2.1.1 *Servitudes/easements*

A servitude (*servidão*) is a right in rem over one piece of land (the servient tenement), in favour of another piece of land (the dominant tenement). The most common examples of servitudes are rights of way and water rights, although other types include the right to graze animals. The content of the servitude must be set out in the title deed and the owner of the servient tenement is entitled to compensation for damage caused by the exercise of the servitude. Servitudes may be created by notarised agreement, and by judicial or administrative decisions. Servitudes may also be created by long usage after 15 years where the right is visibly being used, permanent, in good faith and without registration, and 20 years where the user is in bad faith and the right is not registered. The notarised agreement must be registered to be enforceable against successors in title. There is no maximum duration for servitudes, which may be created for a fixed period or indefinitely, although 20 years' non-use will cause a servitude to expire. Servitudes will also expire upon merger of the dominant and servient tenements.

2.1.2 *Usufruct*

Usufruct (*usufruto*) grants the holder(s) the full and exclusive use and enjoyment of the property of another, for a period of time. It is most commonly used among members of the same family and rarely used for other purposes. The usufructuary may use the property in whatever way he chooses, provided he does not alter the nature of the land or its possible future use. The usufruct is a right in rem, binding successors in title, provided the agreement creating it is notarised and registered. The usufruct is always limited in time and cannot exceed the lifetime of the usufructuary, or a 30-year period where it is granted in favour of a corporate entity. The usufruct may be created by agreement, by will, acquisitive prescription (see 1.4) or by law. The usufruct may be transferred unless specifically excluded by the agreement. The usufruct expires either when the original holder of the right dies or at the end of the term for which the usufruct was granted, unless the grantee is a corporate entity in which case it will terminate after 30 years (or sooner where a shorter term has been agreed). A usufruct may also expire through 20 years' non-use.

2.1.3 *Building rights and dwelling rights*

2.1.3.1 Surface rights (*direito de superficie*) grant a third party the right to erect buildings or to maintain an existing construction or plantation on or below the land belonging to another. During the term of the right, the third party will have absolute ownership of the building or plantation. Surface rights are created by an agreement executed in a notarial deed, by means of a will or by acquisitive prescription; they may also be transferred separately from the land upon which the construction is built or upon which the plantation is cultivated. They can be granted in perpetuity, for the holder's lifetime or for a fixed period. Surface rights are granted for consideration which may be in instalments or in the form of a lump sum. Whenever surface rights are created by agreement, they must be executed in a notarial deed to be valid. To bind third parties, including successors in title to the owner of the freehold, the agreement must also be registered, in which case the right will be in rem. Upon termination, the ownership of the building reverts to the freeholder of the land. Where the term of the surface right comes to an end, the holder of the right is entitled to compensation at value, but unless otherwise agreed the holder of the right may alter or demolish the building. Although not common, surface rights have recently been used for the construction of industrial parks and for underground car parks.

2.1.3.2 Dwelling rights (*direito de uso e habitação*) grant a holder and his family the right to use and enjoy a particular building, or a part of it, belonging to another. Dwelling rights are created by agreement executed in a notarial deed, by will or by law and must be registered in order to bind successors in title to the grantor. They may be created for a fixed period and cannot exceed the lifetime of the holder. They are not transferable either by agreement or by succession. The holder may neither lease the premises over which the right is created nor create a lien over them. Dwelling rights are not commonly used.

2.2 Restrictions on use and other restrictions

There are restrictions on the use of land arising from legal impositions that do not need to be registered and yet bind successors in title. These restrictions arise from the need to balance opposing interests between neighbours, and include the right to object to air emissions, heat and noise emanating from neighbouring properties, where the emissions do not result from a natural use of the property and would cause substantial damage to the adjoining land. There are further restrictions on the construction or deposit of dangerous substances and excavation which might affect adjoining land. Other restrictions on use which might arise include the obligation to grant a temporary right of way to enable construction of neighbouring property, the obligation to allow water to flow on to lower lying land and the restriction upon the opening of doors and windows over adjoining land, which must not be closer than 1.5 metres. Obligations to contribute to repairs and common services will pass to successors in title in the case of transfer of a share in condominium ownership. Public law planning restrictions are commented on in section 8.

2.3 Private mortgages, privileges and charges

Monetary liabilities can be secured on land in a number of ways. Private mortgages (*hipotecas*) are the most common type of mortgages. For further information on mortgages and security in general, see section 7. Judgment debts are secured by a charge over land or privilege (*privilégio creditório imobiliáro*) and are created by implication of law. These privileges are also granted to public authorities, municipalities and government bodies to cover payment of taxes and other liabilities. They take the form of a preferential debt. They grant a right over the property until the creditor receives payment of the debt or repayment of the grant; the beneficiary under this type of charge will take priority over all other creditors. Privileges not only require no prior registration but will prevail over a first mortgage, even where the latter is registered first in time. The right to retain (*direito de retenção*) a property of another is also a way of securing monetary liabilities on land but is only valid if the debt arises from expenses or damages connected to the property; eg upon termination of a tenancy, a tenant may retain the land to secure payment arising from maintenance work carried out by him. The right of pledge over receivables (*consignação de rendimentos*) is a further method for securing monetary liabilities on land. It is an interest in rem granting the holder the right to be paid with the income received from a particular property. The right can be created by court order or by agreement executed in a notarial deed and must be registered to be enforceable against third parties and to bind successors in title. It must be created for a fixed period not exceeding 15 years. A seller may secure the unpaid purchase price on the sale of a property by means of a reservation of ownership (*reserva de propriedade*) which will grant him the right to the outstanding balance where the unpaid price exceeds one eighth of the total. The reservation of ownership must be registered to render the charge enforceable against third parties.

2.4 Contracts and options

Preliminary contracts for sale assume the form of promissory contracts under which the parties undertake to execute a purchase and sale agreement (see further section 4). Promissory contracts may grant an interest in land whenever the parties agree that a right in rem should be granted to the promissory buyer and execute the agreement in a notarial deed and register the agreement in the land register (see section 3). The promissory buyer will then have the right to purchase the property, although the agreement will not be binding upon successors in title unless the agreement is registered. Options or pre-emption rights implied by law are commented on at 1.3.2. Options to purchase land may also be granted by agreement, in order to create an option which will be a right in rem. The agreement must be executed in a notarial deed and registered in order to be binding upon successors in title. Whenever a legal or contractual option to purchase land arises, the owner must give written notice of the sale and its terms to the holders of the option who will then usually have eight days to exercise the option. Whenever the owner of the land fails to give notice, the holder of the option may file a claim against the owner within six months of being made aware of the unnotified sale; the option holder will become the owner of the land provided he pays the purchase price within eight days of the date of service of the claim to the seller and the third party buyers.

2.5 Public or municipal charges

Municipal charges and other public liabilities such as taxes and contributions to social security in the form of privileges are commented on at 2.3.

2.6 Other interests

There is a closed list of rights in rem over land, and it is therefore not possible to create new rights in rem not previously recognised. Other interests in land granting a right in rem are of a public nature and are granted to the state (see further section 8 on planning and building controls).

2.7 Liabilities attaching to land

Liabilities arising out of land which may attach to the owner include breach of restrictions on use imposed to ensure a balance between neighbours' interests (see 2.2). The owner of a building or of a construction which collapses as a result of a construction defect or of negligent repair is liable for damage caused to third parties except where he can prove that he is not personally liable. Other liabilities attaching to the owner or occupier may result from a breach of a contractual obligation or other unlawful act but do not attach to the land itself. Fiscal liabilities attaching to land are commented on in section 11.

2.8 Legal and equitable interests

There is no distinction between legal and equitable interests under Portuguese law.

2.9 Protection of interests

Freehold and other interests granting rights in rem must be registered in order to be enforceable against third parties, including subsequent buyers. There are exceptions to this requirement in the case of privileges, ie judgment debts, public, municipal and social security charges and the right to retain land to secure monetary liabilities (see 2.3).

2.10 Priority of interests

Priority between interests in land of the same category depends upon date of registration. Privileges, ie judgment debts, public, municipal and social security charges, although not registrable, have priority over other interests securing monetary liabilities.

3 TITLE TO LAND

3.1 Proof of title

Title to land is established through registration in the books of the Real Estate Registry Department. The contractual documentation between the parties is only enforceable between the parties. Otherwise, unless an interest is registered, it will not be enforceable against third parties. The property registers contain details of the creation, modification, transfer or extinction of all property rights. Registration creates the certainty required for property transactions and, because the registers are open to the public, it protects the interests of third parties. Title to each building or interest can be found at the registry, including details of the property and any lesser rights or interests in existence. A separate register is also used by the tax authorities for valuation purposes (see 3.2).

3.2 The land register

There are two registers. The property register which establishes legal title is kept with respect to each municipality or parish and ultimate responsibility for it rests with the Justice Minister; the property register kept in the tax departments is administered by the Finance Minister for fiscal purposes.

3.2.1 Descriptions

The descriptions contained in the register set out the definitive boundaries of a property. The entries appear by reference first to municipality, then respective parish and to the plot of land or building, which are then numbered. Some property registers now enable a search by reference to the name of the owner.

3.2.2 Content

The property registers describe the building (or land), and its physical, economic and fiscal details. In each property register, there are preliminary files with descriptions of all immoveable assets and supplementary books in which further facts relating to each particular asset are held. A technique of annotation in the margin next to the descriptions is also used in order to bind the entire entry together. The entry therefore serves to notify the public as to the state of the property and any encumbrances, so that it is impossible to claim ignorance as to its legal situation. Each property has a separate register and applications for entries must be made either by the parties involved or by those having an interest in the register. All applications must be filed in conjunction with the requisite documentation evidencing that the interest to be registered was validly created.

3.2.3 Errors

The registers provide conclusive evidence of the state of a property, although the register may not include all registrable interests (because the entry was not applied for) and the register may contain errors. There are two possible errors that can occur during registration: first, incorrect registration of the terms of the title; and secondly, deficiencies in the title claimed by the applicant. Inaccurate registrations must be rectified by the head of the registry department, as soon as he becomes aware of the irregularity, or upon request by any interested party. Errors resulting from mere incorrect reproduction of the terms of the title are amended on the documents used to make the original entry. If the correction might prejudice the rights of other title holders, however, the agreement of all concerned, or a court order, will be necessary. Errors resulting from deficiencies of title always require the agreement of all interested parties or a court order before correction is made, and correction of the register will not be made if the claimant's title is null and void. Corrections are always made to rectify the error and in principle no compensation is paid to the person against whom the register is rectified.

3.3 Passing of title

Unless title to land is properly registered at the relevant registry, it is not possible to assign or transfer that interest. Formal transfer of the interest will take place upon the agreement to transfer. Formal registration is required in order to enforce the interest against third parties. There is no time limit after which failure to register will render the transfer void. The registration itself is by means of a declaration made by the applicant in a special format that is then presented at the registry with a copy of the notarised deed. Registration is then backdated to the date of application for registration.

4 TRANSACTIONS IN LAND

The most common transactions in land are the sale and purchase of land and the grant of commercial and residential tenancies.

4.1 Procedures

Preliminary investigations as to title, fiscal attachments over the property, the existence of any construction licence or licence to use any building granted by the municipal authority and planning restrictions must be made before entering into any transaction, be it sale or tenancy. Prior to entering into a formal agreement to transfer property, a promissory contract (*contrato promessa de compra e venda*) will be created whereby the parties undertake to execute, at a future date, another contract (the contents of which are set out at this earlier stage). It is commonly used where payment is by instalments or some third party has to fulfil some condition such as the obtainment of finance, or of a construction licence. A promissory contract for sale must take the form of a document signed by both parties and it will then be legally binding between the parties. The signatures of the promissory seller and buyer must be certified in person by a notary, who must check the validity of any construction licence (see section 8). Where the promissory contract is also registered it will be protected for a period of six months, grant rights in rem, and bind successors in title. Upon entering into the promissory contract, the promissory buyer usually gives a deposit. The actual transfer of the property depends upon the execution of a notarial deed (*escritura publica de compra e venda*), which must be prepared by a notary and registered at the real estate registry department (see section 3). Prior to allowing signature of the transfer document, the notary must ensure that the seller has proper title to sell the property. The seller must prove his ownership by showing: a certificate issued by the registry (*certidâo de registro predial*) which also shows whether there are any charges over the property; a document issued by the local tax office indicating that there are no outstanding taxation obligations related to the property (*caderneta predial*); and a construction licence (*licença de construçao*) or a licence to use (*licença de utilzação*) issued by the local municipal authority for any building. Contracts for the sale of property not executed in a notarial deed are null and void. However, if the contract is in writing and has the signatures notarised in the presence of a notary in case of a building or a plot of land, it is possible to infer a promissory contract. Even after the formal contract has been executed by notarial deed, third parties will not be bound until the title has been registered.

4.2 Contract terms

4.2.1 The law implies a warranty for construction defects, pursuant to which a seller is liable for construction defects detected within five years of the date the buyer took possession of the building where the seller has constructed the building or carried out modifications or repairs to it. Within the warranty period, the buyer may claim compensation against construction defects by notifying the seller within a year of the date the defect was detected. If a subsequent owner purchases the building within the warranty period, he will also be entitled to claim under the warranty. A further five-year warranty from the date of possession is implied to protect the buyer to cover the circumstances where the seller makes some misrepresentation or the property transferred is not fit for the purpose it was sold for. The buyer has the right to claim for repairs from the seller or to revoke the sale and claim damages. The claim must be brought within one year of the date of detection and within the warranty period. In spite of the implied warranties the parties should seek protection by express warranties on relevant issues both in the promissory contract and in the definitive deed of sale. The parties must negotiate and enter into the contract in good faith and will be liable in damages to the other party as a result of negotiating and entering into a contract in bad faith. The parties may agree that possession of the property be delivered to the buyer before or after title is passed on the execution of the notarial deed, although it is usually delivered upon the passing of title. The risk passes to the buyer when he takes possession of the property. The full price is usually paid when title is formally passed, although the parties may agree otherwise. Payment in installments may be agreed, in which case the last instalment is usually paid when the formal transfer of title takes place. Failure to meet any of the instalments may result in the acceleration of all outstanding payments. After the formal transfer of title and of physical possession, the seller cannot terminate the contract for non-payment unless otherwise agreed. The rate of interest for late payments is fixed by law at 15 per cent for a commercial sale and 10 per cent for a private sale, unless otherwise agreed between the parties, although an agreed rate cannot exceed the fixed rates by more than nine per cent (or seven per cent in some cases).

4.2.2 Where the final contract is not executed in spite of the promissory contract and deposit, the law provides for penalties for the party in breach. If the promissory buyer breaches the contract, the other party may forfeit the deposit and need not proceed with the sale. If the promissory seller breaches the contract, the promissory buyer has one of three choices:

(a) the right to the termination of the contract and to claim twice the amount of the deposit as compensation;

(b) the right to terminate the contract and seek the return of his deposit and claim the current value of the property deducting the agreed price, if he has already taken possession; and
(c) the right to request a court order for specific performance of the contract.

In addition to this, a creditor with rights under a judicial decision or an executed title, such as an unpaid seller, may request a court order for the seizure of the debtor's assets, although such a claim will not be a privilege so as to take priority over the other debtors.

4.3 Formalities

All contracts regarding the creation and transfer of interests in land must be executed in a notarial deed prepared in writing by a notary public and signed before him in order to be valid. The formalities for tenancies vary according to the purpose of the contract: industrial, commercial and office tenancies are by way of public deed, but residential tenancies only require a written contract. Voluntary mortgages must also be executed by notarial deed and require registration in order to be valid. Once executed the title deed must be registered.

4.4 Fees, costs and taxes

All costs arising from transactions in land are payable by the buyer or by the party to whom the interest is granted, and will include notarial fees, land registry fees and transfer tax, unless the parties agree otherwise.

4.4.1 The agent's commission is paid by the party engaging the agent. Agents tend to charge between two and three per cent of the purchase price for the transaction and their fees are only payable in the event of a successful transaction. Agents may also charge a fixed fee for promotion services which may be charged independently of a successful transaction. Each party pays its own lawyers' fees.

4.4.2 Lawyers use a time charge basis which takes into account the complexity of the case, the means of the client and the practice of the district. Notaries' fees are fixed in the law and may vary from 0.3 per cent to 1 per cent depending on the transaction.

4.4.3 Stamp duty on land transfer is charged at a rate of 0.8 per cent of the price. Land transfer tax charged on the transfer of rural land is charged at eight per cent, whilst on the transfer of buildings, parts of buildings and land for construction it is charged at 10 per cent. No property transfer tax is paid on tenancies, but stamp duty of 10.5 per cent is paid on a figure corresponding to one month's rent.

4.4.4 Property registry fees are charged at an approximate rate of 0.5 per cent of the price paid or the fiscal value of the land or building.

4.4.5 The transaction costs, including notarial and register costs and taxes, are usually in the region of 11 per cent of the value of the transaction although this does not include agents' and lawyers' fees.

4.4.6 Agents' and solicitors' fees attract value added tax (VAT) at a rate of 17 per cent which is levied on services rendered for all types of property and all types of transactions. Property and tenancies are generally exempt from VAT (but see 11.8).

4.5 Professionals' roles

The marketing and sale of the property are usually conducted by estate agents and realty brokers, who play no part in verifying the legality of the transaction. Each party will usually instruct its own lawyer (although a single lawyer may be instructed where there is no conflict of interest), who will conduct searches of the property, obtain all the documentation in relation to it and prepare all the legal documentation required for the transaction, including preliminary agreements, promissory contracts and definitive agreements. Notaries prepare the notarial deed under the lawyers' instructions and verify the legality of construction licences and property titles. Notaries are civil servants and do not act on behalf of the parties. They merely check whether all formalities have been complied with and formalise the documents. The property registry application is usually processed by the buyer's lawyer.

5 LEASES AND OTHER RIGHTS OF OCCUPATION

Contractual tenancy arrangements are of significant economic and social importance, and the legislation focuses on tenant protection. Tenancies are regulated by the Civil Code and by specific legislation for urban tenancies, agricultural and forest tenancies. Urban tenancy agreements may be residential, commercial or industrial or 'professional' when granted to independent professionals (eg lawyers and doctors) for the purpose of setting up their practice. Tenancies may also be mixed, depending on their object and purpose. The maximum duration for the urban tenancy is 30 years and tenancies granted for a longer or indefinite term are reduced to a 30-year term. Tenancies are usually granted for a fixed period and urban tenancies are subject to automatic renewal (see further 5.3). Rural tenancies must be granted for a minimum 10-year period if the tenant is a legal entity and for seven years where the tenant is a physical person, with a maximum term of 30 years. Forest tenancies must be granted for a minimum of 10 years and a maximum of 70 years.

5.1 Rent and other terms

5.1.1 All tenancy agreements must be written documents and all commercial (but not residential) tenancy agreements must be created by notarial deed. The parties in a commercial agreement are free to negotiate rent, as may parties to a residential agreement unless the property belongs to the state, or the tenants are entitled to a new tenancy, or where the rent is subsidised by the state (in which case the rent is established by law). Once the initial rent is fixed for a tenancy, any increase is limited by law. The government establishes the index of rental increases annually, and rents may not be increased beyond this index. Rental increase clauses are valid, but only if they stipulate that the rent is to rise by a value equal to or below that stipulated by the government, except in the case of commercial and industrial tenancy agreements for periods of five years or more and of forest tenancies, in which case the parties may freely stipulate rental increases exceeding the official index. Rural rents are paid annually and may never be paid in advance; forest tenancy rents are paid annually unless otherwise agreed between the parties and may also be paid in advance. The rent of urban tenancy agreements may be paid monthly, fortnightly or weekly and may be paid in advance but not longer than a month in advance. The tenant of an urban tenancy is usually required to give one payment as security. The subletting and assignment of the tenancy will only be permissible in the event of prior approval by the landlord and it is common to include a prohibition clause in the agreement. The assignment of industrial and commercial premises as part of a going concern or business is not subject to prior approval but only to notification within 15 days after assignment. The landlord is responsible for internal and external repairs. Repairs other than those included as the tenant's responsibility may only be executed with the landlord's prior authorisation.

5.1.2 The landlord is generally responsible for repairs to the property, unless otherwise agreed; but the tenant is obliged to return the property at the end of the contract in the same condition as when he took possession, allowing for usual wear and tear. Any extraordinary maintenance, repair and improvement works are normally undertaken by the tenant, unless it is agreed that the repairs are to be the responsibility of the landlord, or are ordered by the local municipality in which case the rent may be increased in order to reflect the property's accrued value. The insurance of a building is compulsory and will be paid for by the landlord. All service costs can be agreed to be the responsibility of the tenant, but the agreement must be in writing. Any default in payment of rent by the tenant as well as other statutory breaches will entitle the landlord to terminate, although such a termination will require a declaration by way of judicial decision. There is no standard tenancy contract, however, the clauses which may be included in the tenancy are restricted by mandatory legal impositions.

5.2 Privity of contract and estate

There is no concept of privity of contract or estate and all rights and liabilities will pass with the property.

5.3 Rent control and security of tenure

5.3.1 The legislation remains very protective of the tenant. If the landlord decides to increase the rent, within the index limit determined by the government, he must inform the tenant in writing with at least 30 days' prior notice. If the tenant does not object to the new rent, it is deemed accepted. The tenant may only object to any new rent demanded by the landlord in accordance with the index set by the government if there are relevant errors in the application of the law. It is not possible to increase rent in excess of the limits set by the government's index except where the landlord is compelled to execute repairs or extraordinary works. For commercial tenancy agreements, the index of rental increases is at different rates to those applicable to residential tenancies. For commercial tenancy agreements for an indefinite term, or those for five years or more, the parties are free to agree rental increases in the agreement. In the case of rural lettings the Agriculture Ministry may establish a table of maximum national rents every two years, taking into consideration the type of crop and the nature of the soil, and these will be the maximum payable.

5.3.2 Decree-Law 321-B/90 regulating residential and commercial tenancies introduced an important change in housing policy and provided greater protection for tenants. Under this legislation, tenancies are automatically renewed, and only the tenant may oppose renewal and terminate the tenancy agreement by means of a prior notice to the landlord, within a certain period before the expiry of the tenancy, the notice period depending on the length of the tenancy. Tenants are only free to terminate tenancy agreements at any time during the tenancy if the tenancy agreement is residential or commercial and is for a term of at least five years, and 90 days' notice is given. The landlord may oppose the automatic renewal of residential and commercial tenancy agreements for terms of at least five years by giving the tenant prior judicial notice one year before the tenancy expires without having to state any justification for that purpose. For all other types of tenancy agreement, the landlord may only oppose the automatic review on grounds such as the need to use the premises for his own purpose or to build up more lettable areas, or terminate the agreement, by means of a court action (*acção de despejo*) based on material statutory breach of the tenant's contractual obligations, such as defaulting on the rent payment, using the building for a purpose other than the one agreed, or some other similar material cause.

5.3.3 Rural tenancy agreements are automatically renewed for successive periods of three years where the tenant is a corporate entity and for successive periods of one year where the tenant is a physical person. There is no automatic renewal for forest tenancies.

5.4 Other legislative restrictions

The various types of tenancy agreements are subject to specific legislative controls on the terms which may be agreed between the parties and which the parties may not contract out of. Apart from those described in 5.3, they include provisions regarding the formalities of tenancy contracts and the tenant's pre-emption right on sale of the property. In addition, the landlord is under a legal obligation to carry out ordinary maintenance repairs and can be ordered to do so by the local municipal authority, in which case the landlord may be entitled to an increase in rent to reflect the value of the works.

5.5 Method of measurement

The method of measurement of premises is the same as generally used in civil engineering. For the purpose of leased premises, these are usually measured in terms of net lettable area.

6 FINANCE AND INVESTMENT SOURCES

Financial activity is conducted through various banks and investment companies with loan finance being the most popular form of finance, although finance leasing is also popular.

6.1 Loan finance

The traditional sources of loan finance are banks, namely the Bank of Portugal (the central bank), commercial banks, investment banks and mutual credit institutions, other credit institutions not authorised to accept deposits, investment companies, leasing and factoring companies, financial companies, such as brokers, asset management companies and investment fund management companies, and other institutions such as insurance companies, pension funds and insurance brokers. Commercial banks finance all sectors and the other credit institutions finance specific sectors. When granting loans, banks and credit institutions take two variables into consideration, the interest rate and the perceived risk. The interest rate varies depending on the risk, which in turn takes into account the mortgagor's financial status and the duration of the loan. Property finance is generally given against security over the property. Usually loans are granted with variable interest rates, with staged repayment of the principal (grace periods to be negotiated) and against a mortgage as security. Interest is paid gross. Companies may borrow money from their shareholders or issue bonds as a way of obtaining loan finance, but shareholders who provide loans do not obtain preferential treatment.

6.2 Investment or equity finance

The stock market is predominantly used to finance manufacturing and commercial companies. Property companies are not commonly financed on the stock market, as they are perceived as being too risky, and their financial statements may not accurately reflect the company's financial standing. Small, privately held companies with interests in property may be financed by their shareholders.

6.3 Mezzanine or mixed funding

Banks and prime lenders generally lend a proportion of the required sum (eg 70–80 per cent) of the value of the property. Other credit institutions may provide the next percentage of finance eg 10 per cent, taking a return by way of a higher interest rate. There are lenders who will provide both prime and mezzanine funding.

6.4 Sale and lease-back

Sale and lease-back arrangements exist, whereby companies who wish to realise their assets in order to release capital, or who wish to finance a new project, may negotiate to sell the property to an investor, often an institution, which will then grant them a lease-back at a market rent and therefore obtain an income from the property.

6.5 Tax leasing

Tax allowances regarding rents are granted to individual taxpayers but only on residential tenancies. Companies may deduct rents for corporate income tax purposes. Tax leasing as a financing mechanism is not commonly used.

6.6 Other types of property finance

It is possible to refer to the joint venture as another type of finance vehicle, as parties can come together, one providing the finance and the other providing the technical know-how for example, but it is not very common in the property market. A different type of property financing is immoveable finance leasing which is arranged for long periods of time with an interest rate defined at the beginning, and the capital paid periodically during the agreed period. At the end of the term, there is a residual value to be paid in order to acquire the asset. Immoveable finance leasing is a common form of property finance and is a concept akin to lease purchase, the property being bought by the financial institution which may either buy the building or buy the land and then enter into a building contract.

6.7 Institutional investment

The main investors in the property market are institutions such as insurance companies and investment funds. The management of the investment funds must be done by management companies. These management companies have as their exclusive object the administration, management and representation of one or more funds within a single market, in this case property funds. In the case of closed investment funds, in which the capital to invest in the acquisition of immoveable values (or moveables) is fixed in the constitution of the funds, the management of the funds may be also carried out by commercial or investment banks and by investment companies. In special cases, the Ministry of Finance may authorise the administration of investment funds by other types of credit institutions. The funds aim to create a diversified portfolio of immoveable assets, which allows the reallocation of risk whilst ensuring a certain return on the investment. It is also possible to incorporate funds to invest in securities. Given the very rigid constraints governing rental contracts there is not much investment in industrial buildings. Residential investment is essentially carried out by some investment funds and the SGII companies (see 6.8). There are few sales of agricultural land; farmers would normally rent the land they wish to cultivate. The pulp industry, however, has in the past acquired large properties in which it has planted trees which are then used in its factories. Recently and as a result of the EU agricultural policy, some companies have acquired small pieces of land with a view to carrying out highly subsidised activities.

6.8 Investors other than institutions

There are also other companies dedicated to investment in property. The SGII (*Sociedade Gestora de Investimento Imobiliário*) has as its main purpose the leasing of immoveable property, bought or constructed by them and the rendering of related services. Other investors in the property market include trading and development companies and private investors.

7 FORMS OF SECURITY

Banks make substantial loans by reference both to the creditworthiness of the customer and securities given. Relationship banking is common but there is no general rule and arrangements vary considerably.

7.1 Mortgages

7.1.1 A private voluntary mortgage (*hypotecas*) is constituted by a notarial deed or by unilateral declaration (eg a will) and all types of mortgages have to be registered to be valid. Mortgages may be legal (granted by law to certain creditors, such as the state and municipalities for the recovery of property tax), judicial (to enforce judgments) or voluntary (created by agreement or unilateral declaration). A mortgage may only be created by the person having title to the interest in the property, and may include someone other than the owner, eg the holder of a surface right, a usufructuary or the holder of concession rights over public assets. Mortgages are characterised by personal liability; hence if a debtor creates a mortgage over one of his assets, and if the proceeds arising from the sale of the mortgaged asset are not sufficient to pay the entire debt, the debtor remains personally liable for the balance of the debt. It is possible to create a mortgage for future or conditional debts. In the case of a future or conditional mortgage, the relevant date of the mortgage is not that of creation of the future debt, nor is it the date of the verification of the condition, but the date of the registration of the mortgage. It is also possible to create a mortgage mentioning only the maximum amount for which the mortgage will provide security, and fixing the precise amount at a later stage. The costs are notarial fees and registration fees (each of 0.3 per cent plus around PTE12,000 for transactions over PTE10,000,000), and stamp duty of 0.5 per cent.

7.1.2 A mortgage grants the creditor the right to the proceeds of sale of a certain immoveable (or equivalent) asset that belongs to the debtor or to a third party, with priority over other creditors. The mortgage will never grant the creditor the right to the ownership of the property or to the right mortgaged where the debt is discharged, and any agreement attempting to convey ownership will be void. If the debtor fails to fulfil his obligation, the creditor may demand enforcement of his right in court by requesting a sale of the mortgaged asset and payment from the proceeds of the judicial sale. The court will first allow the debtor time to make payment before ordinary sale. Enforcement may therefore take some time. The mortgagee may only recover his debt from the proceeds arising from the sale of other assets of the debtor when the proceeds arising from the property or right mortgaged are not sufficient. The mortgage should always be enforced first with the proceeds of sale of the asset mortgaged, and the mortgagor will have a claim if assets other than those providing security are sold first. All other creditors are called to the judicial proceedings to file their claims and the proceeds of sale are distributed to the creditors in order of priority (see 2.10). When the mortgaged asset is damaged or the mortgage becomes insufficient to secure the entire obligation, the creditor has the right to demand substitution by a new mortgage or reinforcement (by extension of the existing mortgage to a greater amount) of the mortgage from the debtor. If the mortgagor does not comply, the mortgagee may demand the immediate fulfilment of the outstanding obligation or, in the case of a future obligation, the registration of the mortgage over other assets of the debtor. Where a mortgagor is under the obligation to insure the mortgaged asset but fails to do so within the agreed time limit or fails to do so at all, the mortgagee has the right to insure the asset himself at the mortgagor's expense. It must be noted, however, that privileges, regarding preferential debts, will take priority even over a first mortgage (see 2.3).

7.2 Floating and other charges

It is not possible to create a floating charge over the wider assets of the mortgagor, or a general fixed charge over all the assets of the mortgagor granting the creditor a priority right in payment, although it is possible to enforce a charge over other assets belonging to the debtor where the security is not sufficient (see 7.1.2). Creditors with no security may nominate any asset belonging to the debtor (if the debtor fails to indicate any assets during the legally prescribed period) and obtain payment with the proceeds of the sale of such an asset after the creditors with security over those assets (who will take priority) have been paid. All forms of security other than the mortgage do not need to be registered in order to be effective, they must merely follow the form prescribed by law. Other charges over land are property privileges, the right to retain and the right of pledge over receivables (see 2.3).

7.3 Bonds and guarantees

Guarantees are usually required jointly or alternatively with mortgages as security. Guarantees may be granted by any physical person, bank or credit institution. Stamp tax at the rate of 0.5 per cent is payable on the sum guaranteed. Guarantees are less formal and cheaper than mortgages. Companies may not grant guarantees unless specifically incorporated for the purpose. The person or bank giving the guarantee undertakes to fulfil the obligation(s) in case of default by the debtor. As the obligations guaranteed are determined, then so may the maximum amount guaranteed be determined. Bank guarantees are very common, whilst guarantees granted by physical persons are less so and are usually given on behalf of small, privately held companies or among members of the same family.

7.4 Credit insurance

Credit insurance is available and is most commonly given up to a certain amount as an alternative to a bank guarantee.

8 PLANNING AND BUILDING CONTROLS

Building standards are established by the government and apply throughout the country. Planning law consists essentially of regional regulations made by government and municipal regulations made by the local municipal authorities but approved by central government and which must comply with the government's central planning requirements.

8.1 Planning authorities

Ultimate control of planning rests with the government and the Ministry of Planning and Regulation of Land. At a local level, the municipal authorities for the area propose planning regulations which require approval and ratification by the national government before implementation by the municipalities.

8.2 Development plans

The 'national plan' defines the overall programme for national and regional action, the major economic objectives and the methods to be used to attain those objectives. Regional plans for the regulation of the territory (PROT) are also prepared by the government. These plans aim to ensure proper and adequate use of land and cover all national territory and adjacent islands. The PROT establishes the general rules of occupation, land use for the area and the planning standards to be used by the area municipal authorities. The government consults the municipalities concerned and then approves the PROT by way of governmental resolution. A PROT must take into account nationally protected areas, eg agricultural land, forests, conservation areas including any protected flora or fauna, as well as industrial centres and infrastructure plans. Municipal planning regulations must be in accordance with both the national and regional plans and will include regulations regarding occupation, use and development within the municipality. The municipal planning regulations establish the classification of land and the zoning of the area, which is based on development objectives, housing needs, social requirements, transportation, communications and infrastructure. Where the municipality is a town, the urban plan establishes the form, the size of the city, the historical buildings in need of protection, the open spaces and the layout of the streets and the infrastructure. Permission for development will only be granted if it complies with the regional and municipal planning regulations in force and the relevant building regulations (see 8.4). The municipalities may veto development proposals or authorise the destruction of works that breach the municipal plan.

8.3 Planning control and procedures

All construction and change of use require municipal licence. The separation of land into plots for construction is subject to another licence granted by the municipality and the legal procedures determining the application differ (see 8.3.1). The municipality assesses fees on urban infrastructure when issuing licences for the separation of land into plots and licences for construction. As the decision whether to grant a licence and the imposition of fees are connected, it may be said that, to a great extent, planning decisions are decided by the municipality according to subjective criteria. Environmental assessments and environmental impact reports may also need to be submitted with the licence application for certain types of proposed development (see 9.5).

8.3.1 The application to obtain a licence for construction (*licença de construçao*) must be filed at the municipality. Before filing the application, the applicant may request a prior opinion on the legal requirements and planning constraints which may apply to the land in question. Proposals for new constructions, reconstruction and alterations of existing buildings must always set out the intended use of the building. Fees are paid if and when the licence is granted. The applicant must have an interest in the land. The municipality must request the opinion of all public entities with specific powers regarding any matter related to the requested licence. The procedure for obtaining a licence for the separation of plots requires the publication of the application and any person may file a claim against the application or request information. Outline applications do not exist and all applications must be detailed.

8.3.2 If the municipality does not make a decision within the time fixed for the type of licence requested, which may vary from 30 to 90 days depending also on whether the locality is urban or rural, the application may be deemed to be tacitly approved. Licences may be granted conditionally. The applicant to whom a licence has been refused may file an appeal to the administrative courts. When refusing a licence, the municipality must justify its decision on certain grounds listed by law. An appellant must invoke illegality of the municipality's decision to refuse the licence as grounds for the appeal.

8.3.3 Licences have a fixed duration, which will be stated on the individual licence, after which they will lapse. Licences attach to the land although the name of the applicant will be mentioned on the licence. Licences pass with the interest in the land and the new owner may request the amendment of the name of the holder of the licence. Developments must be completed once they have commenced.

8.3.4 The municipality may order unauthorised works to cease immediately and has the power to undertake on-the-spot enforcement and to order the demolition of buildings which are in breach of legally applicable planning constraints. Before making an order, the municipality may send a notice to the owner of the building and those affected by the municipal order may appeal against it in the administrative courts. Breaches of planning regulations are subject to fines and are classified as administrative offences. The failure to enforce such orders within the set time limit will not render the use or breach lawful.

8.4 Building standards, control and supervision

Building standards are set out in the urban building general regulations (RGEU) and other specific regulations regarding access, height of buildings, fire and seismic danger which must be complied with in the construction plan submitted by the applicant. The construction plan will be considered by the municipality to see if it conforms with the RGEU before it issues the construction licence. Control over both planning matters and building standards is therefore exercised at the time the construction licence is issued. Inspections of the authorised works are carried out by the municipality which may impose penalties whenever there are deviations from the approved project.

8.5 Protection of buildings of special interest

Public buildings of special architectural, historic and artistic interest are managed by a public entity called the IPPAR. Municipal planning regulations determine the historic areas in each municipality. Buildings located in these areas are subject to restrictions with regard to alteration and demolition works.

8.6 Expropriation and compulsory purchase and compensation

Property may be expropriated on the grounds of legally foreseeable public requirements by an administrative act, which is first notified by publication in the Official Gazette specifying the asset to be expropriated. Once this declaration has been made, the acquiring authority has the right to take possession of the immoveable asset. Expropriation proceedings may only be initiated by the state or by local authorities and only where they have first attempted to find alternative means of satisfying the public requirement. Those concerned should be forewarned, with at least 30 days' prior notice, that the authorities intend to expropriate their assets and will be deemed entitled to the fundamental right of adequate and prompt compensation. Any person affected will then have a right of reversion if the expropriated assets are not employed within two years, and for the purpose for which they were expropriated. Compensation is calculated at the date of declaration of public interest over the property, and interest is added in accordance with the rate of inflation until the expropriation procedure is finalised. The added value arising from expropriation is not taken into account. Where agreement cannot be reached over the expropriation procedure, the parties may resort to litigation, in which case it may take years to complete the procedure and for compensation to be paid.

9 ENVIRONMENTAL MATTERS

The general provisions regulating the environment are comprised in the Environment Protection Law 1987. Environmental protection aims to be preventive and industrial premises and certain developments are required to produce a report on the environmental consequences which the public authorities will take into consideration before relevant licences are issued. Environmental violations are penalised by fines and may give rise to compensation to an injured party. Serious environmental damage may be a strict liability offence. Environmental matters are the responsibility of the Environment Minister.

9.1 Protection against atmospheric and noise pollution

9.1.1 The government has recently introduced a statutory regime for the protection and improvement of the quality of air. The government sets the maximum levels of emissions and recommended levels of certain atmospheric pollutants and has declared certain waters or zones as critical, ie a risk to human health. Monitoring stations have been set up to take readings of pollution levels in large towns as well as near large industrial plants. The open air combustion of industrial and toxic waste is prohibited in urban zones. The installation and expansion of industrial plants emitting atmospheric pollutants are subject to regulations issued by the Environmental Ministry. For all forms of pollution there is a general obligation to remedy the damage caused and to return the environment to its previous state. If this is not done, the polluter will be fined and may be criminally liable.

9.1.2 Protection against noise is regulated by a 1987 Decree, which sets noise levels for industrial and commercial premises as well as those for ground and air traffic. The construction of housing, schools and hospital buildings in areas with very high noise levels is forbidden and is punishable by fines.

9.2 Water pollution

Control of water pollution is regulated by a 1990 Decree which sets the minimum quality requirements for all types of water. The enforcement of legal provisions concerning water quality is carried out by several governmental departments and by the municipalities. Discharges into the ground and neighbouring water courses are subject to the obtainment of a licence from the Environmental Ministry. Discharges into municipal drains require a municipal licence. It is forbidden to discharge polluted waters and waste substances into the sea, rivers and on beaches. As for all forms of pollution, the polluter is under an obligation to return the environment to its original state and will face fines for the failure to do so. Discharges in breach of consent are subject to fines, as are discharges without a licence, although penalties for the latter will be at a higher level.

9.3 Waste storage and disposal

Waste storage and disposal regulations were enacted in 1995 when EC Directives 91/156 and 91/689 were transposed into national law, prohibiting the uncontrolled discharge, deposit and elimination of waste, as well as the transformation or elimination of waste by unauthorised facilities. Those violating the legal provisions will be subject to fines which are substantially greater where the offender is a corporate entity.

9.4 Contaminated land

Contamination registers do not exist at present. Proper enquiries of nearby landfill sites, whether the site was used for waste disposal, whether it was infilled or reclaimed, or whether dangerous materials were used in the construction of any of the buildings may be made where an interest in land is being transferred but are not very common. These enquiries can be addressed to the municipalities. The buyer may carry out any type of enquiry or searches on legal and geological matters regarding the land, although these are more commonly undertaken where the buyer is a developer. The seller is under an obligation to disclose any known defects of the land sold and the disclosure obligation extends to contamination. There is a general obligation not to pollute the environment and to restore a site to its previous condition. The Environmental Ministry is the authority responsible for monitoring, identifying and supervising contamination and its treatment, and has the power to require treatment, and/or clean-up, impose fines and claim compensation. Decontamination and other remedial measures are paid for out of public funds whenever these are carried out by someone other than the polluter.

9.5 Environmental impact assessments

As a result of the EC directive an environmental impact assessment must be carried out prior to any construction or infrastructure project which may have relevant consequences upon the environment. The obtaining of the construction licence (see 8.3) depends upon the outcome of the impact assessment. In the case of construction projects having less effect upon the environment, it is sufficient to file a lesser environmental impact report together with the application to obtain the construction licence.

10 DEVELOPMENT

10.1 Development projects, structures and vehicles

The simplest development will typically involve the purchase of a site by a developer who will use a contractor and sell or lease the building as a whole or in autonomous parts. It is common for developers to find sites both upon request as well as speculatively. On more complex development schemes, it is common to have a number of parties involved, each providing different skills, eg one contributing the financial skills and another the development expertise. On large scale developments each building can be put into a separate company with a management company responsible for the overall development.

10.2 Building contracts and appointment of professionals

10.2.1 Typical forms of building contract

There are two major types of building contract, the private building contract and the public building contract. Private building contracts are regulated by the Civil Code in a fairly generic form. They are contracts for the rendering of services, the object of which is the execution of work for consideration. The contractor must execute the work as agreed, and the owner of the works may supervise if he so wishes, but only if he does not impair the work being carried out. Such supervision is to be done at the expense of the owner. Public building contracts are regulated in great detail by administrative law under a 1993 Decree. The employer has supervisory powers with regard to the execution of the works and may give instructions to the contractor. Generally there is no direct contractual relationship between the owner and the subcontractors and it will be necessary for the contractor to negotiate the terms of the subcontractors' workers.

10.2.2 Common terms

For private building contracts, the price, if it is not agreed in advance, will be determined when it is completed by the usual price charged by the contractor for the particular type of work. The price must be paid when the works are finally accepted as complete by the owner, unless otherwise agreed. The owner may cancel the works at any time during the building contract, but he must indemnify the contractor for the work carried out including his expenses and lost profits. The contractor has right of retention over the works based on non-payment of any instalments by the owner. The owner may check the condition of the work before taking definitive possession of the building. In case of discovery of any defects, the owner must inform the contractor within 30 days. The owner may ask the contractor to undertake repairs if possible; if not he can require the work to be done again. If the defects are not repaired and the work is not carried out again, the owner is entitled to a price reduction and, if the works are unfit for their intended use, the owner may terminate the contract and ask for the return of his money. Building contracts usually provide for the imposition of penalties on the contractor in the event of late completion, otherwise the employer will be entitled to compensation, unless the cause of the delay is outside the contractor's control. In public building contracts, it is possible to stipulate three forms of payment: a global price, itemised prices or a percentage payment. A global price contract is used when the contract's consideration is fixed in advance, in which case it will be the only sum that will be paid for the execution of the work. The only works subject to this price regime are those which lend themselves to accurate estimates of the costs of the materials and the manpower involved. The building contract with itemised prices is used when the remuneration of the contractor results from costs being itemised for each piece of work to be carried out under the contract. Building contracts by percentage occur when the contractor has the obligation to execute the works for a price that corresponds to its cost, plus a percentage to cover the administration charges and normal profit. In case a public authority terminates the contract during construction, the contractor is entitled to compensation for damages and consequential loss. In the event of non-payment the contractor is entitled to termination of the contract; before accepting the works carried out, the employer must examine them and inform the contractor of any defects detected. The contractor is then under an obligation to remedy the defects or otherwise carry out the work again.

10.2.3 Standard form of contracts

There are standard forms of contract used by public authorities, and common forms used within the industry.

10.2.4 Appointment of the professional team

The members of the professional team are usually appointed by the builder and are subsequently approved by the employer together with the builder's contract unless otherwise agreed between the parties.

10.3 Roles of the various parties

The developer and the owner/occupier are usually the same person. The owner normally hires a project manager who acts as his representative and has responsibility for the supervision of the works. This means that he will check, amongst other things, whether the works are carried out in accordance with the plan as well as the quality of the materials used. The project manager is paid under a service contract. Most projects also involve an architect who makes the drawings which form the most important part of the project and which are presented to the municipality for approval. There is often a civil engineer who is responsible for the structure of the building. Quantity surveyors and electrical engineers as well as other types of experts may either be part of the contractor's staff or be subcontracted. In the case of public building contracts, contracts are usually awarded subsequent to a public tender, although this is not always the case for smaller public projects.

10.4 Defects and remedies

10.4.1 In the case of public works, contractors must present a guarantee, fixed at at least five per cent of the total price of the work (or opt for the withholding of 5 per cent of each payment), which will remain in force up to one year, or longer where the type of work justifies this, after the provisory acceptance of the quotation for the work. During this period of one year, if any defect arises which was not detected at the provisional inspection, the owner may use the warranty to correct such defects. The guarantee secures the completion of the works on time and in accordance with the contract terms.

10.4.2 A subsequent owner or occupier, other than the direct contractual employer, may recover the cost of remedying defects from the contractor for a period of five years from the date of completion of the works.

10.5 Defects insurance

If, during the five years subsequent to the conclusion of the project, the building collapses totally or partially, or presents serious problems or defects due to a fault in the soil or the construction, the contractor will be responsible for all damage suffered by the owner. Risk insurance is available as a more viable alternative to suing the contractor. Contractors of public works must comply with certain financial and economic requirements in order to carry out public works, in order to minimise the risk of default.

10.6 Copyright

The architect's work is protected by law, regardless of any registration. Only the architect of the project may authorise construction of the building based on the project. A breach of this right is considered a criminal offence and is subject to a fine. During the construction of a building, the owner of the works may not introduce alterations without previously consulting the architect, despite having the right to supervise construction and carry out all the work phases, to ensure the conformity of the work with the project.

10.7 Fees

Architects and engineers have standard professional fees which are a percentage of the amount involved in the project. These standard fees are set by the professional associations and are relatively high so it is common to negotiate lower fees. The architect's fees reduce with the size of the project and will depend on which of four legal categories of work the project falls within. Overall fees will range from 27.41 per cent on an amount of PTE50,000 to 2.88 per cent on an amount of PTE12 billion.

10.8 Taxes

All construction projects are subject to value added tax at a rate of 17 per cent.

11 TAXES

11.1 Corporation tax

Any company which is resident in Portugal for tax purposes is liable to pay the standard corporation tax on its worldwide profits, subject to relief under any double taxation treaty with the country where its profits originate. All profits of the company are taken into account even if not remitted or sent to Portugal. For corporate income tax purposes, profit and income from property, eg rent, is considered to be profit. A different rate is charged depending upon whether the company is resident, non-resident with a permanent establishment in Portugal or non-resident. A company is considered to be resident in Portugal where its registered office or central management is in Portugal.

11.1.1 Tax rates

Income from property is subject to the standard tax rate of 36 per cent in addition to a municipal surtax (which can range from 0 per cent to 10 per cent of the standard tax rate thus providing for a maximum tax rate of 39.6 per cent) for resident companies and non-resident companies with a permanent establishment, and 25 per cent for non-resident companies.

11.1.2 Computation and administration

Business expenses necessary for the effective management of companies may be deducted when computing income subject to corporate income tax, provided they are properly documented and may include expenses of a revenue or recurring nature if these conditions are complied with. The company itself computes the corporate income tax due by self-assessment in the annual tax return. This tax return must be submitted by 31 May of each year, recording the profits from the preceding tax year ending 31 December. If the company's tax year does not end on 31 December, the return must be submitted within five months following the end of the tax year. Although the system is one of self-assessment, the tax authorities have the power to adjust returns and issue revised assessments.

11.1.3 Depreciation and capital allowances

Most tangible fixed assets used in a business are depreciable for tax purposes if they have useful lives exceeding one year and they progressively diminish in value due to use, technological advances, or to any other reason. Assets worth less than PTE20,000 which do not form an integral part of a larger asset may be fully written off in the year in question. Tax depreciation of fixed assets is normally computed by the straight line method, but the declining balance method may be used for most types of assets if they are acquired new. Typical straight line rates prescribed for tax purposes include two per cent for commercial buildings, five per cent for industrial buildings, 25 per cent for motor vehicles and 12.5–25 per cent for machinery and equipment. Pre-operational expenses may be amortised by the straightline method over three years and patents may be amortised over their useful lives.

11.1.4 Withholding tax

Income from property arising from leases or similar contracts is subject to withholding tax at source at a rate of 15 per cent whenever the tenant is a company or another entity with organised accounts. The withholding tax rate is the same whether the recipient is resident or non-resident, an individual or a company. The withholding tax is payable on account of the final corporate or personal income tax, and is therefore deducted upon calculation of the final tax. Non-resident companies without a permanent establishment are subject to a final tax rate of 25 per cent (see also 14.5).

11.2 Taxes on development value

There are no taxes on development value.

11.3 Taxes on capital gains

There is no separate capital gains tax. Corporate income tax ranging from 36 per cent to 39.6 per cent is levied on both income and capital gains and applies equally to Portuguese resident companies and foreign companies with a permanent establishment in Portugal. Capital gains from the disposal of property benefit from an indexation allowance to ensure that inflationary gains are not taxed and rollover relief where gains are reinvested in fixed assets within the two following accounting years. Foreign companies without a permanent establishment in Portugal are also subject to corporate income tax on capital gains arising from the sale of property located in Portugal, the applicable tax rate being 25 per cent. Capital gains made by individuals on the sale of property are also included as taxable income for personal income tax purposes but, with the exception of land, only 50 per cent of the capital gain is computed.

11.4 Taxes on owner of property

Municipal property tax (*contribuição autárquica*) is levied on the owner, or the holder of a usufruct or a surface right (either a company or an individual, resident or non-resident), of property and assessed on the basis of the registered value of the property. The tax rate is 0.8 per cent for rural properties and from 0.7 per cent to 1.3 per cent for urban properties, the applicable tax rate being established by each municipality. Municipal property tax is assessed annually and paid in April (if the tax amounts to at least PTE30,000 it can be paid in two instalments, one in April and the other in September). Inheritance and gift tax is charged on every gratuitous transfer (by inheritance or gift) of moveable or immoveable property and payable by the recipient of such property. The tax rates are progressive (from 4 per cent up to 50 per cent) depending both on the amount involved and the degree of kinship amongst the parties involved.

11.5 Taxes on occupier

There are no taxes on the occupier.

11.6 Taxes on land transfer

Property transfer tax (*sisa*) is payable on onerous transfers of property, usufruct or surface rights for consideration and is charged to the buyer on the basis of the purchase price. The acquisition of urban property for residential purposes is exempt up to the amount of PTE10,700,000 subject to progressive rates from that amount up to PTE29,700,000 and subject to a single rate of 10 per cent from that amount onwards. The transfer of other urban property and of land for construction is subject to a single rate of 10 per cent and the transfer of rural property to the rate of eight per cent. *Sisa* must be paid before the transfer occurs.

11.7 Wealth taxes

There are no wealth taxes.

11.8 Value added tax

The value added tax (VAT) standard rate is 17 per cent. The transfer of a freehold and of a lesser interest in property is exempted from VAT, which means that VAT inputs cannot be recovered. However the taxpayer can waive this exemption and VAT may then be recovered. In the event of a waiver, the VAT rate applicable is 17 per cent. In order to waive the VAT exemption, the conditions are that the taxpayer must have an accounting system which can identify the income and costs related to each building or lease ('the effective application' method); there must be an agreement between the tenant or the seller regarding the waiver of the VAT exemption; finally, the taxpayer must submit a 'special form' for VAT purposes in which he opts for VAT and selects the effective application method of deduction, accompanied by an application stating the names of the parties involved, the value of the rents or sale price and any other contractual conditions of the business.

11.9 Local and other taxes

There are no other taxes of relevance other than those mentioned.

12 GRANTS AND INCENTIVES

12.1 Subsidies, grants and loans

The government may grant incentives for land acquisitions included in projects in those sectors included in governmental programmes usually subsidised by the EU. These programmes have a limited duration so the investor should obtain information on the programmes being implemented at the time. There are also special incentive programmes for tourism, industry, agriculture and job-creating projects as well as for the repair of leased residential property. Isolated incentives include the subsidy of rents of low income families.

12.2 Tax allowances and reliefs

Foreign entities setting up operations in Portugal have access to a package of financial and tax incentives to be granted in compliance with specific regimes and conditions. These incentives are usually reserved for large investments (in excess of PTE5 billion) which are export orientated. Projects involving less investment may also be awarded with this package of financial and tax incentives provided they are aimed at promoting the globalisation of Portuguese industry. These financial packages are negotiated with the government which then enters into an agreement describing the conditions of the award of the incentives with the investor.

12.3 Other public schemes and incentives

There may be other temporary or passing incentives and the best source of information for these is IAPMEL, Rua Rodrigo da Fonseca, n 73, Lisboa, Portugal.

13 COMPANIES AND BUSINESS ENTITIES

13.1 Limited and unlimited companies

The responsibility of those holding participations (or shareholdings) in companies may be limited to the specific payment of capital or unlimited with regard to the company's liabilities. The different types of company are the share company, the limited liability company and the unlimited liability company.

13.1.1 Share companies (*Sociedades Anónimas, SA*s) must have at least five members. The minimum capital of share companies is PTE5,000,000 and is represented in share certificates. Shares may be bearer shares or nominative and are easily transferred. Share companies have a board of directors or a sole director (provided the share capital is less then PTE30,000,000), and a supervisory board with at least a registered accountant as a member and another as substitute or a sole supervisor who must be a registered accountant and another as substitute. Share companies must be incorporated in a notarial deed and registered and may be privately held or held by the public and listed on the stock exchange, and are widely used as a business entity. Certain types of commercial activities, including banking and financing, may only be carried out by share companies.

13.1.2 Limited liability companies or 'quota companies' (*Sociedades por Quotas, Lda*s) may have just one member if the company is so designated or two or more members and a minimum share capital of PTE400,000. The capital of quota companies is represented by parts or quotas with any amount not less than PTE20,000. The quotas are registered in the commercial registry department under the name of the owner and any transfer of ownership must be registered. Quota companies have one or two directors or a board of directors and may need to have the accounts audited by a registered accountant or a supervisory board where certain limits on turnover, total balance sheet and number of employees are exceeded over two years. Quota companies must be incorporated in a notarial deed and registered at the commercial registry department. Quota companies are widely used as a business entity and have a more flexible structure than share companies and involve fewer structural costs.

13.1.3 Unlimited liability companies (*Sociedade em Nome Colectivo*) must have at least two members and there are no minimum capital requirements. The capital is represented in parts registered in the commercial registry department under the name of the owner. Unlimited liability companies must be incorporated in a notarial deed and registered. Any transfer of parts held in the capital of these companies must be done by notarial deed and the name of the new owner must be registered. The unlimited liability company may have a board of directors or a sole director and will not have a supervisory board. These companies are only used sporadically and are usually family-owned companies as the members will be personally liable for the company's liabilities in the event of the company's assets being insufficient.

13.2 Partnerships

Comandita is akin to partnership and is a mixed liability entity, as some partners have liability limited to the payment of their part in the capital and other partners have unlimited liability. *Comandita* may have its capital represented in parts in the commercial registry (transfers of such parts to be made by notarial deed) or may have the holdings of partners with limited liability represented in shares. The management of these companies is carried out by the partners with unlimited liability except where otherwise set out in the bye-laws. *Comanditas* must be incorporated in a notarial deed and must be registered at the commercial registry. *Comanditas* have separate legal personality and are not commonly used as a form of business entity.

13.3 Other types of business association

13.3.1 Complementary groups of companies (ACE) involve an association of companies or individuals set up for the mutual benefit of their members or to assist them with their activities. The ACE constitutes a separate legal entity from its members. ACEs are set up in an agreement executed in a notarial deed and registered at the commercial registry. The ACEs operate as a company with or without share capital, and with a board of directors, although they may not have the generation of profit as a purpose, and may not purchase an interest in land, hold participations in other companies, or in other ACEs, or be appointed a director of other companies or ACEs.

13.3.2 It is also possible to create a joint venture. Different legal relationships may be established between companies wishing to work together. It is possible to form a contractual relationship (*associação em participação*) whereby one party undertakes to participate in the profits or losses of a predetermined activity undertaken by another company. Companies may also form a group which will be run by common directors for a fixed period; or they may participate in the capital of another company in order to create relationships of total or partial control as well as establish cross-participation. The companies involved are in a group relationship which imposes certain responsibilities upon holding companies.

14 INTERNATIONAL

14.1 Restriction on inward investment

The Foreign Investment Agency (ICEP) aims to promote foreign investment in Portugal. ICEP also functions as a regulatory foreign investment agency, which nowadays serves mainly statistical purposes. Foreign investment operations must be registered with ICEP within 30 days. Foreign investment is encouraged, and there are no restrictions on the introduction of funds into Portugal for any type of operation including the purchase of property; nor are there any restrictions on the ownership of Portuguese property by foreign entities.

14.2 Exchange controls

The repatriation or transfer of funds out of Portugal is free although the bank carrying out the transfer may give information to the Bank of Portugal for statistical purposes.

14.3 Restrictions and registrations on carrying on a business

Foreign investment is encouraged by the government. It is not necessary to have a local investor as an associate. There are no generic restrictions on foreign entities or companies carrying on business in Portugal, although there are specific restrictions on foreign participation in companies with a public service concession.

14.4 Repatriation of income and proceeds of property trading and development

Foreign investors have the right to freely remit dividends and repatriate profits of the sale, after deducting all taxes due (eg withholding tax as set out in 11.1.4), plus any capital gains, without any limitation.

14.5 Withholding tax

Royalties, commissions, rents and interest from bank accounts are subject to withholding tax at source at a rate of 15 per cent. Withholding taxes have been referred to at 11.1.4.

14.6 Double taxation relief

Portugal has entered into a number of double taxation agreements with most European countries, with some relevant exceptions notably the Netherlands and Luxembourg.

CHAPTER 15

The Republic of Ireland

Colin Keane

Partner, McCann, Fitzgerald, Dublin

CONTENTS

1 OWNERSHIP OF LAND 493
2 OTHER INTERESTS IN LAND 495
3 TITLE TO LAND 498
4 TRANSACTIONS IN LAND 500
5 LEASES AND OTHER RIGHTS OF OCCUPATION 503
6 FINANCE AND INVESTMENT SOURCES 505
7 FORMS OF SECURITY 508
8 PLANNING AND BUILDING REGULATION 509
9 ENVIRONMENTAL MATTERS 512
10 DEVELOPMENT 514
11 TAXES 518
12 GRANTS AND INCENTIVES 522
13 COMPANIES AND BUSINESS ENTITIES 523
14 INTERNATIONAL 526

CHAPTER 15

The Republic of Ireland

1 OWNERSHIP OF LAND

The Republic of Ireland, like the United Kingdom, is a common law jurisdiction. Property law is based partly on statute and partly on the common law deriving from the decisions of the Irish courts. Decisions of the United Kingdom courts, although not binding, do still have persuasive authority in the Irish courts. The principal statutes relating to property law are the Landlord and Tenant Law Amendment, Ireland, Act 1860 ('Deasy's Act'), the Vendor and Purchaser Act 1874, the Conveyancing Act 1881, the Settled Land Acts 1882–90, the Registration of Title Act 1964, the Land Act 1965, the Landlord and Tenant (Ground Rents) (No 2) Act 1978 and the Landlord and Tenant (Amendment) Act 1980. A person owns an estate or interest in land which gives him rights and imposes duties. The principal forms of tenure or land ownership are freehold and leasehold.

1.1 Types of tenure

1.1.1 Freehold or absolute ownership

A freehold estate is closest to absolute ownership and confers the right to the land in perpetuity, which can be disposed of by sale, by will or succession on death. The right includes all buildings and structures on the land and the right to everything above and below the land; anything fixed or annexed to the land is treated as part of the land. Land and buildings are not owned separately. The freehold carries with it the ownership of mines and minerals, subject to obtaining a licence to explore and extract. A type of freehold unique to Ireland is the fee farm grant, a cross between a freehold and a leasehold estate. It is a perpetual estate subject to a rent ('fee farm rent') and sometimes to covenants. It is still used in commercial developments where there is a need to reserve the benefit of covenants but at the same time dispose of the property in perpetuity.

1.1.2 Leasehold

A leasehold is less than a freehold estate and involves possession and the exclusive right to use and occupy the property or to receipt of the rents and profits of the land for specified periods, in return for payment either to the freeholder or the holder of the superior lease. A leasehold interest has characteristics of a right in rem but under Irish law is based in contract rather than in tenure. Buildings on leased lands are exclusively for the use and occupation of the leaseholder for the term of the lease but the building will revert to the land on which the building is built upon expiration or earlier determination of the lease (unless, of course, there are statutory or contractual renewal rights). A short-term rack rent (ie open market rental) leaseholder generally cannot dispose of his interest without the permission of his landlord although the latter cannot unreasonably withhold his consent. Long-term ground leases generally do not contain restrictions on alienation. Depending on the market, short-term commercial leases (ie normally up to 35 years) may or may not be granted for a premium (or capital sum) in addition to the annual rack rent. A ground lease of industrial or commercial premises would normally be for a considerably longer term and be for a premium (being the price of the land), in addition to a ground rent. In general, businesses tend towards rack renting rather than freehold or leasehold purchase so as not to tie up capital in land and buildings which could be used as working capital. For further details on leasehold arrangements, see section 5.

1.1.3 Joint ownership

Property may be owned by two or more people at the same time and the co-owners must be treated as a single entity for the purposes of transactions in respect of that land. Joint ownership can be created by agreement or by will. The two main forms of co-ownership are joint tenancy and tenancy in common. In a joint tenancy, each co-owner has an equal right to possession of the land with the other co-owners and when one joint tenant dies his share in the land passes to the surviving joint tenants. If, however, the joint tenant declares severance or disposes of his interest during his lifetime, which he is free to do, the joint tenancy comes to an end. The severed or disposed interest becomes a tenancy in common and the remaining joint tenants continue to hold the interest as joint tenants. A joint tenant therefore cannot, by nature of his interest, dispose of his interest by will leaving his share to someone other than his co-owners. In a tenancy in common, each tenant in common has a distinct and separate interest or share in the property and is free to dispose of the interest at any time and also to leave it to a third party by will.

1.1.4 Condominia

There is no form of condominium ownership in Irish law. Apartments are usually sold by way of long lease in consideration of a premium and a nominal rent. The lease also usually reserves a service charge payable to a management company.

1.1.5 Lesser rights

Lesser rights of occupation or use may be granted by way of licence, eg the right to park cars. However, a licence purporting to grant a right of exclusive possession will usually be construed as a lease even though it may be called a licence. A licence is generally personal to the parties and is not assignable nor does it create any interest in the land itself.

1.2 Legal and beneficial ownership

All property may be held upon trust by the legal owner for a beneficial owner. The interests of a beneficiary are called equitable interests and may arise, eg when the buyer of land under an enforceable contract for sale acquires an immediate equitable interest in it. However, an equitable interest may be defeated by a subsequent buyer of a legal estate in the land who acquires it in good faith and without notice of the prior equitable interest. A beneficiary generally only has rights against the trustees and the income or proceeds of sale. A trust may be expressly established by deed or will providing, eg, for life interests, income for minors or for a class of beneficiaries.

1.3 Restrictions on land ownership and dealing

1.3.1 There are few restrictions on land ownership. Minors (persons under 18) are unable to hold land and consents for the purchase of interests in non-urban land must be obtained by certain non-residents (see further 14.1). Governmental consents are also required for the takeover of companies over certain thresholds relating to value and/or turnover and a failure to do so will render the transaction void. In certain circumstances the acquisition of property over a certain threshold may also require governmental consent under the mergers legislation. There are also overriding public interest limitations on land ownership, which include planning restrictions and compulsory purchase (see further section 8).

1.3.2 Land is generally freely disposable save where there may be statutory restrictions on statutory bodies or local authorities and certain procedures may need to be followed. In the case of charities, the consent of the Commissioners of Charitable Donations and Bequests will usually be necessary. Any disposal of an interest in a family home by one spouse without the prior written consent of the other spouse is void. There are no rights of pre-emption granted to local or public authorities in the event of transactions between private parties.

1.4 Adverse possession

A person who has occupied land for over 12 years by adverse possession has a statutory defence to any claim for possession.

2 OTHER INTERESTS IN LAND

2.1 Servitudes or easements, usufruct, building and dwelling rights

Lesser interests in land include easements and profits à prendre. They are very similar in nature and involve the grant or acquiescence in the acquisition of some right over another person's property.

2.1.1 Servitudes or easements

Easements are express or implied rights created over land for the benefit of other land, such as a right of way or a right to run pipes under land. The right to an easement is appurtenant to and passes with the land which enjoys, or is subject to, that right. For a particular right to amount to an easement it must be sufficiently clearly defined to be capable of express creation. A profit à prendre is a right to enter upon the land of another and remove some part of the natural produce, such as the right to take minerals, turf, fish or game; or the right to graze animals (see also 2.6.1). A profit can be enjoyed independently of ownership of land but is regarded as an interest in land and is frequently related to ownership of a particular piece of land. Certain public rights are very similar to the rights recognised as easements or profits (see 2.6).

2.1.2 Usufruct

There is no such thing as the usufruct but similar mechanisms include the profit à prendre (see 2.1.1) and, for a shorter term, the grazing licence (see 2.6.1).

2.1.3 Building and dwelling rights

Building rights do not exist and it is not legally possible to separate the ownership of land and any building or structure over it. The right of residence is a personal interest which will be registered in the case of registered land (see section 3) and will be recognised by the court where the interest is not registered over unregistered land. The right is personal and cannot be transferred.

2.2 Restrictions on use and other restrictions

Other restrictions on the use of land include public rights, outlined at 2.6.2, and restrictive covenants. Restrictive covenants are conditions that restrict the use of land to protect the value and amenities of another piece of land owned by the covenantee. They are commonly found in leases, and the benefit of both positive and negative covenants will pass to successors in title. Positive obligations, such as repairing covenants, do not bind freehold successors. Public law restrictions under planning and other legislation are commented on in section 8.

2.3 Mortgages and charges

Private mortgages granted for the purpose of securing an indebtedness are dealt with in section 7. A judgment debt can also be registered by the judgment creditor as a judgment mortgage affecting the property. Other private rights include the seller's lien for any unpaid purchase price on the sale of a property which automatically attaches to the property, without the need for registration, if the seller is not paid in full.

2.4 Contracts and options

An option to purchase land or even a contract to purchase does not confer any legal title (which will not pass until the formal conveyance or transfer). However, it will give the holder of the option or the buyer under a contract an equitable interest in the property which is enforceable against third parties. It is necessary to register the option or the contract in the appropriate register according to whether the land is registered or unregistered (see further section 3).

2.5 Public or municipal charges

The cost of government or public bodies carrying out repairs or demolition under various statutes may become a charge on the property. The existence of such a charge would have to be revealed in replies to queries raised by the buyer's solicitor. There is no comprehensive register of such charges or other public rights.

2.6 Other interests

2.6.1 Licence agreements create contractual rights. Such agreements are frequently entered into in relation to agricultural land, eg the contract of conacre, whereby the owner permits a licensee to use land for a season for the purpose of sowing and harvesting a crop. A grazing licence permits the licensee to graze animals on land for a period of 11 months. Rent charges can also be created giving a right to periodic payment from the property and, although rare now, they give an interest in the property binding on successors in title and capable of assignment.

2.6.2 For a right to be a public right it must be capable of being invoked by any member of the public regardless of ownership of any land, eg the right of way over a person's property or the right of the public to fish in the sea, tidal rivers and waters.

2.7 Liabilities attaching to land

Either the owner or occupier of land may incur statutory liability for injuries caused to visitors, licensees and trespassers. Liability can also arise in nuisance for the unreasonable use of one's land to the prejudice of an adjoining owner, or for dangerous escapes, such as under the doctrines set out in the case of *Rylands v Fletcher*, and for injury or damage to passers-by. Statutory liabilities arise for the repair of dangerous structures and for the protection of employees. There are also tax liabilities attaching to land (see section 11).

2.8 Legal and equitable interests

Interests in land are classified as legal or equitable. The latter arise either under a trust or where there has been some imperfection in the formalities of a transaction. All equitable interests may be defeated by a subsequent buyer for value of a legal interest in the land who acquires it in good faith and without notice of the prior equitable interest. All equitable interests require the intervention of the court for their enforcement. It is not possible to protect equitable interests by direct record (see 2.9). It is however possible to register equitable interests in unregistered land in the registry of deeds (see section 3) as long as they are recorded in writing.

2.9 Protection of interests

Title to land is either registered or unregistered and the type of protection available depends on the type of title which is involved (see section 3). In the case of registered land, there are certain rights which must be registered in the land registry to gain protection. These include rights of residence, covenants, leases for life and leases exceeding 21 years, easements and profits à prendre. If such rights are not registered, the right will not be protected against a bona fide buyer for value without notice. Similarly, such rights would need to be registered in the registry of deeds in order to gain protection against a bona fide buyer for value without notice in the case of unregistered land. Where registered land is held on trust by a legal owner for a beneficial owner, the beneficial interest cannot be registered directly, although devices such as inhibitions and cautions equivalent to those found in England and Wales can be used to protect it. By contrast, subject to the limitations of the system regulating unregistered land (see 3.1.2), an equitable interest in unregistered land can be protected by registration in the registry of deeds (see 3.2). Registration in the registry of deeds gives priority to the interest over any preceding or subsequent unregistered interest (legal or equitable). There are a number of burdens which affect registered land without registration, such as public rights and occupational tenancies for terms not exceeding 21 years.

2.10 Priority of interests

Where interests are registered, priority will depend on the date of registration. A registered interest will have priority over an unregistered interest. Priority between unregistered interests will be determined by their date of creation.

3 TITLE TO LAND

3.1 Proof of title

Title to land can be either registered or unregistered.

3.1.1 In the case of registered land the ownership of major interests is recorded in a public register ('the land register') maintained by the land registry. Title is proved by production of an extract from the register in the form of a certified copy folio issued by the land registry although the register itself is conclusive evidence of title. The transfer of registered land or the creation of a charge is perfected only when the appropriate entry on the register is made. In respect of unregistered land a conveyance of a freehold or the grant or assignment of a lease for a term of over 21 years in counties Meath, Carlow and Laois, where registration is now compulsory, will be ineffective unless lodged for registration in the land registry within six months; elsewhere registration is optional.

3.1.2 Title to an estate in unregistered land (where registration is optional) is proved by deducing title over a period of time. The purpose of the register of deeds is to govern priority between documents dealing with the same piece of unregistered land. Unlike the land registry's register of registered land, the register in the registry of deeds does not guarantee the title to the land dealt with by the registered documents nor the validity of the document itself. It is a register of deeds and not of ownership. Registration is not compulsory and is not necessary to perfect a transaction. All memorials (necessary to lodge a document with the registry) are filed in the order in which they are received. In the case of interests in unregistered land title from a conveyance or similar ('good root of title') 40 years old is conclusive, although in practice conveyances of 20 years or more are acceptable for sale purposes.

3.2 Land registers

The central land register is kept in Dublin at the land registry and local offices of the land registry also exist in each county outside Dublin but as it is not possible to obtain a copy of land registry maps from them, all registrations are effected in the Dublin registry. Folios (see 3.2.2) for County Dublin and a few other areas have been computerised and further computerisation is envisaged. There is only one registry of deeds which is in Dublin.

3.2.1 Plans

The land registry maintains maps of all registered land. The boundaries shown on these maps are not seen as conclusive, but registered owners of adjoining land or a registered owner and an owner of adjoining unregistered land can apply to have the boundaries entered on the register as conclusive as between themselves.

3.2.2 Content

The register consists of a series of folios relating to each registered title, in which land is mapped and described. The folio is divided into three parts. The first part describes the land and refers to easements, minerals and boundaries. The second part contains entries of the name, the description and address of the owner and such matters as the classes of owners and titles, devolution of the land, cautions and inhibitions restricting the registration of dispositions. The third records such matters as registered burdens, charges, cautions and inhibitions against dealings with the land. In the case of freehold land, the owner may be registered either as full owner, such as a tenant in fee simple or as a limited owner, such as a tenant for life. A freehold owner may be registered with an absolute, qualified or possessory title, depending upon how satisfied the registrar is with the title shown to him. Burdens affecting the land may and in some cases need to be registered (see 2.9). There is no separate register for burdens and a court order will be required before application to register one of these rights can be made without permission of the registered owner. For those burdens which can affect registered land without registration (see 2.9), the practice is for a seller of registered land to swear a statutory declaration stating that there are no burdens which affect the property being sold and which have not been disclosed.

3.2.3 Errors

Any person who suffers loss because of errors due to the registration of entries obtained by fraud or forgery is entitled to compensation. Where fraud or mistake has occurred, the courts may order rectification of the register.

3.3 Passing of title

The registry of deeds does not play any role in the passing of title, or disposition of unregistered land, and the transaction will only be entered in the registry of deeds if the buyer so chooses to protect his priority. In the case of registered land, the new owner does not have the land vested in him until he is registered as owner. Once registered, he is entitled to the delivery of a land certificate. The buyer can register a priority search which has the effect of 'freezing' the folio for 14 days, granting the buyer protection provided he lodges his transfer within those 14 days. A priority search can be renewed.

4 TRANSACTIONS IN LAND

The most common transactions are the sale and purchase of the freehold, the grant or assignment of a lease, and the creation of a mortgage to secure a loan or other liability.

4.1 Procedures

If the purchase is by way of private negotiation, the end of the negotiations will normally bind the parties in honour only. An exception would be when there is evidence in writing of all the principal terms of the transaction and this is served on or on behalf of the party against whom the transaction is to be specifically enforced. Apart from this legal effect will usually only be given to their agreement when they enter into a formal written contract prepared by solicitors. For unregistered land (see 3.1.2) the seller will produce a good 'root' of title but the buyer's solicitor usually investigates the remainder of the seller's title between the signing of the contract and completion of the sale, when he will also make searches, 'requisitions' on title and check there are no judgments affecting the land. In the case of registered land, title is normally evident from production of a copy folio or land certificate prior to contract. The standard Law Society conditions of sale contain a warranty that all existing buildings on the land were completed in compliance with planning permission and building regulations and that no notices have been served on the seller in respect of the property, which have not been disclosed. The buyer must be satisfied prior to contract as to: planning considerations and the suitability of the development plan for the area (see section 8), and the physical state of the property by means of survey. The sale is completed by the seller signing a document transferring ownership in exchange for the balance of the purchase price. All appropriate title documents are then submitted for stamping at the stamps branch of the revenue commissioners and upon payment of the appropriate stamp duty are filed for registration either in the land registry or in the registry of deeds, as the case may be.

4.2 Contract terms

4.2.1 Parties usually incorporate the Law Society general conditions of sale into their contract. In addition to these general conditions, which the parties may choose to vary, there will be special conditions dealing with title. Special conditions may put the buyer on notice of certain matters where there is perhaps a defect or lack of documentary evidence of title and preclude the buyer from subsequently objecting to that matter. In addition, the contract usually provides for: payment of a deposit (normally 10 per cent of the purchase price); the completion date (often called 'closing date') which, if not specified, is deemed by the standard general conditions to be five weeks after the date of the contract; interest on the balance of the purchase price if the buyer is late in closing the sale; and procedures for service of notice by either party making time of the essence of the contract. The property remains at the seller's risk from the time of the signing of the unconditional contract but the extent of the seller's liability is limited to the amount of the purchase price.

4.2.2 If, after expiration of the notice period (in the general conditions it is 28 days), the sale is not closed then the seller may forfeit the deposit and sue the buyer for damages. Either party may sue for specific performance of the contract.

4.3 Formalities

A contract for the sale of land will not be enforceable unless it is evidenced by some note or memorandum in writing signed by the person against whom it is to be enforced. The written evidence must describe the parties, the property, the price and anything else the parties consider to be important to their agreement. Contracts for the sale of land are generally formal, detailed documents prepared by solicitors.

4.4 Fees, costs and taxes

4.4.1 On a sale of land or grant of a lease the seller or landlord will be responsible for the estate agents' commission. This is usually 2.5 per cent on a sale and 10 per cent of the initial annual rent on a lease where no premium is payable. If the buyer instructs his own agent to find a property he will be responsible for those agent's fees, which are usually negotiated. Estate agents' commission is not usually payable if the transaction does not take place, although with a commercial property a special fee might be negotiated for an abortive transaction.

4.4.2 A solicitor's statutory scale fee for unregistered land titles is one per cent of the purchase price plus IR£100 or otherwise as may be agreed in advance with the client depending on the consideration involved in the transaction, its complexity and the likely time engagement. The statutory scale fee is somewhat less for registered land titles. Some fee is usually charged whether or not the transaction proceeds to completion. In respect of leases, solicitors' fees are usually charged on a sliding scale averaging about five per cent of the initial year's rent. Any provision in an agreement whereby a tenant is made liable for the landlord's solicitor's fees is void as is any provision whereby a buyer is to be liable for the seller's estate agent's fees.

4.4.3 Stamp duty is chargeable on the value of the transaction for sale of land on a sliding scale which rapidly reaches the maximum charge of six per cent once the value exceeds IR£60,000. The rates of stamp duty on residential property (except for certain new dwellings) have been increased to seven per cent (IR£150,001 to IR£160,000), eight per cent (IR£160,001 to IR£170,000), and nine per cent (transactions over IR£170,000). It remains to be seen whether these higher rates will only be temporary. Where the property interest acquired is leasehold, a similar rate of duty is payable on any premium paid by the tenant. In addition, duty is payable on any rent at rates which rise to 12 per cent. The rate of stamp duty is only one per cent where, as is usually the case, the lease is for not more than 35 years. The buyer has the primary obligation to discharge the duty. Where a property holding company is acquired, the rate is only one per cent on the relevant share transfer.

4.4.4 Land registry fees are payable in respect of registered land. For transfers the scale ranges from IR£65–IR£250.

4.4.5 All estate agents' and solicitors' fees attract value added tax (VAT) currently at a rate of 21 per cent.

4.4.6 Stamp duty rates and the VAT rate of 21 per cent on fees are considered to be quite onerous compared to other European countries, but otherwise transaction costs are not exceptional and average six to eight per cent on sales of land inclusive of stamp duty but exclusive of VAT.

4.5 Professionals' roles

The funding of a buyer and the negotiation of the principal terms are usually carried out by estate agents who may be surveyors (members of the Society of Chartered Surveyors in the Republic of Ireland, SCS) or valuers (members of the Irish Auctioneers and Valuers Institute, IAVI). Estate agents who are members of such bodies are covered by their organisations' compensation fund in the event of a claim being made by a client for misappropriation of funds. The deposit on a sale is paid to (and held by) the seller's solicitor, but increasingly the seller's estate agent requests payment of a 'booking deposit' as a token of good faith to be returned if the matter does not proceed. There is no role for a notary as there is in some other European countries and each party will be represented by their own solicitor.

5 LEASES AND OTHER RIGHTS OF OCCUPATION

Leases (also known as tenancies), granting a right in rem, although based on contract, can be for a certain term, ie of fixed length, or periodic, ie from week to week, month to month and so on. They may be created expressly or be implied from the payment of rent on a periodic basis. A tenancy at will exists where there is an intention to create a relationship of landlord and tenant but where the parties have made no express or implied agreement about the duration of the relationship and it can therefore be determined, without notice, by either party at any time. Leases vary in length but leases for terms of 999, 500, 99, 35 years and two years and nine months (and more recently four years and nine months) have traditionally been the most common. Where the intention is effectively to sell the property, leases for longer terms are usually granted, ie 500 years or more, in consideration of a premium and the reservation of a nominal rent. The purpose is usually to reserve certain covenants restricting permitted use and to reserve a service charge payable for services to be provided by the landlord. Such leases are used in the case of sales of apartments, industrial units on an industrial estate and retail stores which are part of a larger development. Where property is let at a full market rent ('rack rent') the lease is usually for a period of anything up to 35 years. If the term is for over 35 years it attracts a much higher rate of stamp duty (six per cent as opposed to one per cent of the annual rent on leases for not more than 35 years). As there are adverse VAT consequences for leases for terms less than 20 years, it is common for leases to be granted for a term of 20 years with a right to break at an earlier point (see further 11.8).

5.1 Rent and other terms

Most modern leases of business premises include a rent review clause enabling the rent to be reviewed periodically (usually every five years) and normally increased in accordance with the prevailing market rates and with provision for determination by a third party (usually a surveyor or estate agent) if the parties cannot agree. Reviews are not index-linked and will be upwards only unless the lease is to a government body which insists on the possibility of a downwards rent review. The tenant is also generally liable for all repairs to the building and to reimburse the landlord the cost of insuring the building. In the case of a lease of part of a building or development, the tenant covenants to pay a service charge which includes a contribution towards the cost of repairs. Notwithstanding any restrictions in a lease, under statute a landlord cannot unreasonably withhold its consent to assignment, subletting, change of use or the carrying out of improvements by a tenant. Leases may be forfeited by the landlord for non-payment of rent or other breach of covenant. Apart from this there are no statutory restrictions on the freedom of the parties to agree the terms of leases of commercial properties. There are also no restrictions in relation to residential tenancies commenced since 1967 (see further 5.3 for limited rent control).

5.2 Privity of contract and estate

Unless the landlord's consent is formally endorsed on the assignment, the original tenant may remain liable for breach of the lease for its duration. Amending legislation has been proposed which would release the original tenant from liability on assignment with the landlord's consent whether or not this consent is actually endorsed on the deed of assignment.

5.3 Rent control and security of tenure

Where a business tenant has been in occupation for three years or more under a tenancy which commenced prior to August 1994, he can claim a new lease for any period up to 35 years. Since 1994, a business tenant whose tenancy commenced after August 1994 must have been in occupation for five years before claiming renewal rights for between 5 and 20 years. Save in the case of office leases, a tenant cannot contract out of these provisions or waive his renewal rights. This has caused complications where both parties want to grant a longer lease without the tenant acquiring landlord and tenant renewal rights as the terms determined by the court under the Act are generally perceived as favouring the tenant. For this reason, it was common for short-term leases to be granted for periods of two years and nine months and, since August 1994, for periods of four years and nine months without the tenant claiming landlord and tenant renewal rights and there may be break options in a lease. Unless peaceful re-entry can be effected, possession cannot be recovered except by court order which may also grant relief against forfeiture upon application by the tenant. A landlord can only refuse to grant a new lease under certain limited circumstances, namely connected with redevelopment or demolition or reconstruction of the buildings in question, and the refusal would require the scrutiny of the court and would entitle the tenant to compensation. There are minimum notice periods for termination of periodic tenancies, eg not less than six months for a yearly tenancy, a month's notice for a monthly tenancy and week's notice for a weekly tenancy. A tenancy for a fixed term does not require any notice of termination save that a tenant claiming a right of renewal must serve a notice claiming such right within three months after the service on the tenant by the landlord of a notice in a prescribed form of the expiration of the term. There are no statutory restrictions in relation to residential tenancies entered into after 1967 although a limited form of residential rent control applies to residential tenancies created prior to 1967 and these are now governed by the Housing (Private Rented Dwellings) Act 1982.

5.4 Other legislative restrictions

New dwellings, but not temporary or holiday accommodation, must comply with certain statutory standards. A landlord of residential accommodation is also obliged to register with the local housing authority. There are also building standards and an obligation to maintain them to standard.

5.5 Method of measurement

The SCS (see 4.5) and the Irish Auctioneers and Valuers Institute, the two largest bodies of property professionals, have prepared a joint code of measurement practice which sets out the basis upon which buildings are measured. Rents are usually expressed by reference to the net internal or net lettable area, which excludes lavatories, staircases and certain other common areas. The gross external area does not generally feature in the calculation of rents save in the case of industrial buildings.

6 FINANCE AND INVESTMENT SOURCES

The approach to property financing is broadly similar to that which applies in England and Wales in terms of the range and types of sources of funding, the techniques adopted and the general legal, market and fiscal environment.

6.1 Loan finance

The traditional sources of loan finance for property are the four main associated or high street banks, supplemented by commercial and merchant banks. While building societies have traditionally concentrated on lending for residential property, a number have recently expanded into commercial lending. The traditional form of debt financing for residential property is the long-term mortgage for between 15 and 25 years. Non-residential property is usually funded by shorter-term debt, typically up to 10 years' duration. The criteria applied by lenders in determining the amount they are prepared to advance include the repayment history of the borrower, the value of the property, the ability of the borrower and/or the property to generate sufficient net income to service the loan and the lender's general view of the strength of property relative to other sectors of the economy. Repayment of the loan may either be by full repayment of the entire amount at the end of the term or by staged amortisation of the capital sum over the term. Interest is generally at a margin over cost of funds, with the cost of funds determined with reference to the Dublin Inter Bank market. The margin charged varies according to the credit-worthiness of the borrower or, if the loan is non-recourse, the quality of the property on which the loan is being secured. The margin also includes an element for Reserve Asset Cost (RAC) which is a levy imposed on all conventional lending by the state controlled Central Bank. Interest rates on borrowing are usually variable and are reviewed either quarterly or half-yearly. A range of Treasury 'products' is, however, available to borrowers wishing to reduce or eliminate their exposure to volatility in interest rates. Companies can borrow money from their shareholders by the issue of loan stock and the holders of such stock may get preferential treatment in relation to dividends.

6.2 Investment or equity finance

Another important source of finance for property is third party investor's equity. A substantial proportion of office, retail and industrial property in the major urban centres is owned by investors and leased on to occupiers. Investors range from large pension funds and assurance companies, property companies (some of which are quoted on the Dublin and London Stock Exchanges) and private individuals. Investors can usually be categorised as tax exempt and taxable. Tax exempt investors, eg pension funds, generally do not borrow to finance the acquisition of property. This is because the cost of borrowed funds with no tax relief is generally higher than the cost of capital to the pension fund. Furthermore pension funds will generally be cash rich and may be uncomfortable with the higher level of risk. Tax paying investors, on the other hand, will generally borrow the maximum possible to fund the acquisition of an investment property using the rental income to service the borrowing cost. There are relatively few property companies quoted on the Dublin Stock Exchange.

6.3 Mezzanine or mixed funding

Larger properties tend to require a mixture of different types of equity and debt finance, possibly ranging across the full risk–reward spectrum. The larger banks have highly developed corporate banking and capital markets operations capable of developing and delivering a custom-designed mixture of funding. The percentage of the value lent will depend on the property and the borrower. A prime lender will normally advance up to 50–75 per cent of the value of the property, whereas the mezzanine lender will lend up to 100 per cent and usually receive a higher rate of interest for the higher risk. The same lender may provide both the prime and mezzanine funding with a higher rate applying to the latter; he may also sometimes take an equity stake.

6.4 Sale and lease-back

This is a common mechanism in order to release capital tied up in property by selling to an investor and taking an immediate leaseback of the property. This is only likely for 'investment grade' property, ie property situated in a well-established location, in good physical condition and not unduly customised by the occupants. The financial status of the tenant must also be strong.

6.5 Tax leasing

Tax paying investors, both private and corporate, are keen to acquire investment properties which carry capital allowances. Hotels and multi-storey car parks and properties located in certain 'designated areas' or 'enterprise zones' carry capital allowances of up to 100 per cent offsettable against taxable income. This has resulted in a range of tax-based lend/lease arrangements whereby occupiers have financed property by taking leases from lending institutions. Those arrangements generally provide for a rent equivalent to interest costs plus capital repayment over the term of the facility. Ownership of the property usually passes from the institution to the tenant at the end of the lease term, generally on payment of a nominal sum. Tax-based leasing is particularly attractive where the occupier has little or no taxable income and therefore no use for the allowances available in respect of the property. A lending institution with tax 'capacity' (ie unsheltered taxable income) can claim the benefit of the allowances available and this benefit is passed on to the occupier/tenant in the form of lower rent or finance costs.

6.6 Other types of property finance

There are no investment vehicles similar to SPOTs or SAPCOs as used in England and Wales as these would infringe existing law relating to unit trusts. However, it is quite common for a group of investors to invest in property through a bare trustee company which holds the legal estate in the property in trust for the investors who hold the beneficial interest as tenants in common.

6.7 Institutional investment

Most investment is undertaken by pension funds and life and general insurance companies. Property usually comprises between 5–10 per cent of most pension funds' portfolios, which is considerably lower than the 15–20 per cent figure of the 1970s. Nevertheless, the decline in the percentage of property holdings stabilised around the mid 1980s. The institutions set the standards which generally apply throughout the prime end of the property market. The dominance of the market by the institutions has been reduced by the large number of private and corporate investors (see 6.8) especially in respect of tax designated properties where capital allowances can be taken advantage of. The general preference of institutional investors is to confine their activities to the prime end of the market in respect of office, retail and industrial property so that the amount of institutional investment in leisure or residential activity is minimal.

6.8 Investors other than institutions

Property companies, some quoted and some private, and private individuals also invest in the property market. Generally they will apply similar standards to those applied by institutional investors regarding length and type of lease and standard of covenant. Much investment by private individuals has taken place in recent years in tax designated areas. There are also a number of overseas investors active in the Irish property market, the majority of whom have traditionally been UK based.

7 FORMS OF SECURITY

Most borrowing for property development is from commercial banks although building societies have begun to lend both to residential and commercial investors. Depending on the perceived quality of the security, certain loans may be non-recourse, but generally lenders are reluctant to lend more than 75 per cent of the value of the property. Generally the banks will look not just at the creditworthiness of the customer but also at the value of the property offered as security.

7.1 Mortgages

If a debenture is not possible (see 7.2), a legal mortgage will usually be granted. In the case of property with unregistered title the legal mortgage is registered in the registry of deeds and, in the case of registered land, a charge is created and registered in the land registry; the entry must detail the property affected but the amount secured need not be specified if it can be expressed as 'all sums due' and care is then taken to have the instrument properly stamped. Mortgages securing not more than IR£20,000 are exempt from stamp duty. Mortgages securing sums in excess of IR£20,000 are liable to stamp duty at IR£1 per IR£1,000 or part of IR£1,000 subject to a maximum duty of IR£500. Registration of a mortgage in the registry of deeds incurs a registration fee of IR£26; in the land registry, the scale fee is between IR£65 and IR£250 (see further section 3 for details of the registration system). The mortgagor retains title to the property and has full use of it but the mortgagee has rights to take possession and exercise a power of sale once the mortgage debt has become due. Alternatively, he can appoint a receiver to manage the property until the loan is repaid. An equitable mortgage can arise where there is no written document evidencing the security; the title deeds or land certificate, if the land is registered, are simply deposited with a verbal expression of the intention to create an equitable mortgage and no registration takes place at either registry. However, such a mortgage can also be in writing and, if so, must be registered in the appropriate register as would be the case with a legal mortgage or charge. An equitable mortgagee has to apply for a court order before it can enforce its security. Details of both legal and equitable mortgages granted by a company must be registered in the companies office within 21 days of creation.

7.2 Debentures

Most lenders will require a mortgage debenture over the property-owning company. This comprises a fixed charge over a particular property and a floating charge over all other assets of the company. This gives the lender the ability to appoint a receiver over the company and not just the property.

7.3 Bonds and guarantees

In certain cases, where the amount of the loan is high in relation to the value of the property, the lender will require a mortgage protection policy or bond to be taken out with an insurance company. This happens more often with residential than with commercial properties. Bonds are a promise to pay a specified sum in the event of a default. They are most commonly used in building contracts and subcontracts. Bank guarantees may also be required, for example where the proposed tenant has not been able to satisfy the landlord as to its creditworthiness. The bank guarantee requires payment of a fee and the lodging of certain security, and will usually be limited in duration.

7.4 Credit insurance

Credit insurance is not a normal feature of property-based lending in Ireland.

8 PLANNING AND BUILDING REGULATION

The main legislation in this area is the Local Government (Planning & Development) Act 1963 (the 1963 Act), as amended.

8.1 Planning authorities

The Minister for the Environment is responsible for overall planning policy and legislation although planning appeals are made to the planning board (see 8.3.2). On a local level, decisions are taken by the local planning authority for the area, ie the county council in rural areas, the corporation in cities and the urban district council in towns. The planning officials dealing with applications are not elected and it is only in the event of a material contravention of a development plan that a resolution by the council will be sought, which will be voted upon by politically elected officials.

8.2 Development plans

Under the 1963 Act, each planning authority is obliged periodically to prepare a development plan for its area setting out the development objectives. The making or variation of a development plan may only be carried out by the elected representatives of the local authority and not by the city or county manager. A local authority may not normally permit development which materially contravenes the development plan unless a special procedure is followed. Before buying a property for a specific purpose it is prudent to check the zoning use of the area under the development plan, to see if planning permission is likely to be granted. In principle, the planning authority is bound to grant a permission where a proposed development is in accordance with the development plan. This is not to say that undesirable conditions may not be attached which may increase the projected cost of the development to the developer.

8.3 Planning controls and procedures

Under the 1963 Act, planning permission is required for all development of land unless that development is exempted development. The definition of development is very broad with the result that almost any kind of building works, including demolition, will require planning permission.

8.3.1 If planning permission is required, an application must be made to the local planning authority together with the appropriate fee. It may be either a detailed application or an outline proposal. The applicant must have an interest in the land to which the application relates or the consent of the owner. Outline permission gives permission, in principle, for the proposed development. Following receipt of detailed plans for the development, the planning authority may grant a full permission. With every application for planning permission, the authority may decide to grant the permission, with or without conditions, or to refuse it, according to the relevant development plan.

8.3.2 If the planning authority fails to notify the applicant of its decision within two months from receipt of the application, the applicant may assume permission by default on the last day of the time limit. An appeal against a decision may be made to the planning board (*an bord pleanála*) by the applicant, or any third party (whether or not that third party has an interest in the land), which may be a pressure group or an aggrieved individual. It has four months from the expiry date for appeals to make its decision although a later date may be designated. A decision of the planning board may be judicially reviewed in the High Court.

8.3.3 Unless a planning permission, whether an outline or detailed permission, is implemented within five years of the granting of the permission it is deemed to lapse. There is no time limit for a detailed application to be made following an outline permission, save that the detailed approval granted subsequently must be implemented within five years of the grant of the outline permission and not the detailed approval. Planning permission attaches to the land and is not personal to the applicant.

8.3.4 Where development has been carried out without planning permission or in breach of the terms of planning permission, the planning authority may serve an enforcement notice on the owner and on the occupier of the land concerned. The notice, which may require specific steps to remedy the non-compliance, must be served within five years of the development being carried out or, in the case of non-compliance with a condition, within five years of the date specified in the condition as the latest date for compliance. If the notice is not complied with within the specified period, the planning authority may carry out the works set out in the notice and recover the cost from the owner of the land; further, a planning authority or any other person (no interest in the land being required), may seek an injunction in the High Court or the Circuit Court requiring cessation of any unauthorised development or use. A failure to comply with the court order can lead to imprisonment.

8.4 Building standards, control and supervision

A developer must also ensure that any regulations in relation to the construction, design and ventilation of a building, and the safety (including fire safety) and welfare of persons entering or inhabiting it, are complied with. Where a fire safety certificate is required, as is generally the case, plans for the proposed work have to be deposited with the local authority for approval and the certificate issued, prior to commencement of the works. Where a building has been, or is being, built in breach of regulations, the local authority may serve an enforcement notice within five years of its completion and it is an offence to breach any of these regulations or enforcement notices served under it. The maximum penalty for such an offence is a fine of IR£10,000 or imprisonment for up to two years, or both. The local authority has power to inspect and test works and take samples but certificates of conformity are not issued by the local authority. There are also strict requirements which require a project supervisor to monitor health and safety during the design and construction stages, and the production of a 'safety file' for the building to be handed over to the buyer.

8.5 Protection of buildings of special interest

A planning authority may include in a development plan proposals to preserve any structure or internal feature of artistic, historic or architectural interest. Notice of such a proposal must be given to the owner and any representation must be taken into account before the development plan is published. Permission will need to be sought for development and a preservation listing provides valid ground for refusal of permission, although there are no special consents which need to be sought and the procedure will be the same as that described in 8.3.1. There are further provisions enabling a planning authority to designate areas of land of outstanding natural beauty, special recreational value or in need of conservation and when considering any planning application, the planning authority must have regard to the designation order.

8.6 Compulsory purchase and compensation

Local and other public or statutory authorities have powers to commence compulsory purchase proceedings for particular purposes. The public authority makes a compulsory purchase order which is published and served upon the owners. The Minister for the Environment will then confirm the order with or without modifications, unless objections have been raised, in which case a public enquiry will be held. Any aggrieved party may challenge a confirmed order in the High Court. The acquiring authority will then serve notice on the owners. Calculation of compensation is complex but will generally reflect the open market value of the land as of the date of notice, without taking the scheme for which the land is being expropriated into account.

9 ENVIRONMENTAL MATTERS

There have been two recent and significant developments in environmental law. The Environmental Protection Agency Act 1992 recognises the need for a comprehensive system of licensing and control for the purpose of environmental protection. The two main aims of the Act are the establishment of the independent Environmental Protection Agency (EPA), and the introduction of a system of integrated pollution control. The EPA is given a number of powers and functions in relation to the monitoring of the quality of the environment, the establishment and maintenance of information relating to the environment and the provision of support and advisory services to ministers of the government, local authorities and the general public for the purposes of environmental protection. One of the most important functions of the EPA will be the granting of integrated pollution control (IPC) licences under the Act.

9.1 Protection against atmospheric and noise pollution

The Air Pollution Act 1987 introduces a system of licensing for the prevention of air pollution during specified industrial activities, such as oil refining or asbestos production. Applications for such licences are made to the relevant local authority. Any breach will give rise to liability in damages. The Act also gives the Minister for the Environment and local authorities a number of powers to control and monitor air pollution. Offences are punishable by a maximum fine of IR£10,000 (together with a fine of up to IR£1,000 for every day on which the offence is continued) and/or up to two years' imprisonment. Authorised persons may enter premises and take samples, carry out inspections or make tests and may not be obstructed in their duties. The Act also imposes civil liability in damages for air pollution where an unauthorised emission causes injury, loss or damage to a person or his property, unless the occupier can prove that the emission was due to an act of God or an act or omission of a third party over whose conduct the occupier had no control and which he could not reasonably have foreseen. Owners of all premises, except private dwellings, are required to use the best practicable means (as published in the minister's directions) to limit and, if possible, prevent emissions from premises.

9.2 Water pollution

The principal statutes in the area of water pollution are the Local Government (Water Pollution) Acts, 1977 and 1990 and it is an offence for any person (including a body corporate) to cause or permit any polluting matter to enter waters. It is also an offence for any person to discharge or cause or permit the discharge of a trade effluent or sewage effluent into waters or sewers without a licence granted by the local authority in whose area the discharge is being made. It is not necessary to show that pollution actually occurred, as mere entry of polluting matters into waters is an offence and punishable by fines of IR£25,000 or five years' imprisonment or both. A court may order termination of the entry or discharge within a specified period, mitigation of the damage caused by the discharge, or compensation to be made payable to the applicant or any other person to mitigate the damage caused. Damages will not be payable if the entry was caused by an act of God or by a third party over whose conduct the occupier had no control and which he could not reasonably have foreseen. A local authority may serve a notice on a person having custody or control of polluting matter directing him to take specified measures to prevent the polluting matter from entering waters. If the notice is not complied with the local authority may take any necessary steps itself at the expense of the person on whom the notice has been served. Notice is not required in urgent cases.

9.3 Waste storage and disposal

The Waste Management Act 1996 is a new framework Act currently awaiting implementation by regulation, which aims to introduce more stringent penalties for offences relating to the control of waste. Under existing domestic law, local authorities ('sanitary authorities') are obliged to maintain and provide adequate sewers and a proper water supply in their area. If a person other than a sanitary authority wishes to provide a waste disposal site it must obtain planning permission and it is an offence to operate without a permit or in breach of it. Each local authority must plan and supervise operations for the disposal of toxic and dangerous waste in its area and the authorisation of the storage, treatment and depositing of such waste. No person, other than the local authority, may carry out the storage, treatment or deposit of toxic and dangerous waste, whether on his own behalf or that of another person, without an appropriate permit issued by a local authority. It is an offence to breach any of the regulations and a fine of up to IR£1,000 or six months' imprisonment, or both, may be imposed. Where any toxic or dangerous waste contains a dangerous substance it may also require a licence under the Dangerous Substances Act 1972.

9.4 Contaminated land

Historically there is no tradition of heavy industry, and the problem of dealing with contaminated land has not arisen to the same extent as in some other countries. Archaeological remains affecting the decision whether to grant permission are more likely to be of relevance to the investor or developer (see 8.5). Therefore it is not common to make enquiries about infilling, reclaiming or the use of dangerous construction materials unless it is evident that such considerations arise and ought to be investigated. Under the Law Society general conditions and under general law, there is no obligation on the seller to disclose contamination of the land. If a buyer has any reason to believe the land might have a history of contamination, then an environmental due diligence might be appropriate leading to warranties being incorporated into the contract for the sale of the land. In the case of a share acquisition it is common practice, where heavy industrial activities were undertaken by the company being acquired, to require environmental warranties covering the existence of and compliance with the conditions attached to environmental licences; to date this has been the only manner in which land contamination has been controlled by the local authorities and the EPA. There are no public registers detailing land which has been put to contaminated use and there are no obligations to clean up contamination specifically except where such obligations might be imposed by contract between the parties to a contract for sale or share purchase agreement. There is no fund available to pay for decontamination or other remedial measures. However, the Waste Management Act 1996 and the implementing regulations which are expected to be made imminently are likely to be used to enable the EPA and the local authorities to require treatment and clean-up of land subject to contamination or both.

9.5 Environmental impact assessments

Where a proposed development will be likely to have a significant effect on the environment, the applicant, when lodging an application for planning permission, may also have to file an environmental impact statement specifying the likely effect on the environment.

10 DEVELOPMENT

10.1 Development projects, structures and vehicles

Many properties are developed by their owners after purchase and obtaining of planning permission. Sometimes the owner/occupier will then sell the property to an investment institution and lease it back on a full repairing and insuring basis for 35 years. To reduce the amount of stamp duty, the owner may transfer the site to the investor before commencing development and the investor will develop the building and then lease it back to the occupier. A considerable proportion of office buildings in Dublin have been speculatively built by developers either alone or in conjunction with an institutional investor without being prelet. If an institution is involved with a developer the transaction may be effected on a prefunding basis. The site is transferred to the institution which then advances the construction cost to the developer, rolls up interest and then pays a balancing figure to the developer on completion of the building or on it being let. This final figure is usually linked to the rental level achieved. Where the developer wishes to retain an ownership interest this has in the past been effected either by a top slice lease or a rent sharing lease. The site is transferred to the institution who then leases it back for, say, 10,000 years reserving a proportion of the occupational rents. In a top slice lease the developer can be left liable for any void in the occupational rents, whereas in a straight rent sharing arrangement the institutional head landlord is only paid a share of the net receivable occupational rents. Since the Finance Act 1991 it is more expensive to put such leases in place as they now attract significant stamp duty whereas previously only nominal stamp duty was paid on a lease where the rent was not ascertainable at the date of execution.

10.2 Building contracts and appointment of professionals

10.2.1 Typical forms of building contract

The majority of construction contracts are awarded on the basis of a fixed price, ie the contractor takes the risk of price fluctuations. In contracts for civil engineering works, particularly in the public sector, the opposite is the case. In general, most types of building contract utilise the traditional arrangement whereby an employer engages a main contractor who may then employ a number of subcontractors. Management contracting, where the management contractor does little or no direct construction work himself, but rather coordinates those who do carry out the work, is not common and has only been adopted for a few larger projects. The contractor is responsible for the works, except where he has undertaken a management role, in which case his obligation is to ensure that the works are executed by the responsible subcontractors within the time programme and within agreed budgets. However, in the event of default by the subcontractor resulting in termination of the contract, the responsibility for the appointment of a new subcontractor will rest with the employer. Often in a medium-sized project, the contractor will perform some or all of the obligations in relation to design as well as doing the building works, so that the contractor will provide the entire package of services. This is known as a 'design and construct' contract, and although the contractor will usually be responsible for the design subcontract works, the employer may have the right and obligation to reappoint the subcontractor.

10.2.2 Common terms

Building contracts can be defined by the price which the contractor will be paid and the method of ascertaining that price. The main types include: the lump sum, where a lump sum is paid to a contractor for completion of the project, although usually instalments are payable by agreement; measurement and value, where the amount of work when completed is measured and valued, in accordance with agreed rates; and cost plus percentage, where the contractor is paid the cost of labour and materials plus an agreed percentage to cover profit and overheads (if properly drafted, the cost plus contract should protect the employer against waste or extravagance on the part of the contractor). The typical contract with a main contractor, whether for construction or civil engineering, or for privately or publicly funded works, provides for a commencement and a completion date. It also provides for stage payments and the contractor may be entitled to determine the contract if a stage payment has not been paid. The employer may be entitled to determine it for a number of reasons, including the suspension of work by the contractor. If the work is not completed by any practical or substantial completion date set out in the contract, liquidated damages (where agreed) are paid unless the contractor is entitled to an extension of time by reason of some factor outside his control. It is becoming increasingly common for a contractor in large projects to guarantee to reach practical completion within a particular budget and/or within a particular time scale in return for a premium reflecting the risks being undertaken.

10.2.3 Standard form of contracts

There are separate types of standard forms of contract. The Institute of Engineers of Ireland (IEI) publishes a standard form of contract for works of civil engineering. Within the category of construction contracts, there are separate standard forms for both privately funded works and publicly funded works. The Royal Institute of the Architects of Ireland (RIAI) publishes standard forms of construction contract. For publicly funded works, the standard form of contract is that for Government Departments and Local Authorities, published in 1982 and known as 'GDLA 82'.

10.2.4 Appointment of the professional team

The architect, engineer and other consultants generally regularise their appointment by way of letter of appointment or a more formal consultancy agreement. The essential points relate to the specification of the personnel to be employed on the project, the scope of work and duties, the fees by way of percentage breakdown for each section of the project and hourly rates for any additional work. The RIAI (see 10.2.3), the Association of Consulting Engineers in Ireland and the SCS (see 4.5) have each drawn up their own standard conditions of engagement, but special conditions can be negotiated and agreed.

10.3 Those involved and their roles

The majority of building contracts are supervised by either an architect or engineer engaged by the employer, depending on the nature of the works. He will owe a duty of care to both parties in respect of the certificate procedures applicable to completion, variations and extensions of time, and will be responsible for the overall design and the administration of the contract on behalf of the employer. He will issue instructions, variations and certificates to the contractor, adjudicating on any requests for extensions of time and, ultimately, certifying completion. Depending on the size and nature of the project, the employer may engage other professional advisers such as a quantity surveyor, mechanical and electrical engineers or a structural engineer. The quantity surveyor assesses the amount of labour and materials required; the mechanical and electrical engineers are responsible for the various systems such as lifts, heating and air-conditioning; and a structural engineer advises on matters such as floor loadings and structural strength. These professional advisers may be engaged directly by the employer. In larger projects, the employer may decide to engage an architect as project manager and design consultant, who, in turn, engages the structural engineer and other requisite consultants as subconsultants. This simplifies communication and the resolving of disputes over defects in the works and their design. The contractor executes the project to the design which has been submitted to him, having first quoted for this, usually on the basis of a competitive tender from a number of different contractors, based on a specification prepared by the architect/engineer with the help of the other consultants. In relation to smaller construction projects, the design work will generally be undertaken by the architect without a consulting engineer or other consultant. Public works contracts are invariably awarded to contractors based on a competitive tender. In private works contracts, while competitive tenders are sought, an employer may seek a quotation from a single contractor and negotiate the contract solely with him.

10.4 Defects and remedies

10.4.1 The building contract should provide for a defects maintenance period, usually 12 months, during which time the contractor is obliged to put right any defects that have arisen. A retention of two per cent to five per cent is deducted from stage payments during the course of the works, depending on the size of the project. When the building has been certified as being practically complete, with a snagging list of minor defects for correction during the defects and maintenance period, the full contract price is then released to the contractor less one half of the retention. That, in turn, is released at the end of the defects liability period upon the issue of a final certificate and the making good of defects.

10.4.2 The liability of a contractor or design team member to a subsequent buyer or occupier of the property is uncertain. The current view is that a subsequent owner or occupier is unable to recover the cost of remedying defects in a building from the original designer or contractor, there being no contractual relationship. Therefore, the designers and the contractor are commonly required to provide collateral warranties to the financier, subsequent owner and/or occupier, acknowledging a direct contractual liability to those parties similar to that owed to the employer. The RIAI has drawn up its own standard form of collateral warranty for use by its members which is gaining acceptance within the industry.

10.5 Defects insurance

Inherent defects or decennial insurance is only available for a very limited number of developments. Where it is available, it does not relieve the contractors of their respective responsibilities and the cover provided is limited and does not include the cost of remedying all defects but only those relating to structural defects. Where such insurance is obtained, the benefit will be passed on to subsequent owners and occupiers.

10.6 Copyright

The copyright in the design of the building remains with the architect or engineer unless agreed to the contrary.

10.7 Fees

The RIAI, the IEI (see 10.2.3) and the SCS (see 4.5) have each included a schedule of fees in their respective standard conditions of engagement, but on large projects, a fee based on a percentage lower than that in the standard conditions of engagement can be negotiated. On average the total professional fees involved in a large project work out at approximately 10 per cent of the project cost.

10.8 Taxes

Value added tax (VAT) is relevant to the construction process and all residential and commercial construction is subject to VAT at the rate of 12.5 per cent. Any contractor tendering for publicly funded projects must ensure that its tax affairs are in order, as failure to produce an appropriate tax clearance certificate from the revenue commissioners prevents a contractor from being awarded such a contract.

11 TAXES

11.1 Corporation tax

A company is only liable to tax on all its worldwide income if it is, or becomes, resident in Ireland. A non-resident company is only liable to tax on profits arising in Ireland. Whether a corporation is resident in Ireland for tax purposes depends on where the actual management and control of the company abides (ie do the board of directors meet in Ireland?), not where it is incorporated.

11.1.1 Tax rates

The rate of corporation tax applicable to resident companies and branches of non-resident companies is 36 per cent, with the first IR£50,000 of taxable income being taxed at 28 per cent. Certain activities, principally manufacturing, attract a reduced 10 per cent tax rate.

11.1.2 Computation and administration

In calculating corporate profits chargeable to tax, the starting point is the profit figure shown in the accounts which is then subject to specific tax computation rules. Generally, expenses of a revenue nature are deductible. The Income Tax Act, 1967 – which also applies to companies subject to corporation tax – only permits the recipient of rental income to deduct rent payable for the premises; any municipal or local authority charges; the cost of any services rendered or goods provided for which no consideration is received, but only where there is an obligation to provide the goods or render the services; the cost of maintenance, repairs, insurance and management, except costs of a capital nature; and interest on borrowed money employed in the purchase or improvement of the premises. The tax system including income tax, corporation tax, VAT and capital tax in Ireland is managed by the revenue commissioners through various divisions. For companies, the preliminary tax calculated on a self-assessment basis is now payable six months after the end of their accounting period.

11.1.3 Depreciation and capital allowances

Only capital expenditure on certain types of buildings may qualify for a tax deduction. Those which qualify include buildings used as factories, mills or docks; multi-storey car parks, and hotels and holiday homes. Buildings which would not normally qualify are included in the capital allowance regime when located in certain tax incentive areas as discussed at 12.2. The rate of allowance is generally a four per cent annual allowance although a rate of 15 per cent per annum with the balance of 10 per cent written off in the final year applies to hotels. The increased allowances of up to 100 per cent applied on a country-wide basis now only apply to certain designated incentive areas. In addition, for all premises, a capital allowances regime for plant, machinery, fixtures and fittings is available. The rates are generally 15 per cent per annum for six years with the balance of 10 per cent written off in the final year. In the case of all capital allowances, the relief given may be subject to a claw-back when the asset is disposed of at a value greater than the tax written down value of the asset concerned.

11.1.4 Withholding tax

The Finance Act 1969 provides for the deduction of tax at source from rents paid for any Irish property to a person whose usual place of abode is outside Ireland. Tax at the standard rate (26 per cent for 1997/98) must be deducted from the gross amount payable. As the deduction is applied to the gross income, it is common for a property manager to be the payee of rental income with expenses being deducted before the net proceeds are paid out of Ireland. In this way, the withholding tax is only paid on the net income. Except where it is paid by an Irish bank or by a Shannon or IFSC company, an interest payment to a non-resident is subject to a withholding tax of 26 per cent if it comprises 'annual interest'. Payments may be made gross if the revenue commissioners issue a clearance to do so where the interest is exempted from Irish tax under the applicable double taxation treaty.

11.2 Taxes on development value

While there are no specific taxes applicable to land gains attributable to potential development use, there are rules under the capital gains tax and income tax codes which can result in the taxation of such gains (see 11.3).

11.3 Taxes on capital gains

The disposal of property situated in Ireland is liable to capital gains tax (CGT) regardless of where the owner is resident. This charge to CGT applies also to the disposal of shares (other than quoted shares) in a company, wherever incorporated, deriving the greater part of their value from property in Ireland. The person by or through whom the consideration is paid, must deduct CGT amounting to 15 per cent of the consideration. This absolute withholding requirement is only relieved where the consideration does not exceed IR£100,000 or the person making the disposal produces a clearance certificate from the revenue. The revenue will only issue a certificate when satisfied that:

(a) the person making the disposal is ordinarily resident in Ireland;
(b) no CGT is payable on the disposal; or
(c) any CGT on the disposal and on any previous disposal by that person has been discharged.

CGT applies normally only on a sale of the asset. However, a deemed disposal includes the case where any capital sum is derived from the property, eg insurance proceeds. Normally, tax is charged on the amount of the net gain to the taxpayer, ie the proceeds minus the cost adjusted for inflation. The rate of CGT is generally uniform at 40 per cent regardless of length of ownership, although a gain on the disposal of shares in small trading companies can qualify for a reduced rate of 26 per cent. The case of gains on development land which are ring-fenced for tax purposes is somewhat different. Development land is land which is sold for more than its current undeveloped use would justify. Inflation relief for the cost of development land is applied only to its current undeveloped use value at the time of acquisition or its base cost at 6 April 1974, if earlier.

11.4 Taxes on owner of property

There are no taxes on the corporate ownership of property. Inheritance or gift tax, under the common scheme of capital acquisitions tax (CAT), is a beneficiary based tax that will fall due if a gift or inheritance comprises property deemed to be situated in Ireland. CAT is charged on the beneficiary (regardless of residence) at progressive rates of up to 40 per cent on the cumulative value of chargeable gifts and inheritances above certain thresholds, which depend on the relationship between the parties. The highest threshold, that between parent and child, is currently IR£185,555. An additional CAT charge at the rate of two per cent in the form of a new probate tax applies to property comprised in a deceased's estate where the net value exceeds IR£10,000 which is situated in Ireland or if the deceased is Irish domiciled at the date of death, wherever the property is situated.

11.5 Taxes on occupier

Residential property tax has been abolished.

11.6 Taxes on land transfer

CAT and CGT are charged on land transfers, as is stamp duty (see 4.4.3).

11.7 Wealth taxes

There are no taxes on the wealth of individuals or companies.

11.8 Value added tax

The government is reviewing value added tax (VAT) on property transactions. In the meantime, short leases, ie less than 10 years, are exempt from VAT unless the landlord elects to waive this exemption (in which case the rate is 21 per cent). He may elect to avoid the charge to him arising on creation of these leases because he will otherwise be deemed to have made a supply to himself on which he will pay VAT. In the case of an outright sale, if the property has been developed since 1972 and the seller had been entitled to a credit for any VAT suffered by him on acquisition or in the course of developing the property, then the sale attracts VAT. If the buyer is himself registered for VAT and does not carry on a VAT-exempt business, he should be able to claim an input credit for this VAT (in effect, a refund). On the grant or the assignment of a new long lease of a building or part of a building which has been developed since 1972, VAT may also be payable. A lease for a term of 10 years or more is deemed to be a supply to the tenant. A lease for less than 10 years gives rise to a self-supply to the landlord (unless he elects to be taxable on rents), while a lease for 10 years or more but less than 20 years, involves both a supply to the tenant and a self-supply to the landlord. The applicable VAT rate is 12.5 per cent and generally this applies to the lowest of: the market value of the property; three quarters of the aggregate rent payable throughout the term of the lease; and the capital sum required to be invested in Irish government gilts to produce a yield equal to the applicable rent. Where the tenant is entitled to a full VAT credit, a joint election can be made by the landlord and tenant that any VAT payable on the lease is payable by the tenant. Because the tenant accounts for this liability and claims a simultaneous deduction for the amount involved, no actual VAT payment is made by the tenant. VAT does apply to all property but it would be rare for agricultural property to have been developed in such a way that would give rise to VAT on a disposal. Also residential property would not normally be sold in the course or furtherance of a person's business. An owner cannot generally elect to charge VAT where he would otherwise be exempt. If an owner is carrying on a vatable activity, then he must charge VAT and be registered for VAT, eg where an insurance company carries on VAT-exempt business when it is dealing with insurance, if it then develops property which is not being used for its insurance business, then it is carrying on a vatable activity and in respect of that activity it must register for VAT, claim input credit and charge VAT on any disposal. The revenue commissioners are responsible for the administration of VAT (see 11.1.2). Appeal commissioners and their determinations can be reheard in the courts as can appeals on points of law.

11.9 Local and other taxes

There are no further taxes of note other than those already referred to.

12 GRANTS AND INCENTIVES

12.1 Subsidies, grants and loans

The Industrial Development Agency (IDA) is the most important governmental agency concerned with the promotion of industrial development in Ireland. As part of its remit, it assesses industrial applicants seeking fixed asset grants. The IDA favours particular sector development such as electronics, pharmaceutical products, health care and food processing. Cash grants are provided for fixed asset investment on items such as site acquisition and development and buildings. The maximum level of grant depends upon whether a project is to be located in a peripheral disadvantaged area or elsewhere (see 12.3). The IDA frequently provides a fully serviced site with planning permission on which an approved undertaking may build its own factory; first year allowance rates of up to 50 per cent are available to owner/occupiers or at rates of up to 25 per cent to landlords, with the balance in each case being allowed at four per cent per annum to a maximum of 100 per cent. It also supports private developers in building advance factories for new industries where promoters do not wish to construct their own premises. The factories may then be rented or purchased from the developers.

12.2 Tax allowances and reliefs

In order to encourage the renewal and development of urban areas, defined areas of cities and certain larger towns have been designated as qualifying for tax-based property incentives. These include an extension of the capital allowance regime, double rent deduction, rates relief and capital expenditure tax write-offs. The usual capital allowance regime applies to a narrowly defined class of buildings. Buildings constructed or refurbished in designated areas qualify for capital allowances if used for a trade or profession at rates from four per cent to 50 per cent depending on the area involved (see 12.3). A person carrying on a trade or profession from qualifying rented premises in a designated area is entitled to a double deduction in calculating taxable profits for rent paid on the premises for a 10-year period. Similarly, no local authority rates are payable in respect of qualifying premises in designated areas for a 10-year period. Since 1981, a scheme has operated in a variety of forms allowing the construction or conversion cost of rented residential accommodation to be deducted from rental income. Also rent subsidies are available when the undertaking is leasing property. The size of these grants or rent subsidies is usually linked to the numbers of jobs created. A further incentive for residential accommodation in the designated areas is that an individual who purchases a qualifying dwelling may deduct 50 per cent of the construction or refurbishment expenditure on that dwelling from his taxable income over a 10-year period. Allowances on the construction and refurbishment of premises used by qualifying companies carrying on certain qualifying service and light industrial activities in urban enterprise areas have been available since 1 August 1994. The allowances at rates of up to 50 per cent are available to owner/occupiers or at rates of up to 25 per cent to landlords. Tenants qualify for the double rent allowance and rates remission.

Finally, expenditure between 1 July 1995 and 30 June 1998 on the construction or refurbishment of tourist accommodation and facilities in designated tourist resort areas qualifies for tax allowances of up to 75 per cent for owner/occupiers and 50 per cent for landlords.

12.3 Other schemes and incentives

Buildings constructed or refurbished in designated areas qualify for capital allowances (see further 12.2 where the various reliefs and allowances available are described in more detail). Apart from two special areas in Dublin, where allowances of up to 100 per cent are available, the final deadline for construction is now set for 31 July 1998 provided that 15 per cent of the total cost of the project has been incurred by 31 July 1997.

13 COMPANIES AND BUSINESS ENTITIES

13.1 Limited and unlimited companies

13.1.1 A company may be unlimited or limited by shares. A private limited company limited by shares is a company whose members' liability is limited to the amount of the shares. It has a share capital and its articles of association restrict the right to transfer shares, limit the number of members to 50 and prohibit invitations to the public to subscribe for shares or debentures. All companies are required to have two directors and file annual returns in the public register at the companies registration office (CRO). This document details the registered office, authorised and issued share capital, shareholders and directors of a company. Private limited companies are required to annex to an annual return, financial statements which may vary in disclosure content, subject to the size of the company. It is also possible to incorporate a company limited by guarantee not having a share capital. Such companies (which are public companies) are normally used as a vehicle through which the activities of a club, association or charity may be carried on, and may seek an exemption from taxation by obtaining charitable status from the revenue commissioners. The members of a company limited by guarantee agree to guarantee the debts of the company up to a certain amount (usually nominal) in the event of a liquidation of the company.

13.1.2 If a company does not satisfy the criteria for a private limited company it will be a public company. One type of public company, the public limited company (plc), must obtain a certificate to commence trading from the registrar of companies and have an issued share capital in excess of IR£30,000 of which 25 per cent must be paid up together with any premium payable thereon. Public companies must have a minimum of seven shareholders with no upper limit. Public companies can be quoted on the Irish Stock Exchange and will be subject to the rules of the stock exchange (the Yellow Book).

13.1.3 Disclosure requirements for unlimited companies are less onerous than those for companies limited by shares or companies limited by guarantee. Certain unlimited companies whose shareholders are limited entities are required to file accounts with their annual returns. Unlimited companies are also exempt from the payment of companies capital duty on share allotments which is normally charged at a rate of one per cent. As a result of this unlimited companies are often used as investment vehicles where a high issued share capital is desired. In part a company's memorandum and articles of association determine what that company may or may not do, although general law principles also apply. The registration requirements of foreign companies are described at 14.3.

13.2 Partnerships

A partnership is the relationship between those carrying on a business in common with a view to profit and is commonly used within those professions, eg medicine and law, not permitted to avail themselves of limited liability. They are regulated by the Partnership Act 1890 (as amended) and are not able to have more than 20 partners (with certain exceptions). There is no incorporation registration procedure for the establishment of a partnership. There may, however, be a requirement to register the partnership name under the Registration of Business Names Act 1963. Unlike companies, a partnership does not have a separate persona from its individual members and this means that each partner pays his own tax on his share of the profits (and is liable for all the debts of the partnership). Formal partnership agreements are common and advisable to set out and regulate the nature of the business and its conduct.

13.2.1 A limited partnership is not a legal entity like a limited company but a form of partnership with a number of special characteristics introduced by the Limited Partnerships Act 1907. A limited partnership is a form of partnership under which certain (but not all) of the partners may have their liability limited to a fixed financial contribution (equivalent to the contribution of capital they made). Such partnerships are required to be registered in the CRO and if not registered they lose the status of limited liability. Any partner who is not a limited partner must be a general partner and will be personally liable for all the debts and obligations of the partnership. Normally the general partner will be a company. A limited partner is not permitted to take an active part in the management of the partnership and, as with ordinary partnerships, each partner is taxed separately on his share of the partnership's profits. Like general partnerships, limited partnerships are normally created by the execution of a formal deed or agreement, a copy of which is required for registration purposes. The Investment in Limited Partnerships Act 1994 created a new form of legal entity, for the purpose of investment in property (real or personal), which is regulated by the Central Bank of Ireland. The number of limited partners that may be admitted to such an investment entity is determined by the general partners and provisions exist for the return of capital to limited partners and the expansion of the type of actions a limited partner may engage in.

13.3 Other types of business association

Companies and partnerships are the two principal forms of association recognised by law and other unincorporated associations have no legal recognition. Unincorporated associations are often used where an umbrella representative organisation is being established by business interests. The association has no legal existence apart from its members. In some instances such umbrella organisations incorporate as guarantee companies without a share capital (see 13.1.1). Note should, however, be made of the position of trusts and joint ventures.

13.3.1 Trusts

The trust has been described at 1.2. It is a simpler vehicle than the company and in certain circumstances can be tax transparent, ie leave the beneficial owner with the tax liability for the property as though it were the true owner, rather than merely a shareholder in a company. This creates a form of ownership somewhere between full ownership and the limited or diluted ownership the individual would have if it merely had shares in the company which owned the property. Because of its flexibility, the concept of the trust has become commonly used in English speaking countries as a way of providing for multiple ownership of assets and for this reason is a useful means of investment, particularly in relation to unit trusts.

13.3.2 Joint ventures

A joint venture is not a separate legal entity recognised by Irish law nor are there specific regulations. The principal document in any joint venture arrangement is the joint venture agreement which is negotiated between the parties. Various vehicles may be used, including trusts, limited partnerships and companies. The agreement will provide, in particular, for the financial contributions of each party, management of the joint venture, the division of profits, the duration of the joint venture, the restrictions and pre-emption terms to apply to the disposal of any party's interest in the venture, and the arrangements for the termination and winding up of the joint venture. There are no particular fiscal regulations for the taxation of joint ventures and the tax treatment will depend on the vehicle used, eg a joint venture company will bear tax on its dividends and distributions as will any other company.

13.3.3 Investment companies

Part 13 of the Companies Act 1990 introduced a new class of company called an investment company. This is a company which holds investments in other companies on behalf of its members. These companies are often referred to as variable capital companies as the actual value of their paid-up share capital must always be equal to the net assets of the company and the company must always be authorised to purchase its members' shares when requested by them. Such companies cannot commence business without being authorised by the Central Bank of Ireland and the Bank has extensive powers to regulate the affairs of such companies.

14 INTERNATIONAL

14.1 Restrictions or consents required for inward investment

There are very few restrictions or consents required on the introduction of funds into Ireland for the purchase of property. However, consent for the purchase of interests in non-urban land has to be obtained from the Department of Agriculture and Food by individuals who do not have their principal place of residence, or by companies not incorporated, in a state which is a member of the EU or a contracting party to the European Economic Area Agreement. Acquisitions without consent are void. Similar requirements and sanctions apply to the subdivision of agricultural holdings.

14.2 Exchange controls

There are no exchange controls or restrictions at present.

14.3 Restrictions and registrations on carrying on a business

Under the Companies Act 1963, a foreign company establishing a place of business in Ireland is required to file certain information in the Companies Registration Office within one month of the establishment of the place of business, including copies of the constituent documents of the company, details of directors and the company secretary, and the name of a person resident in Ireland authorised to accept service of proceedings on behalf of the company.

14.4 Repatriation of income and proceeds of property trading and development

See further 11.3.

14.5 Withholding taxes

Withholding taxes are referred to at 11.1.4.

14.6 Double taxation relief

The Republic of Ireland has separate double taxation treaties with a number of countries.

CHAPTER 16

Scotland

Christine McLintock, Pat Hawthorn and Brandon Nolan

Partners, McGregor Donald, Glasgow

CONTENTS

1 OWNERSHIP OF LAND 529
2 OTHER INTERESTS IN LAND 534
3 TITLE TO LAND 540
4 TRANSACTIONS IN LAND 542
5 LEASES AND OTHER RIGHTS OF OCCUPATION 546
6 FINANCE AND INVESTMENT SOURCES 549
7 FORMS OF SECURITY 550
8 PLANNING AND BUILDING REGULATION 552
9 ENVIRONMENTAL MATTERS 553
10 DEVELOPMENT 555
11 TAXES 556
12 GRANTS AND INCENTIVES 556
13 COMPANIES AND BUSINESS ENTITIES 557
14 INTERNATIONAL 557

CHAPTER 16

Scotland

1 OWNERSHIP OF LAND

This chapter should be read with that on England (and Wales). It outlines the main differences from England rather than setting out the position in full.

Like England, Scotland does not have a codified system of law, but a combination of enacted and common law. Enacted law includes parliamentary statutes, local bye-laws, delegated legislation and EU law. Common law derives from civil law, common law, feudal law, custom and case law. The development of commercial law has been greatly influenced by the law of England but property law has been an exception being derived from Roman and feudal law. Scotland is perhaps the only country where feudalism has survived, albeit in an extremely customised form. Feudal tenure was introduced in medieval times when land was granted to individuals by the Crown in return for homage and service to the King. The feudal relationship between superior and vassal evolved into a means of transferring 'useful ownership' of land to the vassal while reserving development controls in the hands of the superior. The most important statutes are the Land Registers (Scotland) Act 1868, the Conveyancing (Scotland Act) 1874, the Conveyancing and Feudal Reform (Scotland) Act 1970, the Land Tenure Reform (Scotland) Act 1974 and the Land Registration (Scotland) Act 1979. The principal land tenure is feudal tenure. Leasehold tenure is not a separate form of land tenure as such, in that most land the subject of any lease will ultimately be held (by the head landlord) on feudal tenure. In addition a small amount of land is held under non-feudal tenure, being either allodial or udal tenure, a kindly tenancy or a tenancy at will. It is the aim of the Scottish Law Commission that the feudal system be abolished and replaced and it intends to submit a report and draft legislation to the government in the near future.

1.1 Types of tenure

Under the existing system of Scottish feudal tenure, title to land devolves from the Crown. The holder of land from the Crown is said to hold the *dominium plenum* (or whole ownership) akin to freehold ownership under English law. The owner of the *dominium plenum* may transfer or sell his interest as it stands, or alternatively, the land, or part of it, may be feued. Here the ownership of the land to be feued is divided into two parts; the *dominium directum* (or direct ownership or superiority), which the transferor retains, and the *dominium utile* (or useful ownership or *feu*) which is transferred. The owner of the *dominium directum* is the superior. The owner of the *dominium utile* is the vassal or *feuar*. It is normal for the superior to lay down certain restrictions on the use of the property in the feudal grant (known as real conditions or real burdens). The *feuar* is in practical terms the owner of the land, but the superior continues to own the right to enforce the conditions of the feudal grant against the *feuar* and his successors. A *feuar* can, in turn, choose to transfer his ownership in the land, either by outright transfer (thereby substituting a new *feuar* in his place) or by further subinfeudation. In the latter case the transferring *feuar* becomes the immediate or mid-superior of the transferee. There is no limit on the number of permissible superiorities in the feudal chain.

1.1.1 Freehold or absolute ownership

Feufarm and *blench* are the only surviving feudal tenures under which a proprietor of a *dominium utile* of land (the *feuar*) will hold his interest, and there is no longer any substantive difference between the two. Although ownership of land is divided under the feudal system, for most purposes the *feuar* can be treated as the absolute owner of it. Subject to any subsisting conditions contained in the titles to the property (see 2.2) and to any restrictions imposed by statute or common law, the *feuar* has the right to occupy, use and enjoy his property, to exclude others from it and to dispose of the land and any buildings on it (either by further subinfeudation or outright transfer). Anything which is or becomes fixed or annexed to the land or buildings is termed a fixture and becomes part of the land. As a general rule, ownership of the *dominium utile* of land carries with it the right to the soil below and the airspace above the land. However, the law recognises a limited number of 'separate tenements', being heritable property which can be owned and transferred separately from the *solum* of the ground. The most commonly encountered are minerals and the right to fish for salmon. By statute unmined coal is the property of the successors of the recently privatised British Coal Corporation and gold, silver, petroleum and natural gas are reserved to the Crown. In addition, it was very common in the 19th century for superiors to reserve the rights to minerals when feuing land. If such a reservation appears in the title to land which is to be commercially developed the developer will often attempt to buy back the minerals from the superior.

1.1.1.1 The superiority

The owner of the superiority of land (see 1.1) has a less tangible right, namely, to enforce the feuing conditions and (unless already redeemed) to collect *feu* duty. The superiority may be freely transferred by outright transfer but cannot be further divided by feuing. A superiority can, however, be the subject of common ownership (see 1.1.3).

1.1.1.2 Allodial land, kindly tenancies and tenancies-at-will

Allodial property is property owned absolutely without any superior or derivation of rights through the feudal chain back to the Crown. Allodial landholding includes:

(a) land owned by the Crown;
(b) land occupied by kirkyards of the Church of Scotland; and
(c) udal land, the land once held under Norse law in Orkney and Shetland.

Other lands held outside the feudal system include:

(a) manses and glebes of parish ministers; and
(b) lands held under statute (eg lands which are compulsorily purchased).

Kindly tenancies are an anomalous form of hereditary perpetual lease which still survive in the four towns of Lochmaben in Dumfriesshire. Kindly tenants are regarded as holding not as tenants but as full proprietors. Tenancies at will are similar to kindly tenancies and exist by virtue of ancient local custom. They are still to be found in the fishing and rural villages of the north-east of Scotland, in Highland villages and in a mining village in Lanarkshire. Under statute a tenant-at-will may now compulsorily purchase his landlord's interest in the land.

1.1.2 Leases

As in England, a lease may be granted where a right less than absolute ownership is intended. At common law the lease is a personal contract which, though binding on the parties is not binding on the singular successors of the landlord, ie persons (such as creditors or a buyer of the land) who derive a right from the landlord other than through succession on death. The common law has, however, been supplemented by statute and, subject to one important exception, a real right may be conferred by a lease (in the sense that it will be binding against singular successors of the landlord) if:

(a) in the case of a lease of more than one year it is in writing;
(b) the land subject to the lease is capable of separate ownership;
(c) it has a definite termination date;
(d) there is a definite rent which must not be nominal; and
(e) the tenant exercises possession either personally or through, eg a subtenant.

The exception to this rule is leases in an area in which registration of title has become operational (see section 3) and which are capable of enduring for more than 20 years. A tenant under any such lease granted since registration became operational can only obtain a real right by registering his interest in the Land Register. In the case of a lease capable of enduring for more than 20 years (known as a long lease) over land situated elsewhere in Scotland, recording in the General Register of Sasines is optional. However, only a long lease can be registered or recorded and only registered recorded leases can be made the subject of a standard security (the mortgage described at 2.3). A contract which fails to meet the statutory requirements to confer a real right of lease may still be a lease at common law provided certain requirements are met (ie parties in agreement; a right to occupy heritable subjects; a rent or consideration (which need not be definite) and a period of time for which the property is let (which may be in perpetuity). A tenant may only transfer or sublet his interest in a lease if he has an express or implied power to do so (see further section 5).

1.1.3 Joint ownership

There are two forms of co-ownership, joint property and common property.

1.1.3.1 Joint property is confined to the two cases of ownership of land by trustees and ownership by the members of unincorporated associations. Unlike the situation in England, a trust situation is not automatically created as soon as more than one person owns land. In the case of joint property none of the owners has a separate share or interest in the property which can be disposed of or burdened separately or left by way of will. There is a single undivided title held by all of the co-owners. Ownership of the joint property continues only so long as the owner remains a trustee or a member of the association (as the case may be) and upon the death or resignation of an owner his interest transfers automatically to the surviving or remaining owners. Rules of management of joint property are generally provided in the trust deed or the rules of the association, as supplemented in both cases by the general law.

1.1.3.2 If ownership of land is expressly granted to two or more people the result is common property unless the grantees are taking as trustees or members of an unincorporated association. Each owner of common property has title to his own share which he may dispose of or burden by his own act. On the death of one of the owners, his share will pass under his will or be distributed according to the rules of intestate succession. One example of common property is the matrimonial home which is often held in the name of both spouses. Other examples include large housing developments where rights of common property are often conferred in respect of common garden areas and flatted or tenement property (whether used for residential or commercial purposes) where titles often provide for the owners of the individual flats in a tenement to have a right of common property in areas such as the entrance passage, stair and garden. At common law, each owner of common property is entitled to make use of it and to take a rateable share of any profits the property may produce. No one single co-owner can grant a lease or a positive servitude over common property without the consent of the other owners. No alterations can be made to common property without the consent of each co-owner save that necessary repairs or rebuilding can be carried out by one owner who can then recover the cost from his fellow owners pro rata. The common law rules are frequently altered or supplemented by real burdens in the title to property (see 2.2). In the absence of express agreement among co-owners to the contrary, any one co-owner is entitled to realise his share by having the common property divided or, if physical division is impractical, by having the property sold and the proceeds divided. The appropriate mechanism to achieve division and sale is by way of a court action. The right is not available if the parties have agreed to this effect (although such an agreement is not binding on successors) nor is it available in respect of common property which is indispensable, such as a staircase, hall or common access road. There are also statutory rules for matrimonial homes which restrict, but do not exclude, the right to division and sale.

1.1.4 Condominia

Condominium ownership does not exist, although common ownership akin to holding land under a condominium agreement is described in 1.1.3.2.

1.1.5 Lesser rights

If the essential elements of a lease are in existence (ie agreement, heritable subjects, rent, termination date and possession) then the relationship between the parties is as landlord and tenant regardless of what the document says. If, however, any of these requirements are missing, a licence to occupy may be inferred. If possession is exclusive, a contract could be a lease but if it is shared (as in the case of shared business facilities in a business centre) it is more likely to be a licence. The distinction is important since a licence does not prevail against the singular successors of the landlord; if there is no express termination date it may be terminable at the will of the landlord; and the common law rules relating to leases will not apply. It is also important in questions of valuation and rating. Other categories of property rights which provide benefits to the holder more restricted than ownership include liferent, servitude and the statutory occupancy rights in the matrimonial home of a non-entitled spouse or cohabitee (see section 2).

1.2 Legal and beneficial ownership

As a general rule Scots law does not recognise the doctrine of 'legal' and 'equitable' interests in property. If property is held by trustees, full and undivided ownership of trust property is held by the trustees. The right of the beneficiary of the trust is merely a personal right against the trustees and the income and proceeds of the trust property. The right of the beneficiary will usually be effective against the personal creditors, trustees in bankruptcy or liquidators of the trustees and any person who acquires title from the trustees in breach of the trust purposes and for no consideration. However, the title of any person who has acquired an interest in land from trustees for value cannot be challenged on the ground that the disposal by the trustee was contrary to the terms of the trust. Much of the common law of trusts has now been superseded by statute which sets out in detail the general powers of trustees. These statutory powers may be supplemented or restricted by express provision in the relevant trust deed. As in England, trusts can be created expressly or may rarely be implied by law. They are extensively used to make financial provision for families and for pension funds, clubs and charity activities. As Scots law does not recognise 'equitable' securities, trusts have been used by commercial entities as a method of securitisation of assets. Trusts have also been utilised in the setting up of certain timeshare complexes.

1.3 Restrictions on ownership and dealing

1.3.1 As in England, there are few restrictions on the ownership of land. With the exception of mental incapacity, all natural persons aged 16 or over have full capacity to own and transfer property of all kinds; a person under 21 may, however, apply to the court to unravel a 'prejudicial transaction' entered into by him between 16 and 18. A person under 16 can only own land through his guardians as trustees. In theory, a company can only hold land if empowered to do so in its memorandum and articles of association, but statutory protections exist for parties dealing with companies in good faith. While partnerships have separate legal personality, they cannot own property in their own name. While it is possible for a lease of land to be taken in the name of a partnership, it is invariable practice for both ownership and leases of land to be taken in the name of some or all of the partners as trustees for the partnership. A person or body may be restricted from owning land by statute or by its constitution, or as to the terms upon which it acquires or holds land (eg by real burden or conditions enforceable by a superior or a *co-feuar*). There are legislative restrictions on the rights of a landowner which protect the public interest, such as planning and building control regulations, rights of access, conservation of natural beauty or environment and compulsory purchase. There are also restrictions arising to protect private interests such as the laws of nuisance.

1.3.2 With the exception of certain statutory restrictions on bodies such as local authorities, land is generally freely disposable subject to any restrictions contained in the constitution of the transferor or in the title deeds or lease in question. There are statutory restrictions on the operation of pre-emption and redemption clauses in the title to a property (see 2.4). In addition, there are two forms of 'diligence' which can impose restrictions on the ability of a landowner to deal with his land (see 2.3).

1.4 Adverse possession and acquisitive prescription

There are two forms of prescription, positive prescription and negative prescription. Under positive prescription a person with a recorded or registered title to land (albeit challengeable by the true owner) may acquire unchallengeable good title to that land by occupying it openly, peaceably and without judicial interruption for a period of 10 years. Positive prescription cannot run if possession is founded on a deed which is forged or which is invalid. In addition, a real right of positive servitude or a public right of way may be created by 20 years' continuous, open and peaceable possession without judicial interruption. Special rules based on the 20-year prescriptive period also apply to the acquisition of rights (founded on a title) in salmon fishing and in the foreshore. With the exception of a servitude or right of way, possession alone (without the support of a registered title) cannot create a real right in land. Certain rights may also be extinguished by non-use (see 2.1.1)

2 OTHER INTERESTS IN LAND

There are various other interests in land which confer rights less than absolute ownership or possession. The most common are servitudes, real burdens, common interest, liferent, mortgages and matrimonial occupancy rights.

2.1 Servitudes or easements, usufruct, building and dwelling rights

2.1.1 Servitudes

Much of the law of servitudes is derived from Roman law. A servitude is a burden on one piece of land (the servient tenement) whereby the owner must submit to certain uses being exercised over it (a positive servitude) by the owner of another piece of land (the dominant tenement) or must restrain his own use and occupation for the benefit of the owner of the dominant tenement (a negative servitude). A servitude is a real right which is available to successors and derives from ownership of the dominant tenement. Positive servitudes include rights of passage, rights to take or lead water over a servient tenement, rights of pasturage and rights of support. Negative servitudes allow the dominant owner to prevent certain action by the servient owner which might adversely affect the rights to light, air or prospect (eg to restrict the height of buildings). There is a limited number of recognised servitudes. Rights such as shooting and fishing are not servitudes but are merely personal licences. There are four ways of creating a servitude:

(a) express grant (this is the only way a negative servitude can be created);
(b) implied grant, where a servitude is necessary for the comfortable enjoyment of the dominant tenement;
(c) open and peaceable possession or use for 20 years without judicial interruption; and
(d) express or implied reservation when land is divided.

A servitude may be registered or recorded in the appropriate property register (see section 3) if created by express grant but registration is not necessary for its effectiveness (unless contained in a conveyance of land which of itself requires registration, see 2.9). Servitudes can be extinguished by express discharge or renunciation, by confusion (where both tenements come into single ownership), by negative prescription (non-usage or claim) for 20 years, acquiescence, change of circumstances or statute (eg on compulsory purchase). They may also be discharged or varied by the Lands Tribunal for Scotland.

2.1.2 Usufruct

The right of usufruct is not recognised, although there are other mechanisms, eg the liferent (see 2.6.1), which fulfil a similar purpose.

2.1.3 Building and dwelling rights

Building and dwelling rights are not recognised, although there are other mechanisms which fulfil similar purposes (see eg 2.6.3).

2.2 Restrictions on use and other restrictions

2.2.1 Real burdens

Under the feudal system the superior can lay down restrictions on the use of the property by the *feuar*. These restrictions (known as real conditions or real burdens) run with the land and are binding on successors. Real burdens often restrict the use of property or impose maintenance and repair obligations in respect of common areas. Case law establishes seven strict requirements before a condition will be a real burden. To be effective, it must be registered or recorded and contained in full either in a conveyance of the servient tenement or in a separate deed of conditions. In the case of residential developments or multi-occupancy commercial developments, this allows a developer to impose the same feuing conditions on each plot. The conveyance to each such buyer (or *co-feuar*) will often expressly provide for mutual rights of enforcement of the real burdens as between the *co-feuars*. Even in the absence of an express provision, mutual rights of enforcement for *co-feuars* may, in limited circumstances, be implied by law. This is different from England. The creation of real burdens in an outright transfer (as opposed to subinfeudation) is less common. However, if land is subdivided or there is a series of outright transfers of adjacent plots of land subject to similar real burdens, mutual rights of enforcement of the co-disponees may be set out or, in limited circumstances, implied by law. The title deeds to almost every piece of land will contain at least one writ containing real burdens. The right to enforce a real burden can be lost through acquiescence, agreement (any discharge must be registered in the Register of Sasines or the Land Register), by the dominant and servient tenements coming into single ownership, and by compulsory purchase. The Lands Tribunal has the power to vary or discharge real burdens or other real conditions, eg where a change in the character of the land or the neighbourhood renders the obligation unreasonable or inappropriate.

2.2.2 Other rights and remedies of the superior

The concept of a *feuar* paying a yearly sum of money known as *feu* duty for the grant of a *feu* of land to the superior (in addition to any capital sum paid on the grant of the *feu* being made) is of decreasing relevance. Since 1974, it has not been possible to create new *feu* duties and on purchases after that date, the *feu* duty in respect of the property must be redeemed at a figure generally between 10 and 12 times the annual amount. *Feu* duties rarely exceed £10 per annum (with exceptions for large areas). A superior has a range of remedies to enforce real conditions including a court action for specific implement (performance) or interdict (to prevent a breach occurring). If the real conditions have not been complied with or have been breached by a *feuar*, or if *feu* duty has not been paid for five years, the most draconian remedy of the superior (in theory) is to 'irritate' the *feu* and evict the *feuar*. A declaration of irritancy must be sought from the court. The courts are reluctant to allow irritancy if it can be 'purged' and will normally allow the *feuar* (or a mortgagee or other interested party) an opportunity to remedy the breach. If remedy is not possible, the effect of irritancy is that the *dominium utile* reverts to the superior without compensation and all subordinate rights in the land such as those of a mortgagee will be extinguished. It is unusual for superiors of residential property to take a strong interest in enforcing real conditions but the situation is different in relation to commercial estates where the superior may have an active involvement. It is therefore important for the *feuar* (landowner) and any mortgagee to be fully aware of all title conditions.

2.2.3 Common interest and the law of the tenement

Common interest arises by implication of law. It is a real condition, ie a burden on the property of others, rather than a type of ownership. Examples include tenement buildings where, in the absence of common property (see 1.1.3), each flat owner has a right of common interest in those parts of the building which he does not own, and non-feudal rivers and lochs where owners of the river banks can take action to prevent unauthorised intrusion on their water. In the case of a tenement building, if the title deeds do not impose obligations and rights regarding maintenance and repair, the common law of the tenement applies. Under this the owner of the lowest floor owns the soil *(solum)*, foundations and back green subject to a right of common interest for the upper proprietors entitling them to require their maintenance by the lower proprietor and to prevent any injurious alteration. The owner of the highest storey owns the roof and roof space and is responsible for its maintenance, with the lower proprietors having a common interest and right of enforcement. There are similar rules for walls and gables. Common passages and stairs are, however, always held in common property. It is, however, usual for the title deeds to individual flats within a tenement building to provide that each of the flat owners has a right of common property in the soil (*solum*) and the roof to ensure that the maintenance obligation is shared among them.

2.3 Private mortgages and charges

A fixed security or mortgage can only be created over property by way of a statutory standard security. Since 1961 a floating charge can be granted by a company over its assets (including property). Specific comment on standard securities and floating charges is made in section 7. A creditor can attach a debtor's property either in payment or as security of a debt by the 'diligence' known as adjudication. Once an adjudication has been registered in the General Register of Inhibitions and Adjudications, voluntary disposal of the property by the debtor is prohibited and any successor takes title subject to the diligence. Once a court decree is obtained by a creditor in an action of adjudication, the creditor can register the decree in the appropriate property register and the property will vest in the creditor subject to the debtor's right to redeem the debt within a period of 10 years. If no redemption occurs within 10 years, the creditor may raise a further court action to exclude the right of redemption. Alternatively, a creditor may use the 'diligence of inhibition', which is available once an action has been commenced but before any decree is granted. It can therefore be a powerful tool in litigation. Once a notice of inhibition has been registered, any subsequent voluntary deed affecting the property can be avoided at the instance of the inhibiting creditor if his interest is prejudiced. An inhibition prevents any sale or heritable security but generally not a lease.

2.4 Contracts and options

A contract or option for the sale and purchase of property confers no real right or interest only a personal right to enforce the contract which can be defeated eg by a purchaser for value who perfects his title by registration or recording. The creation of real rights in property by registration or recording is considered in more detail at 2.9, 3 and 4.1.5. It may be possible to secure the positive obligations of a landowner under a contract or option relating to land by taking a standard security over the land but there are difficulties in enforcing this. There are statutory restrictions on the operation of pre-emption clauses in *feu* contracts (whenever created) and in dispositions or other deeds executed after 1 September 1974. A superior or other person entitled to the benefit of a pre-emption clause must accept the pre-emption offer within 21 days (or such lesser period provided in the deed) failing which the right is extinguished. In addition, under statute, a redemption clause created after 1 September 1974 (whereby an owner may be obliged to resell the property to a superior or other person) may only be exercised within 20 years of creation.

2.5 Public or municipal charges

Certain government and public bodies such as local authorities can impose charging orders on land in security of payment for statutory works such as common repair schemes or other repairs to or cleaning of dangerous or unsanitary buildings. The charging order is recorded or registered in the relevant property register and attaches to the land.

2.6 Other interests

2.6.1 Other interests and rights in land include the liferent. A liferenter is entitled to any fruits and income deriving from a property during his occupancy during his lifetime only, while the *fiar* receives the capital or the property itself at the end of the liferent. A common arrangement is for a parent to leave the family home in fee to the children while reserving a liferent for the surviving parent. Liferent can be created by express grant (eg in a will) or through a trust.

2.6.2 A public right of way along a definite route may be created by uninterrupted peaceable use for 20 years. It can be lost through disuse or by action of the Secretary of State or local authority. Rights of way (or wayleaves) may also be created by statute or under statutory powers (eg for utilities companies).

2.6.3 There are statutory occupancy rights for non-entitled spouses and co-habitees, ie who have no right of ownership in the matrimonial home, to prevent them being evicted by the entitled spouse and, in certain circumstances, to prevent the matrimonial home from being disposed of. Accordingly it is generally a condition of missives (or contracts, see 4.1.1) that the seller establishes that either there is no non-entitled spouse, or that all occupancy rights have been formally renounced. Similar evidence is required by the Keeper of the Land Register before a statement will be included in the title sheet that there are no subsisting occupancy rights (see section 3).

2.7 Liabilities attaching to land

The statutory regime imposing liabilities on owners and/or occupiers of land, the law of nuisance with regard to unreasonable use of one's land to the prejudice of adjoining owners, and fiscal liabilities in respect of land are much the same as they are in England (see the English chapter, at 2.7). In Scotland the relevant statute regarding liability for injury and damage to visitors or their goods is the Occupier's Liability (Scotland) Act 1960. The doctrine of *Rylands v Fletcher* (to the extent it imposed strict liability until recently for escape of a dangerous thing) does not apply in Scotland where it has always been necessary to prove some degree of fault to succeed in an action of nuisance (see section 9(1)).

2.8 Legal and equitable interests

There is no equivalent to the English law concept of 'equity' and no general distinction between legal and equitable rights. Scots law has a more rigid structure and the distinction is between real rights (enforceable against the world) and personal rights (eg under contract). The principal real rights in land are ownership, rights in security, proper liferent, servitude and lease. Under Scots law, rights in security are not created until they are made real, usually by registration in a public register or by notice being given to interested third parties. Until the real right is perfected, no 'equitable' right in security is conferred. The concept of beneficial interests in property was, however, recognised in the House of Lords case of *Sharp v Woolwich Building Society* (see 2.10 and 3.3).

2.9 Protection of interests

Most real rights in land can only be created by and will not be binding on successors until registration in either the Register of Sasines or the Land Register. The principal exceptions are servitudes and leases which may, or may not, be registered (though long leases in areas operational for land registration purposes which must be registered to create a real right, see 1.1.2). Floating charges granted by Scottish companies over land are registered in the charges register of the grantor at Companies House in Edinburgh and (subject to valid registration, see 7.2) are deemed created on the date of execution of the deed creating the floating charge. A floating charge does not however attach until liquidation or receivership. For the purposes of registration in the Land Register, certain rights, including the servitude interest of the dominant proprietor, most unregistered leases, rights of way, common interest and the interest of the holder of a floating charge, are termed 'overriding' interests. An overriding interest can (but will not necessarily) appear in the title sheet but it is not generally covered by the state indemnity of title provided by land registration. Accordingly important rights can exist which neither appear in the deeds or public records. It is important therefore to include a condition in the sale contract that no such interests exist.

2.10 Priority of interests

2.10.1 In the case of competing interests recordable in the General Register of Sasines (see section 3), priority is generally given to the first to record his interest. With the exception of servitudes, the interest is not created (ie it does not exist) until recording occurs. In the case of title (as opposed to security interests) registrable in the Land Register, the person who is the last to successfully register prevails, although this success may be temporary since if the Land Register is inaccurate it is capable of rectification (see 3.2.3). In both cases, deeds registered on the same day rank equally regardless of the actual time of registration. Servitudes, certain leases and other rights which do not require recording or registration for creation of a real right, rank according to their date of creation. A floating charge is 'created' on the date of execution (although it will be void against any receiver or liquidator unless registered with the registrar of companies within 21 days). A standard security (or mortgage) is 'created' on the date it is recorded in the Register of Sasines or registration in the Land Register, but in order to be enforceable must also be registered with the Registrar of Companies within 21 days of that date. In general, a fixed security which is constituted as a real right before a floating charge has crystallised will have priority. A floating charge can only be granted by a company and can only crystallise, or attach to the assets it purports to cover, on the liquidation of the grantor or on the appointment of a receiver (see 7.3). Secured creditors may, however, agree alternative ranking in a ranking agreement. Unlike the situation in England, ranking agreements which regulate the ranking of fixed and floating charges must also be registered with the Registrar of Companies within 21 days of execution to be enforceable. Provisions in a floating charge prohibiting or restricting the creation of any subsequent fixed or floating security having priority or ranking equally with the floating charge are effective to confer priority on the floating charge even through crystallisation has not yet occurred. Rights in security are dealt with in section 7.

2.10.2 The position has been made less simple by *Sharp v Woolwich Building Society* which gave a buyer priority over the receiver of a seller appointed after payment and delivery of the disposition but before it had been recorded in the appropriate registry. The seller however retains title and the holder of the unrecorded disposition can still be defeated by a bona fide purchaser with a recorded disposition.

3 TITLE TO LAND

3.1 Proof of title

The General Register of Sasines is a comprehensive system of registration of deeds in existence since 1617. Prior to 1979 all deeds conveying or constituting security over land had to be recorded in the Register of Sasines to confer a real right. There is no equivalent in Scotland to the English concept of unregistered land. Statute has now introduced a system of registration of title which will, in time, cover the whole of Scotland and supersede the recording of deeds in the Register of Sasines. The operational areas for land registration to date are the counties of Aberdeen, Fife, Kincardine, Renfrew, Glasgow, Dumbarton, Lanark, Clackmannan, Stirling, Ayr, Dumfries, Wigtown, Kirkcudbright and West Lothian (leaving 19 areas to become operational over the next decade). Unlike the Sasine system, registration in the Land Register confers on the owner a title guaranteed by the state, unless expressly excluded. If an indemnity is excluded, eg because the owner's document of title does not fully encompass the ground occupied, such defects may be remedied by positive prescription (see 1.4). Once an area has become 'operational' certain transactions must be registered in the Land Register to confer a real right. These include new grants of land in *feu*, outright transfers for valuable consideration and all leases of over 20 years. Deeds which do not require land registration, eg gifts can continue to be recorded in the Register of Sasines. The Keeper is unlikely to accept a voluntary registration in a non-operational area except in the case of a substantial building development in an area next due to become operational. The registers are open for inspection by the public.

3.2 The Land Registers

Both property registers, ie the Land Register and the General Register of Sasines are administered in Edinburgh by the Keeper of the Registers of Scotland.

3.2.1 Plans

The Land Register uses ordnance survey maps for identification purposes. In the case of property recorded in the Register of Sasines the extent of the property must be ascertained from any description or plan contained in the title deeds.

3.2.2 Content

The Register of Sasines is divided into counties, and is a title or deed-based system where each deed submitted is copied and recorded in the Register and the original is returned to the owner. Writs are entered into a presentment book in order of presentment and this order determines preferences of title. A separate search sheet is kept for each property providing a history of transactions affecting the property. All title deeds and heritable securities for a piece of land are kept together by the owner or first ranking heritable creditor. The Land Register consists of a title sheet for each interest in a particular area of land. A land certificate is a copy of the title sheet divided into four sections:

(a) the 'property section' describes the property by a reference to a title number and a plan and confirms the type of ownership (eg feudal or leasehold);
(b) the 'proprietorship section' gives the name and address of the current owner or tenant (unlike England details of previous owners/tenants are not shown), the date of registration and the price paid, details of any adverse entry in the Register of Inhibitions and Adjudications, and a statement that there are no subsisting occupancy rights of spouses of former proprietors;
(c) the 'charges section' shows any heritable security affecting the property; floating charges may be noted as an overriding interest; and
(d) the 'burdens section' contains details of all subsisting real burdens and conditions affecting the property (or in the case of the interest of a tenant, the terms and conditions of the lease) and details of any overriding interests to be noted.

Any exclusion of indemnity may be detailed in the proprietorship, charges or burdens sections. A holder of a standard security over land is entitled to a separate charge certificate from the Keeper which, unless excluded, will confer an indemnity. On subsequent dealings, the land certificate together with the new document of transfer or deed creating a real right, are submitted to the Keeper and the land certificate is updated. The land certificate rules and, save where indemnity has been excluded, title deeds and documents of transfer (which will be returned to the owner) can in theory be destroyed. However, they tend to be retained in case of error or omission in the land certificate.

3.2.3 Errors

If information in a title sheet of the Land Register is incorrect, there are provisions for rectification of the register. The discretion of the keeper to rectify is severely restricted for the protection of a registered proprietor in possession. If a person suffers loss either through rectification of the Land Register or through non-rectification of the register he may have a claim of indemnity against the state.

3.3 Passing of title

A transferee does not obtain title to land until the conveyance in his favour is recorded in the General Register of Sasines or registered in the Land Register, as appropriate. Until that time the transferor remains the infeft proprietor and the transferee has only a personal right under the conveyance against the transferor. A buyer may defeat any receiver of the seller after delivery of the disposition to the buyer (see 2.10). With that exception, the transferee is at risk until the recording or registration of the conveyance. There is no protection by way of priority notice. The devices used in conveyancing practice to protect a transferee are outlined in 4.1.5. The date of recording or registration is still, unless the application is rejected or withdrawn, the date when the application is received by the Keeper. Unlike England, there is no time period within which registration in the General Register of Sasines or the Land Register must occur. The sanction for non-recording or non-registration is a failure to obtain a real right until such recording or registration is effected.

4 TRANSACTIONS IN LAND

The most common transactions in respect of land are the sale and purchase of land (by the grant of a new *feu* or outright transfer of an existing *feu*), the grant or assignation of a lease and the creation of a standard security to secure a loan or other liability. A grant of a new *feu* is effected by a document known as a *feu* disposition or *feu* contract. An outright transfer is effected by way of a disposition. In this section reference to a disposition includes reference to a *feu* disposition.

4.1 Procedures

4.1.1 There are normally two, or possibly three, main stages in a transaction for sale or lease. The first is the period up to conclusion of a contract for sale or lease. This contract is commonly entered into by solicitors acting as agents for the parties and is constituted by an exchange or exchanges of letters between the solicitors. The concluded contract is referred to as the 'missives'. The second stage is the period from conclusion of missives until settlement (when the disposition or lease is delivered in exchange for the price and/or first instalment of rent). Occasionally, a tenant will take entry to leased premises before a formal lease is entered into. In these circumstances the fundamental terms will be agreed in the missives and, usually, a draft lease will be annexed. The third stage is the period between settlement and registration or recording of the disposition or lease in the appropriate register when the transferee obtains a real right enforceable against the world.

4.1.2 In a typical sale and purchase, the buyer's solicitor will submit an offer to purchase to the seller's solicitor. The English practice of standard written pre-contract enquiries is not used in Scottish conveyancing practice. There is no standard form of offer but commonly the offer will, in addition to identifying the property and stating the price, include a range of conditions in the nature of warranties intended to elicit information about the property (eg that there are no conditions of title which would adversely affect ownership; the adjacent roads and sewers have been taken over by the local authority; there are no outstanding local authority notices; and alterations have received and comply with appropriate planning permissions, building warrants and completion certificates). Assuming the price to be acceptable, the seller's solicitor will usually respond with a qualified acceptance to the offer, agreeing to make available before settlement the usual clear searches in the relevant property register, the Register of Inhibitions and Adjudications and, if appropriate, the Companies Registry, and delivering the title deeds and any relevant planning permissions to allow the buyer's solicitor to satisfy himself as regards title and planning issues. The missives are not concluded, and the parties are not bound, until all qualifications (in the initial qualified acceptance or any further exchange of letters between the solicitors) have been agreed. To avoid a large number of letters containing terms and conditions, it is not unusual, in the case of commercial property, for an offer to be submitted in draft form for amendment until the offer is in a form acceptable to both parties. The exchange of contracts can then comprise an offer and a straight acceptance.

4.1.3 In a competitive situation, it is normal for prospective buyers to 'note an interest' with the seller's solicitor. The seller will then set a closing date and time by which all offers must be received. There are ethical rules laid down by the Law Society of Scotland with regard to closing dates. The highest offer need not be accepted (indeed all may be rejected) but a solicitor may not, on receipt of the offers, disclose the highest price to one of the lower offerors with a view to eliciting a higher offer. Once missives are concluded, both parties are bound and neither may withdraw without good reason. As a general rule, missives supersede any prior communications. Depending on the complexity of the transaction, missives would normally be concluded within two to three weeks. As there is always the possibility that an offer could be immediately accepted without qualification a buyer should ensure that adequate finance will be available before an offer is made. In many cases property surveys and environmental surveys are also carried out before the offer is made but in commercial transactions missives are often concluded subject to a 'suspensive condition', eg where the buyer is given a limited time to obtain planning permission or building warrants, or environmental or other surveys, failing which the offer is treated as having lapsed. Historically, missives were concluded before title was examined by the buyer or lender but it has now become more common for the preliminary title investigations to take place beforehand.

4.1.4 During the second stage, which can be fairly short, the buyer's solicitor will complete his title examination, finalise any documentation with lenders and review all relevant local authority reports and searches received from the seller's solicitor. In the case of a corporate seller the search in the Companies Registry will disclose any notices relating to liquidation or the like and any registered charges. Searches in the Register of Sasines, the Register of Inhibitions and Adjudications (see further section 3) and the companies registry are generally carried out, on the instructions of the seller's solicitor, by a professional firm of searchers. Reports on the Land Register are provided by the Keeper. The procedure for leases is very similar. In this case, the tenant's solicitor will examine the underlying title of the head landlord and the leases of any intervening principal tenant. Under Scots law, an assignation of the tenant's interest in a lease is not effective until intimation (notice) has been given to the landlord.

4.1.5 After settlement, the buyer's solicitor will procure the stamping of the disposition by the Stamp Office in Edinburgh when stamp duty will be paid. Thereafter the disposition will be sent for recording in the Register of Sasines or registration in the Land Register. There is no equivalent to the English entry of caution or notice nor will a search in the property registers give the buyer any priority. The Register of Sasines (and accordingly any search in it) is always some months behind. Although it is common to request the searchers to also check the computerised Presentment Book (which is only one or two days out of date) this check is not guaranteed by the searchers as being accurate. Writs presented for land registration normally appear in a search made the following day. The Register of Adjudications and Inhibitions is also usually a day or two behind. In the case of the companies registry, it may be up to 21 days after the granting of a floating charge that registration takes place and notice of liquidation or receivership of a company may not appear until seven days after the event. Accordingly, the buyer takes the risk that from the date of the last searches seen before completion to the date he registers his title no other documents or interests are registered to his prejudice and no receiver or liquidator is appointed whose rights could defeat those of the buyer. On a practical level, these risks are dealt with in a number of ways. First, in most cases the seller's solicitor will deliver to the buyer at settlement an undertaking (in a letter of obligation) that no adverse deed will be registered during the risk period and that appropriate clear, up-to-date searches will be provided within an agreed time following settlement. Second, letters of non-crystallisation and/or consent will be obtained from the holders of any registered floating charge. Third, certificates of solvency of a corporate seller are often taken from the directors. Fourth, it is often provided that after delivery of the disposition, the seller holds the title in trust for the buyer. Fifth, the disposition should be recorded or registered as soon as practicable after delivery: in many large commercial transactions this may take place the same day. While these measures are not foolproof, in practice problems are rare. The *Sharp* decision has eliminated one of the risks that used to attach to this final stage (see 2.10).

4.2 Contract terms

4.2.1 Once missives are concluded they will contain few warranties, other than as to the seller's title. Payment of a deposit is unusual but sometimes arises on purchase of a newly built dwelling house. The contract generally provides for payment of interest (generally four per cent above clearing bank base rate) should there be a delay by the buyer. Vacant possession (unless sold subject to lease) will be given on the date of entry in exchange for the price. Risk passes to the buyer on conclusion of missives but commonly the seller will continue to insure until settlement. The principle of *caveat emptor* applies and it is for the buyer to satisfy himself as to any physical or title defects. In a typical sale, the disposition is delivered to the buyer at settlement in exchange for the price. At common law the missives were wholly superseded by delivery of the disposition save to the extent of collateral obligations not relating to the property. The Contracts (Scotland) Act 1997 provides, however, that unfulfilled terms are not now superseded by delivery.

4.2.2 If either party defaults, the other party can apply to the court for an order for specific implement requiring the defaulting party to complete. For a material breach he may be able to resile. Care should be taken before treating missives as at an end without a declaration or declarator of court to that effect. If the buyer discovers some latent defect, there is some doubt whether the buyer can opt to retain the property and claim damages in respect of the difference between the price paid and the actual value (as opposed to reselling and claiming damages for breach of contract). It is therefore common to include this remedy in the missives.

4.3 Formalities

The formalities for contracts and deeds are set out in the Requirements of Writing (Scotland) Act 1995 which sets out more relaxed requirements than before. Contracts relating to land (missives) must be in writing and signed by the principals or their agents but need not be witnessed. Care should therefore be taken that correspondence agreeing the principles of a deal does not inadvertently become a contract. Any such letters should expressly state they are not intended to create contractual relations or commitments. All documents for the creation, transfer, variation or extinction of an interest in land (other than a lease for not more than a year) must be in writing and subscribed by the grantor. If they are to be registered in the Land Register or recorded in the Register of Sasines they should be witnessed by one adult witness in accordance with the provisions of the 1995 Act. A lease for not more than a year can be oral or by informal writing.

4.4 Fees, costs and taxes

The position with regard to fees, costs and expenses (including stamp duty) is similar to that in England (and see the English chapter at 4.4.1, 4.4.3, 4.4.5 and 4.4.6). In Scotland, however, the seller usually meets the cost of all local authority reports and searches. In addition, solicitors' conveyancing fees are not governed by statutory guidelines in Scotland but otherwise section 4.4.2

of the English chapter generally reflects the position. The fees for registration of dispositions in the Register of Sasines and for registration of title in the Land Register are the same and range from a minimum of £22 (for a transaction not exceeding £10,000) to a maximum of £7,500 (for transactions exceeding £5,000,000). The registration fees for standard securities range from £22 (for a security transaction not exceeding £20,000) to £3,750 (for a security transaction exceeding £5,000,000). As regards the role of estate agents, nearly all marketing and sales of land in Glasgow and the West Coast of Scotland are done by estate agents, surveyors or valuers but in the East Coast most marketing and sales of residential property are conducted by solicitors.

5 LEASES AND OTHER RIGHTS OF OCCUPATION

Leases and rights to occupy land fall into three categories:

(a) leases that confer a real right and are binding on successors of the landlord;
(b) leases binding on the parties only; and
(c) personal licences which fall short of the status of a lease.

In the absence of agreement to the contrary, the law will imply definite rights and obligations in the case of the first two. The relationship between the parties to a licence is determined, however, solely by the terms of the licence. The requirements for constitution of a lease and the differences between a lease and a licence are considered in more detail in 1.1.5. As in England, the length of a lease will generally be determined by the purpose of the letting. Historically, ground leases and long leases of 99 or 125 years were granted in towns and cities where subinfeudation was not permitted. Many of these are still in existence and are similar to English leaseholds, having been granted for a capital sum and reserving a nominal annual ground rent. As a result of statutory land tenure reform, however, Scottish landowners are now free to sub*feu* or sell land outright and this type of lease tenure is no longer used in modern practice. Residential accommodation is often let as a short, assured tenancy for a minimum period of between six months and five years (see 5.3), while agricultural land is often let by the year. Post-1974 leases of residential property may not exceed 20 years (including any option to renew). A tenant of a dwelling house protected under the Rents Acts may, however, have security of tenure rights which in practice exceed 20 years. Leases of commercial property are normally for 25 years, particularly where there is an institutional landlord. The 25-year institutional lease is an important phenomenon in the property investment market UK-wide and in the last 50 years it has been imported into Scottish commercial practice to the extent that the pattern of commercial lease holding in England and Scotland is substantially the same. As in England, the value of commercial property is often assessed by yield and, while the yields may differ slightly in the English and Scottish property markets, the market trends are generally similar. While the recession in the property market of the early 1990s was perhaps felt less hard in Scottish cities than in the City of London, it also led to acceptance in the Scottish market of some institutional leases of less than 25 years' duration or 25 year leases with tenant break options. This trend in favour of the tenants continues but is influenced by market forces and the bargaining position of the tenant. One development in the UK which may bring about a dramatic change in the way institutions approach leasing is the private finance initiative (PFI). This is an initiative which is supported in principle by both main political parties to encourage private sector investment in building and infrastructure projects which were formerly developed and funded by the public sector. Many existing and future government buildings and accommodation are to be designed, funded, developed and owned by the private sector and leased back to the government, with the private sector undertaking the management in return for management, maintenance and service charges. This concept is opposite to the concept of a full repairing and insurance lease where the institutional landlord passes all liabilities onto the tenant. Scotland stands to be a major beneficiary of the PFI.

5.1 Rent and other terms

5.1.1 Since, as a matter of practice, the express terms of Scottish commercial leases are similar to their English counterparts the provisions of section 5.1 of the English chapter are generally applicable in Scotland. The important point is that, where any feature is not specifically covered by the terms of the lease, then the Scots law of leases (which apportions the responsibility for the property between the landlord and the tenant) reasserts itself to resolve the situation. In addition, there are some unique features of Scottish commercial leases. In particular, the English statutory framework comprising the Landlord and Tenant Acts does not apply and there are very few statutory restrictions on the terms of the lease or statutory protections for the parties (see further 5.3). The parties to commercial leases are free to negotiate rent, whereas parties to residential and agricultural leases are subject to regulation (see 5.3.1). A Scottish lease will be construed strictly according to its terms. If a Scottish lease states that landlord's consent is discretionary, there is no implied obligation on the landlord to act reasonably in withholding consent. One feature applicable to nearly all leases regardless of the express terms of the lease is 'tacit relocation' whereby if no written notice of termination is given either to or by the tenant within a reasonable time before expiry of the lease, the lease will continue for either the length of the previous contractual period or a year (whichever is the shorter). If at the end of this further year there is no notice of termination from either party (usually 40 days), the lease will be continued for a further year and so on until validly terminated.

5.1.2 For urban unfurnished premises there is a presumption in favour of assignation and subletting without landlord's consent (although this is usually contracted out of). There is no such implied right to assign or sublet in the case of furnished lets and agricultural leases and there are statutory restrictions on assignation and subletting in the case of secure tenancies and assured tenancies of dwelling houses. Where there is no implied or express power to assign and sublet, there can be no alienation without consent. Subleases are not protected so that if a head lease terminates for any reason any sublease granted by the tenant will also usually fall with immediate effect. Unless contracted out of, there is an implied warranty by the landlord that the property is reasonably fit for the purposes for which it is let. There is also an implied obligation on the landlord to keep the property in tenantable repair and wind and watertight condition. It is usual for the landlord to contract out of these provisions and to pass the liability for repairs fully onto the tenant. In the case of a multiple occupancy building, the landlord normally retains liability and control and recovers costs through service charge arrangements. At common law there will be a rent abatement in the event of damage or destruction by an act of God (which will include most of the insured risks) until the property has again been rendered fit for occupation and use: again this is usually contracted out of. There is also a common law presumption that the lease will terminate in the event of total destruction of the leased property as a result of an inevitable accident (eg act of God). This presumption will normally be displaced by contract and the lease will continue notwithstanding damage to or destruction of the property whether by any insured risk or otherwise.

5.1.3 The irritancy (forfeiture) clause in a lease is subject to overriding statutory provisions which provide that, in the case of monetary breaches, a prescribed form of notice must be served on the tenant, giving it 14 days (or any greater period specified in the lease) within which to rectify the breach. Irritancy may be invoked only if payment is not then made. In the case of non-monetary breaches or changes in the status of the tenant (eg liquidation) the landlord will be entitled to irritate the lease only if a fair and reasonable landlord would do so. These provisions cannot be contracted out of. In addition to the normal common law remedies, a landlord has the benefit of the landlord's hypothec under which the landlord can attach moveable items brought onto the leased premises by the tenant (including hired goods) in security of one year's rent.

5.2 No privity of contract

In Scottish leases, there is no privity of contract. After assignation, the assigning tenant normally has no ongoing liability and the ongoing relationship is between the landlord and the new tenant. It is quite normal and institutionally acceptable in Scottish leases for there to be no attempt to impose privity of contract. As a result it is probably easier in Scotland than in England for a landlord to establish that he is acting 'reasonably' in withholding consent to an assignation where this is necessary.

5.3 Rent control and security of tenure

5.3.1 As already mentioned there is very little statutory regulation of commercial leases and the parties are largely free to agree their own terms. There are, however, restrictions on the frequency of rent reviews in agricultural holdings and rent increases may be referred to arbitration. Similar to agricultural holdings are small agricultural holdings under the Small Landowners (Scotland) Acts and crofts regulated by the Crofts (Holdings) (Scotland) Acts both of which give tenants safeguards against rent increases and removal. In the case of residential property, the Rent Acts from the 1970s gave considerable protection to tenants of 'regulated' or 'protected' tenancies such that by the mid 1980s the number of private sector residential properties available for rent had declined substantially. This led to the Housing (Scotland) Act 1988 which introduced a short, assured tenancy similar to that in England. This must be for a term of between six months and five years and, while it gives the tenant limited protection against rent increases, does guarantee recovery of possession by the landlord at the expiry of the term. Many premises, however, remain subject to the old restrictions and may continue to do so until the present occupants, and possibly their immediate families, die.

5.3.2 Tenants of commercial premises have no rights of renewal at the end of the lease except a very limited right to renew for retail tenants contained in the Tenancy of Shops Act 1949 which allows a tenant to make an application to the Sheriff Court for continued occupation for one year which may be granted at the discretion of the sheriff. Unlike in England, in the absence of default or agreement the landlord has no right to recover business premises before the end of the lease on paying compensation to the tenant. Agricultural tenants, however, still enjoy security of tenure and there are currently no proposals for the introduction of Scottish legislation mirroring the English Agricultural Tenancies Act 1995 (which permits fixed-term leases with no rights of succession). The principal statute of relevance is the Agricultural Holdings (Scotland) Act 1991. While it is not possible to contract out of the security of tenure provisions, there are alternatives which do not attract protection, such as a grazing lease for less than one year or a lease (again for less than one year) granted with the prior consent of the Secretary of State.

5.4 Other legislative restrictions

Other than the statutory restrictions on the exercise by a landlord of rights under irritancy (or forfeiture) clauses (see 5.1.3) there are very few regulations affecting lettings.

5.5 Method of measurement

The code of measuring practice referred to in section 5.5 of the English chapter is also used in Scotland.

6 FINANCE AND INVESTMENT SOURCES

The UK property market has access to a variety of financing and investment techniques and these are outlined in section 6 of the English law chapter. It only remains to add that Scotland (principally Glasgow and Edinburgh) now ranks as the third largest finance centre in the European Union (after London and Frankfurt) with upwards of £250 billion of funds under management. With four Scottish-based clearing banks and many Scottish life offices, independent fund managers and investment trusts there are a wide range of funding sources available in Scotland many of which play a significant role elsewhere in the UK.

7 FORMS OF SECURITY

Banking practice tends to be influenced by the state of the UK economy as a whole and the current attitude towards secured lending and relationship banking is briefly detailed in the introduction to section 7 of the English chapter. While in recent years the Scottish clearing banks have taken active steps to encourage relationship banking, there is still an expectation that loans will be secured.

7.1 Mortgages

7.1.1 Since 1970, the only permissible way of creating a fixed security or mortgage over an interest in land is by way of a statutory form of mortgage known as a standard security. The personal debt obligation of the mortgagor may be contained either in the standard security or in a separate document. The right of the creditor is made real by recording of the standard security in the Register of Sasines or registration of the creditor's interest in the Land Register. If granted by a Scottish company or one having a place of business in Scotland but incorporated outside Great Britain, the standard security must also be registered at Companies House within 21 days. Standard conditions, which impose obligations on the mortgagor (eg relating to maintenance and insurance of the property) and which set out the powers and remedies of the mortgagee, are included in the standard security by statute. With the exception of the conditions relating to powers of sale, redemption and foreclosure, the standard conditions may be (and usually are) varied by the parties.

7.1.2 Where a creditor intends to require repayment of the debt secured by a standard security, and failing such repayment, to exercise any of its powers under the standard security, it may serve a calling-up notice in the form prescribed by statute. The period of a calling-up notice is two months, unless shortened by agreement. If the debtor fails to comply with the calling-up notice, the creditor may exercise its rights under the standard security. Those rights include the right to enter into possession and the right to sell the land. A calling-up notice must also be served on all co-obligants or guarantors of the debt secured by the standard security. If a debtor has failed to comply with any of its obligations under a standard security and the default is remediable, a creditor may serve a notice of default. The period of a notice of default is one month. The debtor may, however, remedy the default or object to the notice; or a creditor may, if the debtor is in default under the standard security or has become insolvent, make a direct application to court for a warrant to exercise any of the default remedies he is entitled to. This may be useful where action needs to be taken quickly. Once a creditor is entitled to exercise his power of sale under a standard security, the procedure is quite straightforward. The creditor must simply advertise the sale and take all reasonable steps to ensure that the price is the best which can be reasonably obtained. The sale may be made either by private contract or public auction. A creditor who fails to find a buyer may by application to court foreclose and take title to the secured subjects. There is no ability for a mortgagee to appoint a receiver under a standard security. The statute governing the creation, form and enforcement of standard securities is the Conveyancing and Feudal Reform (Scotland) Act 1970.

7.2 Floating and other charges

An incorporated company (but no one else) can create a floating charge over the whole or any part of its assets or undertaking. The floating charge is a creature of statute and is not immediately effective or enforceable. Rather, it 'floats' over a company's assets entitling the company to deal with the property in the ordinary course of business (but subject to contractual restrictions in the charge document). When the floating charge becomes effective it is said to 'crystallise'. Crystallisation occurs only on the winding up of the company or on the appointment of a receiver. It does not crystallise on the notice of the creditor. The floating charge usually provides that the chargee is entitled to appoint a receiver on a demand being made for payment of sums due or on specified events of default. On crystallisation, a floating charge attaches to the assets of the company covered by the floating charge as if it were a fixed security at the time the charge crystallises, and any such assets re-acquired or coming into the company's hands after crystallisation. The holder of a fixed charge has first call on the proceeds of sale of any assets secured by a fixed charge held by him. By contrast, on the winding up of a company or on the appointment of a receiver, certain debts are preferred to the claims of a floating charge holder. These include money owed to the Inland Revenue for income tax, social security payments and pension scheme contributions, value added tax and remuneration due to employees. Under statute, the holder of a floating charge over 'the whole or substantially the whole' of the property of a company may block the appointment of an administrator (a court-appointed insolvency officer) in respect of that company. As the enforcement of security and loans is suspended on the appointment of an administrator, it has become common for lenders to require borrowers to grant a floating charge over all the assets of the borrower in addition to any standard security which forms the main part of the security cover. If granted by a Scottish company or one having a place of business in Scotland but incorporated outside Great Britain, a floating charge must be registered in the register of charges within 21 days of creation. Failure to register results in the charge being void against any liquidator, receiver or third party creditor of the chargee. A floating change is 'created' on the date of execution of the charging document. Unlike in England, ranking agreements also need to be registered within 21 days of creation.

7.3 Performance bonds and guarantees

The law and practice relating to guarantees are similar in Scotland and England, and section 7.3 of the English chapter is referred to.

7.4 Credit risk insurance

Whilst sometimes available, credit risk insurance can be difficult to obtain.

8 PLANNING AND BUILDING REGULATION

The development and use of land and buildings are subject to control comprised principally within the Town and Country Planning (Scotland) Act 1997.

8.1 Planning authorities

Ultimate control of all matters relating to town and country planning rests with the Secretary of State for Scotland. On a local level, decisions are taken by the local planning authority with ultimate decisions being taken by elected representatives. As a result, planning control can be influenced by political considerations.

8.2 Zoning and development plans

Each local planning authority is required to prepare a structure plan for its area setting out general strategies and policies for the development and use of land. The structure plan is the top tier of the development plan for an area. The second tier is the local plan. Again, each local planning authority must prepare a local plan or plans covering all parts of its area and providing more detailed policies and proposals for the development and use of land in the local area. Statute has introduced greater emphasis on the development plan, similar to that under s 54A of the English Town and Country Planning Act 1990, such that a planning application will be determined in accordance with the development plan unless material considerations indicate otherwise. Therefore, as in England, there is considerable public discussion of the development plan before it is finally adopted.

8.3 Planning control and procedures

The definition of 'development' and the provisions about what does and does not constitute development are similar to those in England although the applicable Use Classes Order is the Town and Country Planning (Use Classes) (Scotland) Order 1989. The provisions detailed in sections 8.3.1, 8.3.2 and 8.3.3 of the English chapter also apply, although the eight-week period within which a local planning authority can make a decision on the planning application can be extended by agreement with the applicant and any appeal against refusal will be made to the Secretary of State for Scotland. Any challenge to the Secretary of State for Scotland's decision is made in the Court of Session. Most appeals are conducted by a reporter from the Scottish Office enquiry reporters' unit. In relation to enforcement (see section 8.3.4 of the English chapter) the time limit of four years where breach consists of building or other alterations or change to use as a single dwelling house is the same in Scotland as in England but the commencement date for the 10-year time limit in the case of any other breach is 25 September 1992. The same types of enforcement action are available to local planning authorities as in England.

8.4 Building standards, control and supervision

Building regulations procedure is similar to that applicable in England although the procedure is governed by the Building (Scotland) Act 1959 as amended.

8.5 Protection of buildings of special interest

The position is similar to England in relation to the listing of buildings and the requirement for listed building consent for alterations and demolition as well as the designation of areas as conservation areas. The listing authority is the Secretary of State for Scotland and administration is in the hands of Historic Scotland.

8.6 Expropriation or compulsory purchase and compensation

The position is similar to England. A public utility or government body can acquire land or an interest in land for a range of public purposes, eg roads or town centre shopping schemes. Subject if appropriate to public enquiry a compulsory purchase order initiated by the purchasing body will be confirmed by central government and the land will be acquired at the market value at the time possession is taken. Private developers may not initiate the process but public bodies sometimes agree to be responsible for the obtaining of the necessary orders as part of projects undertaken with the private sector. Because of the tradition in the UK for private rights to be respected and for full public consultation, it can take a long time for major projects to come to fruition.

9 ENVIRONMENTAL MATTERS

In common with most other European countries there has been an increased awareness of environmental issues and as in England, liabilities for pollution are governed by both statute and common law. As regards common law, liability may arise under the law of delict (the Scottish equivalent of the English tort) where a party is able to demonstrate that a duty of care exists and has been breached, resulting in reasonably foreseeable harm. Liability may also arise in nuisance. The doctrine of *Rylands v Fletcher* (until recently creating possible strict liability for escape of a dangerous thing in England) does not apply. Some degree of fault has always been necessary to succeed in an action for nuisance. In practice, it may be possible to infer fault from the mere happening of an incident and the onus will rest with a defender to show that the nuisance was not his fault. As regards statutory control, most of the statutory provisions referred to in section 9 of the English chapter also extend to, and are in force in, Scotland and subject to certain qualifications set out below, the comments contained in that section are of equal relevance in Scotland. The Scottish Environment Protection Agency (SEPA) rather than the Environment Agency (EA) is the integrated enforcement agency with responsibility for control of water pollution, waste regulation and integrated pollution control, including control of emissions to the atmosphere. Owing to the fact that the National Rivers Authority had historically wider functions than the various Scottish River Purification Authorities, SEPA's mandate is narrower than that of the EA in certain respects. Unlike the EA, SEPA does not have powers in relation to fisheries, navigation and flood defence (although SEPA will be involved in giving flood warnings to local authorities). In other limited respects, SEPA's functions are wider than the EA's. SEPA has acquired the functions of local authorities as enforcing authority in relation to release of substances into the air by virtue of Part I of the Environmental Protection Act 1990. In addition, SEPA will be responsible for drafting a National Waste Strategy. In England and Wales responsibility for the drafting of a National Waste Strategy rests with the Secretary of State. SEPA has the added responsibility for creating smoke control areas and air quality management areas.

9.1 Protection against atmospheric and noise pollution

SEPA now has sole responsibility for policing atmospheric emissions while in England the responsibility is shared between the EA and relevant local authorities.

9.2 Water pollution

The English Water Resources Act 1991 does not apply in Scotland, where the principal statute governing water pollution is still the Control of Pollution Act 1974 as amended. The provisions in Part II of the Control of Pollution Act 1974 prohibiting entry of pollutants into controlled waters (which include coastal, territorial, inland and ground waters) are very similar to the provisions of the Water Resources Act 1991 and section 9.2 of the English chapter can be read as being equally applicable in Scotland subject to substitution of the appropriate statutory references. In addition, the Sewerage (Scotland) Act 1968 regulates intake or discharges into sewerage systems. The regime established by this Act is policed by three recently created water authorities, which are the North, East and West of Scotland Water Authorities.

9.3 Waste storage and disposal

The position set out in sections 9.3 to 9.5 of the English chapter reflects the position in Scotland, save that references to the EA should of course be taken as references to SEPA.

9.4 Contaminated land

See 9.3.

9.5 Environmental impact assessments

As noted in 4.1.3, it is not uncommon in commercial transactions for a buyer to make the receipt of a satisfactory environmental survey by the buyer a suspensive condition of missives for the sale and purchase of land.

10 DEVELOPMENT

The position in Scotland accords substantially with section 10 of the English chapter. The following general observations are made.

10.1 Procurement methods

A common feature of recent fast-track procurement methods is to get the contractor on board at an earlier stage than in a conventional procurement where the works are substantially designed before contract. Design and build over the last decade has been the fastest growth procurement method in Scotland as well as elsewhere in the UK. It now accounts for in excess of one-quarter of all building work carried out. Over the last few years a variant – novated design and build – has emerged as the most significant trend in procurement. In novated design and build the client appoints a design team who work up the design to whatever is considered to be the appropriate level before being novated to the design and build contractor.

10.2 Standard forms

The Scottish Building Contracts Committee (SBCC) publishes a suite of standard form contracts which correspond with those published in England by the Joint Contracts Tribunal (JCT). The SBCC forms incorporate the various JCT Conditions of Contract with appropriate amendments to make the substance and nomenclature of the English conditions conform with the law of Scotland. For example, the appropriate SBCC form for design and build is the Scottish Building Contract with Contractor's Design which incorporates the JCT 1981 Conditions. Some provisions such as those dealing with arbitration are replaced in their entirety, because, unlike England, the law of arbitration in Scotland is based almost entirely on the common law with some statutory intervention.

10.2.1 Prescription and limitation

The English limitation periods have no application in Scotland where prescription operates through passage of time to extinguish legal obligations.

The Prescription and Limitation (Scotland) Acts of 1973 and 1984 stipulate those obligations which are governed by a five-year prescriptive period, those which are governed by a 20-year prescriptive period and those which are imprescriptible. With regard to breach of contractual obligations contained within building contracts the five-year prescriptive period would normally apply. Section 11(3) is of particular importance with regard to latent defect claims. It provides that reparation becomes enforceable from the date when the creditor first became, or could with reasonable diligence have become aware of the loss, injury or damage. Accordingly, in Scotland the prescriptive period is open ended subject to the 20-year (long stop) prescriptive period.

10.2.2 Retention

Most standard forms provide a mechanism where a retention is deducted by the employer to be released upon satisfactory completion of the works. Commonly the retention is stated to be held on a fiduciary basis as trustee for the contractor though stricter requirements exist for the constitution of a trust than in England.

10.3 Recent legislation

Part II of the Housing Grants, Construction and Regeneration Act 1996 introduces a number of the recommendations made by Sir Michael Latham in 1994. Part II is expected to be brought into force in 1998 and the Act will have a significant impact on construction and development throughout the UK.

11 TAXES

Taxation statutes in the UK apply to both England and Scotland. The taxation regime, insofar as it affects property and property owners, is set out in section 11 of the English chapter.

12 GRANTS AND INCENTIVES

There are a number of government and EU funded grants and incentives available in the UK which are aimed at stimulating industrial development to create employment and regenerate those areas where traditional industries have closed down. Overseas investors are treated in the same way as UK-owned firms and there is no discrimination in eligibility. An outline of the grants and incentives available is contained in section 12 of the English chapter. Expert advice and information about grants and financial assistance is available from the Scottish Office Education and Industry Department and Scottish Enterprise (Locate in Scotland) both in Glasgow.

13 COMPANIES AND BUSINESS ENTITIES

Section 13 of the English chapter accurately reflects the position in Scotland. The reader should be aware, however, that there are significant differences between Scots and English law as regards the insolvency, liquidation and receivership of companies, the constitution and management of trusts, and in respect of partnership law.

13.1 Partnerships

While partnerships have a separate legal personality under Scots law it is generally accepted that they cannot hold property in the name of the partnership. Accordingly, partnership property is held in the name of some or all of the partners as trustees on behalf of the partnership.

14 INTERNATIONAL

The position is as set out in section 14 of the English law chapter.

CHAPTER 17

Spain

Victoria Llavero

Gomez Acebo & Pombo

CONTENTS

1 OWNERSHIP OF LAND 561
2 OTHER INTERESTS IN LAND 564
3 TITLE TO LAND 568
4 TRANSACTIONS IN LAND 569
5 LEASES AND OTHER RIGHTS OF OCCUPATION 571
6 FINANCE AND INVESTMENT SOURCES 574
7 FORMS OF SECURITY 576
8 PLANNING AND BUILDING REGULATION 577
9 ENVIRONMENTAL MATTERS 580
10 DEVELOPMENT 582
11 TAXES 586
12 GRANTS AND INCENTIVES 589
13 COMPANIES AND BUSINESS ENTITIES 590
14 INTERNATIONAL 593

CHAPTER 17
Spain

1 OWNERSHIP OF LAND

Under Spanish civil law, there are two distinct legal systems: national law (*derecho estatal*), and local law (*derecho foral*). Since the local law applies only in specific circumstances in autonomous regions of Spain, this chapter covers only the national law. National law is based on a hierarchy of sources of law; the laws, customs, and general principles of law. The most important of these is the law, found principally in the Civil Code. Court decisions are not legal precedent as in common law jurisdictions, but are instead considered persuasive authority. All provisions of the Spanish legal code must respect the essential principles of the 1978 Constitution that property must be regulated by Act of Parliament and comply with its social function. These legal sources establish the different existing types of land ownership and tenancies.

1.1 Types of tenure

1.1.1 Freehold or absolute ownership

Absolute ownership (*propiedad plena*) is the most complete legal right a person may have over land and includes the right of exclusive possession and free disposal, the right to encumber the property by transferring some lesser right to third parties, the right to alter the use of the land and the right to renounce rights over the land, provided it does not prejudice third parties. Absolute ownership gives the owner the right to freely exploit the land, its profits and fruits for his own benefit and the right to everything above and below the land, including any buildings, structures, or anything which is fixed or annexed to the land, subject to the national law. As a general principle, ownership of the land automatically carries with it the ownership of the buildings constructed over it. However, this is subject to any third-party rights which have been granted over the land and any buildings over it may be separately owned where the buildings are constructed and owned by third parties under a surface right (see 2.1.3). A third party may also be granted the right to freely exploit the land, its profits and fruits for his own benefit by the owner.

1.1.2 Leasehold

The notion of leasehold does not exist under Spanish law. Nevertheless, specific legal models of ownership exist and perform a similar function to leasehold (see 2.1.3). Tenancies are mere contractual rights granting no interest in the land. They will be either urban or rural (see section 5). A tenancy is fully transferable, provided this has not been expressly prohibited under the agreement, and can be transferred in whole or in part.

1.1.3 Joint ownership

1.1.3.1 Under the various types of joint ownership (*comunidad de bienes*), two or more individuals or corporations can own land concurrently. Roman joint ownership (*comunidad romana*) exists when two or more joint owners hold property. Their shares may be determined by agreement or through a legal fiction established under the Civil Code. This legal fiction establishes a quota system which fixes the joint owners' respective percentage participation of rights, and their various obligations and duties. In the absence of evidence to the contrary, the quotas are presumed to be equal. A joint owner may enjoy, dispose of and/or relinquish his quota without dividing the land. However, the joint owners have certain pre-emption rights and have the option to buy (*tanteo*) the land for the set price. If the owner does not inform the others about the sale of his interest, the joint owners will then have the legal right to repurchase (*retracto legal*) the property from the third party. The buyer must then be compensated by the joint owner who exercises his right to repurchase, and will receive the sale price and all the costs derived from the purchase agreement. The joint owners have to act unanimously to dispose of or modify the land in any way, but can decide matters of simple administration by a majority. Joint ownership is a voluntary arrangement and can be ended voluntarily. Should one or more of the joint owners decide to terminate the joint ownership they may exercise an *actio comuni dividundo* by which the property is sold and the proceeds distributed among the joint owners.

1.1.3.2 Time-sharing is joint ownership (*multipropiedad*), which exists when various owners have the right to use the property for a given period of time. It is a recent phenomenon, not yet sufficiently developed, and there is no unanimous agreement concerning the legal nature of time-sharing, despite numerous legislative proposals. It is sometimes considered to be a right in rem and at other times a personal obligation. Nevertheless, time-sharing is increasingly being promoted as a tourist commodity and as a special form of joint ownership.

1.1.4 Condominia

Condominium or horizontal property (*propiedad horizontal*) exists where there is a community of proprietors, who exclusively own individual units of a building (such as a flat or office) and who are also joint owners of the building's common areas (such as, eg the stairs, courtyards, garages, corridors, elevators or porter's lodge). In a residential block, for example, the private elements are those apartments with an exit to a common area, which will be owned separately, with all the rights that result from a freehold ownership. The shared ownership over the common areas is governed by the bye-laws of the community of owners and these determine the extent of the communal rights, duties and obligations. There are certain basic norms concerning such rights, duties and obligations laid down in the Civil Code, the Horizontal Property Law, and the community's bye-laws.

1.1.5 Lesser rights

Various rights exist which give a limited right over somebody else's land (*iura in re aliena*). These include servitudes, usufruct and mortgages, which are limited rights in rem. Further comment is made on the former at 2.1.

1.2 Legal and beneficial ownership

Legal and beneficial ownership, as found in trusts of land in common law jurisdictions, does not exist.

1.3 Restrictions on ownership and dealings

1.3.1 Certain individuals cannot acquire assets on their own (such as minors or the incapacitated); for land held on their behalf see 2.8. There are very few restrictions on ownership of land by foreign persons and entities but there are regulations concerning foreign investment into Spain and these are dealt with in more detail in section 14. There are various restrictions on the rights of a landowner, eg those aiming to protect the public interest such as planning regulations or rights of compulsory purchase. There are also some private law restrictions on land ownership which aim to protect private interests such as the laws regulating relations between adjoining landowners.

1.3.2 Every person with full capacity to contract may transfer his rights over property. The law provides that neither minors nor those incapacitated by a judicial court may consent to the terms of a contract. In these cases, the consent of the representative of the child or of the incapacitated person is necessary for the transfer of the land. Also, in special cases such as bankruptcy, the bankrupt is deprived of the management and disposal of his goods and cannot sell the land without judicial intervention. For those with full capacity disposal of the land can be forbidden or made subject to conditions in the public interest by law, by judicial or administrative authority, or by contract, but only temporarily, in order to ensure that land stays in circulation.

1.3.3 Options, private rights of pre-emption and rights of redemption may attach to the land and these are dealt with in more detail in 2.4. Rights of pre-emption generally serve private interests, although there are pre-emption rights in favour of public authorities over protected nature or sports facilities or areas designated for planning purposes.

1.4 Adverse possession or acquisitive prescription

It is possible to acquire ownership of land or other limited rights by acquisitive prescription (*usucapión*) by public, peaceful and uninterrupted possession for 30 years, or 10 to 20 years where the possessor has always acted in good faith, and holds a true and valid title for transfer of the property, but did not actually acquire the ownership (eg, if the person who sold the estate was not its true owner). The possessor must intend to become the owner of the assets, eg the payment of taxes on the land is deemed to be proof of such intent (or animus domini). The possession is interrupted either when the possessor ceases to occupy for more than one year, or by means of a judicial notice given to the possessor. The law provides a summary or judicial proceeding called *interdicto posesorio*, which gives the legitimate possessor a mechanism to defend his possession against disturbances caused by third parties.

2 OTHER INTERESTS IN LAND

This section deals with interests which do not bestow ownership, but merely a limited right over somebody else's land. The most common of these are servitudes, usufruct, options and mortgages.

2.1 Servitudes or easements, usufruct, building and dwelling rights

2.1.1 Servitudes

A servitude (*servidumbres*) is a right over somebody else's land. A servitude will be either predial or personal. A predial servitude is a right in favour of one piece of land (the dominant estate) over another (the servient estate). The right attaches to the dominant tenement and may be enjoyed by anyone occupying the dominant tenement, such as a right of way. It may be enforced against subsequent owners of the servient tenement, provided it has been registered in the property registry (see section 3). An unregistered servitude will only be valid between the contracting parties unless it is apparent. A personal servitude gives a personal right or benefit in favour of an individual, individuals or a community over another´s land. It is enforceable against any subsequent owners of the servient land, subject to registration. Servitudes are also categorised as either voluntary, ie created expressly by act of the parties, or legal. Legal servitudes in turn may be classified as those created by implication of law (civil servitudes), eg where land has no access to a public road and a right of exit is implied in its favour, or those required by reason of public need (administrative servitudes), eg the right to run electricity or telephone cables.

2.1.2 Usufruct

A usufruct is the right of a person (the usufructuary) to use and enjoy the land or other asset in which he has no property title, for a period of time, eg the life of the usufructuary or for a fixed period determined between the parties. In general, the usufructuary may draw a profit or any other benefit from the land and have full use and enjoyment of it, but may not change its substance. This is called a 'proper usufruct'. However, in particular cases, it is also possible to change the usufruct's substance, ie by agreement between the parties or by legal provision, for example the law states that in case of partial loss of the substance of the usufruct, the right of usufruct is reduced to cover the altered object. The Civil Code provides that usufruct may be voluntary or legal. Currently, the only legal usufruct laid down in the Civil Code is the 'surviving spouse usufruct'. Voluntary usufruct may be created by a property owner in favour of another or of himself. In the latter situation, the property owner transfers the land, but retains a usufruct for his own benefit. A usufruct is a right *in re aliena* enforceable against successive owners during the term for which the usufruct is granted, provided it has been registered. An unregistered right of usufruct will only be enforceable between the contracting parties. A usufruct may be transferred and the right will terminate upon expiry of the term for which it was granted.

2.1.3 Building and dwelling rights

2.1.3.1 The surface right (*derecho de superficie*) is an interest in land granted by a property owner to another to cultivate or build on the land. It is a right in rem created by public deed. Where the surface right is created in an urban area, and is granted by the state or a public entity, it may be granted for a maximum term of 75 years; where the same right is granted by a private individual or entity, it may be granted for a maximum of 99 years. Urban surface rights will have to be registered to be valid and binding upon third parties. However in rural areas, surface rights may be granted in perpetuity and the right need not be registered to be valid but will need to be registered to bind third parties. The parties may choose for it to be granted for consideration, in which case the sum must be stated in the registration. Title to land will remain with the property owner but any structure, building or crops on the surface of the land will be owned by the holder of the surface right for the duration of the surface right. At the end of the term, the structure or building on the land will revert to the owner of the land without compensation. However, the holder of the right is entitled to alter or demolish the building. The surface right is transferable and may itself be mortgaged.

2.1.3.2 The dwelling right (*derecho de habitacion*) grants the holder of the right and his family the privilege of occupying the dwelling belonging to a third party. It is created by agreement between the parties and will be regulated by the contractual dispositions set out by them or, by default, under the Civil Code. The dwelling right is temporal and cannot be granted in perpetuity, but only for a fixed period of time, or for the holder's lifetime. The right is not transferable but as it is a right *in re aliena*, it may bind successors in title.

2.2 Restrictions on use and other restrictions

It is possible for absolute owners to enter into restrictions on the use of one piece of land to protect the amenities and value of another piece of land where the parties agree to them. These rights will be enforceable by and between successive owners of the land affected depending on the terms of the agreement entered into. These restrictions will be enforceable between the parties to the agreement, and upon third parties where this is provided for in the agreement itself and the agreement is registered. The validity of the agreement between the parties does not depend on registration.

2.3 Private mortgages, charges and privileges

Monetary liabilities can be secured on land in a number of ways. A mortgage (*hipoteca inmobiliaria*) may be held by a credit institution or private mortgagee in order to secure the performance of a duty (see section 7). The census, which is rarely used, is dealt with in 2.6. It gives certain rights of security. The courts can create a charge over the land to secure judgment debts, such as an attachment. There are also other private rights of security such as the *antichresis* which is an interest in land (rarely used in practice) which grants the creditor the right to obtain the fruits from land owned by the debtor and unlike the mortgage gives the holder of the interest the occupation of the land. Certain debts take the form of privileges, attracting preferred status, eg salaries, insurance premiums and taxes. Their priority, and whether they need to be registered and can take preference over mortgages, depends on each type and on whether they are qualified, special or general privileges.

2.4 Contracts and options

Contracts are dealt with in section 4. An option is an interest over land, granted for a specific period of time, which allows the grantee to purchase the land. The option is irrevocable, may not be altered and the grantor must sell the property on the agreed terms, if the grantee exercises his right of purchase within the contract time stipulated. The option lapses if it is not exercised. The right of pre-emption, which can be granted by contract or law, confers the right to purchase on a third party. The right of redemption allows the acquisition of the property where the pre-emption right has not been honoured.

2.5 Public or municipal charges

Planning restrictions, consents, compulsory purchase orders and public financial charges may be imposed to recover repayment of government grants or to secure tax liabilities. These are controlled by regulations which establish the conditions which must be met and the authorisations which must be obtained by the titleholders. These authorisations must be presented to the property registry when the titleholder applies for the registration of a property, or the registry will deny the registration. There are no special local registers detailing these issues.

2.6 Other interests

Census (*censo*) is an interest which runs with the land and gives the interest holder a right to receive an annual rent. There are three types of census: *census enfitentico, census consignativo* and *census reservativo*. The census is seldom used today and has been replaced by the mortgage or life annuity.

2.7 Liabilities attaching to land

Various duties are provided by law in order to protect public and private interests. The most notable of these is the general duty not to exceed the specific rights granted arising from one's interest in land. For example, the usufructuary cannot sell the full property subject to the usufruct because he is not the owner. Another set of duties exist for occupiers of land to respect a neighbour's right to use and enjoy his own property, including the duty not to create any nuisance which may affect adjoining land. In addition, there are other statutory duties provided by law to protect different administrative interests such as taxes and city planning. Moreover, the Civil Code states that if a building, wall, or any other structure is about to collapse, the owner is obliged to demolish it or to execute the necessary works in order to prevent such collapse. If the owner does not fulfil this obligation, he will be liable for all damage which may be caused by the collapse of all or part of the structure, and the authorities may also demolish the construction at the owner's cost.

2.8 Legal and equitable interests

While the distinction between legal and equitable interests recognised in common law countries does not exist, it is possible to hold land on behalf of another by agreement, and in certain cases by implication of law. With regard to the latter, legal representatives, agents and other third parties may hold land on behalf of another. In addition to this, minors or the mentally incapacitated must have land held on their behalf by their parents, tutors or guardians.

2.9 Protection of rights and interests

Under the civil law, there are two different legal schemes which may be used concurrently or separately to protect any property interest. On the one hand, any possessor of land has the right, depending on the type of interest, to defend himself, through specific legal actions, against claims by another. On the other hand, greater protection may be obtained by an interest holder if his interest is properly registered in the property registry (see section 3) and any rights which are registrable under the Property Registration and Mortgage Act, which include usufruct, servitudes, mortgage and in general all rights over land, are not detrimental to third parties unless registered. Finally, any administrative interest attached to land is protected by law and will be expressly regulated by corresponding administrative regulation providing the system of enforcement.

2.10 Priority of interests

Entry in the property registry will be decisive in determining which interest prevails. Where there is more than one interest in favour of two or more parties, priority depends on date of entry in the registry not creation.

3 TITLE TO LAND

3.1 Proof of title

Title to land can be established by any means admitted by law, principally by production of a public deed granted before a notary public, by writ of execution, and by authentic document of the administration. Property clearly registered in the property registry is protected by the courts on the terms of the law. Title to land that is subject to registration and has not been registered does not confer protection vis à vis third parties. The registry makes registered rights public in order to provide security for the interest holder and prospective interest holders.

3.2 Land registers

The main function of the property registry is to keep a record of the acts, and contracts relating to ownership and other interests in land. It is a registry of titles and to all legal effect it is presumed that all rights in rem registered do exist and belong to their holder as determined by its entries.

3.2.1 Plans

Plans are not registered. The plot in question is identified through a description in the public deed.

3.2.2 Content

Public notification of existing rights is effected by entries made in several official books. The various books reflect what and how real rights affecting property are created, amended, transferred or terminated. All registrations identify the property and persons involved, the nature, scope and value of the right and any conditions attached. Essentially there are two kinds of books: the 'book of registrations' which contains final entries concerning all the rights and interests registrable (ie mortgages, embargoes, usufruct and servitudes), including the description of the property and the owner and owners of the different rights to be registered; and the 'journal book' which contains those rights and interests which the registries have been applied to for registration and which are pending examination by the registrar for final registration.

3.2.3 Errors

Public deeds are studied and reviewed by the property registry clerks before they are finally registered. However, if a mistake is later discovered in any of the registered deeds, it may be corrected through special proceedings, and the court will determine which party must bear the cost of rectification. Where the registrar is responsible for the error, the rectification will be performed free of charge.

3.3 Passing of title

The transfer of an interest in land requires two separate legal acts performed together or almost simultaneously. The first is to enter into a deed which simply grants title in the land and the second is actual or implied delivery of the land. There are different types of implied deliveries and these include:

(a) symbolic delivery, where a particular object, such as a key, is given to the new owner (*traditio simbolica*);
(b) instrumental delivery which occurs automatically when there is execution of a public deed (*traditio suscriptio instrumentorum*);
(c) automatic delivery (*traditio brevi manu*) of the land where the new landowner is already in possession eg a tenant who has bought the land from the landlord and acquired full title; and
(d) *constitutum posesorium* delivery, where a property owner sells the land but reserves a possessory right, such as a usufruct – delivery takes place even though the previous owner remains in possession of the property.

The registration will be backdated to the date of application and will usually be carried out within 15 days.

4 TRANSACTIONS IN LAND

The most common transactions in land are the sale and purchase agreement, the grant of minor property interests and the creation of encumbrances such as mortgages.

4.1 Procedures

The normal steps for creating a sale and purchase agreement are:

(a) searching the property registry looking for any registered encumbrances on the land and establishing the property's planning use;
(b) conducting a survey;
(c) verifying the parties' solvency;
(d) negotiating the agreement and the necessary clauses to ensure performance, eg in cases of deferred payment, the seller may include an undertaking that he may retain a mortgage on the land or request a down payment or deposit (*arras*) to ensure payment of the purchase price;
(e) negotiating which party should pay the transaction costs; and
(f) formalising the sale and purchase agreement in a public deed which is the necessary instrument used to register interests in land at the property registry.

The parties become bound when both have given their consent and the buyer can bring an enforcement action against a party failing to fulfil his obligations. The investigation of environmental issues will usually take place when the parties negotiate the remainder of the clauses and conditions.

4.2 Contract terms

Sale and purchase contracts generally set out the price and terms of the property transfer or sale and the seller will undertake to deliver the property and the buyer to pay some form of consideration. The obligations of a seller and buyer are largely freely negotiable but the contract is limited by various duties and liabilities established by law. The seller must:

(a) maintain the property in good condition from the time the contract is executed until the time the land is delivered to the buyer;
(b) give title to the land and deliver vacant possession;
(c) if the contract is formalised in a public deed, pay the costs of the original deed (copies must be paid for by the buyer);
(d) pay the income of the property to the buyer from the date of the perfection of the contract which will take place with delivery of the property; and
(e) provide guarantees against eviction and latent defects (physical or legal).

After completion of the transaction, if latent defects exist, the buyer may choose to have the purchase price partially refunded or have the contract rescinded and the purchase price and any costs of executing the contract refunded. In addition, the buyer may obtain damages if the seller has deliberately failed to inform the buyer of the latent defects. The buyer must pay the purchase price at the time and in the place and form stipulated. In case of default, the seller may request a court to revoke the contract and award damages. Alternatively, the seller may withhold delivery of the property if payment has not been received. The buyer must also take possession of the property on the date that delivery by the seller should take place. If the buyer does not, the seller may deliver possession to a third-party custodian and free himself from any further responsibility. In addition, the buyer must pay for any necessary improvements to the property, from the time the contract is signed until delivery, and all relevant taxes and fees (see 4.4). The buyer will pay interest for the time between the date of delivery until payment of the purchase price either if agreed between the parties or if the property is income producing and the buyer does not pay the price when required.

4.3 Formalities

All contracts creating an interest in land must be in writing, contain all the material terms and conditions of the transaction and be signed by both parties to the contract or by their agents, who must have specific authorisation (or a power of attorney from the contracting parties). The contracting parties may either request the other to formalise or convert the contract into a public deed, or compel such change by court order. Interests in land are fully protected when all the formalities required for an effective transaction have been completed, and the owner may then defend his rights against any third parties. If the titleholder has not fulfilled all the requirements established by law and then registered his title he will not have protection against bona fide third parties that have registered their title.

4.4 Fees, costs and taxes

4.4.1 Unless otherwise agreed, the seller will pay the agent's commission, his lawyer's fees and most of the notary's fees, whilst the buyer will pay his lawyer's fees, the transfer tax and the property registry's fees. The agent's commission, payable on completion of the transaction, will vary according to market demand and ranges from three to five per cent on smaller transactions and from two to three percent on larger sales. The buyer may hire his own agent to find property or negotiate the purchase and will then pay commission.

4.4.2 Lawyer's fees are usually charged either according to a scale laid down by the local College of Lawyers which varies from one region to another, or on an hourly basis, whether or not the transaction is successful; they are sometimes based on a combination of value and time. When a contract is formalised into a public deed, it must be notarised and the notary will charge a fee payable by the seller. Notary's fees are on progressive scale: 15,000 pesetas for the first million pesetas; 4.5 pesetas per thousand for any amount between one and five million pesetas; and so on, so that eg a sale and purchase of a property at 100 million pesetas will have a notary's fee of 100,000 pesetas.

4.4.3 The rate of transfer tax is generally six per cent and there is generally no stamp duty where transfer tax is payable (see further 11.6).

4.4.4 Registration fees vary according to a progressive scale which depends on the value of the interest to be registered; 4,000 pesetas is charged on the first million pesetas; 1.75 pesetas per thousand on any amount between one and five million pesetas; and 1.25 pesetas per thousand on any amount between five and ten million pesetas.

4.4.5 The total transaction costs vary and will depend on the fees charged by lawyers, notaries and agents as well as taxes. By general standards in Europe they are fairly high but will be split between the parties.

4.4.6 The fees of notaries and lawyers and the commission of agents are subject to value added tax (VAT) and this will also be payable on certain types of transaction, eg on sales by business enterprises (see 11.8).

4.5 Professionals' roles

The parties will be assisted by their own lawyers when the complexity of the transaction makes it necessary. However, it is usual for straightforward transactions to be dealt with exclusively by estate agent and notary public.

5 LEASES AND OTHER RIGHTS OF OCCUPATION

A lease (*arrendamiento*) is a contractual and personal right granting no interest in the land itself. Leases can be either urban or rural and will be governed by their specific legislation and subsidiarily by the Civil Code. Urban leases include commercial, residential and leisure premises, with no maximum length imposed by law so the term will be established by the parties under the agreement. Normally leases do not have a minimum duration. Nevertheless the law allows the tenant in the case of rural and residential leases unilaterally to extend the term of the lease until it reaches a legal limit which in the case of urban leases is five years. The regulation of urban leases will generally depend on whether they were entered into prior to 1985, in which case they will be governed by the Urban Lease Law of 1964; between 1985 and 1994, in which case they will be governed by the so-called 'Boyer Decree'; or after 1994, in which case they will be governed by the Urban Lease Law of 1994. With each generation of lease, the law has introduced greater flexibility for the parties to agree the terms they wish. Public housing is generally regulated by special laws or the Urban Lease Law if no special law exists.

5.1 Rent and other terms

5.1.1 The present rules for urban leases emanate from the Urban Lease Law of 1994. Rental for urban leases is normally paid monthly, in monetary form. Leases entered into since 1994 allow rent to be freely negotiated and usually include a rent review clause (a stabilisation clause) incorporating a procedure for rental increase, whereby the landlord can re-evaluate the rent at any time specified in the lease (but never retrospectively). Rental increases will be linked to the cost of living index but open market reviews reflecting market forces are increasingly common with reference to the retail index or other external measures. However, during the first five years of a residential lease, rent can only be revised yearly in accordance with the cost of living index during the previous 12-month period. From the sixth year of the agreement the revision may follow the system established by the parties or, in the absence of express agreement, the cost of living index. The tenant of an urban residential lease may only sublet or assign the premises with the prior written consent of the landlord up to twice by way of substitution except in the case of members of his family who have been living with him. If the tenant of any commercial urban lease wishes to sublet or assign the premises, he may do so without the prior consent of the landlord, unless expressly prohibited in the lease agreement, provided the landlord is then notified within a month. Limited substitution as for residential leases will be allowed. A subtenant may not himself enter into a sublease under any circumstances. The landlord will retain responsibility for all repairs necessary in order to keep the building fit for the purpose for which it was let, although the tenant will be responsible for any negligent damage. The landlord is entitled to terminate under various circumstances, eg default, unauthorised assignment or change of use or where the tenant is in breach of any other obligation. Deposits equal to one month's rent are required in the case of residential tenancies; tenancies for other uses require a deposit amounting to two months' rent.

5.1.2 Rural leases are those for agricultural, livestock or forest use and extend to any dwellings on such land. Rent is freely negotiable between the parties, may be paid in cash or by way of improvements or repairs to the land and may be reviewed by the parties themselves, or through a court order requested by one of the parties. Rural rents may usually be reviewed after the end of the first year of the lease and will also be increased if the landlord improves the land making an increase in production possible. Alternatively, the rent will be reduced or cancelled if more than half the crop is lost, before being harvested, due to an uninsured risk (ie force majeure or an act of God). Rural leases may not be sublet, nor generally assigned, and any attempt to do so will be invalid although the tenant may pass on the agreement by way of substitution to a spouse or dependant if that person undertakes to perform the same agricultural activities. The landlord is obliged to carry out all repairs which are necessary to maintain the land and/or attached dwellings in conditions appropriate for their use. The landlord may terminate for a number of reasons including default, change of use, and termination of rural activities by the tenant.

5.2 Privity of contract and estate

No doctrine of privity exists.

5.3 Rent control and security of tenure

The Urban Lease Law 1964 allowed an automatic extension of all leases, at the sole discretion of the tenant, his heirs or assignees. The Boyer Decree, however, removed the compulsory nature of this provision and parties are now able to waive this extension, subject to the minimum duration rules which cannot be modified by the agreement of the parties. The landlord may always prevent an extension, even if authorised in the agreement, for a number of reasons which may include his retaining of the premises for his own or his family's use or to demolish the property to erect another on the site (in which case he must give the tenant one year's notice). Since the Boyer Decree, there has been no security of tenure at all, subject to the minimum duration rules, whereas before 1985, all tenants had security of tenure. Rural leases are now specifically regulated by the Law of Rural Leases 1980 and have a minimum duration of six years and the tenant may claim an extension at the end of the lease. The first extension may last for six years and every extension after that may last for three years up to a total of 15 years, after which the lease will automatically terminate.

5.4 Other legislative restrictions

Every lease includes certain mandatory implied legal duties, besides those duties that are freely negotiable between the parties. The tenant is thus obliged to pay rent; use the premises or the land for the purpose originally stated in the lease; keep the premises in good condition; and not conduct any activity on the land that would be illegal, dangerous, immoral, unsanitary or that would cause a nuisance. In return the landlord must respect the tenant's quiet enjoyment of the premises; complete essential repairs; extend the lease in specific circumstances; give rights of pre-emptive purchase to the tenant if he decides to sell; and allow a sublease or assignment in the circumstances described in 5.1.

5.5 Method of measurement

The method of floor measurement is by reference to gross internal floor area.

6 FINANCE AND INVESTMENT SOURCES

6.1 Loan finance

The principal sources of loan finance are the banks, of which there are three main types, all subject to the same regulations. The commercial banks may be industrial or non-industrial with the former specialising in medium and long-term financing and the promotion of new businesses, whilst the latter generally provide traditional banking services. The savings banks (*cajas de ahorros*) provide finance to the public and private sectors, whilst the credit union or credit cooperative (*cooperativas de credito*) is a form of mutual organisation which may now lend up to 15 per cent of total loans to outsiders. Loan finance can also be obtained from mortgage companies (*sociedades de credito hipotecario*), a relatively recent introduction to the financial sector, providing long-term credits for the purpose of house and building purchase. Banks will grant unsecured loans for a maximum amount of eight million pesetas and for a maximum term of five years; in all other cases, banks rely on the borrower's security. The duration of loans can be freely agreed by the parties, but the finance institutions usually limit their maximum duration to 20 or 25 years. Repayment is commonly in the form of fixed and equal instalments calculated as a mixture of interest and capital repayments, and rarely as a single repayment at the end of the term of the loan. Interest rates, which have ranged from 9 to 18 per cent over recent years, can be agreed by the parties, although fixed interest rates are rare, and they are normally floating rates at the MIBOR (Madrid Interbanking Offer Rate) or CECA rate (agreed between the savings banks). Finance institutions often require a guarantee for the repayment of the loan; these may be personal guarantees granted by third persons, or security granted over assets (mortgages or pledges).

6.2 Investment or equity finance

Funds can also be raised from shareholders, privately or through the stock market, through shares or bonds. The stock market is not usually used to raise funds for property except in the case of property investment companies (*inmobiliarias*) and real investment trusts (*instituciones de inversion inmobiliaria*). It is quite common to invest in single-asset property companies. Bonds are often subscribed for by investment banks and institutions such as the *Sociedades de Inversión Inmobiliaria* and *Fondos de Inversión Inmobiliaria* which are similar to mutual funds pooling funds to invest in certain categories of asset such as property and are subject to similar legislative control. There are special tax concessions for investment by these funds in property to be leased to the residential market.

6.3 Mezzanine or mixed funding

The Mortgage Market Act restricts banks, savings banks, mortgage banks, building societies and credit unions from lending more than 70 per cent of the value of the property, or 80 per cent if the loan is for residential property. If further finance is required this will be by way of personal loan attracting a higher rate of interest and not secured on the property. In some cases, this can be provided by the same institution. There is no regulation of the terms of further finance and these will depend upon negotiations between the parties. There are no other means of providing loan finance to cover the gap between equity and primary loans, ie mezzanine finance.

6.4 Sale and lease-back

The sale and lease-back of a property is often undertaken to raise funds and release capital. The business will sell the property to an investor for a capital sum and then lease it back to give the investor an annual return. There is no particular legislative control in this area.

6.5 Tax leasing

There are no schemes commonly adopted by which tax allowances or other benefits can be used to drive or structure transactions.

6.6 Other types of property finance

The leasing industry has grown considerably over recent years to provide users with capital assets which include, not just equipment, but also industrial buildings, warehouses, hotels and offices. At the end of the term, leasing practices will allow for the asset either to return to the landlord, to be purchased for its established residual value by the tenant, or renewal. The landlord may be the manufacturer or supplier, in the case of operational leases, or, more commonly, a leasing company in the case of conventional leases. As part of the credit industry, leasing companies have been subject to a greater degree of regulation as leasing has developed and are the subject of a separate registry since a law of 1988.

6.7 Institutional investment

Recently, there has been a major increase in property investment, largely due to the increase in the free movement of capital. The traditional method of investment remains the acquisition of buildings, either fully let at the date of acquisition or on the more speculative basis that their quality is such that they can readily be let for an acceptable return. Institutional investment has focused strongly on the residential sector under the National Housing Scheme for the construction of residential areas and the sale of housing at reduced prices. The industrial sector has also benefited, with investment principally in the utilities and public services market. The institutions may set the investment criteria for the market to the extent that public subsidies to facilitate the creation of employment or technical improvement may then be granted to those sectors invested in.

6.8 Other investors

Apart from the institutions, the most important investors are private banks and multinational companies. Private investors also play an active role and try to obtain the highest return for their investments, and it is possible for them to invest in sectors where institutional investment is not justified.

7 FORMS OF SECURITY

Only personal loans (usually for consumer goods) are granted without any form of security. Relationship banking exists but a mortgage is usually demanded by financial institutions as security for property finance.

7.1 Mortgages

A mortgage (*hipoteca inmobiliaria*) is the most complete form of security. The mortgage is a right *in re aliena* attaching to the property and can be assigned. A mortgage is granted by its execution before a notary public and its subsequent registration in the property registry. Tax will be paid (at the rate of 0.5 per cent on the amount of the loan should the lender be a bank). Any loan advance should not therefore be released until registration has been completed. The amount secured must either be a fixed sum or a maximum sum (allowing general credit facilities to be made available) and the mortgage must be attached to identified property. The mortgagor retains title to the property and full use of it. The interest rate may be floating provided a maximum is stated. No more than five years' interest (two in some cases) can be secured. An extension of the mortgage, which has to be separately registered, may be required when the mortgagor is in default. There are four principal methods of enforcement:

(a) conventional court proceedings, which allow the mortgagor an opportunity to defend enforcement in full and consequently are generally the slowest method of enforcement;
(b) executive proceedings, which are a more effective court procedure leading to an earlier realisation of the assets;
(c) summary judicial enforcement which is more commonly used and which

leads to a public judicial auction – for this remedy to be available, the deed of mortgage must have specified an address for service for the debtor and an agreed valuation for the property;

(d) notarial enforcement, which is a quick way of enforcing a mortgage and recently introduced, but which has not yet become widely used as it has not been favoured by notaries public, and the mortgage deed must again state an agreed value and specify an agent to represent the debtor at the notarial sale of the property.

For priority between mortgages, see 2.10. Privileges are dealt with at 2.3.

7.2 Floating and other charges

There is no concept of a floating charge which attaches to all the assets of the company or any particular group of assets, although a mortgage may attach inter alia to after-acquired property and improvements, chattels and crops as well as the proceeds of any insurance or compulsory purchase. The charges are valid against the debtor even where they are not registered, although they will require registration if they are to be enforceable against third parties.

7.3 Performance bonds and guarantees

The guarantee of a debt takes the form of a personal guarantee, including a bank or on demand guarantee. The guarantor undertakes to do or pay something due by another in the event that the other party fails to perform. It is only collateral and not a primary obligation, ie it only arises once the party guaranteed has failed to perform the obligation.

7.4 Credit insurance

Special 'caution' insurance (*seguro de caución*) exists whereby the insured party is indemnified by the insurer when the contractor is unable to fulfil all the obligations signed in the guarantee contract. There are other types of insurance, all regulated by the Insurance Contract Law (*Ley de Contrato de Seguro*) which protect against failure of the business, bankruptcy of clients, inability to carry out the project, and *lucro cesante* provides an indemnity where expected profit is not obtained.

8 PLANNING AND BUILDING REGULATION

The Constitution requires the use of land to be regulated in the interests of the community. The planning and building regulations are contained in the Land Use Zoning Act of 1992 which has been seriously affected by a ruling of the Constitutional Tribunal which has repealed more than 200 of its articles; all autonomous regions now have some degree of law-making power. New legislation is being discussed.

8.1 Planning authorities

Responsibility for planning control and zoning at national level lies with the national parliament, which is responsible for enacting a national plan (*plan nacional de ordenación*) although none has been enacted so far. At regional level responsibility lies with the autonomous regions (*comunidades autónomas*) and their parliaments; and at a local level, planning authority lies with local authorities or municipalities. Normally they will only have proposing powers, except in towns where the local population is under 50,000 where they also pass the plan themselves. Planning issues are decided on an administrative basis.

8.2 Zoning and development plans

The national plan is in the course of establishing national guidelines on planning and zoning policy; regional plans (*planes directores territoriales de coordinación*) will establish regional planning policies and zones, whilst the local plans (*planes generales de ordenación urbana* or PGOUs) will regulate local planning policy and land uses. The most important plans are the PGOUs prepared by local government and approved by regional government with extensive public consultation which classify *all* land into different use classifications specifying the possible use and building categories. For urban land, the plan will establish possible future infrastructure, land uses and construction, and a timetable for the implementation of the plan. For land 'fit for development', the plan will only establish a general framework of uses and the main elements of the proposed infrastructure to service these. In the case of land designated as 'not fit for development', the plan will establish measures to preserve the land from development. Legislative measures are being introduced to liberalise the planning and development procedures to increase the land available for development in particular for housing purposes. These plans are supplemented by more specific local plans (eg *planes parciales*, *programas de actuación urbanística* and *estudios de detalle*). Where a specific land use has been established for a determined area, each individual project will require approval by the planning authority and any uses not conforming with the plan will not be permitted; where the intended land use does conform, approval will not be automatic and the plan may indicate other matters with which the project has to conform (eg design and external appearance), before the approval will be granted.

8.3 Planning controls and procedures

All new buildings or constructions, demolition, first use, new utilisation, change of use, modification of the structure or external aspect of the buildings, and any other use listed in the relevant plan require a licence (*licencias urbanísticas*). Minor alterations may not require this.

8.3.1 The Local Government Act of 1985 gives the municipality responsibility for regulating, managing and enforcing zoning laws. The principal method for doing so is the requirement for the *licencias urbanísticas*. Fees payable vary from one locality to another. The applicant must own the land or an interest over the land (eg a surface right, see 2.1.3) or the licence will not be granted.

8.3.2 The time within which a decision regarding an application will be made depends on the work load of the town hall. However, the law establishes time periods after which the licence may be deemed granted. If the licence is denied it is possible to appeal, normally to the same authority who refused it and if it is refused again, there is always the possibility of appealing to the administrative court (*Juzgado de lo Contencioso-Administrativo*) and subsequently to the *Tribunal Superior de Justicia*. In the few cases where the absence of a decision is deemed to be a refusal, the appeal procedure is the same. Any relevant conditions established in the planning regulations may be attached to the licence.

8.3.3 A planning licence will last for a specified time, as established in the plan for the specific works. Licences are always personal and the seller may transfer it to a new owner if he notifies the municipality in writing, otherwise both will be jointly liable for the infringements of the other. Once the development has commenced, the project must be completed within the time limits set out in the plan or licence, or the holder of the licence may be made subject to enforcement proceedings.

8.3.4 If there is an infringement of planning law, the municipality has four years from completion to enforce the regulations contained in the plan. The Zoning Act contains enforcement procedures, entitling the municipality to require any infringing activity to be suspended or to issue 'cease and desist' orders as well as licence compliance orders and, ultimately, to demolish, or expropriate and/or sell any infringing buildings or structures. The municipality may also compulsorily purchase or expropriate the offending land or buildings. In addition, the municipality may bring a civil action for damages. Criminal penalties include six months' to three years' imprisonment and fines.

8.4 Building standards, control and supervision

8.4.1 There are numerous specific regulations concerning how buildings are constructed and how they are designed, eg size of the rooms, ventilation, light and electrical wiring. Building standards will involve prior approval at the time the application for a licence is made. For homes and apartments, a specific licence is required (*cedula de habitabilidad*) which certifies that the apartment or house complies with the standards of hygiene and health required by the regulation. Supervision and inspection are normally carried out once the project is completed and this will be undertaken by the municipality.

8.4.2 In addition to the planning licence (*licencias urbanisticas*) it may be necessary to obtain a first use licence (*permiso de primera utilizacion*) for certain buildings (eg factories, shopping malls or sports halls). For others it may be necessary to obtain an opening licence (*licencia de apertura).* To make certain that construction complies with the plans presented to the authorities an 'opening or use licence' is also needed to open and use the premises.

8.5 Protection of buildings of special interest

Historic buildings, landscape zones, tourist zones, and infrastructures (harbours, roads, railways, energy etc) may be regulated and protected by special plans (*planes especiales*), which establish specific requirements, normally beyond those established in the general plans, in relation to these activities. Where the government designates a site as historic, the municipality must draft a special protection plan, and any castles, churches and palaces within it are automatically placed in a national catalogue of historic buildings. Licences related to special plans have to be granted, but another permit may also be needed from either the central or regional government, depending on the circumstances. The Land Use Zoning Act establishes that owners of buildings or other premises must maintain them in conditions of 'safety, health and repair'. The municipality may also order the execution of repairs or reforms in the façades of buildings. They will be paid for by the owners of the buildings or by the municipality depending upon whether the works required are mere maintenance or improvements for the general benefit.

8.6 Expropriation or compulsory purchase and compensation

The Zoning Act states that when expropriation, which can only be in the public interest, is resorted to, all the land and buildings within a given unit will be expropriated using a complete list of owners and their properties. However, the authorities may decide not to expropriate certain assets. The valuation of the property and requirements for expropriation are governed by specific laws and regulations, which differentiate between expropriation for zoning purposes or for other purposes. Another way in which the authorities can act is through 'execution orders'. Compensation must be for fair value and following the legal procedure and may be appealed against in court.

9 ENVIRONMENTAL MATTERS

The 1978 Constitution recognises the right to a suitable environment and a number of provisions were enacted during the 1980s to comply with EU standards. The responsibility for enacting environmental legislation lies with the central and regional governments, and supervision takes place at regional and local level. Sanctions are either administrative or criminal regardless of the type of pollution and may include fines and imprisonment. Criminal liability only attaches to physical persons and, therefore, the directors and officers of a company may be made liable. Civil liability is based on the principle of fault, and therefore the burden of proof is upon the damaged party to show that the polluter did not take appropriate care to prevent pollution and/or damage. Strict liability, without proof of negligence, is being introduced by the courts to place the burden of remediation on the polluter. A draft act on civil liability for environmental damages is being discussed in parliament and will introduce strict liability.

9.1 Protection against atmospheric and noise pollution

The Air Pollution Act 1972 and subsequent regulatory developments contain provisions intended first to prevent, monitor and eliminate any air pollution, irrespective of source, and secondly to impose thresholds on the emission of toxic substances by private bodies. Potentially polluting activities are listed and there are special requirements regarding installation, prior approval, monitoring and control, which will be the responsibility of the local authorities or municipalities. No distinction is drawn between the polluter, the occupier or the owner. The legislation refers to the 'infringer', and it is possible to find either an existing or previous owner or occupier liable, if there is evidence that he was in breach of the provisions (for lender liability, see 9.4). There is no specific legislation concerning noise pollution, although there are regulatory procedures for approving any undertakings which cause nuisance through insanitary or noxious activities, which would include noise or vibration. The municipalities are entitled to establish their own regulations to prevent noise caused by industrial activities within their municipalities.

9.2 Water pollution

The Water Resources Act 1985 aims to protect inland waters. Any discharges into inland waters require prior authorisation and the payment of levies on a scale according to the category of pollutant. Certain private uses of water are permitted, whilst for others, an administrative authorisation is required. Authorisations are dealt with by the hydrographic confederations which have the power to suspend or revoke authorisations in the event of breach of conditions. A polluter will be subject to fines as well as remediation costs for unauthorised discharges or discharges in breach of authorisation. Either owner or occupier may be made responsible for contamination, and previous and current owners may be held jointly and severally liable (for lender liability, see 9.4). The Sea Coast Act 1988 provides protection for the coastline and regulates the operation of any installations and liquid discharge along the coast. Authorisation is again subject to a levy.

9.3 Waste storage and disposal

The Solid Wastes Act 1975 regulates the planning and monitoring of urban waste collection, treatment and use. Responsibility for the collection and treatment of waste lies with the local councils which manage public landfills. However, subject to appropriate municipal licensing, private landfill is possible. Subsequent legislation in 1986 and 1988 deals with the generation and management of hazardous wastes and sets up appropriate licensing procedures. This legislation caters for matters such as waste-handling, labelling, treatment, consignment and reporting of spillage or loss. Where waste is handled without the requisite licence, the deposit or landfill will be closed immediately and the parties responsible will bear the cost of proper disposal carried out by the authorities. Separate legislation establishes the conditions for storage, labelling and inspection by the Nuclear Security Council of any radioactive waste for which specific authorisations are required.

9.4 Contaminated land

It has become widespread for buyers of interests in land to make the proper environmental enquiries before the transaction takes place which may include an environmental impact assessment under certain circumstances (see 9.5). The seller is under an obligation to make good any hidden defects if the use of the land is affected or its value is decreased. However the seller will be under no obligation to point out manifest defects to the buyer or to draw his attention to defects where the buyer is a member of the profession. In relation to contaminated land, the contracting parties may, however, agree to exempt the seller from any subsequent liability linked to contamination, or the buyer may be indemnified by the seller in this respect. There are no public registers detailing which land has been put to contaminated use, although a list under the 'National Plan for the Remediation of Contaminated Soils' has been drawn up with the intention of preventing further contamination and remediation of existing contaminated sites. There is no fund available for the contamination which the industry must contribute to, although the Remediation Plan does set aside a sum in the region of 132,000 million pesetas for remediation during the period 1995–2005. There are no specific provisions governing soil contamination and remediation, but those contributing to contamination by any activities carried out on the land may be charged with a term of imprisonment of up to four years, a fine and the cost of remediation. Both previous and current owners and occupiers may be responsible and where it is not possible to establish the extent of liability between them, they will be held jointly and severally liable. It is however, extremely unlikely that a lender will be responsible for any breach, and to date there are no cases on this point.

9.5 Environmental impact assessments

Two Decrees of 1986 and 1988 were enacted in order to implement EU Directives. They require certain projects to be the subject of environmental impact assessments, in particular public and private projects involving industrial processes, crude oil refineries, gas installations, power stations, waste storage and disposal sites, dams and transport facilities.

10 DEVELOPMENT

10.1 Development projects, structures and vehicles

Developments are usually undertaken by property companies who buy and develop land, either as a trading activity to sell on, or as a long-term investment to be retained in their own portfolio. Developers will provide finance (either in the form of equity or from external sources) and may undertake construction themselves. Development will be undertaken in one of three ways. First, the landowner and co-owners may personally carry out the development with the landowner financing the project directly. Second, the landowner may contract a third party or developer who will then be in charge of finance and selecting the subcontractors. Third, the building development may be carried out by a contractor which may be a construction company. Commercial loans will often be provided to finance the development.

10.2 Building contracts and appointment of professionals

10.2.1 Typical forms of building contract

The Civil Code sets out general terms and the two most common types of construction contracts are: fixed price contracts (*obra por ajuste o precio alzado*) and modular contracts (*contratos por piezas o por medida*) although the latter is far more commonly used. Some building contracts provide only for the contractor to provide the construction work and the workers, but not the necessary materials. In all types of contract the Civil Code provides that the main contractor will be responsible for the performance of subcontractors. Whether the contractor assumes responsibility for design will be determined by the contract.

10.2.2 Common terms

Under a fixed price contract, the price of the construction is pre-determined with no allowance for inflation or fluctuations. The price may only be adjusted in the event of a variation to the contract works ordered by the developer. Under a modular contract, the contractor will undertake construction in units or stages, and will be paid in accordance with rates or prices specified in the contract. The developer may cancel the contract at any time subject to compensation for costs, work and loss of profits. If the contractor is unable to complete the contract due to some factor beyond his control, the contract can be terminated and the contractor is entitled to the value of the executed construction (often assessed by an expert) and the value of the materials prepared. Public works contracts are regulated separately and contractors are required to provide security for performance in the form of bonds or cash deposits of a minimum of four per cent of the contract price.

10.2.3 Standard forms of contract

There are no generally adopted standard forms of contract or specific regulations applicable to private development projects, but set rules and principles contained in the Civil Code apply to construction contracts (*arrendamiento de obra*) unless the parties agree otherwise.

10.2.4 Appointment of the professional team

The architect and technical architect are appointed under 'assignment forms', governed by the rules in the Civil Code and those issued by professional associations, which are binding on their members. The only Civil Code requirements which the parties cannot contract out of are that there should be provision for a fee in exchange for the services, and the statute of limitation for claiming collection of fees is three years from completion.

10.3 Those involved and their roles

There are several participants in any construction project. Although more common for public works, building contracts may be awarded by tender. Overall responsibility usually rests with the works manager (*director de obra*) usually an architect. Every project must be designed by a qualified technician, a project designer (*proyectista*) appointed by the developer, who will draw up the project documents subject to technical and zoning regulations, and have them certified by the College of Architects (*Colegio Profesional*). All architects have to be registered with the area college, which has considerable supervisory powers. This is a requirement prior to submission of the project documents for municipal approval. Depending on the type of project, the law establishes who is the competent technician. Sometimes, it is the architect himself, perhaps in collaboration with other technicians. Master builders (*aparejadores*) or technical architects (*arquitectos técnicos*) can also be competent for certain projects; engineers may design certain buildings which are not for residential purposes but for purposes in accordance with their specific qualification. The works supervisor (*jefe de obras*) is the technical representative of the contractor at the work site, and must have suitable qualifications or experience. Subcontractors undertake to carry out certain portions of the works, according to the project plan. The works manager (*director de obra*) takes overall control in particular of the technical, aesthetic, planning and environmental aspects of the works. The works execution manager (*director de la ejecución de obra*), usually a master builder or technical architect, is mandatory for certain projects and supervises the execution of the works, technical and quality control. The works manager (*director de obra*) and the works execution manager (*director de la ejecución de obra*) are collectively considered as the managing authority (*dirección facultativa*) in any project. Engineers are usually only employed on civil engineering projects and the quantity surveyor's role is usually undertaken by the architect or technical architect.

10.4 Defects and remedies

10.4.1 Remedies of employer in respect of defects in design and materials

In addition to any criminal or administrative liabilities for personal injury or violation of any statutory codes, the Civil Code provides a remedy against the contractor or architect in the event of building collapse within ten years of construction; but in the case of the architect, liability will only arise if defects are connected with the site or mismanagement of construction. Although the Civil Code refers only to liability for building collapse, this liability has been extended to serious building defects. The courts usually order the contractor or architect to repair the defects or pay for such repair. There are no specific contractual defects or maintenance periods which require the contractor to maintain and/or remedy defects following the completion of the works, other than the warranty period of ten years described.

10.4.2 Remedies of subsequent owners/occupiers other than the contractual employer

The contractor is only liable to the employer, although the Supreme Court has strengthened the protection of the subsequent owners, who can bring an action against the contractor although they were not parties to the original contract. However, this does not extend to the tenant or other third parties.

10.5 Defects insurance

The constructors and architects usually have insurance policies which cover the cost of correcting building defects due to faulty construction, materials or designs. There is no specific insurance available to the building owners and occupiers to cover such defects as an alternative to suing the contractor and the team, however this could in theory be agreed with the insurer. Although feasible under professional liability insurance, the insurance companies are not generally prepared to grant coverage for claims made as a consequence of economic loss due to the final construction not being suitable for its original purpose, without there having been any direct material damage.

10.6 Copyright

The design team owns the copyright in the design drawings, therefore developers need to agree a copyright assignment from the architect. This grants the developer the exclusive right to use the design documents and, save as expressly agreed, the right to grant exclusive authorisations to third parties, and also to prosecute any copyright infringements.

10.7 Fees

The work carried out by architects and technical architects will be subject to fees in accordance with Royal Decrees of 1977 and 1979, which range between 6 and 6.5 per cent of the building costs or less where the construction is larger. Since a Royal Decree of 1996 there are no longer minimum scale fees.

10.8 Taxes

Supplies of goods and services normally bear 16 per cent value added tax (VAT). The VAT rate will be the same for all types of construction. Once the construction work is finished, the developer will execute a deed of declaration of new works (*declaración de obra nueva*) in front of a notary public, which is then registered at the property registry. The execution of this document attracts 0.5 per cent stamp duty, based on the value of the works. The tax on construction, payable by constructors and builders, ranges between two per cent and four per cent of the cost of the works.

11 TAXES

11.1 Corporation tax

Resident companies are subject to corporation tax on their worldwide income (as evidenced by the taxpayer's accounts) and capital gains, whether or not remitted to Spain. Apart from the cases where a Spanish company is not deemed to be fiscally resident in Spain there are few cases where taxation is modified by tax treaties. Non-resident companies operating in Spain through a permanent establishment are subject to corporation tax on their Spanish income and capital gains. For corporation tax affecting Spanish-source income and capital gains obtained by non-resident companies without a permanent establishment see 11.1.4. Resident holding and property companies, and professional firms, are not separately taxed and their income is allocated to their shareholders or partners and taxed in their hands creating tax transparency.

11.1.1 Tax rates

The standard rate of corporation tax, which does not vary according to the size of company, applicable both to income and capital gains is 35 per cent. A lower rate applies to the income of non-resident companies not having a permanent establishment in Spain.

11.1.2 Computation and administration

As a general rule, those expenses correctly deducted under Spanish accounting legislation are allowed for tax purposes. Nevertheless, there are some limitations in respect of specific items of expenditure such as depreciation, bad debts, penalties and fines, gifts, expenses for services rendered to residents of tax havens, and management and R&D fees paid to foreign affiliates. Tax losses may be carried forward for seven years. Since 1 January 1996, deductible expenses need no longer be necessary for, or exclusively incurred on behalf of, the business. Yearly tax returns must be filed with the tax office within six months and 25 days following the end of the fiscal year. At this time, tax must be calculated and paid. The return is open to inspection by the tax authorities within the next five years. Additional assessments raised upon inspection may be appealed to the corresponding regional tax court, in which case the payment obligation may be suspended provided that a suitable guarantee, which must cover the amount in dispute plus the interest for late payment which may be accrued during the litigation process, is lodged with the tax collecting office. Corporation tax pre-payments, on account of the final tax liability, are due in April, October and December.

11.1.3 Depreciation and capital allowances

It is possible to depreciate all income-producing property having a useful life beyond that fiscal year. This depreciation is based on the cost of the assets. Straight line, double declining and sum of digits are all acceptable methods for depreciation. Under the straight line method the total cost may be depreciated over the maximum useful life of the assets, as stated in the chart approved by the Treasury, provided that the rate applied each year does not exceed the chart's established maximum rate. They range between 10 per cent and 12 per cent for plant and machinery, two per cent and four per cent for buildings, and between 10 per cent and 25 per cent for office equipment. A special plan establishing higher rates may be accepted beforehand by the tax authorities in certain cases. Under the double declining method taxpayers may compute depreciation each year by applying twice the maximum established rate to the balance pending amortisation. Special rates of depreciation and capital allowances may be available in the Basque Country and Navarra regions. Tax credits may be available for various categories of investments and expenditure.

11.1.4 Withholding tax

In the absence of a tax treaty, dividends, interest, rents, royalties and compensation for services derived from Spanish sources by non-resident entities without a permanent establishment are subject to Spanish corporation tax at the rate of 25 per cent, which in practice operates as a withholding tax. Income obtained by recipients residing in a tax treaty country is taxable in accordance with the provisions of the treaty. In all cases, rents from a lease of property located in Spain are taxable at the rate of 25 per cent. Dividends paid to parent companies residing in the EU are exempt under the legislation implementing an EU Directive. Interest paid to EU residents is also tax-exempt.

11.2 Taxes on development value

There are no taxes on the increase in value of land due solely to a change in its use or development value.

11.3 Taxes on capital gains

Capital gains made by non-resident entities without a permanent establishment are subject to corporation tax at the same rate applicable to resident companies, namely 35 per cent. In this case 10 per cent of the total agreed price must be withheld by the buyer and paid to the tax office as a payment on account of the final corporation tax liability of the seller. Capital gains arising out of the disposal of fixed assets may be adjusted to take inflation into account. The deductibility of loan interest paid to foreign affiliates is subject to thin capitalisation restrictions. The tax on capital gains resulting from the disposal of fixed assets may be deferred if the proceeds are reinvested in fixed assets within two years (or four years if a reinvestment plan is lodged with the tax authorities). This relief is also available if the purchase of the fixed assets takes place in the year before the transfer of the property.

11.4 Taxes on owner of property

A municipal tax on property (*impuesto sobre bienes inmuebles*) is payable yearly on the ownership of all property including property rights and concessions. It is payable on the cadastral value at the rate of 0.4 per cent for urban property and 0.3 per cent for rural property. The municipality may vary these rates within prescribed limits.

A special annual tax on property owned by non-resident entities (*impuesto sobre bienes inmuebles de entidades no residentes*) is levied at the rate of three per cent on the cadastral value (the administrative valuation) of the property. This tax also applies to other property rights such as usufruct. It does not apply to certain categories of entity not engaged in real estate, such as companies, and public and international bodies. An exemption may also be available to certain entities residing in a country having a tax treaty with Spain.

A municipal tax is levied on the notional increase in the value of urban land upon any transfer of the property, based on values established by the municipality and the number of years that the transferor has retained ownership of the property. It ranges between two and 3.7 per cent per annum. The tax is payable by the seller, in the case of a sale, and otherwise by the donee.

11.5 Taxes on occupier

At present, there are no taxes on occupiers or on occupation.

11.6 Taxes on land transfer

A transfer tax (*impuesto de transmisiones patrimoniales*) is payable by the buyer, levied at the rate of six per cent on the actual value of the property transferred, if the transfer is not subject to value added tax (VAT). The transfer tax also applies to the transfer of shares of companies having more than 50 per cent of their assets in the form of property whenever one shareholder acquires control, direct or indirect, over the company as a result of the transfer. There is no minimum price below which the tax is not payable. Transfers of property subject to VAT and not to transfer tax (see below) also attract stamp tax at a rate of 0.5 per cent if formalised in a notarial deed to be recorded with the property registry.

The lease of urban property attracts stamp duty which is usually paid by the transferee, based on the total rents payable for the duration of the contract, or for six years in the case of contracts for an unlimited duration. Transfer tax is a tax levied on the transfer itself, whereas stamp duty is only payable on the execution of a notarial document which is to be recorded in the property or commercial registry. Note should be made of the tax on the increase in value of the land during the ownership of the seller payable by the seller on transfer (see 11.4).

11.7 Wealth taxes

Impuesto sobre patrimonio is a tax imposed annually on individuals having a net worth in excess of 17 million pesetas, at rates which vary between 0.2 per cent (for the portion of taxable amount under 25 million pesetas) and 2.5 per cent (for the excess over 1,600 million pesetas). Non-resident taxpayers are only taxable on property located in Spain.

11.8 Value added tax

In principle, transfers of property (other than agricultural land and properties where building construction is not permitted) made by business enterprises or professionals and construction are subject to value added tax (VAT), as deliveries of goods, at the rate of 16 per cent or seven per cent, the latter being applicable in the case of dwellings and related garages and annexes. The scope of VAT, however, is restricted by the existence of exemptions such as transfers of land connected with urbanisation plans, under certain circumstances, or second and subsequent transfers of buildings (except those made pursuant to a financial lease or when the buildings are to be rehabilitated or demolished by the acquirer). In these cases, the transaction becomes subject to the transfer tax referred to in 11.6, except if the transferor chooses to waive the exemption and apply VAT to the transfer. Leases of property, other than agricultural property and private dwellings, are subject to VAT (*impuesto sobre el valor añadido*) at the rate of 16 per cent.

11.9 Local and other taxes

Non-resident individuals are taxed on income from Spanish sources in a manner practically identical to that mentioned in 11.1.4.

12 GRANTS AND INCENTIVES

Certain mechanisms have been introduced in accordance with the Constitution to encourage economic development in areas where investment would otherwise be unattractive, and reduce social and economic inequality between regions. These are generally regional incentives in various industries, particularly mining, advanced technology, agriculture, infrastructure, and tourism. In addition, there are various types of assistance available from the EU. Four different types of national incentive zone exist which offer different amounts of assistance, up to 50 per cent of total expenditure. There are further types of zone for which assistance may be available, economic protection zones and special zones. Regional incentives are generally administered by the Ministry of Economy and Finance, though applications may be made to the municipality or the relevant autonomous community.

12.1 Subsidies, grants and loans

Regional incentives include subsidies which are non-refundable and may be conditional. They may involve periodic payments, cover loan interest and/or loan repayments, as well as payments for approved investments. These will generally only be available for developments which benefit the public and/or provide a public service, such as energy production plants or industries located in certain undeveloped areas. A grant may be offered where a subsidy would not be appropriate because there is no public benefit involved but a grant is required in order to make a scheme economically viable, eg offering specific deductions in hiring employees. The government provides assistance through official credit institutions in the forms of loans which must be repaid with interest, or credits which again must be returned with interest, or governmental collateral or security to enable a commercial loan to be obtained from the private sector. These may be the only sources of finance in certain regions for some sectors, such as industry, agriculture, fishing, housing and public services.

12.2 Tax allowances and reliefs

Tax credits are available in respect of amounts spent on new fixed assets (5 per cent), book publication (5 per cent), fostering of exports and overseas marketing (25 per cent), research and development (20 per cent) and staff training (5 per cent) by corporation tax payers. The aggregate of these credits cannot exceed 35 per cent of the annual tax payable. Unused tax credits may be carried forward for five years. Companies established in the Canary Islands enjoy a special, favourable tax treatment, which includes: exemption from transfer tax on formation as well as from any indirect taxes levied on the acquisition of fixed assets during the first three years; 40 per cent reduction of corporation tax related to the sale of goods produced in the Islands; and exemption from corporation tax corresponding to profits allocated to a reserve for investments in the Islands, which may amount to 90 per cent of the undistributed yearly profits. Furthermore, companies formed in the Canary Islands may qualify, subject to certain conditions, as ZEC (*Canary Especial Zone*) companies. The ZEC is an offshore regime whereby profits (other than those resulting from business transactions with the rest of Spain) are subject to one per cent corporation tax and dividend distributions and interest payments to non-residents are tax-free, provided that they are not made to residents in a tax haven.

12.3 Other public schemes and incentives

There are three regions where special incentives may be available, namely the Basque country, Navarra and the Canary Islands.

13 COMPANIES AND BUSINESS ENTITIES

13.1 Limited and unlimited companies

A limited liability company (*sociedad de responsabilidad limitada*, SL) must be incorporated by deed before a notary and registered at the mercantile registry. Its share capital must be divided into cumulative and indivisible *participaciones*. Before transfer of any participation, the other participants and the SL itself have pre-emption rights for 45 days. The company has to have a minimum capital of 500,000 pesetas which must be fully paid up at the time of incorporation, but the consideration need not necessarily be cash. An SL is a separate legal entity, with its own assets and liabilities. The share company or corporation (*sociedad anónima*, SA) was the most common vehicle for the conduct of business, but due to the required minimum share capital (10 million pesetas of which at least 25 per cent must be paid up on incorporation) it is being increasingly replaced by the SL. Non-cash contributions can form part of the share capital, if valued by the mercantile registrar assessor. The company's capital is issued in the form of shares, and unlike the SL, the SA may issue bonds and negotiable securities. Different classes of shares may be created, including bearer shares and non-voting shares with preferential dividend rights. The SA must also be incorporated by notarial deed of incorporation and registered at the mercantile registry. The SA is governed by general shareholders' meetings and there are a number of minority shareholder protections built into the Corporations Act. Both SLs and SAs can be formed with a single shareholder. Another type of company with limited liability for its members is called the *sociedad de garantía recíproca* (SGR) or reciprocal guarantee corporation. The purpose of this financial institution is to provide its members with guarantees in order to help them to obtain bank credit which they might not obtain by themselves. At least four or five of its members must be small and medium businesses, all must belong to the same trade and it must be founded by at least 150 members. The minimum capital is 300 million pesetas, with no upper limit. It must be approved by the Ministry of Economy and Finance, formed by public deed and registered in the mercantile registry and with the Bank of Spain.

13.2 Partnerships

Partnerships can be general (*sociedad colectiva*) or limited (*sociedad comanditaria*). In a *sociedad colectiva* the partners share in the profits and losses of the partnership. Creditors may not take action against individual partners until the assets of the partnership have been liquidated and exhausted. The liability of the partners is unlimited and joint and several at this point, ie one partner may be held liable for all the debts of the partnership, but there is an automatic indemnity from the remaining partners for payments greater than his share. The partnership business should be managed by the partners acting unanimously, although they may delegate certain functions to one or several partners. A partnership is a separate entity from its members, it has full legal personality and has to pay taxes on the profits like any other entity (ie corporations). However, due to the joint and several liability, individual partners may be held liable for the total tax, as is the case with any type of debt. Partnerships (both general or limited) must be incorporated by public deed before a notary public and registered with the mercantile registry. They are regulated by the code of commerce. In a limited partnership, the limited partners are only liable for the partnership debts to the extent of their capital contribution, but play no role in management of the partnership. Only general partners (which can be an SL or an SA) may represent or bind the partnership with third parties. The limited partnership is also a separate entity for tax purposes. Partnerships, both general and limited, are not necessarily included in the special tax transparency regime, since that depends on the activities the entity carries out or the goods it owns. For instance, if more than 75 per cent of the revenues of the fiscal year come from professional activities, such an entity is considered tax transparent, irrelevant of whether it is an SA or a partnership. The partnership limited by shares (*sociedad comanditaria por acciones*) combines features of partnerships and corporations. It is similar to a limited partnership where the limited partners' participation is in the form of shares. The initial share capital must exceed 10 million pesetas, be fully subscribed, and at least 25 per cent paid up. Shares are transferable in the same way as shares in SAs and the management, dissolution and partners' liability are dealt with in the same way as for limited partnerships.

13.3 Other types of business association

13.3.1 The UTE (*union temporal de empresas*) is a type of contractual joint venture, without a legal personality of its own, established for a limited time and for the performance of a specific project. The UTE will involve two or more business entities and can be created with less formality than a joint venture SL or SA. It is often a mere tax vehicle enabling a number of companies to operate together. The joint venture agreement must be registered at the registry of UTEs (at the Ministry of Economy and Finance) and must state the terms of the agreement, the arrangements for distribution of profits and losses, the aim of the venture, the parties involved, and their liability. Liability of the members of the UTE is subsidiary, joint and unlimited. The contract of a UTE creates a new business, without legal personality but acting through a single management, acting under a different name to those of the companies involved, and also with differentiated bye-laws. Creditors must look first to the UTE itself, but if a debt is not fully paid they can claim against any and all of the members, as is the case with general partnerships. This form of joint venture is widely used whenever there is a public project which, due to size, would go beyond the capabilities of a single company. Indeed the administration can require this to be used for a specific project. The UTE ceases to function when its purpose has been completed, or when the term established in its bye-laws expires (a maximum of ten years).

13.3.2 Unincorporated associations do not exist as separate legal entities. However there are associations and foundations, different to business entities and mainly non-profit organisations, which have legal personality and are therefore obliged to pay corporation tax on their income. For historical reasons, the concept of a trust as a separate legal entity is not recognised. Instead, it is considered as a contract, used mainly in inheritance law, and it has many limitations. The main consequence is that although certain goods may be held in trust, the trustee is considered to be the legal owner for all purposes, even tax purposes, so it has no real business or tax advantage.

14 INTERNATIONAL

14.1 Restrictions or consents required for inward investment

A Royal Decree regulates which foreigners may invest in Spanish property and the legal procedure involved. Generally an investment is considered a foreign investment when the origin of the capital being invested is from outside Spain. There is also a presumption, however, that the origin of capital invested by non-resident Spaniards or resident foreigners is domestic unless there is proof to the contrary. Although there are generally few restrictions on the purchase of property by foreigners, some forms of investment (the purchase of property which costs more than 500 million pesetas, or any investment in property by foreign individuals or companies which are located in tax havens) do require administrative 'verification'. The investor must therefore submit a project proposal to the Ministry of Economy and Finance (the Directorate General of Commercial Policy and Foreign Investment, DGPCIE) for authorisation. The application must include: brief details of the investment project; the property to be acquired with a brief description; and the identity of the foreign investor (with various personal details). Unless the administration requests further information, it must give a decision within 30 days. If no decision is forthcoming, the investor may consider the project as verified and may begin it within the next six months (unless a different term is specified). Note should be made of the tax on non-resident companies described at 11.4.

14.2 Exchange controls

As a general rule, there are no restrictions on the introduction of funds into Spain for the purchase of property. Nevertheless, a foreign investor buying property must obtain a bank certificate to prove, for repatriation purposes, that the purchase price in foreign currency (if appropriate) entered Spain. The investor will then have to present the bank certificate and, if necessary, the verification of the DGPCIE, to the notary, before whom the property transfer is formalised, and register it at the local property registry and foreign investments registry.

14.3 Restrictions and registrations on carrying on a business

There are few restrictions on foreign entities or companies carrying on business in Spain other than in certain areas where investments are considered a matter of national security, for example, weapons, telecommunications, air transport, etc in which investments are restricted up to a maximum of 25 per cent and may require governmental approval. Branches of foreign companies, as well as Spanish companies, have to register at the company registry. A branch (*succursal*) is a legal device through which a business entity grants a power of attorney to a Spanish representative who will then register the foreign entity as having a branch in Spain at the Mercantile Registry. The branch is not a separate legal entity in itself.

14.4 Repatriation of income and proceeds of property trading and development

The general rule is that there is complete freedom for non-residents to invest in Spain, notwithstanding the few cases of 'verification' (see 14.1) and the declaration of the foreign investment for statistical purposes. As a consequence of such liberalisation of foreign investments, the investor may transfer freely abroad both the income from its investment and the proceeds of the liquidation of such investment.

14.5 Withholding and other taxes

The different treatment of non-resident companies is dealt with in 11.1.4 and the special tax for non-residents described at 11.4 should be noted.

14.6 Double taxation relief

Spain has double taxation treaties with a number of countries.

CHAPTER 18

Sweden

Rolf Johansson

Partner, Lagerlöf & Leman Advokatbyrå, Stockholm

CONTENTS

1 OWNERSHIP OF LAND 597
2 OTHER INTERESTS IN LAND 601
3 TITLE TO LAND 604
4 TRANSACTIONS IN LAND 605
5 LEASES AND OTHER RIGHTS OF OCCUPATION 608
6 FINANCE AND INVESTMENT SOURCES 612
7 FORMS OF SECURITY 614
8 PLANNING AND BUILDING REGULATION 616
9 ENVIRONMENTAL MATTERS 619
10 DEVELOPMENT 621
11 TAXES 625
12 GRANTS AND INCENTIVES 628
13 COMPANIES AND BUSINESS ENTITIES 629
14 INTERNATIONAL 630

CHAPTER 18

Sweden

1 OWNERSHIP OF LAND

In common with other Scandinavian legal systems, Swedish law is strongly influenced by Romano-Germanic law. The sources of law principally comprise the codes, statutes and preparatory legislative work and reports as an aid to interpretation and also case law, although this is not binding. The principal source relating to property law is the Real Property Code (*Jordabalken*) which came into effect in 1972. It is a relatively recent addition to the Swedish Codes which go back to 1734. The Real Property Code is supplemented by various other statutes and by governmental ordinances on administrative matters. The principal forms of tenure or landownership are ownership and leasehold. Ownership and leasehold are enforceable against all third parties, the distinction between rights in rem and in personam being of little relevance in Sweden.

1.1 Types of tenure

1.1.1 Freehold or absolute ownership

Äganderätt is akin to absolute ownership. It carries with it a right to own, occupy and dispose of the land and any buildings erected on the land by the owner for permanent use. All land is divided into units and ownership is always connected to a registered land unit (see further section 3 on registration of title). A distinction does exist between the land itself and any buildings or structures on the land. Any building (or any other fixed installation) which has been placed on the property by the owner for permanent use is termed an accessory and is considered to be part of the land. Fixtures installed by the landowner in an accessory building, and which are suitable for permanent use in the building, are termed accessories to the building and are also deemed to be part of the property. Examples of fixtures considered to be accessories include lifts, water pipes and radiators. The definition of an accessory is of particular importance, eg when deciding which assets are covered by a mortgage. Buildings and fixtures owned by third parties are deemed to be chattels and will not be defined as accessories, unless and until transferred to the owner of the land. In principle, ownership also carries with it the right to the soil below and the right to the air space above, although the working and winning of minerals may require permission from the county administrative board, and may be granted to someone other than the landowner. Such permission from the authority overrides the rights of ownership of the landowner.

1.1.2 Leasehold

There are different types of lease or tenancy. The leasehold right to land (*Tomträtt*), the land lease (*Arrende*) which is contractual, and other contractual tenancy agreements. The leasehold right to land (*tomträtt*) may be granted where a right less than absolute ownership is intended but it falls very little short of freehold. It is entirely different from the contractual rental agreement and the land lease (*Arrende*) which are described in section 5 and which will not generally be registered. A leasehold will only generally be granted on publicly owned land. The leaseholder essentially has the same legal status as an owner of land and he has the exclusive right to use and occupy the land but may only transfer the lease itself and not the ownership of the land. The leaseholder will be registered in the land register as the owner of the lease and he will have the power to dispose of the lease to any person or entity. He may also mortgage, let and agree to servitudes over the leasehold right. A building which has been placed on the leased land by the leaseholder for permanent use is considered an accessory to and so part of the leasehold right and is covered by a mortgage of the leasehold. A lease is generally granted for an indefinite period against an annual fee based on a small percentage of the land value periodically agreed or determined by the courts. The agreement between the parties (the landowner and the leaseholder) can only be terminated by the landowner, but not before the expiry of a 60-year period. The landowner is barred from discontinuing the leasehold unless he has sound reasons for termination, in which case the landowner is under the obligation to compensate the leaseholder for the value of the leasehold right, including the value of any buildings owned by the leaseholder and placed on the leased land. A lease for a fixed period or a premium is not usual as in common law countries.

1.1.3 Joint ownership

Land may be jointly owned by more than one person and/or entity. However, where land is jointly owned, it is only possible to own a share or percentage of a registered piece of land. An agreement to purchase a physical part of a registered unit of land must be followed within six months by an application for parcelling out of the area (see further section 3 on registration). Rights over the land are exercised by the owners jointly. In accordance with the Joint Ownership Act (*Samäganderättslagen*), any joint owner may at any time demand the sale of the entire property. No pre-emption rights apply. It is common for joint owners of land to set aside the provisions regulating compulsory sale in the Joint Ownership Act by agreement. If such an agreement is intended for business purposes, the provisions on liquidation in the Partnership Act may apply.

1.1.4 Condominia

Apartment blocks are regulated by the Condominium Act (*Bostadsrättslagen*) and may only be owned by the acquisition of a share in a tenant-owner association. Membership of a tenant-owner association is combined with an exclusive right to use a designated unit (flat) in the condominium building without limitation in time. The owner of the whole property will be the tenant-owner association. The potential user of the unit does not own the unit but acquires a share in the association's capital, corresponding to the unit in question. The purchase agreement must be in writing and there are no restrictions on the purchase sum. The potential tenant as a buyer of the share in the association must be granted membership of the association in order to render the purchase of the unit valid. Other legal restrictions, such as pre-emption rights or required consent from the association or its members, do not apply. Standard tenancy agreements without limitation in time are drawn up between the association and the members who are the original tenants and under these agreements, the members/tenants pay a monthly fee to the association to cover the running expenses of the building. A tenant-owner association may also be formed where a building is used for commercial purposes and for buildings containing both residential and commercial units. According to the Condominium Act, legal links between ownership of shares in an association and a designated unit in a building, are prohibited other than through a tenant-owner association.

1.1.5 Lesser rights

Lesser rights including rights to use and enjoy land which do not amount to absolute ownership are dealt with in section 2.

1.2 The role of the trust and the distinction between legal and beneficial ownership

The Anglo-American doctrine of the trust is not adopted by Swedish law. A formal owner of an asset may hold the asset on behalf of and for the benefit of someone else but little protection is provided for the beneficial owner and the concept of nominee or bare ownership is not clearly recognised. The concept has created problems, eg in relation to legal restrictions on landownership. For this reason the separation of legal and beneficial ownership of land is prohibited by statute in some instances, particularly where designed to avoid the restrictions on landownership described in 1.3.

1.3 Restrictions on ownership and dealings

Any subject or company has the right to hold land; if a restriction is contained in the articles of association, this will not affect third parties. A minor or incapacitated person may hold land through custodians. However Swedish banks and financing companies may generally only own land for their own occupation or on a short term basis to protect and enforce their security. The restrictions on foreign ownership of land have been reduced significantly as a result of EU membership. There are, however, some remaining restrictions still imposed on the acquisition by non-nationals of residential and agricultural property which require prior authorisation (see section 14). Furthermore, there are restrictions on the rights of a landowner to protect the public interest, rights of access (see 2.6), planning regulations, preservation of areas of natural beauty and expropriation (see further section 8). The Real Property Code also requires a property owner to respect the interests of neighbours in the way he uses his own property.

1.3.1 Spousal consent

If the seller is married, written consent is required from the spouse (or cohabitant where the property is used as a joint residence) where he wishes to transfer or mortgage the property.

1.3.2 Municipality pre-emption rights

A municipal authority may exercise a right of pre-emption when property situated within its boundaries is for sale, and the property is needed for public purposes. The land registry will give notice to the municipality of the transfer of the property. The seller and the buyer must be informed of the municipality's intention to exercise its right within three months of the day the buyer applies for registration of the transfer. The municipality is barred from exercising its right of pre-emption once the private buyer is actually registered as the landowner. The parties may object to an intended pre-emption, in which case the local authority may have to apply for government permission to exercise the right. The right of pre-emption may be exercised where approval has been granted by government, or by default where the parties have failed to object within the stipulated time. The municipality enters into the agreement on the same terms and conditions as the previous buyer, and save for the purchase price, no refund or damages will be paid to the parties. The parties may ask for a preliminary opinion from the municipality on whether it will be seeking to exercise the pre-emption and if the municipality undertakes to refrain from exercising its pre-emption right, the opinion becomes binding upon the municipality.

1.3.3 Transfers of apartment blocks

On the transfer of property taxed as apartment blocks there is, in principle, no requirement for prior approval from the authorities. However, the transfer of the property does require the parties to notify the municipality of the agreement within two months. The consent of the regional rent tribunal (*Hyresnämnden*) must be sought if the local authority requires this. The consent may be refused for an unsuitable buyer who has previously neglected or violated the Housing Act. The tribunal decision may be appealed against. A failure to notify the municipality in time and a refusal of consent by the tribunal will render the transfer void. The same rules in some situations apply to the buyer of shares in a company which owns an apartment block.

1.3.4 Tenant-owner association's right of first refusal

A tenant-owner association (see 1.1.4) in a building which contains residential accommodation, can be formed if it holds more than three members. If more than 50 per cent of the tenants (all being members of the association) agree to purchase the property, the association may register its interest in acquiring the building in the land registry. The registration is valid for two years after the application is made. Where the registration has been made, during the validity of the registration period, the property owner must make an offer to the association to allow it to buy the property, if he is contemplating the sale of the property. The association may accept the proposal within three months from the date the offer was made, or file an application for an extension of the period, which will then be extended automatically for a further three months. Where the right is not exercised, the property may be sold to a third party, provided the purchase price and the other terms and conditions offered to the buyer are not more favourable than the offer made to the association.

1.3.5 Agricultural land

The transfer of agricultural land requires prior approval by the authorities if the buyer is not an individual, or if the property is in certain designated areas, usually of low population where the intention is to preserve local agricultural communities, although approval is not required if the buyer will be, or is already, living on the land in question.

1.4 Adverse possession

Ownership of land can, in exceptional cases, be acquired by adverse possession (*hävd*). This can only happen in two situations and both require the land to have been registered. Land will be adversely acquired where there has been a transfer which has been registered but is not valid for some reason, and the rightful owner has taken no action to claim the land for 10 years and the registered owner has acted in good faith. Land will also be adversely acquired where someone other than the rightful owner has been registered as the owner of the property in the land register and has been in possession of the land for a minimum of 20 years and the rightful owner has not initiated proceedings to reclaim the land. This second situation does not require good faith.

2 OTHER INTERESTS IN LAND

There are various interests in land which confer a right less than ownership or leasehold. These may be public or private. The most common are contractual leases (dealt with in section 5), mortgages, servitudes and usufruct.

2.1 Servitudes or easements, usufruct, building and dwelling rights

2.1.1 Servitudes

The property owner has the right to encumber his property by granting servitudes (*servitut*) by agreement. A servitude is a right over land (the servient tenement) in favour of other land (the dominant tenement). Servitudes may include rights of access and the right to a water supply. A servitude may also create restrictions on the servient tenement, eg by limiting the size of buildings which may be built on the land. The creation of a servitude must be in writing and comply with certain formal criteria in order to be valid. Servitudes are enforceable by and between successive landowners if they are registered or if their future enforceability is mentioned in the purchase agreement. A servitude may also be created by a land survey authority decision, where in a local authority's opinion a servitude is needed, eg to grant a dominant tenement access to a road, usually as a result of a division or parcelling out of land. For some limited purposes compulsory servitudes may be created, eg to enable the construction of major infrastructure facilities (see 8.6). The actual servitude may not be transferred separately from the land.

2.1.2 Usufruct

Avkomsträtt (usufruct) is a right to take the produce from another's land for a period, eg timber felling rights. The holder of the right may generally use the property in any way he chooses provided that the nature and the use of the land are not altered. The right is limited in time, may be created by an oral agreement, is transferable and may be registered where the creation of the right is by written agreement.

2.1.3 Building and dwelling rights

The building right as recognised under some civil law systems does not exist. However, under the land lease (*Arrende* – which is always contractual and will rarely be registered) it is possible for a landowner to grant a lease to a third party and include provisions in the agreement to the effect that the tenant may build on the land and assume ownership of the buildings for the duration of the lease. When the term of lease comes to an end, several options are available to the parties; the lease may be renewed, the buildings may revert to the landowner who will compensate the tenant or the tenant may dismantle the building. (See section 5 where the terms upon which land leases are granted are dealt with in more detail.)

2.2 Restrictions on use and other restrictions

Property owners may enter into agreements restricting the use of the property. However, unless the agreement meets the requirements for the creation of a servitude, the agreement cannot be registered; though the agreement will still be valid and enforceable between the parties, as long as the party restricting his use of the property is the owner. If the restricting party does not impose the restriction by agreement on the buyer of the property, the agreement will not be enforceable against the subsequent owner and will terminate with the disposal of the property. Public law restrictions under planning and other legislation are commented on in section 8.

2.3 Mortgages

Monetary liabilities can generally only be secured on land by entering into a private mortgage on which comment is made in section 7.

2.4 Contracts and options

When an owner of land contracts to sell the land, but the sale has not been completed, the buyer will have an interest in the land and a right to enforce the contract. This will happen where there is an unconditional contract for sale, or where the conditions in a conditional contract for sale have been fulfilled. A written or oral option over property is not binding or valid.

2.5 Public or municipal charges

Some public and semi-public liabilities can also be secured on property, such as the cost of carrying out road maintenance or land drainage. These obligations are imposed under statute, will not require registration and will take priority over any mortgage registered against the land.

2.6 Other interests

Public access rights (*Allemansrätt*) grant the public the right to pass over or to use any land for recreational purposes provided no risk of damage is caused to the landowner, although residential, commercial, forested and agricultural land which may be damaged by the presence of people or vehicles is expressly excluded.

2.7 Liabilities attaching to land

Liabilities arising out of land may attach either to the owner or occupier or both. There may be statutory liability for physical injury and damage to visitors or their goods, although pure economic loss will only be compensated in tort where there is also criminal liability. Strict liability applies in nuisance for the unreasonable use of one's land to the prejudice of an adjoining landowner, or for dangerous escapes. Under environmental law there is strict liability for various kinds of pollution, provided it is caused by the use of land (see further section 9). For statutory liabilities in respect of the preservation of buildings listed as being of historic or architectural interest, see 8.5. There are also statutory liabilities to protect employees, visitors and/or occupiers. For fiscal liabilities which attach to land, see section 11.

2.8 Legal and equitable interests

Swedish law does not recognise a distinction between legal and equitable interests as in common law jurisdictions. See further 1.2 and 1.3.

2.9 Protection of rights and interests

In order to enforce an interest against the land and subsequent buyers, it is generally necessary to register the interest. Occupational tenancies and land leases can be registered (unless this has been specifically prohibited by the agreement) and are generally enforceable against a subsequent buyer even if they have not been registered, provided they are based on a written agreement and the tenant is in occupation of the premises. Mortgages will need to be protected by registration. Servitudes will normally require registration, and indeed must be registered to be enforceable by and between successors in title and against third parties, unless the seller explicitly excludes registration in the transfer agreement.

2.10 Priority of interests

Priority between rights over land will depend generally on the date of registration, where registrable, not the date of creation. There is however one exception to this, namely that in some situations an older, unregistered right (other than a private mortgage) will take priority over a more recent registered right where the holder of the more recent interest acted in bad faith regarding the existence of the older interest.

3 TITLE TO LAND

3.1 Proof of title

Title to land is established by the signing of the written agreement transferring the land. Although registration is not compulsory for a valid transfer of land, it should be applied for within three months of the transfer, in accordance with the Real Property Code. The consequences of non-registration are dealt with at 3.3. Disposals of land by way of gift will require registration, although other rights in land do not necessarily require registration to be enforceable, see 2.9. The registers are open for inspection to the public and certificates of search (*Gravationsbrevis*) in the form of transcripts may be issued on request. Most of the local land registers in Sweden are computer based and may be accessed on line.

3.2 The land registry and the land register

The land registers are administered by the 100 local land registries.

3.2.1 Plans

The whole of Sweden is divided into land units, which are registered under specific names and codes. Plans are used for the identification of the property and are not definitive as to its boundaries.

3.2.2 Content

The land registers contain information for every parcel of property describing the property and title; the register will show the owner and the leaseholder (where applicable), as well as the purchase price of the most recent transaction and tax value, established on a regular basis by the tax authorities according to objective criteria. It will also reveal any existing bills of mortgage and other entries affecting the land, eg rights of first refusal and other charges, entered to protect third parties' rights. There is no division of the registers, and all the information will be covered under a single entry in the register describing the land or unit, its owner and adverse entries.

3.2.3 Errors

If it is established that an error has been made in the register and loss or economic damage is suffered as a result of detrimental reliance on the register, there are provisions for the rectification of the register, and compensation will be paid to a person against whom the register is rectified.

3.3 Passing of title

Title, for most purposes, passes upon the bill of sale though the rights of ownership are acquired in stages. Failure to register does not make the transfer void. When registration takes place, it will be backdated to the date of the application although a transfer which is not lodged at the land registry within three months will not become technically void. The purchase agreement will be sufficient to establish priority for the buyer over the seller's estate in bankruptcy. An owner with a registered title may create a charge over the property or dispose of the property. Therefore, where a buyer has failed to register the change of title, the seller is still formally capable of creating a charge over the property. Where land is fraudulently sold twice by the same seller, the buyer who applies for registration of title first will have priority over the subsequent buyer, provided he then becomes the registered owner and applies for registration in good faith.

4 TRANSACTIONS IN LAND

The most common transactions in land are the sale and purchase of ownership or leasehold, the grant or assignment of a lease, and the creation of a mortgage to secure a loan or other liability.

4.1 Procedures

4.1.1 It is normal for a sale to take place in two stages, with the first stage usually taking two to four weeks, and the second stage taking place on the day of completion. The first stage will be the negotiation of a contract, which will be combined with certain investigations and enquiries. At this stage, the buyer will raise enquiries concerning the contents of the property and the title, and searches will be made at the land registry and, if the seller is a company, at the companies registry to ensure eg that no liquidator or receiver has been appointed. Enquiries may be made regarding possible local authority pre-emption rights during the first stage of the transaction but can be postponed until registration of title. During this first stage, the buyer will undertake any survey and investigate environmental issues and negotiate any offer of finance. Once the buyer has been satisfied on these issues, he will enter into a binding contract regulating the legal position between the contracting parties.

4.1.2 The second stage will normally take place on the date of the actual transfer of the property as this will usually also be the day the purchase price will be paid, unless otherwise agreed by the parties. Before payment, the parties will meet to confirm the assumption by the buyer of any responsibility, if previously agreed, relating to mortgage repayments, as it is quite common for a buyer to take over the seller's mortgage. The seller will then issue a bill of sale, stating that the transfer of title to the property has been completed and that the purchase sum has been paid. The bill of sale (as well as the contract of sale) must meet all the mandatory requirements (these are dealt with in more detail in 4.3) and serves as a receipt of payment in full. After the purchase contract has been signed but before the second stage has been undertaken, the buyer may protect the contract by his application for registration of his title for the property, which will then be noted in the registry.

4.1.3 There is no need for the notarisation of any transaction, the matter being dealt with entirely between the lawyers to each of the parties with no third party or notary being required to formalise the transaction. Following completion, one of the documents, usually the bill of sale, must be submitted to the land registry at which time it becomes a public document. The municipality may only exercise its right of pre-emption (see 1.3.2) within three months from the buyer's application for registration of the transfer and while the application is still pending. The municipality is barred from taking action once the buyer has actually become the new registered owner of the land. On the transfer of apartment blocks, it is also necessary to notify the municipality of the agreement within two months, which may direct the parties to seek the consent of the regional rent tribunal. A failure to comply with the notification requirements will render the transfer void (see 1.3.3).

4.2 Contract terms

4.2.1 The contract will usually contain warranties and will often stipulate the payment of a deposit, commonly up to 10 per cent of the purchase price, which may, under the agreement, be forfeited to the seller if the transaction does not complete. The contract will also specify the timetable for the date of completion. It will also commonly specify the arrangements for the payment of interest, commonly at eight per cent above the Swedish discount rate, should there be a delay in completion, and vacant possession will be given on completion unless the property is let, when apportionment of service charge, rent and insurance premiums will be required. Risk passes on the transfer date which will be the date of the bill of sale.

4.2.2 The seller is by law only responsible for latent defects in the property, even if he is unaware of these. It is common to have the property inspected by a surveyor before the contract is signed. However, contracts sometimes include clauses whereby the seller excludes liability for latent defects. There are also numerous examples of specific warranties, by which the seller takes responsibility for other defects. Defects detected after the contract date do not entitle the buyer to any remedy. Where the seller is responsible for a defect, the buyer has to give notice within a reasonable time of discovery but is entitled to a corresponding reduction in price. The buyer may also claim damages where there has been negligence or a breach of warranty. An action for termination of the agreement may be brought for a major defect if brought within one year. (This one year limit will not apply if the seller is guilty of gross negligence).

4.2.3 If either party defaults, the other party can apply to the local court for an order of specific performance compelling the defaulting party to complete, or he may treat the contract as repudiated and be entitled to damages. If the buyer delays, the seller can charge interest, and the seller may also often forfeit the buyer's deposit if the buyer fails to complete.

4.3 Formalities

4.3.1 Any contract for the sale of ownership or leasehold must be in writing and signed by both parties or their agents. An oral agreement will not be valid. The contract must include a declaration that the seller conveys the property to the buyer, and the name and the code of the property unit and the purchase price. A failure to witness the seller's signature will not render the agreement void but may cause a delay in the registration procedure. If the seller is an individual and is married or cohabits, written consent will be required from the spouse or partner. Failure to obtain written consent will render the agreement void.

4.3.2 There is no mandatory requirement for a lease agreement for commercial or residential buildings to be made in writing, although written lease agreements are almost always used and either party may request one. It is common to incorporate all the agreed terms into the contract, although complementary oral side agreements are permissible. A written agreement does not have to be registered to be binding.

4.4 Fees, costs and taxes

4.4.1 On a sale of land, the seller will usually pay the agent's commission, although the cost may sometimes be borne by the buyer. The buyer will pay the stamp duty, which will become payable when his title to the property is registered, as well as the land registry fees. Legal costs are borne by each party and usually both sides instruct separate lawyers. The agent's commission will vary according to the agent, the type and value of the property. Fees commonly range from one to five per cent of the sale price, the upper range reflecting commission for small residential property and the lower, commission for large blocks of flats and commercial properties. Where a rent agreement is negotiated by an agent, the commission is commonly 5 to 10 per cent of the first year's rent. Agents' commissions will usually only be payable if the transaction completes.

4.4.2 Lawyers' fees are usually charged whether or not the transaction is successful as the Swedish Bar Association will not normally permit contingency fees. Lawyers' fees are based on a combination of the expertise needed, the value of the property, and time. These are commonly between SEK20,000 and SEK200,000 but may be more.

4.4.3 Stamp duty is charged at 1.5 per cent of the purchase price where the buyer is an individual and at three per cent where it is a company. For 1997, stamp duty is temporarily set down to one-third of the normal rate (a transfer of shares does not affect stamp duty). Alternatively the stamp duty will be based on the rateable value of the property for the year prior to registration of ownership, whichever is the higher. A distinction must be made between leasehold (*tomträtt* as described in 1.1.2) and contractual land leases (see section 5). The transfer of leasehold might trigger stamp duty, whereas the granting of a leasehold will not. Neither the grant nor the transfer of a contractual tenancy will trigger stamp duty.

4.4.4 The land registry will charge minor fees when registering title to the land, for the issue of a bill of mortgage and for other entries in the land register. These fees, which are calculated on a flat rate basis, are relatively low and do not at present exceed SEK1,000.

4.4.5 Total transaction costs involved are usually three to five per cent of the purchase price, although these may vary from one type of property to another.

4.4.6 Agents' and lawyers' fees attract value added tax (VAT), currently at a rate of 25 per cent. This is charged on all property transactions, although exceptions are made where legal services are 'exported', ie rendered on behalf of foreign entities.

4.5 Professionals' roles

The marketing and sale of land are often conducted by estate agents. Estate agents are subject to statutory control and there is a statutory duty to act in the interest of both parties, a breach of which may be actionable. The agent will normally represent the seller and he may draft the contract if the sale is a minor transaction. In major transactions and those concerning commercial property, the contract will usually be drafted by the lawyers (and the parties will usually compete over the initiation of the drafting of the contract). Surveyors will represent the buyer in undertaking a survey of the property and in major transactions each party will be represented by his own lawyer. There is, though, no role for a notary or official, and the land registry processes registration.

5 LEASES AND OTHER RIGHTS OF OCCUPATION

Rights of occupation may take the form of a leasehold, *Tomträtt*, which is described at 1.1.2 and falls little short of freehold, and contractual tenancies, being land leases (*Arrende*) and building leases (*Hyra*). Contractual tenancies are usually in writing but are not required to be. Building leases are described at 5.1 to 5.5 and land leases are described at 5.6.

5.1 Length of term and termination

5.1.1 Commercial tenancies

5.1.1.1 The term of the commercial tenancy may be fixed or continuous. The most common arrangement is to grant a lease for a fixed period of three or five years. There are however many examples of both shorter and longer tenancy periods on the rental market. Industrial buildings are often let for a period longer than three years. In towns and cities the term of the tenancy must not exceed 25 years but in the country a maximum tenancy period of 50 years is allowed. There are no restrictions regarding the minimum term of the tenancy.

5.1.1.2 When the tenancy period is continuous, the tenancy runs for an indefinite time and a party wishing to terminate the tenancy has to give notice nine months in advance, unless a longer notice period is agreed upon by the parties. When the tenancy period is fixed, the term of notice required is still nine months, unless a longer term of notice is agreed upon. Shorter terms of notice are valid only if the fixed tenancy period is less than nine months. The parties are of course free to agree on an immediate termination or surrender at any time.

5.1.2 Residential tenancies

In general, residential tenancies are let for a continuous period. If so, the lease agreement may be terminated by giving notice three months in advance. They may, however, also be let for a fixed period. In such cases, the tenant may give three full calendar months' notice of termination at any time during the tenancy period. The landlord, on the other hand, can only terminate the agreement at the expiry of the tenancy period.

5.2 Rent control and security of tenure

5.2.1 Commercial leases

Unless the landlord has very sound reasons not to prolong the lease, eg tenant default, or a need to occupy the premises for his own purposes, the tenant of commercial premises is entitled to compensation, in principle, for all of his losses, should the landlord give notice of termination and the tenant thus be obliged to vacate. The right to compensation is lost if the landlord offers the tenant a prolongation of the lease on suitable market conditions and the tenant does not accept these. Since the right to compensation is linked to the termination of the lease agreement and depends on the landlord's tender regarding the continuance of the lease, this right is normally referred to as the tenant's indirect right to prolongation of the agreement. A tenant may waive his right to prolongation or compensation in a separate document. Such agreement must be acknowledged by the rent tribunal, unless the lease has lasted for nine months at the time of signing the waiver agreement. However, it is unusual that the tenant's right of compensation is deleted.

5.2.2 Residential leases

If a lease for residential purpose is terminated by the landlord, the tenant, in principle, has the right to prolongation of the lease agreement. This right can only be lost if the tenant has been in breach of the lease agreement in ways specified by law or if the landlord has other sound reasons for the agreement to be terminated. In many cases when the tenant is in breach of contract, he may regain his right to prolongation by remedying his breaches. Non-payment is one obvious reason for a landlord to terminate the lease agreement, but there is a possibility for the tenant to regain the right to prolongation by paying the rent within three weeks from notice of termination. For rare purposes, the tenant of a residential lease may waive his right to prolongation by signing a separate agreement, which must be approved by the rent tribunal, should the lease have lasted less than nine months when the waiver agreement is signed.

5.3 The rent

5.3.1 Commercial leases

5.3.1.1 The parties are free to agree on the rent for commercial premises. Commercial tenants commonly pay extra for heating, value added tax (VAT) (if the tenant is liable for VAT) and property tax. Retail premises and hotels amongst others are sometimes let on a turnover basis and the rent determined as a percentage of the income generated by the tenant at the premises. Usually the rent is linked to changes in the consumer price index of every year. However, such indexation is not allowed if the tenancy period is shorter than three years. The purpose of this is to give the tenant longer tenancy periods. The minimum term requirement for indexation came into force in 1979 and was extended during the 1980s. The legislation was intended to create protection for the tenant from raised rental charges, since the market rent during this period often increased substantially more than the consumer price index.

5.3.1.2 Rent reviews – and renegotiation of other terms and conditions of the tenancy agreement – may be conducted on the potential expiry of the lease period. Notice of rent review must accordingly be given by one of the parties at the same time as notice of termination would have been given if the intention was to end the lease. If a landlord, as a condition for prolonging a commercial lease, demands an excessive rent compared to the market rent, the tenant is entitled to compensation if he does not accept the demanded rent and the lease is thus terminated. However, the right to compensation is waived if the tenant does not submit the matter to the regional rent tribunal (*hyresnämnden*) in accordance with the law concerning prolongation as described in 5.2.1.

5.3.2 Residential leases

5.3.2.1 A party to a residential lease agreement may demand renegotiation with the other party and claim that one or more of the terms and conditions (most commonly the rent) should be amended. Should the other party refuse to change the conditions, the initiator of the negotiations may submit the issue for decision by the rent tribunal. The landlord must follow the tribunal's decision. The rent tribunal will determine the rent for residential apartments according to the legal regulations on utilisation value, which means, as a rule, that the rent must not substantially exceed the rents for residential premises set by the non profit-making, public utility property holders. Therefore, it can be said that there is no free rental market for residential leases.

5.3.2.2 Except by mutual agreement between the landlord and the tenant, the rent can only be changed without the rent tribunal if there is a clause in the lease agreement referring to special institutional negotiations held between representatives of the landlord and a tenant's association. Such negotiations have in practice during recent years resulted in a stable rise in residential rents more or less in accordance with Swedish inflation. The rent for a dwelling cannot be linked to the consumer price index.

5.4 Other conditions

5.4.1 Commercial leases

5.4.1.1 Often, when letting commercial premises, a special standard form contract is used. This standard form has been worked out by the organisations representing landlords and tenants. The parties are free to agree on the responsibility and the duty to pay for the maintenance of the premises. It is not unusual that such responsibility lies upon the tenant. A tenant is not entitled to sublet the entire premises without the landlord's permission. In some cases permission can also be obtained from the rent tribunal. However, parts of the premises can always be sublet without permission if the parties have not agreed otherwise. In principle, a tenant has no right to transfer a tenancy contract without the consent of the landlord. Yet, it is possible to effect an assignment despite the opposition of the landlord if it takes place in connection with the assignment of a business conducted on the premises. Permission from the rent tribunal is required. It is easier to effect an assignment if the lease has lasted longer than three years. There are also other situations where permission from the rent tribunal for the transfer of a tenancy may be obtained. Insurance of the building is usually carried out by the landlord.

5.4.1.2 As regards commercial premises for retailers, it is not unusual that a tenant charges a new tenant a transfer fee ('a fee for the key') when the tenancy agreement is transferred, should the rent be less than a fair market rent and the term be for a fixed period. It is otherwise unusual for a premium to be paid on the transfer or grant of any tenancy. Security for performance such as a bank guarantee is sometimes required.

5.4.2 Residential leases

Standard contracts are often used when letting residences. There are normally few amendments made to such contracts. The tenant is in principle not entitled to sublet the flat without the consent of the landlord. Partial subletting is permitted and the rent tribunal may grant permission for subletting of the whole in some situations. The tenant has a right to transfer the tenancy to his spouse or other relatives living in the flat and in some situations in order to exchange flats with someone else. Permission from the rent tribunal is required. If the tenant dies, the heirs living in the flat may take over the tenancy agreement. It is unlawful both for the former tenant and the landlord to charge a transfer fee to a tenant to whom a residential lease has been transferred. The landlord is also not entitled to charge a fee, except for the rent, for letting a flat. On the other hand, the landlord may pay a tenant to surrender a tenancy contract on a voluntary basis.

5.5 Privity of contract and estate

The doctrine of privity of contract known in common law systems where the original tenant is liable for breaches of contract even after he has assigned the lease agreement to a third party does not apply in Sweden. Such assignment needs the approval of the landlord.

5.6 Land lease

5.6.1 Land lease (*Arrende*) is a lease of the bare land (although it may involve buildings) and may be agricultural (ie for the purpose of farming on the leased land), residential (ie to erect dwellings on the leased land), or commercial (ie to erect buildings for commercial or industrial activities on the leased land). Disputes concerning land leases are settled by the regional tenancies tribunal (*Arrendenämnden*). The buildings erected by the tenant will belong to the tenant. A land lease must be in writing.

5.6.2 The term of an agricultural land lease must be fixed, but there are no limitations as to the minimum time period, unless the lease includes a residence, in which case the period of contract must be at least five years. For residential land leases, the term of contract must not be less than five years. The lease will automatically be extended for another term, unless notice has been given prior to the contractual expiration. The rent must be set as a fixed amount, but it is customary to have clauses indexing the rent.

5.6.3 The legislation applicable to commercial land leases is to a large extent similar to the regulations for commercial tenancies.

5.7 Method of measurement

There are standard regulations set by the professional bodies and generally accepted by the market as to how to take walls, staircases, lavatories etc into consideration when measuring the size of commercial or residential premises. Both net and gross figures may be used, ie either excluding common areas, lavatories, or including the whole floor area wall to wall.

6 FINANCE AND INVESTMENT SOURCES

Swedish banks and finance companies provide finance mainly in the form of loans but also by way of leasing. The other principal source of funds is equity finance.

6.1 Loan finance

The traditional sources of loan finance are the banks, some big insurance companies and finance companies. Conventional loan finance is normally for a fixed term, commonly two, three, five or ten years, with fixed interest although interest rates may be variable, and will commonly provide for repayment by instalments during the term of the loan, extending to 30 years or more in some cases. Interest will be calculated by reference to the lender's own base rate or to the funding cost with a calculated margin, normally between 0.5 to 3 per cent, over the funding cost. Such loans will almost invariably be secured and the security risk is the factor which will influence the banks' willingness to lend. The legal framework for mortgage loans is outlined at 7.1. Small companies will sometimes borrow money from their shareholders, whereas public companies may do so in the form of a convertible debenture. Debenture-holders will normally be given preferential treatment over ordinary shareholders, eg by giving them earlier rights to interest.

6.2 Investment or equity finance

The vehicles for equity or investment finance are somewhat limited. A small, privately held company will be financed by the shareholders providing share capital and sometimes subordinated debentures and warrants. For companies quoted on the stock market the options are more numerous and will, in addition to share capital, include bonds, which are not commonly used, commercial paper or loan stock and convertible debentures and warrants. A number of property holding companies of various sizes and focusing on various geographical regions and types of property are quoted on the Stockholm Stock Exchange.

6.3 Mezzanine or mixed funding

A bank or prime lender will usually take the first security and lend 60–80 per cent of the value of the property. There are lenders who will provide the next 10–20 per cent of the finance and who will take a return by way of a higher interest rate and/or a share in the equity in the property. Equally there are lenders who will provide both prime and mezzanine funding. During the early 1990s, the banks and the finance companies became more reluctant to grant loans related to property investments, although banks and the finance companies are now more willing to grant loans again.

6.4 Sale and lease-back

There are no statutory provisions at present governing sale and lease-back or leasing transactions for property although legislation on the subject is coming into force intended to make the lessee the 'economic owner' of the leased assets, and the lessee would thus be required to account for the property in its balance sheet. However, sale and lease-back arrangements have, for some time, been a popular way for large companies to finance the property from which they conduct business. The most frequently used method is the sale and a subsequent lease-back where the seller/lessor retains an option to repurchase the property. This will either be done directly, in which case the option is not legally enforceable (see 2.4) but the parties trust each other and it is a straightforward arrangement; or indirectly, by purchase through a company, or a partnership created with the single purpose of owning the property.

6.5 Tax leasing

Tax leasing as a property investment vehicle has very little scope in Sweden.

6.6 Other types of property finance

'Securitisation' has recently become increasingly popular with local authorities particularly to finance public sector apartment blocks. The owner of the property issues bonds for which bills of mortgage (see 7.1) are given as security. The advantage of secured bonds, over conventional loan finance, is that the bonds are designed to be quoted on the stock exchange and are therefore more liquid and more easily transferred between investors. While less relevant to the property market, factoring, the selling of a companies' receivables, is another way of raising money.

6.7 Institutional investment

Property is a major area for investment and part of many institutional and pension fund investment portfolios. The life insurance companies and the pension funds are therefore very influential in property management; and the insurance companies will usually set the standards which will apply throughout the market, although the institutional investor does not establish the norm for lease contracts. The long-term management philosophy espoused, ie not merely applying measures for short-term shareholder value at the expense of the company's (or property's) long-term goals and welfare, indicates that the institutions may pay prices that entail negative cash flow and they are reluctant to sell their properties. Institutions and funds seek property in prime locations and in first class buildings. There are normally a variety of commercial buildings and apartment blocks in the institutional property portfolios, but there are institutions specialising in different sectors.

6.8 Investors other than institutions

Other investors on the property market range from property investing quoted companies, normally specialising in the commercial or in the residential sector or a mixture of these sectors, to private investors, normally concentrating on apartment blocks with less flexible rental rates.

7 FORMS OF SECURITY

Swedish banks do not commonly grant loans for property investments by reference to the creditworthiness of a customer alone, and banks will usually demand a mortgage as security. It is very uncommon for loans to be secured solely by the asset, without personal liability on the part of the borrower. The main forms of security used for long-term bank loans are mortgages on property, corporate mortgages (floating charges) or guarantees. Limited company shares, especially in quoted companies, may also be used as security (collateral).

7.1 Mortgages

7.1.1 Only the registered owner of land (or leasehold) can mortgage the property (or leasehold) and, where appropriate, approval of the spouse is required. Mortgages will need to be protected by registration. After an application to the land registry, the owner receives a bill of mortgage for the amount specified. The security is perfected when the bill of mortgage is in the possession of the lender. There is no limit as to the total face value of the bills of mortgage that may be issued. However, the actual value of the bill of mortgage issued is naturally limited to the value of the property. If the full amount of the bill of mortgage is not needed to cover the debt, any excess may be used as collateral for some other debt or obligation. Notice must be served on the existing holder of the bill of mortgage where further security is required, before a second mortgage can take effect. Stamp duty is charged at two per cent of the face value of a bill of mortgage issued by the land registry. Bills of mortgage are always issued by the land registry. The bill of mortgage may then be granted by the landowner as security. Whereas the issue of the bill of mortgage triggers stamp duty, the granting of security does not. Once the loan is repaid the bill of mortgage is returned and can be used again as security for a new loan without additional cost.

7.1.2 The mortgagee can bring an action before the court and claim payment and obtain a declaration that the property is distrained and the property will then be sold by public auction. He may not petition for bankruptcy so long as the security is adequate. A mortgagee may not appoint a receiver. If the land is sold at public auction, a mortgagee (or a second mortgagee) will receive payment on his claim (provided the claim amounts to the face value of the bill or less) and a 15 per cent statutory addition intended to cover any unpaid interest subject to the requirement that the realised value of the assets covers the mortgage in question and the mortgages with higher priority. Any excess proceeds will be paid to the owner or to other creditors. For the priority of mortgages see 2.10.

7.2 Floating and other charges

Swedish law does not provide any system for debentures with specific advantages for property finance or give the debenture holder any right to appoint an administrative receiver or power to stop other creditors from enforcing their claims. Equipment used in the course of business, and trade debtors, may though be used as collateral by registration of a corporate mortgage akin to a floating charge (*företagshypotek*). A corporate mortgage is created by an application to the registration authority (located in Malmö) which will then issue a bill of corporate mortgage. The mortgage normally creates a charge over the entire business of the debtor company in Sweden, but it can also be restricted to a specific part of the company's undertaking. The mortgage will create a charge over all the assets belonging to the company, with the exception of cash, bank deposits, shares and other securities, and assets that may be mortgaged separately, such as ships and land, which never fall within the floating charge. As the specific assets of the company over which the charge is created may change over time, it is only when the mortgage is enforced that it will be possible to determine the actual assets secured.

7.3 Performance bonds and guarantees

It is common for banks and financial institutions to ask for guarantees from a third party. They will be called upon to repay the loan and any interest should there be a default by the borrower, where the borrower's credit worthiness is not adequate, especially in situations where the financed property is held by a subsidiary, although performance guarantees may also be issued by insurance companies and banks. Swedish law does not distinguish between guarantees and bonds and only actual losses will be made good. Due to stamp duty in property transactions, property investing company groups sometimes organise their property investments in such a way that each property unit will be held by a separate limited company or limited partnership. Where private property investments are made through limited companies or limited partnerships, banks may ask for guarantees from the shareholders.

7.4 Credit insurance

There are situations where a credit risk can be insured against. Due to the bankruptcy of some of the credit risk insuring companies in Sweden in the early 1990s, it has become less frequent to use credit insurances to secure property loans in recent years.

8 PLANNING AND BUILDING REGULATION

The development and use of land and buildings is subject to controls comprised within the Planning and Building Act (*Plan-och bygglagen*, PBA). The Management of Natural Resources Act aims to integrate the conservation of natural resources and the concept of sustainable development into planning policy.

8.1 Planning authorities

On a local level, decisions are taken by one of the approximately 300 local municipalities and, as planning decisions are not always taken by elected representatives, planning control is not particularly influenced by political considerations. No administrative body other than the municipalities has the power to make planning decisions, although certain decisions may be taken by the administrative courts where municipality decisions have been appealed against.

8.2 Development plans

8.2.1 Under the PBA, the municipalities prepare and adopt plans regulating the use of land and water for their area. The different kinds of plans are land overviews (*översiktsplan*), area plans (*regionplan*) and detail plans (*detaljplan*). A detail plan sets out the detailed policies and proposals for the development and use of land applicable to a limited area within the local authority's remit (normally a specific district within a town) and is binding on the authorities as well as the individuals during the time period within which the plan is to be accomplished.

8.2.2 The detail plan states a time period ranging from 5 to 15 years during which the plan's objectives may be accomplished. The accomplishment period may be prolonged. The property owner is in principle entitled to a building permit if the development project adheres to the plan and the applicable construction standards. Where development is in theory acceptable outside detail pan areas there is no guarantee that the local building committee will automatically grant the permit, although a landowner may in these circumstances appeal a negative decision. There is no discretion involved on the municipality's part, although small deviations from the plan may sometimes be acceptable. Public discussions will take place before plans are finally adopted.

8.3 Planning control and procedure

Building permits are required from the local authority before starting construction work for all 'development'. The PBA details what constitutes development and what does not. Permits are compulsory for altering, extending or demolishing buildings and installations and for any material change of use of a building or a part of it. The issue of change of use most commonly occurs where the owner of the property wants to change the use of a flat from residential to office use. The PBA also contains provisions with respect to demolition permits and permits regarding ground works. Demolition permits and ground works permits, which may subsequently be changed to building permits, will sometimes be issued to enable the development to commence; applications for these permits will also be dealt with by the municipal building committee (*Byggnadsnämnden*), which is part of the local municipal authority. Certain development will require consent under environmental legislation (see 9.5).

8.3.1 If a building permit is required, applications are sent to the municipal building committee. The applicant need not be the landowner, although if he is not, the permit will not grant him any right against the landowner. Before making a decision, the building committee may sometimes consult neighbours and adjoining landowners, although it should be noted that the building committee has very little discretion with regard to the question of publication. It is possible to apply to the building committee to issue a preliminary statement as to whether a building or an installation requiring a building permit may be permitted on the intended site and is considered an acceptable use of the land.

8.3.2 The decisions of the building committee may be appealed against to the county administrative board, which in turn may be challenged. The right of appeal is confined to those who are regarded as having a formal interest in the decision; this category of people will include neighbours.

8.3.3 A building permit ceases to be valid if the construction works have not been started within two years and completed within five years from the date the permit was granted.

8.3.4 The authorities have no power to force property owners to take positive action to accomplish the plans. If development requiring a building permit is begun without one, the building committee may instigate proceedings requesting the landowner to stop the works and to demolish or restore the building. In principle there is no time limit for enforcement, although in practice where action has not been taken for a number of years, the building committee is unlikely to initiate proceedings but may require the developer to apply for a building permit. The building committee has the power to demand a building fee from the property owner if a building permit is not applied for when one is required. This fee will be four times the standard fee for granting a building permit as a penalty for the work carried out without obtaining a permit. In less serious cases, the building committee may instead decide to demand a special fee amounting to a maximum of SEK1,000. In cases at the most serious end of the scale, the building committee may finally take court action to demand an additional fee amounting to SEK 500 for each square metre of the development, where the project is commenced without a building permit where one is required. Upon completion, the municipality will inspect the finalised development.

8.4 Building standards, control and supervision

In obtaining a building permit, a developer automatically obtains approval of the project's compliance with the construction standards set up by the building committee. This will be dealt with at the same time as the application for the permit (see 8.3).

8.5 Protection of buildings of special interest and building relics

A building which is considered to be of significant cultural and historical value or which is part of an area that is of cultural and/or historic significance, may be declared a building relic (*byggnadsminne*) by the county administrative board which regulates the protection of listed buildings. The owner's obligation is to maintain the building as at the time of listing but the obligation does not extend to restoring the building to its original authentic state and the owner may be entitled to compensation for the extra costs he faces as a result of the restrictions imposed. The Act on Cultural Relics (*Kulturminneslagen*) regulates the precautions to be taken by a developer where churches may be on or near a development site, and also covers measures to be taken where ancient relics are found on a construction site; in some cases excavation costs may be imposed upon the developer.

8.6 Expropriation and compulsory purchase and compensation

For specific reasons, such as the construction of major infrastructure facilities, land needed to carry out a project may be expropriated by compulsory purchase, or by compulsory occupation of the land under a lease or by creation of a compulsory servitude over the land. In principle, a private developer may initiate the process, but only where a public purpose is intended, eg in connection with a transport project or for the construction of industrial plants. Permission to expropriate property is granted by the government or the county administrative board, which will consider the purpose of expropriation. Compensation, considered by the local court for property cases (*fastighetsdomstolen*), will be determined principally on the basis of market value at the time of expropriation but will not include expected increases in value after acquisition. There is no uplift or addition for the inconvenience or disruption. Detailed regulations governing compulsory purchase and compensation are set out in the Expropriation Act.

9 ENVIRONMENTAL MATTERS

The structure of Swedish environmental legislation is complex and many acts overlap. Pollution control is regulated by numerous statutes, but the Environmental Protection Act of 1969 (*Miljöskyddslagen*, EPA) and the Chemical Products Act are the most important, although a new environmental code is to be expected in the near future. The polluting activities to which the EPA applies include the use of land, buildings or other constructions on a site which may harm the environment by the pollution of ground water, air, space and land. The Tort Liability Act (TLA) and the Environmental Tort Liability Act (ETLA) regulate the apportionment of environmental liability. Liability for personal injury, damage to property and pure economic loss is strict where damage has been caused by industrial plants or other installations with a similar potentially hazardous environmental impact. However, liability will not be strict and will be limited to negligence for disturbances which should reasonably be tolerated in the particular locality or as a result of their general occurrence.

The EPA only applies to stationary sources of pollution or nuisances and not to mobile sources. Stationary sources include specific sources such as factories, oil pipes and roads and non-specific sources such as leakage of pollutants from agricultural land and forests. The EPA applies to noise, light and vibrations nuisance provided these originate from a stationary source. Control under the EPA is based upon licensing requirements for specified activities (see 9.2). It is a strict liability criminal offence under the EPA to operate without compliance with the requisite licencing procedure.

The licensing authorities under the EPA are the National Franchise Board for Environmental Protection (*Koncessionsnämnden för miljöskydd*) and the county administrative board (*Länsstyrelsen*). The county administrative board and municipalities have principal responsibility for supervision and their decisions can usually be appealed to the National Franchise Board. A permit is valid for a period of 10 years. During this period, the operator can carry on his commercial activities in accordance with the licensing requirements although new terms may be issued or the licence may be withdrawn, eg in the event of a substantial change of circumstances or considerable technological and scientific improvements. Further controls are imposed in respect of the handling and storage of chemicals under the Chemical Products Act.

9.1 Protection against atmospheric and noise pollution

The EPA integrates controls and so the question of atmospheric and noise pollution is dealt with above.

9.2 Water pollution

The EPA applies to the pollution of water and the licensing requirements (described above) apply equally to water pollution activity.

9.3 Waste storage and disposal

Waste storage and disposal are regulated by the Waste Collection and Disposal Act (*Renhållningslagen*) which requires waste management to be undertaken in such a way as to promote the reuse and recycling of waste where the aim is to save raw materials or energy, or with due regard to environmental conservation. Each municipality is responsible for ensuring that domestic waste in its area is transported to treatment installations whilst observing public health, conservation area and individual interest requirements. The municipality is also to ensure that household waste from its area is finally disposed of by recycling, composting or final disposition. There are further provisions regulating the producer's responsibility for ensuring that waste from packaging is removed, reused, recycled or dealt with as appropriate, as well as various other Acts and ordinances which regulate more specific issues such as the transport of hazardous waste and batteries.

9.4 Contaminated land

The EPA also deals with waste on land. The main principle underpinning the EPA is that anyone engaging in environmentally hazardous activities must implement safety measures, accept restrictions on the way the activities are undertaken and take any precautionary measures that may reasonably be required in order to prevent or remedy disturbances caused by the activity. The EPA also covers activity on a site no longer in use but which has caused the site or its surroundings to become contaminated. Recent case law indicates that an undertaking which ceased its environmentally hazardous activities or transferred its assets prior to 1 July 1988 cannot be held liable for contamination caused before 1988 provided the company operated in accordance with an EPA permit and the permit made no provision for the regulation of future contamination. The EPA seeks to impose the 'polluter pays' principle by imposing liability primarily on the present or latest operator and the obligation to rectify or neutralise the effect of past industrial activity which has led to the contamination of the land. If the operator cannot be found or no longer exists, a past operator or the present owner of the land may, under certain circumstances, be liable for the clean-up costs. A lender or a mortgagee may not be held liable. The main purpose of remediation is not to restore the land to its original condition but to reduce on-going leachate migration and to prevent nuisances occurring. There is no register of contaminated land to assist buyers when making their enquiries, although there is a proposal for its introduction incorporated in the 1996 Committee report preparing a new environmental code.

9.5 Environmental impact assessments

The Management of Natural Resources Act, a general planning Act, imposes the obligation to take both conservation and economic interests into account. An ordinance under this Act applies when decisions are taken under other statutes, including the EPA, and imposes the requirement to undertake environmental impact assessments. An assesment is required for all hazardous activities listed in the Environmental Protection Ordinance (*Miljösskyddsförordningen,* EPO), and which require licence or notification under the EPA. The list includes industrial activities, mining, large agricultural farms, airports and certain military installations.

10 DEVELOPMENT

10.1 Development projects, structures and vehicles

A simple development project might involve the purchase of a site by an owner/occupier, if the land is not already owned by him, with the construction of the premises he requires by his own builder. Alternatively an owner/occupier may approach a developer to arrange both the site and the development. In these circumstances, the developer might undertake the development himself and sell or let it on completion; or do this as project manager or agent for the occupier or investor. A developer may also 'forward sell' the property to an institution, enabling the institution to acquire the site at an early stage, finance the development and then let the building, giving the developer a share in the value or profit. Developments may be funded by the lending banks on straight commercial loans. Speculative development has not generally been undertaken since the recession. In spite of extensive codification generally, construction contracts used for development projects are not subject to any specific legislation, which has resulted in the extensive use of standard forms of contract. As these standard forms are so widely used in Sweden, any discussion of the rights and obligations of the parties involves referring to their content and how they are most commonly used (see 10.2).

10.2 Building contracts and appointment of professionals

10.2.1 Typical forms of building contract

It is common to make a distinction between divided contracts, general contracts and total contracts. In a divided contract, the employer contracts directly with the consultants and the contractors. The consultants and the contractors all have separate agreements with the employer but not with each other. In a divided contract the employer accepts a significant amount of the responsibility for organising, controlling and coordinating the activities on the construction site. In a general contract the employer reaches an agreement with a single contractor, the 'general contractor'. There are two different types of general contract. In the 'pure' general contract, the employer does not enter into any agreements other than with the general contractor and has no influence on the choice of subcontractors. In the case of an 'organised' general contract, the employer invites tenders from different contractors and eventually enters into separate agreements with each different contractor. After he has concluded the agreements, he will transfer these agreements to a single contractor, who will then act as the general contractor and take on the other contractors as subcontractors. In principle, the contractor assumes total liability, and it is usual for the subcontractors not to be under any direct liability to the employer. In a divided and general contract, the employer will be responsible for the design. In a total contract the employer enters only into one agreement with a single contractor and assigns to him the responsibility for the design as well as the construction of the building. Where a total contract covers not only the construction of the building, but also the installations in a plant, the term 'turn key project' is commonly used. The standard form contract (see 10.2.3) provides that fees may be variable or payable in a fixed sum covering the entire project. Variable fees are based generally on a prime cost or other agreed basis.

10.2.2 Common terms

Payment is usually made in instalments during the project. The payment plan normally stipulates that the employer shall pay the contractor 90 (sometimes 95) per cent of the value of the work carried out during the construction phase, in accordance with fixed stages of construction. The remaining payment is released after the approval of the works, upon completion. Where the contract is for a variable fee, the contractor sends the final invoice to the employer within six months from the time of approval of the works. Any later requests for payment need not be acknowledged by the employer and payment may be forfeited. The parties will agree on a time schedule, which the contractor must adhere to. If the work is not completed by the contractual completion date, the agreement will often stipulate that the contractor shall pay liquidated damages to the employer, in which case no other damages will be payable. If the agreement does not include provisions concerning liquidated damages, damages are limited to an amount equal to the contractor's total fee, and may not exceed 10 times the 'base sum' (in 1997, this amounted approximately to

SEK350,000). However, the contractor may be granted an extension of time if the delay is due to factors outside his control, and the effect of which he could not reasonably have mitigated. For provisions regulating the defects and maintenance period, see 10.4.

10.2.3 Standard form of contract

The most frequently used contract between employer and contractor or subcontractor is the General Conditions of Contract for Building and Civil Engineering Works and Building Services, AB 92. These conditions have been published in a number of different versions over the years (for instance AB 54, AB 65 and AB 72), where the number indicates the publication year. AB 92 is published by the Construction Contracts Committee, which consists of representatives from the Organisation of Building Owners and the Organisation of Contractors. The total contract, where the contractor is responsible not only for construction but also for design, is commonly regulated by the General Conditions of Contract for Total Contracts concerning Building and Civil Engineering Works and Building Services ABT 94, although it should be noted that most of the provisions in ABT 94 are identical or similar to those contained in AB 92. Where the employer is an individual consumer, the General Conditions of Agreement for Small House Contracts, ABS 95, is commonly used.

10.2.4 Appointment of the professional team

The standard form of contract normally used in contracts with the various consultants, eg project managers, architects and building engineers, is the 1987 General Rules of Agreement for Architectural and Engineering Consulting Services, ABK 87. These conditions have been prepared by the Construction Contracts Committee representing the clients and the Swedish Association of Consulting Architects and the Swedish Association of Consulting Engineers representing the consultants. They are also used in total contracts between contractor and consultant. The consultant is obliged to define his role and the budget for the job. The fee may be a lump sum or variable usually depending on the hours worked.

10.3 Roles of the various parties

The contractor must provide supervision during the execution of the works and during the design phase, where this is within the scope of the assignment. AB 92 provides that the contractor alone is authorised to direct the execution of the works although the employer has the right to inspect the works at his discretion but these inspections do not limit the contractor's responsibility under the contract. The employer has to be notified when goods and materials are available for inspection. Negotiations concerning variations of design and technical issues during the course of the work will be recorded by the employer and will be checked and signed by the contractor. The standard form contract (see 10.2.4) provides that the consultant is responsible for everything which is required of him for the performance of the assignment in accordance with what is specified in the contract documents, or which otherwise must be regarded as forming part of the assignment.

10.4 Defects and remedies

10.4.1 Under AB 92 the contractor is liable to the employer for negligent damage. Formal inspection is carried out at expiry of the contract period. Defects reported are to be remedied by the contractor. Once the inspector accepts the works there is a two-year warranty period during which the contractor is liable for all defects that appear. After this the contractor is liable for substantial defects caused by his negligence.

10.4.2 The consultant will be liable for any negligent damage he may cause to the employer. ABK 87 (see 10.2.4) assumes that the parties agree on a limitation to the consultant's liability, which is limited to a sum based on the nature and scope of the agreement, and which will be specified in the contract. If no such liability has been agreed upon, the consultant's total liability for damages shall not exceed 100 times the 'base sum' (which in 1997 amounted to approximately SEK3.5 million) at the time the agreement was concluded. Unless otherwise agreed, the consultant will only be liable for damage discovered before the expiry of the defects liability period (normally two years from the date of completion and approval), and claims must be lodged in writing not later than three months after expiry of the limitation period. There is a seven-year limitation period on claims against the contractor, from the date of completion of the development. The normal limitation period and ceiling on damages will be waived where the contractor is guilty of gross negligence, in which case the limitation period will be 10 years.

10.2.3 Defects insurance

The standard form contract AB 92 requires the contractor to take out professional liability insurance as well as an all-risks insurance policy against damage caused to the works, with the employer also named as a party under the policy. Failing this the employer may take out the necessary cover himself at the contractor's expense. The professional liability insurance remains in force during the course of the works to cover the contractor's liability and continues to be valid for two years after the approval of the works to cover any defects in the building discovered during the defects period.

10.6 Copyright

The copyright in the design of the building will occasionally be protected under the Copyright Act but only in the unlikely event that the design falls within the statutory definition of 'intellectual work', meaning 'unique achievement'. Protection under the Act entitles the consultant alone to produce copies of the designs or to build houses according to them, although an owner may alter the buildings using the drawings without his prior consent.

10.7 Fees

Professional fees may be 6 to 8 per cent of the contract sum.

10.8 Taxes

All commercial construction projects are subject to value added tax (VAT) at the Swedish standard rate of 25 per cent. The construction company can choose to account for the VAT due, either on advance payments, or on completion of the contractual work.

11 TAXES

11.1 Corporation tax

Only companies incorporated under Swedish law are considered to be resident in Sweden and liable to Swedish corporation tax on their worldwide profits including capital gains (see 11.3), subject to relief under any double taxation treaty with the country where its profits originate, whether or not those profits are sent to Sweden. Foreign companies will only be taxed on income deemed to derive from Swedish sources. This applies principally to revenue attributable to landownership or to a permanent establishment in Sweden. A proposal to ensure that companies incorporated under foreign law shall be treated as resident in Sweden if their effective management is in Sweden has been delayed. (It should be noted that the 'effective management' requirement is not identical to the requirement of 'central management or control'.)

11.1.1 Tax rates

The rate of corporation tax rate is 28 per cent regardless of the size of the company. The tax is levied on the company's total net profits.

11.1.2 Computation and administration

In calculating its profits, a company can deduct expenses incurred for the purposes of the business of the company. This would extend to fees, commissions and loan interest as well as the usual deductions such as salaries and normal overheads. Taxes on ownership of property (see 11.4) are deductible for income tax purposes provided the property is owned by a business carried on by the taxpayer. Interest is deductible from income, regardless of to whom the interest is payable, and as to payments to companies within the same group, the transfer-pricing rules must be complied with. The tax payable by companies and individuals on income, including capital gains, is dealt with by the local tax authority, as is the calculation of taxes. The assessment is made by the local tax authority based upon a tax return provided by the taxpayer. Assessments are issued and, if unsatisfactory to the taxpayer, may be appealed against. Appeals can be taken to the administrative courts.

11.1.3 Depreciation and capital allowances

Expenditure on buildings must be capitalised and depreciated. Yearly depreciation rates generally follow the recommendations issued by the National Tax Board. Industrial buildings are depreciated at a rate of four to five per cent, buildings used for retail purposes at three per cent, whilst office buildings are depreciated at two per cent. Capital allowances accumulated by depreciation are taken back at the time of sale of the asset in question. Machinery is usually depreciated by the declining balance method. If the taxpayer maintains an adequate accounting record, the maximum depreciation allowance is 30 per cent of the aggregate book value of all assets at the beginning of the financial year, plus cost of assets acquired, less the amount received for assets sold or lost during the financial year. If a straight line depreciation of 20 per cent per annum on all assets results in a lower book value in any one year, the annual depreciation allowance may be increased accordingly. If the taxpayer can prove that the true value of machinery is lower than the result under the previously mentioned methods, depreciation may be allowed to the amount using the real value.

11.1.4 Withholding tax

Dividends paid by a Swedish subsidiary to a shareholder resident abroad are generally subject to a 30 per cent withholding tax on the gross dividend (*kupongskatt*). No withholding taxes are levied on payments of interest or royalties. Sweden has implemented the European Commission Directive under which payment of dividends from a Swedish company to a company holding more than 25 per cent of the share capital in the company is exempt from withholding tax in Sweden provided that the shareholder company is resident within another EU member state.

11.2 Taxes on development value

There are no taxes relating to the increase in value of land due to re-zoning or the value linked to development potential.

11.3 Taxes on capital gains

Any capital gain realised upon sale of property land or profits realised on gains in the value of investment shares of a company owning property will be included in the company's total net income and be subject to the income tax rate of 28 per cent.

11.4 Taxes on owner of property

Property taxes are levied on both individual and corporate owners of land. The tax is based upon a percentage of the rateable value of the premises. The levy on office buildings and other commercial buildings is 1 per cent and 0.5 per cent on industrial buildings. The rate for property housing one or two residential units and apartments is 1.7 per cent. There is no tax levied for the first five years after the completion of the building, and for the following five years the property is subject to 50 per cent of the usual rate. The tax will be set by an annual assessment by the local tax authority which also collects the tax. Certain types of property are exempt. Exemptions generally apply to buildings used for communication purposes such as train stations and buildings owned by certain specified entities, but also extend to school buildings and public buildings. Property which is donated or inherited is subject to gift tax and inheritance tax respectively. The basis for taxation is the rateable value of the property less any consideration from the recipient. The tax rate is progressive and amounts to 30 per cent in the highest bracket.

11.5 Taxes on occupier

There are no taxes levied on tenants, but the commercial tenancy agreement will usually provide that the tenant will reimburse the owner for the property tax.

11.6 Taxes on land transfer

The only direct tax on the transfer of land is stamp duty. This is charged on the price paid at 1.5 per cent for individuals and three per cent for corporate entities, and is payable by the buyer. The stamp duty is, however, reduced to 0.5 per cent for individuals and to one per cent for corporate entities where the purchase agreement was signed between 12 June 1996 and 31 December 1997 and the transfer registered by 31 March 1998 at the latest. There are no exemptions for properties worth less than a certain amount. Stamp duty will be levied where land is transferred within a group of companies although it is not payable on a transfer of shares.

11.7 Wealth taxes

Wealth tax is levied only on individuals resident in Sweden. The wealth tax is 1.5 per cent for net wealth in excess of SEK900,000.

11.8 Value added tax

There is no value added tax (VAT) or transfer tax (other than stamp duty) charged on transfers of land. With regard to rented property, the owner of commercial property may opt to register the premises in which commercial activities are carried out for VAT purposes, provided the tenant is liable for VAT. In this case the owner will charge VAT on rents and may deduct VAT on maintenance, repairs and other expenses as well as building costs. A tenant involved in commercial activities, may also apply for VAT registration of the building where the property is subleased to a subtenant carrying on activities subject to VAT. VAT is also administered by the local tax authority (see 11.1.2). Appeals relating to VAT can be taken to the administrative courts. If the owner disposes of the property within six years of registration for optional VAT, some or all of the VAT deducted will be subject to claw-back. A general VAT rate is levied at 25 per cent which applies also to property, although a reduced rate of 12 per cent applies to hotel rooms and transportation. A VAT rate of six per cent applies to companies providing sports facilities to the general public, which would include, for example, the short-term hire of tennis and badminton courts. The construction company may choose to account for VAT either on advance payments or at the time the work is completed.

11.9 Local and other taxes

There are no other local or other taxes of general application apart from the property taxes referred to above.

12 GRANTS AND INCENTIVES

Both central and local government provide investment incentives in many different forms. Most of these incentives are available to foreign as well as Swedish investors.

12.1 Subsidies, grants and loans

To support lower rent for residential apartments, governmental financial assistance in the form of 'property loan interest aid' is available to landlords and tenant-owner associations in connection with new construction and refurbishment of apartment blocks although this aid is being decreased over the next few years. The National Development Company (*Almi*), provides advisory as well as financial services in the form of loans and bank guarantees, but not state aid, for the benefit of small and medium-size enterprises investing in Sweden. The Fund for Industry (*Industrifonden*) supports promising industrial development projects involving large risks for a company.

12.2 Tax allowances and reliefs

Regional development support is available to Swedish and foreign companies, mainly for industrial activities in designated areas, principally situated in northern Sweden, with high unemployment and low population rates. Investment grants may range up to 50 per cent of the total investment cost. To qualify, the company must demonstrate that there will be a beneficial effect on regional employment and must submit annual reports.

12.3 Other public schemes and incentives

See 12.2.

13 COMPANIES AND BUSINESS ENTITIES

13.1 Limited and unlimited companies

A company is either unlimited or limited by shares, although an unlimited company may only exist in the form of a partnership (see 13.2). Companies limited by shares (*aktiebolag*, AB) are regulated by the Companies Act. Limited companies are the most common form of business entity in Sweden. They are also often the most useful form of association for the foreign investor. A company limited by shares is both a legal and a taxable entity. The shareholders are not personally liable for the company's debts and liabilities beyond the amount which they have to subscribe for their shares. Directors can be made liable for fraudulent or wrongful trading.

13.1.1 There are two types of limited companies, publicly held companies (*publika aktiebolag*) and privately held companies (*privata aktiebolag*). Only publicly held companies may raise capital by selling their shares to the public on the stock exchange and they are required to have a minimum share capital of SEK500,000.

13.1.2 The company is a separate legal entity from the shareholders and directors. It has its own assets and liabilities and is taxed separately under different rules. The purpose of the company is set out in the articles of association, which is a public document registered with the patent and registration office.

13.2 Partnerships

Swedish law distinguishes between three types of partnerships, all of which are subject to the provisions of the Partnership Act. A major distinction is made in the Partnership Act between those partnerships which are registered in the partnership register and those which are not. The parties forming a partnership are allowed substantial freedom in arranging their affairs and most of the provisions of the Partnership Act are permissive. Although it is not necessary, it is recommended that a partnership agreement be in writing.

13.2.1 General partnership

A general partnership (*handelsbolag*, HB) is a legal but not a taxable entity. General partnerships are created by an agreement between two or more persons or legal entities to conduct business jointly as a partnership with a view to profit. All partners are jointly and severally liable for the general partnership's debts and obligations. A former partner will still be liable for the partnership's debts and obligations prior to the disposal of the share. A new partner is also liable for debts and obligations prior to the acquisition of the share. A general partnership must be registered in the public register of partnerships. The partners are subject to taxation for the business conducted by the general partnership and each partner pays his own tax on his share of the profits, depending on how the profits are distributed.

13.2.2 Limited partnership

In a limited partnership (*kommanditbolag*, KB) one or more of the partners have their personal liability for the partnership's debts and obligations limited to a fixed financial contribution to the partnership. However, at least one of the partners must have unlimited liability. The partner(s) whose liability is unlimited to the outside world is called the general partner (*komplimentär*), while the other partners are called limited partners (*kommanditdelägare*). The general partner may be a limited company leaving the limited partners with limited liability while having the advantages, such as separate tax treatment, of partnership. The limited partnership, which must be registered, is generally subject to the same statutory provisions as general partnerships as far as internal matters and third party relations are concerned, although there are other provisions which are only applicable to limited partnerships.

13.2.3 Non-business partnership

There are special regulations in Swedish law applicable to partnerships which do not meet the statutory criteria to constitute a general partnership, eg where the partnership is to be unregistered. A non-business partnership (*enkelt bolag*) is neither a legal nor a taxable entity. Property co-owners (see 1.1.3) may sometimes be regarded as non-business partners.

13.3 Other types of business associations

Companies and partnerships being the principal forms of association recognised by law, other unincorporated associations such as cooperative associations, societies and non-profit associations exist but are not intended for profit-making activities. Note should however be made of the position of joint ventures (see 13.3.2).

13.3.1 Trusts

The use of trusts for business oriented investment in property is very uncommon in Sweden. Foundations exist but trusts in the Anglo-American tradition do not.

13.3.2 Joint ventures

A joint venture in Sweden is an agreement between two or more business enterprises to cooperate through a legal or non-legal entity. Normally the joint venture is conducted through a company limited by shares, a general partnership, a limited partnership, or a non-business partnership. There are no special laws or taxation provisions relating to joint ventures as such.

14 INTERNATIONAL

14.1 Restriction or consents required for inward investment

The rules governing foreign acquisition of Swedish property have been subject to major changes over the last few years to bring Swedish legislation into line with EU obligations, principally by eliminating discrimination on the grounds of nationality. Foreign entities may now acquire shares in Swedish companies or become partners in Swedish partnerships without obtaining prior permission from the authorities. The Foreign Acquisition of Land Act has also been repealed so foreigners no longer need to apply for permission from the government to acquire property in Sweden. However, some restrictions still apply with regard to agricultural property or buildings containing flats, if the buyer is not a Swedish resident or has not been a Swedish resident for at least five years, or if the buyer is a foreign company or association. A company or association registered in Sweden is regarded as resident in Sweden even if any or all owners of the company are a foreign company or a foreign national.

14.2 Exchange control

There are no remaining exchange controls and the Act on Foreign Exchange Control of 1992 is applicable only in the event of Sweden being at war or threatened by hostilities. Reporting requirements to the Bank of Sweden (*Riksbanken*) and the national tax board (*Riksskatteverket*) still exist for statistical purposes and fiscal control. Any payment to and from Sweden amounting to more than SEK75,000 should be made through an 'authorised exchange dealer' (ie any of the major Swedish banks) and should be reported to the Bank of Sweden.

14.3 Restrictions and registrations on carrying on a business

A foreign entity aiming to conduct business in Sweden without creating a Swedish subsidiary must establish a branch (*filial*), unless the entity is an EEIG (European Economic Interest Grouping). Prior to commencing any commercial activity, the branch must be registered with the patent and registration office under a specific name, normally indicating the name of the foreign company, its nationality and the Swedish word for branch (*filial*). The branch will then be subject to Swedish law governing the conduct of business although it will not enjoy the same limited liability as a Swedish subsidiary incorporated as a limited company. Tax regulations also differ according to whether the holding company is resident or not.

14.4 Repatriation of income and proceeds of property trading and development

Under the National Tax Act, a non-resident is liable to income tax on income from land located in Sweden and on any proceeds of sale or capital gains arising from it. However, if the seller is a foreign company, the proceeds of sale of shares in a Swedish company will not be subject to taxation in Sweden. Accordingly, if the foreign corporate investor makes his property investment through a foreign company, capital gains arising from the sale of the company will be tax exempt.

14.5 Withholding taxes

The regulations regarding withholding taxes are outlined at 11.1.4.

14.6 Double taxation relief

Sweden has a multilateral double taxation treaty with the other Nordic countries and bilateral treaties with a number of countries.

CHAPTER 19

Switzerland

D Hochstrasser

Partner, Bar & Kamer, Zurich

CONTENTS

1 OWNERSHIP OF LAND 635
2 OTHER INTERESTS IN LAND 637
3 TITLE TO LAND 641
4 TRANSACTIONS IN LAND 642
5 LEASES AND OTHER RIGHTS OF OCCUPATION 645
6 FINANCE AND INVESTMENT SOURCES 648
7 FORMS OF SECURITY 650
8 PLANNING AND BUILDING REGULATION 652
9 ENVIRONMENTAL MATTERS 655
10 DEVELOPMENT 656
11 TAXES 660
12 GRANTS AND INCENTIVES 663
13 COMPANIES AND BUSINESS ENTITIES 664
14 INTERNATIONAL 667

CHAPTER 19

Switzerland

1 OWNERSHIP OF LAND

Property law throughout Switzerland is governed by the federal Swiss Civil Code (*Zivilgesetzbuch/Code Civil Suisse, CC*). Various private law aspects of property transactions are regulated by the federal Code of Obligations (*Obligationenrecht/Code des Obligations, CO*). As a result of federal codification, the cantons have retained only limited legislative powers. In other areas, however, particularly where zoning and environmental regulation and tax matters are concerned, their powers remain significant. The principal form of tenure is absolute ownership which creates a right in the land itself (a right in rem).

1.1 Types of ownership

1.1.1 Absolute ownership

Absolute ownership (*Eigentum/propriété*) is the most common form of legal title in land and is akin to freehold ownership at common law. It includes the right to use, occupy and dispose of the land and any buildings on it to which the owner has title, subject only to general restrictions imposed by law and to any third party rights which may have been granted, eg building rights or rights of residence (see 2.1). Absolute ownership also carries with it the right to the air space above and to the soil below the surface of the land including any minerals. The landowner is not entitled, however, to prevent any interference above or below his land, if his legitimate interests are not affected.

1.1.2 Leasehold

The principal form of tenure is absolute ownership. Long leases in the Anglo-American tradition granted for a premium or for a capital payment in advance are not used in practice. The most similar mechanism granting a right akin to leasehold is the building right (see 2.1.3). Short leases or contractual tenancy agreements at market rent are, however, commonly used. The tenancy will usually be granted for a rent payable at specified, usually monthly, intervals (quarterly for commercial tenancies). The terms on which tenancies are granted and other aspects of tenancy agreements are dealt with more fully in section 5.

1.1.3 Joint ownership

Ownership in common in the form of joint ownership (*Miteigentum/co-propriété*) is seldom actually used but there are several forms of co-ownership akin to condominia which are of real practical importance. Co-ownership exists where property is owned by more than one person or legal entity. In the absence of regulations to the contrary, they are owners of equal shares in the property and each co-owner may encumber the land in proportion to his share or dispose of his share without the consent of his co-owners. In the absence of a specific agreement between the co-owners, the detailed statutory provisions regulate the decision-making procedure concerning the management of the property. A distinction is made between: (a) day-to-day management which can be exercised by every co-owner, (b) important management decisions which require majority consent (at least half of the co-owners), and (c) decisions concerning aesthetic improvements to the property and the comfort of the residents over and above what is considered standard which require a unanimous vote. The exclusion of a co-owner may be sought by a court order to sell the share in the property. This may be granted if it is considered that the co-owner's conduct amounts to such a breach of his obligations that the other co-owners cannot reasonably be expected to share the ownership of the property with the excluded co-owner any longer.

1.1.4 Condominia

The owners of a condominium (*Stockwerkeigentum/propriété par étages*) have rights of ownership over the common parts, combined with absolute right of ownership of the individual unit or of the entire floor. The relevant statutory provisions detail the rights and duties of the parties, especially as far as maintenance of the building is concerned. These provisions apply by default in the absence of a set of rules agreed by the condominium owners. The provisions dealing with the common parts of the building in a condominium are analogous to those rules which apply to co-ownership. Condominium ownership may apply to all types and groups of buildings.

1.1.5 Lesser rights

It is possible to create lesser rights including those of use or occupation falling short of full ownership which include those rights not binding the land or subsequent owners (a right in personam). Comment is made on these in sections 2 and 5.

1.2 Legal and beneficial ownership

Swiss law does not recognise any concept comparable to the common law trust. Therefore any beneficial ownership will be purely contractual (a right in personam), without a right in rem in the property against the title holder of the land. If that holder disposes of the property in violation of the contractual provisions, the beneficiary is limited to a claim in damages. Although the purchase of property on a fiduciary basis, ie where the buyer's identity is not revealed, and the legal ownership lies with the fiduciary, is considered to be valid, it will be void where it is carried out by the parties in an attempt to circumvent any legal provisions; this is especially the case where a non-resident foreigner intends to acquire property without having the necessary permit (see 14.1). A common way of acquiring a beneficial interest in land is by purchasing shares in a land-holding company; the ownership of the property is then transferred by transfer of the shares.

1.3 Restrictions on ownership and dealing

1.3.1 The most important restrictions on landownership currently in force concern foreign residents and foreign controlled entities which must obtain a permit to acquire an interest in land (see section 14). Otherwise, there are few legal restrictions on landownership. Minors and mentally incapacitated persons may own land, but their rights will be exercised by legal representatives on their behalf. There are some legislative restrictions on the extent of the rights of a landowner, which aim principally to protect the public interest and include planning regulations, rights of access, preservation of natural beauty and compulsory purchase. There are also some restrictions aiming to protect private interests such as the laws of nuisance.

1.3.2 There are specific statutory restrictions on the disposal of land by bodies such as local authorities under public law. Statutory restrictions imposing waiting periods before transferring land to limit speculation and rising prices on the property market have been repealed and no similar enactments are expected in the foreseeable future. Otherwise land is freely disposable subject only to general rules referred to in the relevant sections. There exist no local authority pre-emption rights before a transfer of property is finalised.

1.4 Adverse possession or acquisitive prescription

The importance of the concept of acquisitive prescription (*Ersitzung/ prescription*) creating title in the possessor after a certain period of time is very limited in practice. Nevertheless, if someone is in possession of land for 30 years, in good faith, and the real owner is not listed in the land register or is dead, the possessor may request a court order to register his entry in the land register as owner (see section 3 on registration of title).

2 OTHER INTERESTS IN LAND

There are various interests in land which confer rights less than absolute ownership or possession. These may be public or private and include servitudes, usufruct, mortgages and options.

2.1 Servitudes or easements, usufruct, building and dwelling rights

A landowner may enter into an agreement with any third party creating a servitude, usufruct, right of residence or building right in favour of that person or property. In practice, however, the agreement will often be entered into with an adjoining landowner. In addition to the written form of the underlying agreement (*causa*) and the public notarisation of the agreement, which is required by the Civil Code for some types of servitudes, all of these rights are only valid and enforceable against third parties such as future owners of the property, once they are registered in the file of the property in the land register (see 3.1).

2.1.1 Servitudes

A servitude (*Dienstbarkeit/servitude*) is a right over land (the servient tenement) in favour of other land (the dominant tenement). Servitudes include the right to run services such as drains and cables, rights of access and car parking rights. Unless otherwise determined by the Civil Code, servitudes can be granted in perpetuity or for a lesser period of time.

2.1.2 Usufruct

Usufruct (*Nutznießung/usufruit*) grants the beneficiary the right to possess and use the property in any manner he thinks fit, to take produce from another's land such as rights to fish, but not to treat it in a manner inconsistent with the landowner's substantive rights of ownership. Its term must not exceed 100 years. A usufruct must be registered to be enforceable against successive landowners.

2.1.3 Building rights

A building right (*Baurecht/droit de superficie*) entitles the beneficiary to construct buildings in accordance with the agreement between the parties on the land and to possess and enjoy it for a defined term, which may last up to 100 years. Building rights can be granted over land owned by private as well as public bodies. In the absence of any agreement to the contrary, the right is transferable under contract as well as by succession. The contract granting a right to build must be in writing and notarised. When the term expires the existing buildings revert to the owner of the land who is obliged to pay the beneficiary reasonable compensation for the loss of the buildings. The parties usually agree on a method to determine compensation at the time the contract is entered into. A number of communities (local authorities) have used building rights as a means of offering undeveloped land to the public for the construction of residential housing or offices, whilst retaining a substantial interest in the land, thereby exercising considerably more influence on the development of the site than if the land had been sold.

2.1.4 Dwelling rights

A right of residence (*Wohnrecht/droit d'habitation*) entitles the beneficiary (who must be a person) to occupy a building or an apartment for residential purposes. The right of residence is not transferable and cannot be inherited; in the absence of regulations to the contrary, however, it may be extended to the beneficiary's family, as long as the beneficiary is himself entitled.

2.2 Restrictions on use and other restrictions

Public law restrictions exist under public health legislation, and under zoning and building regulations on which further comment is made in section 8. The provisions of the Civil Code restricting owners from carrying on activities which would encroach upon the enjoyment of adjoining landowners are dealt with in section 9. Restrictions on use may be imposed upon a piece of land by way of negative servitude. The registration and notarisation requirements referred to in 2.1 will apply in order to render the right valid and enforceable against third parties. The negative servitude agreement is invariably entered into with an adjoining landowner, although there are no restrictions on entering into an agreement with any third party.

2.3 Private mortgages, privileges and charges

The Civil Code provides for two slightly different types of mortgage, the actual mortgage (*Grundpfandverschreibung/hypothèque*) and the mortgage note (*Schuldbrief/cédule hypothécaire*). Both types are discussed in more detail in section 7. Other private rights in the nature of security include a seller's statutory mortgage for any unpaid purchase price on the sale of a property if the seller is not paid in full; however the right does not automatically attach to the property, and it is necessary for the seller to file a request for registration of the mortgage within three months of the transfer of ownership. Privileges may attach to land and secure certain debts automatically (see 2.5). See also 10.2.2 where the contractor's statutory mortgage is described in more detail.

2.4 Contracts and options

Options to buy or repurchase (*Kaufsrecht, Rückkaufsrecht/droit d'emption, droit de réméré*) or rights of pre-emption (*Vorkaufsrecht/droit de pré-emption*) may be registered in the land register and become rights in rem. They can be enforced against any successor in title, if and to the extent that they are registered, whether a new transfer has already been registered or not. Unless the transaction is entered in the land register, the buyer is unable to protect his interest. It is therefore important that the buyer ensures the seller signs and files an application for registration in the land register at the same time as the notarisation of the contract.

2.5 Public charges on land

There are also various public liabilities which can be secured on a property such as the non-payment of taxes. Public liabilities do not require registration.

2.6 Other interests

Other interests of an in rem character do not exist. Public rights of access as such do not exist, other than in cases of emergency.

2.7 Liabilities attaching to the land

Liabilities arising out of land may attach either to the owner or occupier or both. There are no private law liabilities attached to the occupier of land although he will be liable if he is an owner/occupier. An owner may be liable under the Code of Obligations, for injury or damage to third parties or their goods caused by construction defects in the building or maintenance neglect and for damage caused to adjoining landowners for the unreasonable use of his land. An owner may also be liable for the repair of dangerous structures. On the other hand, tax liabilities and charges may attach to the occupier of the land in the form of local authority or municipal taxes. However, as the local authorities have a statutory mortgage over the property to secure these liabilities (see 2.5), the owner of the land may become liable for such claims. General comments on tax are made in section 11.

2.8 Legal and equitable interests

This distinction does not exist in Swiss law, and there is no doctrine of equity.

2.9 Protection of interests

For any private interest to be enforceable against the property, it must be protected by registration in the land register (see section 3), although public charges do not need to be registered to be enforceable (see 2.5). In the absence of the requisite registration, an interest can only be enforced as a contractual right against the person or legal entity; as it will not be a recognised right in rem, it will not be enforceable against any subsequent buyer, even if the latter has notice of it. Contractual tenancies may be entered in the land register only by mutual consent of the parties. Under these circumstances, the contractual tenancy becomes a right in rem, a subsequent buyer is bound by the terms of the tenancy agreement and cannot rely on the otherwise applicable provisions regulating the effects of a sale of the property on a tenancy (see 5.3). Where the tenancy remains unregistered, the tenant will have a statutory right to a claim in damages against the subsequent buyer in the event of breach of the tenancy agreement.

2.10 Priority of interests

The relevant date will be the date of registration of the interest and not the date of its creation. The priority between registered interests in land will be determined by the rank of the interest in question. A first rank mortgage therefore entitles the holder to be paid in full, before any subsequent mortgages are paid. If rights of the same rank exist, the proceeds of sale are divided between them. Public charges and mortgages do not have priority over earlier mortgages.

3 TITLE TO LAND

3.1 Proof of title

Title to land can only be established by registration. Every new transfer of ownership requires registration by the new owner. All other interests require protection by registration if they are to be enforceable against subsequent buyers (see 3.2.2). However, in exceptional circumstances, an entry in the land register has mere declaratory effect, eg transfer of title by way of succession, or by court order under the applicable provisions of the Federal Statute on Debt Collection and Bankruptcy (*Schuldbetreibungs- und Konkursgesetz/Loi fédérale sur la poursuite pour dettes et la faillite*). The land registers are open to inspection by the public but only to entities who can demonstrate that they have a valid legal interest in such access. Registration of ownership triggers the tax duties attached to the ownership of property. In this regard, the land registers are used by the tax authorities. Tenements can only be registered by common consent.

3.2 The land register

The land survey register is kept by the responsible cantonal authorities, usually one in every town; villages are sometimes grouped together. The land register is often kept by the notary public.

3.2.1 Plans

All plots of land are divided into cadastral units on the cadastral map and registered under plot numbers in the land survey register. The responsible cantonal authorities maintain these and are also responsible for surveying the land and for determining the boundaries of individual plots of land, which are shown on the official plans.

3.2.2 Content

In the land register (*Grundbuch/registre foncier*) every unit of land has its own file, detailing: ownership; servitudes and usufruct; rights of pre-emption and options to buy or repurchase; land charges granting a right to recurrent payments or services to the beneficiary; priority notices; tenancy agreements; mortgages; and order of priority of rights. The provisions governing the maintenance of the land registers are dealt with under federal legislation (*Grundbuchverordnung/ordonnance sur le registre foncier*), while cantonal law determines which authorities are competent to keep registers and the extent of the land which falls within their jurisdiction. There are provisions for upgrading lesser rights of ownership in the Civil Code that grant ownership to a non-owner who is listed in the land register as owner in good faith after 10 years if there is no challenge as to the possessor's ownership. If someone is in possession of land for 30 years and the real owner is not listed in the land register or is dead the possessor may request a court order to register his entry in the land register as owner.

3.2.3 Errors

There is a legal presumption that the entries in the land register are correct. If there is a false entry in the land register or if for any reason an entry is incomplete, any party relying in good faith on the land register and who suffers damage is fully protected by the provisions on compensation and/or rectification.

3.3 Passing of title

Legal title to land only takes effect by registration of the new owner in the land register. The prerequisite for registration is a notarised agreement between the seller and the buyer, which constitutes the underlying legal ground (*causa*) for acquisition of ownership or any other rights in rem in the land (see section 4). The agreement does not itself convey title but only the right (and obligation) to enter the transfer of title in the register. If the seller refuses to register the transfer, the buyer can bring a lawsuit before the competent judge at the place of the property, who will order the registration, if the contract is found to be valid, binding and enforceable.

4 TRANSACTIONS IN LAND

The most common transactions in land are the sale and purchase of the freehold, the grant of a building right, and the creation of a mortgage to secure a loan from a bank.

4.1 Procedures on sale of property or grant of a building right

4.1.1 It is normal for a sale of property or grant of a building right to take place in two stages and for the whole procedure to take about a month, although this time estimate may vary according to the workload of the notary public. The first stage will consist of the negotiations during which certain preliminary investigations and enquiries will be undertaken. At this stage, the buyer will raise enquiries of the seller or landlord concerning the property. Due to the legal presumption that the land register is correct, a potential buyer can obtain most of the required information about a piece of land from the respective file and his enquiries should therefore focus on issues not recorded in the file. This means that his enquiries should concentrate on the physical state of the building and potential public charges which are not registrable interests. For the same reason, defects in title should not be an issue where the buyer is careful enough to check the identity of the seller. If building rights are being sought, the prospective buyer should ensure that the planned construction and intended use of the buildings are in conformity with the applicable zoning and building laws (see section 8). During this period, the buyer will undertake any survey, investigate environmental issues and negotiate any offer of finance.

4.1.2 This first stage leads to completion, the second stage of the transaction, which takes place when the contract is signed and notarised. Before formal notarisation of the agreement, the transfer of title is not considered valid and cannot be entered in the land register, and the buyer is not entitled to any actual transfer of ownership, ie specific performance (see 2.4) or possession. Following notarisation, registration completing the procedure will take place in the land register as described in 3.3. Possession is usually given and payment made at the time of registration when risk and title will also pass. It should be noted that the register is often in any event kept by the notary public. It is quite common for the buyer to take over existing loans as part of the price.

4.2 Contract terms

4.2.1 The contract will usually contain few warranties, and moreover will usually contain a warranty disclaimer leaving the buyer with the statutory warranty provisions, contained in the Code of Obligations, which cannot be waived. There will be no warranties as to title as the buyer will rely on the registers. The contract will usually stipulate the payment of a deposit, amounting to a small percentage of the purchase price, which is paid when a declaration of intent is entered into, preceding the actual formalisation of the contract in front of the notary public. The declaration of intent will further provide that this deposit will be forfeited to the seller if the transaction does not complete. It will also commonly specify the arrangements for the payment of interest at a rate agreed on by the parties if there is a delay in completion, and vacant possession will be given only when the buyer is entered in the land register as the new owner and the transaction is then considered completed. In the absence of contrary provisions, risk passes to the buyer of the property on the date he is given possession and not at the earlier stage of the declaration of intent. Therefore, the new owner will assume liability for the premiums for the mandatory building insurance that apply in most of the cantons from the date of completion. It is for the buyer to satisfy himself as to whether there are any physical defects or title defects in the property, although investigations regarding the latter are confined to ascertaining the identity of the seller (see 4.1.1). There are statutory obligations in relation to physical defects. Claims for physical defects in the property (such as defects in the building, contamination of the soil, etc) must be brought against the seller within five years after the date of completion of the transaction. Clauses seeking to exclude or limit liability are only valid if the seller did not deceive the buyer as to any defects.

4.2.2 If either party defaults or delays, the other party may be entitled to damages under the general provisions of the Code of Obligations or, if stipulated in the declaration of intent, in accordance with a liquidated damages clause. There is, however, no right to specific performance before notarisation of the contract. The buyer can then obtain an order requiring the contract to be registered. If the buyer delays, the seller can usually charge interest, and in addition, the seller may also forfeit the buyer's deposit if the buyer fails to complete. The seller will also have a statutory mortgage for any unpaid purchase price which will need to be registered within three months.

4.3 Formalities

Contracts for the transfer of ownership of land or any other property rights in rem (including the creation of servitudes, rights of residence and building rights) must fulfil strict formal requirements as a prerequisite to their validity. These contracts (including all material terms) must always be in writing and require public authentication. The authentication has to be undertaken by a competent notary public in accordance with the laws of the canton in the territory in which the property is situated.

4.4 Fees, costs and taxes

4.4.1 The fees of the various professionals involved, ie agent and lawyers, are paid by the party employing the services of the professional in question. The registration and stamp duties are usually split between the parties. It is in the buyer's interest to incorporate a clause to this effect in the purchase contract, because the public authorities have a statutory mortgage for these fees, which would otherwise ultimately have to be borne by the buyer. The agent's commission will vary according to the agent, the type and the value of the property and the particular canton within which the property is located. Fees are regulated under statutes in some cantons, and usually range from one to three per cent of the sale price, although these may be open to negotiation; they are slightly higher for undeveloped land than for houses and apartments. In cantons without specific regulations, a court will decide the fee in the absence of agreement between the parties. Under these circumstances, fees will usually range from two per cent of the purchase price of residential premises, to three per cent or more where building rights are to be granted, with a tendency towards the lower end of the scale in the case of larger transactions. The tariffs of organisations such as the Swiss Association of Real-Estate Brokers (*SVIT*) are not binding, but will usually be referred to in brokerage contracts. The agents' commissions are negotiated on a contingency basis.

4.4.2 Lawyers usually charge their fees on an hourly basis. They are not allowed, in most cantons, to enter into contingent fee arrangements. Nevertheless, the value of the transaction might be one of the factors determining the hourly rate of the attorney. The notary public's fee is determined by cantonal law, and may be calculated either as a percentage of the market value of the property, eg 0.1 per cent of the market value, or at a flat rate, usually between CHF100 and CHF3,000 per transaction.

4.4.3 In most cantons, there is no stamp duty.

4.4.4 The fees charged by the authority responsible for the registration of transactions in the land register vary from canton to canton. They may be from 0.1 per cent to 0.3 per cent of the sale price or of the market value of the right being transferred. Alternatively, they may be charged as a flat fee fluctuating between CHF100 and CHF10,000 per transaction, depending on the value of the right being transferred and the necessary paperwork connected with the registration (see also 11.6).

4.4.5 Switzerland is generally considered to be one of the most expensive countries in the world. Consequently, one might come to the same conclusion when looking at the transaction costs for the acquisition of land. Property values used to be extremely high a few years ago, but have come down considerably since. Nevertheless, they are still quite high when compared to neighbouring countries such as Germany and France. Overall transaction fees in terms of percentage will be relatively low and range around the five per cent mark.

4.4.6 The services of agents, lawyers and notaries are subject to value added tax (VAT) in accordance with the rates described in 11.8. The sale of land and buildings is not subject to VAT.

4.5 Professionals' roles

Although estate agents and land brokers play an important role in practice, their involvement in a transaction is not essential. Brokerage contracts are governed by special provisions contained in the Code of Obligations (*Mäklervertrag/courtage*), which lay down the duties of the parties to such agreements, especially when and under which circumstances a broker is entitled to a fee. Surveyors are not customary in Switzerland, due to the information available from the land register and the cadastral maps. A property transaction does not actually require the involvement of a lawyer because contracts for transactions in land are usually standard contracts that can be drafted by a competent notary public. However, the involvement of lawyers may be important where it is necessary to seek professional advice concerning applicable zoning and building regulation. There is, however, the statutory requirement of a notary public for the mandatory notarisation of the underlying contract of a transaction in land, without which the change of ownership cannot take effect as it cannot be entered into the land register until it has been notarised. The land register application is processed by the public authority which is in charge of the land register.

5 LEASES AND OTHER RIGHTS OF OCCUPATION

The granting of the right to occupy buildings or land over a certain period of time for residential or business purposes in return for the payment of consideration is governed by the provisions of the Code of Obligations on rental agreements (*Mieten/bails*). Due to the fact that 60–70 per cent of the population rent, rather than own, the premises in which they live, and similar figures apply for commercial property, the rental agreement is the single most important type of contract and thus very tightly regulated by mandatory provisions and, as far as termination and variation of the agreement are concerned, strict formal requirements apply. These are dealt with in more detail at 5.3. Tenancies may be concluded either for an indefinite term, which is more common especially for residential purposes, or for a fixed term depending on the purpose of the letting. Tenancy agreements for commercial property are often calculated based on a price per square metre, and rarely by reference to the yield or turnover of the tenant. (For registration and protection of tenancies, see 2.9.)

5.1 Rent and other terms

5.1.1 Indexation is a very common feature for commercial rental agreements but is only permissible where an agreement is concluded for a term of at least five years and the parties have agreed on the official federal consumer price index. In the case of residential property, a limit is imposed on permissible rent rises of four-fifths of the increase in the consumer price index, and any decrease of the index must be taken into account as well. Clauses providing for automatic rent reviews in an upwards only direction no more than yearly are only valid if the agreement is concluded for at least three years and is for a pre-determined annual amount. Both private and commercial tenancies are subject to the provisions in the Code of Obligations. Since a number of these are mandatory, negotiations of tenancy agreements tend to focus on the payable rent, and less on the terms of the agreement. It should be noted that the Code of Obligations distinguishes between residential and commercial tenancies. Whether rent is payable in advance or in arrears, monthly, quarterly or annually and whether a rent deposit is payable is subject to the agreement of the parties. Residential rent is usually paid monthly in advance. As far as rent deposits are concerned, these may not exceed three months' rent in the case of residential property.

5.1.2 Common provisions will relate to the extent to which the tenant may be allowed to alter the premises; if the tenant wishes to carry out improvements to the rented property, he has to request written permission from the landlord and may receive reasonable compensation for his work. The landlord is under the duty to confine any work he undertakes to what is reasonably necessary and the tenant may be entitled to a reduction in rent and damages for disturbance resulting from such works. Small repairs and maintenance are usually paid for by the tenant, although it is common to define the scope of the tenant's duty in the rental agreement, whereas other repairs are usually carried out by the landlord. The tenant may, under certain circumstances, terminate the rental agreement without notice where the apartment is in such a state of disrepair that it can no longer reasonably be occupied, or have the works carried out at the landlord's expense.

5.1.3 The tenant is under no obligation to pay for the cost of insurance. However, it is advisable for a tenant to take out third-party insurance to protect himself against any claim in the event of damage to the property. In the event of default by the tenant or on his becoming insolvent, the statutory terms will provide for the landlord to set a time limit for payment of at least 30 days combined with the threat of termination. Where no payment is forthcoming, the landlord may terminate the rental agreement with 30 days' notice. Termination arising from default or severe violation of the tenant's duties will have the effect of ending his right to apply to the courts for an extension of the rental agreement. Defaults by the landlord, which are usually connected to his duty to repair, may entitle the tenant to terminate the agreement.

5.2 Privity of contract and estate

If a new tenant and the owner are in direct contract (eg if the new tenant pays the monthly rent directly to an account of the owner), it will be considered, after a certain period of time, that the contractual relationship becomes that between the owner and the new tenant. Therefore, a landlord and a tenant respectively will no longer be personally liable on the obligations of the tenancy once they have ceased to be the landlord or tenant.

5.3 Rent control and security of tenure

5.3.1 Rent control is regulated by the courts and tribunals when an action is brought by a tenant. These controls are to be distinguished from the contractual rent reviews described in 5.1.1. The statutory restrictions confine increases in rent by the landlord to where he can show the increase is not abusive under certain narrowly defined circumstances. These include a rise in interest rates, a rise in the landlord's general costs, where it is necessary to bring an existing rent agreement into line with other local rents, and where the suggested increase does not exceed the recommended levels set by organisations representing the interests of landlords and tenants. The tenant may dispute a rent increase before a tribunal (*Schlichtungsbehörde/autorité de conciliation*), which decision may be challenged in the competent cantonal court.

5.3.2 If the rental agreement is made for an indefinite term, it can be terminated by giving the other party at least three months' notice. An official form must be used when giving notice, which must be sent separately to both spouses if an apartment is occupied by a married couple; if these formal requirements are not observed, the termination notice will be void. If the rental agreement is concluded for a fixed term, it expires without further formalities. In both cases, however, the tenant may apply to the court for an extension of the term if he can demonstrate that termination would result in unduc hardship for the tenant or his family, which is not outweighed by the landlord's interests. If the need is urgent, the landlord may terminate the contract by complying with the less onerous statutory notice requirements, instead of the time limits which may be provided in the specific rental agreement. If the tenant seeks a second extension, he has to demonstrate that he took reasonable steps to find alternative accommodation. The maximum permitted extension period is four years for residential and six years for commercial tenancies.

5.3.3 If a property is sold, the tenancy must be taken over by the new owner, regardless of whether it is registered or not. The acquirer has the possibility, though, to terminate the tenancy in accordance with the statutory time limits (instead of being bound to the contractual time limits) if he intends to use the property for his own personal or professional purposes.

5.4 Other legislative restrictions

Agricultural tenancies are subject to a separate restrictive legislation.

5.5 Methods of measurement

Contrary to other countries, it is not usual for residential property to measure the rent by reference to the net internal or external area. This is very common, however, for commercial property which will be measured by reference to the net internal area.

6 FINANCE AND INVESTMENT SOURCES

Due to the relatively stable increase in property prices since the Second World War, banks have perceived very little risk attached to property investment, offering attractive interest rates to investors and have dominated the Swiss property market, although other sources have recently emerged. Property finance is essentially provided in the form of loans.

6.1 Loan finance

6.1.1 Banks provide the most common source of loan finance. All types of banks, eg big international banks, cantonal banks, regional and savings banks and loan associations all lend finance for commercial buildings. The almost non-existent risk attached to property investment has enabled banks to extend loans secured on property with a modest equity ratio which in turn has enabled them to offer very attractive interest rates because they only need to use a small part of their equity to cover the loans. New entrants into the property lending market include insurance companies providing finance for individuals.

6.1.2 Conventional loan finance, as provided by the banks or insurance companies, is usually granted for an indefinite term, with the possibility to request repayment with six months' notice. The borrower has to pay interest, usually semi-annually or annually. In addition, the loan agreement might provide that the loan must be paid back in annual instalments. This is not, however, a statutory requirement. Interest rates will usually be variable, and range between 4.5 and 8 per cent as set by the leading Swiss banks. Nevertheless, as a result of rising interest rates in recent years, more investors have chosen fixed interest rates in the interest of security, usually available for a term of three to six years. Such loans are usually secured (see section 7 for types of security). There is little difference between financing commercial and residential property. One major difference, however, is that in addition to the market value of the property, the expected profit from the business for which the property is acquired will be an important factor for the lender to take into account. Unsecured loans are an exception, and will only be granted to a business with excellent credit ratings or profit expectations.

6.2 Investment and equity finance

If a company is seeking equity finance, for the purpose of acquisition of property, it will either turn to its shareholders, ie private individuals or companies, or, if it is a listed company, use the possibilities granted by the financial markets in Switzerland and/or abroad.

6.3 Mezzanine or mixed funding

A bank or a prime lender will usually grant up to 80 per cent of the loan, if it considers that the loan it is intended to cover reflects the reasonable market value of the property; usually the investor will be required to contribute 20 per cent of the purchase price from his own funds or other sources. If any further loan is made, it will naturally carry a higher risk and there are lenders who will provide a percentage of the remainder of the finance required and take a return by way of a higher interest rate. At present though, the negative impact of the property crash in 1992/93 makes it extremely difficult to obtain any financing beyond 80 per cent of the market value of the property.

6.4 Sale and lease-back

Although leasing has become a very common instrument for financing certain assets such as the purchase of expensive machinery with a limited life span, it is of less significance in the context of property and is not widely used. However, where a sale and lease-back agreement is in place, the property will be sold and subsequently leased-back at a market rent to obtain an income from the property, with an option to re-purchase after the expiry of the term of the agreement.

6.5 Tax leasing

Tax leasing is not a particularly common form of finance vehicle. Like any other investment, investment in property by a company leads to a reduction in the tax burden, if the depreciation provisions are used properly. The possibility of negotiating tax alleviation for investments in areas in need of regeneration varies from canton to canton.

6.6 Other types of property finance

As the banks provide attractive rates of interest, loans secured by way of a mortgage on the property provide the most common method of property finance. Attempts to develop other vehicles such as mortgage funds and securitised mortgage bonds have been investigated but without success.

6.7 Institutional investment

Property is a major (and relatively stable) area of investment. The banks and institutions, or insurance companies, set the standards which apply throughout the market and other investors adopt these to a lesser or greater extent. The institutions will usually be looking for a prime location, a first class building and secure income from a company with a sound credit rating. The recession in the property market in the last three years has reduced the insurance companies' interest in property investment; in order to limit their losses, however, they were forced to take over property in which they had invested by providing finance. The institutional investor has concentrated on commercial investment encompassing the industrial, office and retail sectors although investment in these sectors is presently confined to property in prime locations. An increase in statutory regulation has made investment in residential property today less attractive than it was a few years ago. Nevertheless, apartments of high quality in desirable neighbourhoods might still be considered, if they can be acquired at a reasonable price. Agricultural land is less appealing as a consequence of the high degree of regulation governing agricultural tenancies and the heavily subsidised nature of Swiss agriculture. However, one area which is developing into an important investment sector is the tourist industry, including hotels and other tourist facilities.

6.8 Investors other than institutions

Other investors include trading and development companies and the private investor.

7 FORMS OF SECURITY

Banks do not make substantial loans for the acquisition of land by reference to the creditworthiness of the customer alone, at least as far as residential property is concerned. For businesses, the usual considerations for credits and loans apply and greater emphasis may be placed on the strength of the borrower. In addition to the security instruments discussed in this section, banks may sometimes wish or be willing to have their loan covered by other assets having a value over the amount of the loan.

7.1 Mortgages

7.1.1 There are two slightly different types of mortgages, the actual mortgage (*Grundpfandverschreibung/hypothèque*) and the mortgage note (*Schuldbrief/cédule hypothécaire*). Registration in the land register is a prerequisite for the validity of both types of mortgage. Details of the property and the amount to be secured will be entered; a mortgage may be used to secure any existing, future (in the case of actual mortgages) or contingent debt up to the value of the property. The main difference between the two types is that mortgage notes are negotiable instruments issued to the bearer and are freely transferable, whereas mortgages can only be transferred by written assignment. In addition to this, mortgage notes may not be used to secure future or contingent debts. In both cases, the mortgagor remains personally liable for the secured debt, which is significant where enforcement does not lead to full recovery of the debt. The mortgagor remains entitled to the ownership and occupation of the property. The mortgage covers not only the actual debt, but also includes any interest accrued and the cost of any enforcement proceedings.

7.1.2 To enforce the obligation, the mortgagee will have to apply to the court enforcement office to have a payment order issued. The mortgagor is granted a six-month time limit to clear the debt; a failure to do so will entitle the mortgagee to request the court to make an execution order for sale by public auction. The borrower is protected by the fact that the enforced sale is conducted by a public authority at public auction, which should guarantee a reasonable price. Inevitably however, the prices obtained at public auction are very often inferior to open market prices. The proceeds of sale will primarily be used to cover the costs of the enforcement proceedings, and what remains will be distributed among the secured creditors in accordance with the amount of the claim (including interest and costs) and the rank of the security (see 2.10). Any remaining proceeds will be given to the former owner. The fixed-rank system for mortgages ensures that even if a loan secured by a first mortgage is redeemed, a second mortgage will not move into the first rank and take priority over a later first-rank mortgage, but will remain in the second rank. This will depend on the first-rank mortgage having been registered, the maximum amount secured by the mortgages also being recorded in the register. Under these circumstances, the owner may secure a new loan up to the amount of the previous first mortgage ahead of the second mortgage.

7.2 Debentures

Debentures (*Fahrnisverschreibung/hypothèque mobilière enregistré*) may only be created as a charge over the borrower's moveable property and are of no application in relation to land. The so-called 'floating charge' over non-specifically charged assets is not available as a form of security under Swiss law. Pledges over moveables (*Faustpfand/nantissement*) require a transfer of possession and are not particularly attractive for this reason.

7.3 Performance bonds, guarantees

7.3.1 Where there are no assets over which to secure the loan, it is possible to obtain either a surety (*Bürgschaft/cautionnement*) or a guarantee (*Garantie/porte-fort*), from a third party who will be called upon to repay the loan and any interest should there be a default by the borrower. They can also be used where either the credit of the borrower or the adequacy of the other security is in doubt, or to secure a tenancy default. The difference between these two types of security is that the guarantee is an unconditional undertaking to pay the sum in question by the guarantor which is completely independent of the underlying transaction between the creditor and the borrower; the guarantee will in fact place the third party under the primary obligation to repay the loan in parallel to the borrower (to the extent the borrower does not repay himself). A suretyship is only an obligation to pay in the event of default by the borrower. The validity of the obligation is contingent upon the validity of the contract between the creditor and the borrower. A suretyship is only valid if it is established in writing and, where the third party is an individual, it must be in notarised form. A guarantee, on the other hand, requires no special formalities, although in the light of the strict legal effects which flow from it, a guarantee's enforceability is dependent upon its clarity and precision.

7.3.2 The commercial borrower may choose to assign his business receipts to a bank as security for a loan, although the willingness of a bank to accept the receipts as security depends entirely on the adequacy of the borrower's debtor list.

7.4 Credit insurance

Insurance of credit risks in connection with property is unusual.

8 PLANNING AND BUILDING REGULATION

The development and use of land and buildings are subject to controls comprised within the federal Zoning Act 1979 (*Raumplanungsgesetz/Loi fédérale sur l'aménagement du territoire*) as well as various cantonal and municipal statutes.

8.1 Planning authorities

On a local level, decisions are taken by the local planning authorities for the area, ie the municipalities in both rural and urban areas; the canton will provide the framework for the decisions taken by the municipalities in the cantonal statute enacted by the cantonal parliament and approved by a popular vote (where applicable).

8.2 Plans

The Zoning Act imposes the obligation on the local authorities to prepare specific zoning plans for their area. The cantonal authorities must prepare a utility plan setting out the canton's general planning policies and proposals, by describing the different zones, and how the development and use of land will be regulated within each zone. Zones may comprise protection zones, agricultural zones and building zones, which may be further subdivided into residential building zones, industrial zones and central zones for city centres. The cantons may exercise their discretion and introduce additional categories of zones. There may also be provisions in the utility plan for reserve zones not yet allocated for a particular use. The municipalities may further subdivide the land within such zones. These municipal decisions will have the greatest impact on industrial landowners as they will determine whether building permits will be granted (see 8.3.3) within their locality.

8.3 Planning control and procedures

Generally, it should be noted that all construction activities need a permit, unless they are of such an insignificant nature that they obviously do not affect any of the interests protected by zoning and building laws. In such cases, a mere notice to the authorities is sufficient. In case of doubt as to whether there is development requiring consent, it is possible to submit the documents and plans relating to the proposed development to the relevant local authority. It will issue a preliminary opinion on the matter, by which it will then be bound if a permit is subsequently applied for on the basis of that opinion.

8.3.1 If a building permit is required, an application must be made to the building authority of the municipality where the property lies, together with the appropriate fee. It must give full details of the proposal, in order to demonstrate that the development complies with the zoning plan. The application will then be published in the local official gazette and an opportunity will be given to third parties whose legitimate interests are affected by the proposal to raise their objections. Applications made in respect of land not owned by the applicant have to be accompanied by some kind of evidence that the owner agrees with the intended building project. There is, however, no specific procedure regulating how this should be done.

8.3.2 If a decision is not taken within a reasonable time, recourse to the supervising authority may be made. What will be considered a reasonable time period will vary, depending upon the size and complexity of the specific project. The municipality must then grant the permission subject to conditions or it may refuse the application, stating the reasons for doing so. Both the applicant and any third parties whose rights are affected may appeal the decision to the higher administrative bodies or the courts, depending on the procedural regulations in the particular cantons. Once the decision has been made, it can only be challenged on a point of law or, if the decision is perverse in the light of the actual facts of the case, in the Swiss Federal Supreme Court.

8.3.3 A building permit will (and must) be granted if (a) the proposed type of building and its use consistent with (permitted within) the zone where the development is intended; (b) the property will be connected to all the necessary utilities; and (c) the applicable building regulations will be complied with (see 8.4).

8.3.4 A building permit has to be acted upon within the time limit determined in accordance with cantonal law, which is usually two years. A building permit attaches to the land, and is not personal to the applicant. Once issued, a permit may only be revoked without compensation if it has not been acted upon or if it would be in the public interest.

8.3.5 Breach of building permits may entail financial as well as criminal liability. Where construction has commenced without an application for a permit and where retrospective permission may not be granted, the authority, commonly referred to as the 'building police' when acting in this capacity, has the power to order the removal of the illegal structure. A refusal to comply with the order may result in the authority taking action at the owner's expense. The owner will be granted a time limit within which to comply with the order to remedy a breach. A failure to take remedial action may result in the building police closing the building and a fine. The possibility of appeal and time limits for the owner are governed by cantonal law.

8.4 Building standards, control and supervision

In addition to obtaining a building permit, an applicant must also demonstrate that the proposed development will comply with the requisite building regulations, enacted by the cantons and applied and enforced by the local building authorities. The regulations deal with the design and construction of buildings and the provision of services, fittings and equipment and aesthetic appearance, and as the zoning system requires that a building should be in conformity with its surroundings, the wide discretionary element involved frequently leads to disputes with owners and architects. The regulations also contain powers authorising the authority to supervise the construction works to ensure their conformity with the permit.

8.5 Protection of buildings of special interest

There is specific legislation for the protection of buildings with special historical or architectural value. These buildings are entered into specific registers; the consequence of such an entry is that it is very difficult to obtain permits to alter the appearance of such buildings, not to mention to demolish them. In addition, the zoning laws contain restrictions on building activities in the zones of old quarters of towns and villages that are considered worthy of protection.

8.6 Expropriation and compulsory purchase and compensation

Where land is needed for the construction of major infrastructure facilities, the Swiss Constitution provides that adequate compensation must be paid to an individual or entity whose property rights are affected by measures amounting to expropriation of the interest. Expropriation proceedings can only be initiated by the government or public utilities, and not by private developers. The level of compensation usually reflects the market value of the property. The purpose of the expropriation, eg the construction of a railway line or highway, will usually impose time pressures upon the public authority requesting the expropriation, which may lead to relatively high prices. If the public authority and the owner cannot agree on price (which is not usually the case), the competent administrative body of the canton or the federation, depending on the statutory basis of the expropriation, will decide this. In the latter case, the procedures are cumbersome and may take several years.

9 ENVIRONMENTAL MATTERS

The federal Environmental Protection Act 1983 (*Umweltschutzgesetz/Loi fédérale sur la protection de l'environnement*), provides a basic framework for the control of pollution, including air and noise pollution, soil contamination and dangerous substances. It is the duty of the cantons to implement the Act and not all cantons were particularly quick to respond to the new legislation. The competent authorities responsible for setting standards and enforcement vary from one canton to another. As far as land and property development is concerned, a major role is played by the detailed zoning laws (see section 8), the purpose of which is to preserve the undeveloped areas of Switzerland to maintain land for agricultural and recreational use. As a general rule, environmental liability is based on the 'polluter pays' principle (*Verursacherprinzip/principe du pollueur-payeur*), imposing direct strict liability for any individual or entity causing pollution. In addition to this, the owner of the property may incur secondary liability. However, lender liability has not been recognised to date.

9.1 Protection against atmospheric and noise pollution

The Environmental Protection Act deals in some detail with air pollution as well as excessive noise. New as well as existing structures and buildings must fulfil certain conditions in order to obtain a building permit or a further permit where the use of the site might have an air polluting effect. The conditions apply especially to heating systems, vehicles and fuel emitting structures or plants. The ordinance sets emission limits which may not be exceeded, and provides for periodic inspections. In cases of non-compliance, a time limit is granted to modify or replace the system, beyond which the owner may face both criminal and civil sanctions.

9.2 Water pollution

Similar regulations regarding the protection of water are contained in a separate statute of 1991 (*Gewässerschutzgesetz/Loi fédérale sur la protection des eaux*). They are based on a strict polluter pays principle and provide for damages and criminal sanctions in the event of breach.

9.3 Waste storage and disposal

Federal law regulates waste storage and disposal only in so far as the most dangerous waste is concerned, otherwise the regulation of ordinary waste is delegated to the cantons. In addition, federal law enacts the general principle that waste must be recycled, neutralised or destroyed. Municipal waste is usually incinerated in publicly owned and operated plants, some of which are used for energy regeneration ('waste-to-energy' plants). Onerous charges are levied for the disposal of industrial waste, in accordance with its nature and characteristics. Private households may also be charged a flat rate on a per capita basis for waste disposal; alternatively an increasing number of cantons and municipalities are imposing the purchase of specially designed waste disposal bags on residents for the elimination of domestic waste, the purchase price of which includes an additional waste disposal charge. The rationale underpinning the legislation is the encouragement of waste recycling and the minimisation of its creation by the public.

9.4 Contaminated land

Before purchasing or acquiring an interest in land it is advisable to make proper enquiries regarding any potential environmental liabilities which may arise. The new owner might be held liable for environmental damage caused by a predecessor. There is no general obligation for sellers to disclose any contamination of the land being sold. The existence of such a duty depends on whether the sale contract contains any representations and warranties regarding the existence of contamination. In the absence of warranties, the buyer is well advised to conduct a thorough due diligence investigation. Although federal legislation imposes a duty upon the cantons to keep registers listing contaminated land, these registers have yet to be set up in most cantons and cannot be used as a reliable source of information. An obligation to clean up existing contamination exists to the extent that it threatens the media protected by environmental legislation, eg air, water and ground water amongst others. While the polluter pays principle determines liability under environmental legislation, this is subject to an important exception: if soil contamination is found on a construction site, the party owning the property, who will usually also be the developer, must bear the clean-up costs.

9.5 Environmental impact assessments

The construction of new buildings is subject to detailed provisions regulating the possible impact on the environment that such buildings are allowed to have. For larger projects, a detailed study of such impacts and effects (*Umweltverträglichkeitsprüfung/étude d'impact sur l'environnement*) is required as a prerequisite for a building permit.

10 DEVELOPMENT

10.1 Development projects, structures and vehicles

10.1.1 The most common form of development project is where the owner of a property uses his own property, and finances the building project from his own funds or obtains a mortgage. If the owner is not in a position to undertake sole financial responsibility for a project, he might look to a partner for the provision of finance, with whom he may enter into a joint venture. That partner might be interested in the project for his own business purposes, or might regard it purely as an investment opportunity. The formation of a separate company with a management company responsible for the overall development might facilitate the transfer of the finished project to third parties at some subsequent stage. A further possibility is the involvement at an initial stage of future buyers or tenants who might wish to participate in the construction process to make it more suitable for their specific needs; long-term tenancy agreements would then be concluded between the owner and the future tenants, in order to give tenants the opportunity to get a return on their investment. Common structures for the development of residential property aimed at individuals of modest means are cooperative companies (see 13.1.3).

10.1.2 In addition to the desire to obtain finance at attractive rates and to associate himself with knowledgable and reliable business partners, the owner will also carefully consider the tax implications of any chosen development project structure. If a direct or indirect sale of the property is an unattractive option because it would trigger undesirable tax consequences, an alternative described structure might be used.

10.2 Building contracts and appointment of professionals

10.2.1 Typical forms of building contract

The two most typical forms of building contract used are the work contract and the mandate. The work contract (*Werkvertrag/contrat d'entreprise*), which is the most commonly used in the construction industry, is a contract whereby the contractor is under the obligation to carry out the work and the principal has the duty to pay the price. The essential feature of this contract is that the price to be paid by the principal is only due if the work is carried out and completed as agreed. The contract may be fixed in price, in which case it is stipulated in advance and generally excludes any variation unless unforeseeable circumstances of an exceptional nature intervene impeding completion. Alternatively, the price may be determined in accordance with the value of labour. In the case of fixed price contracts in particular, the contractor will be fully liable. Where he is employed as a general contractor, he has sole responsibility to the owner for the execution of the project, while the other contractors are in a contractual relationship with the general contractor only, and are referred to as subcontractors. By accepting a mandate (*Auftrag/mandat*), the agent is under the duty to carry out the contractually agreed business transactions or services with which he has been entrusted. Any contract that cannot be qualified as a special type of contract, such as a work contract under the Code of Obligations is subject to the provisions on mandate. The essential difference between a work contract and a mandate is that the contractor under the mandate does not give an undertaking to complete the project, but only to use his best endeavours to help the project reach fruition. His liability will be limited, and he may be entitled to remuneration even in cases where he is not able to complete the work. Whereas most contracts in the construction industry qualify as work contracts, mandates will sometimes be used, eg the arrangement between owner and architect, if the architect is not also the project manager.

10.2.2 Common terms

Although the provisions regulating the work contract in the Code of Obligations are applicable to construction contracts, these are not mandatory and will be superseded where the parties choose their own terms of agreement. They may incorporate provisions stipulating the date of completion, consequences of prior termination, damages to be paid in case of default, and the form of payment. In larger projects stage payments are usually provided, which entitle the contractor to draw a percentage of the total price whenever certain defined steps of the construction process have been completed. The most usual arrangement is for a third of the total price to be paid before construction begins, another third to be released during construction and the remaining third to be paid upon completion. More numerous instalments are common for larger developments. The contractor has a statutory mortgage as security for payment for the work undertaken, which he must register within three months of completion of the contractually agreed works (*Bauhandwerkerpfandrecht/hypothèque des entrepreneurs*). A retention as security for performance will only be made by the employer in the case of larger contracts and may range between 10 and 20 per cent. It will be released at the time of acceptance. Compensation in the event of delay is unusual and applies exclusively to large commercial developments. Where compensation is payable, it may be in the form of liquidated damages although there must be a reasonable connection between the delay and the damage suffered, otherwise the court may reduce the amount accordingly, eg if it can be proved no tenants or prospective buyers could have been found even if the development had been completed on time, compensation may be lowered. Extensions of time may be permissible in very limited circumstances, eg for reasons outside the contractor's control, where the contract has a fixed date for completion. Where the contractor has failed to perform his obligations within the time limit, the employer may employ another contractor at the original contractor's expense. Acceptance of the works will be undertaken by the entire team, rather than by an individual member such as the architect.

10.2.3 Standard form of contracts

While the professional organisations provide standard form contracts, the provisions of the Code of Obligations govern the relationship of the parties to the extent that they are not specifically excluded and/or replaced by different provisions.

10.2.4 Appointment of the professional team

The development is executed by one or several contractors in accordance with their agreements signed with the owner. There are terms prepared by the appropriate professional bodies, although the agreements appointing the professional team are entirely negotiable and there is no obligation to adopt the standard terms. The members of the professional team may be paid either by a percentage fee or on a time charge basis. It is common for architects to be paid a fixed price, especially in the case of smaller projects.

10.3 Those involved and their roles

The owner of the land will use a special project manager who will be one of the professionals supervising the project. In addition, the owner will also appoint an architect who will play a crucial role supervising the project in conjunction with the project manager. The architect will be involved from the building permit application stage as he will be expected to provide detailed plans of the proposed development to secure the building permit and to work closely with the construction team and lawyers to ensure the project's compliance with zoning and building regulations. The architect is usually supported by a team of civil, mechanical and electrical engineers who will be in charge of technical aspects, such as lifts, heating and air conditioning. There is no professional similar to a surveyor, whose specific role is to certify competition, variations and extensions of time. This task is fulfilled by whoever is actually in charge of the supervision of the construction work. In larger projects, the owner hires an engineer to fulfil this task as project manager. It is common practice for different contractors to be invited to tender for a project.

10.4 Defects and remedies

10.4.1 If the work performed by the contractor suffers from defects, the owner has the right to either make a deduction from his payment or to request the contractor to remedy the defect, if possible. In addition, the owner is entitled to damages suffered as a consequence of the defect.

10.4.2 A subsequent owner of the building has remedies against the contractor only if they were assigned to him from the previous owner. A statutory core remedy exists which cannot be waived. It will last for a five-year period during which the contractor must remedy the relevant defect.

10.5 Defects insurance

The parties are under a contractual obligation to take out defects insurance. Every architect or contractor has professional liability insurance to provide cover for the cost of remedying defects resulting from any work undertaken. Particularly with regard to large commercial development, it is important to ensure that eventual delays are covered by insurance; where the damage is caused by circumstances beyond the control of the parties, they will not be liable.

10.6 Copyright

The copyright in the design of the building, in so far as it is protected, remains that of the architect. Recent litigation has revealed that it is not clear under what circumstances and to what extent the owner of a building needs the permission of the architect to alter the appearance or design of the building.

However, this question might only arise where buildings have special architectural or aesthetic interest, and will almost certainly never be an issue where standard buildings are concerned. In order to avoid such problems, the inclusion of a protective clause in the architect's contract is advisable.

10.7 Fees

The fees of all the professionals involved in a building project are subject to negotiation and should be agreed in the contracts concluded with the various professionals. Architects and engineers as well as other contractors are members of professional organisations, which have established tariffs which those professionals will try to include in the agreement. Those tariffs do not, however, have any mandatory character, and must not necessarily be accepted by the employer. Overall professional fees will range between 10 and 20 per cent.

10.8 Taxes

All construction work is subject to value added tax as described in 11.8.

11 TAXES

The complexity of the fiscal regime is explained by the federal nature of the Swiss legal system. Taxes vary considerably from one canton to another, where not only different tax rates but also different taxes apply, which can influence the choice of domicile or seat. Each one of the 26 cantons has its own administrative powers in tax and fiscal matters, and confers powers of taxation on the local municipal authorities. There are therefore 27 separate tax jurisdictions and three levels of taxation (federal, cantonal and municipal), although recently passed legislation aims to harmonise and assimilate the tax regimes into a federal taxation system by the year 2001. This section confines itself to a description of the taxation system in very general terms and circumstances may differ in a particular canton.

11.1 Corporation tax

Companies resident in Switzerland for tax purposes are liable to pay federal, cantonal and municipal corporation taxes on their worldwide income; under the federal Direct Tax Law the dividend distributed by a corporation is first subject to graduated corporate income tax and, subsequent to its distribution, income tax at shareholder level. Income attributable to foreign activities is exempt, but nevertheless taken into consideration for determining the rate of taxation. A corporation is considered resident in Switzerland, if it is incorporated in Switzerland or if its place of effective management is in Switzerland.

11.1.1 Tax rates

The current rate of corporate income tax for resident companies ranges from approximately 12 per cent to 35 per cent, according to canton. On the federal, cantonal and municipal level, profit is taxed at graduated rates.

11.1.2 Computation and administration

In calculating its profits, under both federal and cantonal law, a company can deduct expenses of a revenue or recurring nature which are wholly or exclusively incurred for the purposes of the trade of the company. Expenses include fees, commissions and loan interest as well as the usual deductions such as salaries and normal overheads. The tax payable by individuals on income, capital gains as well as the calculation of corporation tax is dealt with by the Cantonal Tax Authority for both federal and cantonal taxes. Taxes may be deductible for federal tax purposes and may also be deductible for cantonal taxes in some cantons. Cantonal taxes are normally calculated on the same basis as federal tax. Federal taxes account for around one third of taxes. The system is one of assessment by the tax administration carried out on the basis of returns of information provided by the tax payer. Assessments are issued and if unsatisfactory to the tax payer may be appealed against. The appeal is initially to the boards of tax appeals (***Rekurskommission/commission** de recours*) and then to the cantonal courts and finally the Federal Supreme Court. It should be noted that the procedural provisions relating to appeals vary significantly from one canton to another. Appeals to the Federal Supreme Court are usually confined to points of law. While it is open to the tax payer to arrange its affairs in such a way as to minimise tax, tax avoidance, any unlawful non-payment or evasion of tax is a criminal offence. Losses may be carried forward for federal tax purposes for seven years; no tax loss carry-back is provided for.

11.1.3 Capital allowances

There is no system in Switzerland allowing for specific deductions from taxes for investments in land (as opposed to other investments). On the other hand, financing costs and capital losses as well as depreciation on property can be deducted as expenses. According to guidelines published by the Federal Tax Administration, no depreciation is generally allowed on the value of land. The standard depreciation rates for buildings range from two to eight per cent per annum, if the tax payer uses the declining balance depreciation method, and from one to four per cent if the straight line depreciation method is used.

11.1.4 Withholding tax

Switzerland levies a withholding tax at a rate of 35 per cent on certain income payments to a non-Swiss resident. Income subject to such withholding includes interest on loans, shareholder dividends, distributions from Swiss investment funds, and interest on bank deposits. No withholding tax is levied on interest paid in connection with conventional loans or grants, royalties on intellectual property rights, licences, management or technical assistance fees. The withholding tax must be deducted from the payment of the dividend or interest, and subsequently charged to the recipient of the income. Swiss residents may recover the withholding tax when they file an income declaration. Non-residents may be entitled to a partial or full refund of Swiss withholding tax where a double taxation treaty exists between Switzerland and their country of residence.

11.2 Taxes on development value

A special tax based on the value of land is levied in 15 cantons. Where cantonal taxes on development value exist, they usually range from 0.05 to 0.2 per cent of the value of the property. Taxes on development land value are not levied at federal level.

11.3 Taxes on capital gains

At federal level, capital gains are taxed in the same way and at the same rate as ordinary business income, whereas capital gains of individuals of a non-corporate nature are not taxed; however, where these result from business assets, they are taxed as ordinary business income. The rate of taxation on the trading profits of a corporate entity or individual is the same at federal and cantonal level. Non-business capital gains are tax-free in most, but not all cantons. However, the regime applicable to capital gains arising is different if they arise from the sale of land (see 11.6).

11.4 Taxes on owner of the property

As mentioned in 11.2, some cantons or municipalities levy special direct taxes on the value of land located in their territory. These taxes are usually imposed in addition to the normal income and net worth or capital taxes to which the owner of the property is subject.

11.5 Taxes on occupier

The occupier of property is not directly liable to taxation. He may, however, be liable for a flat rate charge levied by the municipal authorities for waste disposal and the provision of local amenities. The communal fees and taxes attached to property may, depending on the applicable statute, be levied on the tenant as occupier of the property; however, as these public charges entitle the local authority to a statutory mortgage over the property, this will be of direct relevance to the owner of the property.

11.6 Taxes on land transfer

11.6.1 Most cantons impose a transfer tax on all transfers of title in land including the transfer of all (or the majority) of shares in a land holding company, which is levied either by the canton or the municipalities. The tax is based either on the purchase price or the market value of the property and the buyer and the seller will generally be jointly and severally liable. The rate of taxation varies greatly between 0.1 and 4 per cent.

11.6.2 Some cantons levy an additional tax on the sale of land which comprises part of the private assets of an individual, whereas business profits from the sale of land are taxed at the normal income tax rates; other cantons levy this separate tax on the sale of all land, irrespective of whether it forms part of the private or business assets of a company. The computation varies greatly from one canton to another.

11.7 Wealth taxes

Companies are subject to a federal capital tax at a flat rate of 0.0825 per cent. The cantons also impose a capital tax, but some cantons apply graduated rates. Individuals are subject to a wealth tax at cantonal level, which is graduated according to the net wealth of the individual, and may vary between 0.1 and 0.9 per cent.

11.8 Value added tax

On 1 January 1995, a value added tax (VAT) system (*Mehrwertsteuer/taxe sur la valeur ajoutée*) replaced the old Swiss sales tax. The tax is levied at a rate of 6.5 per cent (2 per cent for certain products covering basic needs, such as food, medicine and newspapers) on goods as well as on services. Any business has to register with the VAT authorities if it provides goods or services in excess of a certain amount. All construction work is subject to VAT as are the services of agents, lawyers and notaries. Tenancies are subject to VAT. The tax payer cannot generally elect to charge VAT where it is not payable.

11.9 Local and other taxes

When a company is incorporated, a one-off stamp duty is levied at the rate of two per cent of the entire authorised share capital. It is also levied at the same rate in cases of capital increases based on the amount by which the share capital of a company is increased. An exception exists for companies with a share capital of less than CHF250,000 which do not have to pay the stamp duty.

12 GRANTS AND INCENTIVES

12.1 Subsidies, grants and loans

In spite of recent shortages of residential housing, no statutory framework has been set up for the provision of grants, subsidies and loans for the development of land because tax incentives have been the traditional vehicle used to encourage investment in land.

12.2 Tax allowances and reliefs

Investment in land may, depending on the canton, be advisable on account of favourable tax treatment. However, the possibility of deducting mortgage payments from income has been significantly reduced in recent years as this mechanism was deemed discriminatory to the large number of residents who rent, rather than own, the property they live in. Some cantons conclude tax agreements with newly established businesses where this may create local employment opportunities and offer tax concessions on newly acquired or newly built sites, thereby enabling new enterprises to have their tax liability significantly reduced over the first few years.

12.3 Other public schemes and incentives

There are currently no other public schemes and incentives, and it seems safe to assume that no such schemes will be introduced in the near future, given the abundance of existing developed property.

13 COMPANIES AND BUSINESS ENTITIES

13.1 Limited and unlimited companies

13.1.1 Share corporations

A company may either be a share corporation, a limited liability company or a cooperative company. The most widespread form of corporate entity is the share corporation (*Aktiengesellschaft/société anonyme*). It is the legal entity used by large public companies, by subsidiaries of multinational corporations, by joint ventures and also by small business units. It also meets the requirements of foreign business interests most effectively. No special licence is required although there are some exceptions which include the banking, insurance and railway sectors. One of the main features of the share corporation is that it is a legal entity distinct from its shareholders, carrying its own company name. The shareholders are not personally liable for the company's debts beyond the amount which they have to subscribe for their shares. There is a minimum requirement that a share corporation should have a minimum share capital of CHF50,000, of which 20 per cent must have been paid up. Only exceptionally will courts pierce the corporate veil and allow creditors to satisfy their claims from the shareholders' assets. The incorporation of the share corporation must be notarised and the corporation comes into existence when it is entered in the commercial register. The formation of a corporation triggers a three per cent stamp tax on the consideration received by the company for the issued shares (which is often equal to the stated capital).

13.1.2 Limited liability companies

A limited liability company (*Gesellschaft mit beschränkter Haftung, GmbH/ société à responsabilité limitée*) is a separate legal entity formed by two or more individuals or companies under a corporate name and with a fixed registered capital for commercial, industrial or other profit-making purposes. Under certain circumstances regulated under statute, the shareholders may be liable for an amount in excess of their shares, but only up to the amount of the registered capital. A limited liability company is a cross between a share corporation and a partnership, but unlike the widely used German GmbH, it does not offer any specific advantages over the corporation and is therefore rarely used.

13.1.3 Cooperative company

A cooperative company (*Genossenschaft/société coopérative*) bears some similarity to a share corporation; the main difference is that its primary purpose is not to make a monetary profit, but to further or secure the special economic interests of its members and is often used to minimise the cost of certain services or goods. A cooperative company, which is a separate and independent legal entity, has no pre-determined capital, because its accessibility to new members is a statutory requirement. Cooperative companies are used in the context of residential buildings, where prospective tenants must acquire a share in the cooperative company in order to be eligible for an apartment and local authorities are more willing to convey public land to entities whose purpose is to offer housing to the public at reasonable prices. The incorporation procedure for a cooperative company is identical to that of a share corporation.

13.2 Partnerships

13.2.1 Ordinary partnership

An ordinary partnership (*Einfache Gesellschaft/société simple*) is the association of two or more individuals based on a contractual agreement. There is no need for any special formal requirements to set up an ordinary partnership; it is usually of a temporary character, as an ordinary partnership is not an independent legal entity, cannot be entered in the commercial register and does not operate under a firm name. All partners remain jointly and severally liable for the liabilities of the ordinary partnership, and pay their own taxes on their share of the profits. As far as property dealings are concerned, ordinary partnerships are only formed for construction projects, which are of limited duration.

13.2.2 General partnership

A general partnership (*Kollektivgesellschaft/société en nom collectif*) is an association of two or more individuals operating under a firm name, forming an independent legal entity based on a partnership agreement between the partners. Although general partnerships are not corporations, they can acquire rights and assume liabilities and the partners' liability towards third parties is unlimited.

13.2.3 Limited partnership

A limited partnership (*Kommanditgesellschaft/société en commandite*) is a general partnership in which (at least) one partner, the so-called general partner, is fully liable for the obligations of the partnership, whereas the other partners' liability may be limited to a fixed financial contribution to the partnership. Unlimited liability to the outside world must be assumed by an individual acting as general partner. Therefore the general partner may not be a company, although there is no restriction on companies (or on individuals) becoming limited partners. The right to take part in the management of the business lies with both limited and general partners.

13.3 Other types of business associations

13.3.1 Foundations

There is no equivalent to the common law concept of trust in Switzerland. A similar function is carried out by the foundation (*Stiftung/fondation*) but this is an unsuitable vehicle for property investment because it must be created by deed, cannot subsequently be modified and is placed under close supervision by the authorities.

13.3.2 Joint ventures

There is no distinct body of law that specifically covers the formation or operation of joint ventures and there is no statutory definition of the term 'joint venture' although there is provision for the contractual joint venture and the joint venture company. The formation of a partnership or of a limited partnership for the purpose of a joint venture is usually excluded, because Swiss law requires that the general partners (not, however, the limited partners) should be individuals, whereas the partners of a joint venture are normally corporations.

13.3.2.1 Contractual joint ventures

Contractual joint ventures are governed by the provisions of the Code of Obligations on ordinary partnerships (*Einfache Gesellschaft/société simple*), although the parties may choose to contract out of most of these provisions. The lack of formal requirements for the creation and termination of a contractual joint venture, the flexibility of its operation, the tax concessions it attracts, its confidentiality and low running costs all contribute to the attraction of the contractual joint venture to the investor where a flexible and temporary structure is required. The major disadvantage is the unlimited liability which attaches to all parties involved and the difficulty involved in the transfer of the contractual interest. A contractual joint venture is therefore principally recommended for short-term projects or projects which do not require a permanent structure.

13.3.2.2 Corporate joint ventures

Joint venture companies are generally incorporated as share corporations (see 13.1). They form an independent legal entity; the relationship between the parties is generally governed by a shareholders' agreement. The major advantages of a joint venture company which will be used whenever a permanent structure needs to be set up, are that it is an independent legal entity, which enables it to enter into agreements and to acquire property, that the liability of the parties is limited to the amount they have to subscribe for their shares, and the interest in the joint venture may be transferred by the sale of the shares. The major disadvantages are the higher costs, the statutory disclosure requirements and formal procedure required to terminate the joint venture, the tax liability, and the lack of flexibility.

14 INTERNATIONAL

14.1 Restrictions or consents required for inward investment

14.1.1 The acquisition of land by foreign residents and foreign controlled entities requires a permit issued by the cantonal authorities under the Acquisition of Immoveables by Persons from a Foreign Country Act 1983 (*Bundesgesetz über den Erwerb von Grundstücken durch Personen im Ausland/ Loi fédérale sur l'acquisition d'immeubles par des personnes à l'étranger*; commonly referred to as the *Lex Friedrich*). A permit is also needed where control over other interests in land is conveyed, including usufruct, building rights and rights of pre-emption, and long-term tenancy agreements. Investment in land holding companies, the assets of which consist primarily of land, is also restricted. However, heirs who inherit land from a Swiss national as well as the immediate family of a resident buyer, do not require prior authorisation.

14.1.2 A foreign controlled entity's right to a permit is very limited and will usually only be granted for the establishment of a permanent place of business. The acquisition by individuals of a secondary residence for recreational purposes is permitted in those cantons (primarily those dependent on tourism) where provision for a limited annual quota of secondary residences has been made. Unlawful acquisitions made in breach of the requisite statutory provisions are void and may lead to the confiscation of the property.

14.1.3 A liberalisation of the restrictions regarding the acquisition of real estate by non-Swiss buyers was rejected on 25 June 1995. Nevertheless, as part of a programme to boost the economy, the Swiss government proposed to Parliament in 1997 to eliminate at least those restrictions in the *Lex Friedrich* which impede foreign business investments in Switzerland. The Parliament voted in favour of that proposal on 30 April 1997. The amended provisions entered into force on 1 January 1998. The major changes are as follows.

14.1.3.1 In order to allow non-Swiss investors the establishment of new production and service facilities, the acquisition of real estate will be exempt from the duty to obtain a permit, if the real property is intended to serve as the regular and established place of business for a commercial or professional activity.

14.1.3.2 The same exemptions take place if the real property serves as residence for a person at the place where that person is legally resident.

14.1.4 Under both of these scenarios, a permit was previously required. No liberalisation will take place with regard to the acquisition of second residences (for vacation purposes) by foreigners.

14.2 Exchange controls

No exchange controls or restrictions are in force at present.

14.3 Restrictions and registrations on carrying on business

Generally, no permits, licences or registration requirements are required to start or carry on business activities in Switzerland, with certain limited exceptions concerning those activities deemed to affect the public interest, such as banking, insurance, and railways.

14.4 Repatriation of income and proceeds of property trading and development

There are no restrictions on the transfer of funds from Switzerland to another country.

14.5 Withholding taxes

Withholding taxes are described at 11.1.4.

14.6 Double taxation relief

Switzerland has concluded double taxation treaties with a large number of European countries as well as with the United States. These treaties limit the withholding tax rates on dividends, interest and royalties. The benefit from double taxation treaties may be forfeited, however, for companies in breach of the statutory provisions regulating the prevention of double taxation treaty abuse.

Index

Austria
absolute ownership
generally, 3
restrictions–
generally, 7
use, on, 7
rights attaching to, 3
acquisitive prescription, 6
adverse possession, 6
building contract
appointment of professional team, 26
development project *see* DEVELOPMENT PROJECT
standard forms, 26
terms, 26
types, 25-6
building rights
availability, 7
duration, 7
generally, 7
protection of interest, 9
registration, 9
termination, effect, 7
building standards, supervision etc, 21-2
buildings of special interest, protection, 22
business controls, restrictions and registration, 33
compulsory purchase, compensation etc, 22
condominium
creation, 5
duration of lease, 15
generally, 4-5
rights attaching to, 4-5
contract for sale
conditional nature of, 11
estate agents' role, 13
fees, costs and taxes, 12-13
formalities, 12
lawyers' role, 13
limits on rights attaching to, 8
procedure, 11
registration, 8
repurchase rights under, 8
rights under, 8
terms, 11-12
transfer date, 12
unconditional, 8
corporation tax
administration, 28
computation, 28
depreciation of capital assets, 28
generally, 27

Austria–*contd*
corporation tax–*contd*
rate, 27
withholding tax, 28
credit insurance, 19
development plan, 20
development project
building contract *see* BUILDING CONTRACT
copyright, 27
defects–
insurance, 27
remedies, 26-7
fees as percentage of overall cost, 27
funding *see* FINANCE
generally, 25
joint venture structure, 25
parties to, 26
taxes *see* TAXES
disposal of land
contract for sale *see* CONTRACT FOR SALE
restrictions, 5-6
succession, by way of, 9
double taxation relief, availability, 33
dwelling rights, protection of interest, 9
environmental protection
atmospheric pollution, 23
contaminated land, 24
damage, liability for, 8
environmental impact assessment, 24-5
generally, 22-3
noise pollution, 23
waste storage and disposal, 24
water pollution, 23-4
exchange control, 32
finance
equity, 17
generally, 18, 25
grants, 30
institutional investment, 18
investment, 17
loan, 16-17
mezzanine or mixed, 17
mortgage *see* MORTGAGE
sale and lease-back, 17
tax leasing, 17-18
floating charge, 19
foreign investment, restrictions and registration, 33
grants, availability, 30
guarantee, 19
immoveables, *meaning*, 3
income, repatriation, 33

Austria–*contd*
inheritance tax, avoiding, 32
interests in land
priority, 9
protection, 9
joint ownership
creation, 4
generally, 4
rights attaching to, 4
termination, 4
joint venture, 32
land
dealing, etc, restrictions on, 5-6
disposal of *see* DISPOSAL OF LAND
liabilities attaching to, 8-9
municipal and public charges, 8
ownership of *see* OWNERSHIP OF LAND
sale of *see* CONTRACT FOR SALE
transactions in *see* TRANSACTIONS IN LAND
land register
content, 10
errors in, 10
inspection, 9
maintenance, 10
plans, 10
leasehold
building rights, 4
generally, 4
rights attaching to, 4
tenancy *see* TENANCY
Leihe, 5
liabilities attaching to land, 8-9
limited company, nature of, etc, 30-31
mortgage
equity finance, 17
generally, 18-19
investment finance, 17
loan finance, 16-17
mezzanine funding, 17
protection of interest, 9
sources of loan finance, 16
types, 7-8, 18
moveables, *meaning*, 3
neighbour disputes
atmospheric pollution, 23
noise pollution, 23
unreasonable use of land, 8
non-resident, restrictions on acquiring interest in land, 32
ownership of land
acquisitive prescription, 6
adverse possession, 6
building rights *see* BUILDING RIGHTS
generally, 3
legal and beneficial ownership, distinction between, 9
main sources of law, 3
restrictions on, 5
tenure, types of–
absolute ownership *see* ABSOLUTE OWNERSHIP
condominium *see* CONDOMINIUM
joint ownership *see* JOINT OWNERSHIP

Austria–*contd*
ownership of land–*contd*
tenure, types of–*contd*
leasehold *see* LEASEHOLD
Leihe, 5
Precarium, 5
trust, role of, 5
partnership, nature of, 31-2
performance bond, 19
personal injury, liability for, 8-9
planning authority, powers etc, 20
planning control
breaches of control, 21
building permits, 20-21
legislative background, 20
procedure, 20-21
pollution *see* ENVIRONMENTAL PROTECTION
Precarium, 5
priority of interests, 9
profits, repatriation, 33
registration
contract of sale, 8
inspection of register, 9
interests requiring, 9
land register *see* LAND REGISTER
restrictions, of, 7
tenancies, 9
transfer on sale, following, 9
sale and lease-back, 17
security
forms of, 18-19
mortgage *see* MORTGAGE
protection of interest, 9
servitude
meaning, 6
creation, 6
duration, 6
generally, 6
personal, 6
real, 6
registration, 9
usufruct *see* USUFRUCT
superaedifikat see BUILDING RIGHTS
tax leasing, 17-18
tax relief
capital allowances, 28
double taxation relief, 33
taxes
capital gains, on, 29
construction projects, on, 27
corporation tax *see* CORPORATION TAX
development value, on, 29
double taxation relief, 33
inheritance tax, avoiding, 32
land transfer, on, 29-30
local tax, 30
occupier, on, 29
owner of property, on, 29
value added tax, 27, 30
wealth taxes, 30
tenancy
duration, 14
legislative restrictions, 16

Austria–*contd*
tenancy–*contd*
maintenance cost etc, 15
measurement, 16
nature, 14
privity of contract and estate, 15
protection of interest, 9
rent–
control, 15-16
determining, 14
payment, 14
reviews, 14
repairs, 15, 16
security of tenure, 15-16
termination, 15
tenure, types of *see under* OWNERSHIP OF LAND
title to land
passing of title, 10
proof, 9
registration *see* REGISTRATION
transactions in land
contract for sale *see* CONTRACT FOR SALE
formalities, 12
procedure, 11
restrictions, 5-6
types, 11
trust, 5, 32
unlimited company, nature of, etc, 30-31
use, restrictions on, 7
usufruct
duration, 7
generally, 6-7
protection of interest, 9
rights attaching to, 6-7

Belgium
absolute ownership
generally, 37
rights attaching to, 37
acquisitive prescription, 39
adverse possession, 39
aid *see* GRANTS
branch, establishment by foreign company, 66
building contract
standard forms, 59
terms, 58
types, 58
building rights
enforceability, 40
generally, 40
nature of right, 40
renewal, 40
building standards, supervision etc, 56
buildings of special interest, protection, 56
business controls
branch operations, 66
inward investment, restrictions or consents required for, 66
repatriation of income etc, 67
restrictions and registration, 67
condominium
creation, 38

Belgium–*contd*
condominium–*contd*
generally, 38
rights attaching to, 38
contract for sale
completion of sale, 44
deposit, payment of, 45
fees, costs and taxes, 46-7
formalities, 46
generally, 41
insurance, duty to effect, 45-6
investigation of title etc, 44
notaries, right to appoint, 45
options and offers, 44
ownership, transfer of, 44
preliminary agreement, 44
private sale agreement, 45
procedures, 43-5
professionals' roles, 47
registration–
duty, payment of, 46
generally, 44
right of first refusal, 45
termination, 44
terms, 45-6
third parties, enforceability against, 46
types of contract, 45
corporation tax
administration, 61
computation, 61
depreciation of capital assets etc, 61
generally, 60
liability to tax, 60
rates, 60
withholding tax, 61
development plan, 54-5
development project
building contract *see* BUILDING CONTRACT
copyright, 60
defects–
insurance, 59-60
remedies, 59
fees, 60
funding *see* FINANCE
generally, 57-8
nature, 57-8
roles of parties, 59
taxes *see* TAXES
double taxation relief, availability, 68
Dutch administration office, nature of, 66
dwelling rights
enforceability, 40
meaning, 40
environmental protection
atmospheric pollution, 57
generally, 56-7
liability without fault, 56-7
noise pollution, 57
penalties, 56
permits, need for, 56
private law remedies, 56
responsibility for, 56
waste storage and disposal, 57

Belgium–*contd*
environmental protection–*contd*
water pollution, 57
exchange controls, 67
finance
equity, 51
generally, 52, 53
hire-purchase, 52
institutional investment, 52
investment, 51
leasing, 52
loan, 51
mezzanine or mixed, 51-2
sale and lease-back, 52
financial aid *see* GRANTS
floating charge, 54
foreign investment *see* BUSINESS CONTROLS
freehold ownership *see* ABSOLUTE OWNERSHIP
grants
availability, 63
Greater Brussels region, business setting up in, 63
income, repatriation, 67
interests in land
priority, 42
protection, 42
joint ownership
accidental, 38
generally, 38
involuntary, 38
rights attaching to, 38
sale of property, 38
termination, 38
voluntary, 38
land
liabilities attaching to, 41-2
protection of rights and interests in, 42
title to *see* TITLE TO LAND
land register
content, 43
errors in, 43
generally, 42-3
plans, 43
leasehold
generally, 37
rights attaching to, 37
tenancy *see* TENANCY
leasing, as a source of finance, 52
liabilities attaching to land, 41-2
limited company, nature of, etc, 63-4
mortgage
family residence, of, 53
formalities, 53
generally, 41
nature, 53
priority, 53
registration, 53
rights under, 53
tax etc on, 53
types, 53
municipal charge, 41
option, 41

Belgium–*contd*
ownership of land
acquisitive prescription, 39
adverse possession, 39
dealing etc, restrictions on, 38-9
generally, 37
legal and beneficial ownership, distinction between, 38
legal and equitable interests, distinction between, 42
restrictions on, 38-9
tenure, types of–
absolute ownership *see* ABSOLUTE OWNERSHIP
condominium *see* CONDOMINIUM
freehold ownership *see* ABSOLUTE OWNERSHIP
joint ownership *see* JOINT OWNERSHIP
leasehold *see* LEASEHOLD
partnership, nature of, etc, 65-6
planning authority, powers etc, 54
planning control
application procedure, 55
authorised development, time for carrying out, 55
generally, 54
permit requirement, 55
violation, 55
priority of interests
generally, 42
mortgages, 53
privilege, 41
profits, repatriation, 67
public charge, 41
rental agreement *see* TENANCY
sale and lease-back, 52
security
forms of, 53-4
mortgage *see* MORTGAGE
servitude
meaning, 39
authentication, need for, 39
creation, 39
generally, 39
registration, 39
transfer of benefit, 39
tax relief
capital allowances, 61
double taxation relief, 68
multinationals, for, 63
taxes
capital gains, on, 61
corporation tax *see* CORPORATION TAX
development value, on, 61
land transfer, on, 62
local tax, 61, 62
owner of property, on, 61-2
registration duty, 62
value added tax, 60, 62
wealth tax, 62
withholding tax, 61, 67

Belgium–*contd*
tenancy
agricultural land, 47
assignment, 48
commercial rental agreement, 50
duration, 47
industrial and warehousing rental agreement, 51
landlords' rights, restrictions on, 47
measurement, methods of, 51
nature of agreement, 47
provisions regulating, 47-8
renewal, 47-8
rent, negotiating, 48
repairs etc, 48
residential rental agreement, 48-9
sale of premises, effect, 48
security, providing, 48
taxes payable on, 48
title to land
passing of title, 43
proof of title, 42
registration *see* LAND REGISTER
transactions in land
contract for sale *see* CONTRACT FOR SALE
fees, costs and taxes, 46-7
formalities, 46
procedures, 43-5
professionals' roles, 47
types, 43
trust, 66
unlimited company, nature of, etc, 65
use
restrictions on, 40
right of, 41
usufruct
meaning, 39
creation, 39
duration, 40
generally, 39-40

Denmark
absolute ownership
generally, 71
rights attaching to, 71
acquisitive prescription, 73
adverse possession, 73
agricultural property
acquiring, 73, 83
lease, duration, 83
building contract
professional team, appointment of, 95
standard forms, 95
terms, 94-5
types, 94
building rights, 74-5
building standards, supervision etc, 91
buildings of special interest, protection, 91
business controls, restrictions and registration, 102-3
compulsory purchase, compensation etc, 91

Denmark–*contd*
condominium
administration, 72
creation, 72
generally, 72
registration, 72
regulation, 72
restrictions, 72
service charges, securing claim for, 76
contract for sale
breach of warranties under, 79
contents, 78-9
delay, 80
deposit, 79
energy consumption certificate, provision of, 79
fees, costs and taxes, 80-1
formalities, 80
generally, 75, 78-9
information, disclosure of, 79
investigation of title, 79
nature of, 75
non-completion, 80
pre-emption rights, 79
procedure, 78-9
professionals' roles, 81
registration, 79
signing, effect, 79
survey, defective, 79
terms, 79
warranties, provision of, 79
cooperative society, 101-2
corporation tax
administration, 97
computation, 97
depreciation of capital assets, 97-8
generally, 97
rates, 97
withholding tax, 98
credit insurance, 88
development plan
contesting, 89
dispensation, granting, 89
interrelationship between plans, 89
preparation and scope, 88-9
revision, 89
types, 88-9
development project
building contract *see* BUILDING CONTRACT
copyright, 96
defects–
insurance, 96
remedies, 96
fees, 96
funding, 94
funding *see* FINANCE
generally, 94
parties to, 94, 96
taxes *see* TAXES
disposal of land
charities, by, 73
public authorities, by, 73

Denmark–*contd*
double taxation relief, availability, 103
dwelling rights, 74-5
easement *see* SERVITUDE
enterprise zone, 100
environmental protection
administration, 91-2
appeal, right of, 92
atmospheric pollution, 92-3
clean technology orders, 92
contaminated land, 93
environmental impact assessment, 94
generally, 91-2
liability, basis for, 92
licensing requirements, 92
noise pollution, 92-3
notification requirements, 92
penalties, 92
powers, 91-2
strict liability, 92
waste storage and disposal, 93
water pollution, 93
exchange controls, 102
finance
equity capital, provision of, 84
generally, 83-4
hire-purchase, 85
institutional investment, 85-6
investment, 84
lease-purchase, 85
loan, 84
mezzanine or mixed funding, 85
mortgage *see* MORTGAGE
partnerships, investment by, 86
sale and lease-back, 85
tax leasing, 85
unit trusts, 85
floating charge, 87
foreign investment, restrictions and registration, 102-3
grants, availability, 100
guarantee, 88
income, repatriation, 103
interests in land, protection, 77
joint ownership
agreement as to, 72
duration, 72
generally, 72
rights attaching to, 72
sale by joint owner, 72
termination, 72
joint venture, 102
land
beneficial interest in, 76
disposal of *see* DISPOSAL OF LAND
liabilities attaching to, 76
ownership of *see* OWNERSHIP OF LAND
restrictions on use, 75
land register
administration, 77
content, 78
errors in, 78

Denmark–*contd*
land register–*contd*
fees, 80
plans, 77-8
leasehold
generally, 71-2
rights attaching to, 72
tenancy *see* TENANCY
liabilities attaching to land, 76
limited company, nature of, etc, 100-101
mortgage
default, remedies, 87
enforcement of security, 87
generally, 86-7
indemnity mortgage, 86, 87
private mortgage, 87
registration, 86, 87
types, 75
non-profit making association, 101-2
non-resident, restrictions on acquiring interest in land, 102
ownership of land
acquisitive prescription, 73
adverse possession, 73
agricultural land, 73
dealing etc, restrictions on, 73
foreign persons, purchase by, 73
generally, 71
legal and beneficial ownership, 72
minors, by, 73
restrictions on, 73, 102
tenure, types of–
absolute *see* ABSOLUTE OWNERSHIP
condominium *see* CONDOMINIUM
freehold *see* ABSOLUTE OWNERSHIP
joint ownership *see* JOINT OWNERSHIP
leasehold *see* LEASEHOLD
urban zone, in, 73
partnership
investment by, 86
nature of, 101
types, 101
performance bond, 88
personal injury, liability for, 76
planning authority, administration etc, 88
planning control
development plan *see* DEVELOPMENT PLAN
fines, appeal against, 90
generally, 88
halt to construction works, ordering, 90
legislative background, 88
permits, applications for, 90
procedures, 90
rectification works, executing, 90
zoning, 88-9
priority of interests
fire insurance premiums, 76
generally, 77
municipal property taxes, 76
public charges, 76

Denmark–*contd*
profits, repatriation, 103
registration
condominium, 72
land register *see* LAND REGISTER
landlord's obligations, 82
mortgages, 86, 87
servitude, 75
title to land, 78
sale and lease-back, 85
sale of land, contract *see* CONTRACT FOR SALE
security
charges generally, 87-8
credit insurance, 88
floating charge, 87
forms of, 86
guarantees, 88
mortgage *see* MORTGAGE
performance bonds, 88
servitude
creation, 74
duration, 74
generally, 74
registration, effect, 75
removal, 75
restrictions, 75
transfer of benefit of, 74
types, 74
stamp duty on contract for sale, 80
summer house, restrictions on acquiring, 73
tax relief
depreciation of capital assets, 97-8
double taxation relief, 103
generally, 100
taxes
capital gains, on, 98
corporation tax *see* CORPORATION TAX
development value, on, 98
land transfer, on, 99
local taxes etc, 99
municipal property taxes, priority, 76
occupier of property, on, 99
owner of property, on, 98
value added tax–
construction costs, on, 97
fees, on, 81
generally, 99
wealth tax, 99
withholding tax, 98, 103
tenancy
agricultural properties, 83
assignment–
non-residential tenancy, 81-2
spouses, between, 82
deposit, payment of, 82
duration, 81
generally, 81
insurance, 82
landlord's obligations, registration and priority, 82
legislative restrictions, 83
measurement, method of, 83

Denmark–*contd*
tenancy–*contd*
privity of contract, 82
rent–
control, 82
determining, 81-2
repairs, 82
security of tenure, 82-3
termination, 82-3
title to land
passing of title, 78
proof of title, 77
registration–
backdating, 78
land register *see* LAND REGISTER
requirements, 78
transactions in land
contract for sale *see* CONTRACT FOR SALE
fees, costs and taxes, 80-1
formalities, 80
procedures, 78-9
professionals' roles, 81
types, 78
trust, prohibition on, 72
unlimited company, nature of, etc, 100-101
usufruct, 74

England and Wales
absolute ownership *see* FREEHOLD
acquisitive prescription, 110
adverse possession, rights acquired by, 110
building contract
professional team, appointment of, 130
standard forms, 129-30
terms, 129
types, 129
building lease, 110
building standards, supervision etc, 125
buildings of special interest, protection, 126
business controls, restrictions and registration, 140
charge
generally, 111
public nature, 111
registration, 111
charging order, application for, 122
compulsory purchase, compensation etc, 125-6
condominium, 108
contract for sale
default, party in, 115
effect, 114
formalities, 115
terms, 115
corporation tax
administration, 132-3
capital allowances, 133
computation, 132
generally, 132
liability to, 132
payment, time-limits, 133
rates, 132

England and Wales–*contd*
corporation tax–*contd*
withholding tax, 133
debenture, 122
development
meaning, 124
planning permission for, 124
development plan, 123-4
development project
building contract *see* BUILDING CONTRACT
copyright, 131
defects–
insurance, 131
remedies, 131
fees as percentage of overall cost, 132
forward selling, 128
funding *see* FINANCE
generally, 128-9
parties to, 130-31
disposal of land, restrictions, 110
double taxation relief, availability, 140
easement
meaning, 110
generally, 110
environmental protection
atmospheric pollution, 126
contaminated land, 127-8
environmental impact assessment, 128
generally, 126
legislative background, 126
noise pollution, 126
waste storage and disposal, 127
water pollution, 127
estate contract, 111
exchange controls, abolition, 140
finance
equity, 119
generally, 128-9
institutional investment, 120-21
investment, 119
loan, 118-19
methods generally, 120
mezzanine or mixed, 119
non-institutional investment, 121
sale and lease-back, 119
tax leasing, 120
types, 118
financial aid *see* GRANTS
floating charge, 122
foreign investment, restrictions and registration, 140
freehold
generally, 107
restrictions on use etc, 111
rights attaching to, 107
grants
availability, 135
English Partnerships, 136
Enterprise Investment Scheme, 137
enterprise zones, 136-7
European Union, assistance from, 137
Regional Enterprise, 136

England and Wales–*contd*
grants–*contd*
Regional Selective Assistance, 136
guarantee, 122-3
income, repatriation, 140
insurance against credit risk, 123
interests in land
equitable, 110, 112
generally, 110-13
legal, 110, 112
minor interests, 112-13
overriding interests, 112
priority, 113
protection, 112-13
joint ownership
death, survivorship on, 108
generally, 108
trust *see* TRUST
joint venture, nature of, etc, 139
land
liabilities attaching to, 112
ownership of *see* OWNERSHIP OF LAND
title to *see* TITLE TO LAND
Land Registry
backdating of registered title, 114
content of registers, 114
errors in, 114
fees, assessing, 115
generally, 113
inspection, 113
plans, 113
title, grades of, 114
types of register, 114
lease of land
deed, need for, 115
leasehold *see* LEASEHOLD
procedure, 114
leasehold
duration, 107
generally, 107-8
rights attaching to, 108
tenancy *see* TENANCY
liabilities attaching to land, 112
licence, creation, 116
limited company, nature of, etc, 138
mortgage
generally, 111, 121-2
priority, 113
protection of interest, 113
registration, 121
types, 121
non-resident, purchase of property by, 140
ownership of land
acquisitive prescription, 110
adverse possession, 110
condominium, 108
dealing etc, restrictions on, 110
equitable interests in land, 108-9
generally, 107
joint ownership *see* JOINT OWNERSHIP
leasehold *see* LEASEHOLD
legal interests in land, 108-9

England and Wales–*contd*
ownership of land–*contd*
restrictions, 110
tenure, types of–
absolute ownership *see* FREEHOLD
freehold *see* FREEHOLD
partnership
limited, 139
nature of, etc, 138-9
performance bond, 123
planning authority, powers etc, 123
planning control
advertisements, 124
development plans, 123-4
enforcement action, 125
legislative background, 123
planning permission, application for, 124-5
profit à prendre
meaning, 110
generally, 110
profits, repatriation, 140
public access over private land, 112
registration
equitable interests, 112
land registry in *see* LAND REGISTRY
mortgage, 113
rentcharge
generally, 111-12
rights attaching to, 111-12
sale of land
contract for sale *see* CONTRACT FOR SALE
fees, costs and taxes, 115-16
land registry fees, 115
procedure, 114
stamp duty, 115
sale and lease-back, 119
security
forms of, 121-3
mortgage *see* MORTGAGE
servitude *see* EASEMENT; PROFIT À PRENDRE
stamp duty, rates, 115
tax relief
capital allowances, 133
double taxation relief, 140
taxes
capital gains, on, 133-4
charge on property, whether, 111
corporation tax *see* CORPORATION TAX
council tax, 134
development value, on, 133
land transfer, on, 134
occupier of property, on, 134
owner of property, on, 134
uniform business rate, 134
value added tax, 116, 135
wealth, on, 134
withholding taxes, 133, 140
tenancy
agricultural property, 117
assignment etc, 117
assured shorthold, 117

England and Wales–*contd*
tenancy–*contd*
business premises, 117-18
commercial accommodation, 116
duration, 116
exclusive possession requirement, 116
forfeiture, 117
generally, 116
legislative restrictions generally, 118
licence, 116
measurement, method of, 118
privity of contract, 117
regulated, protection for, 117
rent–
control, 117
payment in advance, 116
review, 116
residential accommodation, 116
security of tenure, 117-18
terms, 116-17
types, 116
title to land
passing, 114
proof of title, 113
registration *see* LAND REGISTRY
transactions in land
fees, costs and taxes, 116
formalities, 116
professionals' roles, 116
sale of land *see* SALE OF LAND
types, 114
trust
creation, 109
generally, 108
nature of, etc, 139
sale of land by trustees, 109
trustee's role, 109
use, 109
unlimited company, nature of, etc, 138
usufruct, 110

Finland
absolute ownership, rights attaching to, 143
acquisitive prescription, 145
adverse possession, 145
agricultural land, sale of, 145
building contract
professional team, appointment of, 168
standard forms, 168
terms, 167
types, 166-7
building project *see* DEVELOPMENT PROJECT
building rights, 146-7
building standards, control and supervision, 163
buildings of special interest, protection, 163
business controls, restrictions and registrations, 176
compulsory purchase, compensation etc, 163-4
condominium
generally, 144

Finland–*contd*
condominium–*contd*
rights attaching to, 144
contract for sale
disclosure of information, 152
dissolving clause, 153
enforceability, 147
fees, costs and taxes, 154
formalities, 153-4
physical defect in land, 151-2
pre-contract, 151
procedures, 151
rights and obligations under–
excluding, 153
generally, 147, 151-3
risk, passing of, 152-3
suspensive clause, 153
terms, 151-3
cooperative society, 175
corporation tax
administration, 170
capital allowances, 170
computation, 170
depreciation of capital assets, 170
double taxation treaties, effect, 169
generally, 169
liability for, 169
rate, 169
withholding tax, 170
credit insurance, availability, 161
development plan
generally, 162
preparation, 162
types, 162
development project
building contract *see* BUILDING CONTRACT
copyright, 169
defects–
insurance, 168-9
remedies, 168
fees as percentage of overall cost, 169
funding *see* FINANCE
generally, 166
parties to, 168
taxes *see* TAXES
disposal of land, restrictions, 145
double taxation relief, availability, 169, 176
dwelling rights
establishing, 146-7
registration, 147
easement *see* SERVITUDE
environmental protection
atmospheric pollution, 165
contaminated land, 166
environmental impact assessment, 166
generally, 164
legislative background, 164
liability, 164
noise pollution, 165
penalties, imposition of, 164
waste storage and disposal, 165-6
water pollution, 165

Finland–*contd*
exchange controls, 176
finance
banks' willingness to lend money, 159
equity, 159
foundations, by, 160
generally, 158, 160
grants *see* GRANTS
institutional investment, 160
investment, 159
loans, 158-9, 173
mezzanine or mixed, 159
non-institutional investment, 160
sale and lease-back, 160
subsidies, 173
tax leasing, 160
tax relief, 173
floating charge, 161
foreign investment, restrictions, 175-6
forestry land, sale of, 145
grants
availability, 173
generally, 173
guarantee
absolute suretyship, 161
security, as form of, 161
income, repatriation, 176
interests in land
priority, 149
protection, 148
joint ownership
disposal of interest, 144
generally, 144
regulation, 144
rights attaching to, 144
joint venture, 175
land
legal and equitable interests, 148
liabilities attaching to, 148
ownership of *see* OWNERSHIP OF LAND
public access rights, 148
title to *see* TITLE TO LAND
land register
content, 150
errors in, 150
fees, 154
generally, 149
maintenance, 149
plans, 150
leasehold
agreement as to, formalities, 154
generally, 155
nature of, 143
rights attaching to, 143-4
tenancy *see* TENANCY
limited company
formation, 174
generally, 174
liability, 174
minimum share capital, 174
nature of, etc, 174

Finland–*contd*
mortgage
aircraft, over, 161
enforcing, 161
establishing, 161
generally, 147, 161
priority, 149
registration, 161
vehicles, over, 161
vessels, over, 161
non-resident
corporate presence in Finland, establishing, 173
ownership of land, 144-5, 176
restrictions on acquiring property, 175-6
ownership of land
acquisitive prescription, 145
adverse possession, 145
dealing etc, restrictions on, 144-5
foreign ownership, regulation, 176
generally, 143
legal and beneficial interests, 144
minor, by, 145
non-residents, 144-5
public or municipal charges, 147
restrictions, 144-5
restrictions on, 147
tenure, types–
absolute ownership *see* ABSOLUTE OWNERSHIP
condominium *see* CONDOMINIUM
freehold ownership *see* ABSOLUTE OWNERSHIP
joint ownership *see* JOINT OWNERSHIP
leasehold *see* LEASEHOLD
partnership
liability, 174-5
nature of, etc, 174-5
registration, 175
types, 174
performance bond *see* GUARANTEE
planning authority, powers etc, 162
planning control
breaches of control, 163
building permits, 162-3
legislative background, 162
procedures, 162-3
profits, repatriation, 176
public access rights, extent, 148
registration, land registers *see* LAND REGISTER
sale and lease-back, 160
security
forms of, 160-61
mortgage *see* MORTGAGE
servitude
meaning, 146
creation, 146
types, 146
shares, foreign ownership, 175
tax relief
capital allowances, 170
double taxation relief, 169, 176

Finland–*contd*
tax relief–*contd*
generally, 173
taxes
capital gains, on, 171
church tax, 172
corporation tax *see* CORPORATION TAX
development value, on, 171
excise tax, 172
land transfer, on, 171-2
local taxes etc, 172
municipal income tax, 172
occupier, on, 171
owner of land, on, 171
transfer tax, 154
value added tax, 172
wealth taxes, 172
withholding tax, 170
tenancy
duration, 155
legislative restrictions, 155, 157
maintenance of leased property, 156
measurement, 157-8
privity of contract and estate, 156
rent–
control, 156-7
deposit, 156
determining, 155
payment, 155
security of tenure, 156-7
termination, 155, 157
terms, 155-6
transfer, 156
title to land
passing of title, 150, 153
proof, 149
registration *see* LAND REGISTER
trade or business, entities available for carrying on, 173-5
transactions in land
contract for sale *see* CONTRACT FOR SALE
formalities, 153-4
pre-emption rights, 145
procedures, 151
professionals' roles, 154-5
types, 150
use
public access rights, 148
restrictions on, 147
usufruct, 146

France
absolute ownership
generally, 179
rights attaching to, 179
acquisitive prescription, 181
adverse possession, 181
building contract
professional team, appointment of, 202
standard forms, 202
terms, 202
types, 201-2

France–*contd*
building permit
appeal against refusal to grant, 196
application for, 195-6
default, by, 196
generally, 195-7
lapse, 196
necessary, where, 195
private rights, effect on, 197
time-limit for grant of, 196
building rights
duration, 182
enforceability, 182
generally, 182
building standards, control and supervision, 197
buildings of special interest, protection, 197-8
business controls, restrictions and registrations, 209
company, types, 208
compulsory purchase, compensation etc, 198
condominium
administration etc, 180
creation, 180
generally, 180
rights attaching to, 180
contract for sale
binding nature of, 185-6
default, 187
entry into, 185
fees, costs and taxes, 187-8
formalities, 187
generally, 183, 185-6
notarial deed, by, 186
professionals' roles, 188
registration, 186
terms, 186-7
corporation tax
administration, 205
capital allowances, 205
computation, 205
generally, 204-5
liability for, 204
rates, 205
relief from, 207
withholding tax, 205
credit insurance, 194
debenture, 193
development plan, 194-5
development project
building contract *see* BUILDING CONTRACT
copyright, 204
defects–
insurance, 204
remedies, 203-4
fees as percentage of overall cost, 204
funding *see* FINANCE
generally, 201
parties to, 202-3
taxes *see* TAXES
tender for, 203

France–*contd*
easement *see* SERVITUDE
environmental protection
atmospheric pollution, 199
contaminated land, 200
damage, liability for, 198-9
environmental impact assessments, 200
generally, 198-9
noise pollution, 199
waste storage and disposal, 200
water pollution, 199-200
exchange controls, absence of, 209
finance
equity, 191
generally, 192
hire purchase, 192
institutional investment, 192
investment, 191
lease, by, 192
loans, 191
methods generally, 191
mezzanine or mixed, 191
non-institutional investment, 192
sale or lease-back, 192
tax leasing, 192
foreign investment, restrictions, 209
grants, availability, 207
guarantee, 194-5
income, repatriation, 209
interests in land
generally, 181, 183
legal and beneficial interests, 180, 184
priority, 184
protection, 184
joint ownership, 180
joint venture, 209
land
liabilities attaching to, 184
ownership of *see* OWNERSHIP OF LAND
sale of–
contract for sale *see* CONTRACT FOR SALE
pre-emption rights, 181
title to *see* TITLE TO LAND
transactions in *see* TRANSACTIONS IN LAND
leasehold
building right, 180-1
generally, 179-80, 188
tenancy *see* TENANCY
limited company, nature of, etc, 208
loans
availability, 207
generally *see* FINANCE
mortgage
generally, 193
priority, 184
registration, 193
rights under, 193
types, 193
non-resident, restrictions on inward investment etc, 209
option to purchase
generally, 183

France–*contd*
option to purchase–*contd*
rights and obligations under, 186
ownership of land
acquisitive prescription, 181
adverse possession, 181
dealing etc, restrictions on, 180-81
generally, 179
legal and beneficial ownership, 180, 184
legislative background, 179
public and municipal charges, 183
restrictions on, 180-81
tenure, types of–
absolute *see* ABSOLUTE OWNERSHIP
condominium *see* CONDOMINIUM
freehold *see* ABSOLUTE OWNERSHIP
joint ownership, 180
leasehold *see* LEASEHOLD
use, restrictions on, 182-3
partnership, 208-9
planning authority, powers etc, 194
planning control
breaches of control, 197
building permit *see* BUILDING PERMIT
generally, 194
planning procedures, 195-7
transfer, 196-7
priority of interests
generally, 184
mortgages, 184
privileges, 183
privilege
priority, 183
registration, 183
types, 183
profits, repatriation, 209
registry of mortgages and deeds
content of registers, 185
errors in, 185
fees, 188
plans, 185
responsibility for, 184
types of register, 185
sale of land, pre-emption rights, 181
sale or lease-back, 192
security
bonds, 194
credit insurance, 194
debenture, 193
forms of, 193-4
guarantees, 194-5
mortgage *see* MORTGAGE
servitude
meaning, 181
administrative, 181
contractual, 182
creation, 182
enforceability, 181
generally, 181-2
legal, 181-2
negative, 182
termination, 182

France–*contd*
servitude–*contd*
types, 181
subsidy, availability, 207
tax relief
availability, 207
capital allowances, 205
corporation tax, from, 207
double taxation relief, 209
taxes
capital gains, on, 205
corporation tax *see* CORPORATION TAX
development value, on, 205
foreign investors, buildings tax on, 207
land transfer, on, 206
occupier, on, 206
owner of property, on, 206
registration tax, 188
value added tax, 187, 206-7
wealth tax, 206
withholding tax, 205, 209
tenancy
agreement, formalities, 187
agricultural land, pre-emption rights, 181
commercial premises, 189-90
measurement, 190
privity of contract, 190
professional premises, 190
purchaser, binding on, 179
rent and other terms–
commercial premises, 189-90
professional premises, 190
residential premises, 188-90
residential premises, 188-9
security of tenure–
commercial premises, 189-90
professional premises, 190
residential premises, 189
terms, 188-90
transfer, 179
title to land
passing of title, 185
proof, 184
registration *see* REGISTRY OF MORTGAGES AND DEEDS
transactions in land
contract for sale *see* CONTRACT FOR SALE
procedures on sale, 185-6
types, 185
unincorporated association, establishing, 209
unlimited company, nature of, etc, 208
use, restrictions on, 182-3
usufruct
meaning, 182
duration, 182
enforceability, 182
termination, 182
transfer, 182

Germany
absolute ownership
generally, 213

Germany–*contd*
absolute ownership–*contd*
restriction–
generally, 217
use, on, 217
rights attaching to, 213
acquisitive prescription, acquiring title by, 215
adverse possession, acquiring title by, 215
banks
finance provision, 226-7
types, 226
building contract
penalty clause, 238-9
professional team, appointment of, 238
standard form, 238
terms, 237-8
types, 237
building permit
appeal against refusal, 233
application for, 232
construction in absence of, 233
duration, 233
enforcement in case of breach, 233
necessary, where, 232
time-limit for granting, 233
building rights
duration, 216
extent, 216
generally, 216
registration, 216
termination, 216
building standards, control and supervision, 233
buildings of special interest
protection, 233-4
subsidies for renovation, 244
business association, types, 244-7
business controls
inward investment, restrictions or consents required, 247
restrictions and registrations, 247
compulsory purchase, compensation etc, 234
condominium, 214
contract for sale
abstraction, principle of, 220
deposit, payment of, 221
fees, costs and taxes, 222-3
formalities, 222
interests arising thereunder, 217
negotiation, 220
procedures, 220-21
professionals' roles, 223
terms, 221
warranty, breach of, 221
corporation tax
administration, 241
appeal against assessment, 241
computation, 241
depreciation allowances, 241
generally, 240
liability for, 240

Germany–*contd*
corporation tax–*contd*
non-resident's liability for, 240
rates, 240-41
withholding tax, 241-2
credit insurance, as form of security, 230
development
building permit *see* BUILDING PERMIT
planning control, in breach of, 233
development plan
generally, 231-2
preparation etc, 231-2
zoning plan, preparation etc, 231-2
development project
building contract *see* BUILDING CONTRACT
copyright, 240
defects–
insurance, 239
remedies, 239
fees as percentage of overall cost, 240
funding *see* FINANCE
generally, 237
parties to, 238-9
responsibilities, 237
taxes *see* TAXES
disposal of land *see* SALE OF LAND
double taxation relief, availability, 248
dwelling rights, 216
easement *see* SERVITUDE
environmental protection
atmospheric pollution, 234-5
contaminated land, 235-6
enforcement powers, 234
environmental impact assessments, 236
generally, 234
neighbouring land, permissible emissions from, 235
noise pollution, 234-5
waste storage and disposal, 235
water pollution, 235
exchange controls, 247
finance
banks as source of, 226-7
closed-end property funds, 228
equity, 227
generally, 226, 237
grants and incentives, 243-4
institutional investment, 228
investment, 227
leasing arrangements, 228
loan, 226-7
mezzanine or mixed, 227
non-institutional investment, 229
open-end property funds, 228
property finance generally, 228
sale and lease-back, 227
tax leasing, 228
foreign investment, restrictions etc, 247
grants, availability, 243-4
guarantee, as form of security, 230
income, repatriation, 247

Germany–*contd*
interests in land
contract for sale, arising under, 217
first refusal, rights of, 217
generally, 215
legal and beneficial, 218
priority, 219
protection, 218
public and municipal charges, 218
types *see under* OWNERSHIP OF LAND
joint ownership
creation, 214
generally, 214
rights attaching to, 214
termination, 214
transfer of interest, 214
joint venture, 246-7
land
liabilities attaching to, 218
sale of *see* CONTRACT FOR SALE
transactions in *see* TRANSACTIONS IN LAND
land charge
registration, 217
security, as form of, 229-30
land register
content, 219
errors in, 219-20
fees, 223
first refusal, rights of, 217
interests in land, 218
maintenance, 219
plans, 219
presumption of accuracy, 220
priority notice, 220-21
transfer of title, requirements prior to registration, 221
leasehold
duration, 223
generally, 213, 223
tenancy *see* TENANCY
limited company, nature etc, 244-5
mortgage
generally, 229-30
priority, 230
registration, 217, 230
transfer, 230
unspecified sums, as security for, 229
ownership of land
acquisitive prescription, 215
adverse possession, 215
dealings etc, restrictions, 215
generally, 213
leasehold *see* LEASEHOLD
legal and beneficial ownership, 214-15
main sources of law, 213
restrictions, 215
types of ownership–
absolute *see* ABSOLUTE OWNERSHIP
freehold *see* ABSOLUTE OWNERSHIP
joint ownership *see* JOINT OWNERSHIP
types–
condominium, 214

Germany–*contd*
ownership of land–*contd*
types–*contd*
generally, 214
partnership
civil law, 245
commercial, 245-6
silent, 246
performance bond, 230
planning authority, powers etc, 231
planning control
building permit *see* BUILDING PERMIT
generally, 230, 232-3
legislative background, 230
procedures, 232-3
priority of interests, preferential debts, 217
private limited liability company, nature etc, 244-5
privilege, 217
profits, repatriation, 247
public limited liability company, nature etc, 244-5
sale of land
contaminated land, liability for cleaning up, 236
contract for sale *see* CONTRACT FOR SALE
fees, costs and taxes, 222-3
first refusal, rights of, 217
formalities, 222
prerequisites for valid sale, 220
professionals' roles, 223
sale and lease-back, as form of finance, 227
security
credit insurance, 230
floating charges etc, 230
forms of, 229-30
guarantees, 230
land charges, 229-30
mortgage *see* MORTGAGE
performance bonds, 230
servitude
generally, 215-16
limited personal servitude, 216
real servitude, 215-16
types, 215
stock corporation, 244-5
subsidy, availability, 243-4
tax relief
depreciation allowances, 241, 244
double taxation relief, 248
taxes
capital gains, on, 242
corporation tax *see* CORPORATION TAX
development value, on, 242
land tax, 243
land transfer tax, 222-3, 242-3
local etc, 243
occupier, on, 242
owner of property, on, 242
trade income tax, 243
value added tax, 223, 240
wealth tax, 243

Germany–*contd*
taxes–*contd*
withholding tax, 241-2, 248
tenancy
commercial, 223, 225
fixed period agreements, 225
forfeiture, 224
maintenance, 224
measurement, 225
privity of contract and estate, 224
rent–
commercial tenancy, 224
control, 224-5
negotiation, 224
residential tenancy, 224
residential, 223, 224, 225
security of tenure, 225
termination, 223, 225
terms, 224
title to land
passing of title, 220
proof, 219
registration *see* LAND REGISTER
transactions in land
contract for sale *see* CONTRACT FOR SALE
fees, costs and taxes, 222-3
formalities, 222
procedures, 220-21
professionals' roles, 223
types, 220
use
change of, restrictions, 232
restrictions on, 217
usufruct
creation, 216
duration, 216
generally, 216
termination, 216
zoning plan, preparation etc, 231-2

Greece
absolute ownership
generally, 251
rights attaching to, 251
acquisitive possession, 253
adverse possession, 253
building contract
parties to, 275
professional team, appointment of, 274
standard form, 274
terms, 274
types, 273
building permit
appeal against refusal to issue, 269
application for, 268
cancellation, 269
construction in absence of, 269
issue, 268
necessary, where, 268
preliminary control prior to, 268
renewal, 269
time usually taken to grant, 269

Greece–*contd*
building permit–*contd*
time-limit for implementation, 269
transfer of benefit, 269
building right, *meaning*, 254
building standards, control and supervision, 270
buildings of special interest, protection, 270
business controls, restrictions and registration, 283-4
commercial bond, as form of security, 267
compulsory purchase, compensation etc, 270
condominium, 252
contract for sale
breach of warranties in, 258
delay or default, penalties for, 259
deposit, payment of, 258-9
enquiries following, 258
fees, costs and taxes, 259-60
formalities, 259
generally, 255
preliminary contract, 257-8
procedures, 257-8
professionals' roles, 260
purchase price, payment of, 259
registration, 258
signature etc, 258
terms, 258-9
corporation
capital requirement, 281
nature of, etc, 281
corporation tax
administration, 277
computation, 277
depreciation allowance, 277-8
generally, 277
liability for, 277
non-resident companies, 277
rates, 277
withholding tax, 278
credit insurance, as form of security, 267
development plan, 267-8
development project
building contract *see* BUILDING CONTRACT
copyright, 276
defects–
insurance, 276
remedies, 275-6
fees, 276
funding *see* FINANCE
generally, 273
parties to, 275
taxes *see* TAXES
unauthorised, 269-70
disposal of land, restrictions, 253
double taxation relief, availability, 278, 281, 284
dwelling right, rights attaching to, 254
easement *see* SERVITUDE
environmental protection
atmospheric pollution, 271
contaminated land, 272

Greece–*contd*
environmental protection–*contd*
environmental impact assessments, 272-3
generally, 270-71
legislative background, 270-71
liability for pollution etc, 270-71
noise pollution, 271
penalties, 271
pre-authorisation for projects, 271
waste storage and disposal, 272
water pollution, 272
exchange, transfer of property by *see* CONTRACT FOR SALE
exchange controls, 283
finance
antiparochi construction finance, 264
banks as source of, 263
equity, 263-4
financial leasing, 264-5
generally, 263, 265
incentives, 281
institutional investment, 265
investment, 263-4
loan, 263
mezzanine or mixed, 264
property finance, 264-5
sale and lease-back, 264
subsidies, grants and loans, 280
tax leasing, 264
foreign investment, inward investment, restrictions etc on, 283
gift, transfer of property by *see* CONTRACT FOR SALE
grants, availability, 280
guarantee, 267
income, repatriation, 284
interests in land
legal and beneficial interests, 252, 256
priority, 256, 266
protection, 256
joint ownership
creation, 252
generally, 252
rights attaching to, 252
termination, 252
transfer, 252
joint venture
creation, 282
taxation, 282
termination, 282
land
legal and beneficial interests, 256
liabilities attaching to, 255-6
ownership *see* OWNERSHIP OF LAND
public or municipal charges on, 255
restrictions on use etc, 254-5
land register
content, 257
errors in, 257
fees–
mortgage, 266
transfer of property, on, 260

Greece–*contd*
land register–*contd*
generally, 256
plans, 257
types, 256
leasehold
generally, 251
tenancy *see* TENANCY
limited liability company
capital requirement, 281
nature of, etc, 281-2
transfer of corporate participations, 282
loans *see* FINANCE
mortgage
generally, 255, 265-6
prenotation of mortgage, 265-6
priority, 256, 266
registration, 265-6
types, 255
non-resident
acquisition of property by, 283
tax liability–
income, on, 277
transfer of property, on, 279
option, 255
ownership of land
acquisitive possession, 253
adverse possession, 253
dealing etc, restrictions, 252-3
generally, 251
legal and beneficial ownership, 252
legislative background, 251
protection, 256
restrictions, 252-3
types–
absolute ownership *see* ABSOLUTE OWNERSHIP
condominium, 252
joint ownership *see* JOINT OWNERSHIP
leasehold *see* LEASEHOLD
time-share agreements, 252
partnership
creation, 282
generally, 282
taxation, 282
types, 282
planning authority, responsibilities etc, 267
planning control
breach, enforcement where, 269-70
building permits *see* BUILDING PERMIT
development plans, 267-8
generally, 267, 268-70
legislative background, 267
procedures, 268-70
zoning, 267-8
pledge, 265, 266
priority of interests
generally, 256
mortgages, 266
profits, repatriation, 284
sale and lease-back, as source of funding, 264

Greece–*contd*
security
commercial bond, 267
credit insurance, 267
forms of, 265-7
generally, 265
guarantee, 266-7
mortgage *see* MORTGAGE
pledge over moveables, 266
servitude
meaning, 253
creation, 253
generally, 253-4
registration, 253
termination, 254
types, 254
usufruct *see* USUFRUCT
subsidy, availability, 280
tax relief
depreciation allowance, 277-8
double taxation relief, 278, 281, 284
generally, 281
legal acts connected with industrial estate, for, 281
taxes
capital gains, on, 278
corporation tax *see* CORPORATION TAX
development value, on, 278
gift tax, 279
inheritance tax, 279
land transfer tax, 260, 279
local taxes, 280
occupier, on, 279
owner of property, on, 278
shares, on transfer of, 279
value added tax, 260, 276, 280
wealth tax, 279
withholding tax, 278, 284
tenancy
agricultural, 261
duration, 262
generally, 260
legislative restrictions, 262
maintenance etc, 262
measurement, 263
privity of contract and estate, 262
rent–
negotiation, 261
payment, 261
review, 261
security of tenure, 262
subletting, 261
terms, 260-61
transfer, 261
time-share agreement, 252
title to land
passing of title, 257
proof, 256
registration *see* LAND REGISTER
transactions in land
contract for sale *see* CONTRACT FOR SALE
enquiries, making, 258

Greece–*contd*
transactions in land–*contd*
fees, costs and taxes, 259-60
formalities, 259
procedures, 257-8
professionals' roles, 260
types, 257
use, restrictions on, 254-5
usufruct
meaning, 254
creation, 254
duration, 254
generally, 254
zoning, 267-8

Italy
absolute ownership
generally, 287
rights attaching to, 287
acquisitive prescription, 290
building contract
termination, 312
types, 310-11
building permit *see* CONCESSION
building standards
collapse etc, liability for damage caused, 307
control and supervision, 307
environmental matters, 307
health and safety matters, 307
seismic areas, in, 307
buildings of special interest, protection, 307
business association, types of, 316-19
business controls, restrictions and registrations, 320
compulsory purchase, compensation etc, 307
concession
appeal against refusal, 306
benefit attaching to land, 306
duration, 306
grant of, 305
planning application, 305-6
refusal, 306
time-limit for consideration of application, 306
types, 306
condominium, 288-9
contract for sale
building licence, requirement to disclose details of, 306
default etc, 295
fees, costs and taxes, 296
formalities, 296
generally, 291-2
inquiries, 294-5
preliminary contract–
nature of, 291-2
registration, 296
procedures, 294-5
professionals' roles, 296-7
registration, 295, 296
terms, 295

Italy–*contd*
cooperative company, 319
corporation tax
assessment, 314
capital allowances, 314
computation, 314
generally, 313
liability for, 313
rates, 313
withholding tax, 314
credit institution, duty to keep records, 320
credit insurance, 304
development plan
council house plan, 305
general town plan, 304-5
implementation plans, 305
development project
alteration of plans, 310-11
building contract *see* BUILDING CONTRACT
copyright, 313
defects–
insurance, 312
remedies, 311
responsibility for, 311
employment contracts, 311-12
fees as percentage of overall cost, 313
final approval, 311
funding for *see* FINANCE
generally, 310
inspection, right of, 311
materials or labour, unexpected change in cost of, 311
parties to, 312
popular housing, 310
subcontracting, 312
taxes *see* TAXES
variations, 312
double taxation relief, availability, 320
easement *see* SERVITUDE
enfiteusi, 292
environmental protection
atmospheric pollution, 308
building standards regulation, 307
contaminated land, 309
environmental impact assessments, 310
generally, 308
legislative background, 308
noise pollution, 308
waste storage and disposal, 309
water pollution, 309
exchange controls, 320
finance
banks as source of, 299-300
equity, 301
generally, 299, 310
grants and incentives, 316
institutional investment, 301
investment, 301
loan, 299-300
mezzanine or mixed, 301
mutuo, 300
non-institutional investment, 302

Italy–*contd*
finance–*contd*
sale and lease-back, 301
syndication of real estate financing, 300
tax leasing, 301
foreign investment, restrictions, 320
guarantee, nature of, etc, 303-4
income, repatriation, 320
interests in land
generally, 290-93
legal and beneficial interests, 293
priority *see* PRIORITY OF INTERESTS
protection, 293
investment fund, 319
joint ownership
generally, 288
multi-ownership, 288
rights attaching to, 288
termination, 288
time-share, 288
transfer of interest, 288
joint stock company, nature of, etc, 316-17
joint venture, 319
land
liabilities attaching to, 292-3
national industrial park, within, 316
offer of, as incentive to develop, 316
public or municipal charges on, 292
title to *see* TITLE TO LAND
land register
content, 294
contracts to be registered with, 293
errors in, 294
leasehold interests, 297
plans, 293-4
leasehold
generally, 288, 297
registration, 297
tenancy *see* TENANCY
limited liability company, nature of, etc, 317
mortgage
assignment, prohibition on, 302
creation, 302
generally, 291, 302-3
jointly owned property, over, 302
registration, 302-3
third parties, enforcement against, 303
non-resident, restrictions on inward investment, 320
option, *meaning*, 292
ownership of land
acquisitive prescription, 290
dealing etc, restrictions, 289
generally, 287
incapacitated person, by, 289
legal and beneficial ownership, 289
legislative background, 287
minor, by, 289
pre-emption rights, 289
public property, regulation, 289
restrictions, 289

Italy–*contd*
ownership of land–*contd*
tenure, types of–
absolute ownership *see* ABSOLUTE OWNERSHIP
condominium, 288-9
generally, 289
joint ownership *see* JOINT OWNERSHIP
leasehold *see* LEASEHOLD
partnership
commercial, 318
general, 318
generally, 317-19
limited by shares, 319
non-commercial, 318
unlimited, 317-18
planning authority, administration etc, 304
planning control
building permit *see* CONCESSION
generally, 304
legislative background, 304
penalties for breach, 306
planning application, 305-6
procedures, 305-6
response to widespread breaches, 306
priority of interests
generally, 291, 303-4
mortgages, 303
profits, repatriation, 320
sale and lease-back, 301
security
credit insurance, 304
forms of, 302-4
guarantee, 303-4
mortgage *see* MORTGAGE
servitude
meaning, 290
creation, 290
duration, 290
generally, 290
types, 290
subsidy, availability, 316
surface right, 292
tax relief
capital allowances, 314
double taxation relief, 320
taxes
capital gains, on, 314
corporation tax *see* CORPORATION TAX
development value, on, 314
land transfer tax, 315
local etc, 316
occupier, on, 316
owner of property, on, 316
problems inherent in the system, 313
registration tax, 296
value added tax, 296, 313, 315-16
wealth tax, 315
withholding tax, 314, 320
tenancy
affitto, meaning, 298
duties of lessor and lessee, 298

Italy–*contd*
tenancy–*contd*
generally, 288, 297
legislative regulation, 297-8, 299
maintenance etc, 298
measurement, 299
privity of contract and estate, 298
registration, 297
rent–
control, 298-9
determining etc, 297-8
generally, 297-8
premises, for different types of, 297-8
temporary leases, 297
security of tenure, 298-9
subletting etc, 297, 298
terms, 297-8
withdrawal from agreement, 298
title to land
passing of title, 294
proof, 293
registration *see* LAND REGISTER
transactions in land
fees, costs and taxes, 296
formalities, 296
procedures, 294-5
professionals' roles, 296-7
sale of land *see* CONTRACT FOR SALE
usufruct
creation, 291
duration, 291
generally, 291
rights attaching to, 291
tax liability, 316

Luxembourg
absolute ownership
generally, 323
rights attaching to, 323
acquisitive prescription, 325
building contract
parties to, 346
standard form, 346
terms, 346
types, 345-6
building permit
application, 341
conditional authorisation, 341
lapse or loss, 341
refusal, judicial review etc, 341
time-limit for consideration of application, 341
use, time-limits as to, 341
building standards, control and supervision, 342
buildings of special interest, protection, 342
business association, types, 353-5
business controls, restrictions and registrations, 356
charge
floating, 339

Luxembourg–*contd*
charge–*contd*
generally, 327-8, 339
registration, 327
securing, 327-8
compulsory purchase, compensation etc, 342
condominium
maintenance contribution, 327
nature of, etc, 324
contract for sale
fees, costs and taxes, 332-3
formalities, 332
generally, 328, 331
information, disclosure of, 332
notaries public, role of, 332
pre-notarisation procedures, 331
preliminary contract, 331
professionals' roles, 333
terms–
payment, price and manner of, 331
warranties, 331
cooperative society, nature of, etc, 355
corporation tax
administration, 348-9
capital allowances, 349
computation, 348-9
generally, 348
liability for, 348
rates, 348
withholding tax, 349
credit insurance, 340
development plan, nature of, etc, 340-41
development project
building contract *see* BUILDING CONTRACT
copyright, 347-8
defects–
insurance, 347
remedies, 347
fees as part of overall cost, 348
funding *see* FINANCE
generally, 345
incentives, 352-3
industrial areas, state creation of, 353
parties to, 346
taxes *see* TAXES
types of scheme, 345
double taxation relief, availability, 356
dwelling right, 327
easement *see* SERVITUDE
economic interest group, purpose etc, 355
environmental protection
atmospheric pollution, 343
contaminated land, 344
environmental impact assessments, 345
foreign investors, duty to obtain business permit, 343
generally, 343
legislative background, 343
licensing requirements, 343
noise pollution, 344
waste storage and disposal, 344
water pollution, 344

Luxembourg–*contd*
european economic interest group, purpose etc, 355
exchange controls, 356
finance
accommodation-savings contract, 338
equity, 336
generally, 336, 352
government-funded, 352, 353
institutional investors, 338
investment, 336
loan, 336
mezzanine or mixed, 336
non-institutional investors, 338
sale and lease-back, 336
sources, 336
subsidies, grants and loans, 352
tax allowances and reliefs, 352-3
tax leasing, 337
floating charge, creation, 339
foreign investment, restrictions, 356
grants, availability, 352
guarantee, nature of, etc, 339-40
holding company, nature of, etc, 355
income, repatriation, 356
industrial areas, state creation of, 353
interests, priority, 328, 339
interests in land
generally, 326-9
priority, 329
protection, 329
joint ownership
creation, 324
mortgage of interest, 324
rights attaching to, 324
termination, 324
transfer of interest, 324
land
legal and beneficial interests, 329
liabilities attaching to, 329
public or municipal charges over, 328
restrictions on use etc, 327
sale of *see* CONTRACT FOR SALE
title to *see* TITLE TO LAND
transactions in *see* TRANSACTIONS IN LAND
land register
content, 330
errors in, 330
fees, 332
generally, 330
plans, 330
leasehold
generally, 323-4, 333
heritable lease, 327
regulation, 323
tenancy *see* TENANCY
lien
generally, 327-8
public or municipal charges, 328
registration, 328
limited company
private, 353-4

Luxembourg–*contd*
limited company–*contd*
public, 354
mortgage
meaning, 338
creation, 327
disposal and use, 339
generally, 338-9
joint ownership, share in, 324
priority, 328, 339
registration, 339
seizure of land, execution through, 339
types, 338-9
validity of contractual mortgage, 339
non-resident
corporation tax, liability for, 348
inward investment, restrictions, 356
option, 328
ownership of land
acquisitive prescription, 325
generally, 323
legal and beneficial ownership, 325
legislative background, 323
restrictions, 325
tenure, types of–
absolute *see* ABSOLUTE OWNERSHIP
condominium *see* CONDOMINIUM
freehold *see* ABSOLUTE OWNERSHIP
joint ownership *see* JOINT OWNERSHIP
leasehold *see* LEASEHOLD
partnership
civil, 354
commercial, 354
general, 354
generally, 354-5
limited, 354
shares, limited by, 354-5
planning authority, 340
planning control
breach of control, 341
building permit *see* BUILDING PERMIT
generally, 341
legislative background, 340
penalties for infringement, 341
procedures, 341
zoning, 340-41
priority of interests
generally, 329
mortgages, 328, 339
privilege, *meaning*, 327
profits, repatriation, 356
right of use, 327
sale and lease-back, 336
security
bond, 339-40
credit insurance, 340
floating charge, 339
generally, 338
guarantee, 339-40
mortgage *see* MORTGAGE
pledge, 339

Luxembourg–*contd*
servitude
meaning, 326
duration, 326
enforcement, 326
grant, 327
types, 326
sicaf, nature of, etc, 355
sicav, nature of, etc, 355
subsidy, availability, 352
surface right
creation, 326
generally, 326-7
scope, 326-7
tax lien, enforceability, 327
tax relief
capital allowances, 349
double taxation relief, 356
generally, 352-3
holding companies, for, 351-2
investment funds, for, 351
taxes
bankrupt property, on, 350
capital gains, on, 350
corporation tax *see* CORPORATION TAX
development value, on, 349
land transfer, on, 332, 350
occupier, on, 350
owner of property, on, 350
registered lease contracts, on, 350
value added tax, 333, 348, 351
wealth tax, 351
withholding tax, 349
tenancy
agricultural, 335
assignment, 334
commercial, 334, 335
duration, 333
generally, 323-4, 333
heritable lease, 327
industrial, 334, 335
landlord's obligations, 333-4
legislative restrictions, 335
measurement, 336
privity of contract and estate, 335
regulation, 333
rent–
control, 335
generally, 333-5
residential, 334, 335
subletting, 333-4
terms–
agricultural tenancy, 335
commercial tenancy, 334
generally, 333-4
industrial tenancy, 334
residential tenancy, 334
transfer, 324
types of tenancy, 333
title to land
investigation of title, 330
passing of title, 330

Luxembourg–*contd*
title to land–*contd*
proof, 329-30
registration of title *see* LAND REGISTER
transactions in land
fees, costs and taxes, 332-3
formalities, 332
procedures, 331
professionals' roles, 333
restrictions on dealing, 325
sale of land *see* CONTRACT FOR SALE
types, 331
unlimited company, nature of, etc, 353
use
restrictions, 327
right of, 327
usufruct, 326
zoning, 340-41

Netherlands
absolute ownership
generally, 359
rights attaching to, 359
acquisitive prescription, 361
adverse possession, 361
association, nature of, etc, 392
building contract
payments under, 383
professional team, appointment of, 383
standard form, 383
terms, 383
types, 382-3
building permit
application–
appeal against refusal etc, 378
conditional grant, 378
formalities, 378
provisional, 378
time taken to process, 378
breach, enforcement etc, 378-9
expiry, 378
personal nature of, 378
requirement as to, 378
building rights
meaning, 361
creation, 361
duration, 362
generally, 361-2
termination, 362
building standards, control and supervision, 379
buildings of special interest, protection, 379
business associations, types, 390-92
business controls, restrictions and registration, 393
co-ownership
generally, 359-60
rights attaching to, 360
transfer of interest, 360
company
nature, 390-91
types, 390

Netherlands–*contd*
compulsory purchase, compensation etc, 379
condominium, rights attaching to, etc, 360
contract for sale
default, 366
enquiries, pre-contract, 365
fees, costs and taxes, 367-8
formalities, 367
generally, 362
negotiation etc, 365
notarial deed, execution, 366
procedures, 365-6
professionals' roles, 368
registration, 366
survey, 365
terms, 366
cooperative, nature of, etc, 392
corporation tax
administration, 386
capital allowances, 386
computation, 386
generally, 385-6
liability for, 385-6
rates, 386
withholding tax, 386-7
credit insurance, 376-7
development plan
generally, 377
preparation, 377
zoning, 377
development project
building contract *see* BUILDING CONTRACT
copyright, 385
defects–
insurance, 385
postponement of completion, 383
remedies, 384-5
fees, 385
funding *see* FINANCE
generally, 382
parties to, 384
plan, preparation, 382
preliminaries, 382
taxes *see* TAXES
double taxation relief, availability, 393
environmental protection
atmospheric pollution, 380
contaminated land, 381
environmental impact assessments, 381
generally, 380
legislative background, 380
liability, 380
noise pollution, 380
pollution levy, 389
waste storage and disposal, 381
water pollution, 381
exchange controls, 392-3
finance
equity, 373
EU funds, 389
grants and incentives, 389
hire purchase, 373-4

Netherlands–*contd*
finance–*contd*
institutional investment, 374
investment, 373
inward investment, restrictions on, 392
loan, 371-2
mezzanine or mixed, 373
mortgage *see* MORTGAGE
non-institutional investment, 374
sale and lease-back, 373
tax leasing, 373
foreign investment, restrictions on, 392
foundation, nature of, etc, 392
grants, availability, 389
guarantee, 376
income, repatriation, 393
interests in land
generally, 361-4
ownership *see* OWNERSHIP OF LAND
priority *see* PRIORITY OF INTERESTS
protection, 363
registration, 363
joint venture, nature of, etc, 392
land
legal and beneficial interests, 363
liabilities attaching to, 363
ownership *see* OWNERSHIP OF LAND
public or municipal charges, 362
restrictions, 362
transactions in *see* TRANSACTIONS IN LAND
unfenced, 363
use, restrictions, 362
land register
content, 364-5
contract for sale, 366
errors in, 365
location, 364
plans, 364
leasehold
contractual, 359
generally, 368-9
long-term–
meaning, 359
creation, 359
generally, 359
grantors, main, 359
rights attaching to, 359
tenancy *see* TENANCY
limited company
generally, 390-91
private company, 390
shares, limited by, 390
mortgage
creation, 375
default, 375
formalities, 375
generally, 362, 375
loan finance, as source of, 371-2
mutual insurance society, nature of, etc, 392
non-resident, taxation, 386
option, 362

Netherlands–*contd*
ownership of land
acquisitive prescription, 361
adverse possession, 361
dealing etc, restrictions, 361
generally, 359
legal and beneficial ownership, distinction between, 360
restrictions, 361
tenure, types of–
absolute ownership *see* ABSOLUTE OWNERSHIP
condominium, 360
joint ownership *see* CO-OWNERSHIP
leasehold *see* LEASEHOLD
trust, role of, 360
partnership
general, 390, 391
limited, 390, 391
nature of, etc, 391
open and closed, distinction between, 391
planning authority, 377
planning control
breach, enforcement etc, 378-9
building permit *see* BUILDING PERMIT
generally, 377
procedures, 378-9
priority of interests
generally, 364
mortgage, 376
pledge, 376
profits, repatriation, 393
sale and lease-back, 373
security
charges, 375-6
credit insurance, 376-7
forms of, 374-7
generally, 374
guarantees, 376
mortgage *see* MORTGAGE
pledge, 375-6
servitude
meaning, 361
benefit, 361
creation, 361
registration, 361
termination, 361
subsidy, grant of, 389
tax relief
capital allowances, 386
double taxation relief, 393
generally, 389
taxes
building land tax, 388
capital gains, on, 387
corporation tax *see* CORPORATION TAX
development value, on, 387
land transfer, on, 387-8
local taxes, 388-9
occupier, on, 387
owner of property, on, 387
pollution levy, 389

Netherlands–*contd*
taxes–*contd*
value added tax, 368, 388
water authorities, levied by, 389
wealth tax, 387-8
withholding tax, 386-7, 393
tenancy
assignment, 369
generally, 368-9
legislative background, 368, 371
maintenance etc, 369
measurement, 371
premises, different types of, 368-9
privity of contract and estate, 370
rent–
agricultural tenancy, 370
commercial tenancy, 369
control, 370
generally, 369
residential tenancy, 370
review, 369
security of tenure, 370-71
termination, 369, 370
terms, 369
title to land
passing of title, 365
proof, 364
registration *see* LAND REGISTER
transactions in land
fees, costs and taxes, 367-8
formalities, 367
procedures, 365-6
professionals' roles, 368
restrictions, 361
sale of land *see* CONTRACT FOR SALE
types, 365
trust, 360, 391
use, restrictions, 362
usufruct
meaning, 361
creation, 361
generally, 361
termination, 361

Northern Ireland
absolute ownership *see* FREEHOLD
adverse possession, 399
building rights, 399
building standards, control and supervision, 412
buildings of special interest, protection, 413
business associations, 419
charge, registration, 409
companies register
charge, 409
mortgage, 409
company, 419
compulsory purchase, compensation etc, 412-13
condominium, 398
conservation grant, availability, 418

Northern Ireland–*contd*
contract for sale
default, 404
fees, costs and taxes, 404-5
formalities, 404
generally, 400
pre-contract matters, 403
procedures, 403-4
professionals' roles, 405
registration, 403
searches and enquiries, 403
terms, 404
timescale–
commercial property, 403-4
generally, 403
development plan
alteration etc, 410
consultation provisions, 410
generally, 410
inspection, 410
preparation, 410
development project
collateral warranties, 416
defects, collateral warranties as to, 416
generally, 416
limited change of use, 410
planning application *see* PLANNING APPLICATION
easement, 399
enforcement notice, quashing, varying or upholding, 412
environmental protection
atmospheric pollution, 413-14
contaminated land, 415-16
environmental impact assessments, 416
generally, 413
legislative background, 413
liability, 413
noise pollution, 414
waste storage and disposal, 415
water pollution, 414
fee farm grant
nature of, etc, 397
positive obligations, as means of enforcing, 400
recommended ban on future creation, 398
finance
EU funding, 417
generally, 409, 417-18
grants *see* GRANTS
public schemes etc, 418
subsidies, grants and loans, 418
foreign investment, 419
freehold
fee farm grant *see* FEE FARM GRANT
generally, 397-8
sub-farm grant, 397
grants
availability, 418
conservation, 418
EU funding, 417
government loan, 418

Northern Ireland–*contd*
grants–*contd*
industrial development, 418
International Fund for Ireland, 418
tourism amenities, to improve, 418
types, 418
interests in land
generally, 399-401
ownership of land *see* OWNERSHIP OF LAND
priority, 401
protection, 401
joint ownership, nature of, etc, 398
land
interests in *see* INTERESTS IN LAND
legal and equitable interests, 401
liabilities attaching to, 400
public or municipal charges, 400
title to *see* TITLE TO LAND
transactions in *see* TRANSACTIONS IN LAND
use, restrictions on, 399-400
land register
content, 402
errors in, 402
fees, 405
generally, 402
interests not requiring registration, 401
plans, 402
Lands Tribunal, application to, 399
leasehold
duration, 405-6
generally, 398, 405-6
sublease, grant of, 398
tenancy *see* TENANCY
loan, government, 418
mortgage
equitable, 409
generally, 400
registration, 409
non-resident company, registration, 419
option, 400
ownership of land
adverse possession, 399
generally, 397
legal and beneficial ownership, distinction between, 398
legislative background, 397
restrictions, 398-9
tenure, types of–
condominium, 398
freehold *see* FREEHOLD
joint ownership, 398
leasehold *see* LEASEHOLD
partnership, 419
planning application
appeal procedure, 411
conditional grant, 411
deemed refusal, 411
generally, 410-11
grant, 411
limited change of use, 410
necessary, where, 410
outline permission, for, 411

Northern Ireland–*contd*
planning application–*contd*
procedure, 411
public local enquiry, 411
refusal, 411
revocation etc of permission, 411
planning authority, 410
planning control
breach, enforcement, 411-12
development *see* DEVELOPMENT PROJECT
development plan *see* DEVELOPMENT PLAN
legislative background, 410
planning application *see* PLANNING APPLICATION
planning permission *see* PLANNING PERMISSION
procedures, 410-12
use classes legislation, 410-11
planning permission
breach–
demolition, 412
enforcement in case of, 411-12
timescale for implementing, 411
priority of interests, 401
rates
liability for, 417
relief, 417
sale of land *see* CONTRACT FOR SALE
security, forms of, 409
servitude, 399
statutory charges register, 400
tax relief
depreciation allowances, 418
industrial de-rating, 418
rates, on, 417
taxes
generally, 417
rates, 417
value added tax, 405
tenancy
agricultural land, 408
assignment-
consent of landlord, with, effect on liability, 407
landlord's liability, 407-8
tenant's liability, 407
unreasonable withholding of consent, prohibition on, 406-7
business premises, renewal, 408
duration, 405-6
insurance policies, exclusion due to terrorist activities, 406
legislative restrictions, 408-9
maintenance etc, 408-9
measurement, 409
privity of contract and estate, 407-8
protected shorthold, 408
rent–
control, 408
low value residential tenancy, 408
review etc, 406
security of tenure, 408

Northern Ireland–*contd*
security of tenure–*contd*
terms, 406-7
title to land
passing of title, 402-3
proof, 402
registration *see* LAND REGISTER
transactions in land
dealing etc, restrictions, 398-9
fees, costs and taxes, 404-5
formalities, 404
procedures, 403-4
professionals' roles, 405
sale of land *see* CONTRACT FOR SALE
types, 403
trust
number of trustees, 398
trust corporation, 398
use, restrictions, 399-400
usufruct, 399

Norway
absolute ownership
generally, 423
rights attaching to, 423
use, restrictions on, 426
acquisitive prescription, 425
adverse possession, 425
building contract
professional team, appointment of, 444
standard form, 444
terms, 444
types, 443-4
building permit
application, 438-9
conditional grant, 439
development in absence of, 439
duration, 439
necessary, where, 438
refusal of application, 439
timescale for determining application, 439
unnecessary, where, 438
building rights
generally, 426
legislative control, 426
building standards, control and supervision, 439
buildings of special interest, protection, 440
business association, types, 450-52
business controls, restrictions and registrations, 453
company
generally, 450-51
types, 450-51
compulsory purchase, compensation etc, 440
condominium, 424
contract for sale
default, 431
fees, costs and taxes, 431-2
formalities, 431
generally, 426
legislative control, 430

Norway–*contd*
contract for sale–*contd*
marketing of property, 430
pre-contract matters, 430
procedures, 430
professionals' roles, 432
registration, 426, 430
searches and enquiries etc, 430
terms, 430-31
timescale, 430
corporation tax
administration, 446
capital allowances, 447
computation, 446
generally, 446
liability for, 446
rates, 446
withholding tax, 447
credit insurance, 437
development plan
applications in light of, 438
binding nature of, 438
generally, 438
preparation, 438
development project
building contract *see* BUILDING CONTRACT
copyright, 445
defects–
insurance, 445
remedies, 445
fees, 445
funding *see* FINANCE
generally, 443
parties to, 445
taxes *see* TAXES
types, 443
double taxation relief, availability, 453
environmental protection
assessment, 442, 443
atmospheric pollution, 441
contaminated land, 442-3
'emission licence', 441
enforcement provisions, 440-41
generally, 440-41
legislative background, 440-41
liability, 440-41
noise pollution, 441
waste storage and disposal, 442
water pollution, 442
exchange controls, absence of, 453
finance
banks as source of, 434
equity, 434-5
generally, 435-6, 443
grants and incentives, 448-50
institutional investment, 436
investment, 434-5
inward investment, restrictions etc, 452-3
loan–
generally, 434
grants etc *see* GRANTS
mezzanine or mixed, 435

Norway–*contd*
finance–*contd*
non-institutional investment, 436
sale and lease-back, 435
stock exchange, raising funds via, 435
tax leasing, 435
types, 434
foreign investment, restrictions etc, 452-3
grants
generally, 449
nationwide grants, 449
nationwide loan schemes, 449
regional development grants, 449
regional loans, 449
guarantee, 437
income, repatriation, 453
interests in land
generally, 425-8
legal and equitable, 427
ownership of land *see* OWNERSHIP OF LAND
priority *see* PRIORITY OF INTERESTS
protection, 427-8
public access rights, 427
rent charges, 427
joint ownership
generally, 424
legislative control, 424
rights attaching to, 424
joint venture, 452
judgment debt, charging order to secure, 426
land
legal and equitable interests, 427
liabilities attaching to, 427
ownership *see* OWNERSHIP OF LAND
public and municipal charges, 427
restrictions, 426
rights in, 424
title to *see* TITLE TO LAND
transactions in *see* TRANSACTIONS IN LAND
use, restrictions on, 426
land register
content, 429
contract for sale, 430
errors in, 429
fees, 432
leases, 432
limited property rights, 425-6
location, 428
plans, 428-9
leasehold
generally, 423-4, 432
legislative control, 432
office lease, 432
registration of interest, 432
tenancy *see* TENANCY
types, 432
letter of indemnity, 437
licence, 432
lien, unpaid purchase price, for, 426
limited company, nature of, etc, 450
mortgage
generally, 426, 436-7

Norway–*contd*
mortgage–*contd*
nature, 436
priority, 437
registration, 436
rights attaching to, 436-7
non-resident, tax liability, 446
option to purchase
generally, 426
registration, 426
tenant's, 435-6
ownership of land
acquisitive prescription, 425
adverse possession, 425
generally, 423
incapacitated person, by, 425
legal and beneficial ownership, 424
legislative background, 423
minor, by, 425
restrictions, 425
types of tenure–
absolute ownership *see* ABSOLUTE OWNERSHIP
condominium, 424
joint ownership *see* JOINT OWNERSHIP
leasehold *see* LEASEHOLD
partnership
general, 451
generally, 451
internal, 452
legal nature of, 451
limited, 451-2
silent, 452
performance bond, 437
planning authority, 438
planning control
breach, 439
building permit *see* BUILDING PERMIT
development plan *see* DEVELOPMENT PLAN
generally, 437
procedures, 438-9
priority of interests
generally, 428
mortgages, 437
produce, right to use or enjoy, 425
profits, repatriation, 453
public access right, 427
rent charge, 427
sale of land *see* CONTRACT FOR SALE
sale and lease-back, 435
security
charges, 437
credit insurance, 437
guarantee, 437
letter of indemnity, 437
mortgage *see* MORTGAGE
performance bond, 437
types, 436-7
servitude
duration, 426
types, 426
stamp duty, rate, 432

Norway–*contd*
subsidies *see* GRANTS
tax relief
capital allowances, 447
double taxation relief, 453
generally, 450
provincial areas, in designated, 450
taxes
capital gains, on, 447
corporation tax *see* CORPORATION TAX
development value, 447
land transfer, on, 448
municipal tax, 447
occupier, on, 448
owner of property, 447
value added tax, 432, 446, 448
wealth tax, 448
withholding tax, 447, 453
tenancy
agricultural, rights under, 426
legislative control, 432, 433-4
measurement, 434
privity of estate and contract, 433
registration, 432
rent–
control, 433
review provisions, 432-3
restrictions, legislative, 432, 433-4
security of tenure, 433
services, provision of, 433
termination, 433
terms, 432-3
title to land
passing of title, 429
proof, 428
registration *see* LAND REGISTER
transactions in land
fees, costs and taxes, 431-2
formalities, 431
procedures, 430
professionals' roles, 432
restrictions on dealing, 425
sale of land *see* CONTRACT FOR SALE
types, 430
unlimited company, nature of, etc, 450
use, restrictions on, 426

Portugal
absolute ownership
generally, 457
rights attaching to, 457
acquisitive prescription, 460
building contract
copyright, 483
payment, types of, 482
professional team, appointment of, 482
standard forms, 482
termination, compensation on, 482
terms, 481-2
types, 481
building permit *see* MUNICIPAL LICENCE
building rights *see* SURFACE RIGHTS

Portugal–*contd*
building standards, control and supervision, 478
buildings of special interest, protection, 478
business association, types, 487-9
business controls, restrictions and registrations, 489
charge, 462-3
compulsory purchase, compensation etc, 478-9
condominium
meaning, 458
changes, 458
enforcement of horizontal property ownership, 458
generally, 458-9
management of common parts, 459
regulation, 459
time sharing *see* TIME SHARE
contract for sale
binding, whether, 467
breach, 467-8
documentation required, 466-7
fees, costs and taxes, 468-9
formalities, 468
generally, 463
preliminary investigations etc, 466
procedures, 466-7
professionals' roles, 469
promissory contract, 463, 466
proof of ownership, providing, 466
terms, 467-8
warranties, 467
corporation tax
administration, 484
capital allowances, 484
computation, 484
generally, 484
liability for, 484
rates, 484
credit insurance, availability, 476
development plan
breach, destruction of works where, 477
generally, 476-7
preparation, 476
types, 476
development project
building contract *see* BUILDING CONTRACT
defects–
duty to inform, 481
insurance, 483
remedies, 483
fees as percentage of overall cost, 483
generally, 481
parties to, 482
permit for *see* MUNICIPAL LICENCE
taxes *see* TAXES
double taxation relief, availability, 490
dwelling rights, 462
easement *see* SERVITUDE
environmental protection
atmospheric pollution, 479

Portugal–*contd*
environmental protection–*contd*
contaminated land, 480
environmental impact assessments, 480
generally, 479
legislative background, 479
liability, 479
noise pollution, 479
penalties for infringement, 479
waste storage and disposal, 480
water pollution, 479-80
exchange controls, 489
finance
banks as source of, 472
equity, 472
generally, 472
grants and incentives, 487
immoveable finance leasing, 473
institutional investment, 473-4
investment, 472
joint venture *see* JOINT VENTURE
loan, 472
mezzanine or mixed, 472-3
non-institutional investment, 474
sale and lease-back, 473
tax leasing, 473
foreign investment, restrictions, 489
freehold *see* ABSOLUTE OWNERSHIP
grants, availability, 487
group of companies, business association, as a form of, 488-9
guarantee, 475-6
income, repatriation, 490
interests in land
generally, 460-64
legal and equitable, 464
ownership of land *see* OWNERSHIP OF LAND
priority *see* PRIORITY OF INTERESTS
protection, 464
joint ownership
generally, 458
rights attaching to, 458
termination, 458
joint venture
nature of, etc, 489
property finance, as source of, 473
judgment debt, securing, 462
land
liabilities attaching to, 464
ownership *see* OWNERSHIP OF LAND
public or municipal charges, 463
restrictions on use etc, 462
title to *see* TITLE TO LAND
transactions in land *see* TRANSACTIONS IN LAND
land register
backdating of title, 466
content, 465
descriptions in, 465
errors in, 465-6
fees, 468
interest, transfer of, 466

Portugal–*contd*
land register–*contd*
types, 465
leasehold
generally, 457-8
tenancy *see* TENANCY
limited liability company, nature of, etc, 488
mortgage
costs, 474
enforcement, 475
future or conditional debts, 474
generally, 462
insurance of mortgaged asset, 475
liability under, 474
priority, 475
rights under, 475
types, 474
municipal licence
application for–
appeal against refusal, 477
filing, 477
grant, 477
tacit approval, 477
conditional licence, 477
duration, 477
requirement for, 477
transfer of benefit, 477-8
option to purchase, 463
ownership of land
acquisitive prescription, 460
dealings, restrictions, 460
generally, 457
legal and beneficial ownership, 459
legislative background, 457
restrictions, 460
tenure, types of–
absolute ownership *see* ABSOLUTE OWNERSHIP
condominium *see* CONDOMINIUM
freehold *see* ABSOLUTE OWNERSHIP
joint ownership *see* JOINT OWNERSHIP
leasehold *see* LEASEHOLD
partnership, nature of, etc, 488
planning authority, 476
planning control
breach, enforcement procedures, 478
development plan *see* DEVELOPMENT PLAN
generally, 476
municipal licence *see* MUNICIPAL LICENCE
procedures, 477-9
pledge, 463
priority of interests
generally, 464
mortgage, 475
privilege, 462
profits, repatriation, 490
quota company, nature of, etc, 488
sale and lease-back, as source of funding, 473
security
charges, 475
credit insurance, 476

Portugal–*contd*
security–*contd*
floating charge, 475
guarantees, 475-6
mortgage *see* MORTGAGE
types, 462-3, 474-6
servitude
meaning, 461
creation, 461
duration, 461
generally, 461
types, 461
share company, nature of, etc, 487-8
stamp duty, rate, 468
subsidy, availability, 487
surface rights
creation, 461
duration, 461
examples of use, 462
generally, 461-2
termination, 461
tax relief
capital allowances, 484
double taxation relief, 490
foreign investors, for, 487
taxes
capital gains, on, 485
corporation tax *see* CORPORATION TAX
development value, 485
land transfer tax, 468, 486
local taxes etc, 486
occupier, on, 486
owner of property, on, 485
value added tax, 469, 483, 486
wealth taxes, 486
withholding tax, 485, 490
tenancy
creation, 469
duration, 458, 469
formalities, 468
generally, 457-8, 469
legislative restrictions, 471
measurement, 472
privity of contract and estate, 470
regulation, legislative, 469
rent–
control, 470-71
default in payment, 470
negotiation etc, 469-70
repairs etc, 470, 471
rights attaching to, 457-8
rural tenancy agreements–
duration, 469
payment of rent, 470
renewal, 471
security of tenure, 471
service costs, 470
termination, 471
terms, 469-70
types, 469
urban tenancy agreements–
duration, 469

Portugal–*contd*
tenancy–*contd*
urban tenancy agreements–*contd*
rent, payment of, 470
types, 469
time share
duration, 459
execution formalities, 459
generally, 459
registration, 459
rights under, 459
title to land
land register *see* LAND REGISTER
passing of title, 466
proof, 464-5
transactions in land
fees, costs and taxes, 468-9
formalities, 468
procedures, 466-7
professionals' roles, 469
restrictions, 460
sale of land *see* CONTRACT FOR SALE
types, 466
unlimited liability company, nature of, etc, 488
use, restrictions, 462
usufruct
creation, 461
duration, 461
generally, 461
rights under, 461
transfer, 461

Republic of Ireland
adverse possession, 495
bond, as form of security, 509
building contract
delay in completion, 515
parties to, 516-17
payments under, 515
professional team, appointment, 516
standard forms, 516
termination, 515
terms, 515
types, 515
building standards, control and supervision, 511
buildings of special interest, protection, 511
business association, types, 523-5
business controls, restrictions and registrations, 526
company
disclosure requirements, 523-4
statutory duties, 523
types, 523-4
compulsory purchase, compensation etc, 511-12
condominium, nature of, etc, 494
contract for sale
completion of sale, 501
enforcement, 501
fees, costs and taxes, 502

Republic of Ireland–*contd*
contract for sale–*contd*
forfeiture of deposit, 501
formalities, 501
generally, 497
procedures, 500-501
professionals' roles, 502-3
registered land, 500-501
registration, 497
registration following completion, 501
searches etc, 500
terms, 501
unregistered land, 500
corporation tax
administration, 518
capital allowances, 519
computation, 518
generally, 518
liability for, 518
rates, 518
credit insurance, 509
debenture, nature of, 508-9
development plan, 509-10
development project
building contract *see* BUILDING CONTRACT
copyright, 517
defects–
insurance, 517
remedies, 517
fees, 517-18
generally, 514
parties to, 516-17
taxes *see* TAXES
double taxation relief, availability, 526
dwelling right, 496
easement, *meaning*, 496
environmental protection
atmospheric pollution, 512
contaminated land, 513-14
environmental impact assessment, 514
generally, 512
legislative background, 512
noise pollution, 512
waste storage and disposal, 513
water pollution, 512-13
exchange controls, absence of, 526
finance
banks as source of, 505
bare trustee company, investment through, 507
equity, 506
generally, 505
grants and incentives, 522-3
institutional, 507
investment, 506
inward investment, restrictions etc, 526
loan, 505-6
mezzanine or mixed, 506
non-institutional, 507-8
sale and lease-back, 506
tax leasing, 507
tax relief *see* TAX RELIEF

Republic of Ireland–*contd*
foreign investment, restrictions etc, 526
freehold
fee farm grant, 493
generally, 493
rights attaching to, 493
grants, availability, 522
guarantee, 509
income, repatriation, 519-20
interest in land, 495-8
interests in land
legal and beneficial ownership, 495
legal and equitable interests, 498
licence, 494
ownership of land *see* OWNERSHIP OF LAND
priority, 498
protection, 498
investment company, nature of, etc, 525
joint ownership
disposal of interest, 494
generally, 494
rights attaching to, 494
termination, 494
types, 494
joint venture, nature of, etc, 525
land
dealing, restrictions, 495
legal and equitable interests, 498
liabilities attaching to, 497
public or municipal charges, 497
restrictions, 496
title to *see* TITLE TO LAND
transactions in *see* TRANSACTIONS IN LAND
use, restrictions, 496
land register
content, 499-500
errors in, 500
fees–
mortgage, 508
transfer of land, on, 502
location, 499
plans, 499
registrable interests, 498
leasehold
disposal of interest, 494
duration, 494
generally, 493-4, 503
rights attaching to, 493-4
tenancy *see* TENANCY
licence
rights under, 497
types, 497
mortgage
equitable mortgage, 508
generally, 496
registered land, in respect of, 508
registration fee, 508
rights under, 508
stamp duty, whether liable to, 508
unregistered land, in respect of, 508
option to purchase
generally, 497

Republic of Ireland–*contd*
option to purchase–*contd*
registration, 497
ownership of land
adverse possession, 495
generally, 493
legislative background, 493
restrictions, 495
tenure, types of–
absolute ownership *see* FREEHOLD
condominium, 494
freehold *see* FREEHOLD
joint ownership *see* JOINT OWNERSHIP
leasehold *see* LEASEHOLD
partnership
legislative background, 524
nature of, etc, 524
regulation, 524
types, 524
planning authority, 509
planning control
breach, enforcement etc, 510-11
development plan, 509-10
legislative background, 509
planning permission *see* PLANNING PERMISSION
procedures, 510-11
planning permission
application for–
appeal procedure, 510
procedure, 510
time limits, 510
failure to implement, 510
land, attaching to, 510
lapsing, 510
need for, 510
private limited company, nature of, etc, 523
profit à prendre, *meaning*, 496
profits, repatriation, 519-20
public limited company, nature of, etc, 523
public right, *meaning*, 497
sale of land *see* CONTRACT FOR SALE
sale and lease-back, as form of funding, 506
security
bond, 509
credit insurance, 509
debenture, 508-9
guarantee, 509
mortgage *see* MORTGAGE
types, 508-9
stamp duty, rates, 502
tax relief
capital allowances, 519, 523
double taxation relief, 526
generally, 522-3
types, 522-3
taxes
capital gains, on, 519-20
corporation tax *see* CORPORATION TAX
development value, on, 519
land transfer, on, 520
local etc, 521

Republic of Ireland–*contd*
taxes–*contd*
occupier, on, 520
owner of property, on, 520
value added tax, 502, 518, 521
wealth taxes, 520
withholding tax, 519, 526
tenancy
assignment etc, 504
building standards etc, 505
business tenancy, right to renewal, 504
duration, 503
forfeiture, 504
generally, 503
legislative restrictions, 505
measurement, 505
privity of contract and estate, 504
rent–
control, 504
review, 503
repairs etc, 503
residential tenancy, regulation, 504, 505
security of tenure, 504
tax relief, 522-3
terms, 503-4
types, 503
title to land
passing of title, 500
proof of title, 498-9
registered land, 498-9
registration *see* LAND REGISTER
unregistered land, 499
transactions in land
fees, costs and taxes, 502
formalities, 501
procedures, 500-501
professionals' roles, 502-3
restrictions, 495
sale of land *see* CONTRACT OF SALE
types, 500
trust, nature of, etc, 525
unincorporated association, 525
unlimited company, disclosure requirements, 523-4
use, restrictions, 496
usufruct, 496

Scotland
adverse possession, obtaining title to land by, 534
building contract, standard forms, 555
building rights, 535
building standards, control and supervision, 553
buildings of special interest, protection, 553
business association
generally, 557
partnership *see* PARTNERSHIP
charge
floating *see* FLOATING CHARGE
generally, 537
charging order, power to impose, 538

Scotland–*contd*
compulsory purchase, compensation etc, 553
condominium, 532
contract for sale
default, remedies, 545
examination of title etc, 544
exchange, 543
fees, costs and taxes, 545-6
formalities, 545
generally, 537
latent defect in land, discovery of, 545
missives–
conclusion, 542, 543
superseded by delivery of disposition, 545
more than one potential purchaser, offers where, 543
offer to purchase, submission of, 543
post-settlement procedures, 544
procedures, 542-4
qualified acceptance of offer, 543
searches etc, 543, 544
stages, 542
surveys, carrying out, 543
terms, 545
development plan
preparation, 552
public discussion, 552
types, 552
development project
legislation, recent, 556
prescription and limitation, 555-6
procurement methods, 555
retention, 556
standard forms, 555
diligence
generally, 537
inhibition, of, 537
Dominium plenum
blench, 530
division of ownership, 529
feuar–
absolute owner, as, 530
ownership, right to transfer, 529-30
rights, 530
feufarm, 530
nature of, 529
rights attaching to, 529
superiority, owner of–
common ownership *see* JOINT OWNERSHIP
generally, 529-30
mineral rights, 530
rights and remedies, 536
transfer of superiority, 530
dwelling rights, 535
environmental protection
agencies responsible for, 554
atmospheric pollution, 554
contaminated land, 554, 555
environmental impact assessments, 555
generally, 553-4

Scotland–*contd*
environmental protection–*contd*
liability, 553
noise pollution, 554
waste storage and disposal, 554
water pollution, 554
finance
generally, 549-50
grants and incentives, 556
international aspects, 557
private finance initiative, 547
floating charge
creation, 551
crystallisation, 551
priority, 551
registration, 551
rights under, 551
foreign investment, 557
freehold *see* DOMINIUM PLENUM
grants, availability, 556
interests in land
common interest and the law of tenement, 536-7
generally, 532-3, 534-40
legal and beneficial ownership, 533
legal and equitable, 539
liferent, 538
occupancy rights, statutory, 538
ownership *see* OWNERSHIP OF LAND
priority *see* PRIORITY OF INTERESTS
protection, 539
public right of way, 538
real burdens, 535-6
servitude *see* SERVITUDE
superior, rights and remedies, 536
joint ownership
common property, 532
joint property, 531-2
types, 531
land
interests in *see* INTERESTS IN LAND
liabilities attaching to, 538
public or municipal charges, 538
real burdens, 535-6
title to *see* TITLE TO LAND
transactions in *see* TRANSACTIONS IN LAND
use, restrictions on, 535-6
land register
administration, 540
content, 541
disposition–
fees, 546
registration, 544
errors in, 541
fees, 546
inspection, 540
operational areas, 540
plans, 541
types, 540
leasehold
assignment etc, 531
categories, 546-7

Scotland–*contd*
leasehold–*contd*
contract *see* CONTRACT FOR SALE
duration, 546
generally, 531, 546-7
registration, 531
rights attaching to, 531
tenancy *see* TENANCY
licence, 532-3
liferent, creation and nature of, 538
mortgage
calling-up notice, service of, 550
creation, 550
generally, 537
rights and obligations attaching to, 550
standard security, procedures relating to, 550
negative prescription, obtaining title to land by, 534
occupancy right, statutory, 538
option to purchase, 537
ownership of land
adverse possession, 534
generally, 529
incapacitated person, by, 533
legislative background, 529
minor, by, 533
negative prescription, 534
positive prescription, 534
restrictions, 533-4
tenure, types of–
allodial land, 530
condominium, 532
feudal nature, 529-30
freehold *see* DOMINIUM PLENUM
generally, 529-30
joint ownership *see* JOINT OWNERSHIP
leasehold *see* LEASEHOLD
licence, 532-3
tenancy *see* TENANCY
partnership
generally, 557
lease in name of, 533
planning authority, 552
planning control
development plan *see* DEVELOPMENT PLAN
legislative background, 552
procedures, 552-3
planning permission, procedures, 552-3
positive prescription, obtaining title to land by, 534
priority of interests
agreement to alternative ranking, 540
effected, how, 539
floating charge, 551
generally, 539-40
public right of way
creation, 538
loss, 538
registration
floating charge, 551
land register *see* LAND REGISTER

Scotland–*contd*
sale of land *see* CONTRACT FOR SALE
security
credit risk insurance, 551
floating charge *see* FLOATING CHARGE
generally, 550
guarantee, 551
mortgage *see* MORTGAGE
servitude
meaning, 534
creation, 535
generally, 534-5
negative, 535
positive, 534-5
registration, 535
termination, 535
taxes, 556
tenancy
assignment etc, 547
destruction of premises, termination on, 548
forfeiture, 548
irritancy clause, 548
kindly, 530-31
legislative restrictions, 549
measurement, 549
privity of contract, 548
rent–
act of God, abatement following, 548
control, 548-9
negotiation, 547
repairs etc, 548
security of tenure, 548-9
tacit relocation, 547
terms, 547-8
will, at, 531
title to land
passing of title, 542
proof of title, 540
registration *see* LAND REGISTER
transactions in land
fees, costs and taxes, 545-6
formalities, 545
procedures, 542-4
restrictions, 534
sale *see* CONTRACT FOR SALE
types, 542
use, restrictions on, 535-6
usufruct, 535

Spain
absolute ownership
generally, 561
rights attaching to, 561
third-party rights, 561
acquisitive possession, acquiring title by, 563
Basque country, incentives, availability of, 590
building contract
professional team, appointment of, 583-4
standard forms, 583
terms, 583

Spain–*contd*
building contract–*contd*
types, 583
building standards, control and supervision, 579
buildings of special interest, protection, 580
business association
companies, types of, 590-91
generally, 592
partnership *see* PARTNERSHIP
business controls, restrictions and registrations, 593
Canary Islands, incentives, availability of, 590
census
meaning, 566
types, 566
charge, 565-6, 577
compulsory purchase, compensation etc, 580
condominium, 562
contract for sale
default, 570
fees, costs and taxes, 571
formalities, 570
latent defects, discovery, 570
procedures, 569
professionals' roles, 571
terms, 570
vendor's obligations, 570
corporation tax
administration, 586
capital allowances, 586-7
computation, 586
liability for, 586
rates, 586
withholding tax, 587
credit insurance, types etc, 577
development plan
generally, 578
types, 578
zoning, 578
development project
building contract *see* BUILDING CONTRACT
copyright, 585
defects–
insurance, 585
remedies, 584-5
fees as percentage of overall cost, 585
finance *see* FINANCE
generally, 582-3
parties to, 584
taxes *see* TAXES
types, 583
double taxation relief, availability, 594
dwelling right, nature of, etc. 565
environmental protection
atmospheric pollution, 581
contaminated land, 582
environmental impact assessments, 582
generally, 580
liability, 580
noise pollution, 581

Spain–*contd*
environmental protection–*contd*
waste storage and disposal, 581-2
water pollution, 581
exchange controls, 593
finance
banks as source of, 574
equity, 574-5
grants and incentives, 589-90
institutional investment, 575-6
investment, 574-5
inward investment, restrictions, 593
leasing companies, 575
loan, 574
mezzanine or mixed, 575
private investment, 576
sale and lease-back, 575
tax leasing, 575
foreign investment, restrictions etc, 593
grants, availability, 590
guarantee, nature of, etc, 577
income, repatriation, 594
interests in land
census *see* CENSUS
dwelling right, 565
generally, 562
legal and equitable interests, 567
ownership of land *see* OWNERSHIP OF LAND
priority *see* PRIORITY OF INTERESTS
servitude *see* SERVITUDE
surface right, 565
usufruct *see* USUFRUCT
joint ownership
generally, 562
rights attaching to, 562
termination, 562
time-share, 562
transfer of interest in, 562
types, 562
joint venture, UTE, 592
land
interests in *see* INTERESTS IN LAND
liabilities attaching to, 566-7
monetary liabilities secured on, 565-6
public or municipal charges, 566
restrictions on, 565
title to *see* TITLE TO LAND
transactions in land *see* TRANSACTIONS IN LAND
use, restrictions on, 565
land register
content, 568
errors in, 568
fees, 571
generally, 568
plans, 568
leasehold
generally, 561, 571-2
tenancy *see* TENANCY
limited liability company, nature of, etc, 590-91

Spain–*contd*
mortgage
enforcement, 576-7
extension, 576
generally, 576-7
nature of, etc, 576-7
performance of duty, to secure, 565
priority, 567
Navarra, incentives, availability of , 590
option to purchase
generally, 566
lapse, 566
nature of, 566
ownership of land
acquisitive possession, 563
dealings, restrictions, 563
generally, 561
incapacitated persons, by, 563
legal and beneficial ownership, 563
legislative background, 561
minors, by, 563
restrictions on, 563
tenure, types of–
absolute *see* ABSOLUTE OWNERSHIP
condominium, 562
freehold *see* ABSOLUTE OWNERSHIP
joint ownership *see* JOINT OWNERSHIP
leasehold, 561
partnership
generally, 591-2
liability of partners, 591-2
types, 591
planning authority, 578
planning control
breach, enforcement, 579
development plan *see* DEVELOPMENT PLAN
generally, 577
legislative background, 577
licence *see* PLANNING LICENCE
procedures, 578-9
planning licence
appeal against refusal to grant, 579
duration, 579
generally, 578-9
need for, 578
time-limit for consideration of application, 579
transfer, 579
priority of interests
generally, 566
registration, need for, 567
profits, repatriation, 594
sale of land *see* CONTRACT FOR SALE
sale and lease-back, funding, as source of, 575
security
charges, 577
credit insurance, 577
guarantee, 577
mortgage *see* MORTGAGE
types, 565-6, 576

Spain–*contd*
servitude
meaning, 564
registration, 564
types, 564
share company, nature of, etc, 591
subsidy, availability, 589-90
surface right, nature of, etc, 565
tax relief
allowances, 590
Canary Islands, companies in, 590
capital allowances, 586-7
double taxation relief, 594
taxes
capital gains, on, 587
constructions, on, 585
corporation tax *see* CORPORATION TAX
development value, on, 587
land transfer tax, 571, 588
local taxes etc, 589
non-resident, annual tax on, 588
occupier, on, 588
owner of property, on, 587-8
value added tax, 571, 585, 589
wealth tax, 588-9
withholding tax, 587, 594
tenancy
assignment etc, 572
duration, 571-2
generally, 571-2
legislative control, 572
measurement, 574
privity of contract and estate, 573
rent–
control, 573
negotiation, 572
payment, 572
review, 572
rural lease, 572-3
repairs etc, 573
restrictions, 573-4
rural, 572-3
security of tenure, 573
termination, 572, 573
terms, 572-3
transfer, 561
types, 561, 571
title to land
land register *see* LAND REGISTER
passing of title, 569
proof of title, 568
transactions in land
fees, costs and taxes, 571
formalities, 570
procedures, 569
professionals' roles, 571
restrictions, 563
sale of land *see* CONTRACT FOR SALE
types, 569
trust, 592
use
first use licence, 579

Spain–*contd*
use–*contd*
opening or use licence, 579
restrictions, 565
usufruct
meaning, 564
enforcement, 564
termination, 564
transfer, 564
types, 564
zoning
development plans, and, 578
protection of buildings within, 580
responsibility for enforcement, 578

Sweden
absolute ownership
accessories, 597
generally, 597
rights attaching to, 597
adverse possession, acquiring title to land by, 601
building contract
professional team, appointment of, 623
standard from, 623
terms, 622-3
types, 622
building permit
appeal against refusal etc, 618
application for, 617
demolition permit changed to, 617
development in absence of, 618
ground works permit changed to, 617
lapsing, 618
requirement as to, 617
building relic, protection, 618
building right, 602
building standards, control and supervision, 618
buildings of special interest, protection, 618
business association
companies, types of, 629
joint ventures, 630
partnership *see* PARTNERSHIP
trusts, 630
business controls, restrictions and registrations, 631
charge, as form of security, 615-16
compulsory purchase, compensation etc, 619
condominium, 598-9
contract for sale
agricultural land, transfer, 601
apartment blocks, transfer, 600
bill of sale, issuing, 606
default or delay, 606-7
deposit, payment of, 606
enquiries etc, 605
fees, costs and taxes, 607-8
formalities, 607
generally, 602
latent defects, liability for, 606
mortgage, taking over, 605-6

Sweden–*contd*
contract for sale–*contd*
municipal pre-emption rights, 600
negotiation, 605
post-completion matters, 606
pre-emption, municipality's right of, 600, 606
procedures, 605-6
professionals' roles, 608
registration, 602
registration, application for, 606
spousal consent, 600
tenant-owner association's right of first refusal, 600-601
terms, 606-7
corporation tax
administration, 625
capital allowances, 625-6
computation, 625
generally, 625
liability for, 625
rates, 625
withholding tax, 626
credit insurance, 616
development plan
generally, 617
preparation, 617
public discussion, 617
types, 617
development project
building contract *see* BUILDING CONTRACT
copyright, 624
damages for failure to complete, 622-3
defects–
insurance, 624
remedies, 624
funding *see* FINANCE
generally, 621-2
parties to, roles of, 623
payment provisions, 622
professional team, appointment of, 623
taxes *see* TAXES
time schedule, agreement on, 622
double taxation relief, availability, 632
environmental protection
atmospheric pollution, 619, 620
contaminated land, 620-21
environmental impact assessments, 621
generally, 619-20
legislative background, 619-20
liability, 619
licence–
authorities, 619
withdrawal, 620
noise pollution, 619, 620
waste storage and disposal, 620
water pollution, 619, 620
exchange controls, 631
finance
banks as source of, 612
equity, 613
generally, 612, 621

Sweden–*contd*
finance–*contd*
grants and incentives, 628
institutional investment, 614
investment, 613
inward investment, restrictions etc, 630-31
loan, 612-13
mezzanine or mixed, 613
non-institutional investment, 614
property loan interest aid, 628
regional development support, 628
sale and lease-back, 613
securitisation, 614
tax leasing, 614
foreign investment, restrictions, 630-31
grant, availability, 628
guarantee, 616
income, repatriation, 631-2
interests in land
building right, 602
generally, 601-4
legal and equitable interests, 603
mortgage *see* MORTGAGE
ownership of land *see* OWNERSHIP OF LAND
priority *see* PRIORITY OF INTERESTS
protection, 603
public access rights, 603
public or municipal charges, 603
registration, 603
servitude *see* SERVITUDE
usufruct, 602
joint ownership, land in, 598
joint venture, 630
land
interests in *see* INTERESTS IN LAND
liabilities attaching to, 603
restrictions on, 602
title to *see* TITLE TO LAND
transactions in *see* TRANSACTIONS IN LAND
use, restrictions on, 602
land register
administration, 604
content, 604
errors in, 604-5
fees, 608
mortgage, 615
plans, 604
leasehold
contract for *see* CONTRACT FOR SALE
creation, 598
duration, 598
generally, 598, 608
land lease, 612
rights attaching to, 598
tenancy *see* TENANCY
termination, 598
transactions *see* TRANSACTIONS IN LAND
limited company, nature of, etc, 629
mortgage
buyer taking over seller's mortgage, 605-6
corporate, 615-16
enforcement, 615

Sweden–*contd*
mortgage–*contd*
generally, 602, 615
registration, 603, 615
spousal consent, 615
who can mortgage, 615
non-resident
acquiring property in Sweden, 630-31
company treated as resident, proposals as to, 625
restrictions on acquiring property, 599
ownership of land
adverse possession, 601
generally, 597
incapacitated person, by, 599
legal and beneficial ownership, distinction between, 599
legislative background, 597
minor, by, 599
restrictions, 599
tenure, types of–
absolute *see* ABSOLUTE OWNERSHIP
condominium, 598-9
freehold *see* ABSOLUTE OWNERSHIP
joint ownership, 598
leasehold *see* LEASEHOLD
trust, role of, 599
partnership
general, 629
generally, 629
limited, 630
non-business, 630
types, 629
planning authority, 616
planning control
breach, enforcement provisions, 618
building permit *see* BUILDING PERMIT
development plan *see* DEVELOPMENT PLAN
generally, 616
procedures, 617-18
priority of interests
generally, 604
land fraudulently sold twice, where, 605
profits, repatriation, 631-2
registration
interest in land, 603
land register *see* LAND REGISTER
sale of land *see* CONTRACT FOR SALE
sale and lease-back, as form of finance, 613
security
charges, 615-16
credit insurance, 616
guarantees, 616
mortgage *see* MORTGAGE
types, 614-16
servitude
meaning, 601
creation, 601
enforcement, 601
registration, 603
rights attaching to, 601
transfer, 601

Sweden–*contd*
stamp duty, payment, 607-8
subsidy, 628
tax relief
capital allowances, 625-6
double taxation relief, 632
generally, 628
taxes
capital gains, on, 626
corporation tax *see* CORPORATION TAX
development value, on, 626
foreign company's liability for, 625
land transfer tax, 627
local taxes etc, 628
occupier, on, 627
owner of property, on, 626-7
value added tax, 608, 625, 627-8
wealth tax, 627
withholding tax, 626, 632
tenancy
commercial tenancy–
duration, 608-9
maintenance etc, 611
rent provisions, 610
security for performance, 611
security of tenure, 609
subletting, 611
termination, 609
transfer, right to, 611
generally, 608
measurement, 612
occupational, registration, 603
privity of contract and estate, 612
residential tenancy–
death of tenant, 611
duration, 609
rent provisions, 610-11
security of tenure, 609-10
subletting, 611
surrender, 611
termination, 609
transfer, right to, 611
title to land
passing of title, 605
proof of title, 604
registration *see* LAND REGISTER
transactions in land
agricultural land, transfer, 601
apartment blocks, transfer, 600, 606
fees, costs and taxes, 607-8
formalities, 607
municipal pre-emption rights, 600, 606
procedures, 605-6
professionals' roles, 608
restrictions, 599
sale of land *see* CONTRACT FOR SALE
spousal consent, 600
tenant-owner association's right of first refusal, 600-601
types, 605
trust, 630
unlimited company, nature of, etc, 629

Sweden–*contd*
use, restrictions on, 602
usufruct, 602

Switzerland
absolute ownership
generally, 635
rights attaching to, 635
acquisitive prescription, acquiring title to land by, 637
building contract
breach, 658
delay, compensation for, 658
extension of time under, 658
professional team, appointment of, 658
standard form, 658
terms, 658
types, 657-8
building permit
appeal against refusal to grant etc, 653
application for, 653
breach, 654
environmental impact assessment, need for, 656
grant–
conditional grant, 653
mandatory grant, 653
non-personal nature of, 653
revocation, 653
time limit for acting on, 653
building right
generally, 638
grant–
generally, 638
procedures on, 642-3
rights under, 638
transfer, 638
building standards, control and supervision, 654
buildings of special interest, protection, 654
business association
companies, 664-665
foundations, 666
joint venture *see* JOINT VENTURE
partnership *see* PARTNERSHIP
business controls, restrictions and registrations, 667
compulsory purchase, compensation etc, 654-5
condominium, 636
contract for sale
completion, 643
declaration of intent, entering into, 643
default or delay, 643-4
defects, claims for, 643
deposit, payment of, 643
enquiries etc, 642-3
existing loans, buyer taking over, 643
fees, costs and taxes, 644-5
formalities, 644
negotiations, 642
procedures, 642-3

Switzerland–*contd*
contract for sale–*contd*
professionals' roles, 645
terms, 643-4
transfer, seller refusing to register, 642
unpaid purchase price, statutory mortgage for, 644
cooperative company
development of cheap residential property, involvement in, 657, 665
nature of, etc, 665
corporation tax
administration, 661
capital allowances, 661
computation, 661
generally, 660
liability for, 660
rates, 661
withholding tax, 661-2
credit insurance, 652
debenture, 651
development project
building contract *see* BUILDING CONTRACT
building permit *see* BUILDING PERMIT
cooperative companies' involvement, 657
copyright, 659-60
defects–
insurance, 659
remedies, 659
fees, 660
funding *see* FINANCE
generally, 656-7
parties to, 659
tax implications, consideration of, 657
taxes *see* TAXES
types, 656-7
disposal of land *see* TRANSACTIONS IN LAND
double taxation relief, availability, 668
dwelling right, 638
environmental protection
atmospheric pollution, 655
contaminated land, 656
environmental impact assessment, 656
generally, 655
legislative background, 655
liability, 655
noise pollution, 655
waste storage and disposal, 655-6
water pollution, 655
exchange controls, absence, 667
finance
banks as source of, 648
equity, 649
generally, 648, 649, 656-7
grants and incentives, 663-4
institutional investment, 650
investment, 649
inward investment, restrictions etc on, 667
loan, 648
mezzanine or mixed, 649
non-institutional investment, 650

Switzerland–*contd*
finance–*contd*
sale and lease-back, 649
tax leasing, 649
foreign investment, restrictions etc, 667
foundation, 666
guarantee, 651-2
income, repatriation, 668
interests in land
building right *see* BUILDING RIGHT
dwelling right, 638
generally, 637-41
legal and equitable, 640
ownership of land *see* OWNERSHIP OF LAND
priority *see* PRIORITY OF INTERESTS
protection, 640
servitude, 638
types, 637
usufruct, 638
joint ownership
creation, 636
decision-making procedure, types of, 636
exclusion of co-owner, 636
generally, 635-6
rights attaching to, 636
joint venture
contractual, 666
corporate, 666-7
generally, 666
land
liabilities attaching to, 640
non-resident attempting to acquire, restrictions, 667
privilege attaching to, 639
public charges on, 639
public law restrictions, 639
restrictions on, 639
sale of *see* CONTRACT FOR SALE
title to *see* TITLE TO LAND
transactions in *see* TRANSACTIONS IN LAND
use, restrictions on, 639
land register
content, 641-2
errors in, 642
fees, 644-5
inspection, 641
location, 641
plans, 641
responsibility for, 641
tax duties, registration triggering, 641
leasehold
generally, 635, 645-6
tenancy *see* TENANCY
limited liability company, nature of, etc, 664-5
mortgage
enforcement, 651
fixed-rank system, 651
generally, 639, 650-51
priority, 651
purpose, 651
registration, 650

Switzerland–*contd*
mortgage–*contd*
rights under, 651
statutory, 658
types, 639, 650
unpaid purchase price, for, 644
non-resident
acquisition of property, restrictions etc, 667
permit to acquire land, 667
option to purchase
enforcement, 639
generally, 639
registration, 639
ownership of land
acquisitive prescription, 637
generally, 635
incapacitated persons, by, 637
legal and beneficial ownership, 636-7
legislative background, 635
minors, by, 637
restrictions, 637
tenure, types of–
absolute ownership *see* ABSOLUTE OWNERSHIP
condominium, 636
joint ownership *see* JOINT OWNERSHIP
leasehold *see* LEASEHOLD
transfer–
contract for sale *see* CONTRACT FOR SALE
formalities, 644
partnership
general, 665
limited, 665-6
ordinary, 665
planning authority, 652
planning control
breach, 654
building permit *see* BUILDING PERMIT
generally, 652
legislative background, 652
procedures, 653-4
zoning plans, 652
priority of interests
generally, 640-41
mortgages, 640-41, 651
public charges, 640-41
profits, repatriation, 668
sale and lease-back, as form of finance, 649
security
assignment of business receipts as, 652
credit insurance, 652
debentures, 651
guarantee, 651-2
mortgage *see* MORTGAGE
surety, 651-2
types, 639, 650
servitude, 638

Switzerland–*contd*
share corporation, nature of, etc, 664
stamp duty, incorporation, on, 663
surety, 651-2
tax relief
capital allowances, 661
double taxation relief, 668
generally, 664
taxes
capital gains, on, 662
corporation tax *see* CORPORATION TAX
development value, on, 662
generally, 660
land transfer tax, 662-3
local taxes etc, 663
occupier, on, 662
owner of property, on, 662
value added tax, 645, 663
wealth tax, 663
withholding tax, 661-2, 668
tenancy
agricultural, legislative restrictions, 648
default by landlord, 647
duration, 646
generally, 645-6
improvements, 646
insurance, 646
measurement, 648
privity of contract and estate, 647
rent–
control, 647
indexation, 646
payment, 646
reviews, 646
repairs, 646
sale of property, effect on tenancy, 647
security of tenure, 647
termination, 646-7
terms, 646-7
title to land
passing of title, 642
proof of title, 641
registration *see* LAND REGISTER
transactions in land
building right, procedures on grant of, 642-3
fees, costs and taxes, 644
formalities, 644
local authorities, by, 637
professionals' roles, 645
restrictions, 637
sale of land *see* CONTRACT FOR SALE
types, 642
trust, absence of concept, 666
use, restrictions, 639
usufruct, 638
zoning, 652